SUCCESSFUL
COLLEGE
WRITING

KATHLEEN T. McWHORTER

Niagara County Community College

bedford/st.martin's
Macmillan Learning

Boston | New York

For Bedford/St. Martin's

Vice President: *Leasa Burton*
Program Director for English: *Stacey Purviance*
Senior Program Manager: *Karita F. dos Santos*
Director of Content Development: *Jane Knetzger*
Executive Development Editor: *Jane Carter*
Development Editor: *Cara Kaufman*
Assistant Editor: *Paola García-Muñiz*
Director of Media Editorial: *Adam Whitehurst*
Advanced Media Editor: *Angela Beckett*
Marketing Manager: *Amy Haines*
Senior Director, Content Management Enhancement: *Tracey Kuehn*
Senior Managing Editor: *Michael Granger*
Senior Digital Content Project Manager: *Ryan Sullivan*
Senior Workflow Project Manager: *Paul Rohloff*
Production Supervisor: *Robert Cherry*
Director of Design, Content Management: *Diana Blume*
Interior Design: *Cenveo® Publisher Services*
Cover Design: *William Boardman*
Director of Rights and Permissions: *Hilary Newman*
Text Permissions Researcher: *Elaine Kosta, Lumina Datamatics, Inc.*
Photo Permissions Editor: *Angela Boehler*
Photo Researcher: *Krystyna Borgen, Lumina Datamatics, Inc.*
Director of Digital Production: *Keri deManigold*
Media Project Manager: *Emily Brower*
Editorial Services: *Lumina Datamatics, Inc.*
Copyeditor: *Angela Morrison*
Indexer: *Christine Hoskin*
Composition: *Lumina Datamatics, Inc.*
Cover Images: *(bottle) New Africa/Shutterstock; (sunglasses) clu/Getty Images; (headphones) Nirut Punshiri/EyeEm/Getty Images; (pen) Gen Sadakane/EyeEm/Getty Images; (smartphone) hudiemm/E+/Getty Images; (backpack) Billion Photos/Shutterstock*
Printing and Binding: *LSC Communications*

Library of Congress Control Number: 2020943226

ISBN 978-1-319-24509-2 (Student Edition)
ISBN 978-1-319-38733-4 (Loose-Leaf Edition)

Printed in the United States of America.

2   3   4   5   6   25   24   23   22

Acknowledgments

Text acknowledgments and copyrights appear at the back of the book on pages 793–94, which constitute an extension of the copyright page. Art acknowledgments and copyrights appear on the same page as the art selections they cover.

Contents

Paul Bradbury/OJO Images/
Getty Images

PART ONE

An Introduction to Reading, Writing, and Learning in College 1

iii

PART TWO

Strategies for Writing Essays 101

mantinov/Shutterstock.com

4 Prewriting: How to Find and Focus Ideas 102

WRITING QUICK START 102

PART THREE

Patterns of Development 223

WILDLIFE GmbH/Alamy

PART FOUR

Reading and Writing Arguments   515

PART FIVE

Writing with Sources 569

Joelle Sedlmeyer/Photolibrary/
Getty Images

PART SIX

Academic and Business Applications 665

ThomasVogel/E+/Getty Images

24 ▶ Reading and Writing about Literature 666

WRITING QUICK START 666

Thematic Contents

Preface

Other texts assume that first-year composition students already possess the basic skills they will need to succeed in college, but my own experience tells me that this is not true. That is why I wrote *Successful College Writing*. It uses a unique, highly visual, student-centered approach to teach students the reading and study skills they need while guiding them through the writing strategies and activities that form the core of composition instruction. The overwhelmingly positive response to the first seven editions demonstrates that *Successful College Writing* fulfills an important need.

The eighth edition continues to meet students where they are and get them where they need to go by building on one of the text's core strengths: its integration of writing and reading instruction as two aspects of the same process. Through consultation with instructors across the country, in-depth conversations with several instructors who run or have run co-requisite (or ALP) programs, and a rethinking of the way annotations are handled, I have worked hard to make the eighth edition more accessible and better than ever at helping instructors address the needs of first-year college students at a variety of levels of preparedness. Achieve with *Successful College Writing* also helps instructors meet students where they are and get them where they need to go by providing an online course space with tools to help create a supportive writers' community in the classroom, whether their classes are in person or online.

New to the Eighth Edition

The main goal of the revision—based on feedback from experienced instructors familiar with the needs of today's students—was to provide additional support for students who may be underprepared for first-year composition while not neglecting the needs of more college-ready students. With that in mind, this edition pays special attention to academic reading and writing, with the goal of making the kind of reading and writing students are expected to do in college less scary and more doable.

Achieve with *Successful College Writing*

A dedicated composition space paired with trustworthy content, Achieve with *Successful College Writing* helps instructors engage students in new ways. Developed to support best practices in commenting on drafts—and co-designed with teachers and students from across the country—Achieve is a flexible, integrated suite of tools for designing and facilitating writing assignments, with actionable insights that make students' progress toward outcomes clear and measurable.

- **Diagnostics** generate individualized study plans and personalize students' learning, allowing instructors to differentiate instruction.
- **Pre-built, fully customizable assignments** support the book's approach—all with rubrics and draft goals that can be used as is or tailored to individual needs. Each editable writing assignment is based on the Guided Writing Assignments in *Successful College Writing*.

- **A peer review tool** helps students use feedback productively and helps instructors facilitate the process.
- **A revision plan tool** helps students chart a concrete path to improvement.
- **Reflection prompts** facilitate transfer of learning to other writing assignments.
- **Source Check** alerts writers to potential originality issues and links them to revision help—before they submit a final draft.
- **A built-in e-book** provides point-of-need instruction and support as students draft, review, revise, and reflect.
- **Easy-to-read dashboards** show submissions, progress, and trends that can inform instructors' lesson plans.

For details, visit **macmillanlearning.com/college/us/englishdigital**. See pages xxxiii–xxxiv for packaging options.

Additional Help for Underprepared Students and Their Instructors

Underprepared students will benefit from new Just-in-Time Tips. These tips, which accompany professional readings following the Guided Writing Assignment in Parts 3 and 4, call students' attention to challenging features in the reading and offer strategies for understanding and thinking critically about them. They complement the annotations that appear with the first professional reading and offer underprepared students strategies they can transfer to other college reading assignments. They enhance or supplement the skills highlighted in the "Just-in-Time Guide to Reading and Responding" following Chapter 3.

In the Instructor's Annotated Edition, I have also added ALP tips to help instructors new to the co-requisite (or ALP) model adapt or supplement the content in *Successful College Writing* to meet the needs of underprepared students. *Successful College Writing* has more material than most instructors can cover in a single semester, so these tips point out activities (such as the "Essay in Progress" writing assignments) that could be used instead in the ALP section. These tips also offer suggestions for activities (such as applying the "How Writers Read" boxes) that could be used in workshop-style class meetings for drafting or revising students' writing. (Instructors who do not use the Instructor's Annotated Edition can also find these teaching tips in Achieve, Macmillan's online courseware.)

To assist instructors new to teaching the co-requisite section, *Instructor's Resource Manual for Successful College Writing* includes two especially helpful chapters: one on teaching the co-requisite course and another on developing a course plan for the co-requisite section. Both are written by Jamey Gallagher of the Community College of Baltimore County, where the ALP program was started.

More Coverage of Academic Writing— Appropriate for All New College Students

Because even well-prepared students sometimes struggle with college-level expectations, new "Academic Writing" sections in Part 2 offer extra help with the kinds of writing tasks students are expected to produce in college. For example, these sections

- guide students as they paraphrase, summarize, and quote from sources
- help students learn to introduce, present, and explain material borrowed from sources while avoiding plagiarism

- help students write appropriate titles, introductions, and conclusions
- demonstrate how to maintain a tone that is appropriate to academic writing—without losing an individual voice

These "Academic Writing" sections, in conjunction with the content in Part 5 ("Writing with Sources"), prepare students to explore a topic and produce source-based writing.

New "Explore, Research, Write" assignments, which appear following selected professional readings in Parts 3 and 4, scaffold academic, source-based writing by providing students with vetted, reliable, and relevant sources from which they can draw information and ideas to supplement and inform their own thinking and writing.

A *Student's Companion for Successful College Writing* (which appears both in a stand-alone book and in Achieve with *Successful College Writing*, Macmillan's online course space) also includes "Sentence Guides for Academic Writers," which can be incorporated into the work of the course. These guides show students how to join the academic conversation by presenting the ideas of others, agreeing with another writer and adding ideas of their own, disagreeing appropriately, and making clear where a source stops and students' commentary begins.

Popular and Scholarly Reading Selections on Topics That Matter

As with each edition, I have worked hard to curate a selection of readings—by both students and professionals—that will challenge, engage, provide springboards for writing, and offer effective examples of each pattern of development. The eighth edition includes seventeen new professional reading selections and three new essays by student writers. New reading selections include

- classic and new voices, from Joan Didion's "The Santa Ana" to an excerpt from Tara Westover's bestseller *Educated* to a personal narrative by William Peeples, a prisoner in a maximum security prison in Illinois
- relevant topics, such as what makes some people especially gullible (by Scientia Professor Joseph Paul Forgas), how we can protect ourselves from phony "friends" online (by cyber security expert Arun Vishwanath), and how to spot fake news (by Eugene Kiely and Lori Robertson of FactCheck.org)
- just plain fun essays like Jan Diehm and Amber Thomas's comparing men's and women's pockets

New student essays in the eighth edition include

- Darnell Henderson's "From Screens to Gardens: An Antidote to Digital Overload"
- Mya Nunnally's classification essay "Science Fiction: Three Forms, Many Fans"
- Thai Luong's cause-and-effect essay "Why Ban Single-Use Plastics?"

Proven Features of *Successful College Writing*

While I have worked hard to reimagine some aspects of *Successful College Writing*, I have also maintained many of the features that instructors and students have found effective from past editions. Every chapter of *Successful College Writing* continues to provide practical, student-oriented instruction and abundant guidance and support for inexperienced writers.

Practical, Step-by-Step Writing Assignments

The eighth edition of *Successful College Writing* still provides the tools students need to understand writing as a flexible, multifaceted process, with writing assignments—in the text and pre-built and fully customizable in Achieve—supporting the book's approach.

- **Part 1** begins this process by emphasizing the importance of reading and writing as a tool for mastering complex information and ideas, and applying them to new situations. It also alerts students to the expectations their college instructors will have for them as readers, thinkers, and writers, including how they read, think, and respond critically to texts and images. The "Just-in-Time Guide to Reading and Responding" (at the end of Part 1) provides students with the survival reading skills they need to understand and fully engage with college-level texts in a handbook format, and bite-sized responses allow students to dip into the guide and get back to their assigned reading quickly.
- **Part 2** provides detailed coverage of the writing process—from choosing and narrowing a topic and generating ideas to developing and supporting a thesis, drafting essays and paragraphs, revising, editing, and proofreading. Each chapter in Part 2 includes plenty of skill-building exercises (many of them collaborative); "Essay in Progress" activities that lead students through each step in writing an essay; and sample essays that follow student writers Latrisha Wilson, Darnell Henderson, and Kate Atkinson through the various stages of drafting and revision.
- **Parts 3 and 4** cover the patterns of development that students encounter most frequently in college and on the job. Graphic organizers offer students a visual guide to the structure of selections in each pattern and provide a scaffold for students as they draft their own essays. Each Guided Writing Assignment provides a writing prompt and walks students through the writing process, emphasizing activities for generating and evaluating ideas, developing a thesis, organizing and drafting the essay, and revising and editing that essay, including a flowchart for revising and tips for editing sentences and words in each pattern. In Achieve with *Successful College Writing*, these assignments appear pre-built, with draft goals and rubrics; instructors can use them as is or customize them to meet the needs of the course.
- **Part 5** provides in-depth instruction for writing a research project, including information about finding useful and reliable sources, synthesizing information and ideas from sources to support the writer's ideas, and incorporating and documenting material borrowed from sources.
- **Part 6** covers writing in academic and business settings, from writing about literature, taking essay exams, and creating a portfolio to making presentations and writing résumés, job application letters, and business emails.

Appealing, Helpful Visuals

Because inexperienced writers are often more comfortable with images than with text, *Successful College Writing* continues to employ a visual approach to writing instruction.

- **Writing Quick Starts** jumpstart each chapter, providing engaging images for students to respond to in writing, introducing them to the main topic of the chapter, and promoting metacognition by asking students to consider what they already know about writing in each mode.
- **Graphic Organizers**—charts that display relationships among ideas—offer tools both for analyzing readings and for planning and revising essays, and they present students with a more visual alternative to traditional outlines.
- **Guided Writing Assignments**—in a streamlined, step-by-step, visual format—walk students through the process of writing essays in each of the rhetorical modes. These same writing assignments also appear in Achieve, Macmillan's online courseware, embedded in writing tools that help students do the work of the course and help instructors respond easily and effectively.
- **Revision Flowcharts** help students read and revise their own essays systematically as well as review the essays of their peers.
- **Numerous figures, photographs, boxes, and bulleted lists** throughout the text reinforce key points and summarize information.

Improving Reading Skills: A Five-Pronged Approach

Recognizing that students frequently enter first-year writing courses without the active and critical reading skills they need to succeed in first-year composition and other college courses, *Successful College Writing* supports students with a five-pronged approach to improving their reading skills that will also help students become better writers:

1. **Overt reading instruction** in Chapters 2 and 3, in the "Just-in-Time Guide to Reading and Responding," and in the "How Writers Read" boxes. Chapter 2 includes a "Guide to Active Reading" and a "Guide to Responding to a Reading," and Chapter 3 offers detailed coverage of reading both text and visuals critically. The "Just-in-Time Guide" offers support that students can dip into as needed and lets them get right back to their reading, and the "How Writers Read" boxes throughout help students recognize that reading and writing are two sides of the same coin.
2. **Graphic Organizers** in Parts 2, 3, and 4 that help students recognize the structure of the essay
3. **Activities to foster critical reading** following readings in Parts 3 and 4 and in LearningCurve, Bedford/St. Martin's adaptive quizzing program. (Activities on eleven core topics are available in Achieve with *Successful College Writing*, which can be packaged with the textbook or purchased on its own; for more information, see pp. xxxiii–xxxiv.)
4. **Collaborative activities** to enhance critical reading
5. **Peer review–style activities and revision flowcharts**, which can be used alone or with classmates to emphasize reading and thinking critically

Over the years, my work with students has convinced me that skills taught in isolation are seldom learned well or applied, so each of the chapters on the patterns of development in Parts 3 and 4 reinforces the reading skills taught in Part 1 and elsewhere. As students develop their writing skills by producing a particular type of essay, they simultaneously learn practical strategies for reading that type of essay.

Comprehensive Coverage of Research and Documentation

Because finding, evaluating, and incorporating information and ideas from useful sources is so central to academic success, *Successful College Writing* provides three full chapters (Part 5) on writing with sources, including a careful discussion of accidental plagiarism and paraphrasing without "patchwriting," using information and ideas from sources to support the writer's own ideas, and documenting sources in MLA and APA styles (including updated APA citations using the new seventh edition of the *Publication Manual of the American Psychological Association*). New sections on academic writing and writing from sources also appear throughout Part 2.

Thorough Reference Handbook

The handbook in Part 7 covers basic grammar, sentence problems, punctuation, mechanics, and spelling and includes

- hand-corrected examples to make needed revisions easy to understand
- marginal definitions of key grammatical terms
- helpful revision flowcharts and summary boxes
- sentence and paragraph exercises

Because issues multilingual writers face are also often issues for native speakers and writers, I have folded the coverage of ESL troublespots into the main body of coverage in the handbook in this edition.

The handbook also reinforces students' learning with plenty of opportunities for practice: with exercises in the text, with additional exercises keyed to the handbook in *A Student's Companion for Successful College Writing* (a supplement for students who may need a little extra support), and with additional practice through LearningCurve, Bedford/St. Martin's adaptive quizzing program (available in Achieve with *Successful College Writing*).

Attention to Outcomes

Successful College Writing helps students build proficiency in the four categories of learning that writing programs across the country use to assess student work:

- rhetorical knowledge
- critical thinking, reading, and composing
- processes
- knowledge of conventions

For a table that correlates the Council of Writing Program Administrators (WPA) outcomes to features of *Successful College Writing*, see pages xxxvi–xli.

A Student's Companion for Successful College Writing

A Student's Companion for Successful College Writing is designed specifically to help students succeed in first-year composition. The text includes

- **coverage of important college success strategies**, including building confidence, managing time, and writing ethically and responsibly

- **nine chapters on writing in the patterns of development** that include tons of fun activities (like MadLibs) to help students read actively and critically and to develop thoughtful, college-level essays and new reading activities that can be used with any of the selections in *Successful College Writing* or supplementary readings supplied by instructors. These reading activities include previewing or "getting the gist" activities, paraphrasing practice, attention to purpose and audience, and much more.
- **"Sentence Guides for Academic Writers,"** designed to help students join the academic conversation, showing them how to present information from sources, present their own views, and put the two together to amplify a writer's views or reject those views appropriately
- **editing practice**, tailored to the instructional content in Chapters 6, 7, 9, and the handbook in *Successful College Writing*

Acknowledgments

This edition benefited from the experience of those instructors who reviewed the seventh edition and the manuscript for the eighth edition. I am grateful for their thoughtful comments and helpful advice: Raphael Bennett, Broward College; Jacqueline Bollinger, Erie Community College; Leah Creque, Morehouse College; Jaime Manuel Flores, Waukesha County Technical College; Ellen Gilmour, SUNY University at Buffalo; Elizabeth Hardy, Mayland Community College; Michele Hardy, Prince George's Community College; Sheena Hernandez, Garden City Community College; Elizabeth Jones, Wor-Wic Community College; Dianna Just, Northeastern Oklahoma A&M College; Julie Karey, Columbia College; Gus LaFosse, Kilgore College; Marissa McKinley, Indiana University of Pennsylvania; James Minor, South Piedmont Community College; James Ortego, Troy University–Dothan; Andrew Preslar, Lamar State College–Orange; James D. Richey Jr., Tyler Junior College; Portia Scott, Kilgore College; and Lisa Tittle, Harford Community College.

A number of instructors also kindly agreed to provide feedback on draft content and how to improve it. My thanks go out to Raphael Bennett, Broward College–Central; Jacqueline Bollinger, Erie Community College; Floyd Brigdon, Trinity Valley Community College; Debra Farve, Mt. San Antonio College; Jaime Manuel Flores, Waukesha County Technical College; Keith Freeman, Morehouse College; Jason Graves, Kilgore College; Seonae Ha-Birdsong, Northeastern Oklahoma A&M College; Julia Harper, Wor-Wic Community College; Jen Jacobs, Harford Community College; Gus LaFosse, Kilgore College; Andrew Preslar, Lamar State College–Orange; Melissa Reddish, Wor-Wic Community College; Jennifer Richardson, Northern Virginia Community College; James T. Richey Jr., Tyler Junior College; Portia Scott, Kilgore College; Wei Yan, St. Louis Community College–Forest Park; and Gwendolyn Whitehead, Lamar State College–Orange.

Additional thanks go to the instructors who provided feedback on *A Student's Companion for Successful College Writing*: Debra Airheart, Trinity Valley Community College; Lynda Brooks, Kilgore College; Quanisha Charles, Jefferson Community and Technical College–Downtown; Rachel Dobrauc, Waukesha County Technical College; Debra Farve, Mt. San Antonio College; Heather Shea Fitch, Kilgore College;

Jaime Manuel Flores, Waukesha County Technical College; Heidi Johnsen, LaGuardia Community College; James T. Richey Jr., Tyler Junior College; Lucas Shepherd, Tyler Junior College; and Wei Yan, St. Louis Community College–Forest Park.

I also want to thank Elizabeth Gruchala-Gilbert for her research assistance (Seattle Pacific University); Carolyn Lengel, Heather Fitch (Kilgore College), and Andrew Preslar (Lamar State College–Orange), with help from Debra Farve (Mt. San Antonio College), for all their hard work on *A Student's Companion for Successful College Writing*, a supplement for students in co-requisite (or ALP) classes or for anyone who needs a little extra help developing ideas, drafting, and revising an essay; and Jamey Gallagher for writing material on teaching a co-requisite (or ALP) course alongside a freshman writing course for the instructor's manual.

I especially want to thank Kathy Tyndall for her valuable assistance in helping me revise portions of the manuscript, including the apparatus following the readings and the annotations in the Instructor's Annotated Edition, and for her help in revising the instructor's manual and writing the quizzes for reading comprehension and summary practice.

Many people at Bedford/St. Martin's have contributed to the creation and development of *Successful College Writing*. Each person with whom I have worked is a true professional. Each demonstrates high standards and expertise, and each is committed to producing a book focused on student needs.

My thanks to Leasa Burton, vice president for humanities at Bedford/St. Martin's, for her tireless efforts to helm the ship; Stacey Purviance, program director for the English group at Bedford/St. Martin's, for overseeing this project and making valuable contributions to its revision; and Karita dos Santos, senior program manager, for her forthright advice and valuable assistance in making some of the more difficult decisions about the book and her untiring efforts to champion this book. Special thanks go to Adam Whitehurst, director of media editorial for the humanities; Angela Beckett, advanced media editor; and Emily Brower, media project manager, for their thoughtful work on Achieve. I also appreciate the advice and guidance that marketing manager Amy Haines has provided at various junctures in the revision of this text. Paola García-Muñiz, assistant editor, has helped improve and prepare the manuscript in innumerable ways. Ryan Sullivan, senior digital content project manager, deserves special recognition for his herculean efforts in guiding this revision through the production process.

I owe the largest debt of gratitude to Jane Carter, my development editor, for her valuable guidance and assistance in preparing this revision. Her careful editing and attention to detail have strengthened the eighth edition significantly. She helped me to reinforce the book's strengths and retain its focus on providing extra help to students.

Finally, I must thank the many students who inspired me to write this book and the many students whose writing I have been delighted to include, especially Darnell Henderson, Mya Nunnally, and Thai Luong, whose talent produced the three new student essays in the eighth edition. From my students I have learned how to teach, and they have shown me how they think and learn. My students, then, have made the largest contribution to this book, for without them I would have little to say and no reason to write.

Kathleen T. McWhorter

Bedford/St. Martin's Puts You First

From day one, our goal has been simple: to provide inspiring resources that are grounded in best practices for teaching reading and writing. For more than 35 years, Bedford/St. Martin's has partnered with the field, listening to teachers, scholars, and students about the support writers need. We are committed to helping every writing instructor make the most of our resources.

How Can We Help *You*?

- Our editors can align our resources to your outcomes through correlation and transition guides for your syllabus. Just ask us.
- Our sales representatives specialize in helping you find the right materials to support your course goals.
- Our learning solutions and product specialists help you make the most of the digital resources you choose for your course.
- Our Bits blog on the Bedford/St. Martin's English Community (**community .macmillan.com**) publishes fresh teaching ideas weekly. You'll also find easily downloadable professional resources and links to author webinars on our community site.

Contact your Bedford/St. Martin's sales representative or visit **macmillanlearning.com** to learn more.

Print and Digital Options for *Successful College Writing*

Choose the format that works best for your course, and ask about our packaging options that offer savings for students.

Print
- **Paperback student edition.** To order the paperback version of *Successful College Writing*, Eighth Edition, use ISBN 978-1-319-24509-2. To order the paperback version packaged with Achieve, use ISBN 978-1-319-38847-8. To order the paperback version packaged with *A Student's Companion for Successful College Writing*, use ISBN 978-1-319-38851-5.
- **Loose-leaf edition.** This format does not have a traditional binding; its pages are loose and hole punched to provide flexibility and a lower price to students. To order the loose-leaf edition of *Successful College Writing*, use ISBN 978-1-319-38733-4. The loose-leaf edition can be packaged with Achieve for additional savings. To order the loose-leaf packaged with Achieve, use ISBN 978-1-319-38936-9.
- **A *Student's Companion for Successful College Writing* (Lengel/Fitch).** This student supplement is designed specifically to help underprepared students succeed in first-year composition. To order *A Student's Companion for Successful College Writing*, use ISBN 978-1-319-35731-3. To order *Successful College Writing*, Eighth Edition, packaged with *A Student's Companion*, use ISBN 978-1-319-38851-5.

Digital

- **Achieve with *Successful College Writing*.** Achieve puts student writing at the center of your course and keeps revision at the core, with a dedicated composition space that guides students through drafting, peer review, source check, reflection, and revision. Fully editable pre-built assignments support the book's approach and an e-book is included. For details, visit **macmillanlearning.com/college/us/englishdigital**.
- **Popular e-book formats.** For details about our e-book partners, visit **macmillanlearning.com/ebooks**.
- **Inclusive Access.** Enable every student to receive their course materials through your LMS on the first day of class. Macmillan Learning's Inclusive Access program is the easiest, most affordable way to ensure all students have access to quality educational resources. Find out more at **macmillanlearning.com/inclusiveaccess**.

Your Course, Your Way

No two writing programs or classrooms are exactly alike. Our Curriculum Solutions team works with you to design custom options that provide the resources your students need. (Options below require enrollment minimums.)

- **ForeWords for English.** Customize any print resource to fit the focus of your course or program by choosing from a range of prepared topics, such as Sentence Guides for Academic Writers.
- **Macmillan Author Program (MAP).** Add excerpts or package acclaimed works from Macmillan's trade imprints to connect students with prominent authors and public conversations. A list of popular examples or academic themes is available upon request.
- **Mix and Match.** With our simplest solution, you can add up to 50 pages of curated content to your Bedford/St. Martin's text. Contact your sales representative for additional details.
- **Bedford Select.** Build your own print anthology from a database of more than 800 selections, or build a handbook and add your own materials to create your ideal text. Package with any Bedford/St. Martin's text for additional savings. Visit **macmillanlearning.com/bedfordselect**.

Instructor Resources

You have a lot to do in your course. We want to make it easy for you to find the support you need—and to get it quickly.

- **Instructor's Annotated Edition of *Successful College Writing*, Eighth Edition,** includes the full student edition of the text as well as possible answers to all the activities in the text and teaching tips for both first-year composition and any ALP/co-requisite sections. To order an examination copy of the Instructor's

Annotated Edition, use ISBN 978-1-319-35730-6. (Answers and tips are also available in Achieve as a downloadable PDF.)

- **Instructor's Resource Manual for Successful College Writing, Eighth Edition,** is available as a PDF that can be downloaded from the book's catalog page at **macmillanlearning.com** and is also available in Achieve. The instructor's manual offers a wide variety of tips, strategies, and approaches, allowing instructors to choose the methodology that is compatible with their teaching style and philosophy. It includes chapters on teaching with *Successful College Writing*, designing a course plan for first-year composition (with sample plans and syllabus), teaching and designing a co-requisite (or ALP) writing class (by Jamey Gallagher, Community College of Baltimore County), assessing student writing, teaching as an adjunct instructor, using the writing center, finding resources for teaching composition, administering two provided writing assessment tests, and more.

- **Lecture Slides for Successful College Writing, Eighth Edition,** outlines the instructional content in Parts 1–4 of the text and includes key graphic organizers and revision flowcharts.

Features of *Successful College Writing*, Eighth Edition, Correlated to the Writing Program Administrators (WPA) Outcomes Statement (2014)

Desired Student Outcomes	Relevant Features of *Successful College Writing*
RHETORICAL KNOWLEDGE	

Desired Student Outcomes	Relevant Features of *Successful College Writing*
Learn and use key theoretical concepts through analyzing and composing a variety of texts.	• Chapter 1 covers successful learning strategies in general and for the writing class in particular; it also covers expectations for reading and writing in college. • Chapter 2 offers advice for reading academic and other challenging texts, including instruction on active reading (including previewing) and reading to respond (annotating, summarizing, and keeping a response journal). • Chapter 3 offers advice for reading texts and visuals critically, including analyzing the author's ideas; language; and assumptions, generalizations, or omissions, as well as reading photos and graphics actively and critically. • New sections on academic writing throughout Parts 1 and 2 offer students extra help with the kinds of writing they are expected to produce in college. • Chapters in Parts 3 and 4 include reading selections for a variety of audiences, from popular to more scholarly (see, for example, "Why Are Some People More Gullible Than Others?" by Scientia Professor of Psychology Joseph Paul Forgas), followed by scaffolded apparatus to help students read actively and critically; Guided Writing Assignments that help students craft essays using a variety of rhetorical modes; annotated student essays that provide useful examples of successful college writing; and "Using [Mode] in College and the Workplace" boxes at the beginning of each chapter in Parts 3 and 4. • New "Explore, Research, Write" assignments (following the professional reading selections in Chapters 13–18 and 20) provide students with vetted reading selections and ask them to use those selections to practice writing from sources. • Part 5 offers advice for writing using sources and citing sources in MLA and APA style. • Part 6 offers advice about writing in specific academic contexts (Chapter 24, "Reading and Writing about Literature," and Chapter 25, "Essay Examinations and Portfolios") and about writing in the workplace (Chapter 26, "Multimedia Presentations and Business Writing").
Gain experience reading and composing in several genres to understand how genre conventions shape and are shaped by readers' and writers' practices and purposes.	• Chapter 1 covers reading a syllabus and highlights the expectation that students will both read and produce writing in a variety of genres, from abstracts to research projects. • Part 2 includes several new sections on academic writing to help students learn to read academic texts like writers and apply what they learn to their own writing. • Chapters 19 and 20 cover reading and writing arguments. • Chapter 23 covers writing a research project, with example research projects in MLA and APA style. • Chapter 24 instructs students in reading literature and writing literary analyses and includes a sample essay. • Chapter 25 covers writing essay examinations and compiling portfolios, with a sample essay answer, sample portfolio contents, and reflective letter. • Chapter 26 covers creating multimedia presentations using PowerPoint and Prezi presentation slides, writing résumés and job application letters, and writing in electronic media for business.
Develop facility in responding to a variety of situations and contexts calling for purposeful shifts in voice, tone, level of formality, design, medium, and/or structure.	• Chapter 2 includes a new section on reading digital text and provides a list of strategies for reading digital text. Chapter 2 also includes coverage of analyzing the author's tone. • Chapter 3 covers reading critically, particularly by paying attention to the author's use of language. • The chapters in Part 2 include new sections on academic writing, including one in Chapter 8 that emphasizes maintaining an appropriate tone in academic writing, without sacrificing voice. • Chapter 9 offers instruction on editing words and sentences, including editing to create an appropriate tone and level of diction.

Desired Student Outcomes	Relevant Features of *Successful College Writing*

RHETORICAL KNOWLEDGE

	• Chapter 23 covers appropriate formats for writing a paper using sources in MLA and APA style.
	• Chapter 26 covers appropriate business writing formats and styles for résumés, job application letters, and electronic business correspondence. It also covers appropriate design and formatting of slides in presentation software, such as PowerPoint and Prezi.
	• Achieve* includes tutorials in critical reading and digital writing. LearningCurve includes activities in critical reading, topic sentences and supporting details, topics and main ideas, and issues of correctness.
Understand and use a variety of technologies to address a range of audiences.	• Chapter 2 includes a new section on reading digital text, and provides a list of strategies for reading digital text effectively.
	• Chapter 9 discusses computer-aided proofreading, including the pitfall of relying too heavily on spell-check and grammar-check software.
	• Achieve* offers tutorials in documenting and working with sources in both MLA and APA style, as well as tutorials in making multimedia presentations, job searching, and personal branding.
Match the capacities of different environments (e.g., print and electronic) to varying rhetorical situations.	• Chapter 2 includes a new section on reading digital text and provides a list of strategies for reading digital text successfully.
	• Chapter 22 covers researching online.
	• Chapter 23 covers using appropriate formats (MLA or APA) for writing a paper using sources.
	• Chapter 25 covers using print and digital portfolios for assessment and learning.
	• Chapter 26 covers planning, drafting, and delivering a multimedia presentation using visual aids (objects and presentation slides), whether face-to-face or via the Web; creating effective résumés and job application letters, whether printed or uploaded electronically; and using electronic media for business writing.
	• *Instructor's Resource Manual for Successful College Writing*, Eighth Edition (for instructors), covers teaching and learning online.
	• Achieve* offers tutorials on digital writing (including photo and audio editing), making presentations, word processing, using online research tools, and job search/personal branding.

CRITICAL THINKING, READING, AND COMPOSING

Use composing and reading for inquiry, learning, critical thinking, and communicating in various rhetorical contexts.	The entire book is informed by the connection between reading critically and writing effectively, but see the following sections:
	• Chapter 1 covers the importance of reading and writing for college success and the distinctive qualities and demands of academic reading and writing.
	• Chapter 2 covers reading actively and understanding and responding to reading in writing.
	• Chapter 3 covers thinking critically about text and images by analyzing the author's ideas, use of language, assumptions, generalizations, and omissions; synthesizing ideas; and analyzing photographs and graphics by reading them actively and critically.
	• The "Just-in-Time Guide to Reading and Responding" provides a useful reference for students who need help with reading, developing college-level vocabulary, highlighting appropriately, and preparing for a discussion of a reading selection.
	• Part 2 includes new "Academic Writing" sections that offer help with the kinds of writing tasks students are expected to produce in college.
	• Parts 3 and 4 cover thinking critically about the features of the genre, including analyzing and evaluating a reading in the chapter's pattern, and synthesizing ideas across readings. The apparatus following the reading selections in the latter part of each chapter provide activities that walk students through the process of analyzing the reading.
	• Achieve* offers tutorials and activities in LearningCurve on reading critically.

Desired Student Outcomes

Relevant Features of *Successful College Writing*

CRITICAL THINKING, READING, AND COMPOSING

Desired Student Outcomes	Relevant Features of *Successful College Writing*
Read a diverse range of texts, attending especially to relationships between assertion and evidence, to patterns of organization, to interplay between verbal and nonverbal elements, and to how these features function for different audiences and situations.	• Chapter 1 includes coverage of expectations for academic reading and writing and why improving one's reading and writing skills is crucial. • Chapter 2 focuses entirely on strategies for reading and responding to text and visuals. This chapter also now includes coverage of reading digital texts effectively. • Chapter 3 includes coverage of assessing evidence, distinguishing between fact and opinion, and the roles patterns of development and synthesis and illustrations (photographs and graphics) play in writing. • Chapter 4 includes coverage of the importance of purpose, audience, point of view, genre, and medium in reading and writing. • Chapter 5 emphasizes the importance of supporting a thesis with evidence, including incorporating visuals as evidence. • Chapter 6 focuses on the relationship between a paragraph's topic and use of supporting evidence. • Chapter 8 includes coverage of tone, including a new section on crafting an appropriate tone in academic writing—without losing the writer's individual voice. • Parts 3 and 4 focus on a pattern of organization, with each including a section that asks students to consider the role of the audience and situation. Readings in these chapters range from popular (see "I'm Not Leaving until I Eat This Thing" and "Pockets") to accessible scholarly selections (see "The Psychology of Stuff and Things," "His Marriage and Hers: Childhood Roots," and "Why Some People Are More Gullible Than Others"). Where appropriate, activities following the readings also ask students to think critically about the relationship between text and visuals. • Chapter 19 covers supporting an arguable claim, evidence and appeals, and responses to alternative views. • Chapter 23 addresses appropriate tone for essays written for academic audiences and the role of reasons and evidence in supporting the writer's ideas.
Locate and evaluate (for credibility, sufficiency, accuracy, timeliness, bias, and so on) primary and secondary research materials, including journal articles, essays, books, databases, and informal electronic networks and Internet sources.	• Chapter 3 focuses on analyzing a selection critically, including assessing the quality of the evidence and the author's use of language to discover bias or faulty reasoning. • Chapter 19 asks readers to attend to reasons, evidence, and appeals when reading arguments. • Chapter 21 emphasizes choosing appropriate source types for the project (primary vs. secondary source; scholarly, popular; books vs. articles vs. media sources); evaluating sources for relevance, including timeliness and appropriateness for the audience; and reliability, including fairness and objectivity, verifiability, and bias. • Chapter 22 provides instruction on using library resources, including using key words effectively for searching catalogs and databases, using and choosing appropriate research tools such as subject guides and government documents, and conducting field research.
Use strategies—such as interpretation, synthesis, response, critique, and design/redesign—to compose texts that integrate the writer's ideas with those from appropriate sources.	• Chapter 2 covers a variety of strategies, including synthesis, analysis, response, and critique in its "Guide to Responding to a Reading." • Chapter 3 covers using analysis of an author's ideas, language, and assumptions/generalizations/omissions to read critically. • The chapters in Part 2 now include "Academic Writing" sections that help students write effectively for an academic audience, including guiding students as they paraphrase, summarize, and quote from sources and helping students learn to introduce, present, and explain material borrowed from sources while avoiding plagiarism. • Chapters 11–18 each include a "How Writers Read" box that challenges students to analyze and evaluate the readings in the chapter's rhetorical mode and a "Synthesizing Ideas" box that asks students to make connections among readings. The apparatus following reading selections in the second half of each chapter also includes activities for analyzing the writer's technique, thinking critically about the rhetorical mode, and responding to the reading.

Desired Student Outcomes	Relevant Features of *Successful College Writing*

CRITICAL THINKING, READING, AND COMPOSING

- Chapters 13–18 and 20 now include "Explore, Research, Write" activities that supply three reading selections and ask students to draw on those selections to write an essay.
- Chapter 22 covers evaluating notes and synthesizing sources.
- Chapter 23 covers integrating information from sources with the students' own ideas as well as integrating quotations, paraphrases, and summaries while avoiding plagiarism.
- Tutorials in documenting and working with sources are available in Achieve.*

PROCESSES

Develop a writing project through multiple drafts.

- The chapters in Part 2 pay close attention to the writing process: Chapter 4 focuses on finding and focusing ideas; Chapter 5, on developing and supporting a thesis; Chapter 6, on writing focused, well-supported paragraphs; Chapter 7, on organizing and drafting an essay; Chapter 8, on revising an essay for content and organization, including benefits and processes of peer revising; Chapter 9, on reading and revising a draft critically. One student's writing process, from idea generation through revision, is depicted across the chapters in Part 2, while two other student essays (by Darnell Henderson and Kate Atkinson) demonstrate parts of the writing process.
- The Guided Writing Assignments in Parts 3 and 4 walk students through the writing process for each of the rhetorical modes.
- Chapter 25 coverage of developing a portfolio emphasizes the importance of demonstrating and reflecting on the writing process.
- Achieve* puts student writing at the center of the course and keeps revision at the core, with a dedicated composition space that guides students through drafting, peer review, source check, reflection, and revision.
- *A Student's Companion for Successful College Writing* (ISBN 978-1-319-35731-3) offers additional writing activities to help students build a fully developed essay in each of the modes. *A Student's Companion* is available as a stand-alone text or as a student-facing resource in Achieve.*

Develop flexible strategies for reading, drafting, reviewing, collaborating, revising, rewriting, rereading, and editing.

- Chapter 1 introduces the idea of learning strategies to help students adapt their approach to the needs of the assignment or discipline.
- Chapter 2 offers a "Guide to Active Reading" that asks students to preview, activate background knowledge and write guide questions, highlight key points, and make connections among ideas. It also includes a "Guide to Responding to a Reading" that asks students to summarize to check their understanding, annotate and synthesize to connect the writer's ideas with their own, and analyze and evaluate the reading. Finally, the chapter walks students through the process of writing a response essay, from devising ideas to revising, editing, and proofreading.
- Part 2 provides an overview of the writing process, with activities and student samples punctuating the process. It also includes coverage and models to help students participate in and benefit from peer review.
- The Guided Writing Assignments in Parts 3 and 4 offer pattern-specific coverage of prewriting, drafting, revision, editing, and proofreading.
- Chapter 25 includes coverage of developing a portfolio, emphasizing the importance of demonstrating and reflecting on the student's writing process.
- *A Student's Companion for Successful College Writing* (ISBN 978-1-319-35731-3), a new supplement, offers reading activities for each mode and rubrics for each of the Guided Writing Assignments in the text. Students can use these rubrics to assess their own writing or the writing of their peers.
- Achieve* puts student writing at the center of the course and keeps revision at the core, with a dedicated composition space that guides students through drafting, peer review, source check, reflection, and revision.

*Achieve is available on its own (with a complete e-book) or packaged with the print text. See pp. xxxiii–xxxiv for details.

continued

Desired Student Outcomes	Relevant Features of *Successful College Writing*
PROCESSES	
Use composing processes and tools as a means to discover and reconsider ideas.	• Chapter 2 walks students through the process of writing a response essay based on techniques of active reading, critical reading, and reading-to-write strategies such as annotating an essay and keeping a response journal. • Chapter 3 asks students to read, analyze, and evaluate the author's ideas, using strategies such as analyzing the author's language (denotation vs. connotation), figurative language, and tone; and analyzing generalizations and omissions. • Chapter 8 focuses on revising for big-picture issues, the thesis, supporting evidence, organization, and development. The chapter also introduces peer revision and responding to the instructor's comments as strategies for revising. • Parts 3 and 4 offer pattern-specific coverage of prewriting, drafting, revision, editing, and proofreading. • Chapter 25 emphasizes the importance of demonstrating and reflecting on the student's writing process in the context of creating a portfolio. • Part 5 chapters cover writing a research project, including planning, finding, and evaluating sources; drafting and synthesizing information to support the writer's own ideas; revising the research project; and citing sources in a style that is appropriate to the discipline. Student samples in these chapters provide appropriate models for college-level research projects.
Experience the collaborative and social aspects of writing processes.	• Opportunities to work collaboratively appear in exercises throughout the book (see, for example, the "Working Together" activities), with additional ideas for collaboration suggested in the teaching tips in the Instructor's Annotated Edition. (These tips are also available as a downloadable PDF in Achieve* with *Successful College Writing*.) • Chapter 4 provides instruction for brainstorming in groups. • Chapter 8 includes coverage of peer review and tips for getting the best results from collaborative editing. • Chapter 6 of *Instructor's Resource Manual for Successful College Writing* offers tips on managing the peer review process. (The instructor's manual is available as a free download from the instructor's tab on the *Successful College Writing* catalog page at **macmillanlearning.com** and also in Achieve.*)
Learn to give and to act on productive feedback on works in progress.	• Chapter 8 includes coverage of peer review, tips for getting the best result from the process, and using the instructor's comments to revise. • The chapters in Parts 3 and 4 provide Guided Writing Assignments, offering pattern- and genre-specific advice on peer review and revision, with revision flowcharts that can be used to guide the peer-review process or revision by individual writers. • Chapter 6 of *Instructor's Resource Manual for Successful College Writing* offers tips on managing the peer review process. • *A Student's Companion for Successful College Writing* (ISBN 978-1-319-35731-3) offers rubrics for each of the Guided Writing Assignments in the text. Students can use these rubrics to assess their own writing or the writing of their peers. For packaging options, see p. xxxiii.
Adapt composing processes to a variety of technologies and modalities.	• The entire book assumes that students will be using technology for writing and research. • Chapter 1 emphasizes the importance of avoiding the distractions that can arise from multitasking and provides advice for managing online courses responsibly. • Chapter 21 provides special tips for evaluating resources in a digital landscape. • Chapter 22 provides searching strategies for online research, including searching of catalogs and databases, searching for information online, and using citation managers for managing the research process; it also gives instruction on organizing notes regardless of the medium in which they were taken. • Chapter 23 gives instruction on avoiding plagiarism by cutting and pasting carelessly. • Chapter 26 covers making multimedia presentations, using PowerPoint or Prezi, making a Web-based presentation, submitting a résumé and cover letter online, and using electronic media (such as email, Twitter, and Facebook) for business. • Achieve* offers tutorials on digital writing, including photo and audio editing, making presentations, word processing, using online research tools, and job search/personal branding.

*Achieve is available on its own (with a complete e-book) or packaged with the print text. See pp. xxxiii–xxxiv for details.

Desired Student Outcomes	Relevant Features of *Successful College Writing*

KNOWLEDGE OF CONVENTIONS

Develop knowledge of linguistic structures, including grammar, punctuation, and spelling, through practice in composing and revising.	• Chapter 9 covers writing concisely, varying sentences, editing to create an appropriate tone and level of diction, choosing appropriate words, and editing to avoid errors of grammar, punctuation, and mechanics. • The Guided Writing Assignments in Parts 3 and 4 offer pattern- and genre-specific advice about editing and proofreading. • The handbook in Part 7 provides instruction in correcting errors of grammar, punctuation, mechanics, and spelling. • Achieve* provides access to LearningCurve, adaptive game-like quizzing that provides opportunities for learning to identify and correct common writing problems. • *A Student's Companion for Successful College Writing* (ISBN 978-1-319-35731-3) includes additional exercises for Chapters 6, 7, and 9 and the handbook.
Understand why genre conventions for structure, paragraphing, tone, and mechanics vary.	• Chapter 1 highlights differences in expectations for writing as students move from high school to college, including expecting to find differences among genres and disciplines. • Chapter 9 covers editing to create an appropriate tone and level of diction, whether the level is informal, popular, formal, or academic, and choosing words that are appropriate to the audience and purpose.
Gain experience negotiating variations in genre conventions.	• The chapters in Part 2 discuss various aspects of academic writing and how it differs from writing for a popular audience. For example, Chapter 5 discusses choosing evidence that is appropriate for an academic audience; Chapter 7 includes coverage of writing effective introductions, conclusions, and titles for an academic audience; and Chapter 8 emphasizes the importance of crafting a tone that is appropriate to an academic audience. • The beginning of each chapter in Parts 3 and 4 includes a box highlighting how the rhetorical mode could be used in college and in the workplace; a range of readings so students gain experience reading selections written for sophisticated popular audiences as well as more academic audiences (see "The Psychology of Stuff and Things," by Christian Jarrett, for example); and apparatus following the readings in the second half of each chapter to help students gain experience in negotiating variations in the conventions. • Chapter 26 highlights style choices that are appropriate for writing in a business context.
Learn common formats and/or design features for different kinds of texts.	• Chapter 23 highlights variations in formatting depending on expectations in the discipline for which the text was created. • Chapter 26 covers formatting expectations for PowerPoint and Prezi slides, business writing formats for résumés, job application letters, and other forms of electronic business writing. • Achieve* provides tutorials on photo and audio editing, creating presentations, and personal branding.
Explore the concepts of intellectual property (such as fair use and copyright) that motivate documentation conventions.	• Chapter 23 covers concepts underlying plagiarism, including common knowledge.
Practice applying systematic citation conventions to a range of source material in students' own work.	• Chapter 24 covers documenting sources in MLA and APA styles. • Achieve* offers tutorials in documentation and working with sources.

How Writers Read

How Readers Write

Paul Bradbury/OJO Images/Getty Images

PART ONE

An Introduction to Reading, Writing, and Learning in College

1 Reading and Writing for College Success

vm/E+/Getty Images

In this chapter
you will learn to

- discover the factors that contribute to college success
- develop learning strategies to improve your reading and writing skills
- understand what academic reading and writing involves
- grasp the importance of improving your reading and writing skills

Writing Quick Start

ANALYZE   This photograph shows a college student studying. What factors might explain why this student does (or does not) excel academically?

WRITE   Write a paragraph based on your experiences with education up to this point that explains which factors you think contribute to (or detract from) academic success. Be specific: You might discuss tasks that students need to know how to perform, offer tips, identify pitfalls, or consider nonacademic factors, such as jobs and family responsibilities.

CONNECT   What factors did you identify as contributing to college success? Some you may have mentioned include the following:

▶ being motivated and organized

▶ completing all assignments

▶ focusing on a task to study and learn

▶ having good instructors

▶ performing well in class and on exams

▶ knowing how to write papers and essay exams

All of these skills, and many others, contribute to academic success. This chapter begins with a reading that discusses several key factors that contribute to college success. The remainder of the chapter presents numerous strategies to help you develop the skills you need for success in all your college courses and in your writing class in particular.

Factors That Contribute to Success

Read "The New Marshmallow Test," the article that follows. As you read, highlight the main points the writer is making about multitasking and academic success, and write notes, questions, and comments in the margin about your own media multitasking habits and your ability to devote your undivided attention to class lectures and course materials during your study time. You'll be glad you did!

READING

The New Marshmallow Test: Students Can't Resist Multitasking

Annie Murphy Paul

Annie Murphy Paul is a contributing writer for *Time* magazine and often writes about learning and its improvement. She also blogs about learning at CNN.com, Forbes.com, and HuffingtonPost.com and has written several books, including *The Cult of Personality*, which explores the historical quirks of how personality tests were developed and critiques their value; *Origins: How the Nine Months before Birth Shape the Rest of Our Lives*, a book about the science of prenatal influences; and *Brilliant: The New Science of Smart*.

1   Living rooms, dens, kitchens, even bedrooms: Investigators followed students into the spaces where homework gets done. Pens poised over their "study observation forms," the observers watched intently as the students—in middle school, high school, and college, 263 in all—opened their books and turned on their computers.

2   For a quarter of an hour, the investigators from the lab of Larry Rosen, a psychology professor at California State University–Dominguez Hills, marked down once a minute what the students were doing as they studied. A checklist on the form included: reading a book, writing on paper, typing on the computer—and also using email, looking at Facebook, texting, talking on the phone, watching television, listening to music, surfing the Web. Sitting unobtrusively at the back of the room, the observers counted the number of windows open on the students' screens and noted whether the students were wearing earbuds.

3   Although the students had been told at the outset that they should "study something important, including homework, an upcoming examination or project, or reading a book for a course," it wasn't long before their attention drifted: Students' "on-task behavior" started declining around the two-minute mark as they began responding to arriving texts or checking their Facebook feeds. By the time the 15 minutes were up, they had spent only about 65 percent of the observation period actually doing their schoolwork.

Attending to multiple streams of information and entertainment while studying, doing homework, or even sitting in class has become a common behavior among college students.   JHU Sheridan Libraries/Gado/Contributor/Archive Photos/Getty Images

Rosen's study, published in the May 2013 issue of *Computers in Human Behavior*, is part of a growing body of research focused on a very particular use of technology: media multitasking *while learning*. Evidence from psychology, cognitive science, and neuroscience suggests that when students multitask while doing schoolwork, their learning is far spottier and shallower than if the work had their full attention. They understand and remember less, and they have greater difficulty transferring their learning to new contexts. So detrimental is this practice that some researchers are proposing that a new prerequisite for academic and even professional success—the new marshmallow test of self-discipline—is the ability to resist a blinking inbox or a buzzing phone.

4

The media multitasking habit extends into the classroom. While most middle and high school students don't have the opportunity to text, email, and surf the Internet during class, studies show the practice is nearly universal among students in college and professional school. One large survey found that 80 percent of college students admit to texting during class; 15 percent say they send 11 or more texts in a single class period.

5

During the first meeting of his courses, Rosen makes a practice of calling on a student who is busy with his phone. "I ask him, 'What was on the slide I just showed to the class?' The student always pulls a blank," Rosen reports. "Young people have a wildly inflated idea of how many things they can attend to at once, and this demonstration helps drive the point home: If you're paying attention to your phone, you're not paying attention to what's going on in class." Other professors have taken a more surreptitious approach, installing electronic spyware or planting human observers to record whether students are taking notes on their laptops or using them for other, unauthorized purposes.

6

In a study involving spyware, for example, two professors of business administration at the University of Vermont found that "students engage in substantial multitasking behavior with their laptops and have non-course-related software applications open and active about 42 percent of the time." Another study, carried out at St. John's University in New York, used human observers stationed at the back of the classroom to record the technological activities of law students. The spies reported that 58 percent of second- and third-year law students who had laptops in class were using them for "non-class purposes" more than half the time. Texting, emailing, and posting on Facebook and other social media sites are by far the most common digital activities students undertake while learning, according to Rosen. That's a problem, because these operations are actually quite mentally complex, and they draw on the same mental resources—using language, parsing meaning—demanded by schoolwork.

7

David Meyer, a psychology professor at the University of Michigan who's   8
studied the effects of divided attention on learning, takes a firm line on the brain's
ability to multitask: "Under most conditions, the brain simply cannot do two
complex tasks at the same time. It can happen only when the two tasks are both
very simple and when they don't compete with each other for the same mental
resources. An example would be folding laundry and listening to the weather
report on the radio. That's fine. But listening to a lecture while texting, or doing
homework and being on Facebook—each of these tasks is very demanding, and
each of them uses the same area of the brain, the prefrontal cortex."

Young people think they can perform two challenging tasks at once, Meyer   9
acknowledges, but "they are deluded," he declares. It's difficult for anyone to
properly evaluate how well his or her own mental processes are operating, he
points out, because most of these processes are unconscious. And, Meyer adds,
"there's nothing magical about the brains of so-called 'digital natives' that keeps
them from suffering the inefficiencies of multitasking. They may like to do it, they
may even be addicted to it, but there's no getting around the fact that it's far better
to focus on one task from start to finish."

Researchers have documented a cascade of negative outcomes that occurs   10
when students multitask while doing schoolwork. First, the assignment takes
longer to complete, because of the time spent on distracting activities and because,
upon returning to the assignment, the student has to refamiliarize himself with
the material.

Second, the mental fatigue caused by repeatedly dropping and picking up a   11
mental thread leads to more mistakes. Third, students' subsequent memory of
what they're working on will be impaired if their attention is divided. As the
unlucky student spotlighted by Rosen can attest, we can't remember something
that never really entered our consciousness in the first place. And a study last
month showed that students who multitask on laptops in class distract not just
themselves but also their peers who see what they're doing.

Fourth, some research has suggested that when we're distracted, our brains   12
actually process and store information in different, less useful ways. In a 2006
study in the *Proceedings of the National Academy of Sciences*, Karin Foerde of the
University of Texas–Austin and two colleagues asked participants to engage in a
learning activity on a computer while also carrying out a second task, counting
musical tones that sounded while they worked. Brain scans taken during Foerde's
experiment revealed that different regions of the brain were active under the two
conditions, indicating that the brain engages in a different form of memory when
forced to pay attention to two streams of information at once. The results suggest,
the scientists wrote, that "even if distraction does not decrease the overall level of
learning, it can result in the acquisition of knowledge that can be applied less
flexibly in new situations."

Finally, researchers are beginning to demonstrate that media multitasking   13
while learning is negatively associated with students' grades. In Rosen's study,
students who used Facebook during the 15-minute observation period had lower
grade-point averages than those who didn't go on the site. Meyer, of the University of Michigan, worries that the problem goes beyond poor grades. "There's a

definite possibility that we are raising a generation that is learning more shallowly than young people in the past," he says. "The depth of their processing of information is considerably less, because of all the distractions available to them as they learn."

Given that these distractions aren't going away, academic and even professional achievement may depend on the ability to ignore digital temptations while learning—a feat akin to the famous marshmallow test. In a series of experiments conducted more than forty years ago, psychologist Walter Mischel tempted young children with a marshmallow, telling them they could have two of the treats if they put off eating one right away. Follow-up studies performed years later found that the kids who were better able to delay gratification not only achieved higher grades and test scores but were also more likely to succeed in school and their careers.   14

Two years ago, Rosen and his colleagues conducted an information-age version of the marshmallow test. College students who participated in the study were asked to watch a 30-minute videotaped lecture, during which some were sent eight text messages while others were sent four or zero text messages. Those who were interrupted more often scored worse on a test of the lecture's content; more interestingly, those who responded to the experimenters' texts right away scored significantly worse than those participants who waited to reply until the lecture was over.   15

The ability to resist the lure of technology can be consciously cultivated, Rosen maintains. He advises students to take "tech breaks" to satisfy their cravings for electronic communication: After they've labored on their schoolwork uninterrupted for 15 minutes, they can allow themselves two minutes to text, check websites, and post to their hearts' content. Then the devices get turned off for another 15 minutes of academics. Over time, Rosen says, students are able to extend their working time to 20, 30, even 45 minutes, as long as they know that an opportunity to get online awaits. Device-checking is a compulsive behavior that must be managed, he says, if young people are to learn and perform at their best.   16

Understanding the Reading

1. **Main Idea** Explain the author's main point in your own words.
2. **Effects** According to the reading selection, what are some short-term effects of multitasking while studying? What may be some long-term effects?
3. **Comparison** What was the original marshmallow test, and what did it show? How would the new marshmallow test work?

Responding to the Reading

1. **Collecting Data** Explore your media multitasking habits by trying to replicate Larry Rosen's investigation. For one hour while you are studying, use the following categories to mark down once every fifteen minutes what you are doing as you study:

- ☐ reading a book
- ☐ writing on paper
- ☐ typing on the computer
- ☐ playing computer games
- ☐ reading and writing texts
- ☐ posting or liking posts on Instagram or Snapchat (or another social media site)
- ☐ watching television or streaming videos
- ☐ listening to music
- ☐ surfing the Web

2. **Analysis** At the end of the hour, analyze your findings.
   - What percentage of your one-hour study time did you devote to studying?
   - How long were you able to go without a distraction?
   - What was your primary distraction?
3. **Assessment** Write a paragraph or two explaining how well you think you "learned" what you were studying and what lessons you will take away from this exercise. What changes will you make in your study habits (if any), and how will you make them?

Adopt Success Strategies for All Your Courses

"The New Marshmallow Test" showed that focusing on what you're studying both inside and outside the classroom contributes significantly to your success in college. There are also other strategies for college success that will help you read, write, and learn more effectively and efficiently. These strategies are presented in this section.

Use Effective Learning Strategies

The more you know about how learning works, the easier learning becomes. The following section summarizes some tried-and-true, practical learning strategies based on verbal learning theory. Applying them will make many tasks you face in college easier—especially those in your writing classes.

Focus your attention. As you learned from reading "The New Marshmallow Test" at the beginning of the chapter, you cannot learn if your mind is wandering. Use the following strategies to direct your concentration to the task at hand:

- **Work at peak periods of attention.** Identify the time of day or night that you are most efficient and focused. Avoid working when you are tired, hungry, or distracted, if you can.
- **Vary your activities.** Do not complete, say, three reading assignments consecutively. Instead, alternate assignments: for example, read, then write, then work on math problems, then read another assignment, and so on. Use writing to keep you mentally alert and physically active. Highlight, annotate, and take notes as you read.

- **Don't work too long on any given task.** It is better to space out your study. Don't work on an essay draft for four hours. You will accomplish more if you spread out your work into two, two-hour sessions.
- **Challenge yourself with goals and deadlines.** Before beginning an assignment, estimate how long it should take and work toward completing it within that time limit.
- **Keep a to-do list.** When you are working on an assignment, stray thoughts about other pressing things (getting your car repaired, planning a birthday party for your mother) are bound to zip through your mind. When these thoughts occur to you, jot them down so that you can unclutter your mind and get back to work.

Reward yourself.   As Professor Rosen (in "The New Marshmallow Test") suggests, use a fun activity, such as texting a friend or getting a snack, as a reward for reaching your goal or completing your assignment.

See the Just-in-Time Guide to Reading and Responding following Chapter 3 for more help with deciding what to learn.

Decide what to learn and how to learn it.   It is difficult to learn something unless you intend to. Try drawing the front of a one-dollar bill. Most likely you could not provide much detail. Why? You never intended to learn it, despite the many bills you have handled.

You cannot learn every detail in this or any other textbook. Learning will occur more easily if you decide what you need to focus on. Some instructors may help you decide what is important by providing grading rubrics that make the criteria of evaluation clear. Others may not, but you can develop your own sense of what strong and weak work looks like by asking your instructor for examples and then making a list of the features that make one piece of writing work better than another.

Learning theory shows that you shouldn't learn everything the same way. You shouldn't study mathematics the same way you study art history. Similarly, you may not write an essay for your composition class the same way you would write a lab report for your biology class. Analyze each writing assignment you are given; understand the *genre*, or type of writing, you are expected to produce; and decide the best strategies to complete it.

Use metacognition.   Metacognition is self-awareness of how your reading, writing, and learning is going. It involves monitoring and assessing what is working and what is not, and experimenting with approaches to learning. Writing is a gradual process, but you will learn to write better if you are aware of strategies that work and those that don't. While writing, take time to ask yourself whether what you are doing is producing the results you expect. If not, make changes. You may discover, for example, that when planning an essay, outlining is too rigid but free-flowing brainstorming works much better.

For more about mapping and outlining, see "Discovering Ideas to Write About" in Chapter 4 and "Organizing Your Supporting Details" in Chapter 7.

Group and organize information.   New information is more easily learned if it is organized or grouped into chunks. The graphic organizers used throughout this book (see Graphic Organizer 11.2, p. 246) help you see an essay as a whole, rather than as numerous individual pieces. Outlining and mapping or clustering are also effective means of organizing information.

Practice, review, and respond.   Rereading and rote memorization are two of the most ineffective ways to learn. Instead, interact with the information by applying it, discussing it, and evaluating it. The writing activities throughout this book enable you to learn writing skills through practice, review, and response. Peer review (assessing your writing and that of your classmates) is another tool that can help you hone your skills for assessing your own writing.

For more about peer review, see Chapter 8.

Activate prior knowledge.   It is difficult to store new, unfamiliar pieces of information in your memory and then retrieve them when needed. Activating prior knowledge can help you connect new learning to something that you already know. That's why previewing techniques such as asking and answering questions based on the headings in a reading selection aid learning. You can also connect a new essay you are reading with something you've experienced or learned about in another class. For example, if you are reading an essay on language change and the evolution of new words entering the English language, you might think of the new and recently coined terms you just learned in a computer science class. In this book, the headnotes that precede each reading provide helpful background information.

For more about this topic, see the "Preview" section (p. 22) in Chapter 2.

Synthesize your learning.   **Synthesis** is a way to extend and reinforce your learning. It means pulling together ideas from your reading assignments, your class lectures, and your own experience. It involves analyzing similar or competing ideas and using them to extend or challenge your understanding. It may also involve connecting ideas to your own experience to see the practical consequences of an idea. For example, if after reading "The New Marshmallow Test" earlier in this chapter you considered your own media multitasking or completed the checklist in the "Responding to the Reading" section, then you were synthesizing the reading with your own experience. During a biology class lecture on genetics, you might write a note connecting the topic of trait inheritance with your personal family history. In an American history class, you might read a letter from a freed slave, a diary of a plantation owner, and a speech by an abolitionist and then write about what life as an enslaved person was like prior to the Civil War.

Use Your Course Syllabus

The most important document you will receive in your first week of class is your course **syllabus**, a document that describes how the course operates and directs you through your class. A typical syllabus includes information on required texts, attendance and plagiarism policies, the grading system, course objectives, weekly assignments or readings, due dates, and dates of exams. A sample syllabus is shown in Figure 1.1. Here are some tips for using a syllabus to maximize your learning and your course grade:

- **Read the syllabus carefully at the beginning of the course.** Check it regularly so that you are prepared for class.
- **Ask your instructor any questions you may have about the syllabus, course structure, deadlines, and expectations about course objectives.** Note the answers on the syllabus or in your course notebook.

- **Mark all deadlines on your planner, including the intermediate dates you will need to meet your deadlines.** For example, include not only the due date for a paper, but also the date by which you will need to complete the research and the date by which you will need to complete the first draft in order to have time to revise thoughtfully.
- **Pay close attention to the course objectives.** These outline what you are expected to learn in the course. Papers and exams will measure how well you meet them.
- **Make sure you can access the syllabus.** Print a copy and keep it in your notebook or save a copy on your computer, tablet, or smartphone.

FIGURE 1.1   Excerpted Sample Syllabus for a College Writing Course

I. General Information

Course Title: English Composition I	*Course Number:* ENG 161	*Semester:* Fall
Instructor: John Gillam	*Phone:* (724) 555-7890	
Email: gillam@indiana.edu	*Office Hours & Location:* MWF 3–5 English Department offices in Ryan Hall	

This is a good way to contact your instructor.

Important: Be sure to use them.

II. Text

McWhorter, Kathleen T. *Successful College Writing.* 8th ed., Bedford, 2021.

III. General Course Objectives

Planning and organizing are expected.

1. The student will learn to organize his or her thoughts into a meaningful written work.

2. The student will easily recognize and correct grammatical mistakes.

Learning to write for an academic audience is important.

3. The student will become familiar with the conventions of academic writing.

4. The student will be able to read and respond critically to print and digital text.

You will be graded on these.

IV. Specific Course Objectives

Learn these strategies.

1. The student will write papers using the following strategies: description, illustration, process analysis, comparison and contrast, classification and division, and cause and effect.

Correctness counts: Allow time for proofreading.

2. The student will edit and proofread for errors in grammar, punctuation, mechanics, and spelling.

Read assignments carefully.

3. The student will be tested on reading comprehension.

Learn about documentation.

4. The student will write a research paper using appropriate documentation.

5. The student will critically analyze readings that use specific writing strategies.

6. The student will use the Internet as a tool for research.

EXERCISE 1.1 ▸ **GETTING THE MOST FROM YOUR SYLLABUS**

Review the syllabus that your writing class instructor distributed. Write a paragraph describing your expectations and concerns about your writing course based on the syllabus. Be sure to answer the following questions:

1. What are you expected to learn in the course?
2. What kinds of essays will you write?
3. What are the grading and attendance policies?
4. Is class participation expected and required? Is it part of your grade?
5. Is research required? Is Internet use required or expected?

V. Classroom Procedures

Absences: The student is responsible for attendance. Attendance affects performance, and all students are expected to take part in class discussions and peer-review sessions. Each student is expected to be present and is responsible for class notes and assignments. If absent, the student is responsible for arranging an appointment with the instructor to discuss the notes and assignments missed.

Attendance is essential.

Format for papers: Papers must be typed double-spaced using a 12-point font. Be sure to keep a copy of each assignment for yourself.

VI. Disability Statement

If you need to have special arrangements made due to a physical or learning disability, please notify the instructor as soon as possible. (Disclosure of the type of disability is not required.)

Don't hesitate to ask for needed services.

VII. Grading

All papers must be turned in on the due date. Late papers will be lowered one letter grade. No papers will be accepted after the last day of class. If you do not understand the grade assigned to a paper, see me immediately. You are encouraged to save all papers in a folder to enable you to keep track of progress and compute your own grade.

Meeting deadlines is essential.

The instructor encourages questions.

Keep a copy of assignments.

VIII. Tentative Schedule

Week of Sept. 3:	Course Introduction
	Ch. 1 (Reading and Writing for College Success)
	Ch. 2 (Active Reading and Responding)
Week of Sept. 10:	Writing Assessments
	Ch. 3 (Thinking, Reading, and Writing Critically)
	Ch. 4 (Prewriting)
	Ch. 5 (Developing and Supporting a Thesis)
Week of Sept. 17:	Ch. 7 (Drafting an Essay)
	Ch. 12 (Description)
	Draft of Essay #1 due
Week of Sept. 24:	Ch. 13 (Illustration)
	Draft of Essay #2 due

Read these chapters the first week. Your instructor may not remind you of reading assignments or due dates, so check the syllabus weekly.

Writing assignments are noted.

Avoid Procrastination

Procrastination is putting off things that need to be done; you know you should work on an assignment, but you do something else instead. To avoid procrastination, try these tips:

- Develop a schedule at the beginning of each week in which you allot time to complete each assignment due that week.
- Divide each task into manageable parts.
- Avoid making excuses. It is easy to say you don't have enough time to get everything done, but often that is not true.
- Avoid escaping into routine tasks such as shopping, cleaning, or doing your laundry rather than completing the task.

Demonstrate Academic Integrity

Demonstrating academic integrity means conducting yourself in an honest and ethical manner. It involves avoiding the obvious forms of classroom dishonesty such as copying homework, buying a paper on the Internet, and cheating on exams or helping others do so. It also means not plagiarizing, using the ideas or language of others—deliberately or unintentionally—without giving credit. An example of intentional plagiarism is cutting and pasting information into your paper from the Internet without indicating that it is borrowed. Unintentional plagiarism occurs when you use language too similar to that of the original source, inadvertently omit a citation, or forget to place quotation marks around a quotation.

To learn how to avoid unintentional plagiarism, see "Avoid Plagiarism" in Chapter 23.

Consult Your Instructors

Don't be afraid to take advantage of your instructor's office hours. Most instructors will happily work with you to understand a reading or an assignment and to provide information on research, academic decisions, and careers in their fields. But you need to take the initiative. Find out when your instructors hold office hours, and if invited, use their email addresses to communicate.

Listen Carefully, Take Notes, and Participate in Class

Classroom participation involves both listening and speaking. Because you learn so much through listening, learning to listen carefully and critically—grasping what is said and discussing, questioning, and responding to what you hear—is a crucial success strategy.

Listen carefully and critically. Did you know that you can process information faster than speakers can speak? As a result, your mind has time to wander while listening. Try using the following suggestions to maintain your attention in the classroom and prepare to respond:

- **Focus on the lecture.** Arrive promptly for class, shut off distracting media (your phone and your Web applications), sit toward the front of the room (not among a group of friends), and maintain eye contact with the speaker—all will make you feel more involved and less likely to drift off mentally.
- **Try to anticipate the ideas the speaker will address next.** Doing so will keep your mind active.

- **Maintain an open mind.** It is easy to shut out ideas and opinions that do not conform to your own values and beliefs. Try to avoid evaluating a message as positive or negative until it is complete and understandable, and strive to understand the speaker's viewpoint, even if you think you disagree.
- **Identify and assess the speaker's main point and key supporting evidence.** Once you've identified the speaker's thesis, or main point—it is likely to be repeated in different forms throughout the presentation—consider the speaker's reasons and evidence: Has enough support been supplied? Is the evidence relevant? Are the reasons logical?
- **Take notes.** Create an informal outline to keep track of the key points and the main reasons and evidence the speaker offers. After class, flesh out your notes while your memory is fresh.

Participate in class. You can learn more from your classes if you participate fully in class. Ask questions when you need information and clarification, and answer questions posed by the instructor to demonstrate and evaluate your knowledge and express interest in the class. Use the following tips to strengthen your questioning and answering skills:

- **As you read assignments, jot down questions to ask in class—don't worry if they seem silly or unimportant.** Bring your list to class, and use it when your instructor invites questions. And don't apologize for asking; other students probably have the same questions but are reluctant to ask them.
- **Speak out.** Stop worrying about what your friends and classmates will think. If you're nervous about participating in class, composing your response before volunteering to answer may give you confidence.
- **Focus on critical questions.** Instead of asking factual questions, think about how the information can be used, how ideas fit together, how things work, what might be relevant problems and solutions, or what the long-term value and significance of the information are.

EXERCISE 1.2   IMPROVING YOUR LISTENING AND CLASS-PARTICIPATION SKILLS

Review the advice given above. Then choose at least three points to apply in the next two lectures you attend for one of your other courses. Finally, write a paragraph reflecting on what you learned from the experience.

EXERCISE 1.3   WORKING TOGETHER

Working with a classmate, brainstorm a list of questions you could ask about the content presented in this chapter.

Learn to Manage Stress

Stress is a natural reaction to the challenges of daily living, but if you are expected to accomplish more or perform better than you think you can, stress can become overwhelming. As a successful student, you need to monitor your stress. Take the "How Stressed Are You?" quiz on the next page to assess your stress level.

Quiz: How Stressed Are You?	Always	Sometimes	Never
1. I worry that I do not have enough time to get everything done.	☐	☐	☐
2. I regret that I have no time to do fun things each week.	☐	☐	☐
3. I find myself losing track of details and forgetting due dates, promises, and appointments.	☐	☐	☐
4. I worry about what I am doing.	☐	☐	☐
5. I have conflicts or disagreements with friends or family.	☐	☐	☐
6. I lose patience over small annoyances.	☐	☐	☐
7. I seem to be late, no matter how hard I try to arrive on time.	☐	☐	☐
8. I have difficulty sleeping.	☐	☐	☐
9. My eating habits have changed.	☐	☐	☐
10. I find myself needing a cigarette, drink, or prescription drug.	☐	☐	☐

You can use stress to motivate yourself to start a project or assignment, or you can let it interfere with your ability to function mentally and physically. If you answered "Always" or "Sometimes" to more than two or three items in the "How Stressed Are You?" quiz, you may be reacting to stress negatively. Here are some effective ways to change your thinking and habits to reduce stress:

- **Establish your priorities.** If college is more important than your part-time job, for example, request a work schedule to accommodate your study schedule. If someone asks you to take on an extra shift that will cut into study time, be selfish and say no.
- **Simplify your life by making fewer choices.** For example, instead of deciding what time to set your alarm clock each morning, get up at the same time each weekday.
- **Focus on the positive.** Instead of saying, "I'll never be able to finish this assignment on time," ask yourself, "What do I have to do to finish this assignment on time?"
- **Separate work, school, and social problems.** Create mental compartments for your worries. Don't spend class time thinking about a work problem. Deal with problems at the appropriate time.
- **Keep a personal journal.** Relieve stress by writing down your worries, but include notes about how you can resolve those problems, too.

Manage Online Courses Responsibly

Online courses are convenient, but they require more self-direction and ability to work alone than face-to-face classes do. Here are some tips for succeeding in online courses:

- **If possible, avoid taking online courses during your first term in college.** Once you are familiar with college expectations, you will be better prepared to take an online course.
- **Study for online courses as you do for face-to-face classes.** Most students who fail online courses do so because they fall hopelessly behind on reading and assignments. Even if a class does not meet at a specified time, build study time for the course into your schedule to avoid procrastinating on classwork.
- **Plan on doing a lot of reading and writing.** In addition to reading assignments and papers, you will also need to read posts from your professor and other students and contribute to written class "discussions."
- **Write thoughtful posts, and use appropriate language online.** Make it easy for classmates and your instructor to read your posts. Think through what you want to say, and use correct spelling and grammar. Besides adding your own ideas, respond to earlier posts, and be polite, even when you disagree with an earlier comment. Finally, be sure to reread your comments before posting them.

Don't Let Nonacademic Problems Interfere with Success

The reason large numbers of students drop out of college has nothing to do with academics. These students would be able to handle the work if only nonacademic problems—from erratic work schedules and child-care difficulties to financial problems and family conflicts—did not interfere. These kinds of problems can result in missing classes or coming to class unprepared and failing to turn in assignments on time (or at all), which can all lead to low grades.

Your campus does have resources to help you. If personal problems are interfering with your performance at school, the first thing to do is talk to your instructors. Once they understand your circumstances, most instructors will do everything they can to help you succeed. Then seek help from student services, such as the financial aid office, the health center, the counseling center, and commuter service centers. These services are usually free. (You are already paying for them through your tuition.) Your campus's Web site will list the services available and indicate where to find them.

Academic Reading and Writing: What Should You Expect?

An important part of doing well with any task is knowing ahead of time what it involves. The list below explains expectations for reading and writing in college.

- **Expect your reading and writing to become less personal and more academic.** Most of your reading and writing in college will be informative or persuasive.

Informative writing presents information in an objective, nonpersonal way; **persuasive writing** attempts to convince readers to act or to understand a text or an event in a certain way.

For help with revising, see Chapter 8; for help with editing and proofreading, see Chapter 9 and the Handbook at the back of this book. See the Just-in-Time Guide for suggestions on learning vocabulary.

- **Expect to read and write in different forms, or genres.** Academic reading and writing assignments may include specialized types, or **genres**, from scholarly articles and scientific studies to abstracts and research projects. Each genre has its own conventions. For example, lab reports have a specific purpose (to report the results of a laboratory experiment), format (including sections with headings such as *Introduction, Materials and Methods, Results/Data,* and *Conclusions*), and style of writing (brief, factual, and concise). As you encounter new genres, study samples that can serve as models for your own writing.
- **Expect to use standard American English and the language of the discipline.** College students are generally expected to avoid slang, present their ideas clearly and accurately, and write in complete and grammatically correct sentences. They are also expected to understand and use the specialized vocabulary of the field, words like *photosynthesis* and *homeostasis* in biology, or *allegory* and *personification* in literature. You may need to consult a specialized dictionary, encyclopedia, or database for help with unfamiliar terms.

For more on reading actively and critically, see Chapters 2 and 3.

- **Expect to read, write, and think critically.** In college, instructors will expect you to go beyond merely repeating what you hear in class or read in the textbook; they will expect you to demonstrate understanding by being able to draw your own inferences based on what you have learned; synthesize, or combine, information to support your ideas; and apply ideas to new situations.

For guidance in identifying, locating, using, and citing scholarly sources, see Part 5.

- **Expect to read, use, and document scholarly sources.** Instructors expect you to locate and use books and articles written by experts and published in scholarly journals and by university presses. Whether you quote, summarize, or paraphrase words and ideas from sources, your instructors will expect you to credit them by including an in-text citation and a list of works cited (or references).

Why Improve Your Reading and Writing Skills?

Most college students ask themselves these two questions:

1. How can I improve my grades?
2. How can I improve my chances of getting a good job after college?

The answer to both questions is the same: Improve your reading and writing skills. Here are three reasons why doing so will be worth the time and effort:

1. **Reading and writing help you learn and remember.** In general, the more senses you use in learning, the more easily you learn and the more you will remember. You take in information visually while reading, and you engage your sense of touch as you put your pen to paper while writing. (Evidence suggests that

handwriting is more effective than typing at solidifying memory.) Taking notes, outlining, summarizing, and annotating enhance learning by engaging your attention and getting you to think about the subject matter as you connect, define, and evaluate ideas.

2. **Reading and writing help you think and solve problems.** Reading makes the ideas of experts available to you, and writing forces you to think through issues in a sustained way, define issues or problems, and see new aspects of them. For example, one student had a father-in-law who seemed hostile and uncooperative. The student described her problem in an email to a friend: "He looks at me as if I'm going to take his son to the end of the earth and never bring him back." When she reread what she had written, she realized that her father-in-law might resent her because he was afraid of losing contact with his son. She looked for ways to reassure her father-in-law and strengthen their relationship. Writing about the problem helped the student define it and discover ways to solve it.

3. **Reading and writing skills enable you to communicate effectively.** Employers consistently want the "total package"—both technical knowledge *and* strong oral and written communication skills—in recent college graduates. Why? Because in almost all jobs, you can expect to read and write plenty of letters, email messages, and reports to customers, colleagues, and supervisors. Because your writing course offers both immediate and long-range benefits, it is one of the most important college courses you will take.

Adopt Success Strategies for Your Writing Class

You have already learned some general strategies for success in college. The section below presents strategies that will help you in your writing class.

Start with a Positive Attitude toward Reading and Writing

You have the ability to be a strong reader and a successful writer. To approach your writing course with a positive attitude and get the most out of it, use the following suggestions:

1. **Think of reading and writing as processes.** Reading a complex text requires more than just reading it through once; it requires prereading, annotating, and critical analysis to understand it fully. Writing, too, is not a single act of getting words down on paper. It is a series of steps—planning, organizing, drafting, revising, and editing and proofreading—all of which can be done in whatever order makes sense and repeated as needed. (Most writers go back and forth among these steps.)

2. **Be patient.** Writing improves with practice. On some days, writing will be easier than on other days, but as you draft and revise your essays, your writing will improve in small ways that build on one another. Build in extra time for completing writing assignments.

3. **Understand how your instructor will assess your writing.** Some instructors may have a rubric, or list of characteristics with examples at different levels of success; others may be willing to share past examples of successful writing.

Use the College Writing Center

Writing centers generally provide trained student tutors and professional staff, who may help you do the following:

- understand an assignment
- analyze a reading selection
- organize your ideas
- revise a draft
- use appropriate format and documentation
- understand errors on a graded paper

However, do not expect them to interpret a reading, write your paper, or correct all of its errors. When you visit the writing center, be sure to bring the following:

- your assignment
- all drafts of your essay
- any articles or essays to which the assignment refers
- paper and pen or pencil

Get the Most out of Writing Conferences

Many writing instructors require writing conferences with individual students to discuss the student's work and his or her progress in the course. If the conferences are optional, be sure to schedule one.

The following tips will help you get the most out of a writing conference:

1. **Reread recently returned papers and notes from previous conferences ahead of time.** Your instructor's comments should be fresh in your mind.

2. **Arrive prepared and be on time or a few minutes early.** Bring copies of the essay you are currently working on, as well as previously graded papers.

3. **Allow your instructor to set the agenda.** Still, you should be prepared to ask questions.

4. **Take notes on your instructor's comments and suggestions.** Take them during the conference, if doing so is not distracting, or immediately after.

5. **Revise the draft essay you and your instructor discussed.** The revision will go most smoothly if you revise while your instructor's suggestions are still fresh in your mind.

Keep a Writing Journal

Keeping a **writing journal** will help improve your writing by giving you a judgment-free place to practice and an opportunity to reflect on what you're learning. In your journal, you can experiment with voice, topics, or approaches to a topic; comment on a reading selection or assignment; record your impressions and observations; or explore relationships among people or ideas. It can also be a good source of topics for writing assignments. Here's how to get started:

1. **Write in a spiral-bound notebook or create a computer file.** Date each entry.
2. **Set aside five to ten minutes for journal writing each day.** You don't need a long block of time; instead, you can write while waiting for a bus or for class to start.
3. **Concentrate on capturing your ideas, not on being grammatically correct.** Try to write correct sentences, but don't focus on grammar and punctuation.

WRITING ACTIVITY 1

Write a journal entry describing your reaction to something you learned in one or more of your classes this term. For example, you might write about how you could apply it or how it relates to something else you already know about.

2

Active Reading and Responding

GILLES SABRIE/The New York Times/Redux

Writing Quick Start

ANALYZE   Assume you saw this photo with the caption "A Street in China: Technology at Work" on an online news site. What technology does the photo illustrate? What feelings does it elicit? What issues does it raise? What information does the caption add?

WRITE   After you have studied the photograph, draft a paragraph explaining its relevance to the lives of Chinese citizens. Be specific in your response.

CONNECT   To explain the photograph, you had to think beyond the obvious. You first had to understand that the photo depicted East Asian people—from children to the aged—being subjected to facial recognition software. Then you had to consider the caption: "A street in China: technology at work." The caption tells you that this facial recognition technology is "at work" in China, but it does not tell you the nature of this "work." You need to put all these details together to decide on the main point of the photograph and perhaps read the article to learn what kind of work the software is being put to.

Reading words involves a similar process of comprehension and evaluation. You must not only understand what the author *says*, but you must also determine what the author *means*. Both parts of the process are essential. This chapter will focus on understanding, interpreting, and responding to what you read, while Chapter 3 will consider how to analyze, evaluate, and think critically about the text and images you read.

A Guide to Active Reading

To read effectively, especially on the college level, students must engage words actively to understand how they work together to express ideas. To clarify the distinction between active and passive, think of sports fans watching a game. Diehard fans cheer some players and boo others, evaluate plays and calls, and shout out advice. By contrast, nonfans let the game take its course with little or no personal involvement or reaction and may well not even recall the score after the game is over.

HOW WRITERS READ ▶ ACTIVE VERSUS PASSIVE READING		
	PASSIVE READING	**ACTIVE READING**
BEFORE READING	Passive readers simply begin reading without considering the author or topic.	Active readers preview, or familiarize themselves with, the text; they think about what they already know about the author and subject; and they form questions to guide their reading.
WHILE READING	Passive readers read without asking themselves questions about what they're reading and without engaging actively with the text.	Active readers read the essay while looking for answers to questions and key elements, and they highlight key points and work to understand passages they find challenging.
AFTER READING	Passive readers simply close the book when they're finished and most likely forget most of the details they have read.	Active readers check and consolidate their learning and make connections by reviewing headings and highlights, paraphrasing difficult passages, and drawing graphic organizers.

Like fans of a sports team, active readers get involved with the material they read. They become active participants by questioning, thinking about, and reacting to ideas using the process outlined in Graphic Organizer 2.1. In fact, it is this kind of active involvement in what they read that helps effective readers understand and remember a selection long after they finish the page. The sections that follow explain in detail each of the steps in reading actively.

Active readers achieve understanding and recall by engaging with the material *before* they read, *while* they read, and *after* they read. This chapter will explain what to do at each stage, and the readings throughout this book will guide you in applying these techniques at each stage.

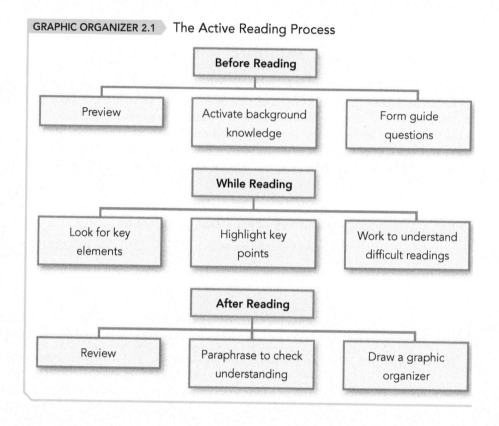

GRAPHIC ORGANIZER 2.1   The Active Reading Process

Before Reading: Write to Preview and Create Guide Questions

To read actively, start your reading by preparing your mind: Preview the selection and write guide questions to help you discover what the reading is about and focus your mind on the topic.

Preview

Previewing is a quick way of familiarizing yourself with an essay's content and organization. It helps you decide what you need to learn, and it has a number of other benefits as well:

- It helps you get interested in the material.
- It helps you concentrate on the material because you have a mental outline of it before you begin reading and therefore know what to expect.
- It helps you remember more of what you read.

To preview a reading selection, use these guidelines:

1. **Read the title, subtitle, headnote, and author.** The title and subtitle may tell you what the reading is about. Check the author's name to see if it is one you recognize. Read the headnote to glean important background information about the author, topic, and publication in which the reading originally appeared.
2. **Read the introduction or the first paragraph.** These sections often provide an overview of the selection.
3. **Read any headings and the first sentence following each one.** Taken together, headings often form a mini-outline of the selection. The first sentence following a heading often explains the heading further.
4. **For selections without headings, read the first sentence in a few of the paragraphs on each page.**
5. **Look at the photographs, tables, charts, and drawings.**
6. **Read the conclusion or summary.** A conclusion draws the selection to a close and may repeat the main idea (or thesis) of the essay and the key supporting ideas, providing a summary.
7. **Read any end-of-assignment questions.** These questions will help focus your attention on what is important and what you might be expected to know after you have read it.

Remember to read *only* the parts of an essay that are listed. The following essay has been highlighted to illustrate the parts you should read while previewing. Preview it now.

`READING`

American Jerk: Be Civil, or I'll Beat You to a Pulp

Todd Schwartz

Todd Schwartz is a writer based in Portland, Oregon. A longer version of this essay originally appeared in the *Oregon Humanities Review* in 2008 under the title "The Great Civility War." The version below was published in 2009 in the *Utne Reader.*

It was the most civil of times, it was the least civil of times, it was the age of politeness, it was the age of boorishness, it was the epoch of concern, it was the epoch of who cares, it was the season of hybrid, it was the season of Hummer, it was the spring of Obama, it was the winter of hate speech . . . 1

With apologies to Mr. Dickens (or not: screw him), we have arrived at simultaneously the most and least civil moment in U.S. history. A moment when a roomful of even relatively evolved people will react with discomfort to an off-color joke about people of color—and when those same people have no compunction whatsoever about loudly ignoring one another as they blather into their cell phones. 2

We have never been more concerned about the feelings of minority groups, the disabled, and the disadvantaged. Yet we have never been less concerned about the feelings of anyone with whom we share the road, the Internet, or the movie theater. 3

Political correctness holds such sway that holidays go unnamed for fear of insulting or excluding someone. Schools won't let teachers use red pens to correct papers, because little Ethan's or Emily's self-esteem might be bruised. No one is 4

Corbis/VCG/Getty Images

"poor," but many are "socioeconomically disad-vantaged." Civility and thoughtfulness in speech have never been so complete or so codified.

All of which is well intentioned and mostly a wonderful thing. I'm all for being polite and caring and Golden Rule-ish. Sadly, like a lovely field of wildflowers—which in reality is filled with blood-sucking ticks and noxious pollen—we live oh-so-politely in what must certainly be the rud-est era in recorded history. Maybe even prehistory. 5

Neanderthals were probably nicer to each other than we are. 6

Pick your poison: reality television, slasher movies, video games, online porn, cell phones, automated answering systems, giant assault vehicles for trips to the grocery store, car stereos played at volumes easily heard on Jupiter, web-powered copyright infringement, people who will not shut their inane traps in movie theaters, and, lord help us, now even people who won't shut their inane traps during live theater. 7

We're all talking to someone all the time, but it's ever more rarely to the people we are actually with. Our cell phones blare ringtones that no one else wants to hear. We love to watch TV shows about the stunningly predictable results of hand-feeding a grizzly bear or lighting a stick of dynamite with a cigarette. We also love shows where people lie to others for money and programs where snarky, slightly talented folks say vicious things to hopeful, and usually more talented, contestants. 8

Civility rules, friends. 9

Civility is dead, jerks. 10

Why? I have a few theories. 11

The first is that America is in the same position as Rome found itself in about 420 CE, meaning that we've reached the peak of our civilization and now everything is going to Tartarus in a chariot. We're too far from our food and energy sources, and fewer and fewer of the Druids and Visigoths like us anymore. So we desperately cling to a patina of civility while we grab a snack and watch large, toothy predators devour people. 12

The second is that sunlight contains tiny spores that lodge in the cerebellum, making the infected believe they are the center of the universe. 13

My final and somewhat less cutting edge theory is that a large percentage of people are just clueless, distracted, and self-absorbed, unable to process concepts such as spatial awareness (for example: when you are walking in the same direc-tion with several hundred people in, say, an airport terminal, DON'T JUST STOP IN THE MIDDLE OF THE FLOW!). 14

But I digress. 15

I am not here to judge whether being civil and considerate is somehow better than being a mindless dillweed. You must make that choice for yourself. We inhabit the most civil of times and the least—and I completely honor and respect your freedom to choose your side in the Great Civility War. 16

Just don't get in my way. I'm on my cell in the Escalade, and I can't be bothered. 17

| EXERCISE 2.1 | TESTING YOUR RECALL AFTER PREVIEWING |

Based only on your preview of the essay "American Jerk," indicate whether each of the following statements is true or false. If most of your answers are correct, you will know that previewing helped you gain a sense of the essay's context and organization. (For the answers to this exercise, see the last page in this chapter.)

_____ 1. The reading is primarily about civility and the lack of it.
_____ 2. The author blames the Internet for our society's lack of civility.
_____ 3. The author suggests that political correctness does not go far enough.
_____ 4. People are often not intentionally rude but simply are distracted or unaware.
_____ 5. Society is unconcerned about minorities.

Activate Your Background Knowledge and Experience

After previewing, take time to discover what you already know or have experienced about the topic. For example, after previewing the essay in Chapter 1 on multitasking, think of how and when you multitask and whether it has helped you to be (or hindered you from being) productive and efficient. Think of situations when you have observed others multitasking and whether it seemed effective. Activating your prior knowledge will make the reading more meaningful, more interesting, and easier to remember.

| EXERCISE 2.2 | ACTIVATING YOUR KNOWLEDGE AND EXPERIENCE |

Activate your knowledge and experience about the ideas presented in "American Jerk" by listing three situations that demonstrate civility or the lack of it.

Form Questions to Guide Your Reading

Asking and answering questions will strengthen your comprehension and recall of the material. Before you begin reading, devise questions about the selection based on sections you previewed. Then, as you read, answer those questions. The following examples will help you start devising your own questions:

Essay Titles	Questions
"Part-Time Employment Undermines Students' Commitment to School"	Why does part-time employment undermine commitment to school?
"Human Cloning: Don't Just Say 'No'"	What are good reasons to clone humans?

Headings	
"Types of Territoriality"	What are the types of territoriality?
"Territorial Encroachment"	What is territorial encroachment, and how does it occur?

Not all essays lend themselves to these techniques. In some essays, you may need to dig deeper into the introductory and final paragraphs to form questions. Look again at your preview of "American Jerk." Using the introductory paragraphs of that essay, you might decide to look for answers to this question: *Why is the author, Todd Schwartz, negative toward Americans?*

EXERCISE 2.3   **FORMING GUIDE QUESTIONS**

List three questions that you expect to be able to answer after reading "American Jerk."

While Reading: Write to Think and Interact with the Text

While you are reading, be sure to think about and interact with the reading, figuring out which ideas are important and which are less so by

For more about annotating, see "Generate and Record Ideas" later in this chapter.

See the Just-in-Time Guide for tips on mastering challenging words and expanding your vocabulary.

- identifying and examining key elements
- highlighting key points
- making marginal notes, called *annotations*, about any ideas that occur to you (Annotation may be done more completely on a second read, after you have finished reading, understand the gist, and are ready to delve deeper.)

As you read, figure out the meaning of unfamiliar vocabulary and be prepared to strengthen your comprehension of challenging reading assignments.

Look for Key Elements

As you read, pay particular attention to the following key elements:

For more about introductions and conclusions, see Chapter 7.

For more about thesis statements, see Chapter 5.

To learn more about topic sentences and supporting details, see Chapter 6.

1. **The title and subtitle.** Although you read these while previewing, now examine them to determine how the title and subtitle relate to the subject and what they reveal about the author's point of view.
2. **The introduction.** The opening paragraph or paragraphs often provide background information, announce the topic, and grab the reader's attention.
3. **The author's main point.** Look for a **thesis statement** that directly expresses the one big idea that the essay explains, explores, or supports. Writers often place the thesis in the first or second paragraph to let readers know what lies ahead. But the thesis may appear at the end of an essay or may be implied or suggested rather than stated directly.
4. **The support and explanation.** Usually, each paragraph in the body of an essay supports the author's main point. Look at each paragraph to determine what it is about—the paragraph's main idea may be stated in a **topic sentence**—and

consider how it relates to the thesis. Take note of the kinds of evidence the author supplies, such as facts and statistics, examples, anecdotes, or comparisons.

5. **The conclusion.** The essay's final paragraph or paragraphs often restate the author's main point or offer ideas for further thought.

The parts you examine when you read are those you use when you write. You'll learn much more about each part of an essay in Chapters 4–7.

Now read "American Jerk," paying attention to the marginal notes that identify and explain its various parts.

American Jerk: Be Civil, or I'll Beat You to a Pulp

Todd Schwartz

Todd Schwartz is a writer based in Portland, Oregon. A longer version of this essay originally appeared in the *Oregon Humanities Review* in 2008 under the title "The Great Civility War." The version below was published in 2009 in the *Utne Reader*.

It was the most civil of times, it was the least civil of times, it was the age of politeness, it was the age of boorishness, it was the epoch of concern, it was the epoch of who cares, it was the season of hybrid, it was the season of Hummer, it was the spring of Obama, it was the winter of hate speech . . .

With apologies to Mr. Dickens (or not: screw him), we have arrived at simultaneously the most and least civil moment in U.S. history. A moment when a roomful of even relatively evolved people will react with discomfort to an off-color joke about people of color—and when those same people have no compunction whatsoever about loudly ignoring one another as they blather into their cell phones.

We have never been more concerned about the feelings of minority groups, the disabled, and the disadvantaged. Yet we have never been less concerned about the feelings of anyone with whom we share the road, the Internet, or the movie theater.

Political correctness holds such sway that holidays go unnamed for fear of insulting or excluding someone. Schools won't let teachers use red pens to correct papers, because little Ethan's or Emily's self-esteem might be bruised. No one is "poor," but many are "socioeconomically disadvantaged." Civility and thoughtfulness in speech have never been so complete or so codified.

All of which is well intentioned and mostly a wonderful thing. I'm all for being polite and caring and Golden Rule-ish. Sadly, like a lovely field of wildflowers—which in reality is filled with bloodsucking ticks and noxious pollen—we live oh-so-politely in what must certainly be the rudest era in recorded history. Maybe even prehistory.

Neanderthals were probably nicer to each other than we are.

Pick your poison: reality television, slasher movies, video games, online porn, cell phones, automated answering systems, giant assault vehicles for trips to the

Marginal notes:

Title and subtitle: Suggest idea of conflict over behavior

1   **Introduction:** Illustration suggests contradictory attitudes.

2   **Main idea:** Thesis states main idea and refers to Dickens, who used "It was the best of times, it was the worst of times" in his novel *A Tale of Two Cities*.

3   **Support:** Offers examples of contradictory attitudes toward groups

4

5

6

7   **Support:** Provides examples of rudeness

grocery store, car stereos played at volumes easily heard on Jupiter, web-powered copyright infringement, people who will not shut their inane traps in movie theaters, and, lord help us, now even people who won't shut their inane traps during live theater.

Support: More examples

We're all talking to someone all the time, but it's ever more rarely to the people we are actually with. Our cell phones blare ringtones that no one else wants to hear. We love to watch TV shows about the stunningly predictable results of hand-feeding a grizzly bear or lighting a stick of dynamite with a cigarette. We also love shows where people lie to others for money and programs where snarky, slightly talented folks say vicious things to hopeful, and usually more talented, contestants.   8

Contradictions: Refer back to information and introduce reasons to follow

Civility rules, friends.   9
Civility is dead, jerks.   10
Why? I have a few theories.   11

Support: First reason

The first is that America is in the same position as Rome found itself in about 420 CE, meaning that we've reached the peak of our civilization and now everything is going to Tartarus in a chariot. We're too far from our food and energy sources, and fewer and fewer of the Druids and Visigoths like us anymore. So we desperately cling to a patina of civility while we grab a snack and watch large, toothy predators devour people.   12

Support: Second reason

The second is that sunlight contains tiny spores that lodge in the cerebellum, making the infected believe they are the center of the universe.   13

Support: Third reason

My final and somewhat less cutting edge theory is that a large percentage of people are just clueless, distracted, and self-absorbed, unable to process concepts such as spatial awareness (for example: when you are walking in the same direction with several hundred people in, say, an airport terminal, DON'T JUST STOP IN THE MIDDLE OF THE FLOW!).   14

But I digress.   15

Conclusion: Affirms thesis statement and ends on a humorous note

I am not here to judge whether being civil and considerate is somehow better than being a mindless dillweed. You must make that choice for yourself. We inhabit the most civil of times and the least—and I completely honor and respect your freedom to choose your side in the Great Civility War.   16

Just don't get in my way. I'm on my cell in the Escalade, and I can't be bothered.   17

Highlight Key Points

As you read, you will encounter many new ideas, some more important than others. You will agree with some and disagree with others. Later, as you write about what you have read, you will want to return to the main points to refresh your memory. To locate and remember these points easily, read with a highlighter or pen in hand.

Caution: Highlighting is an active reading strategy *only* when you use it to distinguish important ideas from less important ideas, so be selective. (If you highlight every idea, none will stand out.) The following guidelines will make your highlighting as useful as possible:

1. **Before you begin reading, decide what kinds of information to highlight.** What types of tasks will you do as a result of your reading? Will you write a paper, participate in a class discussion, or take an exam? Think about what you need to know, and tailor your highlighting to the needs of the task.
2. **Read first; then highlight.** First read a paragraph or section; then go back and mark what is important within it. This approach will help you control the tendency to highlight too much.
3. **Highlight key elements, words, and phrases.** Mark the thesis statement, the topic sentence in each paragraph, important terms and definitions, and key words and phrases that relate to the thesis. While you read, you may also want to jot down any ideas that you do not understand or record your own thoughts about the author's ideas. These activities are part of the process of annotation, covered later in the chapter in the section on responding to reading.

EXERCISE 2.4   **HIGHLIGHTING KEY POINTS**

Reread "American Jerk," highlighting as you read.

Work to Understand Difficult Readings

Some readings are straightforward, but much of the reading you'll do in college will be challenging. The subject matter may be complex, the sentences and paragraphs may be long or involved, or the writer may use difficult or unfamiliar vocabulary. Whatever the problem, however, you know you must complete the assignment. The Just-in-Time Guide to Reading and Responding following Chapter 3 provides tips for overcoming challenges in your reading. Dip into it to find useful solutions whenever you find yourself facing reading challenges.

Read Digital Text Differently

A growing body of research demonstrates that online reading is not only strikingly different from reading a printed text; it is also more challenging and needs to be approached with a different set of skills. Consider the following differences between print and online texts:

1. **Print text is linear; digital text is multidirectional.** When reading print text, your eye moves from left to right and top to bottom, with only an occasional photo or

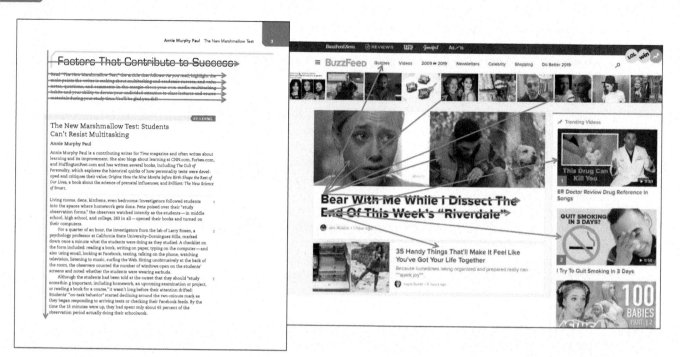

graphic interrupting the flow. Digital text, on the other hand, has images, side-bars, links, and other distractions that encourage you to move around the screen and from screen to screen in just about any order. It is hard to know where to begin reading and where to stop.

2. **Print and digital text differ in the types of reading they encourage.** Online readers tend to skim texts rather than read them. Their eyes move across the top of a page looking for information or interesting bits and then scan down the left edge of the page, noting what appears there. Their eyes tend to skate across the text without really interacting with it or responding to the ideas they encounter. Critical analysis and response suffer, and digital readers tend to forget the details and lose the sequence of ideas and logical structure of an argument. Research substantiates that comprehension is stronger when reading print text than when reading digital text.

3. **Readers of print and digital text face different mental challenges as they read.** While reading, both print and digital readers must decide what is and is not important, but digital readers face decisions that print readers don't. These include

   - whether to ignore the links, follow them now, or check them out later
   - where the most important information appears on the screen
   - what material (like sidebars and ads) can be skipped, should be skimmed, or should be read carefully

   Digital readers, then, often have to work harder to make sense of what they're reading.

4. **Sources are cited differently.** Compare the following excerpts. How do they differ? To cite sources, print text includes footnotes or in-text citations with a list of works cited at the end. In contrast, digital texts often have embedded links that direct readers to additional sources or references, combining reading and research into a single process. While links can be extremely useful and convenient, they also lure readers away from what they are reading, interrupting the flow of ideas and diverting attention from the content at hand.

For more about in-text citations and lists of works cited, see "Document Your Sources: MLA Style" in Chapter 23.

---

3 Success and Likeability

In 2003, then Columbia Business School professor Francis Flynn and New York University professor ~~...~~derson ran an experiment to text ~~...~~ of men and women in the workplace.[1] They ~~...~~ a Harvard Business School case study about a real-life entrepreneur named Heidi Roizen. The case described how Roizen became a successful venture capitalist by using her "outgoing personality . . . and vast personal and professional network [that] included many of the most powerful leaders in the technology sector."[2]

[1] A discussion and analysis of this study were provided by Professor Francis H. Flynn in discussion with the author, June 22, 2011.

[2] To read this case study, see Kathleen McGinn and Nicole Tempest, *Heidi Roizen*, Harvard Business School Case Study #9-900-229 (Boston: Harvard Business School Publishing, 2009).

Print text: Uses footnotes to cite sources

Likability and Success Hardly Go Hand-in-Hand

by Marianne Cooper

APRIL 30, 2013

Save   Share   ❸ Comment   нH Text Size   Print $8.95 Buy Copies

In their blog post, "New Research Shows Success Doesn't Make Women Less Likeable," Jack Zenger and Joseph Folkman conclude . . . that "likeability and success actually go together remarkably well for women." As a sociologist who focuses on gender, work, and family it is always nice for me to hear when things are going well for women at work.

Digital text: Uses links for more information and to cite sources

(*Left*) From Sheryl Sandberg's *Lean In* (2013); (*right*) from *Harvard Business Review* (2013)

Strategies for Reading Digital Text

Because digital text is different from print, it must be read differently. Use these strategies to read digital text actively and critically:

- **Expect to spend as much—or more—time reading digital text.** Since it's more work to read digital text, you'll need to slow down and reread the parts that matter most.

- **Define your purpose for reading and make decisions about what—and how—to read.** Decide what you need to read based on your purpose. Are you reading an article to discuss in class, studying for an exam, or looking for information to support a claim you're making in a research project? If you're looking for a

(continued)

fact or verifying something you already know, you'll read a lot differently than if you're trying to understand, interpret, analyze, or compare.

- **Preview (or browse) before reading online text.** Take a few minutes to understand the page's organization and features before diving in. Decide, too, whether to mentally filter out graphics, inserts, color, and so forth. Remember, these "add-ons" make reading online a more complex mental process.

- **Avoid skipping and skimming.** When you are reading for ideas, rather than to locate a specific fact, read everything as you would in a print text. Read a digital article through once before checking any links. Then decide which, if any, promise to deliver what you need.

- **Remember that reading is not learning.** Check your comprehension as you go and review after reading. Annotate the article if the platform allows (or make notes on paper, if it doesn't). Paraphrasing, taking notes, writing outlines, drawing maps, and summarizing are crucial to retention.

- **Think critically.** It is easy to glide through digital content without analyzing and evaluating the ideas presented. Be sure to subject the information to close scrutiny.

- **Use reputable sources and learn to spot the tell-tale signs of disinformation.** (See "Detect Disinformation" in Chapter 3 and "Evaluate Sources" in Chapter 21.)

EXERCISE 2.5   **READING DIGITAL TEXT**

Imagine you are working on a research paper on artificial intelligence and want to find information on the risks associated with facial recognition software. Find three to four different types of sources on the topic, such as an article from an online magazine or newspaper, a chapter or excerpt from a book, a blog post, and a scholarly article from a database your library subscribes to. (If you need help finding sources, consult Chapter 22 or ask a librarian at your school for help.) Then write a paragraph comparing what you found. You might address the following questions:

a. How do the sources differ in format and layout?
b. Which of the sources include links? Which (if any) include in-text citations to sources? Are the links important and useful in the digital material you located? What about the in-text citations?
c. What sections or portions of the digital page contain the most important information?
d. What sections, if any, did you skip? Why did you decide to skip them?

After Reading: Review and Organize to Consolidate Understanding

When you finish reading an assignment, it may be tempting to close the book, periodical, or browser window and move immediately to another task. However, doing so increases the likelihood that you will forget most of what you have read because you will not have had time to process the material. The following strategies will help get you ready to write about what you have read.

Review to Consolidate Your Understanding

Review immediately after you finish reading to pull all the ideas in the reading together and make them stick in your mind. You will probably also discover more about how the ideas are connected. Reviewing should not take much time; your goal is to touch on each main point one more time, not to embark on a long and thorough study. To review material after reading, use the same steps you used to preview the reading. (See "Before Reading" earlier in this chapter.) Pay particular attention to the following elements:

- the headings
- your highlighting
- your annotations
- the conclusion

Write new annotations about ideas or connections that come to you or become clearer as you review.

Draw a Graphic Organizer to Examine Relationships among Ideas

Think of a graphic organizer as a means of tracking the author's flow of ideas. Your graphic organizer should include all of the key elements of an essay listed on pages 26–27. Graphic Organizer 2.2 shows a sample format for a graphic organizer. A graphic organizer for "American Jerk" appears in Graphic Organizer 2.3. Work through the organizer, rereading the essay paragraph by paragraph at the same time.

Paraphrase to Check Your Understanding

Earlier in the chapter you learned to form questions to guide your reading. The process of **paraphrasing** key passages—answering your guide questions by putting ideas and information from the text into your own words and sentences—will help you check your understanding: If you are unable to restate what you have read in fresh words and sentences, you probably do not fully understand it.

For more about paraphrasing, see Chapter 22.

GRAPHIC ORGANIZER 2.2   Key Elements to Include

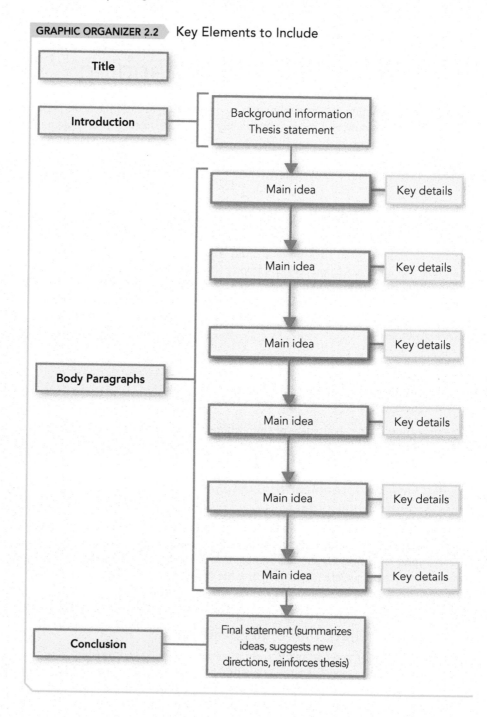

GRAPHIC ORGANIZER 2.3 "American Jerk"

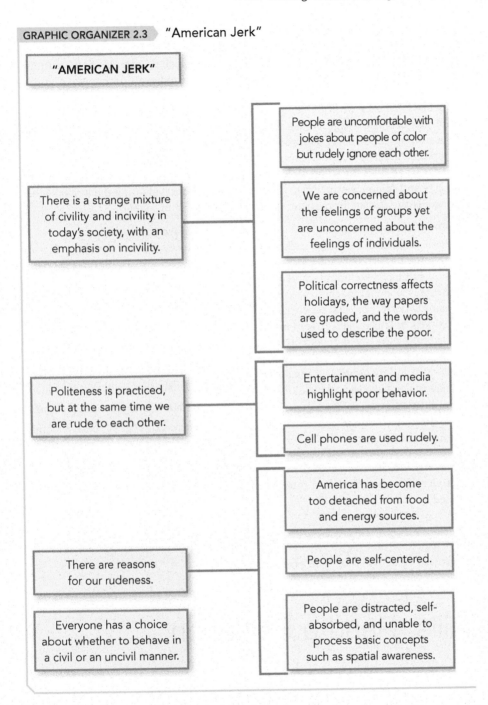

"AMERICAN JERK"

There is a strange mixture of civility and incivility in today's society, with an emphasis on incivility.

- People are uncomfortable with jokes about people of color but rudely ignore each other.
- We are concerned about the feelings of groups yet are unconcerned about the feelings of individuals.
- Political correctness affects holidays, the way papers are graded, and the words used to describe the poor.

Politeness is practiced, but at the same time we are rude to each other.

- Entertainment and media highlight poor behavior.
- Cell phones are used rudely.

There are reasons for our rudeness.

- America has become too detached from food and energy sources.
- People are self-centered.
- People are distracted, self-absorbed, and unable to process basic concepts such as spatial awareness.

Everyone has a choice about whether to behave in a civil or an uncivil manner.

Paraphrasing is especially useful when reading academic writing that may contain challenging ideas expressed in unfamiliar academic jargon and complicated sentence and paragraph structures. The paraphrasing you do can also help you think through, make sense of, and connect key ideas and avoid overquoting when writing about the text.

Below is an excerpt from "The American Jerk" alongside student Karen Vaccaro's paraphrase of this passage. Notice how Vaccaro puts the author's ideas into her own words and sentences, using quotation marks to set off a key term she defines but cannot replace. She cannot avoid using all terms from the original—after all, the paraphrase does address the same topic—but she does her best to avoid using Schwartz's language and sentence structures, and she refrains from evaluating the writer's ideas. (The words she repeats from the original are highlighted in yellow.)

Original Paragraph

Political correctness holds such sway that holidays go unnamed for fear of insulting or excluding someone. Schools won't let teachers use red pens to correct papers, because little Ethan's or Emily's self-esteem might be bruised. No one is "poor," but many are "socioeconomically disadvantaged." Civility and thoughtfulness in speech have never been so complete or so codified.

Paraphrase

Schwartz claims that "political correctness," the effort to avoid offending members of disadvantaged groups, has become so extreme that referring to the poor as *poor*, commenting on students' writing in a way that makes the errors stand out, or even wishing someone a merry Christmas is practically forbidden. Our words and behavior, he argues, are now totally controlled by concern for the feelings of others.

Note that the ideas do not have to appear in the same order as the original, the author's exact words are not used, and interpretation or reaction to what the author says is omitted.

EXERCISE 2.6   **WRITING A PARAPHRASE**

Paraphrase paragraph 5 of "The American Jerk."

Apply Your Skills: Read a Selection Actively

The following reading selection will give you an opportunity to practice the active reading strategies you have just learned in this chapter. It will also be used as the reading assignment on which to base a response essay described in the following section.

Before Reading

1. **Preview.** Preview the reading using the steps listed in the "Before Reading" section earlier in this chapter, and answer the following questions:
   - What issue will the reading address?
   - Do you expect the author to offer examples of the issue? Why or why not?

2. **Connect.** Activate your knowledge and experience on the topic by answering the following questions:
   - Do you usually evaluate a friend request before accepting it? Why or why not?
   - Have you ever encountered a fake social media profile? If so, how did you spot it?
   - In your opinion, what would motivate someone to create fake social media profiles?

While Reading

Highlight the key elements of the essay. Make marginal notes of any ideas that come to mind as you read.

READING

Why Do So Many People Fall for Fake Profiles Online?

Arun Vishwanath

This essay originally appeared on the Web site *The Conversation* on September 20, 2018. *The Conversation* is an international online media outlet that publishes academic and scientific content related to news and current affairs. Dr. Arun Vishwanath, the author of this reading, is a widely published cybersecurity and online deception expert.

1   The first step in conducting online propaganda efforts and misinformation campaigns is almost always a fake social media profile. Phony profiles for nonexistent people worm their way into the social networks of real people, where they can spread their falsehoods. But neither social media companies nor technological innovations offer reliable ways to identify and remove social media profiles that don't represent actual authentic people.

2   It might sound positive that over six months in late 2017 and early 2018, Facebook detected and suspended some 1.3 billion fake accounts (Wagner and Molla). But an estimated 3 to 4 percent of accounts that remain ("Fake Accounts"), or approximately 66 million to 88 million profiles (Murphy), are also fake but haven't yet been detected. Likewise, estimates are that 9 to 15 percent of Twitter's 336 million accounts are fake (Confessore et al.; Confessore and Dance; Newberg).

3   Fake profiles aren't just on Facebook and Twitter, and they're not only targeting people in the U.S. In December 2017, German intelligence officials warned that Chinese agents using fake LinkedIn profiles were targeting more than 10,000 German government employees ("German Spy Agency"). And in mid-August, the

Israeli military reported that Hamas was using fake profiles on Facebook, Instagram and WhatsApp to entrap Israeli soldiers into downloading malicious software (Gross et al.).

Although social media companies have begun hiring more people and using artificial intelligence to detect fake profiles, that won't be enough to review every profile in time to stop their misuse. As my research explores, the problem isn't actually that people—and algorithms—create fake profiles online. What's really wrong is that other people fall for them.   4

My research into why so many users have trouble spotting fake profiles has identified some ways people could get better at identifying phony accounts—and highlights some places technology companies could help.   5

People Fall for Fake Profiles

To understand social media users' thought processes, I created fake profiles on Facebook and sent out friend requests to 141 students in a large university. Each of the fake profiles varied in some way—such as having many or few fake friends, or whether there was a profile photo. The idea was to figure out whether one or another type of profile was most successful in getting accepted as a connection by real users—and then surveying the hoodwinked people to find out how it happened.   6

I found that only 30 percent of the targeted people rejected the request from a fake person. When surveyed two weeks later, 52 percent of users were still considering approving the request. Nearly one in five—18 percent—had accepted the request right away. Of those who accepted it, 15 percent had responded to inquiries from the fake profile with personal information such as their home address, their student identification number, and their availability for a part-time internship. Another 40 percent of them were considering revealing private data.   7

But Why?

When I interviewed the real people my fake profiles had targeted, the most important thing I found was that users fundamentally believe there is a person behind each profile. People told me they had thought the profile belonged to   8

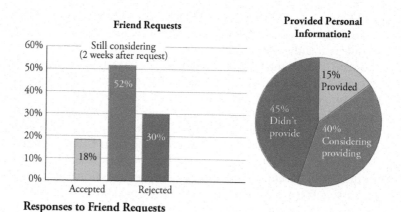

Responses to Friend Requests

someone they knew, or possibly someone a friend knew. Not one person ever suspected the profile was a complete fabrication, expressly created to deceive them. Mistakenly thinking each friend request has come from a real person may cause people to accept friend requests simply to be polite and not hurt someone else's feelings—even if they're not sure they know the person.

In addition, almost all social media users decide whether to accept a connection based on a few key elements in the requester's profile—chiefly how many friends the person has and how many mutual connections there are. I found that people who already have many connections are even less discerning, approving almost every request that comes in. So even a brand-new profile nets some victims. And with every new connection, the fake profile appears more realistic, and has more mutual friends with others. This cascade of victims is how fake profiles acquire legitimacy and become widespread (Vishwanath, "Diffusion of Deception"). 9

The spread can be fast because most social media sites are designed to keep users coming back, habitually checking notifications and responding immediately to connection requests. That tendency is even more pronounced on smartphones (Vishwanath, "Habitual Facebook Use")—which may explain why users accessing social media on smartphones are significantly more likely to accept fake profile requests than desktop or laptop computer users. 10

Illusions of Safety
And users may think they're safer than they actually are, wrongly assuming that a platform's privacy settings will protect them from fake profiles. For instance, many users told me they believe that Facebook's controls for granting differing access to friends versus others also protect them from fakers. Likewise, many LinkedIn users also told me they believe that because they post only professional information, the potential consequences for accepting rogue connections on it are limited. 11

But that's a flawed assumption: Hackers can use any information gleaned from any platform. For instance, simply knowing on LinkedIn that someone is working at some business helps them craft emails to the person or others at the company. Furthermore, users who carelessly accept requests assuming their privacy controls protect them imperil other connections who haven't set their controls as high. 12

Seeking Solutions
Using social media safely means learning how to spot fake profiles and use privacy settings properly. There are numerous online sources for advice—including platforms' own help pages. But too often it's left to users to inform themselves, usually after they've already become victims of a social media scam—which always begins with accepting a fake request. 13

Adults should learn—and teach children—how to examine connection requests carefully in order to protect their devices, profiles and posts from prying eyes, and themselves from being maliciously manipulated. That includes reviewing connection requests during distraction-free periods of the day and using a computer rather than a smartphone to check out potential connections. It also involves identifying which of their actual friends tend to accept almost every friend request from anyone, making them weak links in the social network. 14

These are places social media platform companies can help. They're already creating mechanisms to track app usage and to pause notifications (Constine), helping people avoid being inundated or needing to constantly react. That's a good start—but they could do more.   15

For instance, social media sites could show users indicators of how many of their connections are inactive for long periods, helping people purge their friend networks from time to time. They could also show which connections have suddenly acquired large numbers of friends, and which ones accept unusually high percentages of friend requests.   16

Social media companies need to do more to help users identify and report potentially fake profiles, augmenting their own staff and automated efforts. Social media sites also need to communicate with each other. Many fake profiles are reused across different social networks. But if Facebook blocks a faker, Twitter may not. When one site blocks a profile, it should send key information—such as the profile's name and email address—to other platforms so they can investigate and potentially block the fraud there too.   17

Links

Confessore, Nicholas, and Gabriel J. X. Dance. "Battling Fake Accounts, Twitter to Slash Millions of Followers." *The New York Times*, 11 July 2018, www.nytimes.com/2018/07/11/technology/twitter-fake-followers.html.

Confessore, Nicholas, et al. "The Follower Factory." *The New York Times*, 27 Jan. 2018, www.nytimes.com/interactive/2018/01/27/technology/social-media-bots.html.

Constine, John. "Facebook Prototypes Tool to Show How Many Minutes You Spend on It." *TechCrunch*, 22 June 2018, techcrunch.com/2018/06/22/your-time-on-facebook.

"Fake Accounts." *Community Standards Enforcement Report*, Facebook, 2019, transparency.facebook.com/community-standards-enforcement#fake-accounts.

"German Spy Agency Warns of Chinese LinkedIn Espionage." BBC, 10 Dec. 2017, www.bbc.com/news/world-europe-42304297.

Gross, Judah Ari, et al. "After Facebook, Hamas Turns to Instagram to Lure IDF Soldiers, Army Says." *The Times of Israel*, 15 Aug. 2018, www.timesofisrael.com/after-facebook-hamas-turns-to-instagram-to-lure-idf-soldiers-army-says.

Murphy, Bill, Jr. "Facebook Says It Disabled Almost 1.3 Billion Fake Accounts. And the Numbers Only Get More Insane from There." *Inc.*, www.inc.com/bill-murphy-jr/facebook-says-it-disabled-almost-13-billion-fake-accounts-and-numbers-only-get-more-insane-from-there.html. Accessed 8 Aug. 2019.

Newberg, Michael. "As Many as 48 Million Twitter Accounts Aren't People, Says Study." CNBC, 10 Mar. 2017, www.cnbc.com/2017/03/10/nearly-48-million-twitter-accounts-could-be-bots-says-study.html.

Vishwanath, Arun. "Diffusion of Deception in Social Media: Social Contagion Effects and Its Antecedents." *Information Systems Frontiers*, vol. 17, no. 6 (Dec. 2015), pp. 1353–67, doi: 10.1007/s10796-014-9509-2.

Vishwanath, Arun. "Habitual Facebook Use and Its Impact on Getting Deceived on Social Media." *Journal of Computer-Mediated Communication*, vol. 20, no. 1 (Jan. 2015), pp. 83–98, doi: 10.1111/jcc4.12100.

Wagner, Kurt, and Rani Molla. "Facebook Has Disabled Almost 1.3 Billion Fake Accounts over the Past Six Months." *Vox*, 15 May 2018, www.vox.com/2018/5/15/17349790/facebook-mark-zuckerberg-fake-accounts-content-policy-update.

After Reading

Working together.   In groups of four to five students, discuss possible tell-tale signs of fake social media profiles. If needed, do an Internet search to find samples of fake profiles or tips on how to identify a fake profile. Groups should share their findings with the class.

A Guide to Responding to a Reading

Responding to a reading is usually the next step after careful, active reading. **Response** is a process of synthesizing, analyzing, evaluating ideas, reflecting on, and sometimes writing about what you read. When an instructor gives a reading assignment, some form of response is always required. For example, you might be expected to discuss it in class, analyze it on an essay exam, or research the topic further and report your findings. By responding to material, you understand and learn it better. Of course, you may go back and forth, returning to active reading as part of forming a response.

A common assignment is a **response essay**, which requires you to read a selection, analyze it, and write about some aspect of it. Figure 2.1 shows the process of responding to an assignment. It begins with summarizing to check your understanding, moves to creating and organizing a response, and culminates in producing a response, often a written one.

For an example of a student's response essay, see Karen Vaccaro's "'American Jerk'? How Rude! (but True)" at the end of this chapter.

FIGURE 2.1   Responding to a Reading

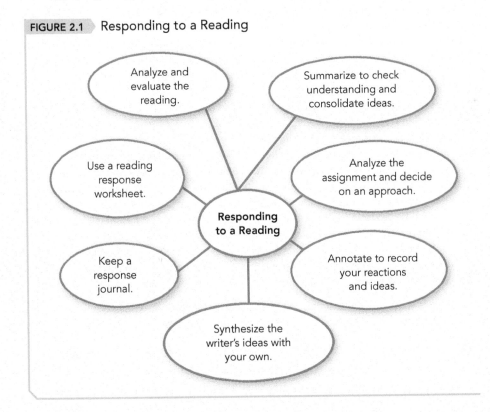

- Analyze and evaluate the reading.
- Summarize to check understanding and consolidate ideas.
- Use a reading response worksheet.
- Analyze the assignment and decide on an approach.
- **Responding to a Reading**
- Keep a response journal.
- Annotate to record your reactions and ideas.
- Synthesize the writer's ideas with your own.

Many tools and strategies will help you create a reasoned and effective response to what you read. These include analyzing the assignment, annotating and synthesizing your ideas with those of the author, and using a response worksheet or a response journal to analyze and evaluate the reading. A good way to start is first to summarize the selection.

Summarize to Consolidate Ideas

A **summary** is a brief restatement of just the major ideas of a reading in your own words and sentences. Writing a summary forces you to decide what is important and enables you to see how ideas relate and connect. Summarizing can also improve your retention and recall of the material. To prepare for discussing a reading in class or writing about it in a response paper or on an exam, writing a summary is a good first step. If you have difficulty writing a summary, you will know you do not fully understand the reading. As you summarize, you may also find that your own thoughts about the reading begin to take shape.

These guidelines will help you write an effective summary:

See the section on highlighting in the Guide to Active Reading earlier in this chapter.

1. **Review your highlighting.**
2. **Start your summary with an opening sentence that states the author's thesis in *your own words*.** The thesis is the most important idea that the entire essay addresses or explains. Include the author's name and the title of the selection you are summarizing.
3. **Include the author's most important supporting ideas.** Use either highlighted topic sentences or marginal summary notes as a guide for what to include. Be sure to use your own words and sentence patterns—not those of the author.
4. **Present the ideas in the order in which they appear in the original source.** Use transitions (connecting words and phrases, such as *first, next,* or *as a result*) as you move from one major supporting idea to the next.
5. **Reread your summary to determine whether it contains enough information.** Your summary should include the selection's main ideas and key supporting points. (Your opinions do not belong in a summary.) A good rule of thumb is that a summary should be about one-fifth the length of the original, but whether this will be too much or too little will depend on the source you are summarizing and your purpose in writing the summary. (A summary may be just one or two sentences in a response essay or research project but may be almost a third of the length of the original if you are using it as a study tool for a complex reading you will be tested on.)

Here is a sample summary by Karen Vaccaro, the student whose response essay, "'American Jerk'? How Rude! (but True)," can be found at the end of this chapter:

The writer expresses Schwartz's thesis in her own words.

The order of ideas parallels the order in Schwartz's essay.

In "American Jerk," Todd Schwartz claims that, although people believe they are acting politely, rudeness and incivility are on the rise. We overdo political correctness, yet we behave rudely to everyone around us. The author believes that because our civilization has evolved to the point that we are no longer concerned with basic survival, we can act selfishly while pretending to be civil. The author also contends that people often are not intentionally rude but instead are simply distracted and self-absorbed. The bottom line is that people must choose their own behavior and decide how they will act.

Many students keep a journal in which they write summaries and other responses to what they've read. These journal entries can serve as useful sources of ideas for writing papers.

The writer continues to use her own words—not those of Schwartz.

ESSAY IN PROGRESS 1 ▶ WRITING A SUMMARY

This assignment is the first step of a five-part essay-in-progress assignment. The steps lead you through the process of developing and writing a response essay. The writing assignment is as follows:

> Write a two- to three-page paper in response to "Why Do So Many People Fall for Fake Profiles Online?" earlier in this chapter (or an essay assigned by your instructor). Choose one problem, question, or issue that the essay addresses and detail your response to it.

As part of the above assignment, complete each of the following tasks:

1. **Review** Reread your highlighting for the reading.
2. **Organize** Draw a graphic organizer of the reading.
3. **Summarize** Write a brief one-paragraph summary of the reading.

Analyze the Assignment and Decide on an Approach

Before beginning your response, make sure you understand the parameters of the assignment.

- **The task.** Will you be discussing the reading selection in class to consolidate your understanding? Review your annotations and any notes you wrote while reading, and bring any ideas or questions you might have about the selection to class.
- **Your purpose.** Will you be analyzing it for an essay exam as a way of demonstrating your command of issues or themes you have studied in class? Consider themes or topics you have discussed in class or in other readings, and think about how the reading selection relates.
- **Instructor expectations.** Will you be writing a response to demonstrate your understanding and analysis as well as your ability to write a clear, cohesive

essay? Consider the direction or approach you should take, the length your instructor expects, and whether you are expected (or allowed) to do additional research, as well as how best to organize and develop the response. If you are uncertain about your instructor's expectations, be sure to ask.

ESSAY IN PROGRESS 2 ▸ ANALYZING THE ASSIGNMENT

Essay in Progress 1 gives the following assignment:

> Write a two- to three-page paper in response to "Why Do So Many People Fall for Fake Profiles Online?" earlier in this chapter (or an essay assigned by your instructor). Choose one problem, question, or issue that the essay addresses and detail your response to it.

Write a paragraph in which you identify the task, your purpose, and your instructor's likely expectations.

Generate and Record Ideas: Annotating, Synthesizing, Analyzing, and Evaluating

Once you have created and organized ideas from the reading, it is time to generate and create your own ideas. This involves synthesizing, keeping a response journal, and analyzing and evaluating.

Annotate to Record Your Impressions

For more about keeping a journal, see Chapter 1.

When you **annotate** a reading assignment, you jot down your questions and reactions to the reading in the margins or in a reading journal. Think of your annotations as a personal response to the author's ideas. You can annotate while you read, but your most useful annotations will often come after an initial reading, as you reread and review the material. You may want to go back to reread and annotate a selection once you have an idea of what you will be writing about. Your annotations can take many forms:

- important points (such as the thesis) to which you react intellectually or emotionally
- places where you want or need further information
- passages that reveal the author's reasons for writing
- passages that raise questions or that intrigue or puzzle you
- ideas you agree or disagree with or that seem inconsistent
- themes or ideas that relate to a topic you may want to write about

Karen Vaccaro's response to "American Jerk" appears at the end of this chapter.

Later, as you write about or discuss the reading, your annotations will help you focus on major issues and questions. A portion of Karen Vaccaro's annotations on "American Jerk" are shown below.

Sample Annotations

Civility rules, friends.

Civility is dead, jerks.

A reference to A Tale of Two Cities, a novel about the French Revolution. Is Schwartz implying that Americans are ready to revolt?

Why? I have a few theories.

The first is that America is in the same position as Rome found itself in about 420 CE, meaning that we've reached the peak of our civilization and now everything is going to Tartarus in a chariot. We're too far from our food and energy sources, and fewer and fewer of the Druids and Visigoths like us anymore. So we desperately cling to a patina of civility while we grab a snack and watch large, toothy predators devour people.

Tartarus = Hell. Fall of Rome: Are things really so bad now? Romans kept slaves!

Is this such a bad thing? We have time to relax and think.

Rome's "neighbors"?

Patina = only on the surface

The second is that sunlight contains tiny spores that lodge in the cerebellum, making the infected believe they are the center of the universe.

My final and somewhat less cutting-edge theory is that a large percentage of people are just clueless, distracted, and self-absorbed, unable to process concepts such as spatial awareness (for example: when you are walking in the same direction with several hundred people in, say, an airport terminal, DON'T JUST STOP IN THE MIDDLE OF THE FLOW!).

Schwartz's main point. My boyfriend gets distracted by his phone—a lot! (I do, too, sometimes.)

ESSAY IN PROGRESS 3 ▶ ANNOTATING

Reread "Why Do So Many People Fall for Fake Profiles Online?" or the reading your instructor assigned. Annotate the essay as you reread.

Synthesize the Writer's Ideas with Your Own

One way to start ideas flowing for a response is to connect, or **synthesize**, the ideas expressed in the reading with your own ideas, knowledge, and experiences. Doing so builds a bridge between your ideas and the author's. You may have begun synthesizing ideas as you annotated, but to synthesize more formally, follow these steps:

1. **Look for useful information in the essay that you could apply or relate to other real-life situations.** Think of familiar situations or examples that illustrate the subject. For example, for "American Jerk," which considers incivility in society, you might write a journal entry about incivility among college students.

2. **Think beyond the reading.** Recall other material you have read and events you have experienced that relate to the reading. In thinking about "American Jerk," for example, you might recall the behavior of students in the classroom, as described in the reading "The New Marshmallow Test" from Chapter 1. How does student use of digital technology in the classroom relate to the topic of civility, for example?

3. **Use the key-word response method for generating ideas.** Choose one or more key words that describe your initial response, such as *angered, amused, surprised, confused, annoyed, curious,* or *shocked.* Then write for five to ten minutes without stopping in response to your word. You can explain your response or offer examples to support your reaction. Try approaching the reading from many different perspectives. Here is the result of Karen Vaccaro's key-word response to "American Jerk":

Possible topic 1: How generations create their own values

Possible topic 2: How behavior changes with changes in technology

Possible topic 3: How bad is rudeness in comparison with evils of earlier times?

After reading "American Jerk," I felt annoyed and insulted. I agree that the world has changed because of cell phones, but I don't think that these changes have made people ruder. Each generation creates its own rules and values, and the cell-phone generation is doing that. If media and entertainment were horrible and insulting, then people wouldn't watch them. Humans are evolving, and our expectations have to evolve with technology. Some people do act like they are polite when they actually do rude things all the time. But really, are things as bad as he claims? Isn't enslaving people a lot worse than talking on the phone when out with a friend?

ESSAY IN PROGRESS 4   **SYNTHESIZING IDEAS**

Use synthesis to draw connections between the ideas expressed in "Why Do So Many People Fall for Fake Profiles Online?" or the reading your instructor assigned and your own ideas and experiences.

Analyze and Evaluate the Reading

After you see a movie, you ask a friend, "What did you think of it?" Your friend may praise the plot, criticize the acting, or comment on the characters' behavior. Your friend is analyzing the film, breaking the film down into its component parts and assessing how well they work together. When you analyze a reading, you may focus on any aspect of the selection, such as how the author tries to reach his or her intended readers by choosing evidence readers will respond to, offering reasons they can accept, or using a tone readers will find appealing. When you evaluate a reading, you consider the author's fairness or accuracy, the effectiveness of the presentation, the quality of the supporting evidence provided, and the relevance of the selection to your purpose. Numerous techniques for both analysis and evaluation are explored in detail in Chapter 3.

An effective starting point for analysis and evaluation is to devise critical questions. Asking critical questions and then answering them is a useful method for analysis and for discovering ideas for a response. Critical questions go beyond what the author said and explore what he or she meant. These questions may focus on the implications, practicality, accuracy, and application of the author's ideas, for example. Here are three sample questions and the answers that Karen Vaccaro wrote after reading "American Jerk":

Possible topic: How to teach politeness and effective methods

Can we turn the tide and find a way to return to a polite society?

I think that adults emphasize politeness less than in the past. Parents and teachers hardly try to instill it in children. People no longer have to learn etiquette. To improve manners would require us to rethink how we raise and educate children.

Is technology causing people to be less civil, or is it just an excuse?

Technology has changed the way that people communicate with one another.

Possible topic: The effects of technology on human behavior

Technology makes it easier to have less personal contact with others, but it does not encourage rudeness. It's possible to use technology and still be civil to other people.

Is American society actually worse than it used to be, as Schwartz seems to claim? While horrible things still happen here, we no longer have slavery or segregation; women, gay people, and nonwhites have much more freedom and opportunity.

Possible topic: The contrast between the evils of the past and the "evils" of present-day rudeness

ESSAY IN PROGRESS 5 ▶ **WRITING CRITICAL QUESTIONS**

Write critical questions in response to the reading you are preparing to write about. As you read the essay a second time, record additional reactions that occur to you. Some students prefer to use a different color of ink to record their second set of questions. (Refer to the sample student annotation on p. 45.)

Keep a Response Journal

A **response journal** is a section of your writing journal in which you record reactions or questions that arose as you annotated. Experiment with the following two ways to organize a response journal entry to discover the one that works better for you.

For more about keeping a journal, see Chapter 1.

Map or cluster format.   On a blank page, write, outline, draw, or create a diagram to express your reactions to an essay. This open-page format encourages you to let your ideas flow freely. Figure 2.2 shows Karen Vaccaro's open-page response journal entry for "American Jerk." This entry suggests several possible topics to write about: identifying generational differences in defining civility, determining standards for civility, and recognizing subjectivity in evaluating behavior.

Response-to-quotations format.   Divide several pages of your journal into two columns or create a table with two columns. On the left, jot down five to ten quotations

FIGURE 2.2   Sample Open-Response Journal Format

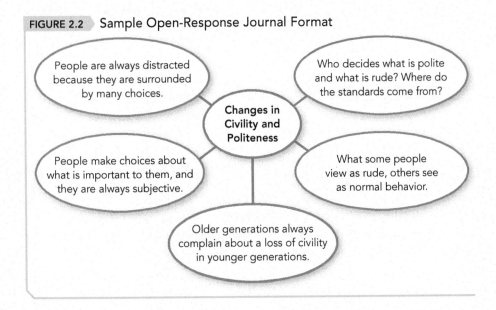

FIGURE 2.3   Sample Response-to-Quotations Journal Format

Possible writing topics are noted.

Quotations	Responses
"A moment when a roomful of even relatively evolved people will react with discomfort to an off-color joke about people of color—and when those same people have no compunction whatsoever about loudly ignoring one another as they blather into their cell phones" (para. 2).	This statement implies that racial jokes and talking on your cell phone are somehow on the same level of rudeness.
"No one is 'poor,' but many are 'socioeconomically disadvantaged'" (para. 4).	There is a distinction between "poor" and "socioeconomically disadvantaged," and it's an important one. The first term has to do with money, but the second one also has to do with culture and opportunities.

Topic: Types or degrees of rudeness

Topics: Contrast between/ meaning of "socioeconomically disadvantaged" and "poor"

that state an opinion, summarize a viewpoint, and so forth. On the right, write your response to each quotation. You might explain it, disagree with or question it, relate it to other information in the reading or in another reading, or tie it to your experiences. The two-column format forces you to think actively about an essay while you question what you have read and draw connections. It also provides possible ideas to write about in a response paper. Be sure to keep track of where in the reading you found the quotations so you can cite them properly. Figure 2.3 provides an example of the response-to-quotations format.

For more on paraphrasing, see Chapter 22 or the section on paraphrasing earlier in this chapter.

You may find it useful to make a third column for a paraphrase of the quotation. Paraphrasing forces you to think about the meaning of the quotation, and ideas for writing may come to mind as a result.

ESSAY IN PROGRESS 6   **WRITING A RESPONSE JOURNAL ENTRY**

For "Why Do So Many People Fall for Fake Profiles Online?" or another essay chosen by your instructor, write a response in your journal using the map or cluster format or the response-to-quotations format.

Use a Reading-Response Worksheet

A reading-response worksheet guides and records your response while directing your thinking. Figure 2.4 shows the format of a response worksheet.

FIGURE 2.4   Reading-Response Worksheet

Reading-Response Worksheet

Title: _"American Jerk"_

Author: _Todd Schwartz_

First Impressions: _The article is funny, but a little extreme. I agree that some people are_
very concerned about political correctness, while others feel free to flaunt their racism, but
are these the same people?

Summary: _In "American Jerk," Todd Schwartz argues that people believe they are acting_
politely, while rudeness and incivility are on the rise. Schwartz claims that since we don't have
to fight for our survival, we can act selfishly while pretending to be civil and that people are
often rude because of their self-absorption. We can choose not to be rude.

Connections to Your Own Experiences: _We've all experienced road rage, cell phones_
ringing/texting at the movies or with friends. On the other hand, political correctness
has led to trigger warnings in school, teachers not using red pen for fear of hurting
students' feelings, and parents even being afraid to discipline their kids and owners—their
dogs.

Analysis (issue, aspect, feature, problem): _Schwartz seems to think we're ruder now_
than ever. But are we? Were slave holders polite to the people they "owned"? And is it the
same people who are being overly politically correct and rude? I'm not sure his argument
holds up.

Useful Quotations: _"We're all talking to someone all the time, but it's ever more rarely_
to the people we are actually with" (para. 8). Relate this to the lack of civility and manners.

Write a Response Essay

A response essay presents an organized and focused discussion of the content of the reading assignment.

Determine the Content and Focus of Your Response Essay

Your response essay may include a brief summary of the reading assignment and use quotations and paraphrases as evidence. However, most of your response should focus on interpreting and evaluating what you have read. Your essay should be focused; it should not present unrelated reactions to the reading or jump from idea to idea. Focus your response on

- one key idea
- one primary question the essay raises
- one major issue it explores

For example, suppose your instructor asks you to read an article entitled "Advertising: A Form of Institutional Lying," which argues that advertisements deceive consumers by presenting half-truths, distortions, and misinformation. Your instructor then asks you to write a two-page paper responding to the essay but gives you no other directions. In writing this paper, you might take one of the following approaches:

- Evaluate the evidence and examples the author provides, and determine whether the evidence is relevant and sufficient to support the claim.
- Discuss the causes or effects of deception in advertising that the author overlooks. (You may need to consult other sources to take this approach.)
- Evaluate the assumptions the author makes about advertising or consumers.

Follow the Steps for Writing a Response Essay

For more about writing and supporting a thesis, see Chapter 5.

For more about drafting an essay, see Chapter 7.

For more about revising an essay, see Chapter 8.

Make sure your sentences are clear, concise, and varied, and your words are accurate, specific, and appropriate. Then use the suggestions in "Proofread Carefully" in Chapter 9 to catch any remaining typos or formatting errors.

Use the following steps as a guide when writing response essays:

1. **Reread the writing you did in response to the selection.** Look for related ideas. Try to find ideas that fit together to produce a viewpoint or position toward the reading. (Do not attempt to cover all your ideas. Your essay should not analyze every aspect of the essay. Instead, you should focus on one feature or aspect.)
2. **Write a sentence that states your central point.** This sentence will become your thesis statement. It should state what your essay will assert or explain.
3. **Collect ideas and evidence from the reading to support your thesis.** Use quotations, paraphrases, and summaries to call attention to the writer's key points and examples.
4. **Organize your ideas into essay form.** Your essay should have a title, introduction, body, and conclusion.
5. **Revise your essay.** Be sure that all your ideas support your thesis, you have explained your ideas clearly, and you have provided support from the reading for each one.
6. **Edit your sentences and words, and proofread for accuracy and correctness.**

Refer to the Reading Clearly and Correctly

Writing a response essay requires that you make direct references to the reading itself. There are three ways you can do this:

1. You can **summarize** the author's ideas and then comment on them.
2. You can **paraphrase** the author's ideas and then respond to them.
3. You can include a **direct quotation** and then discuss it.

Choose the techniques most appropriate to your audience and purpose. (In a given paper you might use all three.) Be sure to use them to support your own ideas. You might, for example, look back at your response-to-quotations journal and find a quotation to support one of your major points. Or you might find a sentence you highlighted and paraphrase it. Or you may find that it would be helpful to summarize examples or details the author gives to support a main point.

Regardless of which techniques you use, it is essential that you make it clear you are using the author's ideas, not your own. If you fail to do so, you might be accused of plagiarism, unfairly using an author's ideas without acknowledging them.

To learn more about plagiarism, see Chapter 23.

Notice in the student essay that follows how Vaccaro uses introductory comments to signal she is using the author's ideas:

- She introduces a summary by saying "In his article 'American Jerk,' Todd Schwartz claims . . ." (para. 1).
- She introduces a paraphrase by stating, "Schwartz is right when he says . . ." (para. 2).
- She introduces a quotation by writing, "Schwartz writes . . ." (para. 3).

Also notice that for each reference to the reading, Vaccaro includes an in-text citation in parentheses following the borrowed material. Her in-text citations contain information on how to locate the material she used.

You can learn more about how to select, integrate, and cite sources in Chapters 7, 22, and 23.

ESSAY IN PROGRESS 7 ▶ **WRITING A RESPONSE ESSAY**

Write a two- to three-page paper in response to "Why Do So Many People Fall for Fake Profiles Online?" (or whichever essay you've been writing about in previous Essay in Progress activities in this chapter). Choose one question or issue that the essay addresses and detail your response to it. Use the steps listed above and the ideas you generated in Essays in Progress 3–6 to develop your essay.

STUDENTS WRITE

"American Jerk"? How Rude! (but True)

Karen Vaccaro

Karen Vaccaro wrote the following essay in response to "American Jerk." As you read, notice how Vaccaro analyzes Schwartz's points about civility and the lack of it in our society.

Introduction: Identifies the article Vaccaro is responding to and summarizes Schwartz's main point

Vaccaro's <u>thesis</u> statement indicates how her ideas differ from Schwartz's.

Vaccaro includes a quotation and agrees with Schwartz.

Vaccaro paraphrases Schwartz and offers examples from her own experience of lack of concern.

Vaccaro connects Schwartz's ideas to her own experience and affirms his ideas.

In his article "American Jerk," Todd Schwartz claims that Americans today are both the most and the least civil we have ever been. Although the painful truth in these observations is a bit hard to take, Schwartz eases the reality by providing a great deal of humorous relief. <u>Schwartz's claim is an apt one, and most of his observations about our current culture are accurate, but some of his observations and accusations are broad generalizations that don't always hold true.</u>   1

"We have never been more concerned about the feelings of minority groups, the disabled, and the disadvantaged," Schwartz writes in paragraph 3, and he is right. We have become a culture obsessed with being PC (politically correct). I often carefully choose and often second-guess the words I use to describe anyone of a different race or physical or mental ability, for fear of offending anyone. And yet many people I encounter seem hardly concerned about offending me. Schwartz is right when he says that our society lacks a concern about the feelings of others with whom we share places and experiences, giving highways, the Internet, and theaters as examples. Cyclists seem to have taken over city streets and even shout insults at me when I am walking in a crosswalk (and they are breaking the law by ignoring a red light). Despite many methods used to discourage theater goers from using their phones, audience members text and leave their ringers on during films, concerts, and plays. In fact, last week I was at a live theater performance, and in the middle of an important scene, a cell phone rang in the audience—twice.   2

In another example of how (overly) civil we've become, Schwartz writes, "Schools won't let teachers use red pens to correct papers because . . . self-esteem might be bruised" (para. 4). This reminded me of the teaching internship I did while studying abroad in China one semester. I taught an English writing course to Chinese high school students. One day I was marking up the students' papers with a red pen (as I thought teachers were supposed to do). Another American teacher said, "I thought teachers weren't supposed to mark students' papers with red pens anymore." I asked if red was offensive to Chinese students. "No," she answered. "Some of my teachers back home in America said it's because red is a harsh color that really stands out from the black and white." "Well, yes, I thought that was the point," I said.   3

"But it can make some students feel bad," she responded. "That's the silliest thing I've ever heard," I said as I went back to marking my students' papers with the red pen. Have we become so "civil" that we're afraid to teach students? Don't young men and women come to class expecting to learn something, knowing that at some point they will need to be corrected to see their mistakes so that they can truly learn?

Then there are the less civil aspects of our culture, as Schwartz so accurately points out. We Americans have become obsessed with reality television shows that often take advantage of the misfortune and embarrassment of others. In addition, "giant assault vehicles" (para. 7) dwarf other cars on the road, guzzle gas, often take up more than one parking space, and seem unnecessary on city streets in a time of environmental awareness and concern. Furthermore, we are so interested in our technological gadgets that we ignore real human-to-human interactions. "We're all talking to someone all the time," Schwartz writes, "but it's ever more rarely to the people we are actually with" (para. 8). I have noticed that my boyfriend often whips out his iPhone. Even when we're walking and talking, catching up after days of not seeing one another, he's playing a new game, downloading a new app, or texting with friends. I myself can be guilty of this rude behavior. Sometimes I am spending time with one friend but will be texting another friend. I know it's rude, but I do it anyway (usually because the friend I'm with is doing the same thing and therefore it seems okay). We no longer realize how rude it is to divide our attention between two sources instead of giving our friend or loved one our full, undivided attention.

4

Vaccaro identifies another of Schwartz's points that she agrees with and admits that she is guilty of it as well.

Where I must disagree with Schwartz, though, is his sweeping, unfounded statement that we are now living in "what must certainly be the rudest era in history" (para. 5). Really? Are we ruder than people who enslaved others and denied them any and all rights, including the right to be treated like human beings and not animals? Are people who refuse to "shut their inane traps" (para. 7) ruder than people in the time of segregation? It might be easy to convince ourselves that the present must be the rudest time in our history, since it is freshest in our minds, and we know it very well. But if Schwartz took time to flesh out his observations and accusations with concrete examples, he might rethink such a generalization.

5

Vaccaro moves to points with which she disagrees.

Conclusion: Vaccaro points out the value of Schwartz's article.

> Even if it doesn't fix the problems it calls attention to, Schwartz's entertaining and witty article forces us to stop and think about how contemporary American culture straddles the line between civility and rudeness. Many of his examples illustrate the hypocrisy of our behaviors and ways of thinking. Ultimately, Schwartz is correct in his claim that "we have arrived at simultaneously the most and least civil moment in U.S. history" (para. 2). I doubt, though, that Neanderthals—with their barbaric weapons and primitive hunting instincts—"were probably nicer to each other than we are" (para. 6).

6

Work Cited

Schwartz, Todd. "American Jerk: Be Civil, or I'll Beat You to a Pulp." *Successful College Writing*, 8th. ed., by Kathleen T. McWhorter, Bedford/St. Martin's, 2021, pp. 27–28.

Analyzing the Writer's Technique

1. Express Vaccaro's thesis (central point) in your own words.
2. What kinds of information does Vaccaro include to support her thesis?
3. Where would additional examples help Vaccaro support her thesis?

Responding to the Reading

1. Vaccaro admits to texting one friend while spending time with another. Are you also guilty of acts of incivility? If so, describe one.
2. What steps or actions could be taken to build Americans' awareness of their lack of civility?
3. Do you agree or disagree that our culture is obsessed with political correctness? Give examples to support your answer.
4. Write a journal entry describing an act of incivility that you have observed or experienced that particularly disturbed or annoyed you.

Answers, Ex 2.1
1. T
2. F
3. F
4. T
5. F

Thomas Imo/Photothek/Getty Images

3

Thinking, Reading, and Writing Critically

Writing Quick Start

ANALYZE Suppose your sociology instructor shows you this photo of a pile of old mobile phones in a scrap heap in Ghana and asks you to write an analysis of what you see and what you think it means. Now imagine that your computer science instructor asks you to write an analysis of the same photograph.

WRITE Draft two paragraphs describing the photograph and analyzing its significance from these two different perspectives. How do your two paragraphs differ in word choice, content, and point of view?

CONNECT As you analyzed and wrote about the photo, you not only had to question, evaluate, and respond critically, but you also chose words and ideas that helped to express your point of view in a way that was appropriate to your audience. In this chapter you will learn strategies for thinking, reading, and writing critically that you can apply to reading essays, newspaper and magazine articles, textbook selections, works of literature, and visuals, including photographs and graphics, and that you can apply to essays and other college assignments you write.

Analyzing What You Read

We live in a world of overload, surrounded by news, opinions, advertisements, and other kinds of information everywhere we look (or listen). Sometimes the information we encounter presents ideas fully and fairly. More often, writers and speakers present only their own views on a topic, without fully exploring the range of positions. And sometimes writers and speakers present their positions in such a way as to make their viewpoint sound like the only logical option. So it is important to assess carefully the ideas and information we encounter. And since writers may not always be aware when unfair bias creeps in, it is also important to assess carefully the way you present your own ideas, making sure that you have presented them clearly and fairly. As you read and respond to academic writing in a variety of disciplines, you will be called upon to interpret, assess, and integrate ideas from a variety of sources. Your instructors will expect you to go beyond understanding a text to analyze it, evaluate it, and think critically about it. This chapter will help you extend the skills you practiced in Chapter 2 to become sophisticated readers and writers.

Analyze the Author's Ideas

To analyze an essay, begin by examining the author's ideas closely and critically. This involves knowing what the author *says*, and, more important, it involves making inferences about what the author *means*. It also involves examining the supporting evidence an author offers, distinguishing between fact and opinion, and identifying bias.

Make Reasonable Inferences

An **inference** is a reasonable guess based on the available facts and information, including content directly provided in the reading. Inferences are logical connections between what the writer states directly and what he or she implies. Consider the following situation:

> You have been attending your history class all semester; you participate in class and your interest in history is evident. Your scores on three exams were 95, 97, and 99, out of 100. You wrote one paper for the class and got an A on it. It is the end of the semester, your instructor has just announced the date of the final exam, and she asks you to stop and talk to her after class. During the class, the instructor also mentions some summer internships that she recently learned about.

In this situation, you are confident that you are passing the course. So what might she want to talk to you about? One reasonable inference is that it has something to do with the final exam, since it was just announced. Another possible inference is that she may want to encourage you to apply for one of the internships she mentioned.

Here are some guidelines for making reasonable inferences:

1. **Understand the author's purpose and literal meanings.** Before you can make reasonable inferences, you need a clear understanding of the author's purpose and the reading's thesis statement, main ideas, and supporting details.

2. **Pay attention to details.** Sometimes details offer a hint regarding what the writer has implied or left unsaid. When you notice a striking or unusual detail, ask yourself: Why is this detail included? For example, read the following passage:

> Maria attends college, has a full-time job, takes care of her two children, cooks dinner for her family every night, and pays taxes. She doesn't look like an illegal immigrant, but this is how the U.S. government classifies her.

What is the writer's reason for including the detail about Maria's immigration status? Perhaps the writer is implying that undocumented workers are just like everyone else: They go to school, work, and have families. You might also reasonably infer that the writer disagrees with or questions this classification.

3. **Consider the facts.** Consider the complete set of facts provided in the reading. What is the writer trying to suggest with these facts? What conclusions do the complete set of facts support? Suppose a writer presents the following facts:

> Dr. Tannenbaum is an old-school doctor. His staff greets you by name and offers you a cup of coffee when you arrive for your appointment. A receptionist answers the phone and returns all calls promptly. Dr. Tannenbaum talks to you as if you're a human being, not just a medical chart, and he'll make house calls if you live alone and have no transportation to his office.

From these sentences, the conclusion is clear: The writer considers Dr. Tannenbaum an excellent doctor who treats his patients with respect.

4. **Examine word choices.** A writer's choice of words often conveys his or her feelings toward the topic. Look for words that are heavy with connotations (or associations) and ask yourself why the writer chose these words. For example, in the paragraph about Dr. Tannenbaum, the author uses the adjective *old-school* to imply a traditional doctor who cares about his patients. Readers can sense that the writer intends to contrast "old-school doctors" with doctors who use "new-fangled" approaches, of which the author likely disapproves.

5. **Support your inference with specific evidence.** Valid inferences are based on fact, context, and personal experiences. Be sure you have ample evidence to back up any inference you make. It would be incorrect to infer that Dr. Tannenbaum is highly skilled at diagnosing rare illnesses, for example, based on the information presented.

EXERCISE 3.1   **MAKING REASONABLE INFERENCES**

Read the following excerpt from "American Jerk" in Chapter 2 and answer the questions that follow.

> Pick your poison: reality television, slasher movies, video games, online porn, cell phones, automated answering systems, giant assault vehicles for trips to the grocery store, car stereos played at volumes easily heard on Jupiter, web-powered copyright infringement, people who will not shut their inane traps in movie theaters, and, lord help us, now even people who won't shut their inane traps during live theater.

We're all talking to someone all the time, but it's ever more rarely to the people we are actually with. Our cell phones blare ringtones that no one else wants to hear. We love to watch TV shows about the stunningly predictable results of hand-feeding a grizzly bear or lighting a stick of dynamite with a cigarette. We also love shows where people lie to others for money and programs where snarky, slightly talented folks say vicious things to hopeful, and usually more talented, contestants.

1. What reasonable inferences can you make about the author's opinion of the typical American? Provide three adjectives that the author would use to describe Americans.
2. Which specific words or phrases in the selection provide hints regarding the author's attitude toward "American jerks"?
3. What details are particularly revealing about Americans' behavior?

HOW READERS WRITE **IMPLIED MEANINGS**

Put yourself in your readers' position: As you write, consider the inferences your readers are likely to draw from what you write. To avoid confusion, misunderstanding, or misinterpretation, be sure to:

- **State accurately and precisely what you want readers to understand.** If you only suggest an idea, some writers may miss it. Others may misinterpret it. As a result, they may take away a meaning you did not intend.

- **Define your terms.** If a term, such as *masculinity*, has many possible shades of meaning, define the term as you intend to use it.

- **Choose your terms carefully.** Terms may convey not only their dictionary meaning (or *denotation*) but may also be associated with feelings. For example, both *slender* and *skinny* mean thin, but *slender* has positive overtones while *skinny* has negative ones.

- **Be careful when leaving readers to draw their own conclusions.** If you choose to leave an idea unstated, only implying what you mean, be sure that the examples or evidence you supply can lead only to the conclusion you intend.

For more about connotation versus denotation, see "Consider Denotation versus Connotation" later in this chapter.

Assess the Evidence

In general, the most reliable information is based on solid *evidence*. When reading or writing, carefully assess the evidence provided:

- Is it reliable?
- Does the evidence support the writer's assertions?
- Has enough evidence been provided to make a strong case?

The following list of pros and cons will help you determine the reliability of some of the most common types of evidence.

Type	Pros	Cons
Personal experience or examples	• Can be powerful: No one understands an experience, for example, like a person who has lived it.	• Is subjective: Two people can experience the same event very differently. • Not enough to support a broad generalization.
Eyewitness reports	• May be powerful: Witnesses often have strong convictions that their memories are reliable.	• Are often inaccurate: Many studies have shown that memory is easily influenced. • May be subjective: If two people see a man running from a burning building, one may think, "What a lucky man! He escaped from the burning building," while the other may think, "That man started the fire."
Surveys	• May be highly reliable when conducted by experienced researchers who collect responses from a wide array of subjects.	• May be misleadingly worded or administered inconsistently, or may include responses from too narrow a spectrum of respondents.
Data and statistics	• Tend to be collected by academic researchers and members of professional research organizations who try to be as objective and accurate as possible.	• Can be used in ways that hide the truth. Example: A soda company may claim that "90% of the people in a taste test preferred our cola to the competitor's." This may be true, but consider how many subjects were tested, whether the test was run in a neutral location, and so on.
Evidence from scientific experiments and studies	• Usually considered highly reliable because they are based on the scientific method, a set of procedures that researchers follow to investigate their hypotheses and test the results of other experiments and studies.	• May apply to only a narrow range of cases. • Can be influenced by uncontrollable factors. Example: Studies on drug safety are often contradictory. • May reflect the economic or political biases of scientists conducting the study; occasionally, results may be falsified or outcomes misrepresented.

For more about analyzing data in graphics, see "Analyze Graphics" later in this chapter.

HOW READERS WRITE ▶ EVIDENCE

One of your main responsibilities as a writer is to provide reliable and sufficient evidence to support your thesis. As you select data and evidence to support your ideas, think critically about:

- **Your audience.** Evidence that may convince one audience may be unconvincing to another. For example, a medical doctor may not be persuaded by anecdotal experiences of a remedy's effectiveness, while a group of patients may be more receptive to personal stories.

- **Your purpose.** Your purpose may influence the type of supporting evidence you provide in your essay. If your purpose is to explain the process of flying a drone, then you need accurate step-by-step facts and procedures. If your purpose, however, is to persuade readers that drones are a threat to safety, then you need reasons why drones can be hazardous and statistical evidence demonstrating that injuries and accidents have occurred as a result of the use of drones.

EXERCISE 3.2 ▶ EVALUATING STATEMENTS

Consider each of the following statements and the context in which it is made. List what types of information are missing that would help you weigh the evidence and evaluate the claim being made. What further types of evidence would you need to accept or reject the statement?

1. On the label of a bag of cookies: "CONTAINS 45% LESS FAT and 0 grams of TRANS FAT!"
2. In a printed campaign flyer for mayoral candidate Mary Johnson: "My opponent, Joe Smith, has been accused of serious conflicts of interest in the awarding of city contracts during his term as mayor."
3. In large print on the cover of a book you see online: "'This novel is a . . . wild and exciting . . . ride through the rough-and-tumble days of the Gold Rush . . . full of . . . adventure and excitement. . . . Memorable.'—*New York Times*"

Distinguish Fact from Opinion

In order to determine whether an opinion has been adequately supported by facts, first you must be able to distinguish facts from opinions. The chart below will help.

Definition	Examples
Facts are objective statements of information that can be verified—that is, their truth can be established with evidence. Facts can be checked in trustworthy sources such as online dictionaries and Web reference sources such as refdesk.com.	• Many people who smoke marijuana do not go on to use more dangerous drugs. • Texting while driving has caused many accidents.

Opinions are subjective—that is, they differ by individual. They make a claim based on attitudes, feelings, or beliefs. These claims cannot be established definitely as either true or false, at least at the present time. Often they put forth a particular position or agenda.	• Marijuana use will probably be legalized in all fifty states by 2025. • People who text while driving should be fined and have their driver's licenses revoked.

When writers want to limit the extent of a claim, they often use qualifying words and phrases. For example, an expert on government debt may write, "*It seems likely that* Social Security payments will decline for future generations of Americans." Using such words and phrases limits the writer's responsibility for providing solid evidence to support the claim and allows other viewpoints to be acceptable.

HOW READERS WRITE ▸ FACT AND OPINION IN ACADEMIC WRITING

Facts are important to include in all types of academic writing. Including your opinions may or may not be appropriate, however.

Omit personal opinions from informative writing, unless they are specifically asked for. Examples of informative writing include summaries, paraphrases, lab reports, and research reports.

Include personal opinions in persuasive writing. Examples of persuasive writing include response papers, book or movie reviews, interpretations or analyses for history or literature classes, and proposals. When personal opinions are included, be sure to support them with evidence, reasons, or explanations.

EXERCISE 3.3 ▸ DISTINGUISHING BETWEEN FACTS AND OPINIONS

Label each of the following statements as fact (*F*) or opinion (*O*):

1. The best symphonies are shorter than twenty minutes.
2. About half the population of Uruguay lives in Montevideo.
3. More women earned doctoral degrees in engineering in 2020 than in 2000.
4. Private companies should not be allowed to operate concessions inside our national parks.
5. The mountains of northern Idaho contain the most scenic landscapes in the country.

EXERCISE 3.4 ▸ WRITING FACTS AND OPINIONS

For two of the following topics, write one statement of fact and one statement of opinion:

1. voter turnout rates in presidential elections
2. alternative energy solutions
3. the Super Bowl

Detect Disinformation

Also known as *fake news*, **disinformation** is false information that is deliberately presented to mislead listeners and readers. Often, it is written plausibly, appeals to readers' preconceived notions, and is damaging to an organization, person, or product. Disinformation may be written by overzealous promoters of political or ideological positions; those seeking power, authority, or political gain; or those out to make a quick buck (or all three). Occasionally, the term *fake news* is used to mislead by those who wish to discredit an unfavorable report.

Most often, disinformation is spread through Web sites and social media. *Influencers*—people and organizations with thousands of real (or fake) followers—may share and reshare it (wittingly or not). Innocent readers may also share it with friends and family.

Creators of fake news use a variety of techniques to get unsuspecting readers to accept disinformation:

- They use misleading headlines, visuals, or graphics to hoodwink readers.
- They create fake sites with a similar design and URL to that of a legitimate site.
- They use real people or legitimate sources without their knowledge or approval.
- They edit, revise, or rewrite content (without permission) from legitimate sources to suit the writer's purpose.
- They take quotations or content out of context to create a deceptive impression.

For example, in January 2017, BuzzFeed reported on a site that used photos of physicist Steven Hawking, along with an "interview" in a synthesized voice similar to that used by Hawking, to promote a financial trading site in which unsuspecting users could lose thousands of dollars instantly. The fake news story appeared on a site that used CNN's logo and a similar URL (CNN's URL is CNN.com; the fake news site used CNN-trading.com). The headline on the site promised "A Computer Code Unlike Any Other" and included the byline of a nonexistent reporter. The fabricators even created a fake Facebook page and a fake news article for the fake reporter they created. (To read more about the deception, visit www.buzzfeed.com/jamesball/fake-news-site-uses-professor-stephen-hawking-to-sell-get-ri.)

Disinformation can be spread verbally, but it can also be spread visually, using photographs and videos. For example, a visual can be doctored or fabricated: A person's face can be superimposed on another person's body, photographs and videos can be cropped, the rate of speech can be changed, or new video or photographic details can be added. Or the original material can be edited: A photograph of a person can be cut and pasted to appear in any location the fabricator chooses, videos can be spliced to combine pieces from two videos as if they were from a single event, brief portions of a video can be removed from a full video to misrepresent the speaker's message, or a portion of a speech can be omitted to alter what the speaker actually said.

Strategies for Identifying Disinformation

Disinformation is often deliberately disguised as legitimate information. Use the following strategies, in addition to those provided for evaluating a source's reliability in Chapter 21, to detect untrustworthy information:

- **Scrutinize the domain, URL, and Web site format.** Untrustworthy sites may use a URL that differs only in domain name (*.com.co* rather than *.com*, for example). For a time, the fake site *ABCnew.com.co*, for example, was sucking in readers trying to get to the legitimate *ABCnews.com* Web site. Or they may take advantage of *typosquatting*, buying a common misspelling of a popular Web site's URL (*yuuotube.com*) to snag viewers.

- **Verify facts and be suspicious of facts published in only one source.** Most reliable information is published in a variety of sources. Google a questionable fact to see if it appears in several other sources that do not refer to the source you are using, or check facts using nonpartisan fact-checking sources like Factcheck.org or Snopes.com.

- **Check the "About Us" section.** Reputable Web sites present information about their organization, including their mission, leadership, ethics, and contact information. Be suspicious if the site lacks an "About Us" section or if that section is vague; doesn't name key figures in the organization; or uses reactionary, self-congratulatory, or melodramatic language.

- **Be alert for attention-grabbing headlines.** Known as *clickbait*, headlines like "5 Things Politicians/Doctors/Lawyers Don't Want You to Know—Number 3 Will Blow Your Mind" or "You Can Lose 20 Lbs in Just 4 Weeks by Eating This" entice you to click on them to continue reading. They often exaggerate or misrepresent the content presented.

- **Be skeptical of unnamed sources, researchers, surveys, or polls.** Credible sources identify their sources so you can verify the information presented and locate further data.

- **Evaluate images.** Visuals that accompany print content should clearly and accurately illustrate or supplement the print information. Writers of disinformation often do not create their own images; instead they "borrow" (steal) them from other sites. Check their legitimacy by clicking on the image and searching Google for it.

EXERCISE 3.5 ▶ **IDENTIFYING DISINFORMATION**

Below is a "news" story originally found online. Read the story and consider the questions in the margins. Then write a paragraph or two answering the following questions:

1. What techniques do the authors of this site use to convince readers the site is legitimate?
2. What do the authors do to make this article seem exciting and sensational?
3. How would you go about confirming a story like this?

1. Who is the author of this article?

2. Why is this page of *The Sun* inserted in the photograph?

3. What is the purpose of this statement? What action or behavior does it encourage?

5. What additional details about the location would be helpful?

6. How likely is it that a lab technician would be quoted? Does the quotation seem realistic? Why or why not?

9. Is this an authentic publication?

10. How, when, and where was this statement released?

4. By what process was this referred to the FBI? Why would the CIA be involved?

7. After reading this paragraph, what would you say is the author's attitude toward the FBI? Why?

8. Could President Nixon have "made this possible" in 1977? When was President Nixon in office?

NOW 8 NEWS
First in News

ABOUT

HOT TOPICS | THOUSANDS ATTENDED MIAMI GAY FESTIVAL; SEVERAL LATER TESTED POSITIVE FOR CORONAVIRUS

HOME   NEWS

Dead Body Of Homeless Man Turns Out To Be The Legendary Elvis Presley

The Sun
HE WAS 42 AND ALONE
KING ELVIS DEAD

POSTED BY: NOW8NEWS

Sharing is caring!

SAN DIEGO, California – A homeless man said to be around 80 years old was found deceased under a tree in San Diego, California. Nobody exactly knew the man's identity, but friends and people that frequent the area referred to him as Jessie. Investigators preformed a DNA test in the nationwide DNA database, and the results have shocked the nation. 'Jessie Doe's' DNA results matched that of Elvis Aaron Presley, who was thought to have died in 1977.

Lab technician Robert Brensdale said he and his lab assistant, Madeline Hedgespeth, laughed when the name popped up. *"We thought somebody, somewhere, somehow in the system pulled the greatest and most elaborate prank on us ever, we both laughed with hysteria for about an hour,"* Bresndale told Jerry Hardin of the Hollywood Word, a new entertainment publication based out of Los Angeles.

Brensdale and Hedgespeth then went to their superior with laughter, as if he were the one behind this "prank". They were told to simmer down and stay quiet, that this was no laughing matter. From there, the results went up the ladder to the FBI and CIA.

Now, weeks later, FBI spokesperson Philip Hunter has revealed that the deceased man's body was actually the body of Elvis Presley, who had been in the witness protection program since 1977.

The FBI has released this statement:

"Mr. Presley was placed in the program under a voluntary basis, but he was not a witness to any crime. Upon meeting President Nixon, the two became great friends, and Mr. Presley wanted out of his life, he wanted to be an unknown, so President Nixon made this possible. Yes, it is official – Elvis Presley was really alive all that time, and only a handful of people knew it, most of which are no longer with us."

His body will officially be laid to rest at his original burial site in the Meditation Garden at Graceland mansion at 3764 Elvis Presley Boulevard in Memphis, Tennessee. The date has not yet been announced.

Analyze the Author's Language

Authors often convey their message through the language they use, choosing words to create impressions, express feelings, even shape the readers' attitudes and feelings toward the topic. When analyzing language, be sure to consider denotative versus connotative meanings, figurative language, and euphemisms and doublespeak, as well as the writer's overall tone.

Consider Denotation versus Connotation

A **denotation** is the literal meaning of a word. For example, the denotation of the word *talking* is "expressing ideas using speech." A **connotation** is the set of additional meanings or associations that a word has taken on. Often a word's connotation has a much stronger effect on readers or listeners than its denotation does. The manner in which a politician talks to his or her audience might be described as "responding to ideas" (which carries a positive connotation), "discussing ideas" (which is an objective-sounding statement of fact), or "lecturing" or "ranting" (which give readers a negative impression). As you read, ask yourself, "What effect is the writer's word choice likely to have on readers?"

EXERCISE 3.6   **ANALYZING DENOTATION AND CONNOTATION**

For each of the following words, think of one word with a similar denotation but a positive connotation and another word with a similar denotation but a negative connotation.

▶ Group (of people): positive connotation, *audience*; negative connotation, *mob*

1. choosy
2. cheap
3. smart
4. bold
5. walk

Assess Figurative Language

Figurative language is language used in a nonliteral way to create a striking impression. For example, "The teenage boy tore into his sandwich like a hyena into a fallen zebra" creates a stronger image and conveys a more meaningful description than "He ate his sandwich quickly." The four common types of figurative expressions are:

1. **Personification.** Giving an object human qualities or characteristics. For example, in the sentence, "The urn glared at me from the mantelpiece," an urn (an inanimate object) is made to seem ominous.
2. **Symbolism.** Using one thing to represent something else. For instance, the White House is often considered a symbol of the United States. For many people, a car symbolizes freedom.
3. **Simile.** Comparing two items using the word *like* or *as*. For example, in *Peter Pan*, J. M. Barrie describes Mrs. Darling's mind with the following simile: "Her romantic mind was like the tiny boxes, one within the other, that come from the puzzling East."
4. **Metaphor.** Comparing two objects without using the word *like* or *as*. For example, Shakespeare wrote in *Romeo and Juliet*, "But soft, what light through yonder window breaks? / It is the east and Juliet is the sun." Here the speaker compares Juliet to the sun.

Most writers use figurative language to add color and shades of meaning to their writing. Carefully chosen, figurative language can persuade or convey a certain impression. For example, a political party may use powerful patriotic images, such as the

White House or the bald eagle, to convey the idea that their agenda is "what's right for America." In the quote from *Peter Pan* above, the author uses figurative language to convey a strong impression of Mrs. Darling: Her mind is "romantic" (which may connote "unrealistic" or "out of touch"), and it is similar to tiny boxes within boxes from the "puzzling East." Through this simile, Barrie implies that Mrs. Darling's thought processes are puzzling, even to the people who know her.

When you encounter figurative language, ask yourself the following questions:

- How does it affect the writer's tone?
- Does it advance the author's agenda?
- Does it reveal bias?
- Is the author using figurative language to inform and delight or to hide something?

EXERCISE 3.7 ▸ **RECOGNIZING SIMILES AND METAPHORS**

Identify each of the following excerpts as a simile or metaphor and explain the items being compared. What is the tone of each excerpt? How does the figurative language help to convey a particular impression?

1. "She entered with ungainly struggle like some huge awkward chicken, torn, squawking, out of its coop." —Sir Arthur Conan Doyle, "The Adventure of the Three Gables"
2. "Her father had inherited that temper; and at times, like antelope fleeing before fire on the slope, his people fled from his red rages." —Zane Grey, *Riders of the Purple Sage*
3. "Shall I compare thee to a summer's day? / Thou art more lovely and more temperate." —William Shakespeare, Sonnet 18

HOW READERS WRITE ▸ **FIGURATIVE LANGUAGE**

Figurative language can freshen and energize your writing, or, if used inappropriately, confuse readers and lead to misunderstanding. When using figures of speech, consider your audience.

- **What meaning, detail, or nuance will the figure of speech add?** That is, how will the figure of speech enhance the reader's experience or understanding?
- **Will your audience understand the comparison or reference?** For the figure of speech to be effective, your readers will need a basic understanding of all terms used. For example, if you write a simile comparing an embarrassed friend with Hester Prynne (from Nathaniel Hawthorne's *The Scarlet Letter*), your point may be lost if your audience has never read this book.
- **Will the comparison appeal to your readers?** If you compare something sacred and valued by your audience to something commercial and entertaining, you may alienate them. For example, comparing a Gothic cathedral with a castle at Disneyland might offend some readers.

See "Do You Use Fresh, Appropriate Figures of Speech" in Chapter 9 for more about using figures of speech in your writing.

Identify Euphemisms and Doublespeak

A **euphemism** is a word or phrase that is used to avoid a word that is unpleasant, embarrassing, or otherwise objectionable. For example, many people think it is more considerate to say that a loved one "passed away" rather than "died." Many people prefer the terms *disabled* and *person with disabilities* to the word *handicapped*.

Doublespeak is a type of euphemism that uses deliberately unclear or evasive language to sugarcoat an unpleasant reality. As a critical thinker you should always be alert for it, particularly when reading about business and politics. For example, a government spokesperson may say that it is engaging in "enhanced interrogation" when it is actually torturing prisoners; a corporation may tell employees that the company will be "smartsizing" instead of saying that some of them will be laid off.

Euphemisms and doublespeak use roundabout, indirect, or neutralized language to avoid stating the facts directly. Any time you encounter such language, your critical-thinking skills should kick into gear. Ask yourself questions like these:

- What is the author trying to prevent me from knowing?
- Why is the author hiding something: to spare my feelings, avoid personal embarrassment, or hide something nasty about the author or the group the author represents?

EXERCISE 3.8　　**RECOGNIZING EUPHEMISMS AND DOUBLESPEAK**

Answer each of the following questions:

1. The media often report about people from other countries who come to the United States without permission from the U.S. government or who stay here after their permission to visit has expired. Two terms are used to refer to these people: *illegal aliens* and *undocumented immigrants*. Discuss which term seems to have a more negative connotation and which seems more neutral. Why does each term carry the connotations it does? Is the more neutral term a euphemism? Why or why not?
2. Working with a classmate, brainstorm a list of euphemisms and doublespeak currently in use in the media. Be prepared to share your list with the class.

Analyze the Author's Tone

Tone refers to how a writer sounds to readers, and it is influenced by how the writer feels about his or her topic and readers and the language the writer uses to convey that attitude. Tone is constructed primarily by

- choosing words with the appropriate connotation
- using figurative language effectively
- using euphemism and doublespeak
- using stylistic features such as sentence patterns and length to lend emphasis

For more on sentence patterns and length, see "Analyze Your Sentences" in Chapter 9.

Using these strategies effectively, a writer can communicate surprise, disapproval, disgust, admiration, gratitude, or amusement. These are just a few of the words commonly used to describe tone; Table 3.1 lists many others. Recognizing an author's tone will help you interpret and evaluate the message and its effect on you.

TABLE 3.1 Words Commonly Used to Describe Tone

angry	detached	impassioned	objective
arrogant	earnest	indignant	sarcastic
bitter	forgiving	informative	serious
compassionate	frustrated	joyful	sympathetic
condescending	hateful	mocking	worried

HOW READERS WRITE ▶ **TONE**

Finding the most appropriate and effective tone to use in a piece of writing requires you to think critically about the characteristics of your audience and determine what would be clear, understandable, and appealing to them. In choosing a tone, consider the following:

- **Knowledge of the subject.** A helpful, supportive tone may be best if your readers are unfamiliar with the subject. However, if your readers are knowledgeable about your subject, they may regard a helpful, supportive tone as demeaning or insulting.

- **Background and experience.** Consider your readers' gender, education, professional position, age, and so forth in analyzing what tone would be most appropriate. For example, a lighthearted, familiar tone might not be appropriate for an academic paper intended for your professor or other scholars in the field.

- **Attitudes and beliefs.** If your audience agrees with your position on an issue, a passionate, highly partisan tone may be welcome, but if your audience disagrees, a passionate tone may offend or alienate your readers.

EXERCISE 3.9 **ANALYZING TONE**

Read each of the following statements and describe its tone. Which words in the statement provide clues to the tone? (Refer to Table 3.1 if necessary.)

1. Do you eat canned tuna? Then you are at least partially responsible for the deaths of thousands of innocent dolphins, which are mercilessly slaughtered by fishermen in their quest for tuna.

2. The penalty for creating and launching a computer virus should include a personal apology to every person who was affected by the virus, and each apology should be typed—without errors!—on a manual typewriter.

3. Piles of solid waste threaten to ruin our environment, pointing to the urgent need for better disposal methods and strategies for lowering the rate of waste generation.

4. All poets seek to convey emotion and the complete range of human feeling, but the only poet who fully accomplished this goal was William Shakespeare.

EXERCISE 3.10   EXPERIMENTING WITH TONE

Consider the following situation: A developer has received permission to bulldoze an entire city block filled with burned-out tenement buildings and abandoned factories. In their place, the developer is going to build a community of three hundred upscale condominiums for people who work in the city and want to live close to their jobs.

Write three different sentences (or paragraphs) that react to this news. Make the tone of your first sentence *outraged*. Make the tone of your second sentence *joyful*. Make the tone of your third sentence *nostalgic*.

Analyze the Author's Assumptions, Generalizations, and Omissions

Authors make decisions or take shortcuts that can influence readers' understanding. For example, they make assumptions and generalizations, and they decide which information to include or exclude. As a critical reader and writer, analyze the author's assumptions and assess whether the generalizations the author makes are fair and whether he or she omits any information that is important to a full understanding of the subject.

Recognize the Author's Assumptions

An **assumption** is an idea or principle the writer accepts as true and makes no effort to prove. Often the writer implies assumptions rather than stating them directly.

Some assumptions are fair and reasonable; others are not. For example, it is reasonable to assume that most of the people who read *People* magazine are interested in celebrities. It is not reasonable to assume that readers of *People* magazine are Republicans.

Assumptions can be based on any combination of the following:

- anecdotal evidence
- facts
- opinions
- values and beliefs
- personal experiences
- background

Writers often make assumptions at the beginning of an essay and then base the rest of the essay on that assumption. If the assumption is false or cannot be proven, then the ideas that flow from it may also be incorrect. For instance, the following excerpt begins with an assumption (highlighted) that the writer makes no attempt to prove or justify:

> Childbirth is a painful experience, intolerable even with appropriate medications. In response to this pain, modern women should accept the painkillers offered to them by their doctors. Why be a martyr? You have to suffer sleepless nights because of your child for the rest of your life; bring them into this world on your terms—pain free. Women should not be embarrassed or reluctant to request anesthesia during labor.

The author assumes that all women find childbirth intolerably painful and then argues that women should request anesthesia during labor. But if the writer's initial assumption is false, much of the argument that follows should be questioned.

As you read, look for assumptions the author takes for granted, and then decide whether these assumptions are realistic and reasonable by asking questions like these:

- Are these assumptions supported by facts?
- Does the writer use terms that have more than one meaning or interpretation? Would the writer's preferred definition be acceptable to most readers?
- How do the writer's assumptions reinforce or challenge social norms (or standards)?
- What effects do these assumptions have on the essay? Whose interests are served?
- What information, beliefs, or values, if any, would raise doubts about this assumption?

The answers to these questions will help you determine whether arguments or opinions based on these assumptions make sense. If you disagree with some of the assumptions in a source, check other sources to obtain different viewpoints.

HOW READERS WRITE ▷ **ASSUMPTIONS**

In your writing, you will undoubtedly make assumptions that reflect your own beliefs and traditions. But be on the lookout for assumptions that may not be shared.

- **Be sure your assumptions are reasonable and supportable.** You may assume, for example, in an essay on how to overcome rising college costs, that a college education is valuable and worthwhile. Recognize, however, that while most readers would agree with this assumption, some may not.

- **If readers are likely to disagree with your assumption, include evidence that validates your assumption.** You could offer statistics showing, for example, that on average a college education increases lifetime earnings.

EXERCISE 3.11   IDENTIFYING ASSUMPTIONS

Identify the assumption(s) made in each of the following statements:

1. Computer users expect Web sites to entertain them with graphics, sound, and video.
2. In response to the problem of ozone depletion, the U.S. Environmental Protection Agency has designed various programs to reduce harmful emissions. It wants to stop the production of certain substances so that the ozone layer can repair itself over the next fifty years.
3. Only the routine vaccination of all children can eliminate the threat of serious disease and ensure optimum public health. These shots should be administered without hesitation. Parents must have full confidence in their doctors on this matter.
4. Since so many athletes and coaches approve of the use of performance-enhancing drugs, these substances should be allowed without regulation.
5. Because they recognize that meat consumption is environmentally damaging, environmentalists are often vegetarians.

EXERCISE 3.12   IDENTIFYING ASSUMPTIONS IN A READING

Reread "American Jerk" in Chapter 2. What assumptions does the author make in the first four paragraphs of the essay?

Assess the Author's Generalizations

A **generalization** is a claim based on one or more specific examples and applied more widely. Many writers generalize to argue a point, and generalizations may be reasonable or not. They are unreasonable when they are based on too little evidence or when all the variables are not taken into consideration (hasty generalization) and also when the conclusion is applied more widely than the evidence supports (sweeping generalization). Consider the following example: A woman who feels unfulfilled in her emotional life divorces her husband, leaves her children, and decides to travel the world. As she travels, she learns more about herself and falls in love with a new man. Based on this one woman's experience, it would be a sweeping generalization to assume that all women in search of a richer emotional life should leave their husbands and children to travel the world.

Most generalizations, however, are not so clearly reasonable or unreasonable. Imagine you are reading an article by a writer who argues that cars should be prohibited in congested cities. To support this claim, the writer cites studies showing the benefits of banning cars in three European cities. Is such a generalization fair? The reader must decide whether these three case studies provide *sufficient* evidence for such a generalization.

When assessing generalizations, ask yourself the following questions:

- How many examples has the author provided?
- Are these examples representative of the situation? That is, do the examples represent most people's experiences?
- Can the generalization be proved scientifically? In other words, is there a scientific consensus about the generalization?

For more about reasoning—and errors in reasoning—see "Defect Faulty Reasoning" in Chapter 19 and "Effective Arguments Are Logical" in Chapter 20.

Generalizations can provide many ideas for your own writing. An informative essay might look at the evidence supporting and contradicting a generalization. A persuasive essay might argue that an assumption is unreasonable or unfair.

HOW READERS WRITE ▷ **GENERALIZATIONS**

Ask yourself these questions to analyze the generalizations you make in your own writing.

- **Is it logical?** Is your generalization one that most reasonable people would accept? For example, most would not accept the generalization "Because Dr. Harper is young, she is bound to be a good doctor," because age is not commonly associated with medical competence.

- **Is it supportable?** Can you provide concrete and convincing evidence that will encourage your readers to accept your generalization? For example, you would find it difficult if not impossible to support the claim "Every college student is primarily interested in obtaining a high-paying job," because you could not find out what every single college student's goals are.

EXERCISE 3.13 ▷ **IDENTIFYING GENERALIZATIONS**

Label each of the following statements fact (*F*) or generalization (*G*). Indicate what support or documentation would be necessary for you to evaluate its accuracy.

1. Many women want to become pilots.
2. Elephants can vocalize at frequencies below the range of human hearing.
3. In certain parts of the Red Sea, the temperature of the water can reach 138 degrees Fahrenheit.
4. Most people who live in San Diego are associated with the U.S. Navy.
5. People all over the world showed sympathy by donating money to Serbian refugees.

Look for Purposeful Omissions

Writers and speakers sometimes mislead by omission.

- They leave out essential information, background, or context, or include only the details that favor their position.
- They adopt the passive voice (*a decision was made*) to avoid taking or assigning responsibility for an action.
- They use vague nouns and pronouns (*they are bleeding our city's coffers dry*) to avoid specifying exactly what or whom they are referring to.

Consider an article written by a parent who has home-schooled her children. As an advocate of home schooling, she is likely to emphasize her children's educational progress and her own sense of personal fulfillment achieved by teaching her children. However, she may omit information—for example, that home-schooled children sometimes feel lonely or isolated from their peers. She also may refer to home schooling as "better" for children without specifying exactly what it is better than (her local public school, public schools in general, or any kind of school) or in what ways it is better.

Regardless of what you are reading, ask yourself the following questions to be sure you are getting full and complete information:

- Has any important information or contradictory evidence been omitted? What, if anything, am I not being told?
- Is it clear to whom actions or thoughts are being attributed? If not, why not?
- Is there another side to this argument or aspect to this topic that I should consider?
- Based on my own knowledge and experience, how do I evaluate this material?

To answer these questions, you may need to do some additional reading or research.

EXERCISE 3.14 IDENTIFYING PURPOSEFUL OMISSIONS

Read the following scenarios and determine what information is being withheld from you. What additional information do you need to determine whether you are being misled?

1. You see a TV ad for a fast-food restaurant that shows a huge hamburger topped with pickles, onions, and tomatoes. The announcer says, "For a limited time, get your favorite burger for only ninety-nine cents!"
2. You open your mailbox and find a letter from a credit-card company. The letter invites you to open a charge card with no annual fee and offers you instant credit if you return the attached card in a postage-paid envelope.
3. You are shopping online for an exercise bike and find one that appears to be a good deal. The site states that it requires some assembly, shipping and handling charges may apply, and seat cushion style may vary.

EXERCISE 3.15 IDENTIFYING BIAS IN A READING SELECTION

Reread the excerpt from "American Jerk" in Exercise 3.1. Using the techniques described in "Analyze the Author's Language," write a paragraph explaining whether you detect hidden bias in the selection or whether the writer makes clear that he is expressing only one viewpoint among others. If you detect bias, point to purposeful omissions or other strategies (such as his word choices) the writer uses to hide his biases. If you do not, explain why you feel the excerpt is not biased.

Use the Patterns of Development to Think and Read Critically

The patterns you will learn to identify and use in Part 3 suggest useful questions for critical reading, questions that highlight aspects of the reading selection you might not otherwise have considered. Each chapter in Part 3 includes a box called "How Writers Read." These boxes explore in depth the concerns critical readers and thinkers should address as they analyze and evaluate readings using each pattern.

Use Synthesis to Think and Read Critically

For more about synthesis, see "Work with Sources: Evaluate Your Notes and Synthesize" in Chapter 22.

At times you may realize that you do not have sufficient knowledge or experience to analyze and evaluate an author's ideas. In such cases, you may need to locate additional sources to fill in the gaps, provide additional viewpoints, challenge the author's assumptions or speculations, or offer more detailed evidence. When you synthesize information from sources to assess or challenge a writer's assumptions or claims, you must do two things:

1. Synthesize, or merge, information from sources with your existing, but limited, knowledge and experience.
2. Test the evidence or claims from the original reading against your own experience and what you've learned from the new sources.

Use the following questions as guidelines:

- **On what do two or more of the sources agree?** On what, if anything, do they disagree?
- **What new information or perspectives did you encounter?** Did they reinforce or challenge information or ideas in the other source(s)?
- **In what ways do the new sources help you understand the original reading?** Do they provide context, expand upon a topic, or challenge the writer's interpretation, for example?

EXERCISE 3.16 ▸ **SYNTHESIZING YOUR SKILLS**

As a cumulative activity and to synthesize all the critical-thinking strategies you have learned in this chapter, refer to the reading "Why Do So Many People Fall for Fake Profiles Online?" in Chapter 2, to answer the following questions:

1. Do a brief online search to evaluate Arun Vishwanath's qualifications to write about fake profiles online. Explain why he is or is not qualified to write on this topic.

2. What types of evidence does Vishwanath use to support his ideas? Give several examples, and explain in a sentence or two whether the evidence is relevant.

3. Identify at least three statements of fact and three statements of opinion Vishwanath makes.

4. Identify at least five words with positive or negative connotations.

5. Describe the author's tone. What effect does the tone have on you as a reader? How effective do you find it?

6. Identify at least one assumption the author makes.

7. What generalizations does the author make? List two.

8. What additional information would you need to evaluate Vishwanath's claims?

9. Based on your analysis, do you think Vishwanath seems fair or biased? Write a paragraph justifying your answer.

Reading Visuals Critically

Visuals appear everywhere—on television and in movies; in magazines, newspapers, text-books, and presentation slides; on signs, flyers, and billboards; in print and online. They may appear on their own, but often they are combined with text to make a message even more effective. Visuals are used so widely because they can convey information and impressions, sell products and ideas, raise questions, and trigger emotions. Because they are so powerful, make sure you study them as carefully as you read, analyze, and evaluate written text. You should also choose them carefully when you use them in your own writing.

For more about how to incorporate a visual into an essay, see "Academic Writing: Integrating Evidence from Sources" in Chapter 5.

Take a look at Figure 3.1 (on p. 76), for example. This is a public service advertisement (PSA) from the National Highway Safety Transportation Administration. What did you notice first? Perhaps you noticed "Distraction Is Deadly: 3,166." Or perhaps you noticed the photograph of the tombstone engraved with the letters *Smh*, an abbreviation for "shaking my head," an expression often used in text messages to express disdain for something so stupid that words alone cannot convey it. Or maybe you noticed the headline "U Drive. U Text. U Pay."

Whatever you noticed first, second, or third, when you put the text and images together, you recognized the purpose of the ad: to encourage readers not to text while driving. The design, the colors, and the headline contrasting with the tombstone image—together these elements make a dramatic statement about the dangers of texting while driving. By combining words and images, this PSA makes the issue of texting while driving much more compelling and engaging than it would have been with written text alone.

FIGURE 3.1   Distracted Driving Claims Lives

Distracted Driving

Overview

Distracted driving is dangerous, claiming 3,166 lives in 2017 alone. NHTSA leads the national effort to save lives by preventing this dangerous behavior. Get the facts, get involved, and help us keep America's roads safe.

Share: f   🐦   in   ✉

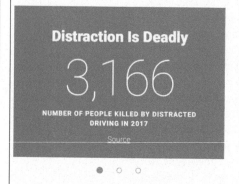

Distraction Is Deadly

3,166

NUMBER OF PEOPLE KILLED BY DISTRACTED DRIVING IN 2017

Source

● ○ ○

According to the National Highway Traffic Safety Administration, distracted drivers killed more than 3,000 people in 2017. The highest rate of distracted driving occurred among those fifteen to nineteen years old. National Highway Traffic Safety Administration

Analyze Photographs

Use these guidelines when reading photographs and any words (captions, labels, slogans, text) that accompany them.

1. **Preview the visual.** What is its main subject? What did you notice first, and how did it affect you?
2. **Study the visual as a whole, and then examine its parts.** What is its focal point? What details appear in the foreground and the background? (Translating the photo into words may be helpful.) Is it a close-up or a distance shot? (Close-ups may reveal emotions; distance shots provide more context.)
3. **Read the caption and any accompanying text, consider the context, and make connections.** What information about time, place, or subject is provided? What does the author want to emphasize? How does the photo relate to the ideas presented in the surrounding text? What happened before or after the photo was taken? Is any other context provided?
4. **Determine the author's purpose and intended message.** Is the purpose to inform, amuse, shock, persuade, or some combination of these or other motives? Is the photo intended to elicit a powerful reaction from viewers or to provide information?

What do you learn when you apply these guidelines to the photograph in Figure 3.2, which is taken from a communications textbook?

FIGURE 3.2 Reading Happens Anytime, Anywhere

Glow - Hola/Glow - Hola/Superstock

EXERCISE 3.17 ANALYZING A TEXTBOOK PHOTO

Apply the guidelines for analyzing photos above to the photo in Figure 3.3, which is taken from an economics textbook. Then answer these questions:

1. Describe your first impression of the photo.
2. Summarize what is happening in the photo. What details convey this impression? Is it a close-up or distance shot? What is revealed (or hidden) about the subject of the photograph as a result?
3. What does the caption or any context contribute to your understanding of the photo? (This photograph appeared in an economics textbook in a chapter titled "Factor Markets and Distribution of Income.")
4. Why did the author include this photo? Does it reveal any assumptions or biases?
5. Does the photo look staged, edited, or touched up? If so, what details convey this impression?
6. Does the photo achieve the author's purpose? What other kinds of photos or visuals might the writer have used to make the same point? (Provide reasons or use details from the photograph to support your claim.)

FIGURE 3.3 The Value of a Degree

If you have doubts about completing college, consider this: Factory workers with high school diplomas earn much less than college graduates. The present discounted value of the difference in lifetime earnings is as much as $1 million. Monika Graff/The Image Works

Analyze Graphics

Graphics organize and condense information, making lengthy or complicated data and concepts easier to understand. Writers use many types of graphics; the purpose of each of the common types is summarized in Table 3.2.

TABLE 3.2 Graphics and Their Purposes

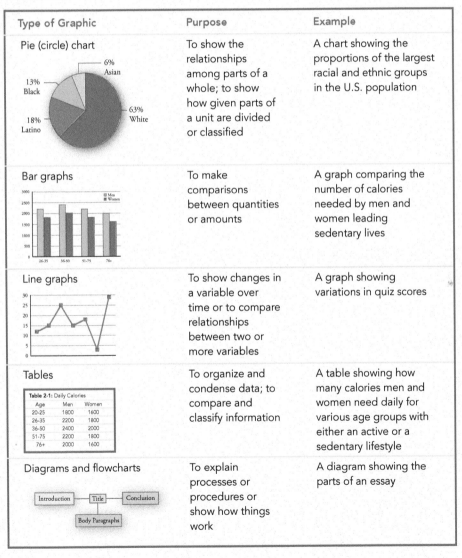

Type of Graphic	Purpose	Example
Pie (circle) chart	To show the relationships among parts of a whole; to show how given parts of a unit are divided or classified	A chart showing the proportions of the largest racial and ethnic groups in the U.S. population
Bar graphs	To make comparisons between quantities or amounts	A graph comparing the number of calories needed by men and women leading sedentary lives
Line graphs	To show changes in a variable over time or to compare relationships between two or more variables	A graph showing variations in quiz scores
Tables	To organize and condense data; to compare and classify information	A table showing how many calories men and women need daily for various age groups with either an active or a sedentary lifestyle
Diagrams and flowcharts	To explain processes or procedures or show how things work	A diagram showing the parts of an essay

Use these guidelines when analyzing graphics and any words (captions, labels, slogans, text) that accompany them:

1. **Preview the table or chart.** Read the title and caption (if any) and look quickly at the table or chart. What is it supposed to show?
2. **Look at the headings (of tables/charts), labels (of figures), and legends (of charts/figures) to determine how the data are organized.** The headings and labels should indicate the variables. The legend (or guide to the colors, symbols, terms, or other information) should show what is being analyzed. A scale shows how measurements should be read.
3. **Read the caption (if any) and any discussion of the graphic in the text, and make connections.** Does the text explain why the graphic was included or what it is intended to show? (If not, make your own connections between the text and graphic.) To understand a complicated graphic, you may need to study the text and graphic carefully several times. Read the whole explanation in the text before looking back at the graphic.
4. **Study the data to try to identify trends or patterns.** Note unexpected changes (such as sudden increases or decreases in amounts), surprising statistics, or unexplained variations. Summarize any trends and note any patterns you find. Writing will crystallize the idea in your mind, and your notes will be useful for review.
5. **Check the source of the data.** Are the data from a reliable source? Are they up to date?

EXERCISE 3.18 ► ANALYZING A TABLE

Use the guidelines above to analyze Table 3.3.

TABLE 3.3 ► Book Reading Habits, 2018 (by Age)

Age	18–29	30–49	50–64	65+
Read book in any format	84	74	71	67
Read a print book	75	67	65	63
Read an e-book	34	31	20	15
Listened to an audiobook	23	22	15	12

SOURCE: Data from Andrew Perrin, "FactTank: Nearly One-in-Five Americans Now Listen to Audiobooks," Pew Research Center, 8 Mar. 2018, www.pewresearch.org/fact-tank/2018/03/08/nearly-one-in-five-americans-now-listen-to-audiobooks

EXERCISE 3.19 **WORKING WITH TABLES AND FIGURES**

Study the figure below, which converts some of the data from Table 3.3 into a line graph, and answer the questions that follow.

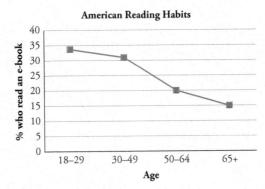

1. Compare this figure with Table 3.3. What variables does this figure use? Which data from that table were used to create this figure?
2. What title would you give this figure? The title should accurately describe the information conveyed by the figure.
3. Write a caption for this figure that accurately describes the trend(s) it shows.

EXERCISE 3.20 **WRITING ABOUT GRAPHICS**

Examine the graphics that accompany the reading "Why Do So Many People Fall for Fake Profiles Online?" in Chapter 2 (or another reading chosen by your instructor). Then write a paragraph explaining their purpose, describing their organization, and discussing the trends or patterns they show.

Think Critically about Photos and Graphics

Just as you should critically examine all the words you read, you should also critically examine all visuals that accompany a reading. Photographs and graphics may reflect bias or distort information, either intentionally or unintentionally. For example, an author may choose more or less powerful or flattering photographs demonstrating support or criticism of a person or issue (see Figure 3.4, p. 82).

Or an author may crop a photo to distort the viewer's perception (see Figure 3.5, p. 82). The first photo in the series shows only a gun barrel, apparently pointing at the head of the wounded soldier (the focal length appears to have been shortened); the last photo shows only the soldier being given water from a canteen; only the photo in the middle shows both the gun and the canteen.

When reading graphics, consider also whether showing the data in a different type of graphic would change the reader's perception of the information. Compare Figure 3.6 (p. 83) with Exercise 3.19. How does showing the data in a bar graph change your perception of the data?

FIGURE 3.4   The Power of Pictures

Simone Biles, American gymnast   AP Images/Melissa J. Perenson/CSM

FIGURE 3.5   Cropping Photographs to Affect Viewers' Reactions

AP Images/Itsuo Inouye

FIGURE 3.6 Shaping Readers' Perceptions through Depiction of the Data

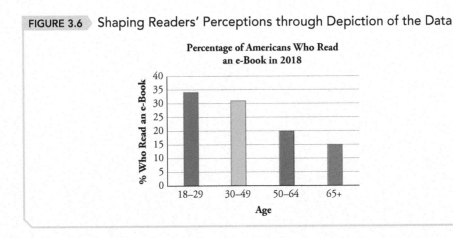

Percentage of Americans Who Read an e-Book in 2018

Finally, consider whether the scale or units of measurement are misleading in any way. Reducing the scale, for example, can make differences seem huge, and expanding the scale can make them seem tiny. Compare the bar graph in Figure 3.7 with that in Figure 3.6. The data used in both charts are the same, but because the chart in Figure 3.6 reduces the scale, the difference between the groups appears more dramatic than it is.

FIGURE 3.7 Misleading by Adjusting the Scale

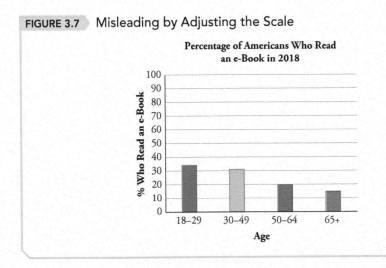

Percentage of Americans Who Read an e-Book in 2018

Be especially careful when pictures are used in graphics instead of lines or bars (Figure 3.8). The labels in this graphic clearly indicate that more U.S. households own dogs (36.5%) than own cats (30.4%). But the relative size of the two animals suggests that the percentage difference is much greater than 6.1% (36.5–30.4%). If you looked only at the images, you might assume that dog ownership is much greater than it really is. You might

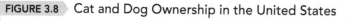

FIGURE 3.8   Cat and Dog Ownership in the United States

30.4% of U.S. households   36.5% of U.S. households
own at least one cat   own at least one dog

SOURCE: Data from American Pet Products Association, American Veterinary Medicine Association, and the Humane Society of the United States. humanesociety.org/issues/pet_overpopulation/facts/ pet_ownership_statistics.html, avma.org/KB/Resources/Statistics/Pages/Market-research-statistics-US -pet-ownership.aspx. *(cat)* © Benjamin Simeneta/Shutterstock.com; *(dog)* © ARTSILENCE/Shutterstock.com

also reasonably conclude that there are more pet dogs than pet cats in the United States, but the labels indicate that the pictures represent households that own *at least one* cat or dog. Some households may own two, six, or even ten cats. In fact, as of 2013 the American Pet Products Association estimates that there were over 10 million more pet cats than pet dogs in the United States. But you wouldn't know this from a glance at this graphic.

Oli Scarff/Getty Images

Just-in-Time Guide to Reading and Responding

Many of the reading assignments for your college courses will be straightforward. Some, however, may make you throw your up hands and say, "I can't handle this!" This guide will help you overcome the obstacles you face and find answers to the questions you have. This guide is the help you need, just in time. Because reading and writing are two sides of the same process, much of what you learn in this Just-in-Time Guide can be flipped and applied to issues you encounter as a writer.

1   Getting Started

Each time you begin a new reading, you are starting from scratch. What do you do if you're having difficulty getting started?

1a If I don't know anything about the subject, what should I do?

Having even a small amount of background knowledge will help you orient yourself to the reading, which will help you learn more. Use these two key strategies: Preview the reading, and Google the topic.

1. **Preview the reading.** You learned to preview in Chapter 2. It is a fast and easy way to become familiar with the reading's content and organization, and it gives you a good sense of what the selection is about. If you're having trouble getting started (or even if you're not), begin by previewing.

2. **Google the topic, especially unfamiliar terminology.** To find needed background information, look for sources that are written for the beginner or novice and that come from a credible source. For example, suppose your biology instructor assigns a chapter titled "Biodiversity." A quick Web search will help you learn the basic meaning of *biodiversity* ("the variety of life in a particular habitat"). *Note:* Many other search engines can be as effective as Google. Try using Ask.com, WebCrawler, and Yahoo if Google doesn't return the results you want. Also, if you're a visual learner, try searching YouTube for videos that provide background information on your topic.

For more about credibility, see Chapter 21.

1b What can I do to keep my mind on an unappealing topic or selection?

All readings are not equally interesting. How do you stay focused on dry, technical reading assignments, especially when you're not particularly interested in the topic?

1. **Ask and answer questions.** Create a dialogue with the text. By asking and answering questions about the reading, you turn the reading into a quest for information. You can base your questions on titles or chapters or sections, like so:

Chapter Title or Section	Questions
Psychological Disorders	What is a psychological disorder?
Supply and Demand	What are supply and demand?
The Human Development Index	What is the human development index, and what does it measure?

2. **Be active: write, think, talk aloud, draw diagrams.** Read with a pencil in your hand. Take notes in the margins, sketch out important concepts, or write a response at the top or bottom of the page. Get up, walk around the room, and talk to yourself about what you've read to get ideas flowing.

3. **Predict what will come next.** Writers provide signals (transitions and repetition) to prepare you for what's coming next. Watch for these cues. When you see one, stop for a moment to predict what the author is about to say:

> Nonverbal communication means communication that takes place without words or sounds. Body language is a key form of nonverbal communication. For example, standing with your arms crossed can send a signal that you are feeling mistrustful, insecure, or uncomfortable.

Expect an illustration of body language to follow.

4. **Brainstorm with classmates.** Talk with your classmates to clarify concepts and form study groups. In your study group, prepare for exams by trying to figure out which questions will be on the exam. If a group member comes up with a question that you can't answer, write it down and ask your instructor during the next class session.

5. **Relate the author's ideas to your own experience.** You will learn the material more effectively and have a better sense of its relevance if you can relate the ideas you are reading about to your own life or experience. Consider this example from a sociology textbook:

> A (dyad) is a group of two people, the smallest possible social group.

My parents are a dyad. So is any couple.

1c How can I figure out what I am supposed to learn from an assignment?

Your instructor and your course materials (such as your syllabus or textbook) can help you determine what exactly you need to learn from each assignment:

1. **Take cues from your instructor.** Often your instructor will identify the goals for each assignment. If you're not sure of your instructor's expectations, ask.

Your Instructor Says . . .	Clue: What You Should Learn
"Read the excerpt from Maya Angelou's *I Know Why the Caged Bird Sings* and come to class prepared to discuss it."	A discussion generally centers on key ideas, so you know that you are not expected to memorize every detail in the reading selection.
"Read the chapter on sensation and perception, and be ready for a pop quiz."	Read for main ideas, because most pop quizzes test on major concepts, not tiny details.
"Come to the lab knowing all the bones in the human arm."	Memorize *all* the bones in the arm, not just a few of them.

2. **Refer to the syllabus.** Determine how each assignment matches the course goals or learning objectives on the syllabus, and spend more time on readings that directly relate to each of those objectives. If you are unsure of the goal of any given assignment,

For more about how to use a syllabus, see Chapter 1.

don't be shy about asking your instructor. Do *not* ask "Will this be on the test?"—which implies that you care only about the right answers and not about gaining knowledge or learning. Rather, ask "What should I be able to do after reading this assignment?"

3. **Use learning objectives.** Learning objectives often appear in textbooks, either at the beginning of the chapter (as in this text) or at the beginning of each new section. They often begin with imperative verbs (commands) like *describe, list, explain, define, compare, summarize,* or *analyze.* As you complete each section, make sure you can do exactly what the learning objective says you must do.

Learning Objective	What You Must Do
Apply broken windows theory to the experience of New York City in the 1980s.	Show *how* New York City used broken windows theory in the 1980s. Being able to *define* broken window theory is not enough to accomplish this objective.
List and *explain* the four key elements of management.	Identify each of the four key components of management (planning, organizing, leading, and controlling) *and* describe what each one is or does.

1d What should I do when an assignment has me feeling overwhelmed or completely lost?

Sometimes, despite your best efforts, you feel completely defeated by an assignment. No matter how hard you try, you can't make any progress—but you still have to complete it. What should you do?

1. **Read the headnote or chapter introduction.** Both provide invaluable pathways into the reading.
   - A *headnote* is brief information about the assignment that appears after the author and title, but before the reading itself. Headnotes are often included with essays or literature. They provide key biographical information about the author, along with some context about the reading.
   - A *chapter introduction* often includes a *vignette,* or story, or a visual that helps to set the stage for the chapter. Many students are tempted to skip the chapter introduction because they think, "I just want to get on with it." Skipping chapter introductions is a mistake, because they often include interesting examples that bring concepts to life.
2. **Read the items that follow the reading.** A highly effective way to prepare yourself for a reading assignment is to preview the end-of-chapter material.
   - Lists of **key terms** identify essential vocabulary.
   - **Summaries and comprehension, discussion, and critical-thinking questions** signal which material is most important in the chapter.

Core Concepts Summary

2.1 THE ATOM IS THE FUNDAMENTAL UNIT OF MATTER.

Atoms consist of positively charged protons and electrically neutral neutrons in the nucleus, and negatively charged electrons darting around the nucleus. page 2-1

The number of protons determines the identity of an atom. page 2-2

Protons and neutrons together determine the mass of an atom. page 2-2

Protons and electrons determine the charge of an atom. page 2-3

Negatively charged electrons travel around the nucleus in regions called orbitals. page 2-3

The periodic table of the elements reflects a regular and repeating pattern in the chemical behavior of elements. page 2-3

2.2 ATOMS CAN COMBINE TO FORM MOLECULES LINKED BY CHEMICAL BONDS.

Electrons that occupy the outermost energy level (shell) of an atom (valence electrons) determine its ability to combine with other atoms to form molecules. page 2-4

A covalent bond results from the sharing of electrons between atoms to form molecular orbitals. page 2-4

A polar covalent bond results when two atoms do not share electrons equally as a result of a difference in the ability of the atoms to attract electrons, a property called electronegativity. page 2-5

Core concepts summary, pp. 2–19, from Morris, James, et al., *How Life Works*, W. H. Freeman, 2013

3. **Talk to your instructor.** When all else fails, ask your instructor for help. He or she may be able to recommend background readings or study aids, refer you to the tutoring center, and offer other tools that will help you. Do not be afraid to approach your instructors; they are there to help you learn.

2   Learning Words

Words are the building blocks of language; they are the keys to both reading and writing more effectively. As a college student, you will encounter many unfamiliar words.

2a   Do I need to learn every unfamiliar word?

The answer is no! (This is not the answer you expected, right?) It is impossible to learn all the words in the English language. Instead, focus on learning vocabulary that you will need to write effectively in your classes (including essay exams).

Each academic discipline has its own vocabulary, a set of terms that is unique to the field or that is used in a specific way. For example, in psychology, you may need to learn terms such as *placebo effect* ("improvement resulting from the belief that medicine is effective") or understand the specialized meaning of the word *extinction* ("the gradual weakening of conditioned behavior").

Classical Conditioning | 189

Extinction and Spontaneous Recovery

Once learned, can conditioned responses be eliminated? Pavlov (1927) found that conditioned responses could be gradually weakened. If the conditioned stimulus (the ringing bell) was repeatedly presented *without* being paired with the unconditioned stimulus (the food), the conditioned response seemed to gradually disappear. Pavlov called this process of decline and eventual disappearance of the conditioned response **extinction.**

Pavlov also found that the dog did not simply return to its unconditioned state following extinction (see Figure 5.2). If the animal was allowed a period of rest (such as a few hours) after the response was extinguished, the conditioned response would reappear when the conditioned stimulus was again presented. This reappearance of a previously extinguished conditioned response after a period of time without exposure to the conditioned stimulus is called **spontaneous recovery.** The phenomenon of spontaneous recovery demonstrates that extinction is not unlearning. That is, the learned response may seem to disappear, but it is *not* eliminated or erased (Archbold & others, 2010; Rescorla, 2001).

■ **extinction** (in classical conditioning) The gradual weakening and apparent disappearance of conditioned behavior. In classical conditioning, extinction occurs when the conditioned stimulus is repeatedly presented without the unconditioned stimulus.

■ **spontaneous recovery** The reappearance of a previously extinguished conditioned response after a period of time without exposure to the conditioned stimulus.

Extinction and spontaneous recovery definition; marginal definitions, p. 189, from Hockenbury & Hockenbury, *Psychology*, 6e, Worth, 2013

KEY TERMS

learning, p. 184

conditioning, p. 184

classical conditioning, p. 186

unconditioned stimulus (UCS), p. 186

unconditioned response (UCR), p. 186

conditioned stimulus (CS), p. 186

conditioned response (CR), p. 186

stimulus generalization, p. 188

stimulus discrimination, p. 188

higher order conditioning, p. 188

extinction (in classical conditioning), p. 189

Key terms, p. 228 (1st col. + heading), from Hockenbury & Hockenbury, *Psychology*, 6e, Worth, 2013

You can recognize the terms you need to learn because

- **Your instructor will use them.** She may emphasize or define terms in class: "Make sure you understand the key elements of *Pavlovian conditioning*." Or she may repeat them or list them on a lecture slide. Record these terms in your class notes and code them so that you can find them easily for study and review.
- **Your textbook will define them.** These terms may appear in the text (in **boldface** or *italics*, as in the example on p. 89), in the margin, in a list of key terms at the end of the chapter, or in a glossary at the end of the book.
- **They appear in research articles or reports in scholarly journals.**

2b What should I do if I don't know the meaning of a word?

1. **Pronounce it.** By pronouncing the word *magnific* aloud, you may hear part of the word *magnify* and know that it has something do with enlargement. This general meaning may give you enough information to continue reading. (*Magnific* means "large, imposing, or impressive.")
2. **Look for context clues to meaning.** These clues may appear within the sentence or in surrounding sentences.

Type of Clue	Example
Definition or Synonym	*introduced* is a synonym for "prefaced" The poet *prefaced*, or <u>introduced</u>, her reading with a personal story.
Example	These examples suggest that opiates are painkilling drugs. *Opiates*, such as <u>methadone, oxycodone, and morphine</u>, are often misused and abused.
Contrast/ Opposites	The underlined phrase provides a term opposite in meaning to the phrase in italics. In certain societies children are always *on the periphery*, <u>never the center</u>, of family life.
Inference	Your experience helps you understand that *fracas* means "scuffle" or "brawl." After the playoff game, a *fracas* broke out among hometown fans of the losing team.

Be sure to confirm that you have figured out the correct meaning by substituting the meaning in the sentence and checking that it makes sense.

3. **Use word parts.** Many words are made up of *prefixes* (beginnings), *roots* (middles), and *suffixes* (endings) that have specific meanings. By looking at its parts, you may be able to figure out the meaning of an unfamiliar word. Understanding the word parts will make the word easier to remember, too.

Prefix +	Root +	Suffix =	New Word
three	color	pertaining to	having three colors
tri	chrom	atic	trichromatic

If you are studying the sciences, you will find word parts essential in learning a vast number of new vocabulary words. In anatomy and physiology, for example, if you learn that *hypo* means "below" or "deficient," you can figure out words such as *hypodermis* (the lowest layer of the skin), *hypocalcemia* (calcium deficiency), *hypoglycemic* (low blood sugar), *hypotension* (low blood pressure), and so forth.

4. **Use a dictionary.** Dictionaries are no longer huge, clunky books that sit on library stands—they now appear online and as smartphone apps, and most of them are free. Many e-readers, including Amazon Kindle, have built-in dictionaries that allow you to click on a word and pull up its definition. Even Microsoft Word has a built-in dictionary that you can access by highlighting a word and right-clicking on it.

Some online dictionaries such as Merriam-Webster.com feature an audio button that you can "push" to hear the word pronounced out loud. Most dictionaries also provide the word's *etymology* (origin and history), which can be useful in helping you learn the word.

Because accessing a dictionary is now so easy, you might think a dictionary should be your first line of defense, but if you find many unfamiliar words in a passage, looking up every one may not be practical. You are also more likely to learn a word if you try pronouncing it, looking for context clues, or analyzing its parts before turning to a dictionary.

5. **Make marginal notes.** When you figure out the meaning of a new word or look it up, jot its meaning in the margin so you don't forget it. Writing down the word's meaning also helps to cement it in your memory.

2c Which online resources are useful for vocabulary development?

The following resources are reliable and trustworthy:

- Merriam-Webster.com is a reliable online dictionary that offers audio pronunciation and etymology, as well as definitions, synonyms, and antonyms.
- Refdesk.com is an online reference source that provides factual information about people, places, and events. (This site is chock-full of links, so stay focused on finding what you need.) You will find the links to dictionary.com and Merriam-Webster at the center of the page, under the category "More Word of the Day."

2d How can I learn the words I need to know?

The key to learning any new word is to use it. Experts estimate that you need to use a word five to ten times before you learn it, so practice using new vocabulary at every opportunity as you speak and write.

- **Be sure you know how to pronounce the word.** Use online dictionaries to hear the word's correct pronunciation. Many people are reluctant to use a word if they are uncertain about its pronunciation.
- **Think of two synonyms and one antonym for the word.**
- **Use the word in a sentence or two.** Write the sentences down.
- **Draw diagrams.** Creating diagrams that show relationships between terms may be helpful. For example, in biology, you might draw the following map to help you remember the three bodily sense systems.

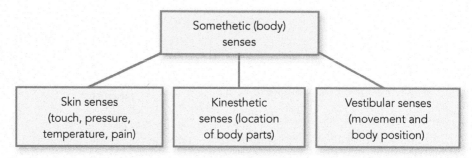

- **For technical, specialized, or challenging terminology, use flash cards.** Write the word on the front of an index card, and write its meaning (and pronunciation) on the back, or use one of the many online sites that enable you to create electronic flash cards. (Note: Writing your own flash cards may work better than typing them or using preprinted ones.) The secret to success in using flash cards is to test yourself to determine which words you have learned and which need further study.

Mike Enright

3   Reading Paragraphs: Main Ideas

Paragraphs are the building blocks of good writing. Here are some strategies for understanding the key idea of any paragraph.

3a How do I identify the topic of a paragraph?

The one general subject discussed in the paragraph is its **topic**. Every sentence in the paragraph explains or discusses this topic. Consider this paragraph:

> <u>Weather forecasts have become as sensationalistic as any story in *The National Enquirer* or on TMZ.</u> Weather is a fact of life across the globe, and each year the TV news reports (sometimes for hours at a time) on bouts of severe weather, including thunderstorms, blizzards, hurricanes, and tornadoes. Meteorologists — especially those on TV — make a habit of acting as if every snowstorm, heavy rainstorm, or hurricane is going to destroy thousands of homes, kill millions of people, and cause billions in damage. These forecasts whip people up into a frenzy of fear when the truth is that most storms cause fairly little damage in isolated areas. The highest cost of these storms is the emotional toll that sensationalized forecasts take on people who stay glued to the TV set listening to the weatherpeople predicting the end of the world.

Topic sentence

The topic of this paragraph is *sensationalistic weather forecasts*. Each sentence in the paragraph is related to this topic.

3b How do I find the topic sentence?

The topic of a paragraph is often found in a **topic sentence**, which states the paragraph's main idea. Often, the topic sentence is the first sentence of the paragraph, but sometimes it comes in the middle of the paragraph and sometimes at the end. Use the following strategies to find the topic sentence:

1. **Distinguish between general and specific.** The topic sentence is usually the most general sentence in the paragraph, while all the other sentences offer specific support for the topic sentence. Analyze the structure of the paragraph to determine which sentence is the most general. That sentence is the topic sentence.

   General

   Specific

   > <u>Weather forecasts have become as sensationalistic as any story in *The National Enquirer* or any celebrity-scandal story on TMZ.</u> Weather is a fact of life across the globe, and each year the TV news reports (sometimes for hours at a time) on bouts of severe weather, including thunderstorms, blizzards, hurricanes, and tornadoes. Meteorologists—especially those on TV—make a habit of acting as if every snowstorm, heavy rainstorm, or hurricane is going to destroy thousands of homes, kill millions of people, and cause billions in damage. These forecasts whip people up into a frenzy of fear, terror, and anxiety when the truth is that most storms cause fairly little damage in isolated areas.

2. **Look for a sentence that introduces the topic.** When you read a how-to paragraph, for example, the sentence that precedes the first step is often the topic sentence, as in the following paragraph:

   Topic sentence

   > Buying a new car is a nerve-racking experience for many people, but it doesn't have to be. <u>You can follow a few simple steps to get the car you want for the right price.</u> First, do your research on the Internet. Find out the invoice price and whether the manufacturer is offering any special incentives to the dealer. Next, go to the dealership and announce, "I want to buy a car today." You will receive instant and close attention. Third, use the broken-record method of negotiating by saying the same thing over and over again: "I want to pay $X for this car."

3. **Ask questions.** You can ask two simple questions that together will help you identify the topic sentence:
   - *If I had to choose a title for this paragraph, which one or two words would I use?*
   - *What sentence in the paragraph makes the main point about the topic I identified in my title?*

3c How do I figure out the implied main idea of a paragraph?

Sometimes paragraphs do not include a topic sentence. In those paragraphs, you must infer the main idea from the content. Consider the following paragraph:

> The United States is a democracy, but almost half of the U.S. population (44% to be exact) does not <u>vote</u> in presidential elections. Data exist for <u>voter turnout</u> in 170 of the world's nations; the United States ranks at #120 on the list. Only 20% of young people (ages 18–24) bother to <u>cast a vote</u> in any election. In local (city) elections, as few as 10% of registered <u>voters show up at the polls</u>. Almost 25% of American adults have not even <u>registered</u> to vote.

Use repeated words and ideas to identify the implied main idea.

How can you determine the implied main idea?

1. **Find the topic.** Whether the paragraph states its main idea directly or not, a paragraph is always a collection of sentences on a single topic. To identify the topic, notice its frequent repetition of related terms or ideas. Then you ask yourself, "What is the one idea that is repeated in the paragraph?" The answer is clear: *Low voter turnout in the United States.*

2. **Decide what the writer wants you to know about the topic.** You can think of the implied main idea as the general idea that is supported by the specifics. In the paragraph about voter turnout, the author has provided shocking statistics about the lack of voter turnout in the United States. All of the sentences point to the general implied main idea: "Although the United States is a democracy in which voting is essential to the political process, there is widespread apathy among American voters, and many do not bother going to the polls."

4   Reading Paragraphs: Details

The sentences that support a paragraph's main idea are its **details**. Not all details are equally important.

4a How do I know which details are worth remembering?

Sometimes everything in a paragraph looks important; other times, nothing seems worth remembering. You may be right in both cases.

1. **Sometimes none of the details is essential to learn and remember.** In the following paragraph, all the detail sentences are just examples. Not any one is important in itself to remember, but together they do give you a better sense of the author's main point. You could highlight one to jog your memory, or just mark "ex" in the margin.

> <u>**Criticism** refers to materials that respond to and evaluate a particular work</u>. A film critic may write a movie review examining the plot and characterization, as well as the cinematography. A magazine review may evaluate a new mystery novel by comparing it to others of the same genre. A scientist may respond to a recently published research study on immunotherapy, challenging its methodology.

Topic (or main idea) sentence

Examples

2. **Sometimes the paragraph contains only important details, details that** *directly* *explain* **or** *support* **the main idea.** Pay attention to all of these.

Topic (or main idea) sentence

Key details

> McClelland, a well-known Harvard psychologist, hypothesized that human behavior is motivated by three distinct psychological needs. The need for affiliation involves seeking to be liked by others and held in high regard by them. The need for power urges people to influence or seek control over others. The need for achievement involves reaching both realistic and idealistic goals.

3. **Some paragraphs contain secondary details that explain more about the important details.** Secondary details are not essential to remember.

Secondary details

> McClelland, a well-known Harvard psychologist, hypothesized that human behavior is motivated by three distinct psychological needs. The need for affiliation involves seeking to be liked by others and held in high regard by them. Those motivated by the need for affiliation enjoy working with others and work well in groups. The need for power urges people to influence or seek control over others. For these individuals, status and prestige are important; some may tend to be showy and ruthless. The need for achievement involves reaching both realistic and idealistic goals. Those motivated to achieve seek evaluation and feedback about their ideas and skills and tend to seek challenge.

4. **Use transitions to guide you from primary detail to primary detail.** Notice how the writer uses the transitions "first," "second," and "finally" to lead you from one reason to the next.

Transitions

> Within human communication, silence is the absence of speech, but it, too, can carry meaning. First, silence can be a weapon used against others; think of it as a kind of punishment. After a quarrel, a spouse may refuse to speak to his or her partner, communicating anger or disappointment. Second, the lack of speech may express emotion. Refusing to speak may indicate lack of cooperation or defiance. Imagine a silent child pouting, for example. Finally, silence can suggest shyness or discomfort. A person new to a group may be silent until he or she learns what the group accepts and expects.

Other common transitions include *for example,* *in conclusion,* *meanwhile,* and *however.* You can find a list of the most commonly used transitions in Table 6.1 (p. 154).

4b What should I do if I don't understand a sentence or a detail?

1. **Keep reading!** Sometimes the rest of the paragraph or selection will provide the clues you need to make sense of the confusing detail, or you may realize that you really don't need that particular detail to fulfill your purpose. If, after reading the whole selection, you still don't understand a detail that seems important, first figure out any unfamiliar words. (See 2. Learning Words.) Then try to express the detail in your own words.
2. **Look for and pay attention to examples.** Examples often make complicated or difficult concepts clear and easy to understand.

How will entry or exit by other firms affect the profits of a typical existing firm? Because the differentiated products offered by firms in a monopolistically competitive industry compete for the same set of customers, entry or exit by other firms will affect the demand curve facing every existing producer. If new gas stations open along a highway, each of the existing gas stations will no longer be able to sell as much gas as before at a given price.

Challenging text

Example that clarifies and explains

5   Reading Essays and Textbook Chapters

The two most common reading assignments in college courses are essays and textbook chapters. Use the following strategies to plan your reading schedule and complete your assignments on time.

5a   What should I do if I just can't get started on the assignment?

Sometimes assignments are intimidating. The key to getting started is to make the assignment manageable.

1. **Divide the task into doable pieces, and work in time blocks.** A typical textbook chapter is twenty to thirty pages long. A long essay or journal article may be fifteen to twenty pages long. To make a long, complicated text more manageable, start by previewing the assignment, looking for breaks indicated by headings, numbers, or some other element. Then read one chunk at a time, perhaps over several days.

2. **Reward yourself when you complete the task.** Give yourself a small treat, such as a healthy snack or a half hour of YouTube, to motivate you to finish.

5b   How can I keep from getting lost in a difficult and lengthy reading assignment?

1. **Review previously read material before beginning new material.** Take a moment to flip through the previous chapter or review your class notes. Doing so will activate your memory and orient you to the new assignment. This strategy is particularly helpful when you are moving from one discipline to another—for example, when you have just completed your philosophy reading and must now move on to your economics assignment.

2. **Look for patterns.** The author of your assignment may have used a specific pattern in each section of the chapter you are reading. For example, each major section in an economics textbook may be organized in this manner:

- heading
- key terms and definitions
- examples
- graphical analysis
- application to the real world
- comprehension questions

By identifying this pattern, you get into the flow of reading the chapter. You know what to expect, and you train your brain to learn the concepts according to the system the author has set up. Trust the author's system of organization! Most textbook authors are expert teachers, and they write their books to maximize students' ability to learn the material. Also look for patterns of text development and the transitions that signal them. For an overview of these patterns, see Chapter 10.

3. **Create an overview (an outline, graphic organizer, or a diagram) and refer to it frequently.** Research shows that taking notes (especially by hand) while reading increases comprehension and learning. On a separate sheet of paper, draw a diagram of each main section or create a point-by-point outline or graphic organizer. If you are a visual learner, try drawing a branching diagram or idea map.

For more about creating an outline or graphic organizer, see Chapter 2 and Chapter 7.

5c How can I be sure I am understanding what I read?

Have you ever finished reading an essay and thought, "What did I just read? My mind is a complete blank." Don't worry—it happens to everyone occasionally. Fortunately, two useful strategies can help:

1. **Express each idea in your own words.** After reading each main section of a textbook chapter or essay, write out the main idea in your own words. Do not simply copy topic sentences from the text. By restating the key idea in your own words, you test your own understanding of the material. If you can't accomplish this task, you didn't really understand what you read. Reread the section and try again to capture the main idea before moving on to the next section. (Essays may have no section breaks. In this case, stop every few pages to summarize what you've read.)

2. **Test yourself.** Use the textbook features—such as the learning objectives at the start of the chapter or the key concepts at the end of the chapter—to test yourself. If the book provides an answer key, use it to check your work, not to avoid doing the work. (The latter strategy will come back to bite you at exam time.) If your text lacks learning objectives or a list of key concepts, turn headings into questions and then make sure you can answer those questions correctly. Use the results of your self-testing to determine which materials need further study or review.

6 Reviewing

Students frequently think that rereading is a great tool for learning, but other strategies, like those listed below, often work better.

6a Should I reread assigned chapters or reading selections to review?

You may need to reread challenging assignments to understand them. But don't make a habit of rereading all of your assignments from start to finish to review.

1. **Reread only for a specific purpose.** Comprehension improves when you identify main ideas and key supporting details, not when you reread the entire assignment.

To ensure that you have understood a difficult paragraph, it makes sense to reread the paragraph. But by the time you finish the assignment, you should reread only sections and only for a specific purpose—for example, to find a piece of information, to review a concept you find challenging, or to check your understanding of a particular topic.

2. **Use alternative strategies for review.** Rather than rereading the entire assignment, try these strategies:
   - **Test yourself by anticipating exam questions.** Make up questions based on headings or visual aids, and write the answers to them.
   - **Write, highlight, annotate, paraphrase, or summarize.** Take your pick; each can be useful, depending on the situation.
   - **Memorize key information when you have to.** Sometimes there is no substitute for simple memorization. Use flash cards to help you memorize key vocabulary. Also develop memory tricks, or *mnemonics*, to aid in recall. For example, many students use the name "Roy G. Biv" to remember the colors of the rainbow: red, orange, yellow, green, blue, indigo, and violet. Or they use the acronym HOMES to remember the names of the Great Lakes: Huron, Ontario, Michigan, Erie, Superior. Develop a set of mnemonics that work for you.

6b How can I remember what I just read?

Immediate review and periodic review are the keys to learning and then retaining information.

1. **Review right after you read.** When you're done reading the assignment, don't simply close the book and move on. Rather, spend five to ten minutes flipping through the selection, rereading your notes, and gauging your understanding of the material. Keep a list with two columns: "Material I Understand and Remember" and "Material I Need to Review and Practice." Use this list to aid in periodic review.

2. **Review what you've read periodically (say, once a week).** The best way to keep information in your memory is to review it periodically. If six weeks will elapse between your first reading of the assignment and the test, spend a bit of time (perhaps half an hour) in each of those six weeks reviewing your notes. Then, the night before the test, you will not need to cram in order to relearn the material.

3. **Write to consolidate information.** By writing out information, you will remember and learn it better. Research shows that writing by hand aids recall better than typing on a computer does.

6c How can I prepare for a quiz on a reading assignment?

Try these strategies:

1. **Highlight and annotate as you read, and review your highlighting and annotations.** For guidelines on how to highlight and annotate effectively, see Chapter 2.

2. **Outline or summarize the reading.** Draw a graphic organizer or create an outline to help you understand the reading's content, organization, and key points. Write a one-paragraph summary in your own words, and then evaluate your summary: Ask

yourself, "Would this summary tell someone who has not read the essay what the essay is about?" For detailed instructions on outlining and drawing a graphic organizer, see Chapter 7; for detailed instructions on summarizing, see Chapter 2.

3. **Test yourself by predicting and answering questions.** Write actual questions and practice answering them within a certain period of time. Doing so not only gives you practice at writing a timed response, but it also pushes you to identify the ideas you've learned and those you need to brush up on. (Quizzes will most likely focus on key points rather than secondary or unimportant details.)

6d How can I prepare for class discussions based on a reading assignment?

Often, your instructor will use the reading assignment as the basis for a class or group discussion. The instructor will often say something like, "Be prepared to discuss this essay during our next class session."

1. **Make marginal notes as you read.** Jot down your reactions in the margins, engaging in a "conversation" with the assignment. Write not only about agreements, but also about disagreements, examples from your own life or other classes, and further thoughts on the topic. Then review your annotations after you've completed the assignment.

2. **Write in your journal.** A response journal is a section of your writing journal in which you record summaries of readings, along with your reactions to and questions about those readings. Chapter 2 provides details about two useful formats: the open-page format and the two-column format.

6e What should I do if I highlight practically everything?

Too much highlighting is a common error. Here are some tips for highlighting just the right amount of your reading assignment:

1. **Determine what you need to know.** Highlight only main ideas and important details. If you have trouble identifying main ideas, see section 4a of this guide, "How do I know which details are important and worth remembering?" As a general rule, do not highlight full sentences, and highlight no more than one-quarter of a page. Limiting your highlighting forces you to sort more important from less important ideas, and this sorting process enhances learning.

2. **Read a paragraph or short section first; then go back and highlight it.** By doing so, you give yourself time to identify what's important. Use headings and boldfaced key terms to help you determine what should be highlighted. Consider using different highlighting colors for different types of information—for example, use yellow for key vocabulary and definitions and blue for key examples. (Make sure you use colors that are easy to read through.)

3. **Compare your highlighting with a classmate's.** Determine which of you has a more effective method of highlighting, and then adapt your highlighting methods accordingly.

4 Prewriting

How to Find and Focus Ideas

Geri Lavrov/Photographer's Choice/Getty Images

In this chapter you will learn to

- choose and narrow a topic
- consider purpose, audience, point of view, genre, and medium
- discover ideas to write about

Writing Quick Start

ANALYZE Study the photo on this page. What is happening? What do you think this person could be reacting to?

WRITE Jot down whatever comes to mind. You might write about times when you've felt the same emotions you think the person is expressing, or about times when you've seen others express strong emotions in public. Try to write nonstop for at least five minutes. Don't stop to evaluate your writing or worry about grammar. Just record your thoughts.

CONNECT You have just used **freewriting**, a method of discovering ideas about a topic by writing without stopping for a set period of time. Read over what you wrote. Suppose you are now asked to write an essay about joy or exuberance. Do you see some starting points and usable ideas in your freewriting?

Generating ideas, considering your writing situation (your purpose, audience, point of view, and genre), and choosing and narrowing a topic are all part of the writing process, as illustrated in Graphic Organizer 4.1. Although writing is often described as a step-by-step process, writers often move back and forth between the steps and return to an earlier step to cut and paste material they previously developed. This movement is designated by arrows pointing in both directions in the graphic organizer.

GRAPHIC ORGANIZER 4.1   An Overview of the Writing Process

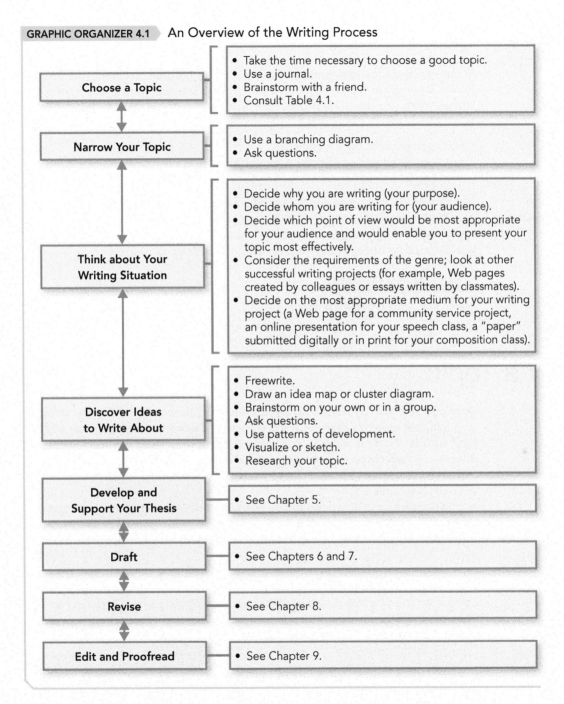

Choose a Topic
- Take the time necessary to choose a good topic.
- Use a journal.
- Brainstorm with a friend.
- Consult Table 4.1.

Narrow Your Topic
- Use a branching diagram.
- Ask questions.

Think about Your Writing Situation
- Decide why you are writing (your purpose).
- Decide whom you are writing for (your audience).
- Decide which point of view would be most appropriate for your audience and would enable you to present your topic most effectively.
- Consider the requirements of the genre; look at other successful writing projects (for example, Web pages created by colleagues or essays written by classmates).
- Decide on the most appropriate medium for your writing project (a Web page for a community service project, an online presentation for your speech class, a "paper" submitted digitally or in print for your composition class).

Discover Ideas to Write About
- Freewrite.
- Draw an idea map or cluster diagram.
- Brainstorm on your own or in a group.
- Ask questions.
- Use patterns of development.
- Visualize or sketch.
- Research your topic.

Develop and Support Your Thesis
- See Chapter 5.

Draft
- See Chapters 6 and 7.

Revise
- See Chapter 8.

Edit and Proofread
- See Chapter 9.

Choose a Topic

In some writing situations, your instructor will assign the topic. In others, your instructor will allow you to choose your own topic, perhaps selecting from a number of possibilities. When you choose your own topic, don't just grab the first one that comes to mind. Rather, look for a topic that

- is appropriate to the assignment
- you know something about or want to learn about
- will maintain your interest

For more on keeping a journal, see Chapter 1.

In addition to Internet browsing to search for a topic, don't overlook topics discussed in your classes or related to your entries in your writing journal, daily activities such as sports or social events, programs you've heard or seen on radio or television, or the world around you: people, objects, and social interactions.

> **ESSAY IN PROGRESS 1**
>
> List at least three broad essay topics.

Narrow a Topic

Once you have chosen a topic, narrow it to make it manageable within the required length of your essay. For example, if you are assigned a two- to four-page essay, a broad topic such as divorce is too large. However, you might write about one specific cause of divorce or its effects on children. *Skipping this step is one of the biggest mistakes you can make.* You can waste a great deal of time working on an essay only to discover later that the topic is too broad.

To narrow a topic, limit it to a specific part or aspect. Two techniques—branching and questioning—will help you. The idea-generating techniques covered later in the chapter ("Discover Ideas to Write About," pp. 111–19) may also be used to narrow a broad topic.

Use a Branching Diagram

Start by writing your broad topic at the far left side of your paper or computer screen. Then subdivide the topic into three or more subcategories or aspects. Here is an example for the broad topic of wild-game hunting.

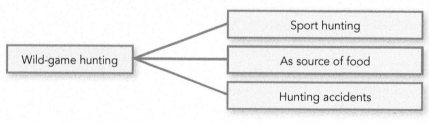

Then choose one subcategory and subdivide it further, as shown here.

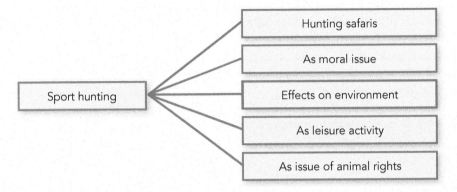

Continue narrowing the topic in this way until you feel you have found one that is interesting, appropriate to your assignment, and manageable. The following example shows narrowed topics that would be workable for a two- to four-page essay on the effects of sport hunting on the environment.

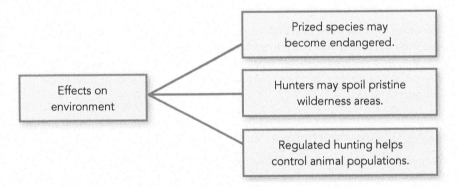

Note: Did you notice that as the narrowing progressed, the topics changed from words and phrases to statements of ideas? Once you begin planning, researching, and drafting your essay, you may need to narrow your topic even further.

EXERCISE 4.1 ▸ BRANCHING

Use branching diagrams to narrow three of the following broad topics to more manageable topics for a two- to four-page essay.

1. School lunches
2. Alternative energy sources
3. Manned space travel
4. Campaign finance rules
5. Air travel safety measures

ESSAY IN PROGRESS 2

Narrow one of the broad topics you chose in Essay in Progress 1 to a topic manageable for a two- to four-page essay.

Ask Questions to Narrow a Broad Topic

Use questions that begin with *who, what, where, when, why,* and *how* to narrow your topic. Questioning will lead you to consider and focus your attention on specific aspects of the topic. Here is an example of questioning for the broad topic of divorce.

Questions	Narrowed Topics
Why does divorce occur?	• Lifestyle differences as a cause of divorce • Infidelity as a cause of divorce
How do couples divide their property?	• Division of assets after a divorce
Who can help couples work through a divorce?	• Role of friends and family • Role of mediator • Role of attorney
What are the effects of divorce on children?	• Emotional effects of divorce on children • Financial effects of divorce on children
When might it be advisable for a couple considering divorce to remain married?	• Couples who stay together for the sake of their children • Financial benefit of remaining married

Sometimes you may need to ask additional questions to limit the topic sufficiently. The topic "emotional effects of divorce on children," for example, is still too broad for a brief essay. Asking questions such as "What are the most common emotional effects?" and "How can divorcing parents prevent emotional problems in their children?" can lead to more specific topics.

EXERCISE 4.2   **QUESTIONING**

Use questioning to narrow three of the following subjects to topics that would be manageable within a two- to four-page essay.

1. Senior citizens
2. Mental illness
3. Environmental protection
4. Cyberbullying
5. Reality TV shows

Think about Your Writing Situation

Once you have decided on a manageable topic, you are ready to consider your writing situation: your purpose, audience, point of view, genre, and medium.

Determine Your Purpose

A well-written essay should have a specific purpose or goal. There are three main purposes for writing:

1. **To *express* yourself:** For example, to express the writer's feelings about an incident of road rage that he or she observed
2. **To *inform* your reader:** For example, to inform readers about the primary causes of road rage
3. **To *persuade* your reader:** For example, to persuade readers to vote for funding to investigate the problem of road rage in the community

To identify your purpose, ask yourself the following questions:

1. Why am I writing this essay?
2. What do I want this essay to accomplish?

Some essays can have more than one purpose. An essay on snowboarding, for example, could be both informative and persuasive: It could explain the benefits of snowboarding and urge readers to take up the sport because it is good exercise.

Consider Your Audience

Considering your **audience** (the people who will read your essay) is an important part of the writing process. Many aspects of your writing—how you express yourself, which words you choose, which details and examples you include, which types of sentences you use, and what attitude you take toward your topic—depend on the audience. Your **tone** (how you sound to your audience) is especially important. If you want your audience to feel comfortable with your writing, you need to write in a manner that your readers can understand and that appeals to them.

For more on tone, see "Analyze the Author's Language" in Chapter 3.

If you were describing a student orientation session to a friend, you would use a different tone and select different details than you would if you were describing the orientation in an article for the student newspaper.

Telling a Friend	Writing for the Student Newspaper
Remember I told you how nervous I am about attending college in the fall? Well, guess what? I went to my student orientation over the weekend, and it was much better than I expected. I even met one of my teachers! Professor Yi was so nice and down-to-earth that now I'm starting to get excited about going to college.	College student orientations are often thought to be stuffy affairs where prospective students attempt to mix with aloof professors. For this reason, I am pleased to report that the college orientation held on campus last weekend was a major success and not a pointless endeavor after all. Along with my fellow incoming first-year students, I was impressed with the friendliness of instructors and the camaraderie that developed between students and faculty.
Language: Casual	**Language:** More formal
Sentence structure: Shorter sentences	**Sentence structure:** Longer sentences
Tone: Familiar, friendly	**Tone:** Serious, formal

How to consider your audience.   As you consider your audience, keep the following points in mind:

- **Your readers are not present and cannot observe or participate in what you are writing about.** If you are writing about your apartment, for example, they cannot visualize it unless you describe it in detail.
- **Your readers do not know everything you know.** They may not have the same knowledge about and experience with the topic that you do, so you will have to define specialized terms, for example, if readers are unlikely to know what they mean.
- **Your readers may not share your opinions and values.** If you are writing about raising children and assume that strict discipline is undesirable, for example, some readers may not agree with you.
- **Your readers may not respond in the same way you do to situations or issues.** Some readers may not see any humor in a situation that you find funny. An issue that you consider only mildly disturbing may upset or anger some readers.

For a helpful list of questions you can ask to analyze your audience, consult the box below.

Analyzing Your Audience

When analyzing your audience, ask yourself the following questions:

- **What does my audience know (or not know) about my topic?** If you are proposing a community garden project to an audience of city residents who know little about gardening, you will need to describe the pleasures and benefits of gardening to capture their interest.
- **What is the education, background, and experience of my audience?** If you are writing your garden-project proposal for an audience of low-income residents, you might emphasize how much money they could save by growing vegetables, and if you are proposing the project to middle-income residents, you might stress how relaxing gardening can be and how a garden can beautify a neighborhood.
- **What attitudes, beliefs, opinions, or biases are my audience likely to hold?** Suppose your audience believes that most development is harmful to the environment. If you are writing an essay urging your audience to sponsor a new community garden, consider emphasizing how the garden will benefit the environment and decrease development.
- **What tone do my readers expect?** Suppose you are writing to your local city council urging council members to approve the community garden. Although the council has been stalling on the issue, your tone should be serious and not accusatory. As community leaders, the council members expect to be treated with respect.
- **What tone will help me achieve my purpose?** If you are writing to your city counselor to urge her to support the community garden, a respectful tone is more likely to achieve your goal than a hostile one.

Considering your audience when it is composed of one person: your instructor.   Instructors occasionally direct students to write for a particular audience, such as readers of a certain magazine or newspaper, but you can often assume that your main audience is your instructor. In most cases, it is best to write as if your instructor were unfamiliar with your topic. Instructors want to see if their students understand the topic and can write and think clearly about it. For academic papers, provide enough information to demonstrate your knowledge of the subject (including background information, definitions of technical terms, and relevant details), make sure your essay is clear and understandable, maintain a reasonable tone, provide evidence from sources that are appropriate to your discipline, and treat alternative views fairly.

EXERCISE 4.3   **CONSIDERING YOUR AUDIENCE**

1. Write a one-paragraph description of a current television commercial for a particular product. Your audience is another college student.
2. Write a description of the same commercial for one of the following writing situations:
   a. An assignment in a business marketing class: Analyze the factors that make the advertisement interesting and appealing. Your audience is a marketing instructor.
   b. A letter to the company that produces the product: Describe your response to the advertisement. Your audience is the consumer relations director of the company.
   c. A letter to your local television station: Comment favorably on or complain about the advertisement. Your audience is the station director.

Choose a Point of View

Point of view is the perspective from which you write an essay. There are three types: first, second, and third person. In choosing a point of view, consider your topic, your purpose, and your audience. Think of point of view as the "person" you become as you write.

- **First person** uses first-person pronouns (*I, me, mine, we, ours*). First person is often effective and appropriate in an essay narrating an event in which you participated. For formal essays, many instructors prefer that you not write in the first person.
- **Second person** uses second-person pronouns (*you, your, yours*). Second person is appropriate when giving directions, as in an essay explaining how to build a fence: "First, *you* should measure. . . ." Sometimes the word *you* may be understood but not directly stated, as in, "First, measure. . . ." Many textbooks, including this one, use the second person to address student readers; however, many instructors prefer that you avoid using the second person in formal essays.
- **Third person** uses people's names and third-person pronouns (*he, she, it*). Third person is prevalent in academic writing. It is less personal and more formal than first person and second person. Think of the third person as public rather than private or personal. The writer reports what he or she sees.

EXERCISE 4.4   **POINT OF VIEW**

Working with a classmate, discuss which point of view (first, second, or third person) would be most appropriate in each of the following writing situations:

1. An essay urging students to participate in a march against hunger to support a local food drive
2. A description of a car accident on a form that your insurance company requires you to submit in order to collect benefits
3. A paper for an ecology course on the effects of air pollution caused by a local industry

---

Consider the Genre and Medium

Genre is a term used to classify types of text—for example, laboratory reports, proposals, or blog posts. Each genre has its own conventions, or ways of doing things. A laboratory report, for example, has a specific purpose: To inform readers about how an experiment was conducted so that it can be repeated and to tell readers the results. It takes the third-person point of view, uses technical language, and includes the sections *Introduction, Methods, Results,* and *Discussion.*

To write effectively you need to understand the conventions of the genre and follow them closely. Reviewing samples of effective writing in the genre, either by classmates or those posted on reliable Web pages, can be helpful.

Medium refers to the means through which ideas are expressed and information conveyed. In your writing class, your primary medium will be printed text, but your essays may include visuals, and if assignments are submitted or viewed electronically, you may also include audio or visual files, animations, or hyperlinks to Web sites. Be sure to choose a medium that suits your purpose and your audience. (For example, consider whether your readers will have high-speed Internet access when reading your assignment.) Also consider the conventions of the genre in which you are writing.

HOW WRITERS READ   **ANALYZING THE AUTHOR'S PURPOSE, AUDIENCE, POINT OF VIEW, AND GENRE**

Considering the author's purpose, audience, point of view, and genre can help you read effectively and sharpen your critical-thinking skills.

BEFORE READING
- Previewing to determine the selection's **genre** will help you decide which sections are most important. Knowing what you're expected to know or write about will allow you to read to find that information.

WHILE READING
- Pay attention to **purpose, audience,** and **point of view.** Depending on the purpose and audience, a writer may not always feel the need to provide complete information. Point of view may hint at the writer's slant or bias.

AFTER READING
- Identify the author's **purpose** and the **audience** for whom an essay is written and use this information to evaluate the reliability and sufficiency of the evidence provided and to identify possible biases.

Discover Ideas to Write About

Discovering ideas to write about is a process of gathering all of your separate but related ideas on a topic and fitting them together. For example, you may know a lot about biking, but all your knowledge is not stored in one place in your brain: Verbal information is stored in one place; sensory impressions are stored in another. Be sure to draw on both. Table 4.1 shows the ideas one student developed on bicycling, providing a wealth of ideas to write about on the topic.

TABLE 4.1 ▶ Synthesizing Your Ideas on a Topic

To Discover Ideas, Draw Upon Your . . .	Example Topic: Bicycling
Verbal knowledge: Facts, dates, numbers, concepts, definitions, reasons, and so forth	Types of bikes, costs, speeds, repairs, convenience, bike races
Personal knowledge: Events you have experienced	A bike trip to Yellowstone National Park, pedaling to school
Mental images: Pictures in your mind, recollections of images on television, videos	A mental image of the first bike you rode; a video of the Tour de France
Sensory impressions: Recollections of tastes, smells, touch, and sound	The feel of wind in your face as you ride, the roar of a truck coming up behind you
Motor skills: Memory of physical actions	Keeping your balance, steering, braking, changing gears

In the following sections, you will learn a number of specific strategies for discovering and recording ideas to write about. Depending on your preferences, you will probably find that some strategies work better than others. Experiment with each before deciding which will work for you. You may also find that the technique you choose for a given essay may depend on your topic.

Freewrite

When you use freewriting, you write for a specific period of time, usually five to ten minutes. Freewriting allows you to explore ideas and make associations, jumping from one idea to another. If nothing comes to mind, just write the topic, your name, or "I can't think of anything to write" until something occurs to you. The following tips will help you:

- **Write or type nonstop.** Writing often forces thought, so keep going, even after you think you have nothing more to say.
- **Don't be concerned with grammar, punctuation, or spelling.**
- **Write or type fast!** Try to keep up with your thinking. (Most people can think faster than they can write or type.)
- **Record ideas as they come to you** and in whatever form they appear—words, phrases, questions, sentences—or pictures and doodles.

- **If you are freewriting on a computer, darken the screen** so that you are not distracted by errors, formatting issues, and the words you have already written.

When you are done, reread your freewriting, and highlight or underline ideas that seem useful. Look for patterns and connections: Do several ideas together make a point, reflect a sequence, or suggest a larger, unifying idea? Here is an excerpt from one student's freewriting on the broad topic of violence in the media:

> There seems to be a lot of <u>violence</u> in the media these days, particularly on TV. For example, last night when I watched the news, the camera man showed people <u>getting shot in the street</u>. What kind of people watch this stuff? I'd rather watch a movie. It really bothered me because people get so turned off by such an ugly, <u>gruesome scene</u> that they <u>won't want to watch the news</u> anymore. Then we'll have a lot of <u>uninformed citizens</u>. There are too many already. Some people do not even know who the vice president of the U.S. is. A negative thing—the media <u>has a negative impact</u> on any person or group who wants to do something about violence. And they create <u>negative impressions of minority and ethnic groups</u>, too. If the media shows one Latino man committing a crime, viewers falsely assume <u>all Latinos</u> are criminals. It's difficult to think of something positive that can be done when you're surrounded by so much violence. It's all so overwhelming. <u>What we need</u> is not more coverage of violence but <u>viable solutions</u> to the violence we have. The media coverage of violent acts only serves to make people think that this <u>violence is a normal state of affairs and nothing can be done</u> about it.

A number of subtopics surfaced from this student's freewriting:

- the media's graphic portrayal of violence
- the negative effect of media violence on viewers
- the media's portrayal of minority and ethnic groups

Any one of these topics could be narrowed to a manageable topic for an essay.

EXERCISE 4.5   **FREEWRITING**

Set a clock or timer for five minutes and freewrite on one of the following broad topics. Then review and highlight your freewriting, identifying usable ideas with a common theme that might serve as a topic for an essay. Starting with one of the potential topics from your freewriting, freewrite for another five minutes to narrow your topic further and develop your ideas.

1. Job interviews
2. Instagram
3. How to be self-sufficient
4. Pressures on college students
5. Hip-hop music

Draw a Map or Cluster Diagram

Mapping, or **clustering**, is a visual way to discover ideas and relationships. To create a map, do the following:

1. Write your topic in the middle of a blank sheet of paper and draw a box or circle around it. (Consider using a graphics program such as bubbl.us or smartdraw.com.)
2. Think of ideas that are related to or suggested by your topic. As you think of them, write them down in clusters around the topic, connecting them to the topic with lines (Figure 4.1). Think of your topic as a tree trunk and the related ideas as branches.
3. Draw arrows and lines or use highlighting to show relationships and connect groups of related ideas.
4. Think of still more ideas, clustering them around the ideas already on your map.

The sample map in Figure 4.1 was done by a student working on the topic of the costs of higher education. In this map, the student compared attending a local community college and attending an out-of-town four-year college. A number of different subtopics evolved, including the following:

- transportation costs
- social life
- availability of degree programs
- room and board costs

Mapping may appeal to you if you prefer a spatial method of dealing with information and ideas or if you like to devise your own structure or framework within which to work.

FIGURE 4.1 Sample Map

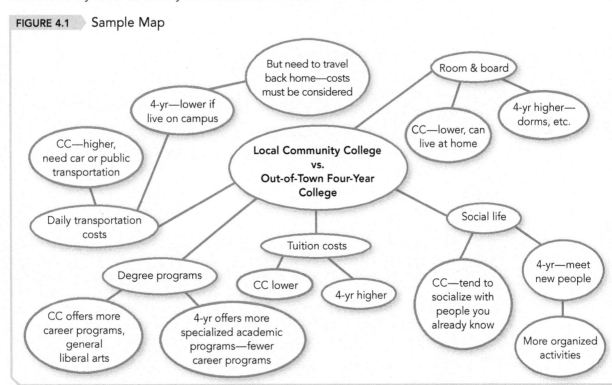

MAPPING

Narrow one of the following topics. Then draw a map of related ideas as they come to mind.

1. Presidential politics
2. Daydreaming
3. Tattoos
4. Cable TV
5. Year-round schooling

Brainstorm

When you **brainstorm**, you list everything that comes to mind when you think about your topic: facts, impressions, emotions, and reactions. Record words or phrases rather than sentences, and give yourself a time limit; this will force ideas to come to your mind faster. If you use a computer, you might use bullets or the indent function to brainstorm.

The following example shows a student's brainstorming on the narrowed topic of the disadvantages of home schooling. Three clusters of topics are evident.

Topic: Disadvantages of Home Schooling

❶ Parent may not be an expert in every subject.

❷ Libraries may not be easily accessible.

❷ A wide range of equipment or resources may not be available.

❶ Child may be confused by parent playing the role of teacher.

❸ Child does not learn to interact with other children.

❸ Child does not learn to compete against others.

❶ Parents may not enforce standards.

❶ Parents may not be objective about child's strengths and weaknesses.

❶ Child may learn only parent's viewpoint and not be exposed to a wide range of opinions.

❷ Special programs (art, music) may be omitted.

❷ Services of school nurse, counselors, reading specialists may not be available.

❶ Limitations of parents

❷ Unavailable services/ resources

❸ Problems of social development

Once you select a cluster to focus on, you can do further brainstorming to generate ideas about your narrowed topic.

Brainstorming is more structured than freewriting because you focus only on the topic at hand instead of writing whatever comes to mind. It is flexible because you can use it to generate ideas or narrow a topic. It also works when it is done in groups of two or three classmates. Use a chalkboard or whiteboard in an empty classroom, share a large sheet of paper, sit together in front of a computer screen, or use networked computers. Say your ideas aloud as you write. You'll find that your classmates' ideas will trigger more of your own.

EXERCISE 4.7   BRAINSTORMING

Choose one of the following subjects and narrow it to a manageable topic for a two- to four-page paper. Then brainstorm, either alone or with one or two classmates, to generate ideas to write about.

1. Value of music
2. National parks
3. Credit-card fraud
4. Texting
5. Web advertising

Ask Questions

Earlier in this chapter, you learned to ask questions to narrow a topic, but you can also ask questions as a way to discover ideas about a topic. Working either alone or with a classmate, write down every question you can think of about your topic. Focus on ideas, not correctness. Don't judge or evaluate ideas as you write. It may help to imagine that you are asking an expert on your topic anything that comes to mind.

Here is a partial list of questions one student generated on the narrow topic of the financial problems that single parents face:

How can single parents afford to pay for day care?

How do single parents find time to attend college to improve their employability and earning power?

How can women force their former husbands to keep up with child support payments?

Beginning a question with "What if . . ." is a particularly good way to extend your thinking and look at a topic from a fresh perspective. Here are a few challenging "What if . . ." questions about the financial situation of single parents:

What if the government provided national day care or paid for day care?

What if single parents were not allowed to deduct more than one child on their income tax?

What if single parents were entitled to special tax rebates?

Another way to stimulate your thinking is to ask questions that approach the topic from a number of different perspectives. For the topic of the increased popularity of health foods, you could write questions about human motivation to purchase, marketing strategies, or nutritional value, for instance.

After devising a number of questions, you may want to write tentative answers, or *hypotheses*. If you need to conduct research, you can use these hypotheses as a guide.

To learn more about using research questions, see "Plan Your Research Project" in Chapter 21.

EXERCISE 4.8 ▶ **QUESTIONING**

Working either alone or with a classmate, choose one of the following topics, narrow it, and write a series of questions to discover ideas about it:

1. The campus newspaper
2. Learning a second language
3. Financial aid regulations
4. The minimum wage
5. Government aid to developing countries

Use the Patterns of Development

In Parts 3 and 4 of this book, you will learn nine ways to develop an essay or a paragraph:

- narration
- description
- illustration
- process analysis
- comparison and contrast
- classification and division
- definition
- cause and effect
- argument

These methods are often called *patterns of development.*

In addition to providing ways to develop an essay or a paragraph, the patterns of development may be used to generate ideas about a topic. Think of the patterns as doors through which you gain access to your topic. The list of questions in Table 4.2 will help you approach your topic through these different "doors." For any given topic, some questions work better than others. If your topic is voter registration, for example, the questions listed for definition and process analysis would be more helpful than those listed for description.

EXERCISE 4.9 ▶ **PATTERNS OF DEVELOPMENT**

Use the patterns of development to generate ideas on one of the following topics. Refer to Table 4.2 (p. 117) to form questions based on the patterns.

1. Buying only American-made products
2. Community gardens in urban areas
3. How high-speed trains would change travel
4. The spread of viruses
5. Effects of computer hacking

Visualize or Sketch

Visualizing or **sketching** may be effective ways to discover ideas about your topic. To visualize a person, for example, close your eyes and picture that person in your mind. Imagine what he or she is wearing and what his or her facial expressions and gestures might look like.

TABLE 4.2   Using the Patterns of Development to Explore a Topic

Pattern of Development	Questions to Ask
Narration (Chapter 11)	What stories or events does this topic remind you of?
Description (Chapter 12)	What does the topic look, smell, taste, feel, or sound like?
Illustration (Chapter 13)	What examples of this topic are particularly helpful in explaining it?
Process Analysis (Chapter 14)	How does this topic work? How do you do this topic?
Comparison and Contrast (Chapter 15)	To what is the topic similar? In what ways? Is the topic more or less desirable than those things to which it is similar?
Classification and Division (Chapter 16)	Of what larger group of things is this topic a member? What are its parts? How can the topic be subdivided? Are there certain types or kinds of the topic?
Definition (Chapter 17)	How do you define the topic? How does the dictionary define it? What is the history of the term? Does everyone agree on its definition? Why or why not? If not, what points are in dispute?
Cause and Effect (Chapter 18)	What causes the topic? What are its effects? How often does it happen? What might prevent it from happening? What may happen because of it in the short term? What may happen as a result of it over time?
Argument (Chapters 19 and 20)	What issues surround this topic?

One student who was investigating the topic of extrasensory perception (ESP) decided to use the questions for definition and cause and effect. Here are the answers she wrote:

Definition (How can my topic be defined?)

- ESP, or extrasensory perception, is the ability to perceive information not through the ordinary senses but as a result of a "sixth sense" (as yet undeveloped in most people).
- Scientists disagree on whether ESP exists and how it should be tested.

Cause and Effect (What causes my topic? What may happen because of it?)

- Scientists do not know the cause of ESP and have not confirmed its existence, just the possibility of its existence.
- Some people with ESP claim to have avoided disasters such as airplane crashes.

Here is what one student "saw" when visualizing a shopping mall. Possible subtopics are annotated.

Possible subtopics:
Tour-group shopping

Teenage behavior

Body piercing
Mother-daughter bonding

> As I walked through the local mall, I crossed the walkway to get to Target and noticed a large group of excited women all dressed in jogging suits; they were part of a shopping tour, I think. I saw a tour bus parked outside. Across the walkway was a bunch of teenagers, shouting and laughing and commenting on each other's hairstyles. They all wore T-shirts and jeans; some had body adornments—pierced noses and lips. They seemed to have no interest in shopping. Their focus was on one another. Along the walkway came an obvious mother-daughter pair. They seemed to be on an outing, escaping from their day-to-day routine for some shopping, joking, and laughing.

The technique of sketching, or storyboarding, uses a series of sketches to show a sequence of events or relationships among ideas. Some students may find it easier to draw sketches than to formulate ideas in words; then, once the ideas are on paper in sketch form, they can be converted to text.

EXERCISE 4.10   **VISUALIZING AND SKETCHING**

Visualize one of the following situations. Make notes on or sketch what you "see." Include as many details as possible.

1. A couple obviously "in love"
2. A class you recently attended
3. The campus snack bar
4. A traffic jam
5. A sporting event

Academic Writing: Researching Your Topic

For more about finding, using, and citing sources, see Chapters 21 and 22; to learn more about avoiding plagiarism, see Chapter 23.

Research can help you devise and explore topics for any assignment. Reading what others have written about your topic may suggest new approaches, reveal issues or controversies, and help you determine what you already know (or do not know) about the topic. But in academic writing, research can be vital. Reading what others have said about your topic can help you recognize where you stand on a debate, identify where other researchers have fallen short, or alert you to gaps you can fill with your own research.

Take notes while reading sources, and be sure to record the publication data you will need to cite each source (author, title, publisher, page numbers, and so on). If you use ideas or information from sources in your essay, you must give credit to those sources of the borrowed material. Make sure to avoid simply cutting and pasting material from your sources directly into your notes to avoid plagiarizing inadvertently. Plagiarism, even by accident, carries serious penalties.

HOW WRITERS READ	USING PREWRITING STRATEGIES TO STRENGTHEN UNDERSTANDING
	The numerous prewriting strategies you use as a writer can also help you understand and remember more of what you read.
BEFORE READING	• Use **freewriting** or **brainstorming** to discover what you already know about the subject of the essay you are about to read.
WHILE READING	• Use **questioning** to interact with the author and read critically. • **Look for patterns** to help you interact with the text and connect ideas.
AFTER READING	• Draw a **map or graphic organizer** to help you organize and consolidate the content of the essay. It is also a useful strategy for study and review.

EXERCISE 4.11 RESEARCHING A TOPIC

Do library or Internet research to generate ideas on one of the narrowed topics listed here:

1. Reducing the federal deficit
2. Preventing terrorism in public areas
3. Controlling children's access to the Internet
4. A recent local disaster (flood, earthquake)
5. Buying clothing on eBay

EXERCISE 4.12 PREWRITING

Choose two prewriting techniques discussed in this chapter that appeal to you. Experiment with each method by generating ideas about one of the topics from the previous exercises in the chapter. Use a different topic for each prewriting technique you choose.

ESSAY IN PROGRESS 3

Keeping your audience and purpose in mind, use one of the prewriting strategies discussed in this chapter to generate details about the topic you narrowed in Essay in Progress 2.

STUDENTS WRITE

In this and the remaining five chapters of Part 2, we will follow the work of Latrisha Wilson, a student in a first-year writing course who was assigned to write about surveillance and loss of privacy.

Wilson decided to use questioning to narrow her topic and freewriting to generate ideas about her narrowed topic. An example of her questioning follows:

Latrisha Wilson's Questioning

<u>What are some examples of surveillance in the US?</u>

Cameras in retail stores and at bank cash machines

Cell-phone surveillance and tracking

Airport security checkpoints

Online surveillance

Nanny cams

Traffic cameras and street corners

GPS devices worn by people on probation

Undercover police

Cameras in government buildings

Cameras on school buses

Wilson decided to explore further the types of surveillance commonly conducted in the United States. She did so by asking another question:

<u>Which of these types of surveillance are the least "obvious"?</u>

1. Undercover police

   They disguise their identity.

   They often become friends with the people they are investigating.

   They participate in drug deals.

   Oftentimes, their family members do not even know about their assignments.

   They become the "bad guy" in order to get the "bad guy."

2. Online surveillance

   Who is hiding behind our computer screens?

   Valuable information about us is gathered from the Web.

   Lots of information is gathered without our consent.

   Google studies Gmail accounts for key words and sells the information to companies.

   Information on Facebook is also sold to marketers.

After looking over the answers to her questions, Wilson decided to focus on types of surveillance. The following excerpt from her freewriting shows how she started to develop her topic:

Latrisha Wilson's Freewriting

I feel like I have no privacy. Just the other day I read how the mayor of my city brags of his new plan to put surveillance cameras on all the big street corners. There are already lots of traffic and security cameras. Soon there won't be anywhere I can walk without being monitored by some government employee sitting behind his desk. My life is like a movie anybody can watch. A reality tv show. If I'm not breaking the rules, what right does anyone have to track me? I'm not even safe going online. Netflix and YouTube keep suggesting movies to me. Stores where I have only shopped once keep emailing me about their new products. I get so much junk mail that Gmail just created a folder in my inbox just for "promotions." And right beside my inbox I see all those ads targeted specifically to me. If I write my mom "happy birthday," the next day I see ads for places to buy birthday hats. That's really creepy. I use Google for everything but that doesn't give them the right to pour through all my messages in search of information they can sell. I thought Google was a free service. To the mayor I'm just a potential criminal and to Google I'm just a potential consumer. What happened to my right to privacy?

As you work through the remaining chapters of Part 2, you will see how Wilson develops her tentative thesis statement in Chapter 5, a specific paragraph in Chapter 6, her first draft in Chapter 7, and her final draft in Chapter 8. In Chapter 9, you will see a paragraph from her final draft, edited and proofread to correct sentence-level errors.

5

Developing and Supporting a Thesis

"Let me just charge it for ten more seconds."

Jon Adams/The New Yorker Collection/The Cartoon Bank

Writing Quick Start

ANALYZE   Study the cartoon on this page, which pokes fun at an everyday experience.

WRITE   Working alone or with one or two classmates, draft a statement that expresses the main point of the cartoon. Your statement should not only describe what is happening in the cartoon but also state the idea that the cartoonist is trying to communicate to his audience.

CONNECT   The statement you have just written is an assertion around which you could build an essay. Such an assertion is called a *thesis statement*. Developing a thesis is an important part of the writing process shown in Graphic Organizer 5.1, which lists the skills presented in this chapter while placing them within the larger context of the writing process.

GRAPHIC ORGANIZER 5.1   An Overview of the Writing Process

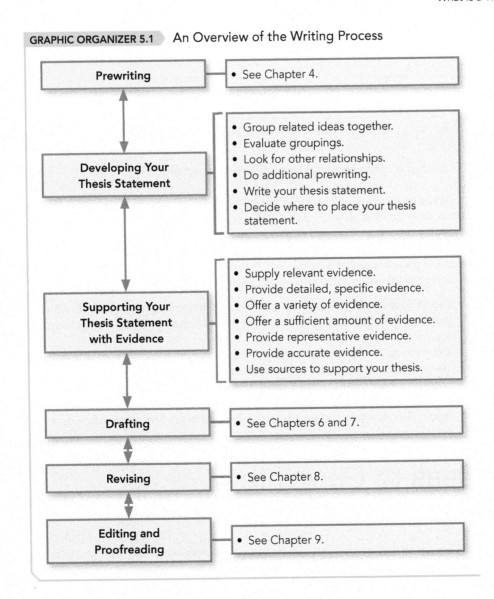

| Prewriting | • See Chapter 4. |

Developing Your Thesis Statement
- Group related ideas together.
- Evaluate groupings.
- Look for other relationships.
- Do additional prewriting.
- Write your thesis statement.
- Decide where to place your thesis statement.

Supporting Your Thesis Statement with Evidence
- Supply relevant evidence.
- Provide detailed, specific evidence.
- Offer a variety of evidence.
- Offer a sufficient amount of evidence.
- Provide representative evidence.
- Provide accurate evidence.
- Use sources to support your thesis.

| Drafting | • See Chapters 6 and 7. |

| Revising | • See Chapter 8. |

| Editing and Proofreading | • See Chapter 9. |

What Is a Thesis Statement?

A **thesis statement** is the main point of an essay. It is usually expressed in a single sentence. An effective thesis statement should accomplish three goals. It should

1. introduce your narrowed topic
2. reveal what your essay is about
3. state the point you will make about that topic

It may also forecast how the essay will be organized.

Here is a sample thesis statement:

```
         ┌──── topic ────┐              ┌──────── position ──────────┐
Playing team sports, especially football and baseball, develops skills and

  ┌──────────────────────────────────┐
qualities that can make you successful in life because these sports

              ┌──────────── forecast ────────────┐
demand communication, teamwork, and responsibility.
```

When you write, think of a thesis statement as a promise to your reader. The rest of your essay delivers on your promise. The example thesis promises the audience that by reading this essay, they will discover how football and baseball players learn communication, teamwork, and responsibility and how these skills and qualities contribute to the players' success in life.

Keep the following guidelines in mind as you develop your thesis statement:

For more on prewriting, see Chapter 4.

- **Expect your thesis statement to evolve during prewriting.** Exploring your topic may lead you to discover a new focus or a more interesting way to approach your topic.

For more on conducting research, see Chapter 22.

- **Expect to do research to revise your thesis.** You may need to do some reading or research to learn more about your topic or tentative thesis.

For more on drafting and revision, see Chapters 7 and 8.

- **Expect to revise your thesis as you draft and revise your essay.** You may write several versions of a thesis statement before you find one that works, and you may revise your thesis as you gather and organize supporting evidence, draft, and revise your essay.

Synthesize Ideas to Generate a Working Thesis Statement

Coming up with a working thesis statement involves reviewing your prewriting to determine how some or all of the ideas you discovered fit together:

1. **Review your prewriting, group together details on the same topic, and write a one- or two-word headline for each group.** A student working on the topic of intelligence in dogs noticed in her brainstormed list that the details could be grouped into two general categories: (1) details about learning and (2) details about instinct. Here is how she arranged her ideas:

Learning	Instinct
follow commands	females deliver and care for puppies
read human emotions	avoid danger and predators
get housebroken	seek shelter
serve as guide dogs for blind people	automatically raise hair on back in response to aggression

2. **Decide which group(s) of ideas best represents the focus your paper should take.** Sometimes, one group of details will be enough to develop a working thesis. Other times, you'll need to use the details in two or three groups. The student working on a thesis for the topic of intelligence in dogs evaluated her grouped details and decided that learning provided enough material to write about.

3. **Determine whether your thesis should be primarily informative, persuasive, or expressive.** For example, an informative essay may explain the measures taken in one's community to prepare for and prevent school shootings, a persuasive essay may argue that specific steps need to be taken to avoid such shootings, and an expressive essay may recount feelings and responses to a practice drill that simulated a school shooting.

4. **Consider whether you have enough relevant details.** If your list of details is thin, you may not have enough details to come up with a good working thesis. Delete any details that do not work, and use prewriting to generate more ideas, trying a different prewriting strategy from the one you used previously. A new strategy may help you see your narrowed topic from a different perspective. If your second prewriting does not produce better results, consider refocusing or changing your topic.

> **ESSAY IN PROGRESS 1**
>
> If you used a prewriting strategy to generate details about your topic in response to Essay in Progress 3 in Chapter 4, review your prewriting, highlight useful ideas, and identify several sets of related details among those you have highlighted.

Draft a Working Thesis Statement

Use the following guidelines as you draft, evaluate, and revise your working thesis:

1. **An effective thesis makes an assertion.** Rather than stating a simple, obvious fact, a thesis should take a position, express a viewpoint, or suggest your approach toward the topic.

Lacks an Assertion	Hollywood movies, like *Loving* and *Rocketman*, are frequently based on true stories.
Revised: Makes an Assertion	Hollywood movies, like *Loving* and *Rocketman*, manipulate true stories to cater to the tastes of the audience.

2. **An effective thesis is specific.** Provide as much information as possible about your main point.

Too General	I learned a great deal from my experiences as a teenage parent.
Revised: More Specific	From my experiences as a teenage parent, I learned to accept responsibility for my own life and for that of my son.

EXERCISE 5.1 **IDENTIFYING AND REVISING THESIS STATEMENTS THAT LACK SPECIFIC ASSERTIONS**

First, determine which of the following draft thesis statements are effective and which make a simple statement of fact or are overly general. Then revise each unsatisfactory thesis, making it into an effective thesis for a brief (two- to four-page) college writing assignment.

1. Students overspend during the holiday season.
2. The viewers were moved by pictures of the devastation in Haiti following Hurricane Matthew.
3. Academic integrity is a problem on college campuses because many students cheat on assignments.
4. Taking a class online can be convenient, but succeeding in online classes requires self-discipline and motivation.
5. As a result of taking care of her family's dog, Adrian developed a strong desire to rescue abandoned pit bulls.

EXERCISE 5.2 **IDENTIFYING AND REVISING OVERLY GENERAL THESIS STATEMENTS**

First, determine which of the following thesis statements are too general for a brief (two- to four-page) college-level writing assignment. Then narrow the overly general thesis statements using the strategies for narrowing topics discussed in Chapter 4.

1. Unfortunately, discrimination exists in many forms in today's society.
2. The demands of my job undermined my relationship with my family.
3. The experience of living in a dorm provides students with opportunities to develop valuable people skills that will serve them well throughout their lives.
4. Violent storms can have devastating effects on communities.
5. Although it seemed unwise at the time, postponing college was one of the wisest decisions I ever made.

3. **Focus on one central point.** Limit your essay to one major idea.

Focuses on Several Points	This college should improve its tutoring services, sponsor more activities of interest to Latino students, and speed up the registration process for students.
Revised: Focuses on One Point	To better represent the student population it serves, this college should sponsor more activities of interest to Latino students.

4. **Offer an original perspective on your topic.** If your thesis seems dull or ordinary, it probably needs revision. Search your prewriting for an interesting angle on your topic.

Too Ordinary	Many traffic accidents are a result of carelessness.
Revised: More Interesting	An automobile accident can change a driver's entire approach to driving.

IDENTIFYING AND REVISING THESIS STATEMENTS THAT FOCUS ON SEVERAL POINTS

The following thesis statements focus on more than one central point. Revise them so that each focuses clearly on only one point.

1. In order to be more successful in college, students must learn time management strategies, curtail their social life during the week, and learn to balance work and school obligations so that they are able to enjoy all parts of their life.

2. The Internet has revolutionized the way friends communicate, but it has also made children more sedentary, which has had negative health effects, and it has also made people in the workforce more solitary, which has undermined teamwork.

3. Movie theaters continue to attract viewers to new releases, although many of them are simply remakes of older movies and ones that appeal only to those who like graphic violence.

4. Although the tornado destroyed the entire town and seriously injured hundreds of people, the local townspeople grew closer as they tended to the injured, helped to rebuild houses, and shared their financial resources with one another.

5. Although the company has made strides in repairing its reputation in the community, it still needs to pay its employees a fair salary, restructure management, and conduct business with more reputable vendors.

5. **Avoid making an announcement.** Don't use phrases such as "This essay will discuss" or "The subject of my paper is." Instead, state your main point directly. (Note that some disciplines do encourage writers to announce their thesis statements directly, but in the humanities it is frowned upon. Check with your instructor if you are not sure.)

Makes an Announcement	The point I am trying to make is that people should not be allowed to smoke on campus.
Revised: States Main Point Directly	The college should prohibit smoking on campus.

6. **Use your thesis to preview the organization of the essay.** Consider using your thesis to mention the two or three key concepts on which your essay will focus, in the order in which you will discuss them.

Lacks Preview	A charity fund-raising event requires careful organization and planning.
Revised: Previews Organization	A charity fund-raising event requires careful organization and planning, including choosing a venue, gathering materials, managing costs, and publicizing the event.

EVALUATING THESIS STATEMENTS

Working in a group of two or three students, discuss what is wrong with each of the following thesis statements. Then revise each thesis to make it more effective.

1. In this paper, I will discuss the causes of asthma, which include exposure to smoke, chemicals, and allergic reactions.
2. Spinning classes are an enjoyable form of exercise.
3. The crime rate is falling in many U.S. cities.
4. Living in an apartment has many advantages.
5. Children's toys can be dangerous, instructional, or creative.

ESSAY IN PROGRESS 2

Keeping your audience in mind, select one or more of the groups of ideas you identified in Essay in Progress 1. Write a working thesis statement based on these ideas.

Place the Thesis Statement Effectively

Your thesis statement can appear anywhere in your essay, but it is usually best to place it in the first paragraph as part of your introduction. When your thesis appears at the beginning of the essay, your readers will know what to pay attention to and what to expect in the rest of the essay. If you place your thesis later in the essay, you need to build up to it gradually in order to prepare readers for it.

HOW WRITERS READ   **IDENTIFYING AND USING THE THESIS STATEMENT**

Just as you express the main point of an essay in a thesis statement, so do most of the writers you will read in this text and in your other assigned reading. The strategies here will help you identify the thesis statement and use it to guide your reading.

BEFORE READING
- Preview the title, introduction, and conclusion to identify the subject of the reading, and then predict the thesis the writer may develop.

WHILE READING
- Identify the actual thesis. Does it confirm your prediction? If you have trouble identifying the thesis, ask yourself, "What is the most important idea the writer wants to express about the subject?" Then look for a sentence that states this point.
- Use the thesis statement to help you draw a blueprint of the essay: Think of the thesis statement as the roof; how do the reasons and key evidence the writer supplies support the thesis?

AFTER READING
- Paraphrase the thesis. If you cannot, this is a sign that you do not really understand the essay. (You may suffer from what psychologists of learning call the "illusion of knowing.") Reread the selection, or consult the "Just-in-Time Guide to Reading and Responding" for help.

In narrative or descriptive essays, writers may not state the thesis directly. Instead, the thesis may be strongly implied by the details. Although some professional writers use an implied thesis, academic writers, including professors and students, generally state their thesis directly. Check with your instructor if you are unsure whether you need to include an explicit thesis.

Support Your Thesis Statement with Evidence

After you have written a working thesis statement, the next step is to develop evidence that supports your thesis. **Evidence** is any type of information, such as examples and anecdotes, facts and statistics, or expert opinion, that will convince your reader that your thesis is reasonable or correct.

Tailor the Evidence to Your Writing Situation

Your writing situation—that is, your purpose, audience, point of view, genre, and medium—will determine which types of evidence will be most effective. For example:

- If your purpose is to persuade, using comparison and contrast to highlight advantages and disadvantages, giving examples of problems, citing statistics to support your claim, and using quotations from experts may help make your argument convincing.
- If your audience is unfamiliar with your topic, providing definitions, historical background, an explanation of a process, and factual and descriptive details may be necessary.

Table 5.1 (p. 130) lists various types of evidence and gives examples of how each type could be used to support a working thesis on acupuncture. **Note:** Many of the types of evidence correspond to the patterns of development discussed in Parts 3 and 4.

| EXERCISE 5.5 | CHOOSING THE BEST EVIDENCE FOR YOUR WRITING SITUATION |

1. In groups of two or three students, discuss and list the types of evidence that could be used to support the following thesis statement for an informative essay:

   The need to become financially independent is a challenge for many young adults and often causes them to develop social and emotional problems.

2. For each audience below, discuss and record the types of evidence that would offer the best support for the preceding thesis.
   a. Young adults
   b. Parents of young adults
   c. Counselors of young adults

TABLE 5.1 Types of Evidence Used to Support a Thesis

Working Thesis:	Acupuncture, a form of alternative medicine, is becoming more widely accepted in the United States.
Types of Evidence	**Example**
Definitions	Explain that in acupuncture, needles are inserted into specific points of the body to control pain or relieve symptoms.
Historical Background	Explain that acupuncture is a medical treatment that originated in ancient China.
Explanation of a Process	Explain the principles on which acupuncture is based and how scientists think it works.
Factual Details	Explain who uses acupuncture, on what parts of the body it is used, and under what circumstances it is applied.
Descriptive Details	Explain what acupuncture needles look and feel like.
Narrative Story	Relate a personal experience that illustrates the use of acupuncture.
Causes or Effects	Discuss one or two theories that explain why acupuncture works. Offer reasons for its increasing popularity.
Classification	Explain types of acupuncture treatments.
Comparison and Contrast	Compare acupuncture with other forms of alternative medicine, such as massage and herbal medicines. Explain how acupuncture differs from these other treatments.
Advantages and Disadvantages	Describe the pros (nonsurgical, relatively painless) and cons (fear of needles) of acupuncture.
Examples	Describe situations in which acupuncture has been used successfully—by dentists, in treating alcoholism, for pain control.
Problems	Explain that acupuncture is not always practiced by medical doctors; licensing and oversight of acupuncturists may thus be lax.
Statistics	Indicate how many acupuncturists practice in the United States.
Quotations	Quote medical experts who attest to the effectiveness of acupuncture.

Collect Evidence to Support Your Thesis

Select one or more of the following suggestions to generate evidence that supports your thesis:

1. Create a two-column worksheet; list types of evidence in the left column and provide examples that support your thesis in the right column. Collect evidence only for the types that are appropriate for your thesis.

2. Picture yourself speaking to your audience. What would you say to convince your audience of your thesis? Jot down ideas as they come to you.

3. Develop a skeletal outline of major headings. Leave plenty of blank space under each heading, and fill in ideas about each heading as they come to you.

4. Draw a graphic organizer of your essay, filling in supporting evidence as you think of it.

5. Discuss your thesis statement with a classmate; try to explain why he or she should accept your thesis as valid.

For more on outlining and drawing a graphic organizer, see Chapter 7.

ESSAY IN PROGRESS 3

Using the preceding list of suggestions and Table 5.1, generate at least three different types of evidence to support the working thesis statement you wrote in Essay in Progress 2.

Choose the Best Evidence

In collecting evidence in support of a thesis, you will probably generate more than you need. Consequently, you will need to identify the evidence that (1) best supports your thesis and (2) best suits your purpose and audience:

1. **Make sure the evidence is relevant.** All of your evidence must clearly and directly support your thesis. Irrelevant evidence will distract and puzzle (or annoy) your readers. If your thesis is that acupuncture is useful for controlling pain, you would not need to describe other alternative therapies.

2. **Provide specific evidence.** Avoid general statements that will not help you make a convincing case for your thesis. For instance, to support the thesis that acupuncture is becoming more widely accepted by patients in the United States, citing statistics that demonstrate an increase in the number of practicing acupuncturists in the United States over the past five years would be most convincing. (You may need to return to your prewriting or conduct research to find evidence for your thesis.)

3. **Offer a variety of evidence.** Using different kinds of evidence increases the likelihood that your evidence will convince your readers. If you provide only four examples of people who have found acupuncture helpful, for instance, your readers may conclude that four people's experiences do not mean that acupuncture is becoming more popular nationally. If you also provide statistics and quotations from experts, however, more readers will be likely to accept your thesis. Using different types of evidence also enhances your credibility, showing readers you are well informed about your topic. The "Types of Evidence" checklist below lists a number of evidence types. Use it to determine whether the evidence you are offering is varied enough.

4. **Provide a sufficient amount of evidence.** The amount of evidence you need varies according to your audience and your topic. To discover whether you have provided enough evidence, ask a classmate to read your essay and tell you whether he or she is convinced. If your reader is not convinced, ask him or her what additional evidence is needed.

5. **Provide representative evidence.** Do not provide unusual, rare, or exceptional situations as evidence. Suppose your thesis is that acupuncture is widely used for various types of surgery. An example of one person who underwent painless

heart surgery using only acupuncture will not support your thesis unless the use of acupuncture in heart surgery is common. Including such an example would mislead your reader and may bring your credibility into question.

For more about choosing reliable evidence, see Chapter 20. For more on conducting, incorporating, and citing research, see Chapters 21 and 22.

6. **Provide accurate evidence from reliable sources.** Do not make vague statements, guess at statistics, or make estimates. For example, do not simply say that many medical doctors are licensed to practice acupuncture in the United States or estimate the number. Instead, find out exactly how many U.S. physicians are licensed for this practice.

Checklist: Types of Evidence

Use this checklist to make sure you are offering a variety of evidence in support of your thesis.

☐ Historical background

☐ Factual details (facts, statistics)

☐ Narration (a story or anecdote)

☐ Descriptive details (details that appeal to the senses)

☐ Examples

☐ Explanation of a process

☐ Comparison and contrast

☐ Classification

☐ Definitions

☐ Causes or effects

☐ Advantages or disadvantages

☐ Problems

☐ Quotations

Academic Writing: Choosing Evidence

For most kinds of academic writing, certain types of evidence are preferred over others. In general, your personal experiences and opinions are not considered as useful as more objective evidence such as facts, statistics, historical background, and expert testimony.

Suppose you are writing an academic paper on the effects of global warming. Your observations about climate changes in your city would not be considered adequate or appropriate evidence to support the idea of climate change as an effect of global warming. To support your thesis, you would need to provide facts, statistics, and expert testimony on climate change in a wide geographic area and demonstrate their relationship to global warming.

ESSAY IN PROGRESS 4

Evaluate the evidence you generated in Essay in Progress 3. Select the evidence that you could use to support your thesis in a two- to four-page essay for a college class.

Academic Writing: Integrating Evidence from Sources

For many academic writing assignments, you will use evidence from sources to support your thesis. You can include source information in three ways: as a quotation, a paraphrase, or a summary.

1. A **quotation** uses the exact words of your source. Use a quotation when the information or idea cannot be as clearly, accurately, or compellingly expressed in your words (for example, if you are borrowing information that is highly technical or conveyed in a particularly engaging way).
2. A **paraphrase** expresses an author's idea in your own words and sentences. Use a paraphrase when the information and ideas are important, but the exact wording is not.
3. A **summary** condenses a passage into a concise format, capturing the main point and leaving out the details. Use a summary when you want to convey the gist of the information.

You should mostly use paraphrases and summaries to make sure your voice predominates; quotations should be used sparingly.

Regardless of whether you quote, paraphrase, or summarize a source, introduce a source with a signal phrase (or attribution). A **signal phrase** includes

- the author's name
- a verb that reflects the "move" the author is making

For more information about paraphrasing and summarizing effectively, see Chapter 22; to learn more about integrating quotations effectively, see Chapter 23.

Also include enough information about the source for your readers to understand its value and a page reference so that readers can find the information for themselves if they're interested in learning more. Later references to a source in a signal phrase can include just the author's last name.

Examples

Olivia Berafato, a professor of chemical engineering, explains . . . (p. XX).

Constitutional law attorney Alan Dershowitz argues that ". . ." (p. XX).

In her book *You Just Don't Understand*, linguist Deborah Tannen theorizes . . . (p. XX).

Once you present and cite source information, make clear what it means, why it is relevant, and how it supports the point you are making. You must also give credit to all those from whom you borrow information and ideas by including a source citation in your list of works cited or references.

See the section "Academic Writing: Crafting a Research 'Sandwich'" (Chapter 6) for a sample research paragraph. Chapter 23 provides additional information about citing sources in the text and in a list of works cited or references.

Incorporate Visuals into an Essay

Today's readers are used to seeing more than words on a page, and since your task is to engage readers and communicate meaning effectively, using appropriate visuals may help. Visuals can enhance your essay and contribute to its meaning by

- offering an example
- conveying information more clearly or concisely than you could in words
- eliciting a response or reaction from readers
- providing emphasis
- sparking interest

Of course, including visuals is not appropriate in every writing situation, nor is a visual a substitute for an explanation. And including a visual that is merely decorative is rarely appropriate, especially in academic writing. (Your instructor can advise you if you are unsure about whether including a visual is appropriate.)

The excerpt from a student essay in Figure 5.1 (p. 135) illustrates how to use a visual effectively and how to integrate it into an essay. The photograph in the sample page in Figure 5.1 achieves several purposes:

- It offers an example of altruism among animals of different species.
- It creates visual interest.
- It lends emphasis to the essay's thesis—that animals exhibit emotions, including altruism.

Select Appropriate Visuals

See Chapter 3, for more about reading visuals actively and critically.

Use the following guidelines to choose effective and reliable visuals:

1. **Use visuals to illustrate important ideas in your essay.** Illustrations should offer support for your thesis or the topic sentence of the paragraph in which they appear. For example, you might include a photograph of a painting you are analyzing or a visual example that supports the point you are making in a paragraph (as in the sample page in Figure 5.1). You may also include a chart, table, or graph that allows you to convey a large amount of data clearly and succinctly.

2. **Use visuals that are appropriate given your audience.** Use visuals that are appropriate to your writing situation and that your audience will understand and appreciate. (For example, it would be inappropriate to include visuals that are merely decorative in a college essay.) Visuals should be avoided if they require prior knowledge your audience lacks or they make a point that could be more easily conveyed in words.

3. **Use visuals that are consistent with your method of development.** For example, a descriptive essay might include a photograph, a comparison-and-contrast essay might include a bar graph, a classification or division essay might include a table or pie chart, and a process essay might feature a diagram or flowchart.

4. **Avoid misleading visuals.** Make sure the data used to create charts and graphs are reliable and that photographs do not distort or misrepresent the subjects. Visuals from sources such as well-respected news organizations or government agencies are generally reliable.

To incorporate a visual effectively within your essay, reference the visual (*for example, see Fig. 1*) and briefly explain its intended message. Place the visual as close after the reference in the text as possible to ensure readers can connect the visual with the part of the text in which it is discussed. Include the figure number and a brief explanatory caption below.

One final word of caution: Unless the visual is a photograph you took or a graphic created from data you collected, you must credit the source. For academic papers, include complete source information at the end of the caption (unless your instructor provides other instructions).

FIGURE 5.1 Integrating Visuals into an Academic Essay

Sympathy and caring have been noted in non-primate species as well. Researchers have found that young barn owls are "impressively generous" toward each other, saving portions of their food for smaller and hungrier owls (Angier). Likewise, the *Nature* episode "Animal Odd Couples" documents a number of instances in which animals of one species have cared for animals of another. In one example, Jack, a goat, led Charlie, a blind horse, around the ranch where they lived *every day for sixteen years*, until Jack's death (Fig. 1). The animals' caretaker even compared Jack to the television character Lassie, describing how Jack got human help to rescue Charlie after he became trapped in a grove of trees following a microburst of wind.

Identifies source

Introduces and explains the visual

Includes figure number (abbreviated "Fig." in MLA style) in text and caption

Fig. 1. Seeing is believing: Jack leading Charlie (a blind horse). Film still from "Animal Odd Couples" (27:23), *Nature* (PBS, 7 Nov. 2012).

What makes this example particularly noteworthy is that the animals were of different species. Had the goat been helping another goat, it would be easy to assume that the act of caring was the result of what scientists call *genetic altruism*, animals helping others of their own species because there is something in it for them—namely, the assurance that their kin (and, therefore, their genes) will continue. This theory certainly provides an adequate,

Topic sentence supports thesis/references example

STUDENTS WRITE

In the Students Write section of Chapter 4, you saw how Latrisha Wilson narrowed her topic and generated ideas for her essay on surveillance. You also saw how she explored types of surveillance as they affect her privacy. After reviewing her responses to questions about her topic and her freewriting, Wilson drafted the following working thesis.

> These new digital technologies have both benefits and drawbacks.

She realized that her thesis was overly general and too broad, so she did more freewriting and brainstorming to help her recall details about types of surveillance. Here's an excerpt from her brainstorming:

- Spies like James Bond are no longer necessary. Movies and video games fool us into believing they are, but mainly spying is done by computers.
- The National Security Agency (NSA) watches everything we do on the Internet and everything we say on our phones.
- Edward Snowden, the NSA whistleblower, was a newsmaker. He exposed the NSA's secret surveillance.
- Google has access to everything about us, and they sell the information to other companies.
- If we want to communicate through a screen or a phone, we have to give up our privacy.
- We seldom are asked for our consent to share information about ourselves.
- Twitter, Flickr, YouTube, Facebook, and other new media also provide lots of information about our daily lives, and not just to our "friends."
- Because we enjoy sharing our lives and learning about the lives of others, we forget about where the information is going.
- In reality, we have very little privacy if we use digital devices.

After brainstorming, she decided that she should focus on the drawbacks of digital communications technology. She narrowed her thesis even further to focus on the subtle forms of surveillance new communications technology enable:

> Often advertised as free services, new ways of communicating put us under more invasive but less obvious forms of surveillance.

READING

Internet Addiction

Greg Beato

The following essay by Greg Beato was first published in 2010 in *Reason*, a magazine that offers updates on current developments in politics and culture from a libertarian perspective. Beato, a contributing editor for *Reason*, supports the essay's thesis with a variety of evidence. As you read, highlight the thesis statement and notice the types of evidence used to support it.

Before Reading

1. **Preview** Use the steps listed in the "Preview" section in Chapter 2.
2. **Connect** What does *addiction* mean in this context, and what kinds of Internet use does Beato mean?

While Reading Pay particular attention to Beato's thesis and the evidence he provides to support it.

In 1995, in an effort to parody the way the American Psychiatric Association's hugely influential *Diagnostic and Statistical Manual of Mental Disorders* medicalizes every excessive behavior, psychiatrist Ivan Goldberg introduced on his website the concept of "Internet Addiction Disorder." Last summer Ben Alexander, a 19-year-old college student obsessed with the online multiplayer game *World of Warcraft*, was profiled by CBS News, NPR, the Associated Press, and countless other media outlets because of his status as client No. 1 at reSTART, the first residential treatment center in America for individuals trying to get themselves clean from Azeroth, iPhones, and all the other digital narcotics of our age.

At reSTART's five-acre haven in the woods near Seattle, clients pay big bucks to detox from pathological computer use by building chicken coops, cooking hamburgers, and engaging in daily therapy sessions with the program's two founders, psychologist Hilarie Cash and clinical social worker and life coach Cosette Rae. With room for just six addicts at a time and a $14,500 program fee, reSTART isn't designed for the masses, and so far it seems to have attracted more reporters than paying clients. When I spoke with Rae in May, she said "10 to 15" people had participated in the 45-day program to date.

Still, the fact that reSTART exists at all shows how far we've progressed in taking Dr. Goldberg's spoof seriously. You may have been too busy monitoring Kim Kardashian's every passing thought-like thing on Twitter to notice, but Digital Detox Week took place in April, and Video Game Addiction Awareness Week followed on its heels in June. Internet addiction disorder has yet to claim a Tiger Woods of its own, but the sad, silly evidence of our worldwide cyber-bingeing mounts on a daily basis. A councilman in the Bulgarian city of Plovdiv is ousted from his position for playing *Farmville* during budget meetings. There are now at least three apps that use the iPhone's camera to show the world right in front of you so you can keep texting while walking down the street, confident in your ability to avoid sinkholes, telephone poles, and traffic. Earlier this year, 200 students taking a class in media literacy at the University of Maryland went on a 24-hour media fast for a group study, then described how "jittery," "anxious," "miserable," and "crazy" they felt without Twitter, Facebook, iPods, and laptops. "I clearly am addicted," one student concluded, "and the dependency is sickening."

In the early days of the Web, dirty talk was exchanged at the excruciatingly slow rate of 14.4 bits per second, connectivity charges accrued by the hour instead of the month, and the only stuff for sale online was some overpriced hot sauce

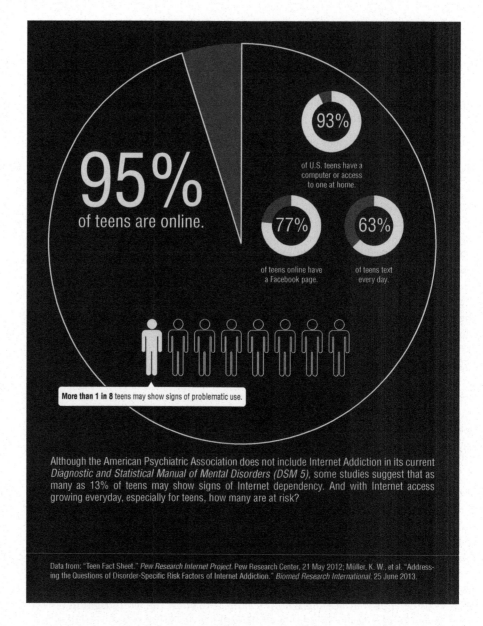

95% of teens are online.

93% of U.S. teens have a computer or access to one at home.

77% of teens online have a Facebook page.

63% of teens text every day.

More than 1 in 8 teens may show signs of problematic use.

Although the American Psychiatric Association does not include Internet Addiction in its current *Diagnostic and Statistical Manual of Mental Disorders (DSM 5)*, some studies suggest that as many as 13% of teens may show signs of Internet dependency. And with Internet access growing everyday, especially for teens, how many are at risk?

Data from: "Teen Fact Sheet." *Pew Research Internet Project.* Pew Research Center, 21 May 2012; Müller, K. W., et al. "Addressing the Questions of Disorder-Specific Risk Factors of Internet Addiction." *Biomed Research International,* 25 June 2013.

from a tiny store in Pasadena. It took the patience of a Buddhist monk, thousands of dollars, and really bad TV reception to overuse the Web in a self-destructive manner. Yet even then, many people felt Ivan Goldberg's notes on Internet addiction worked better as psychiatry than comedy. A year before Goldberg posted his spoof, Kimberly Young, a psychologist at the University of Pittsburgh, had already begun conducting formal research into online addiction. By 1996 the Harvard-affiliated McLean Hospital had established a computer addiction clinic, a professor at the University of Maryland had created an Internet addiction support group, and *The New York Times* was running op-eds about the divorce epidemic that Internet addiction was about to unleash.

Fifteen years down the line, you'd think we'd all be introverted philanderers   5
by now, isolating ourselves in the virtual Snuggie of *World of Warcraft* by day and stepping out at night to destroy our marriages with our latest hook-ups from AshleyMadison.com. But the introduction of flat monthly fees, online gaming, widespread pornography, MySpace, YouTube, Facebook, WiFi, iPhones, netbooks, and free return shipping on designer shoes with substantial markdowns does not seem to have made the Internet any more addictive than it was a decade ago.

In 1998 Young told the Riverside *Press-Enterprise* that "5 to 10 percent of the 52   6
million Internet users [were] addicted or 'potentially addicted.' " Doctors today use similar numbers when estimating the number of online junkies. In 2009 David Greenfield, a psychiatrist at the University of Connecticut, told the *San Francisco Chronicle* that studies have shown 3 percent to 6 percent of Internet users "have a problem." Is it possible that the ability to keep extremely close tabs on Ashton Kutcher actually has reduced the Internet's addictive power?

Granted, 3 percent is an awful lot of people. Argue all you like that a real   7
addiction should require needles, or spending time in seedy bars with people who drink vodka through their eyeballs, or at least the overwhelming and nihilistic urge to invest thousands of dollars in a broken public school system through the purchase of lottery tickets. Those working on the front lines of technology overuse have plenty of casualties to point to. In our brief conversation, Cosette Rae tells me about a Harvard student who lost a scholarship because he spent too much time playing games, a guy who spent so many sedentary hours at his computer that he developed blood clots in his leg and had to have it amputated, and an 18-year-old who chose homelessness over gamelessness when his parents told him he either had to quit playing computer games or move out.

A few minutes on Google yields even more lurid anecdotes. In 2007 an Ohio   8
teenager shot his parents, killing his mother and wounding his father, after they took away his Xbox. This year a South Korean couple let their real baby starve to death because they were spending so much time caring for their virtual baby in a role-playing game called *Prius Online*.

On a pound-for-pound basis, the average *World of Warcraft* junkie undoubtedly   9
represents a much less destructive social force than the average meth head. But it's not extreme anecdotes that make the specter of Internet addiction so threatening; it's the fact that Internet overuse has the potential to scale in a way that few other addictions do. Even if Steve Jobs designed a really cool-looking syringe and started distributing free heroin on street corners, not everyone would try it. But who among us doesn't already check his email more often than necessary? As the Internet weaves itself more and more tightly into our lives, only the Amish are completely safe.

As early as 1996, Kimberly Young was promoting the idea that the American   10
Psychiatric Association (APA) should add Internet addiction disorder to the *Diagnostic and Statistical Manual of Mental Disorders (DSM)*. In February, the APA announced that its coming edition of the *DSM*, the first major revision since 1994, will for the first time classify a behavior-related condition—pathological

gambling—as an "addiction" rather than an "impulse control disorder." Internet addiction disorder is not being included in this new category of "behavioral addictions," but the APA said it will consider it as a "potential addition . . . as research data accumulate."

If the APA does add excessive Internet use to the DSM, the consequences will   11
be wide-ranging. Health insurance companies will start offering at least partial coverage for treatment programs such as reSTART. People who suffer from Internet addiction disorder will receive protection under the Americans with Disabilities Act if their impairment "substantially limits one or more major life activities." Criminal lawyers will use their clients' online habits to fashion diminished capacity defenses.

Which means that what started as a parody in 1995 could eventually turn   12
more darkly comic than ever imagined. Picture a world where the health care system goes bankrupt because insurers have to pay for millions of people determined to kick their Twitter addictions once and for all. Where employees who view porn at work are legally protected from termination. Where killing elves in cyberspace could help absolve you for killing people in real life. Is it too late to revert to our older, healthier, more balanced ways of living and just spend all our leisure hours watching *Love Boat* reruns?

Examining the Reading

1. **Definition** Define the term *Internet addiction*.
2. **Examples** What are some examples of dangerous behavior caused by Internet addiction?
3. **Meaning** Why does adding Internet addiction to the DSM have important social consequences?
4. **Vocabulary** Define each of the following words as they are used in the essay: *parody* (para. 1), *pathological* (2), *nihilistic* (7), *lurid* (8), and *specter* (9).

Analyzing the Writer's Technique

1. **Thesis** State the author's thesis in your own words. Then, using the guidelines on pages 125–28, evaluate the effectiveness of the thesis.
2. **Rhetorical Situation** To what audience does Beato address this essay? What purpose does the essay fulfill? How do you think the writing situation affects the author's choice of evidence?
3. **Support** Cite one paragraph from the essay in which you think the author provides detailed, specific information. Explain why you chose that paragraph. Does it support the thesis? Why or why not?

Visualizing the Reading

In the chart below, supply an example of each type of evidence the author has used in the reading. The first one has been done for you.

Type of Evidence	Example
Historical Background	Website parody of the *DSM* in 1995 included Internet addiction and 1996 McLean Hospital program for Internet addiction
Descriptive Details	
Statistics	
Examples	
Comparison and Contrast	
Quotations	

Thinking Critically about the Reading

1. **Sources** Evaluate the sources that Beato uses to support his thesis. Are they trustworthy and reliable?
2. **Tone** Describe the author's tone. How does the tone affect your response to the reading?
3. **Opinion** Identify at least one statement of opinion in paragraph 9. Does the author offer evidence to support the opinion?
4. **Connotation** What is the connotation of the word *junkies* in paragraph 6? Identify at least four other words in the selection with strong positive or negative connotations.
5. **Evaluation** How useful are the anecdotes in paragraphs 7 and 8 as evidence?

For more about connotation and tone, see "Analyze the Author's Language" in Chapter 3 and "Analyze Your Word Choice" in Chapter 9; for more about distinguishing facts and opinions, see "Distinguish Fact from Opinion" in Chapter 3.

Interpreting a Graphic

1. **Meaning** The text below the large pie chart on page 138 reports that "13% of teens may show signs of Internet dependency," and the pictogram says that "more than 1 in 8 teens may show signs of problematic use." What is the difference between the terms *dependency* and *problematic use*?
2. **Source** How reliable do the sources for this graphic seem? What other sources might you use for a paper on Internet dependency among teens?

Responding to the Reading

1. **Audience** How do you think this essay would change if the author wrote it for *Parents* magazine?
2. **Discussion** Why do you think the number of people addicted to the Internet has actually lessened since 1998? What might it mean that the American Psychological Association is not ready to include Internet addiction in the DSM? What does this say about the disorder?

3. **Journal** In your journal, write about ways you use the Internet that may not be healthy. How does it negatively affect your life? Do you feel it has more positive than negative effects on your life? Explain.

Working Together

1. Imagine that you and a classmate are authors of an advice column for your college newspaper. Write a letter responding to a reader who asked for advice about kicking her Internet addiction. Working with your partner, draft a one-paragraph reply, suggesting steps the person can take to break free of her addiction. Be creative in your response. Be prepared to share your advice with the class.

2. Working with two or three of your classmates, spend five to ten minutes brainstorming a list of positive and negative effects of Internet use among college students. Then write a thesis statement based on the ideas you generated. Compare your list with the lists of other groups in the class.

DanielBendjy/iStock/Getty Images

6
Writing Effective Paragraphs

Writing Quick Start

ANALYZE The photograph above shows an annual event popular in many cities around the world, the Gay Pride Parade. Study the photograph and consider the mood or feelings of those participating in the event.

WRITE Draft a sentence that captures the feelings you can identify in the photograph. Then write several more sentences that explain what details in the photograph reveal the feelings exhibited by the crowd.

CONNECT In much the same way as a photograph does, a paragraph makes an overall impression, or main point, and includes details that support this main point. Your first sentence, or **topic sentence**, states the main idea, and the other sentences you write provide the details that support it.

In this chapter you will learn to

- understand the structure of a paragraph
- write effective topic sentences
- select details that support the paragraph's main idea
- use transitions and repetition effectively

143

Structure Your Paragraphs Effectively

A paragraph is a group of connected sentences that develop a single idea about a topic. Each paragraph in your essay should support your thesis and contribute to the overall meaning and effectiveness of your essay.

A well-developed paragraph contains

- a well-focused topic sentence
- specific supporting details
- transitions and strategic repetition that show how the ideas are related, within and across paragraphs.

When writing a paragraph using sources, you may need to include an additional sentence that interprets or explains the evidence provided in the paragraph.

For a paragraph to develop a single idea, it must have **unity**: It must stay focused on one idea, without switching or wandering from topic to topic. A paragraph also should be of a reasonable length, neither too short nor too long. Short paragraphs are often underdeveloped; long paragraphs may be difficult for readers to follow. Note that what is an appropriate length may change across genres (or types) of writing—college essays usually have longer paragraphs than newspaper articles, and scholarly articles usually have longer paragraphs than college essays.

Here is a sample paragraph from a college textbook with its parts labeled:

Topic sentence: Main idea

Repetition: Key terms

Transitions: Guideposts

Audiences gather with varying degrees of willingness to hear a speaker. Some are anxious to hear the speaker, and may even have paid a substantial admission price. The "lecture circuit," for example, is a most lucrative aspect of public life. But whereas some audiences are willing to pay to hear a speaker, others don't seem to care one way or the other. Other audiences need to be persuaded to listen (or at least to sit in the audience). Still other audiences gather because they have to. For example, negotiations on a union contract may require members to attend meetings where officers give speeches.

—DeVito, *The Essential Elements of Public Speaking*

Notice how the writer repeats the words *audience(s)* and *speaker,* along with the synonyms *lecture* and *speeches,* to help tie the paragraph to the idea in the topic sentence. To visualize the structure of a well-developed paragraph, see Graphic Organizer 6.1.

Write Effective Topic Sentences

A **topic sentence** is to a paragraph what a thesis statement is to an essay. Just as a thesis announces the main point of an essay, a topic sentence states the main point of a paragraph. In addition, each paragraph's topic sentence must support the thesis of the essay. An effective topic sentence should be focused, support the thesis, and be placed appropriately (usually at the beginning of the paragraph).

GRAPHIC ORGANIZER 6.1   The Structure of a Paragraph

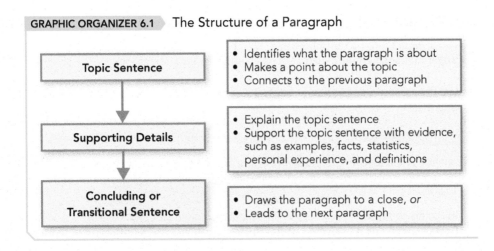

A Topic Sentence Should Be Focused

A topic sentence should make clear what the paragraph is about (its topic) and express a view or make a point about the topic.

⎯⎯⎯⎯ topic ⎯⎯⎯⎯
Shocking behavior by fans, including rudeness and violent language,

⎯⎯⎯⎯ point about topic ⎯⎯⎯⎯
has become common at many sporting events.

A topic sentence should use specific and detailed language to tell readers what the paragraph is about. Vague, general, or unfocused statements should be avoided.

Unfocused   Some members of minority groups do not approve of affirmative action.

Focused   Some members of minority groups disapprove of affirmative action because it implies that they are not capable of obtaining employment based on their own accomplishments.

Unfocused   Many students believe that hate groups shouldn't be allowed on campus.

Focused   The neo-Nazis, a group that promotes hate crimes, should not be permitted to speak in our local community college because they encourage hostility toward Jewish, nonwhite, and immigrant students and community members.

If you have trouble focusing your topic sentences, review the guidelines for writing an effective thesis statement in Chapter 5, many of which also apply to writing effective topic sentences.

A Topic Sentence May Preview the Organization of the Paragraph

A topic sentence may suggest the order in which details are discussed in the paragraph, so readers know what to expect.

Teaching employees how to handle conflicts through both

┌───── detail 1 ─────┐   ┌ detail 2 ┐
anger management and mediation is essential in high-stress jobs.

Readers can expect a discussion of anger management first, followed by a discussion of mediation.

EXERCISE 6.1   **WORKING WITH TOPIC SENTENCES**

Revise each of the following topic sentences to make it focused and specific. At least two of your revised topic sentences should also preview the organization of the paragraph.

1. In society today, there is always a new fad or fashion in clothing.
2. People watch reality television shows because they find them irresistible.
3. Body art is popular.
4. Procrastinating can have a negative effect on your success in college.
5. In our state, the lottery is a big issue.

A Topic Sentence Should Support Your Thesis

Each topic sentence must in some way explain the thesis or show why the thesis is believable or correct. For example, this sample thesis could be supported by the topic sentences that follow it:

Thesis   Adoption files should not be made available to adult children who are seeking their biological parents.

Topic Sentences

- Research has shown that not all biological parents want to meet with the sons or daughters they gave up many years before.
- If a woman gives up a child for adoption, it is probable that she does not ever intend to have a relationship with that child.
- Adult children who try to contact their biological parents often meet resistance and even hostility, which can cause them to feel hurt and rejected.
- A woman who gave up her biological child because she became pregnant as a result of rape or incest should not have to live in fear that her child will one day confront her.

All of these topic sentences support the thesis because they offer valid reasons for keeping adoption files closed.

EXERCISE 6.2   **USING TOPIC SENTENCES TO SUPPORT A THESIS**

For each of the following thesis statements, identify the topic sentence in the list below it that does not support the thesis.

1. To make a marriage work, a couple must build trust, communication, and understanding.
   a. Knowing why a spouse behaves as he or she does can improve a relationship.
   b. People get married for reasons other than love.

    c. The ability to talk about feelings, problems, likes, and dislikes should grow as a marriage develops.

    d. Marital partners must rely on each other to make sensible decisions that benefit both of them.

2. Internet sales are capturing a larger market share relative to in-store sales.

    a. Internet retailers that target a specific audience tend to be most successful.

    b. The convenience of ordering any time of day or night has increased Internet sales.

    c. Many customers use PayPal for online purchases.

    d. Websites that locate and compare prices for a specified item make comparison shopping easier on the Internet than in retail stores.

A Topic Sentence Should Be Strategically Placed

The beginning of the paragraph is the most common and often the best position for a topic sentence: You state your main point, and then you explain it. The topic sentence tells readers what to expect in the rest of the paragraph, making it clear and easy for them to follow.

> Advertising is first and foremost based on the principle of visibility—the customer must notice the product. Manufacturers often package products in glitzy, even garish, containers to grab the consumer's attention. For example, one candy company always packages its candy in reflective wrappers. When the hurried and hungry consumer glances at the candy counter, the reflective wrappers are easy to spot. It is only natural for the impatient customer to grab the candy and go.

Topic sentence: Appears at beginning of paragraph

When one or two sentences are needed at the beginning of a paragraph to smooth the transition from one paragraph to the next, the topic sentence may follow these transitional sentences.

> However, visibility is not the only principle in advertising; it is simply the first. A second and perhaps more subtle principle is identity: The manufacturer attempts to lure the consumer into buying a product by linking it to a concept with which the consumer can identify. For instance, Boundaries perfume is advertised on television as the choice of "independent" women. Since independent women are admired in our culture, women identify with the concept and therefore are attracted to the perfume. Once the consumer identifies with the product, a sale is more likely to occur.

Topic sentence: Appears after transitional sentence, before example

If you want to present convincing evidence before stating your point about the issue, you may want to save your topic sentence until the end of the paragraph. This allows readers to draw their own conclusions based on the details you have provided. This strategy is common in argumentative writing (especially when readers may not be sympathetic to the writer's position).

> The saying "Guns don't kill people; people kill people" is deceptive in the same way that the statement "Heroin doesn't kill people; people kill themselves"

is deceptive. Naturally, people need to pull the trigger of a gun to make the gun kill other people, just as it is necessary for people to use heroin for it to kill them. However, these facts do not excuse us from the responsibility of keeping guns (or heroin) out of people's hands as much as possible. People cannot shoot people unless they have a gun. <u>This fact alone should persuade the government to institute stiff gun control laws.</u>

Topic sentence: Follows evidence

ESSAY IN PROGRESS 1

For an essay that you have written for this or another class, evaluate each of your topic sentences for content and placement. Revise as needed to make each more effective.

HOW WRITERS READ   **PARAGRAPHS**

Use these strategies to understand and remember what you read:

WHILE READING

- Identify the paragraph's topic, or main idea, and the position or point of view the writer wants to express about the topic. (This is usually conveyed by the topic sentence, but may be implied.)
- Use transitional words and phrases to guide you from one detail to another and to alert you when the author moves on to a new idea. Transitions may even signal what kind of idea (an example, a contradictory fact, a further explanation) is to follow and which supporting ideas are most important.

AFTER READING

- Test your understanding and recall of the paragraph's main point by paraphrasing the topic sentence (expressing it in your own words) without looking at the paragraph.

Include Supporting Details

In addition to including well-focused topic sentences, effective paragraphs are unified and well developed—they provide relevant details that support the main point.

Effective Paragraphs Have Unity

A paragraph has unity when all of the sentences directly support the topic sentence. Including details that are not relevant to the topic sentence makes your paragraph unclear and distracts your reader from the point you are making. To identify irrelevant details, evaluate each sentence by asking the following questions:

1. Does this sentence directly explain the topic sentence? What new information does it add?
2. Would any essential information be lost if this sentence were deleted? (If not, delete it.)
3. Is this information distracting or unimportant? (If so, delete it.)

The following sample paragraph lacks unity. As you read it, try to identify the sentences that do not support the topic sentence.

Paragraph Lacking Unity

(1) <u>Much of the violence we see in the world today may be caused by the emphasis on violence in the media.</u> (2) More often than not, the front page of the local newspaper contains stories involving violence. (3) In fact, one recent issue of my local newspaper contained seven references to violent acts. (4) There is also violence in public school systems. (5) Television reporters frequently hasten to crime and accident scenes and film every grim, violent detail. (6) The other day, there was a drive-by shooting downtown. (7) If the media were a little more careful about the ways in which they glamorize violence, there might be less violence in the world today and children would be less influenced by it.

Topic sentence: Main idea

Although sentences 4 and 6 deal with the broad topic of violence, neither is directly related to the main point stated in the topic sentence. Both should be deleted.

EXERCISE 6.3 **PRACTICING PARAGRAPH UNITY**

Alone or in a group of two or three students, read each paragraph and identify the sentences that do not support the double underscored topic sentence.

1. (a) <u>Today many options and services for the elderly are available that did not exist years ago.</u> (b) My grandmother is eighty-five years old now. (c) Adult care for the elderly is now provided in many parts of the country. (d) Similar to day care, adult care provides places where the elderly can go for meals and social activities. (e) Retirement homes for the elderly, where they can live fairly independently with minimal supervision, are another option. (f) My grandfather is also among the elderly at eighty-two. (g) Even many nursing homes have changed so that residents are afforded some level of privacy and independence while their needs are being met.

2. (a) <u>Just as history repeats itself, fashions have a tendency to do the same.</u> (b) In the late 1960s, for example, women wore miniskirts that came several inches above the knee; some forty years later, the fashion magazines are featuring this same type of dress, and many teenagers are wearing them. (c) The miniskirt has always been flattering on slender women. (d) I wonder if the fashion industry deliberately recycles fashions. (e) Men wore their hair long in the hippie period of the late 1960s and 1970s. (f) Today, some men are again letting their hair grow. (g) Beards, considered "in" during the 1970s, have once again made an appearance.

Effective Paragraphs Are Well Developed

A well-developed paragraph should include enough supporting details to demonstrate that the topic sentence is accurate and believable. Compare the two paragraphs below.

Underdeveloped Paragraph

Email and texting are important technological advances, but they have hidden limitations, even dangers. It is too easy to avoid talking to people face to

Does not explain why email and text messaging are important

Does not provide any evidence of how or why they can be addictive

face. Emailing and texting can be addictive, too. Plus, they encourage ordinary people to ignore others while typing on a keyboard.

Developed Paragraph

States reason that emailing and texting are disadvantageous

Provides further information about the addictive qualities of texting and email

Explains the qualities of face-to-face interaction that are absent from email and texting

Email and texting are important technological advances, but they have hidden limitations, even dangers. While email and texting allow fast and efficient communication and exchange of information, they provide a different quality of human interaction. It is too easy to avoid talking to people. It is easier to click on a phone number and text a friend to see if she wants to meet for dinner than it would be actually to talk to her. In fact, using these services can become addictive. For example, some students on campus are obsessed with checking their email and sending, reading, or checking for texts many times throughout the day, even during class lectures and small group discussions. They spend their free time texting with acquaintances across the country while ignoring interesting people right in the same room. There is something to be said for talking with a person who is sitting next to you and responding to his or her expressions, gestures, and tone of voice.

The first paragraph has skeletal ideas that support the topic sentence, but it does not explain those ideas. The second paragraph fleshes out the ideas by providing examples and explanations.

To discover if your paragraphs are well developed, ask yourself the following questions:

To learn more about prewriting strategies, see Chapter 4; for more on research, see Part 5; for a list of evidence that can be used to support a paragraph, see Table 5.1.

- Have I provided enough evidence to achieve my purpose?
- Have I given my readers enough information to make my ideas understandable and believable?
- Have I provided the amount and type of evidence that readers of a college essay will expect?
- Do I jump quickly from one idea to another without explaining each idea first? (Reading your essay aloud, or asking a friend to do so, can help you hear gaps.)

To develop your paragraphs further, you can use a prewriting strategy or do some research to find supporting evidence for your topic sentence. The same types of evidence that can be used to support a thesis can be used to develop a paragraph.

EXERCISE 6.4   **USING EVIDENCE TO DEVELOP A PARAGRAPH**

Use Table 5.1 (p. 130) to suggest the type or types of evidence that might be used to develop a paragraph based on each of the following topic sentences:

1. Many people have fallen prey to fad diets, risking their health and jeopardizing their mental well-being.
2. One can distinguish experienced soccer players from rookies by obvious signs.
3. To begin a jogging routine, take a relaxed but deliberate approach.
4. The interlibrary loan system is a fast and convenient method for obtaining print materials from libraries affiliated with the campus library.
5. Southwest Florida's rapid population growth poses a serious threat to its freshwater supply.

USING DETAILS TO DEVELOP A PARAGRAPH

Create a well-developed paragraph by adding details to the following paragraph:

> Although it is convenient, online shopping provides a less satisfying experience than shopping in an actual store. You don't get the same opportunity to see and feel objects. Also, you can miss out on other important information. There is much that you miss. If you enjoy shopping, turn off your computer and support your local merchants.

Effective Paragraphs Provide Supporting Details and Arrange Them Logically

The evidence you provide to support your topic sentences should be concrete and specific. Specific details interest your readers and make your meaning clear and forceful. Compare the following two examples:

Vague

Many people are confused about the difference between a psychologist and a psychiatrist. Both have a license, but a psychiatrist has more education than a psychologist. Also, a psychiatrist can prescribe medication.

General statements do not completely explain the topic sentence.

Concrete and Specific

Many people are confused about the difference between psychiatrists and psychologists. Both are licensed by the state to practice psychotherapy. However, a psychiatrist has earned a degree from medical school and can also practice medicine. Additionally, a psychiatrist can prescribe psychotropic medications. A psychologist, on the other hand, usually has earned a Ph.D. but has not attended medical school and therefore cannot prescribe medication of any type.

Concrete details make clear the distinction between the two terms.

To make your paragraphs concrete and specific, use the following guidelines:

1. **Focus on *who, what, when, where, how,* and *why* questions.** Ask yourself these questions about your supporting details, and use the answers to expand and revise your paragraph.

   Vague   Some animals hibernate for part of the year. (What animals? When do they hibernate?)

   Specific   Some bears hibernate for three to four months each winter.

2. **Name names.** Include the names of people, places, brands, and objects.

   Vague   When my sixty-three-year-old aunt was refused a job, she became an angry victim of age discrimination.

   Specific   When my sixty-three-year-old Aunt Angela was refused a job at Vicki's Nail Salon, she became an angry victim of age discrimination.

3. **Use action verbs.** Select strong verbs that help your readers visualize the action.

Vague	When Silina came on stage, the audience became excited.
Specific	When Silina burst onto the stage, the audience screamed, cheered, and chanted, "Silina, Silina!"

4. **Use descriptive language that appeals to the senses (sight, sound, smell, taste, touch).** Words that appeal to the senses help your readers feel as if they are observing or participating in the experience you are describing.

Vague	It's relaxing to walk on the beach.
Specific	I unwound as I walked in the sand, breathing in the smell of the salt water and listening to the rhythmic sound of the waves.

5. **Use adjectives and adverbs.** Carefully chosen adjectives and adverbs in your description of a person, place, or experience can make your writing more concrete.

Vague	As I weeded my garden, I let my eyes wander over the meadow sweets and hydrangeas, all the while listening to the chirping of a cardinal.
Specific	As I slowly weeded my perennial garden, I let my eyes wander over the pink meadow sweets and blue hydrangeas, all the while listening absent-mindedly to the chirping of a bright red cardinal.

For more on organization, see Chapter 7.

The details in a paragraph should also follow a logical order. You might arrange the details from most to least (or least to most) important, in chronological order, or in spatial order.

EXERCISE 6.6   **PROVIDING CONCRETE, SPECIFIC DETAILS**

Alone or in a group of two or three students, revise and expand each sentence in the following paragraph to make it specific and concrete. Feel free to add new information and new sentences, and be sure to arrange the supporting details logically.

> I saw a great concert the other night in Dallas. Two groups were performing. The music was great, and there was a large crowd. In fact, the crowd was so enthusiastic that the second group performed an hour longer than scheduled.

For the essay you worked with in Essay in Progress 1, evaluate the supporting details you used in each paragraph. Revise as necessary to make each paragraph unified and logically organized. Make sure you have provided concrete, specific details.

Academic Writing: Crafting a Research "Sandwich"

In academic writing, supporting paragraphs generally follow a standard "sandwich" pattern: The writer's own ideas are like the bread—they begin and end the paragraph—and the evidence is like the filling (the turkey, peanut butter, or what have you).

Think of the top "slice" as the writer's main point (or claim)—what the paragraph will be about. This top section (which can be just one sentence or several sentences) may also provide a transition from the previous paragraph, put the source in context, or tell readers why the claim is important.

The "filling" (the middle portion of the paragraph) presents the evidence that supports the writer's claim. This information may come from one source, several sources, or the writer's own research study or experiment.

See Chapter 5 and Chapter 23.

The bottom "slice" (the last part of the paragraph) holds the "sandwich" together by commenting on, interpreting, or discussing the research information. This part of the paragraph makes clear what the evidence means, why it is relevant, and how it supports the writer's point.

Here is an example from paragraph 2 of Arun Vishwanath's essay "Why Do So Many People Fall for Fake Profiles Online?" in Chapter 2.

> <u>When I interviewed the real people my fake profiles had targeted, the most important thing I found was that users fundamentally believe there is a person behind each profile.</u> People told me they had thought the profile belonged to someone they knew, or possibly someone a friend knew. Not one person ever suspected the profile was a complete fabrication, expressly created to deceive them. Mistakenly thinking each friend request has come from a real person may cause people to accept friend requests simply to be polite and not hurt someone else's feelings—even if they're not sure they know the person. (para. 2)

Author's claim

Evidence from author's research

Significance of research

In some academic writing, this sandwich pattern may occur over several paragraphs, or an entire section, instead of just a single paragraph. Keep this pattern in mind the next time you are asked to use evidence to support your point—and the next time you read a selection based on research.

Use Transitions and Repetition

All the details in a paragraph must fit together and function as a connected unit of information. When a paragraph has **coherence**, its ideas flow smoothly, allowing readers to follow its progression with ease. Two useful devices for linking details are transitions and repetition of key terms.

TABLE 6.1 Commonly Used Transitional Expressions

Type of Connection	Transitions
Logical Connections	
Items in a series	then, first, second, next, another, furthermore, finally, as well as
Illustration	for instance, for example, namely, that is
Result or cause	consequently, therefore, so, hence, thus, then, as a result
Restatement	in other words, that is, in simpler terms
Summary or conclusion	finally, in conclusion, to sum up, all in all, evidently, actually
Similarity/agreement	similarly, likewise, in the same way
Difference/opposition	but, however, on the contrary, nevertheless, neither, nor, on the one/other hand, still, yet
Spatial Connections	
Direction	inside/outside, along, above/below, up/down, across, to the right/left, in front of/behind
Nearness	next to, near, nearby, facing, adjacent to
Distance	beyond, in the distance, away, over there
Time Connections	
Frequency	often, frequently, now and then, gradually, week by week, occasionally, daily, rarely
Duration	during, briefly, hour by hour
Reference to a particular time	at two o'clock, on April 27, in 2010, last Thanksgiving, three days ago
Beginning	before then, at the beginning, at first
Middle	meanwhile, simultaneously, next, then, at that time
End	finally, at last, eventually, later, at the end, subsequently, afterward

Transitions are words, phrases, or clauses that lead your reader from one idea to another. Think of transitions as guideposts, or signals, of what is coming next in a paragraph. Some commonly used transitions are shown in Table 6.1, which groups transitions according to the type of connections they show.

In the two examples that follow, notice that the first paragraph is disjointed and choppy because it lacks transitions. The revised version is more coherent and therefore easier to follow.

Without Transitions

Most films are structured much like a short story. The film begins with an opening scene that captures the audience's attention. The writers build up tension, preparing for the climax of the story. They complicate the situation by revealing other elements of the plot, perhaps by introducing a surprise or additional characters. They introduce a problem. It will be solved either for the betterment or to the detriment of the characters and the situation. A resolution brings the film to a close.

With Transitions

    Most films are structured much like a short story. The film begins with an opening scene that captures the audience's attention. Gradually, the writers build up tension, preparing for the climax of the story. Soon after the first scene, they complicate the situation by revealing other elements of the plot, perhaps by introducing a surprise or additional characters. Next, they introduce a problem. Eventually, the problem will be solved either for the betterment or to the detriment of the characters and the situation. Finally, a resolution brings the film to a close.

Notice that the repetition of key terms (*film[s]*, *writers*), as well as pronouns that stand in for the key terms (*they* for *writers*), also lends coherence to the paragraph.

Repetition: Key terms

Transitions: Guideposts

ESSAY IN PROGRESS 3

For the essay you worked with in Essay in Progress 2, evaluate your use of transitions within each paragraph, adding them where needed to make the relationship among your ideas clearer.

STUDENTS WRITE

Chapters 4 to 7 show Latrisha Wilson's progress in planning and drafting an essay on surveillance. Below you can see her first-draft paragraph (also included in Chapter 7 as part of her first draft essay), and her revision to strengthen the paragraph.

First-Draft Paragraph

    Surveillance can refer to a thrilling activity, like the kind of spying on foreign terrorists that goes on in James Bond movies. But the truth is that most spying is done by surveillance computers. And then there is surveillance by drones. Edward Snowden bounced around for weeks from one airport to another, and lived for a while in the Moscow airport, eating who knows what and sleeping who knows where. The NSA seems to be able to do whatever it wants without having to answer to anyone or suffer any consequences. But we can't say the same for whistleblowers. Just look what they did to Chelsea Manning! The US government aggressively pursued Snowden. The NSA is more and more aggressively protecting its own secrecy, by punishing whistleblowers, and lying to Congress, and it seems as if they are more concerned about themselves than the people they are spying on.

Transition needed

Need to explain who Snowden is, what he did, and when; also add transition to make connection clear

Snowden's travels irrelevant

Need to explain what NSA is, what it did

Relevance of Chelsea Manning unclear; explain or delete

Detail needed to support claim about spying by surveillance computers in topic sentence

Revised Paragraph

When the word *surveillance* comes up, people think of some thrilling and dangerous activity, like the spying on foreign terrorists that goes on in James Bond movies. But in the U.S. today, most spying isn't done by handsome secret agents out to save the world; it's done by surveillance computers, and they monitor U.S. citizens, not just foreign terrorists. For example, consider what we learned from the whistleblower Edward Snowden, who sacrificed his career as a contractor for the National Security Agency (NSA) to alert the public to the deals the NSA makes with companies like Microsoft, Facebook, and Verizon to collect personal information and monitor everything their customers do on the Internet or speak into a smartphone.

Analyzing the Writer's Technique

1. **Topic Sentence** Identify Wilson's topic sentence. How did she strengthen it in her revision?
2. **Details** What irrelevant details did she delete?
3. **Transitions** What transitions did she add to provide coherence?
4. **Repetition** What words are repeated, thus contributing to coherence?
5. **Further Revision** What further revisions do you recommend?

READING

Black Men and Public Space

Brent Staples

Brent Staples is a journalist who has written numerous articles and editorials as well as a memoir, *Parallel Time: Growing Up in Black and White* (1994). He holds a Ph.D. in psychology and is a member of the *New York Times* editorial board and a regular contributor to its Commentary section. This essay, first published in *Harper's* magazine in 1986, is a good model of a well-structured essay. As you read the selection, highlight or underline the author's thesis.

Before Reading

1. **Preview** Use the steps listed in the "Preview" section in Chapter 2.
2. **Connect** What is public space, and how does our society expect us to behave there?

While Reading Pay particular attention to how Staples structures his paragraphs.

My first victim was a woman—white, well dressed, probably in her early twenties. 1
I came upon her late one evening on a deserted street in Hyde Park, a relatively
affluent neighborhood in an otherwise mean, impoverished section of Chicago. As
I swung onto the avenue behind her, there seemed to be a discreet, uninflammatory distance between us. Not so. She cast back a worried glance. To her, the young-
ish black man—a broad six feet two inches with a beard and billowing hair, both
hands shoved into the pockets of a bulky military jacket—seemed menacingly
close. After a few more quick glimpses, she picked up her pace and was soon running in earnest. Within seconds she disappeared into a cross street.

That was more than a decade ago. I was twenty-two years old, a graduate 2
student newly arrived at the University of Chicago. It was in the echo of that terrified woman's footfalls that I first began to know the unwieldy inheritance I'd
come into—the ability to alter public space in ugly ways. It was clear that she
thought herself the quarry of a mugger, a rapist, or worse. Suffering a bout of
insomnia, however, I was stalking sleep, not defenseless wayfarers. As a softy
who is scarcely able to take a knife to a raw chicken—let alone hold one to a
person's throat—I was surprised, embarrassed, and dismayed all at once. Her
flight made me feel like an accomplice in tyranny. It also made it clear that I
was indistinguishable from the muggers who occasionally seeped into the area
from the surrounding ghetto. That first encounter, and those that followed, sig-
nified that a vast, unnerving gulf lay between nighttime pedestrians—particularly women—and me. And I soon gathered that being perceived as dangerous
is a hazard in itself. I only needed to turn a corner into a dicey situation, or
crowd some frightened, armed person in a foyer somewhere, or make an errant
move after being pulled over by a policeman. Where fear and weapons
meet—and they often do in urban America—there is always the possibility of
death.

In that first year, my first away from my hometown, I was to become 3
thoroughly familiar with the language of fear. At dark, shadowy intersections, I
could cross in front of a car stopped at a traffic light and elicit the *thunk, thunk,
thunk, thunk* of the driver—black, white, male, or female—hammering down the
door locks. On less traveled streets after dark, I grew accustomed to but never
comfortable with people crossing to the other side of the street rather than pass
me. Then there were the standard unpleasantries with policemen, doormen,
bouncers, cabdrivers, and others whose business it is to screen out troublesome
individuals *before* there is any nastiness.

I moved to New York nearly two years ago and I have remained an avid night 4
walker. In central Manhattan, the near-constant crowd cover minimizes tense one-
on-one street encounters. Elsewhere—in SoHo, for example, where sidewalks are
narrow and tightly spaced buildings shut out the sky—things can get very taut
indeed.

After dark, on the warrenlike streets of Brooklyn where I live, I often see 5
women who fear the worst from me. They seem to have set their faces on neutral,
and with their purse straps strung across their chests bandolier-style, they forge

ahead as though bracing themselves against being tackled. I understand, of course, that the danger they perceive is not a hallucination. Women are particularly vulnerable to street violence, and young black males are drastically overrepresented among the perpetrators of that violence. Yet these truths are no solace against the kind of alienation that comes of being ever the suspect, a fearsome entity with whom pedestrians avoid making eye contact.

It is not altogether clear to me how I reached the ripe old age of twenty-two   6
without being conscious of the lethality nighttime pedestrians attributed to me. Perhaps it was because in Chester, Pennsylvania, the small, angry industrial town where I came of age in the 1960s, I was scarcely noticeable against a backdrop of gang warfare, street knifings, and murders. I grew up one of the good boys, had perhaps a half-dozen fistfights. In retrospect, my shyness of combat has clear sources.

As a boy, I saw countless tough guys locked away; I have since buried several,   7
too. They were babies, really—a teenage cousin, a brother of twenty-two, a childhood friend in his mid-twenties—all gone down in episodes of bravado played out in the streets. I came to doubt the virtues of intimidation early on. I chose, perhaps unconsciously, to remain a shadow—timid, but a survivor.

The fearsomeness mistakenly attributed to me in public places often has a   8
perilous flavor. The most frightening of these confusions occurred in the late 1970s and early 1980s, when I worked as a journalist in Chicago. One day, rushing into the office of a magazine I was writing for with a deadline story in hand, I was mistaken for a burglar. The office manager called security and, with an ad hoc posse, pursued me through the labyrinthine halls, nearly to my editor's door. I had no way of proving who I was. I could only move briskly toward the company of someone who knew me.

Another time I was on assignment for a local paper and killing time before an   9
interview. I entered a jewelry store on the city's affluent Near North Side. The proprietor excused herself and returned with an enormous red Doberman pinscher straining at the end of a leash. She stood, the dog extended toward me, silent to my questions, her eyes bulging nearly out of her head. I took a cursory look around, nodded, and bade her good night.

Relatively speaking, however, I never fared as badly as another black male   10
journalist. He went to nearby Waukegan, Illinois, a couple of summers ago to work on a story about a murderer who was born there. Mistaking the reporter for the killer, police officers hauled him from his car at gunpoint and but for his press credentials would probably have tried to book him. Such episodes are not uncommon. Black men trade tales like this all the time.

Over the years, I learned to smother the rage I felt at so often being taken for a   11
criminal. Not to do so would surely have led to madness. I now take precautions to make myself less threatening. I move about with care, particularly late in the evening. I give a wide berth to nervous people on subway platforms during the wee hours, particularly when I have exchanged business clothes for jeans. If I happen to be entering a building behind some people who appear skittish, I may walk by, letting them clear the lobby before I return, so as not to seem to be following them. I have been calm and extremely congenial on those rare occasions when I've been pulled over by the police.

And on late-evening constitutionals I employ what has proved to be an   12
excellent tension-reducing measure: I whistle melodies from Beethoven and
Vivaldi and the more popular classical composers. Even steely New Yorkers
hunching toward nighttime destinations seem to relax, and occasionally they
even join in the tune. Virtually everybody seems to sense that a mugger
wouldn't be warbling bright sunny selections from Vivaldi's *Four Seasons*. It is
my equivalent of the cowbell that hikers wear when they know they are in bear
country.

Examining the Reading

1. **Paraphrase** Explain what Staples means by "the ability to alter public space" (para. 2).
2. **Details** Staples considers himself a "survivor" (para. 7). To what does he attribute his survival?
3. **Examples** What does Staples do to make himself seem less threatening to others?
4. **Vocabulary** Explain the meaning of each of the following words as it is used in the reading: *uninflammatory* (para. 1), *unwieldy* (2), *vulnerable* (5), *retrospect* (6), and *constitutionals* (12).

Analyzing the Writer's Technique

1. **Unity** Analyze paragraph 3 of "Black Men and Public Space." Does it have a topic sentence, and if so, where is the topic sentence placed? Does this paragraph effectively support Staples's thesis? Do all the supporting details seem concrete and specific? Why or why not?
2. **Supporting Details** Identify several places in the essay where Staples uses specific, concrete supporting details effectively. Explain your choices.
3. **Transitions and Repetition** Cite several examples of effective transitional strategies. Write a paragraph explaining how they lend coherence to the essay. Identify any places in the essay where you think Staples could have made connections between paragraphs clearer.

Thinking Critically about the Reading

1. **Word Choice** Why did Staples choose the word *victim* in paragraph 1? What connotations does it have? What images does he create through its use?
2. **Fact and Opinion** Highlight the facts about what Staples sees during his night walks, and underline his opinions about what he sees. Evaluate the evidence for his interpretations and opinions and consider the following question: Is he also prejudging people?
3. **Sources** What other kinds of sources might Staples have considered in formulating his views? How would including such sources have changed his essay?
4. **Tone** Describe the tone of the essay. What effect does the tone have on you as a reader? How effective do you find it?
5. **Omissions** What information has Staples omitted that would help you further understand his thesis, if any?

Responding to the Reading

1. **Reaction** Why is Staples's whistling of classical music similar to hikers wearing cowbells in bear country?
2. **Discussion** In what other ways can an individual "alter public space"?
3. **Journal** Do you think Staples should alter his behavior in public to accommodate the reactions of others? Write a journal entry explaining whether you agree or disagree with Staples's actions.
4. **Essay** Staples describes himself as a "survivor" (para. 7) of the streets he grew up on. In a sense, everyone is a survivor of certain decisions or circumstances that, if played out differently, might have resulted in misfortune. Write an essay that explains how and why you or someone you know is a survivor.

Robert Nickelsberg/Archive Photos/Getty Images

7
Drafting an Essay

In this chapter you will learn to

- structure an essay effectively
- organize supporting details
- write effective introductions, conclusions, and titles

Writing Quick Start

ANALYZE   The photograph here shows a person using a bike-sharing program. A number of such programs have sprouted up across the country and even on some college campuses.

WRITE   Working alone or with a classmate, compose a sentence that states your opinion of this type of initiative and how likely a bike-sharing program would be to succeed in your area or on your campus. Then brainstorm evidence to support your opinion. Number your best evidence 1, your second-best evidence 2, and so on. Finally, write a paragraph that begins with the sentence you wrote and includes your evidence.

CONNECT   The paragraph you just wrote could be part of an essay on how cities and towns are trying to become more environmentally sustainable. To write an essay, you would need to do the following:

   ▶ Do additional prewriting and research to learn more about this topic.
   ▶ Write a thesis statement and develop supporting paragraphs.
   ▶ Write an effective introduction and conclusion.
   ▶ Choose a good title.

This chapter will guide you through the process of developing an essay as part of the writing process shown in Graphic Organizer 7.1.

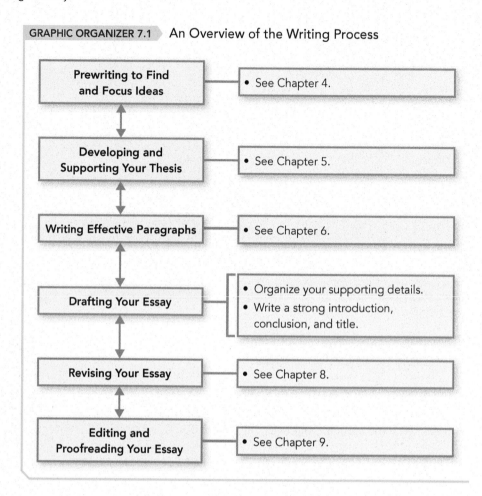

GRAPHIC ORGANIZER 7.1   An Overview of the Writing Process

- Prewriting to Find and Focus Ideas
  - See Chapter 4.
- Developing and Supporting Your Thesis
  - See Chapter 5.
- Writing Effective Paragraphs
  - See Chapter 6.
- Drafting Your Essay
  - Organize your supporting details.
  - Write a strong introduction, conclusion, and title.
- Revising Your Essay
  - See Chapter 8.
- Editing and Proofreading Your Essay
  - See Chapter 9.

Organize Your Essay Effectively

Think of an essay as a complete piece of writing, with a title, an introduction and thesis statement, several body paragraphs supporting the thesis, and a conclusion. (See Graphic Organizer 7.2.)

For more on developing a thesis and selecting evidence to support it, see Chapter 5.

The body of your essay contains the paragraphs that support your thesis. Before you begin writing these paragraphs, decide on the method of organization you will use. Three common ways to organize ideas are most-to-least (or least-to-most) order,

GRAPHIC ORGANIZER 7.2   The Structure of an Essay: Parts and Functions

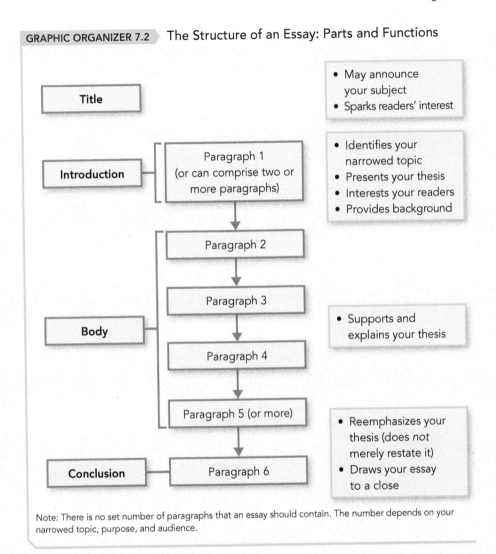

Note: There is no set number of paragraphs that an essay should contain. The number depends on your narrowed topic, purpose, and audience.

chronological order, and spatial order. To decide which to use, consider your topic and how it can be most logically and most compellingly presented.

Use Most-to-Least (or Least-to-Most) Order

When you choose this method of organizing an essay, you arrange your supporting details moving gradually from most to least (or least to most) important, familiar, or interesting. If you need to entice readers or expect they will read only the beginning of your essay, you might include your strongest evidence first. If readers are interested in the topic and likely to read on, you might hold your most memorable evidence for last. You can visualize these two options as follows:

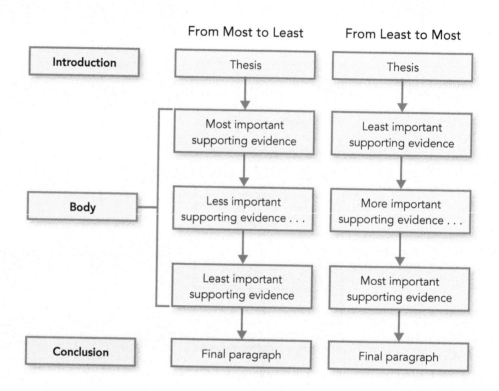

	From Most to Least	From Least to Most
Introduction	Thesis	Thesis
Body	Most important supporting evidence	Least important supporting evidence
	Less important supporting evidence . . .	More important supporting evidence . . .
	Least important supporting evidence	Most important supporting evidence
Conclusion	Final paragraph	Final paragraph

The revised draft of Darnell Henderson's essay appears later in this chapter.

A student, Darnell Henderson, devised this thesis statement: "In a time when children are constantly plugged into the virtual world, working in school gardens can help them develop social-emotional skills, learn by doing, and make positive connections to the natural world." He identified three benefits that support this thesis:

- Gardening fosters face-to-face interpersonal skills.
- Time outside positively affects children's well-being.
- Gardens provide applications to many school subjects.

Henderson then decided to arrange the supporting evidence from most to least important.

Most to Least Important

Paragraph 2: Working together builds interpersonal communication skills.

Paragraph 3: Students learn by doing in a variety of school subjects.

Paragraph 4: Working outdoors has positive benefits.

For each of the following narrowed topics, identify several qualities or characteristics that you could use to organize details in most-to-least or least-to-most order. For each, would you choose most-to-least or least-to-most order? Why?

1. Three Web sites where you shop
2. Three friends
3. Three members of a sports team

4. Three fast-food restaurants
5. Three television shows

Use Chronological Order

When you arrange your supporting details in **chronological** (or time) **order**, you put them in the order in which they happened, beginning the body of your essay with the first event and progressing through the others as they occurred. Chronological order is commonly used in narrative essays (essays that tell a story or recount events) and process analyses (essays that explain how something works or is done).

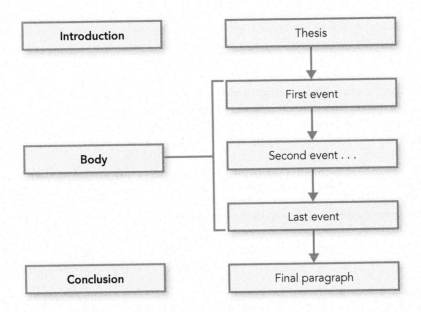

Suppose that Henderson, in writing about the benefits of school gardens, decides to explain his thesis by discussing student participation in a school garden from planting through harvest. In this case, he might organize the events chronologically (in the order in which they occur), demonstrating student involvement at each stage.

EXERCISE 7.2 ▸ WORKING WITH CHRONOLOGICAL ORDER

Alone or with a classmate, identify at least one thesis statement from those listed below that could be supported with paragraphs organized in chronological order. Explain how you would use chronological order to support this thesis.

1. European mealtimes differ from those expected by many American visitors, much to the visitors' surprise and discomfort.
2. Despite the many pitfalls that await those who shop at auctions, people can find bargains if they prepare in advance.
3. My first day of kindergarten was the most traumatic [or exhilarating] experience of my childhood, one that permanently shaped my view of education.
4. Learning how to drive a car increases a teenager's freedom and responsibility.

Use Spatial Order

When you use **spatial order**, you organize details about your subject by location. Spatial organization is commonly used in descriptive essays (essays that portray people, places, and things) as well as in classification and division essays (essays that explain categories or parts). Consider, for example, how you might use spatial order to support the thesis that movie theaters are designed to shut out the outside world and create a separate reality within. You could begin by describing the ticket booth, then the lobby, and finally the theater. Similarly, you might describe a place from right to left or from inside to outside. Darnell Henderson, writing about the benefits of school gardens, could describe the garden's plantings from front to back or left to right, for example.

Visualize spatial organization by picturing your subject in your mind or by sketching it. "Look" at your subject systematically—from top to bottom, inside to outside, front to back. Cut it into imaginary sections or pieces and describe each piece. Here are two possible options for visualizing an essay that uses spatial order:

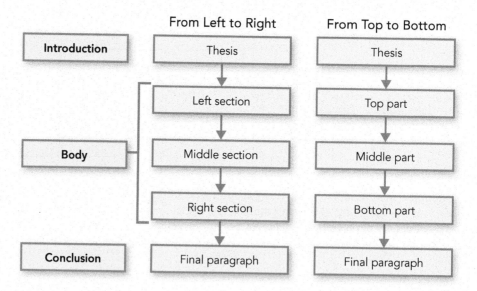

> **EXERCISE 7.3** ▶ **WORKING WITH SPATIAL ORDER**

Alone or with a classmate, identify one thesis statement listed below that could be supported by means of spatial organization. Explain how you would use spatial order to support this thesis.

1. Our family's yearly hiking trip provides us with a much-needed opportunity to renew family ties.
2. The Civic Theatre of Allentown's set for Tennessee Williams's play *A Streetcar Named Desire* was simple yet striking and effective.
3. Although a pond in winter may seem frozen and lifeless, this appearance is deceptive.
4. A clear study space can cut down on time-wasting distractions.

> **ESSAY IN PROGRESS 1** ▶

Choose one of the following activities:

1. Using the thesis statement and evidence you gathered for the Essay in Progress activities in Chapter 5, choose a method for organizing your essay.
2. Choose one of the following narrowed topics:
   a. Positive or negative experiences with computers
   b. Stricter (or more lenient) regulations for teenage drivers
   c. Factors that account for the popularity of action films
   d. Safety in public high schools
   e. Advantages or disadvantages of driverless cars

Then, using the steps in Graphic Organizer 7.1, prewrite to produce ideas, develop a thesis, and generate evidence to support the thesis. Next, choose a method for organizing your essay (from most-to-least/least-to-most, chronological, or spatial order). Explain briefly how you will use that method of organization.

Prepare an Outline or a Graphic Organizer

After you have written a thesis statement and chosen a method of organization, take a few minutes to create an outline or graphic organizer of the essay's main points in the order you plan to discuss them. This is especially important when your essay is long or complex. Outlining or drawing a graphic organizer can help you see how ideas fit together and may reveal places where you need to add supporting information.

Outlining. There are two types of outlines: informal and formal. An **informal (or scratch) outline** uses key words and phrases to list main points and subpoints. Below is an informal outline of Darnell Henderson's essay later in this chapter. Recall that Henderson chose to use the most-to-least-important method of organization.

Sample Informal Outline

<u>Thesis</u> In a time when children are constantly plugged into the virtual world, working in school gardens can help them develop social-emotional skills, learn by doing, and make positive connections to the natural world.

<u>Paragraph 1</u> Introduction

<u>Paragraph 2</u> Students benefit from face-to-face communication.

- Screens keep students apart and focus students inward.
- Gardens offer physical space in which students can interact.
- Research shows students who garden have better communication skills.

<u>Paragraph 3</u> Gardening provides opportunities for hands-on learning.

- Experiential learning involves learning by doing, such as when students learn to calculate the surface area of the garden and when they learn about plant growth cycles through a year of gardening.
- Experiential learning makes learning direct and exciting.

<u>Paragraph 4</u> Working outdoors improves students' well-being.

- Research demonstrates time outside lowers stress, improves concentration, and gives sense of calm.
- Time outside is antidote for digital addiction.

Formal outlines use Roman numerals (I, II), capital letters (A, B), Arabic numbers (1, 2), lowercase letters (a, b) and indentation to designate levels of importance. Formal outlines fall into two categories:

- *Sentence outlines* use complete sentences.
- *Topic outlines* use only key words and phrases.

Here is a sample topic outline that a student wrote for an essay for her interpersonal communication class:

Sample Formal (Topic) Outline

First Topic
  First Subtopic
    First Detail
    Second Detail
      Detail or Example
      Detail or Example
  Second Topic
    First Detail

    Second Detail

I. Types of listening
  A. Participatory
    1. Involves the listener responding to the speaker
    2. Has expressive quality
      a. Maintain eye contact
      b. Express feelings using facial expressions
  B. Nonparticipatory
    1. Involves the listener listening without talking or responding
    2. Allows speaker to develop his or her thoughts without interruption

All items at the same level should be equally important, explain or support the topic or subtopic under which they are placed, and be grammatically parallel.

For more on parallel structure, see Chapter 9.

Not Parallel

I. Dietary Problems
   A. Consuming too much fat
   B. High refined-sugar consumption

Parallel

I. Dietary Problems
   A. Consuming too much fat
   B. Consuming too much refined sugar

If your instructor allows, you can use both phrases and sentences within an outline, as long as you do so consistently. You might write all subtopics (designated by capital letters A, B, and so on) as sentences and all supporting details (designated by 1, 2, and so on) as phrases, for instance.

Preparing a graphic organizer. Think of a graphic organizer as an outline in visual form. Graphic Organizer 7.3 shows the graphic organizer that Darnell Henderson

GRAPHIC ORGANIZER 7.3 Sample Graphic Organizer

To learn more about creating a graphic organizer, see Chapter 2.

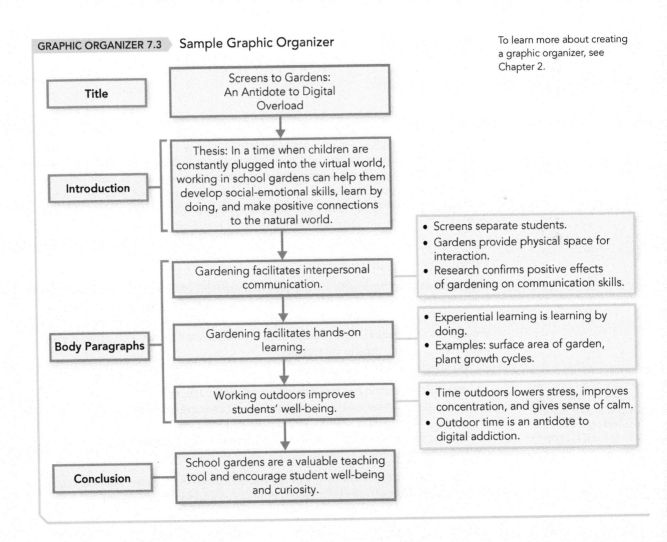

created for his essay. Notice that it follows the most-to-least important method of organization, as did his informal outline shown earlier.

Whether you use an outline or a graphic organizer, begin by putting your working thesis statement at the top of a page and listing your main points below. Leave plenty of space between main points. While you are filling in details that support one main point, you will often think of details or examples to use in support of a different one. As these details or examples occur to you, jot them down under or next to the appropriate main point on your outline or graphic organizer.

> ### ESSAY IN PROGRESS 2
>
> For the topic you chose in Essay in Progress 1, prepare an outline or draw a graphic organizer to show your essay's organizational plan.

Write Your Introduction, Conclusion, and Title

When you write an essay, you don't have to start with the title and introduction and write straight through to the end. Some students prefer to write the body of the essay first and then return to the introduction. (Often your true thesis emerges only in the conclusion.) Others prefer to write a tentative introduction as a way of getting started. Some students think of a title before they start writing; others find it easier to add a title when the essay is finished. Regardless of when you write them, the introduction, conclusion, and title are important components of a well-written essay.

Write a Strong Introduction

Introductions often start with a fairly general statement of the topic and narrow their focus until they reach the thesis statement at the end of the paragraph. However you begin, your readers should be able to form an expectation of what the essay will be about from this section. Because the introduction creates a first, and often lasting, impression, take the time to get it right.

An effective introduction should

For more about tone, see "Analyze the Author's Tone" (Chapter 3) and "Are Your Tone and Level of Diction Appropriate?" (Chapter 9).

- establish your topic and indicate your focus, approach, and point of view
- set the tone of your essay—how you "sound" to your readers and what relationship you have with them
- interest your readers and provide any background information they may need
- present your thesis statement

Notice how each of the two sample introductions that follow, both on sexual harassment, creates an entirely different impression and set of expectations.

Introduction 1

Sexual harassment has received a great deal of attention in recent years. From the highest offices of government and the military to factories in small towns, sexual harassment cases have been tried in court and publicized on national television for all Americans to witness. **This focus on sexual harassment has been, in and of itself, a good and necessary thing.** However, when a first-grade boy makes national headlines because he kissed a little girl of the same age and is accused of "sexual harassment," the American public needs to take a serious look at the definition of sexual harassment.

Sets tone: Tone is reasonable yet with mild sense of disbelief

Engages readers/provides background: Grabs readers' attention with provocative example

Thesis: Thesis prepares readers for an essay that examines definitions of sexual harassment and perhaps offers one

Introduction 2

Sexual harassment in the workplace seems to happen with **alarming frequency**. As a woman who works part time in a male-dominated office, I have **witnessed at least six incidents** of sexual harassment aimed at me and my female colleagues on various occasions **during the past three months alone.** For example, in one incident, a male coworker repeatedly made kissing sounds whenever I passed his desk, even after I explained that his actions made me uncomfortable. A female coworker was invited to dinner several times by her male supervisor; each time she refused. The last time she refused, he made a veiled threat: "You obviously aren't happy working with me. Perhaps a transfer is in order." These incidents were not isolated, did not happen to only one woman, and were initiated by more than one man. My colleagues and I are not the only victims. Sexual harassment is on the rise and will continue to increase unless women speak out against it loudly and to a receptive audience.

Sets tone: Tone is outraged, angry

Engages readers/provides background: Provides specific, distressing examples

Thesis: Thesis prepares readers for an essay that suggests ways women can speak out against sexual harassment

An introduction can be difficult to write. If you have trouble, return to it later, once you have written the body of your essay. As you draft, you may think of a better way to grab your readers, set your tone, and establish your focus.

The following suggestions for writing a strong introduction will help you capture your readers' interest:

1. **Ask a provocative or disturbing question, or pose a series of related questions to direct readers' attention to your key points.**

   Should health insurance companies pay for more than one stay in a drug rehabilitation center? Should insurance continue to pay for rehab services when patients consistently put themselves back into danger by using drugs again?

2. **Begin with a dramatic or engaging anecdote or an example that is relevant to your thesis.**

   The penal system sometimes protects the rights of the criminal instead of those of the victim. For example, during a rape trial, the defense attorney can question the victim about his or her sexual history, but the prosecuting attorney is forbidden by law to mention that the defendant was charged with rape in a previous trial. In fact, if the prosecution even hints at the defendant's sexual history, the defense can request a mistrial.

3. **Offer a quotation that illustrates or emphasizes your thesis.**

   As Indira Gandhi once said, "You cannot shake hands with a clenched fist." This truism is important to remember whenever people communicate with one another but particularly when they are attempting to resolve a conflict. Both parties need to agree that there is a problem and then agree to listen to each other with an open mind. Shaking hands is a productive way to begin working toward a resolution.

4. **Cite a little-known fact or shocking statistic.**

   Recent research has shown that the color pink has a calming effect on people. In fact, a prison detention center in western New York was recently painted pink to make prisoners more controllable in the days following their arrest.

5. **State a commonly held misconception, and correct this misconception in your thesis.**

   Many people have the mistaken notion that social media platforms offer users protection against contact from fake sites. In fact, although most platforms offer some protections, they do not protect users against many scams and bogus contacts.

6. **Describe a hypothetical situation.**

   Suppose you were in a serious car accident and became unconscious. Suppose further that you slipped into a coma, with little hope for recovery. Unless you had a prewritten health-care proxy that designated someone familiar with your wishes to act on your behalf, your fate would be left in the hands of doctors who knew nothing about you or your preferences for treatment.

7. **Compare your topic with one that is familiar or of special interest to your readers.**

   The process a researcher uses to locate a specific piece of information in the library is similar to the process an investigator follows in tracking a criminal; both pose a series of questions and follow clues to answer them.

Write an Effective Conclusion

Write a **conclusion** that brings your essay to a satisfying close. For most essays, your conclusion should reaffirm your thesis without directly restating it. For lengthy essays, you may want to summarize your main points. Shorter essays can be ended more memorably and forcefully by using one of the following suggestions:

1. **Take your readers beyond the scope and time frame of your essay.**

   For now, then, the present system of community policing seems to be working in reducing crime and increasing citizen satisfaction with police services. In the future, however, it may be necessary to form stronger partnerships with community leaders to monitor and reduce high-tension situations.

2. **Remind readers of the relevance of the issue or suggest why your thesis is important.**

> As stated earlier, research has shown that the seat-belt law has saved thousands of lives. These lives would almost certainly have been lost had this law not been enacted.

3. **Offer a recommendation or urge your readers to take action.**

> To convince the local cable company to eliminate pornographic material, concerned citizens should organize, contact their local cable station, and threaten to cancel their subscriptions.

4. **Discuss broader implications not fully addressed in the essay (but do not introduce a completely new issue).**

> When fair-minded people consider whether the FBI should be allowed to tap private phone lines, the issue inevitably leads them to the larger issue of First Amendment rights.

5. **Conclude with a fact, quotation, anecdote, or example that emphasizes your thesis.**

> The next time you are tempted to send a strongly worded text, consider this fact: Your friends and your enemies can forward those messages, with unforeseen consequences to you.

Introductions and Conclusions: Common Mistakes to Avoid

In your introduction, don't . . .

make an announcement. Avoid opening comments such as "I am writing to explain . . ." or "This essay will discuss . . ."

prolong your introduction unnecessarily. An introduction that is longer than two paragraphs will probably sound long-winded and make your readers impatient.

discourage your readers from continuing. Statements such as "This process may seem complicated, but . . ." may make your readers apprehensive.

use a casual, overly familiar, or chatty tone, especially in academic writing. Openings such as "You'll never in a million years believe what happened . . ." are generally not appropriate for college essays.

In your conclusion, don't . . .

make an announcement or restate your thesis directly. Statements like "In my essay I have shown . . ." are dull and mechanical.

introduce major points or supporting evidence. Reasons and evidence that support your thesis belong in the body of your essay.

apologize or weaken your stance. Do not say, for example, "Although I am only twenty-one, . . ." or back down after criticizing someone by saying "After all, she's only human."

use standard phrases. Don't use phrases such as "To sum up," "In conclusion," or "It can be seen, then." They are routine and tiresome.

Write a Good Title

The title of your essay should indicate your topic and prepare readers for what follows. Titles such as "Baseball Fans" or "Gun Control," which just indicate the topic, provide readers with little information or incentive to continue reading.

topic   position

<u>Why</u> State Lotteries Are an <u>Unfair</u> Tax on the Poor

↑   ↑

suggests a cause-effect analysis   suggests an argument

For more on writing situations, see Chapter 4.

For other writing situations—depending on your purpose, audience, point of view, genre, and medium—your title may be direct, informative, witty, intriguing, or a combination of these. The following suggestions will help you write effective titles.

- **Ask a question that your essay answers.**

    Who Plays the Lottery?

- **Use alliteration.** Repeating initial sounds often produces a catchy title.

    Lotteries: Dreaming about Dollars

- **Use a play on words or a catchy or humorous expression.** This technique may work well for less formal essays.

    Playing to Lose

- **Use a brief quotation.** You will likely need to mention the quotation in your essay and indicate there who said it and where.

    The Lottery: "A Surtax on Desperation"?

EXERCISE 7.4   **WRITING TITLES**

For each of the following essays, suggest a title. Use each of the above suggestions at least once.

1. An essay explaining tenants' legal rights
2. An essay opposing drug testing on animals
3. An essay on the causes and effects of road rage
4. An essay comparing fitness routines
5. An essay discussing the right to vote in America

Academic Writing: Introductions, Conclusions, and Titles

Because academic writing follows a consistent format, introductions, conclusions, and titles likewise have standard features. An **introduction,** which often is more than one paragraph, typically has the following four parts:

1. Identification of the topic
2. Review of key findings by other researchers and where they fell short or left a gap

3. Explanation of the need for the writer's research, how it extends the research of others, or how it fills gaps
4. Presentation of the thesis, which explains the purpose of the paper

Since academic writers are addressing other scholars in their field, they generally do not try to grab interest with a snappy anecdote or a compelling quotation. They assume that their readers will be interested in where their research fits into a broader program, so they use a factual, informative tone in the introduction and throughout the paper.

A **conclusion**, which again may extend beyond a single paragraph, typically has the following four parts:

1. Affirmation of the thesis
2. Synthesis and discussion of findings: what the writer's findings mean, how they compare with other research projects in the same area, how the writer's research builds on or goes beyond previous research
3. Limitations of the writer's research: what the research did not prove
4. Areas for further study

The conclusion often tells readers why the research was important and why it matters; consequently, the conclusion is often worth reading before reading the entire paper.

A **title** in an academic essay is intended to be factual and descriptive of the paper's contents. Think of it as a succinct summary of the main point of the paper. It tells readers exactly what to expect in the paper. It is not intended to be cute, catchy, or humorous.

| EXERCISE 7.5 | EVALUATING INTRODUCTIONS, CONCLUSIONS, AND TITLES |

The following student essay by Darnell Henderson on school gardens as an antidote to digital overload was written using Graphic Organizer 7.3, earlier in this chapter. Read the essay and answer the questions that follow.

STUDENTS WRITE

From Screens to Gardens: An Antidote to Digital Overload

Darnell Henderson

Today, children spend more time than ever indoors on computers, game   1
consoles, and smart phones, raising concerns about digital and social
media addiction and the problems they cause: shorter attention spans,
depression, and even difficulty sleeping (Feiler). To counter this digital
overload, many schools are embracing school gardens. School gardens help
youngsters overcome the toxic effects of too much screen time by providing

students with opportunities to learn from the world around them. In a time when children are constantly plugged into the virtual world, working in school gardens can help them develop social-emotional skills, learn by doing, and make positive connections to the natural world.

Where screens often serve to separate children from their peers and draw their focus into virtual relationships, gardens provide a space where students can work together on the physical task of growing food. Studies show that students who participate in garden programs have better interpersonal and cooperative skills, as well as a better self-understanding ("Benefits"). Taking responsibility as a group for the well-being of living plants makes students communicate with one another and solve problems together, thereby building important social skills, as well.

Gardening also provides an opportunity for hands-on learning. The garden connects readily to most school subjects through practical everyday lessons. Experiential learning, or "learning by doing," is a teaching strategy often used to help children engage more with new knowledge by having to put it to use (Hausburg and Gudenkauf). Children often learn how to calculate surface area from a textbook, but seeing a garden before them and being asked to calculate how much space there is to grow tomatoes, peppers, or corn creates a richer understanding of that mathematical concept. Growing plants from seed to flowering and fruiting stage and then eating those different plant parts is a science class taken to the next level. For schools, gardens represent a valuable opportunity to reinforce many curriculum standards with firsthand experience, making learning more direct and exciting.

Problem-solving in real life contexts improves such social skills, but doing so outdoors amplifies the effect on children's well-being. Imagine a group of children bent over desks under fluorescent lights at equally spaced desks versus crouched around a garden, hands in the soil, sun on their shoulders. Research supports that time in nature helps children lower their stress, strengthen their ability to focus, and maintain a sense of calm (Suttie). Time outside is an antidote to the effects of digital addiction, and incorporating it into the school day creates a better environment for learning and teaching alike.

Technology is by no means essentially harmful to kids or their learning. Used the right way, it can be another effective teaching tool in schools.

2

3

4

5

But when technology overuse at home leaves children scatterbrained, disinterested, and disconnected from the world around them, school gardens can bring back their sense of wonder and community. School is ultimately a place for growth, and school gardens can grow not only food, but also healthy, curious young people. As children come of age in an era of increasing distance from the natural and even the physical world, gardens have become a more valuable teaching tool than ever before.

Works Cited

"Benefits of School-Based Community Gardens: A Compilation of Research Findings." Slow Food USA, n.d., www.slowfoodusa.org/contents/sdownload/3591/file/Benefits-of-School-Gardens-Denver-Urban-Gardens.pdf. Accessed 17 July 2019.

Feiler, Bruce. "When Tech Is a Problem Child." *The New York Times*, 19 Nov. 2016, www.nytimes.com/2016/11/20/fashion/children-technology-limits-smartphones.html.

Hausburg, Taylor, and Sarah Gudenkauf. "Getting Started with Experiential Learning." *Edutopia*, George Lucas Educational Foundation, 17 Apr. 2019, www.edutopia.org/article/getting-started-experiential-learning.

Suttie, Jill. "The Surprising Benefits of Teaching a Class Outside." *Greater Good Magazine*, The Greater Good Science Center at the University of California, Berkeley, 14 May 2018, greatergood.berkeley.edu/article/item/the_surprising_benefits_of_teaching_a_class_outside.

Analyzing the Writer's Technique

1. Assess Henderson's introduction: How effectively does it prepare the reader for the balance of the essay? Does it capture your interest as a reader? Why or why not?
2. Highlight Henderson's thesis statement. What angle on the topic does it offer?
3. What method(s) does Henderson use to arrange his details logically within paragraphs?
4. Assess Henderson's conclusion. Does it effectively draw his essay to a close? Why or why not?
5. Assess Henderson's title. Does it provide you with enough incentive to want to keep reading (assuming that the fact that it was assigned is not sufficient)? How could you change it to make it more compelling to you and your classmates?

ESSAY IN PROGRESS 3

Using the outline or graphic organizer you created in Essay in Progress 2, write a first draft of your essay.

HOW WRITERS READ   **ESSAYS**

Seeing a reading assignment as a whole, rather than as a series of individual sentences and paragraphs, makes it easier to recall and make sense of what you just read. Use these strategies to get the most out of what you read:

BEFORE READING

- Activate your prior knowledge, establish an intent to remember, and prepare your brain to learn by previewing the essay, reading the headnote, brainstorming to discover what you already know about the topic, and reading the questions or assignments that follow the essay.

WHILE READING

- Read actively and critically by highlighting key ideas and making notes in the margins about your questions and reactions, analyzing how the essay is organized, and assessing the author's purpose and perspective on the topic. (This may require you to reread the selection.)

AFTER READING

- Reinforce and extend your learning by drawing a graphic organizer or outlining the selection (this will confirm your understanding and consolidate your memory) and devising critical questions that will help you analyze the author's language, assess the evidence he or she provides, recognize assumptions or omissions, and synthesize the author's ideas with your own.

STUDENTS WRITE

The Threats of Surveillance (Draft)

Latrisha Wilson

The first draft of an essay by Latrisha Wilson follows. Wilson used her freewriting (Chapter 4) and her working thesis (Chapter 5) as the basis for her draft, adding details that she came up with by doing additional brainstorming. Because she was writing a first draft, Wilson did not worry about correcting the errors in grammar, punctuation, and mechanics. (You will see an excerpt from her revised draft and her final draft in Chapter 8, and an excerpt that shows Wilson's final editing and proofreading in Chapter 9.)

There are plenty of new ways to talk to friends and family. We can communicate by talking on our iPhones, but there are dangers there. Our conversations can be recorded, and the GPS function on the phone allows our whereabouts to be tracked. We can chat on Skype, Gmail, Facebook message, and read each other's Twitter or Blog posts. And then there are security cameras that record our every move. These new digital technologies are incredibly useful; however, they also come at a hidden cost.

Surveillance can refer to a thrilling activity, like the kind of spying on foreign terrorists that goes on in James Bond movies. Bond used high-tech devices and gadgetry to carry out his missions. But the truth is that most spying is done by surveillance computers. And then there is surveillance using drones. Edward Snowden bounced around for weeks from one airport to another, and lived for a while in the Moscow airport, eating who knows what and sleeping who knows where. The NSA seems to be able to do whatever it wants without having to answer to anyone or suffer any consequences. But we can't say the same for whistleblowers. Just look what they did to Chelsea Manning! The US government aggressively pursued Snowden. The NSA is more and more aggressively protecting its own secrecy, by punishing whistleblowers, and lying to Congress and, it seems as if they are more concerned about themselves than the people they are spying on.

The NSA isn't the only organization to be spying on us. You got companies like Google and other companies doing it to. The next time you pull up your Gmail account, go to your inbox and click on a message. Do you see all those advertisements to the right of your inbox? There directly related to the message you are reading. (I wish my mom "Happy Birthday!" and now I see ads for places to buy birthday hats. This creepy connection is because Google is a major online marketing business, and it automatically scans all of our e-mails for keywords and phrases all at the same time. Companies are paying Google tons of money to record our search histories and pore over our personal messages. Spokesmen for Google reassure us that only computers, no human beings, are reading our e-mails.

Google and other corporations could do more do inform it's users about privacy concerns. How much personal information are we giving away when we make an account with G-mail, Facebook, or Netflix? What kind of controls keep employees at this companies from accessing our viewing histories, profiles, or private communications? Its never easy to tell. The terms are long legal documents written in a lingo your everyday person doesn't want to bother to decipher. We just check a box.

Well, what's the big deal? I have nothing to hide from neither the   5
government nor companies like Google and Facebook. Neither do I, I would say in response. But I don't like the idea of having people I don't know constantly looking over my shoulder. When I'm writing a Facebook message to my boyfriend, do I need to worry about getting blackmailed by some Facebook employee, who got bored on a break and decided to do some browsing? Less and less is there any kind of privacy, online or in real life.

Analyzing the First Draft

1. **Title and Introduction** Evaluate Wilson's title and introduction.
2. **Thesis** Evaluate Wilson's thesis statement.
3. **Support** Does Wilson provide adequate details in her essay? If not, which paragraphs need more detail? What additional information might she include?
4. **Organization** How does Wilson organize her ideas?
5. **Conclusion** Evaluate the conclusion.

Working Together

Using the template in Graphic Organizer 7.3 as a model, work with two or three of your classmates to create a graphic organizer for the article "Black Men and Public Space" in Chapter 6. Then come up with an alternate title (one that will spark your readers' interest). Be prepared to share your title and explain why your group chose it.

Roberto Westbrook/Blend Images/Getty Images

8
Revising Content and Organization

Writing Quick Start

ANALYZE Study the photograph above, paying attention to the details. What is happening, where, and why?

WRITE Now draft a few sentences summarizing what you think is happening, and then add details to your original sentences to describe the photo more fully. After you add these details, will it be easier for a reader who has not seen the photo to picture what is happening in it?

Exchange papers with a classmate and examine how your classmate organized the ideas. Look for parts that you find confusing and that need more detail. Write down your comments for your classmate. Finally, using your own comments and those of the classmate who examined your list, make changes to improve your own description of the photograph.

CONNECT When you changed your list, did you include more details from the photo? Leave some unimportant details out? Change or rearrange any details? If so, you *revised* the description of the photo. **Revision** is a process of making changes to improve what your essay says and how you say it. Revising an essay works in much the same way as the revision of your list did. As Graphic Organizer 8.1 shows, revision is an essential part of the writing process.

In this chapter you will learn to

- ask key questions to revise
- work with your classmates to revise
- use your instructor comments to revise

GRAPHIC ORGANIZER 8.1   An Overview of the Writing Process

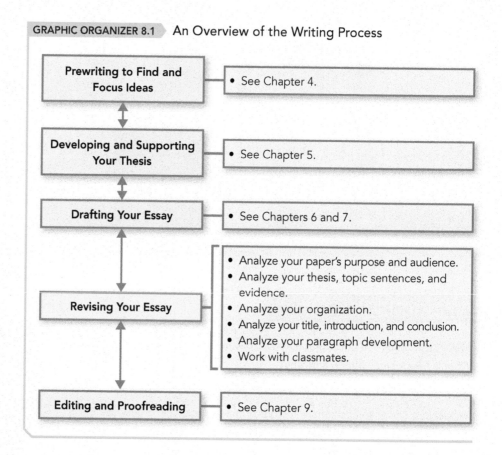

Prewriting to Find and Focus Ideas
- See Chapter 4.

Developing and Supporting Your Thesis
- See Chapter 5.

Drafting Your Essay
- See Chapters 6 and 7.

Revising Your Essay
- Analyze your paper's purpose and audience.
- Analyze your thesis, topic sentences, and evidence.
- Analyze your organization.
- Analyze your title, introduction, and conclusion.
- Analyze your paragraph development.
- Work with classmates.

Editing and Proofreading
- See Chapter 9.

Why Revise?

A thorough, thoughtful revision can change a C paper to an A paper! Revising can make a significant difference in how well your paper

- achieves your purpose.
- expresses your ideas to your intended audience.
- reflects your reader's expectations of your genre.

This difference is why most professional writers—and successful student writers—revise frequently and thoroughly.

Revising is not a process of correcting surface errors, such as spelling mistakes or punctuation errors. Rather, it is a process of looking at your *ideas* and finding ways to make them clearer and easier to understand. This may mean adding, eliminating, or reorganizing key elements within the essay, even revising your thesis statement and refocusing the entire essay.

The amount of revision you need to do depends in part on how you approach writing. For example, some students take a highly structured approach to writing. They plan in detail what they will say before they draft. Others may dash off a draft as ideas come to mind. A well-planned draft usually requires less revision than one that was spontaneously written. Regardless of how carefully planned an essay may be, any first draft requires at least some revision.

Use Effective Revision Techniques

The following techniques will help you evaluate and revise your essays:

- **Allow time between drafting and revising, so you can approach your essay from a fresh perspective.** Try to leave enough time to set your draft aside overnight if possible.
- **Listen for problems as you or a friend reads your draft aloud.** Listening carefully can help you identify awkward wording, vague or overused expressions, or main points that are unclear or lack adequate support. A reader less familiar with the text than you may also slow down when reading or misread confusing passages, providing a hint for areas that need revision.
- **Ask a classmate to read and comment on your paper.** This process, called *peer review*, is discussed in the section "Work with Classmates to Revise Your Essay," later in this chapter.
- **Look for consistent problem areas in your writing.** Develop a checklist of common problems—such as confusing organization or a lack of concrete supporting details—by listing issues from several essays you have written; then check for these problem areas as you revise.
- **Read a printed copy.** You will be able to analyze and evaluate your writing more impartially, and you can write marginal annotations, circle troublesome words or sentences, and draw arrows to connect details more easily.
- **Draw a graphic organizer or outline your draft.** A graphic organizer or outline allows you to see how your thesis and topic sentences relate to one another and helps you evaluate content and organization. If you spot a problem, such as a detail or an example that does not support a topic sentence, write notes to the right of your organizer (or outline), as shown in Graphic Organizer 8.2.

For more about creating a graphic organizer, see the sections "Draw a Graphic Organizer to Examine Relationships among Ideas" in Chapter 2 and "Prepare an Outline or a Graphic Organizer" in Chapter 7.

Ask Key Questions for Revision

To identify broad areas of weakness in your essay, ask yourself these five key questions:

1. Does my essay clearly convey a purpose, address an appropriate audience, and follow the conventions of the genre?
2. Does my essay include a clear, well-focused thesis and provide enough reasons and evidence to support the thesis?
3. Does each paragraph include a clear main idea (usually stated in a topic sentence) and enough details to develop the idea fully?
4. Do the ideas in my essay fit together logically?
5. Does my essay have a strong introduction, a strong conclusion, and an appropriate title?

After identifying areas that need reworking, refer to the self-help flowcharts that follow.

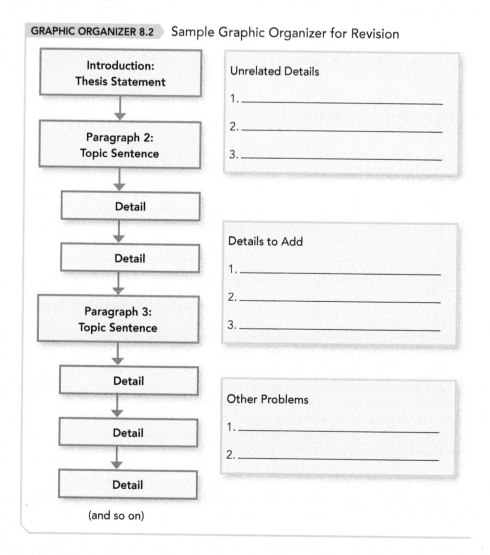

GRAPHIC ORGANIZER 8.2 Sample Graphic Organizer for Revision

Analyze Your Purpose and Audience

For more about purpose, see Chapter 4; for more about developing a thesis, see Chapter 5.

First drafts often lack focus. They may go off in several directions rather than have a clear purpose. For instance, one section of an essay on divorce may inform readers of its causes, and another section may argue that it harms children. A first draft may also contain sections that appeal to different audiences. For instance, one section of an essay on counseling teenagers about drug abuse might seem to be written for parents; other sections might be more appropriate for teenagers.

To determine if your paper has a clear focus, write a sentence stating what your essay is supposed to accomplish. If you cannot write such a sentence, your paper probably lacks a clear purpose. To find a purpose, reread your draft. Does one purpose predominate? If so, revise the sections that do not fit in. If not, do some additional thinking or brainstorming, listing as many possible purposes as you can think of and revising to address the purpose you find most appropriate.

To determine if your essay is directed to a specific audience, write a few sentences describing your intended readers. Describe their knowledge, beliefs, and experience with your topic. If you are unable to do so, focus on a particular audience and revise your essay with them in mind.

For more about assessing your audience, see Chapter 4; for more about tone and level of diction, see Chapter 9.

ESSAY IN PROGRESS 1

Evaluate the purpose and audience of the draft essay you wrote in Essay in Progress 3 in Chapter 7 or another essay that you have written. Make notes on your graphic organizer or annotate your outline.

Academic Writing: Analyze Your Tone

When revising a piece of academic writing, check to make sure that you have adopted a clear, direct, and informative tone. Tone reflects your attitude toward the topic and audience and is created by the words you use. Are there any unnecessary multisyllabic words that are not especially appropriate to the context? Have you thrown in jargon to make your writing seem more sophisticated? Have you determined whether terms that your readers may not know can be replaced by more familiar terms? If not, have you included a brief definition?

As with any good writing, language is important. Pay attention to the denotation (literal meaning) and connotation (emotional resonance) of the words you have chosen. Also be sure to use the most concrete and specific words that convey your meaning. In particular, most academic writing should avoid the following language issues:

- **Emotional or inflammatory language.** For example, change "The proposal is outrageous!" to "The proposal did not include the financial estimates necessary to assess its validity."
- **Slang, figurative, or informal expressions.** For example, change "The teenager spilled the beans" to "The thirteen-year-old confessed to having lied about where she went and who she was with on Friday evening."
- **Contractions.** Change words like "it's" to "it is" and "shouldn't" to "should not."
- **Broad unsubstantiated generalizations.** For example, change "All existing plans should be abandoned" to "The plan to reduce funding for public higher education institutions in New York state should be abandoned."
- **First-person (*I, me*) and second-person (*you, your*) language.** Unless the writer is conveying a personal experience, the first person is generally inappropriate in academic writing, although this may vary from discipline to discipline. The second person is appropriate to instructional content but not to academic writing.

To get a sense of what is an appropriate tone for your essay, look at other academic sources written on the topic, or consult your instructor or a writing center tutor.

Analyze Your Thesis, Topic Sentences, and Evidence

Use Figure 8.1 to examine your thesis statement, topic sentences, and evidence.

ESSAY IN PROGRESS 2

Using Figure 8.1, evaluate the thesis statement, topic sentences, and evidence of the essay you began assessing in Essay in Progress 1 above. Make notes on your graphic organizer or annotate your outline.

FIGURE 8.1 Flowchart for Evaluating Your Thesis Statement, Topic Sentences, and Evidence

QUESTIONS

REVISION STRATEGIES

1. Does your essay have a thesis that identifies your topic and position and suggests your slant? (To find out, state your thesis; then highlight the sentence in your draft that comes closest to what you just said. If you cannot find such a sentence, you probably do not have a well-focused thesis.)

 NO ▶

- Reread your essay and answer this question: What is the essay's one main point?
- Write a thesis statement that expresses that main point.
- Revise your paper to focus on that main point.
- Delete parts of the essay that do not support your thesis statement.

 YES ▼

2. Do your readers have the background they need to understand your thesis? (To find out, ask someone unfamiliar with your topic to read your essay, and get feedback.)

 NO ▶

- Answer *who, what, when, where, why,* and *how* questions to discover more background information.

 YES ▼

3. Have you presented enough evidence to support your thesis? (Place a ✔ beside the evidence that supports your thesis. For paragraphs with few ✔ s, ask yourself: Do they need more evidence to be convincing?)

NO ▶

- Use prewriting strategies or do additional research to discover more supporting evidence.
- Evaluate this new evidence and add the most convincing evidence to your essay.

 YES ▼

4. Does each topic sentence logically connect to and support the thesis? Read the thesis, and then read each topic sentence. Revise when the connection is not obvious.

NO ▶

- Rewrite the topic sentence so that it clearly supports the thesis.
- If necessary, broaden your thesis so that it encompasses all your supporting points.

 YES ▼

5. Is your evidence specific and detailed? Reread paragraphs where you placed ✔ s. Does each item answer one of these questions: *Who? What? When? Where? Why? How?* For paragraphs with few or no ✔ s, add more detailed evidence.

 NO ▶

- Answer *who, what, when, where, why,* and *how* questions to discover more detailed evidence. Name names, give dates, and specify places.
- Use action verbs and descriptive language, including carefully chosen adjectives and adverbs.

Analyze Your Organization

Your readers will not be able to follow your ideas if your essay is not unified. To assess your essay's unity, examine its organization. Your graphic organizer or outline will help you discover any flaws.

See Chapter 7 to learn more about preparing a graphic organizer; organizing your essay effectively; and writing a strong introduction, conclusion, and title.

You can also ask a classmate to read your essay and explain how it is organized. If your classmate cannot describe your essay's organization, it probably needs further work. Use one of the methods in Chapter 7 or one of the patterns of development described in Parts 3 and 4 to reorganize your ideas.

Analyze Your Introduction, Conclusion, and Title

The following questions can help you evaluate your introduction, conclusion, and title:

1. **Will your introduction interest your readers and provide needed background information?** If your essay jumps into the topic without preparing readers for it, your introduction needs to be revised. Ask the questions *who, what, when, where, why,* and *how* to determine the background information your readers will need. Then use the suggestions in Chapter 7 to create interest.

2. **Does your conclusion draw your essay to a satisfactory close, reinforce your thesis statement, and follow logically from the introduction?** If not, try imagining yourself explaining the significance or importance of your essay to a friend, and use this explanation to rewrite your conclusion. Then use the suggestions for writing conclusions in Chapter 7 to add interest.

3. **Does your title accurately reflect the content of your essay?** Write a few words that "label" your essay. Mine your thesis for a few key words that can serve as part of your title. Finally, use the suggestions in Chapter 7 to help you write a title.

HOW WRITERS READ ▶ YOUR OWN WRITING	
	When you are revising, you are expected to analyze and evaluate your own writing. The most effective way to do this is to treat your own writing as if it were someone else's. These steps can help:
BEFORE READING	• Take a break: You will be better able to create the distance you need to be objective. • Preview your essay: Do the title, introduction, headings (if any), and conclusion together provide an effective overview?
WHILE READING	Assume you know nothing more about the subject than what you have written in the essay. • Are there points where you would be confused? • Would you need more information to be convinced?
AFTER READING	Ask yourself these "so what?" questions: • Did the essay enrich your understanding of the topic? (If not, you may need to provide more or better evidence.) • Did the essay show that the topic matters—to you and to your readers? (If not, you may need to reconsider your tone or even your thesis.)

ESSAY IN PROGRESS 3

Evaluate the organization of your essay in progress. Make notes on your draft copy.

Analyze Your Paragraph Development

Each paragraph in your essay must fully develop a single idea that supports your thesis. (Exception: Each paragraph of a narrative essay focuses on a separate part of the action; see Chapter 10.) In a typical first draft, paragraphs are often weak or loosely structured. They may contain irrelevant information or lack a clearly focused topic sentence.

See Chapter 6 for more on paragraph development.

Study each paragraph in conjunction with your thesis statement. Then consider whether your topic sentence supports your thesis and whether the reasons and evidence in the paragraph support the topic sentence. You may need to delete or combine some paragraphs, rework or reorganize others, or move paragraphs to more appropriate placement in the essay. If you need to supply additional information to support your thesis, you may need to add paragraphs to the draft. Use Figure 8.2 to analyze and revise your paragraphs.

ESSAY IN PROGRESS 4

Using Figure 8.2, examine each paragraph of your essay in progress, and make notes on your draft.

Academic Writing: Check Your Use of Sources

When writing from sources, it is important to check that you have incorporated them effectively and cited them correctly. Regardless of whether you have paraphrased, summarized, or quoted the work of others, the following list of questions will help you evaluate your use of sources:

1. **Is information or ideas from the source captured accurately?** Check that paraphrases and summaries accurately reflect the author's ideas. Double-check quotations to be certain that they match the original source exactly, including punctuation.

2. **Is the source cited correctly, using in-text citations and a list of works cited?** For more information about citing sources in MLA and APA style, see Chapter 23.

3. **Are signal phrases used to integrate borrowed information and ideas into your own writing?** Signal phrases (*Professor X argues . . .*) not only work as transitions to make your flow of ideas smoother, but they also help readers recognize where borrowed material ends and your own ideas and interpretation begin. Signal phrases that also indicate the author's relevant background (*Professor X, a psychologist who has written widely on Stockholm syndrome, . . .*) let readers know that the author is an authority and lend credibility to your writing.

FIGURE 8.2 Flowchart for Evaluating Your Paragraphs

QUESTIONS   REVISION STRATEGIES

1. Does each paragraph have a clear topic sentence that supports the thesis? <u>Underline</u> the topic sentence in each paragraph. Then evaluate whether the topic sentence makes a statement that supports the main idea of the essay.

 NO ▶

- Revise a sentence within the paragraph so that it clearly states the main point.
- Write a new sentence that supports the thesis and states the main point of the paragraph.

 YES ▼

2. Do all sentences in each paragraph support the topic sentence? To find out, read the topic sentence and each supporting sentence in turn.

 NO ▶

- Revise supporting sentences to make their connection to the topic sentence clear.
- Delete any sentences that do not support the topic sentence.

 YES ▼

3. Does the paragraph offer adequate explanation and supporting details? Place ✔ s beside supporting details. Then ask yourself: Will readers want or need to know anything else?

NO ▶

- Add more details if your paragraph seems skimpy.
- Use either the *who, what, when, where, why,* and *how* questions or the prewriting strategies in Chapter 4 to generate the details you need.

 YES ▼

4. Will it be clear to your reader how each sentence and each paragraph connects to those before and after it? (To find out, read your paper aloud to see if it flows smoothly or sounds choppy.)

 NO ▶

- Add transitions where they are needed. Refer to the list of common transitions in Table 6.1.

4. **Do the sources support your own ideas?** Reread to be sure that each time you use a source, you have made clear why it is used and how it supports your own ideas. Think of supporting paragraphs like a sandwich, with your own ideas and interpretations acting as the bread, and information from sources as the stuffing in between.

5. **Is too much source material used?** Make sure you have not overused sources and skimped on stating and explaining your own ideas. As a check, literally highlight your own ideas. If more than half of your essay is not highlighted, you have used too many sources.

Work with Classmates to Revise Your Essay

Many instructors ask students to use **peer review**, a process in which two or more students read and comment on one another's papers. Working with classmates is an excellent way to get ideas for improving your essays and your approach to the writing process. Peer review can also hone your critical reading skills. The suggestions that follow will help writers and reviewers get the most from peer review.

Find a Good Reviewer

Your instructor may pair you with another class member or let you find your own reviewer, either a classmate or someone outside class. If you can select your own reviewer, use these tips:

- Select a classmate who is attentive in class, so he or she will be familiar with the assignment and with what you have learned so far in the course. If you need to find someone outside of class, choose a person who has already taken the course, preferably someone who did well in it.
- Avoid choosing close friends; they are not necessarily the best reviewers because they may be reluctant to offer criticism or may be too critical. Instead, choose someone who is serious, skillful, objective, and willing to spend the time needed to provide useful comments.
- If your college has a writing center, ask a tutor in the center to read and comment on your draft.
- Use more than one reviewer if possible, so you can get several perspectives.

Get Helpful Advice

To get the greatest benefit from peer review, use the following suggestions:

1. **Provide readable copy.** A typed, double-spaced draft is best.
2. **Do some revision yourself first.** Think through your draft, and try to fix obvious problems. The more developed your draft is, the more helpful your reviewer's comments will be.
3. **Offer specific questions or guidelines.** Give your reviewer a copy of the "Questions for Peer Reviewers" below, and add other questions that you want answered. You might also give your reviewer one of the revision flowcharts in this (or another) chapter.
4. **Be open to criticism and new ideas.** Try not to be defensive. Look at your essay objectively, seeing it from your reader's perspective.
5. **Don't feel obligated to accept all of the advice you are given.** A reviewer might suggest a change that will not work well in your paper or wrongly identify something as an error. If you are uncertain about a suggestion, discuss it with your instructor or other reviewers.

Questions for Peer Reviewers

1. What is the purpose of the essay?
2. Who is the intended audience?
3. What expectations are associated with this genre?
4. Is the introduction fully developed?
5. What is the main point or thesis? Is it easy to identify?
6. Does each paragraph offer a clear topic sentence and relevant and convincing evidence to support the main point? Where is more evidence needed? (Identify specific paragraphs.)
7. Is each paragraph clear and well organized? Are transitions needed to connect ideas within paragraphs?
8. Is the organization easy to follow? Where might it be improved, and how? Are transitions needed to connect ideas between paragraphs?
9. Does the conclusion draw the essay to a satisfying close?
10. What do you like about the draft? What could be improved? Underline or highlight passages that are unclear or confusing.

Give Helpful Advice

Reviewers should be honest but tactful. Criticism is never easy to accept, so keep your reader's feelings in mind. These tips will help you provide useful comments:

1. **Read the draft through twice before making any judgments or comments.**
2. **Focus on the main points and how clearly they are expressed.** If you notice a misspelling or a grammatical error, you can circle it, but correcting errors is not your primary task.
3. **Offer praise.** It helps the writer to know what is effective as well as what needs improvement.
4. **Be specific.** For instance, instead of saying that more examples are needed, tell the writer which ideas in which paragraphs are unclear or unconvincing without examples. Suggest useful examples in each case.
5. **Use the Questions for Peer Reviewers above as well as any additional questions that the writer provides to guide your review.** If the essay was written in response to an assignment in one of the chapters in Part 3 or 4, consult the revision flowchart in that chapter.
6. **Write notes and comments directly on the draft.** At the end of the essay, write a note that summarizes your overall reaction, pointing out both strengths and weaknesses. Here is one reviewer's sample final note:

> Overall, I think your paper has great ideas. It definitely held my interest, and the example about the judge proved your point well. But it could be organized better. The last three paragraphs don't seem connected to the rest of the essay. Maybe better transitions would help. Also the conclusion just repeats your thesis statement. It needs to be developed more.

7. **Use the Comments feature or insert comments in brackets or in a different color following the passage.** Make it easy for the writer to find and delete your comments after reading them.

8. **Do not rewrite paragraphs or sections of the essay.** Instead, suggest how the writer might revise them.

> **ESSAY IN PROGRESS 5**
>
> Give your essay in progress to a classmate to read and review. Ask your reviewer to respond to the Questions for Peer Reviewers. Revise your essay using your revision outline, Figures 8.1 and 8.2, and your reviewer's suggestions.

Use Your Instructor's Comments

The comments your instructor provides are an important resource to use in revising your essays. You can use them not only to revise an essay but also to improve your writing throughout the course.

Revise an Essay Using Your Instructor's Comments

Often your instructor's comments provide a road map for you to begin your revision. An essay by a student, Kate Atkinson, appears in Figure 8.3. Her assignment was to write an essay defining a specialized term, and Kate chose "guerrilla street art" as her subject. In the margin, Kate's instructor comments on a range of elements in the essay, including the effectiveness of the introduction, paragraph unity and development, word choice, and source citations. (Because this was a draft, Kate's instructor did not comment on errors, such as misspellings and capitalization mistakes, that Kate will correct while editing and proofreading.) Kate read the comments carefully and used them to revise her essay. Her final draft appears in Chapter 17.

FIGURE 8.3 Using Your Instructor's Comments to Revise Your Essay

Guerrilla Street Art: Definition Essay Rough Draft

Comment [KM1]: Good opening sentence. It gives readers a reason for wanting to know more about it and challenges them to look for it.

Guerrilla street art is everywhere, if you look for it. There are countless examples in the small college town where I grew up, where the dense population of college students and artists breeds creativity. Just around the corner from my school there are stickers littering sign posts, colorful graffiti tags on exposed

Comment [KM2]: This term is not yet defined. I know it is defined later, but readers will wonder what it is now. Perhaps choose a different example here?

brick walls, homemade posters advertising local bands at the bus stop, and a cheerful Dr. Seuss character stencilled on the sidewalk. These small works of art can go easily unnoticed, but they bring an unexpected vibrancy to the city that is

1

unique. Guerrilla street art is any unauthorized art in a public space. By taking art out of the traditional context, guerrilla street artists create controversy and intrigue by making art free and accessible to a broad audience.

Graffiti is unauthorized writing or drawing on a public surface. It dates back [2] centuries and artists have been know to use chalk, markers, paint, and even carving tools to inscribe their messages on public property. Common techniques used by street artists today include graffiti, stenciling, poster art, sticker art, and wheat pasting. Graffiti is so common that it is difficult to travel far in most urban settings without coming across a word or image scrawled in spray paint on a public a surface. Stenciling is a form of graffitti in which artists use pre-cut stencils to guide their work, and pre-made stickers and posters are popular because they can be quickly appled and are easy to mass produce. "Wheat pasting" refers to the use of a vegetable-based adhesive to adhere posters to walls. Using a less common technique called "yarn bombing," crafty artists knit colorful sheaths of wool and acrylic and wrap them around telephone poles and park benches. The finished pieces are eye-catching and unusual, but not permanent or damaging to public property.

The various motives behind guerilla street art are as diverse as the artwork itself [3] and range from social and political activism to self-promotion of the artist. Artist embellish telephone poles with colorful yarn or train carriges with ornate murals as a way to reclaim and beautify public space. Others use public space as a billboard to advocate for a cause. An example of street art as propaganda is artist Shepard Fairey's iconic image of Barack Obama. The simple design combines a striking red, white, and blue portrait of Obama with the word "Hope." With the nod of approval from Obama's campaign team, Fairey and his team dispersed and glue, stencilled, and tacked the image onto countless public surfaces across the US until it became an important facet of the campaign. The picture itself is powerful, but what made it even more effective as a campaign tool was the distribution of the image by supporters and the youth appeal that it garnered as a result.

Street Art is also an easy way for new artists to gain notoriety without revealing [4] who they really are. A tag, which is an artists signature or symbol, is the most prevalent type of graffitti. Before the Obama campaign, Shepard Fairey gained international acclaim for a sticker depicting wrestler Andre the Giant and the word "Obey." The image soon became his tag and can be found in almost all of his work, making it instantly recognizable. The anonymity of street art also gives artists the freedom to express themselves without fearing the judgement of their peers. At worst, this freedom can result in crude or offensive inscriptions on public property but at best, it can produce bold statements.

(continued on next page)

Comment [KM3]: This is your thesis, but it is not very detailed. What about combining it with the following sentence to create a stronger thesis?

Comment [KM4]: This sentence defining graffiti is almost the same definition as your definition of guerrilla street art in para. 1.

Comment [KM5]: The paragraph is about graffiti-writing or drawing. Do wheat pasting and yarn bombing fall into this category? If so, can you expand the definition to fit them? Or are they other forms of guerrilla street art? If so, I'd put them in a separate paragraph.

Comment [KM6]: This is a strong topic sentence.

Deleted: for

Comment [KM7]: Are all causes propaganda? You might want to choose a different word here or introduce propaganda and a separate motive first.

Comment [KM8]: Add source citation.

(Figure 8.3 continued)

Comment [KM9]: This sentence leads me to believe that the para. will be about secrecy, but midway through the topic seems to switch to reasons for street art's appeal. Maybe make this part into a separate paragraph?

Comment [KM10]: Add source citation.

Comment [KM11]: I am glad you raised this question. I kept wondering about it all along as I read the essay. Can you raise it earlier? And should you try to answer this knotty question of "What is art"? Maybe just recognize that the question exists?

Due to the illicit nature of their art, the street artist community is shrouded in secrecy.   5
In the film "Exit through the Gift Shop," a documentary by notorious British street
artist Banksy, hooded figures in ski masks are shown scaling buildings and perched
precariously on ledges, armed with spray cans and buckets of industrial paste and always
on the lookout for the police. Despite his celebrity, Banksy has managed to keep his identity
anonymous and his face is never shown in the film. It is common for street artists to be
arrested for trespassing and vandalism, and the risk and intentional disobience involved in
street art adds to its appeal, especially amoung young people. Another appeal of guerrilla
street art is that it is comtemporary and can be enjoyed without a visit to a museum. It is free
and encourages the belief that art should be accessible and available to everyone. It is also a
movement that anyone can take part in and that challenges traditional standards of art.

Guerrilla street art has blossomed from and underground movement to a cultural   6
phenomenon. At the very least, it brings up the controversial questions of what
constitutes art, and whether public space is an appropriate place for it. It brings
beauty and intrigue to urban spaces that would otherwise go unnoticed and it is a
tool for artists to exercise freedom of speech and expression.

EXERCISE 8.1   **COMPARING A FIRST DRAFT AND A FINAL DRAFT**

Either alone or in small groups, compare Kate Atkinson's rough draft with her final
draft in Chapter 17. Make a list of the changes she made to her essay in response
to her instructor's comments. Also, put a checkmark next to any problems that recur
throughout the first draft of the essay.

Use Your Instructor's Comments to Improve Future Essays

When you receive a graded essay back from an instructor, it is tempting to note the
grade and then file away the essay without reading any accompanying notes or suggestions. To improve your writing, however, take time to study each comment. Use the
following suggestions to improve future essays:

- **Reread your essay at least twice.** It takes more than one reading to process
  numerous comments on a wide range of topics. Read your essay once to note
  grammatical corrections. Then read it a second time to study comments about
  organization or content.
- **If you did not get a high grade, try to determine why.** Was the essay weak in
  content, organization, or development?
- **Make sure you understand (and can correct) each grammatical error.** If you
  cannot, check a grammar handbook or ask a classmate. If you still do not
  understand your error, check with your instructor.

- **Record grammar errors in an error log.** When you proofread your next essay, look carefully for each type of error.
- **Using Figures 8.1 and 8.2, highlight or mark weaknesses that your instructor identified.** When writing your next essay, refer back to these flowcharts. Pay close attention to the areas you had trouble with as you revise your next paper.
- **If any comments are unclear, first ask a classmate if he or she understands them.** If not, talk to your instructor, who will be pleased that you are taking time to study the comments.

EXERCISE 8.2   **USING YOUR INSTRUCTOR'S COMMENTS ON A DRAFT**

If your instructor has returned a marked-up first draft to you, read the comments carefully. Then draw a line down the middle of a blank sheet of paper. On the left, write the instructor's comments; on the right, jot down ways you might revise the essay in response to each comment. Put a checkmark next to any problems that recur throughout your essay; these are areas to which you will want to pay particular attention in your future writing.

‹ STUDENTS WRITE

After writing her first draft, which appears in Chapter 7, Latrisha Wilson used the guidelines and revision flowcharts in this chapter to guide her revision. For example, she decided that she needed to focus more on how communications technologies allow greater surveillance. She added details and examples, including a visual to show what she was describing.

Wilson asked a classmate to review her essay. A portion of his comments is shown below.

Reviewer's Comments

I like your topic. It's current and interesting, but maybe your thesis could be more specific? Maybe it should focus on how new ways of communicating put us at risk of surveillance? Or you could revise your intro to focus on whistleblowers (that's what your first body paragraph talks about), but you'd need to add a lot of information. Since I have gmail and instagram, I'd like to know more about how those sites use our personal information to make money, and maybe you could include a screenshot of a gmail page to show where the ads are. That might be helpful for the 5 people in the world (like the teacher?) who don't have gmail accounts. The only other thing that I think may be a problem is the tone. It's kind of casual for an essay for class. Maybe you could make your tone more formal?

Using her own analysis and her classmate's suggestions, Wilson created a graphic organizer (Graphic Organizer 8.3) to help her decide how to revise her draft. She used the format for an illustration essay (Graphic Organizer 13.1) provided in Chapter 13.

GRAPHIC ORGANIZER 8.3   Graphic Organizer for Latrisha Wilson's Revision Plans

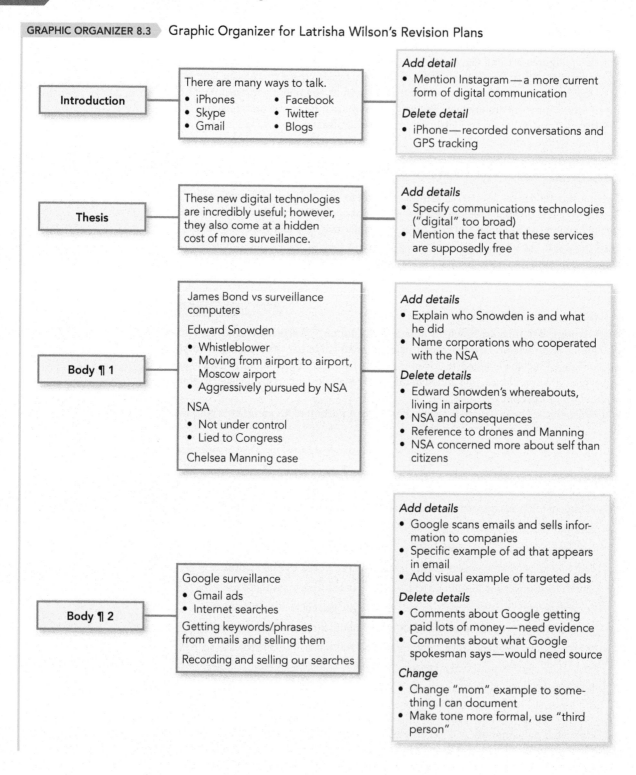

Introduction

There are many ways to talk.
- iPhones
- Skype
- Gmail
- Facebook
- Twitter
- Blogs

Add detail
- Mention Instagram—a more current form of digital communication

Delete detail
- iPhone—recorded conversations and GPS tracking

Thesis

These new digital technologies are incredibly useful; however, they also come at a hidden cost of more surveillance.

Add details
- Specify communications technologies ("digital" too broad)
- Mention the fact that these services are supposedly free

Body ¶ 1

James Bond vs surveillance computers

Edward Snowden
- Whistleblower
- Moving from airport to airport, Moscow airport
- Aggressively pursued by NSA

NSA
- Not under control
- Lied to Congress

Chelsea Manning case

Add details
- Explain who Snowden is and what he did
- Name corporations who cooperated with the NSA

Delete details
- Edward Snowden's whereabouts, living in airports
- NSA and consequences
- Reference to drones and Manning
- NSA concerned more about self than citizens

Body ¶ 2

Google surveillance
- Gmail ads
- Internet searches

Getting keywords/phrases from emails and selling them

Recording and selling our searches

Add details
- Google scans emails and sells information to companies
- Specific example of ad that appears in email
- Add visual example of targeted ads

Delete details
- Comments about Google getting paid lots of money—need evidence
- Comments about what Google spokesman says—would need source

Change
- Change "mom" example to something I can document
- Make tone more formal, use "third person"

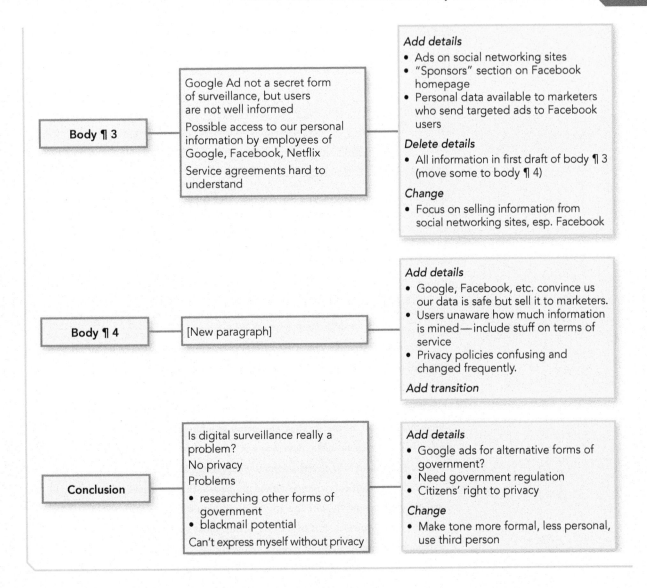

After creating the graphic organizer, Wilson revised her first draft. A portion of her revised draft, with her revisions indicated using the Track Changes function of Microsoft Word, follows.

Revised Draft

Do we need to talk? There are plenty of exciting new ways to ~~talk to friends and family.~~ do it. We can ~~communicate by talking~~ text, FaceTime on our iPhones, gchat on Google,

~~Facebook message,~~ and read each other's Twitter feed or blog posts, or share pictures on Instagram or Snapchat. ~~but there are dangers there. Our conversations can be recorded, and the GPS function on the phone allows our whereabouts to be tracked. We can chat on Skype, Gmail, Facebook message, and read each other's Twitter or Blog posts. And then there are security cameras that record our every move.~~ These new digital technologies are incredibly useful; however, they also come at a hidden cost. Often advertised as free services, new ways of communicating put us under more invasive but less obvious forms of surveillance.

Before Wilson submitted her final draft, she read her essay several more times, editing it for sentence structure and word choice. She also proofread it to catch errors in grammar and punctuation as well as typographical errors. (A portion of Wilson's revised essay, with editing and proofreading changes marked, appears in Chapter 9.) The final version of Wilson's essay follows.

Final Draft

No Place Left for Privacy

Do we need to talk? There are plenty of exciting new ways to do it. We can text, FaceTime on our iPhones, gchat on Google, Facebook message, or read each other's Twitter feed or blog posts, or share pictures on Instagram or Snapchat. These new digital technologies are incredibly useful; however, they also come at a hidden cost. Often advertised as free services, new ways of communicating put us under more invasive but less obvious forms of surveillance.   1

When the word *surveillance* comes up, people think of some thrilling and dangerous activity, like the spying on foreign terrorists that goes on in James Bond movies. But in the U.S. today, most spying isn't done by handsome secret agents out to save the world; it's done by surveillance computers, and they monitor U.S. citizens, not just foreign terrorists. For example, consider what we learned from the whistleblower Edward Snowden, who sacrificed his career as a contractor for the National Security Agency (NSA) to alert the public to the deals the NSA makes with companies like Microsoft, Facebook, and Verizon to collect personal information and monitor everything their customers do on the Internet or speak into a telephone.   2

The NSA, of course, isn't the only organization spying on us. Another kind of surveillance, which doesn't make top press, is the eavesdropping   3 that Google and other communication service providers regularly do on their users. Google software, for example, automatically scans the content of all Gmail for keywords and phrases that then must get sold or rented to other companies because users of Gmail regularly see targeted advertisements related to what they've written about: If a user wishes her friend "Happy Birthday!" she now sees advertisements for party clowns and birthday packages. (See fig. 1.)

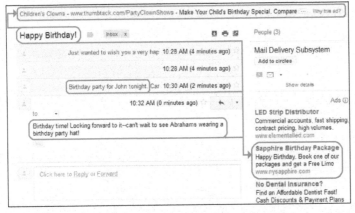

Fig. 1. Birthday email string leads to birthday advertising

Advertisers pay social networking sites to do something similar, which is why users might have noticed that section of "sponsors" to the right of their Facebook homepage. Everything public on a typical person's profile page—their age, relationship status, favorite music, education history—is available to marketers (for a price), so they can send their ads to specific people.   4

In this way, Facebook, Google, and other digital service providers sell advertisers intimate data about us, while also attempting to convince us that all our personal data is safe. Most people have little to no idea how much data they give up when they get on the Internet. How would they? Facebook and Google constantly change their privacy policies, and the terms-of-service agreements are long legal documents written in a language which your everyday person doesn't have the time or energy to decipher. So they just check a box.   5

"What's the problem?" you might say. "I have nothing to hide from either the government or companies like Google and Facebook." But think   6 about it for a few minutes: When researching a political science paper on alternate forms of government, will typing words like "anarchism" or "Marxism" into a search box set off warning signals at the NSA or trigger Google to send advertisements for *The Anarchist's Handbook* (which might set off warning signals)? To honestly express ourselves, we need privacy. But less and less is there any kind of space for it online, where most of us read, write, and communicate. There needs to be some space online where all our activity is not recorded and sold (or taken by government agencies). But unless more rules and regulations are put in place to govern the behavior of Internet service providers and governmental data miners, privacy will become a thing of the past, and people will forget that they are not just consumers, but also citizens with rights, like the right to privacy.

Analyzing the Revision

1. **Revision** Identify the major revisions that Wilson made from the earlier draft in Chapter 7. Explain why you think she made the changes she did. Are there other changes she could have made to make the final draft even better?
2. **Introduction and Conclusion** Examine Wilson's introduction and conclusion. In what ways are they more effective than the introduction and conclusion in her first draft? What additional improvements could she make?
3. **Details** Choose one paragraph, and compare the details provided in it with those in the corresponding paragraph of the first draft. Which added details are particularly effective, and why?
4. **Tone** Consider the differences in tone between Wilson's first draft and her revised draft. What changes affected her tone? (List three.) Given that she was writing this essay for a college course and that her instructor was her main audience, how effective is the tone of the revised essay?

Working Together

In groups of two or three classmates, use the questions below to analyze paragraph 6 (or another paragraph) from the essay "The New Marshmallow Test: Students Can't Resist Multitasking" (in Chapter 1) or another essay.

- What is the topic sentence of this paragraph?
- How is the paragraph organized?
- What transitions does the author use in the paragraph?
- What action verbs (if any) does the author use in the paragraph? (Give an example.)
- Does the author use descriptive language (language that appeals to the senses)? If so, give an example of such language.

Be prepared to share your responses with the rest of the class.

NO FISHING/NO ADMITTANCE TO NON – SYNDICAT MEMBERS TACKLE WILL BE SEIZED TRESSPASSERS PROSERCUTED ZERO TOLLERANCE

9
Editing Sentences and Words

Writing Quick Start

ANALYZE   The photo on this page shows a sign with errors of grammar and punctuation. Read carefully to identify all the errors, and then correct them.

WRITE   In a few sentences, describe how errors like these affect viewers' reaction to the message and their opinion of the sign's creator.

CONNECT   When you identified errors in the sign and corrected them, you edited and proofread it. **Editing** and **proofreading** are processes of examining individual sentences and words and correcting them as needed so that each conveys the intended meaning accurately, concisely, and in an interesting and appropriate way. These are the last steps in the writing process (see Graphic Organizer 9.1), and they are crucial. Because you are almost finished with your assignment, you may be tempted to hurry through or skip editing and proofreading altogether. But as this Writing Quick Start demonstrates, careful editing and proofreading will always pay off in the end because an error-free essay is important to conveying your message effectively and establishing a positive relationship with your reader. This chapter will help you sharpen your sentences; refine your word choice; and correct errors with grammar, punctuation, and spelling that can annoy readers or obscure your meaning.

In this chapter you will learn to

- analyze and edit your sentences for wordiness; repetition of type, length, and pattern; parallelism; and weak verbs

- analyze and edit your word choice for tone, level of diction, overly general word choice, and use of clichés

- proofread effectively

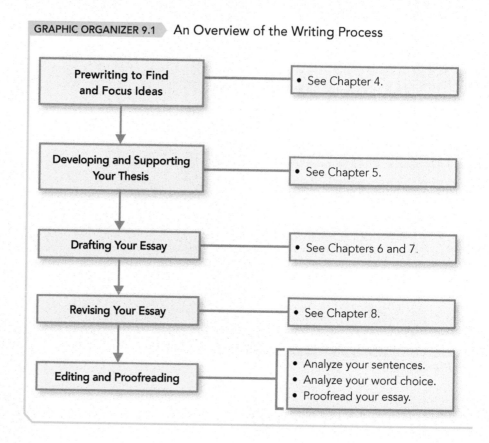

GRAPHIC ORGANIZER 9.1   An Overview of the Writing Process

| Prewriting to Find and Focus Ideas | • See Chapter 4. |

| Developing and Supporting Your Thesis | • See Chapter 5. |

| Drafting Your Essay | • See Chapters 6 and 7. |

| Revising Your Essay | • See Chapter 8. |

| Editing and Proofreading | • Analyze your sentences. • Analyze your word choice. • Proofread your essay. |

Analyze Your Sentences

Effective sentences should have four important characteristics:

1. They should be clear and concise.
2. They should be varied.
3. They should use parallel structure for similar ideas.
4. They should contain strong, active verbs.

When using information or ideas from sources to support your claims, your sentences should also do one more thing:

5. They should introduce and identify the source clearly and smoothly.

Are Your Sentences Concise?

Concise sentences convey their meaning in as few words as possible. Use the following suggestions to make your sentences concise:

   1. **Avoid wordy expressions.** Omit words and phrases that contribute little or no meaning. If a sentence is clear without a particular phrase or if the phrase can be replaced by a more direct word or phrase, take it out or replace it.

- ~~In the near future,~~ ^A^ another revolution in computer technology is bound to occur~~/~~ ^soon.^

- ~~In light of the fact that~~ ^Since^ computer technology changes ~~every month or so,~~ ^monthly,^ software upgrades are ~~what everybody has to do.~~ ^necessary.^

2. Eliminate redundancy. Look for places where you have repeated an idea unnecessarily by using different words that have the same meaning.

- ~~My decision to choose~~ ^Choosing^ accounting as my major will lead to steady, rewarding employment.

- Teenagers use slang to establish ~~who they are and what~~ their identity ~~is~~.

3. Eliminate unnecessary sentence openings. Look for words you have expressed indirectly or tentatively. As you revise, edit to make them more direct.

- ~~It is my opinion that~~ ^F^ast-food restaurants ^should^ avoid oversized portions.

- ~~Many people would agree that~~ ^S^ electing nutritious snacks is a priority for health-conscious people.

4. Eliminate unnecessary adverbs. Using too many **adverbs** can weaken your writing. Adverbs such as *extremely*, *really*, and *very* add nothing and can weaken the words they modify. Notice that the following sentence is stronger without the adverb.

An **adverb** modifies a verb, an adjective, or another adverb.

- The journalist was ~~very~~ elated when he learned that he had won a Pulitzer Prize.

Other adverbs, such as *somewhat*, *rather*, and *quite*, also add little or no meaning and are often unnecessary.

- The college president was ~~quite~~ disturbed by the findings of the Presidential Panel on Sex Equity.

5. Eliminate unnecessary phrases and clauses. Wordy phrases and clauses make it difficult for readers to find and understand the main point of your sentence. This problem often occurs when you use too many **prepositional phrases** and clauses that begin with *who*, *which*, or *that*.

A **prepositional phrase** is a group of words that begins with a preposition and includes the object or objects of the preposition and all their modifiers: *above the low wooden table.*

- The ^students'^ complaints ~~of students in the college~~ encouraged the dean to create additional parking spaces.

- The ~~teenagers who were~~ ^teenage^ mall walkers disagreed with the ^newspaper^ editorial ~~in the newspaper that supported the~~ ^supporting^ shopping mall regulations.

6. Avoid weak verb-noun combinations. Weak verb-noun combinations such as *wrote a draft* instead of *drafted* or *made a change* instead of *changed* tend to make sentences wordy.

- The attorney ~~made an assessment of~~ ^{assessed} the company's liability in the accident.
- The professor ~~gave a lecture~~ ^{lectured} on Asian American relations.

EXERCISE 9.1

Edit the following sentences to make them concise:

1. Due to the fact that Professor Wu assigned twenty-five math problems for tomorrow, I am forced to make the decision to miss this evening's lecture to be given by the vice president of the United States.
2. In many cases, workers are forced to use old equipment that needs replacing despite the fact that equipment malfunctions cost the company more than the price of new machines.
3. Chick-fil-A is one of the best examples of a fast-food restaurant that everyone pays way too much attention to.
4. The president of Warehouse Industries has the ability and power to decide who should and who should not be hired and who should and who should not be fired.
5. The soccer league's sponsor, as a matter of fact, purchased league jerseys for the purpose of advertisement and publicity.

HOW WRITERS READ ▶ **SENTENCES AND PARAGRAPHS**

Sentences and paragraphs that are unclear, vague, or repetitious can be confusing (and annoying). Fortunately, most of your college reading assignments will have been carefully edited, but you may encounter poor writing on the job, on personal Web sites, and even in some periodicals.

When you encounter material that contains numerous grammatical or spelling errors or that uses dull, stilted, or unclear language, take the time to check the reliability of the content carefully: Lack of care in writing and editing can often be a sign of sloppy thinking, and authors who do not take the time to present their ideas in clear, correct prose may not have taken the time to think through or research their topic fully.

Are Your Sentences Varied?

Sentences that are varied will help hold your reader's interest and make your writing flow more smoothly. Vary the type, length, and pattern of your sentences.

How to vary sentence type.   There are four types of sentences: *simple, compound, complex,* and *compound-complex.* Each type consists of one or more clauses. A **clause** is a group of words with both a subject and a verb. There are two types of clauses:

- An **independent clause** can stand alone as a complete sentence.
- A **dependent clause** cannot stand alone as a complete sentence. It begins with a subordinating conjunction (for example, *because* or *although*) or a relative pronoun (for example, *when, which,* or *that*).

A brief summary of each sentence type and its clauses appears in Table 9.1.

TABLE 9.1 Sentence Types

Sentence Type	Clauses	Example
Simple	One independent clause and no dependent clauses	Credit-card fraud is increasing in the United States.
Compound	Two or more independent clauses and no dependent clauses	Credit-card fraud is increasing in the United States, and it is costing retailers millions of dollars.
Complex	One or more dependent clauses and one independent clause	Because credit-card fraud is increasing in America, consumers must become more cautious.
Compound-complex	One or more dependent clauses and two or more independent clauses	Because credit-card fraud is increasing in America, consumers must be cautious, and retailers must take steps to protect consumers.

Use the following suggestions to vary your sentence types:

1. Use simple sentences for emphasis and clarity. A **simple sentence** contains only one independent clause, but it is not necessarily short. It can have more than one subject, more than one verb, and several modifiers.

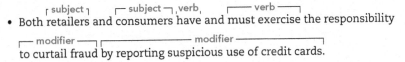

- Both retailers and consumers have and must exercise the responsibility to curtail fraud by reporting suspicious use of credit cards.

A short, simple sentence can be used to emphasize an important point or to make a dramatic statement.

- Credit-card fraud is rampant.

If you use too many simple sentences, however, your writing will sound choppy and disjointed.

Disjointed	It was a cold, drizzly spring morning. I was driving to school. A teenage hitchhiker stood alongside the road. He seemed distraught.
Better	I was driving to school on a cold, drizzly spring morning when I saw a teenage hitchhiker standing alongside the road. He seemed distraught.

Coordinating conjunctions (*and, but, or, nor, for, so, yet*) connect sentence elements that are of equal importance.

A **conjunctive adverb** is a word (such as *also, however,* or *still*) that links two independent clauses.

A **correlative conjunction** is a word pair (such as *not only . . . but also*) that works together to join elements within a sentence.

2. Use compound sentences to show relationships among equally important ideas. A **compound sentence** consists of two or more independent clauses joined in one of the following ways:

- With a comma and **coordinating conjunction**:

  – Leon asked a question, *and* the whole class was surprised.

- With a semicolon:

  – Graffiti had been scrawled on the subway walls; passersby ignored it.

- With a semicolon and a **conjunctive adverb**:

  – Each year thousands of children are adopted; *consequently,* adoption service agencies have increased in number.

- With a **correlative conjunction**:

  – *Either* the jury will reach a verdict tonight, *or* it will recess until Monday morning.

In each example, both clauses are equally important and receive equal emphasis.

You can also use compound sentences to explain *how* equally important ideas are related. For example, you can use different coordinating conjunctions to show the relationship between two important related ideas. (See Table 9.2 below.)

TABLE 9.2   **Selecting Coordinating Conjunctions to Convey Relationships**

Coordinating Conjunction	Relationship	Example
and	Additional information	The three teenage vandals were apprehended, *and* their parents were required to pay damages.
but, yet	Contrast or opposition	No one wants to pay more taxes, *yet* taxes are necessary to support vital public services.
for, so	Causes or effects	Text messages can disrupt a student's concentration, *so* turning your cell phone off in class is essential to learning.
or, nor	Choices or options	Quebec may become a separate country, or it may settle its differences with the Canadian government.

3. Use complex sentences to show that one or more ideas are less important than (or subordinate to) another idea. A **complex sentence** consists of one independent clause and at least one dependent clause. Either type of clause may come first. When the dependent clause comes first, it is usually followed by a comma. When the independent clause comes first, a comma is usually not used:

- Because the dam broke, the village flooded.
- The village flooded because the dam broke.

In the preceding sentences, the main point is that the village flooded. The dependent clause explains *why* the flood happened. A dependent clause often begins with a *subordinating conjunction* that indicates how the less important (dependent) idea is related to the more important (independent) idea. Table 9.3 lists some subordinating conjunctions and the relationships they suggest.

TABLE 9.3 ▶ **Selecting Subordinating Conjunctions to Convey Relationships**

Subordinating Conjunction	Relationship	Example
as, as far as, as soon as, as if, as though, although, even though, even if, in order to	Circumstance	*Even though* cable television has expanded, it is still unavailable in some rural areas.
because, since, so that	Causes or effects	*Because* the movie industry has changed, the way theaters are built has changed.
before, after, while, until, when	Time	*When* prices rise, demand falls.
whether, if, unless, even if	Condition	More people will purchase hybrid cars *if* these cars become less expensive.

Dependent clauses can also begin with a relative pronoun (*that, who, which*).

- Many medical doctors *who are affiliated with a teaching hospital* use interns in their practices.

To see how complex sentences can improve your writing, study the following two paragraphs:

Original
    Are you one of the many people who has tried to quit smoking? Well, don't give up trying. Help is here in the form of a nonprescription drug. A new nicotine patch has been developed. This patch will help you quit gradually. That way, you will experience less severe withdrawal symptoms. Quitting will be easier than ever before, but you need to be psychologically ready to quit smoking. Otherwise, you may not be successful.

Monotonous use of simple and compound sentences

Revised
    If you are one of the many people who has tried to quit smoking, don't give up trying. Help is now here in the form of a nonprescription nicotine patch, which has been developed to help you quit gradually. Because you experience less severe withdrawal symptoms, quitting is easier than ever before. However, for this patch to be successful, you need to be psychologically ready to quit.

Varied sentence types convey relationships among ideas.

4. Use compound-complex sentences occasionally to express complicated relationships. A **compound-complex sentence** contains one or more dependent clauses and two or more independent clauses.

- If you expect to study medicine, you must take courses in biology and chemistry, and you must prepare for four more years of study after college.

Use compound-complex sentences sparingly. When overused, they make your writing hard to follow.

EXERCISE 9.2

Combine each of the following sentence pairs into a single compound or complex sentence:

1. A day-care center may look respectable. Parents assume a day-care center is safe and run well.
2. In some states, the training required to become a day-care worker is minimal. On-the-job supervision and evaluation of day-care workers are infrequent.
3. Restaurants are often fined or shut down for minor hygiene violations. Day-care centers are rarely fined or closed down for hygiene violations.
4. More and more mothers have entered the workforce. The need for quality day care has increased dramatically.
5. Naturally, day-care workers provide emotional support for children. Few day-care workers are trained to provide intellectual stimulation.

How to vary sentence length.   If you vary sentence type, you often automatically vary sentence length as well. Simple sentences tend to be short, while compound and complex sentences tend to be longer. Compound-complex sentences tend to be the longest.

You can use sentence length to achieve a specific effect: Short sentences tend to be sharp and emphatic; they move ideas along quickly, creating a fast-paced essay. In the following example, a series of short sentences creates a dramatic pace:

- The jurors had little to debate. The incriminating evidence was clear and incontrovertible. The jury announced its verdict with astonishing speed.

Longer sentences, in contrast, move the reader more slowly through the essay. Notice that the lengthy sentence in this example suggests a leisurely, unhurried pace:

- While standing in line, impatient to ride the antique steam-powered train, the child begins to imagine how the train will crawl deliberately, endlessly, along the tracks, slowly gathering speed as it spews grayish steam and emits hissing noises.

How to vary sentence pattern.   A sentence is usually made up of one or more subjects, verbs, and modifiers. **Modifiers** are words (adjectives or adverbs), phrases, or clauses that describe or limit another part of the sentence (a noun, pronoun, verb, phrase, or clause). Here are some examples of modifiers in sentences:

Words as Modifiers	The *empty* classroom was unlocked. [adjective]
	The office runs *smoothly*. [adverb]
Phrases as Modifiers	The student *in the back* raised his hand.
	Schools should not have the right *to mandate community service*.
Clauses as Modifiers	The baseball *that flew into the stands* was caught by a fan.
	When the exam was over, I knew I had earned an A.

As you can see, the placement of modifiers may vary, depending on the pattern of the sentence.

1. Modifier last: subject-verb-modifier. The main message (expressed in the subject and verb) comes first, followed by information that clarifies or explains the message.

┌── subject ──┐┌ verb ┐┌── modifier ──┐
- The instructor walked into the room.

In some cases, a string of modifiers follows the subject and verb.

┌── subject ──┐┌── verb ──┐   ┌── modifier ──
- The salesperson demonstrated the word-processing software, creating and

deleting files, moving text, creating directories, and formatting tables.

2. Modifier first: modifier-subject-verb (periodic sentences). Information in the modifier precedes the main message, elaborating the main message but slowing the overall pace. The emphasis is on the main message at the end of the sentence.

┌────────── modifier ──────────┐┌ subject ┐ verb
- Tired and depressed from hours of work, the divers left the scene of the accident.

Use periodic sentences sparingly: Too many will make your writing sound stiff and unnatural.

3. Modifier in the middle: subject-modifier-verb. The modifier interrupts the main message and tends to slow the pace of the sentence. The emphasis is on the subject because it comes first in the sentence.

┌── subject ──┐┌────────── modifier ──────────┐ verb
- The paramedic, trained and experienced in water rescue, was first on the scene of the boating accident.

Avoid placing too many modifiers between the subject and verb in a sentence. Doing so may cause your reader to miss the sentence's key idea.

4. Modifiers used throughout.

┌────────── modifier ──────────┐┌────────── subject ──────────┐
- Because human organs are in short supply, awarding an organ transplant,

┌────────── modifier ──────────┐   ┌── verb ──┐
especially hearts and kidneys, to patients has become a controversial issue,

┌────────── modifier ──────────┐
requiring difficult medical and ethical decisions.

By varying the order of subjects, verbs, and modifiers, you can give emphasis where it is needed as well as vary sentence patterns as shown in the following paragraphs:

Original

Monotonous use of same subject-verb-modifier pattern

Theme parks are growing in number and popularity. Theme parks have a single purpose—to provide family entertainment centered around high-action activities. The most famous theme parks are Disney World and Disneyland. They serve as models for other, smaller parks. Theme parks always have amusement rides. Theme parks can offer other activities such as swimming. Theme parks will probably continue to be popular.

Revised

Ideas come alive through use of varied sentence patterns.

Theme parks are growing in number and popularity. Offering high-action activities, theme parks fulfill a single purpose—to provide family entertainment. The most famous parks, Disney World and Disneyland, serve as models for other, smaller parks. Parks always offer amusement rides, which appeal to both children and adults. Added attractions such as swimming, water slides, and boat rides provide thrills and recreation. Because of their family focus, theme parks are likely to grow in popularity.

EXERCISE 9.3

Add modifiers to the following sentences to create varied sentence patterns:

1. The divers jumped into the chilly waters.
2. The beach was closed because of pollution.
3. Coffee-flavored drinks are becoming popular.
4. The dorm was crowded and noisy.
5. The exam was more challenging than we expected.

Academic Writing: Are Sources Introduced Clearly and Integrated Smoothly?

Whenever you paraphrase, summarize, or use quotations to present ideas or information from a source, you will need to introduce the borrowed material. This brief introduction should convey why you are incorporating it—who the author is, what kind of work the borrowed material is from, or another brief explanation of why the borrowed material is relevant.

One strategy for working this kind of information into your writing is to include it as a modifier. Instead of tacking on a second sentence, add information about the author or the work from which you are borrowing as a phrase or clause following the author's name:

┌─────────────── phrase describing author's credentials ───────────────┐
Vishwanath, a researcher on fake social media profiles and president and chief
└───┘
technologist at Avant Research Group, argues that parents should teach their

children to protect themselves by carefully assessing social media connection

("friend") requests (p. 39).

This strategy allows you to incorporate the information readers need right where they need it.

For each of the sentence groups that follow, write one sentence that incorporates relevant information about the author. You do not need to include all the information provided; choose the information that best shows why readers should accept the statement as true. An example is provided for you.

Sentences to Combine   How students are labeled can affect their success in school.

Adam Alter is an assistant professor of marketing and psychology at New York University. Alter's research focuses on decision making.

▶ According to Adam Alter, a professor who studies decision making, how students are labeled can affect their success in school.

1. Bystanders of bullying can be divided into three groups: "confederates," who egg bullies on; the "co-victims," or the next in line to be bullied; and the "isolate," those who try to remain uninvolved.
   Ian Rivers is a professor of human development at Brunel University.
   Rivers is an expert on bullying.

2. A study reveals that *Pawn Stars* is the TV show viewers of all political persuasions most love to hate.
   Johanna Blakley is the director of research and managing director of the Norman Lear Center, a research center that focuses on the effect entertainment has on society.
   Blakley is an expert on the media habits of liberals and conservatives.

3. In general, parents do not discuss emotions (except anger) with their sons, so boys tend to grow up without being as aware of their emotions as girls are.
   Daniel Goleman has a Ph.D. in behavioral and brain sciences.
   Goleman has written three books on emotional intelligence.

4. Children as young as age two already have a sense that some items belong to them.
   Christian Jarrett has a Ph.D. in psychology.
   Jarrett writes for the British Psychological Society's magazine *The Psychologist*.

5. Human beings have a tendency to accept information at face value, especially when it reinforces beliefs they already hold.
   Joseph Paul Forgas is Sciencia Professor of Psychology at the University of New South Wales in Australia.
   Forgas studies how interactions with other people change in response to intellectual and emotional processes.

Are Your Sentences Parallel in Structure?

Parallelism means that similar ideas in a sentence are expressed in similar grammatical form. It means balancing words with words, phrases with phrases, and clauses with clauses. Parallel sentences flow smoothly and make your thoughts easy to follow. Study the following sentence pairs. Which sentence in each pair is easier to read?

- The horse was large, had a bony frame, and it was friendly.
- The horse was large, bony, and friendly.

- Maria enjoys swimming and sailboats.
- Maria enjoys swimming and sailing.

In each pair, the second sentence sounds better because it is balanced grammatically. *Large*, *bony*, and *friendly* are all adjectives. *Swimming* and *sailing* are nouns ending in *-ing*.

The following sentence elements should be parallel in structure:

1. **Nouns in a series**
   - A thesis statement, ~~that is clear,~~ ^{clear} strong supporting paragraphs, and ~~a~~ ^{an interesting} conclusion ~~that should be interesting~~ are all elements of a well-written essay.

2. **Adjectives in a series**
   - The concertgoers were rowdy and ~~making a great deal of noise.~~ ^{noisy.}

3. **Verbs in a series**
   - The sports fans jumped and ~~were applauding.~~ ^{applauded.}

4. **Phrases and clauses within a sentence**
   - The parents who supervised the new playground were pleased ~~about~~ ^{that} the preschoolers ~~playing~~ ^{played} congenially and that everyone enjoyed the sandbox.

5. **Items being compared**
   - It is usually better to study for an exam over a period of time than ~~cramming~~ ^{to cram} the night before.

EXERCISE 9.5

Edit the following sentences to eliminate problems with parallelism:

1. The biology student spent Saturday morning reviewing his weekly textbook assignments, writing a research report, and with lab reports.
2. The career counselor advised Althea to take several math courses and that she should also register for at least one computer course.
3. Three reasons for the popularity of fast-food restaurants are that they are efficient, offer reasonable prices, and most people like the food they serve.
4. Driving to Boston is as expensive as it is to take the train.
5. While at a stop sign, it is important first to look both ways and then proceeding with caution is wise.

Do Your Sentences Have Strong, Active Verbs?

Strong, active verbs make your writing lively and vivid. By contrast, *to be* verbs (*is*, *was*, *were*, *has been*, and so on) and other **linking verbs** (*feels, became, seems, appears*)—which connect a noun or pronoun to words that describe it—can make your writing sound dull. Linking verbs often contribute little meaning to a sentence. Whenever possible, use stronger, more active verbs.

"To Be" Verb	The puppy *was* afraid of thunder.
Action Verbs	The puppy *whimpered* and *quivered* during the thunderstorm.
Linking Verb	The child *looked* frightened as she boarded the bus for her first day of kindergarten.
Action Verbs	The child *trembled* and *clung* to her sister as she boarded the bus for her first day of kindergarten.

To strengthen your writing, use active verbs rather than passive verbs as much as possible. A **passive verb** is a form of the verb *to be* combined with a past participle (*surprised, chosen, elected*). In a sentence with a passive verb, the subject does not perform the action of the verb but instead receives the action. By contrast, in a sentence with an **active verb**, the subject performs the action.

Passive	It *was claimed* by the cyclist that the motorist failed to yield the right of way.
Active	The cyclist *claimed* that the motorist failed to yield the right of way.

Notice that the first sentence emphasizes the action of claiming, not the person who made the claim. In the second sentence, the person who made the claim is the subject.

Unless you decide deliberately to deemphasize the subject, try to avoid using passive verbs. On occasion, you may need to use passive verbs, however, to emphasize the object or person receiving the action.

- The Johnsons' house *was destroyed* by the flood.

Passive verbs may also be appropriate if you do not know or choose not to reveal who performed an action. Journalists often use passive verbs for this reason.

- It *was confirmed* late Tuesday that Senator Kraemer is resigning.

EXERCISE 9.6

Edit the following sentences by changing passive verbs to active ones, adding a subject when necessary:

1. Songs about peace were composed by folk singers in the 1960s.
2. The exam was thought to be difficult because it covered thirteen chapters.
3. For water conservation, it is recommended that low-water-consumption dishwashers be purchased.
4. The new satellite center was opened by the university so that students could attend classes nearer their homes.
5. In aggressive telemarketing sales calls, the consumer is urged by the caller to make an immediate decision before prices change.

For your essay in progress (the one you worked on in Chapters 6, 7, and 8) or any essay you are working on, evaluate and edit your sentences.

Analyze Your Word Choice

Each word in your essay contributes to your essay's meaning. Consequently, when you are revising, be sure to analyze your word choice, or **diction** (see Figure 9.1). The words you choose should suit your purpose, audience, tone, and genre. This section describes four aspects of word choice to consider as you evaluate and revise your essay:

1. Tone and level of diction
2. Word connotations
3. Concrete and specific language
4. Figures of speech

FIGURE 9.1   Flowchart for Evaluating Your Word Choice

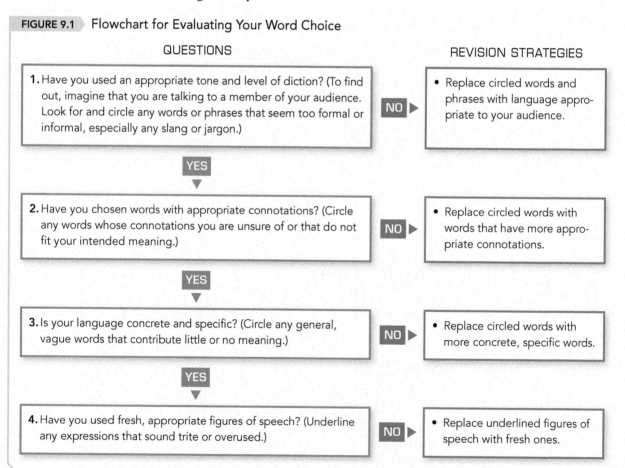

QUESTIONS

REVISION STRATEGIES

1. Have you used an appropriate tone and level of diction? (To find out, imagine that you are talking to a member of your audience. Look for and circle any words or phrases that seem too formal or informal, especially any slang or jargon.)

NO ▶
- Replace circled words and phrases with language appropriate to your audience.

YES ▼

2. Have you chosen words with appropriate connotations? (Circle any words whose connotations you are unsure of or that do not fit your intended meaning.)

NO ▶
- Replace circled words with words that have more appropriate connotations.

YES ▼

3. Is your language concrete and specific? (Circle any general, vague words that contribute little or no meaning.)

NO ▶
- Replace circled words with more concrete, specific words.

YES ▼

4. Have you used fresh, appropriate figures of speech? (Underline any expressions that sound trite or overused.)

NO ▶
- Replace underlined figures of speech with fresh ones.

Are Your Tone and Level of Diction Appropriate?

Imagine that as a technician at a computer software company, you discover a time-saving shortcut for installing the company's best-selling software program. Your supervisor asks you to describe your discovery and how it works for two audiences—your fellow technicians at the company and customers who might purchase the program. Would you say the same thing in the same way? Definitely not. Your writing would differ not only in content but also in tone and level of diction. The writing addressed to the other technicians would be technical and concise, explaining how to use the shortcut and why it works. The writing directed to customers would praise the discovery, mention the time customers will save, and explain in nontechnical terms how to use the shortcut.

Tone refers to how you sound to your readers. Your word choice should be consistent with your tone. When writing to the technicians, you would use a direct, matter-of-fact tone. When writing to the customers, your tone would be enthusiastic. There are three common **levels of diction**: formal, popular, and informal.

For more about tone, see "Analyze the Author's Tone" in Chapter 3.

HOW WRITERS READ ▶ TONE	
	Tone contributes to and affects meaning, and tone can be a sign of the writer's approach or attitude toward the subject. Use these strategies to identify tone:
BEFORE READING	• Read the headnote to get a sense of where the writer commonly publishes; academic writers and writers who contribute to serious newspapers (like *The New York Times*) often strive for a serious, neutral tone.
WHILE READING	• Pay attention to the title, which often sets or at least provides a clue to the writer's tone. • Read the introduction with care. Writers often try to capture the reader's attention in the introduction, so it is often a place where the writer's attitude toward the topic is clearest. • If you see a word, phrase, or sentence that clearly establishes the tone (because, for example, it uses words with rich connotations), highlight or annotate it for later reference.
AFTER READING	• Think about how the selection's tone shaped your response to the essay. Did the tone make the reading seem trustworthy, sarcastic, concerned, or mean-spirited, for example? Did it enhance or undermine your trust for the writer? • Consider how tone and purpose are related. Given the writer's purpose, did the tone seem appropriate?

Formal diction.   The **formal** level of diction is serious and dignified. Think of it as the kind of language that judges use in interpreting laws, presidents employ when greeting foreign dignitaries, or speakers choose for commencement addresses. Formal diction is often written in the third person, tends to include long sentences and multisyllabic words, and contains no slang or contractions. It has a slow, rhythmic flow and an authoritative, distant, and impersonal tone. Here is an example taken from *The*

Federalist, No. 51, a political tract written by James Madison in 1788 to explain constitutional theory:

> It is of great importance in a republic, not only to guard the society against the oppression of its rulers, but to guard one part of the society against the injustice of the other part. Different interests necessarily exist in different classes of citizens. If a majority be united by a common interest, the rights of the minority will be insecure.

Formal diction is also used in scholarly publications, operation manuals, and most academic fields. Notice in the following excerpt from a chemistry textbook that the language is concise, exact, and marked by specialized terms, called *jargon*, used within the particular field of study. The examples of jargon are in italics.

> A *catalyst* is classified as *homogeneous* if it is present in the same *phase* as that of the *reactants*. For reactants that are *gases*, a *homogeneous catalyst* is also a *gas*.
>
> —Atkins and Perkins, *Chemistry: Molecules, Matter, and Change*

Popular diction.   **Popular**, or casual, diction is common in magazines and newspapers. It sounds more conversational and personal than formal diction. In popular diction, sentences tend to be shorter and less varied than in formal diction. The first person (*I, me, mine, we*) or second person (*you, your*) may be used. Consider this example taken from a popular arts magazine, *Paste*:

> "Concert for George" pays tribute to not only one of the greatest musicians in history, but one of the freakin' Beatles.
>
> —Wyndham Wyeth, "The 11 Best Concert Films"

Informal diction.   **Informal** diction, also known as *colloquial language*, is the language of everyday speech and conversation. It is friendly and casual. Contractions (*wasn't, I'll*), slang expressions (*selfie, YOLO, tat*), sentence fragments, and first-person and second-person pronouns are all common. Informal diction should not be used in essays and academic writing, except when it is part of a quotation or a block of dialogue. Also inappropriate for essays and academic writing is the use of language shortcuts typically used in email and texting. These include abbreviations (*u* for *you, r* for *are*) and emojis (☺).

Here is an example of informal diction. Notice the use of the first person, slang expressions, and a loose sentence structure.

> This guy in my history class is a psycho. He doesn't let anybody talk but him. I mean, this guy interrupts all the time. Never raises his hand. He drives us nuts—what a loser.

Diction in academic writing.   When you write academic papers, essays, and exams, you should use formal diction and avoid flowery or wordy language. Here are some guidelines:

- Use the third person (*he, she, it*) rather than the first person (*I, we*), unless you are expressing a personal opinion.
- Use standard vocabulary, not slang or a regional or ethnic dialect.

- Use correct grammar, spelling, and punctuation.
- Aim for a clear, direct, and forthright tone.

One of the most common mistakes students make in academic writing is trying too hard to sound "academic." Be sure to avoid writing stiff, overly formal sentences, using big words just for the sake of it, and expressing ideas indirectly.

Inappropriate Diction

Who among us would be so bold as to venture to deny that inequities are rampant in our ailing health- and medical-care system? People of multiethnic composition overwhelmingly receive health care that is not only beneath the standard one would expect, but even in some cases threatening to their very lives. An abundance of research studies and clinical trials prove beyond a doubt that a person of non-European descent residing in the United States of America cannot rely on doctors, nurses, physician assistants, nurse practitioners, and other health-care workers to provide treatment free of invidious discrimination.

Language is stiff and pompous.

Revised Diction

Who can deny that inequities are common in our ailing medical care system? Racial and ethnic minorities receive health care that is substandard and in some cases life-threatening. Many research studies and clinical trials demonstrate that minorities in the United States cannot rely on doctors, nurses, physician assistants, nurse practitioners, and other health-care workers to provide unbiased treatment.

Language is formal but clear.

EXERCISE 9.7

Revise the following informal statement by giving it a more formal level of diction:

My first trip to Los Angeles was amazing! We hung out with surfer dudes and seals in Malibu, checked out Marilyn Monroe's hand prints outside Grauman's Chinese Theatre, bumped into Donald Duck at Disney Land, and a whole lot more. Really, we couldn't have had a more awesome vacation.

Do You Use Words with Appropriate Connotations?

Many words have two levels of meaning—a denotative meaning and a connotative meaning. A word's **denotation** is its precise dictionary definition. For example, the denotative meaning of the word *mother* is "female parent." A word's **connotation** is the collection of feelings and attitudes the word evokes—its emotional colorings or shades of meaning. A word's connotation may vary from one person to another. One common connotation of *mother* is a warm, caring person. Some people, however, may think of a mother as someone with strong authoritarian control. Similarly, the phrase *horror films* may conjure up memories of scary but fun-filled evenings for some people and terrifying experiences for others.

For more about analyzing connotative meanings, see "Consider Denotation versus Connotation" in Chapter 3.

Since the connotations of words can elicit a wide range of responses, be sure the words you choose convey only the meanings you intend. In each pair of words that follows, notice that the two words have a similar denotation but different connotations:

artificial/fake   firm/stubborn   lasting/endless

EXERCISE 9.8

Describe the different connotations of the three words in each group of words.

1. crowd/mob/gathering
2. proverb/motto/saying
3. prudent/penny-pinching/frugal
4. token/gift/keepsake
5. display/show/expose

Do You Use Concrete Language?

Specific words convey much more information than general words. The following examples show how you might move from general to specific word choices:

General	Less General	More Specific	Specific
store	department store	Sears	Sears at the Galleria Mall
music	popular music	country rock music	Taylor Swift's "ME!"

Concrete words add life and meaning to your writing. In each of the following sentence pairs, notice how the underlined words in the first sentence provide little information, whereas those in the second sentence provide interesting details.

General	Our <u>vacation</u> was <u>great fun</u>.
Concrete	Our <u>rafting trip</u> was filled with <u>adventure</u>.

General	The <u>red and white flowers</u> were blooming in our yard.
Concrete	<u>Crimson and white petunias</u> were blooming in our yard.

Suppose you are writing about a shopping mall that has outlived its usefulness. Instead of saying "a number of stores were unoccupied, and those that were still in business were shabby," you could describe the mall in concrete, specific terms that would enable your readers to visualize it.

The vacant storefronts with "For Rent" signs plastered across the glass, the half-empty racks in the stores that were still open, and the empty corridors suggested that the mall was soon to close.

Revise the following sentences by adding concrete, specific details:

1. The book I took on vacation was exciting reading.
2. The students watched as the instructor entered the lecture hall.
3. The vase in the museum was an antique.
4. At the crime scene, the reporter questioned the witnesses.
5. Although the shop was closed, we expected someone to return at any moment.

Do You Use Fresh, Appropriate Figures of Speech?

A **figure of speech** is a word or phrase that makes sense imaginatively or creatively but not literally. For example, if you say "the movie was *a roller coaster ride*," you do not mean the movie was an actual ride. Rather, you mean it was thrilling, just like a ride on a roller coaster. This figure of speech, like many others, compares two seemingly unlike objects or situations by finding one point of similarity.

Fresh and imaginative figures of speech can help you create vivid images for your readers. However, overused figures of speech can detract from your essay. Be sure to avoid **clichés** (trite or overused expressions) such as *blind as a bat, green with envy, bite the bullet,* or *sick as a dog.*

Three common figures of speech are simile, metaphor, and personification. A **simile** uses words such as *like* or *as* to make a direct comparison of two unlike things.

The child acts *like a tiger.*

The noise in a crowded high school cafeteria is as deafening *as a caucus of crows.*

A **metaphor** also compares unlike things but does not use *like* or *as.* Instead, the comparison is implied.

That child is a tiger.

If you're born in America with black skin, you're born in prison.

—Malcolm X, "Interview"

Personification describes an idea or object by giving it human qualities.

A sailboat devours money.

In this example, the ability to eat is ascribed to an inanimate object, the sailboat.

When you edit an essay, look for and eliminate overused figures of speech, replacing them with creative, fresh images. If you have not used any figures of speech, look instead for descriptions that could be improved by using a simile, a metaphor, or personification.

For more on figures of speech, see "Description Uses Comparison" in Chapter 12.

Invent fresh figures of speech for two items in the following list:

1. Parents of a newborn baby
2. A lengthy supermarket line or a traffic jam
3. A relative's old refrigerator
4. A man and woman obviously in love
5. Your team's star quarterback or important player

For the essay you worked on in Essay in Progress 1, use Figure 9.1 to evaluate and edit your word choice.

Proofread Carefully

When you are satisfied with your edited words and sentences, you are ready for the final step of the writing process—*proofreading*. By proofreading, you make sure your essay is error free and presented in acceptable manuscript format. Your goals are to catch and correct surface errors—such as errors in grammar, punctuation, spelling, and mechanics—as well as keyboarding or typographical errors. An essay that is free of surface errors gives readers a favorable impression of the essay and of you as its writer.

Spotting errors is easier when working with a clean, printed copy, so start with a fresh printout. Do not attempt to work with a previously marked-up copy or on a computer screen. Be sure to double-space the copy to allow room to mark corrections between lines.

Use the following suggestions to produce an error-free essay:

1. **Review your paper once for each type of error.** Because it is difficult to spot all types of surface errors simultaneously, read your essay several times, each time focusing on *one* error type—errors in spelling, punctuation, grammar, mechanics, and so on. Then read once more, focusing on just the errors you make most often. (Keep a list of your most common errors in your writing journal, and update it as each assignment is returned.)
2. **Read your essay backward, from the last sentence to the first.** Reading in this way will help you spot errors without being distracted by the flow of ideas.
3. **Use the spell-check and grammar-check functions cautiously.** The spell-check function can help you spot some—but not all—spelling and keyboarding errors. For example, it cannot detect the difference in meaning between *there* and *their* or *to* and *too*. Similarly, the grammar-check function can identify only certain kinds of errors and is not a reliable substitute for a careful proofreading.
4. **Read your essay aloud.** By reading aloud slowly, you can catch certain errors that sound awkward, such as missing words, errors in verb tense, and errors in the singular or plural forms of nouns.
5. **Ask a classmate to proofread your paper.** Another reader may spot errors you have overlooked.

STUDENTS WRITE

Recall that Latrisha Wilson's essay, "No Place Left for Privacy," was developed, drafted, and revised in the Students Write sections of Chapters 5, 6, 7, and 8. Below is a body paragraph from a second draft of Wilson's essay with her final editing and proofreading changes shown. The reasons for each change, identified by number, are noted in the margin. The final draft of Wilson's essay, with these changes incorporated into it, appears in the "Students Write" for Chapter 8 (pp. 198–200).

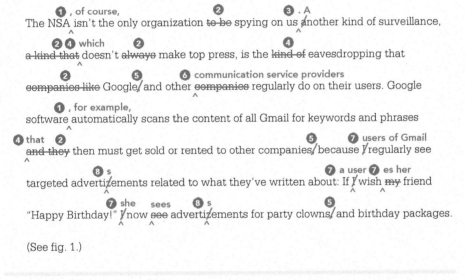

(See fig. 1.)

PART THREE

Patterns of Development

10

An Introduction to Patterns of Development

Vova Pomortzeff/Alamy

Writing Quick Start

ANALYZE   Study the photograph. It presents an unusual situation, and there are numerous possible interpretations of what is happening.

WRITE   After identifying your writing situation (your purpose, or reason for writing; the audience you are trying to reach; the genre, or type, of text you will create; and the medium in which the text will be read), write a paragraph explaining one possible scenario that explains what is happening.

CONNECT   Because the photograph is open to interpretation, there are numerous ways you could plan, develop, and organize your paragraph. For example, if you wanted to express your thoughts and feelings to your friends, you might have texted them a story about what the people in the photograph are doing or how they got there (*narration*). If you were writing an exam for your biology instructor, you might have described the changes in the physiology of the woman in response to environmental cues (*process analysis*) or analyzed the differences in responses of the woman and the group of people observing her (*comparison and contrast*). If you were writing a response to the photograph for a composition class, you might have described how the winter scene looked, felt, and sounded from the perspective of the scantily clad woman or one of the furred and booted group of observers (*description*).

Likewise, in many writing situations, you have a wide range of choices of what to write about and how to write it. This chapter explains how to use patterns of development to organize both your ideas and how you express them.

Many paragraphs and essays use specific **patterns of development** (also called **rhetorical modes**, or just **modes**) like narration, process analysis, and comparison or contrast, because they help the writer to

- devise a strong thesis or topic sentence
- select appropriate evidence
- create a unified paragraph or essay

The patterns also help readers learn and remember by, say, comparing something they know well with something unfamiliar or describing a place they've never been so that they can picture it.

While some authors write essays that focus mainly on a single mode, many others create essays from paragraphs in a variety of patterns, choosing among the patterns that will best help them achieve their goals. In the chapters in Parts 3 and 4, you will read essays that focus mainly on one mode but may also use a variety of patterns to supplement the main one. As you read these essays and write your own mixed-mode essay later in this chapter, think about how writers use patterns to achieve their goals.

Understand the Patterns of Development

The most common patterns of development are

- narration
- description
- illustration (or exemplification)
- process analysis
- comparison and contrast

- classification and division
- definition
- cause and effect
- argument

Narration Tells a Story

Narration uses a sequence of events—a story—to make a point. The following excerpt from a narrative essay tells the story of one man's experience with the police:

Example   Friday for me usually means a trip to the bank, errands, the gym, dinner, and then off to the theater. On this particular day, I decided to break my pattern of getting up and running right out of the house. Instead, I took my time, slowed my pace, and splurged by making strawberry pancakes. Before I knew it, it was 2:45; my bank closes at 3:30, leaving me less than 45 minutes to get to midtown Manhattan on the train. I was pressed for time but in a relaxed, blessed state of mind. When I walked through the lobby of my building, I noticed two light-skinned Hispanic men I'd never seen before. Not thinking much of it, I continued on to the vestibule, which is separated from the lobby by a locked door.

—Alton Fitzgerald White, "Right Place, Wrong Face" (para. 5, p. 244)*

*Text Credit: Alton Fitzgerald White. "Rag Time, My Time." *The Nation*, November 10, 1999. Copyright © 1999 The Nation. All rights reserved. Used under license.

When to use it. Use narration when you want readers to learn something by experiencing an episode or sequence of events. In the Writing Quick Start, you could use narration to tell a story of how the people in the photos got to their location. You might begin with their decision to go out walking and end at the moment the photo was taken.

Description Creates a Word Picture

Description uses words that appeal to the five senses. The following excerpt from a descriptive essay uses words that appeal to the senses to convey the appearance of a homeless man:

Example   He sat on the sidewalk, leaning with his back against the side of a brick building, wearing a filthy, gray tank-top and dingy cargo pants with rips in the knees. His hair was dirty and wild, barely restrained by a flimsy elastic tie. He wasn't begging; his exposed knees were pulled up to his chest and his head was cradled in his arms, hidden from view. His shoulders shook slightly from quiet sobs but he didn't bother anyone passing him on the sidewalk.

—Maia Nault, "Sometimes, We Give" (para. 6, p. 289)

When to use it. Use description when you want to emphasize the sensory aspects of an object or experience. In the Writing Quick Start, you could use description to convey in detail what the winter landscape looked, sounded, felt, or even smelled like.

Illustration Explains with Examples

Illustration uses examples to explain unfamiliar topics, concepts, or terms. In the following excerpt from an illustration essay, the author provides a specific example (*illustration*) to support his thesis that road rage represents a decline in civilized society:

Example   A most amazing example of driver rage occurred recently at the Manhattan end of the Lincoln Tunnel. We were four cars abreast, stopped at a traffic light. And there was no moving even when the light had changed. A bus had stopped in the cross traffic, blocking our paths: it was a normal-for-New-York-City gridlock. Perhaps impatient, perhaps late for important appointments, three of us nonetheless accepted what, after all, we could not alter. One, however, would not. He would not be helpless. He would go where he was going even if he couldn't get there. A Wall Street type in suit and tie, he got out of his car and strode toward the bus, rapping smartly on its doors. When they opened, he exchanged words with the driver. The doors folded shut. He then stepped in front of the bus, took hold of one of its large windshield wipers and broke it.

—Martin Gottfried, "Rambos of the Road" (para. 8, p. 315)

When to use it. Use illustration when you want to provide specific, sometimes extended, examples to support your thesis statement. You could use the photo in the Writing Quick Start as inspiration for an essay about how global warming is changing the environment; you might cite average temperatures over the last fifty years and provide examples of how changes have affected plants and animals.

Process Analysis Explains How Something Works or Is Done

Process analysis explains step by step how something works, is done, or is made. In the following excerpt from a how-to essay, the writer describes her process for writing restaurant reviews:

Example   I used to write food reviews for *California* magazine before it folded. . . . First, I'd go to a restaurant several times with a few opinionated, articulate friends in tow. I'd sit there writing down everything anyone said that was at all interesting or funny. Then on the following Monday I'd sit down at my desk with my notes and try to write the review. Even after I'd been doing this for years, panic would set in. I'd try to write a lead, but instead I'd write a couple of dreadful sentences, XX them out, try again, XX everything out, and then feel despair and worry settle on my chest like an x-ray apron. . . . Finally, I would pick up my one-inch picture frame, stare into it as if for the answer, and every time the answer would come: all I had to do was to write a really shitty first draft of, say, the opening paragraph. And no one was going to see it.

—Anne Lamott, "Shitty First Drafts" (para. 5, p. 348)

When to use it.   Use process analysis when you want to provide step-by-step instructions or a part-by-part analysis. In the Writing Quick Start, you might discuss the physiological changes a swimmer in the polar bear club would experience before, during, and after an icy plunge.

Comparison and Contrast Shows Similarities and Differences

Writers compare or contrast to examine closely what two things have in common or what their differences are. Many essays use both comparison and contrast. In the following excerpt, the authors compare one aspect of the differences between pockets in men's and women's jeans:

Example   Predictably, skinny jeans, which more closely hug the hips, have smaller front pockets for both men and women, but the gap between women's and men's jeans is still noticeable in both skinny and straight styles. On average, women's skinny jean pockets were 3.5 inches (48%) shorter and 0.3 inches (6%) narrower than men's skinny jeans. Women's straight jean pockets were 3.4 inches (46%) shorter and 0.6 inches (10%) narrower.

—Jan Diehm and Amber Thomas, "Pockets" (para. 6, p. 385)

When to use it.   Use comparison and contrast to provide an in-depth analysis that explores the similarities and/or differences between two or more people, places, things, experiences, concepts, arguments, and so on. In the Writing Quick Start, there is opportunity to compare physiological differences between the woman in the swimsuit and her companions in heavy coats and hats.

Classification Categorizes Items, and Division Separates an Item into Parts

Classification sorts people, things, or ideas into groups; division takes a single item and breaks it down into parts. In the following excerpt from a classification essay, the writer classifies bystanders of bullying into three categories:

Example   Together with colleagues from Boston College in the United States (V. Paul Poteat) and York St. John University in the United Kingdom (Nathalie Noret), I have attempted to better understand the "mindset" of the bystander, in the hope that it will provide me with further clues as to why bullying continues, despite forty years of research and intervention. In essence, this research has resulted in a recasting of the role of the bystander into three very distinct types of pupil: the confederate, the co-victim, and the isolate. These three types are very different from the pupil who does not engage; these are pupils who are desperate to avoid the torment being meted out on their classmate. This is not rocket science, but it does highlight a flaw in much of the research that has gone before: Without taking into account the experiences of bystanders, we may have underplayed the lasting impact that bullying can have on individuals and the school community.

—Ian Rivers, "Empower Pupils to Beat the Bullies" (para. 2, p. 440)

When to use it.   Use classification or division when you want to look closely at the subcategories or parts of a particular topic. In the Writing Quick Start, you might classify people in terms of how likely they are to indulge in extreme sports, such as swimming in icy waters.

Extended Definition Explains How a Term Is Used or What It Means

An extended definition explains in detail how a term is used or differentiates among its shades of meaning. To define a term fully, writers frequently need to use other patterns of development as well. In this example, the writer not only defines the term *gullibility* briefly; he also uses illustration (the April Fools' example), comparison and contrast (gullibility versus credulity), and cause and effect (the realization that it's April Fools' Day causes skepticism to take hold).

Example   Gullibility is a tendency to be easily manipulated into believing something is true when it isn't. Credulity is closely related, a willingness to believe unlikely propositions with no evidence behind them. April Fools' tricks often work because they exploit our baseline inclination to accept direct communications from others as reliable and trustworthy. When a colleague tells you the boss wants to see you immediately, the first, automatic reaction is to believe them. Once we realize this is April 1, a more critical mindset will increase our threshold of acceptance and trigger more thorough processing. Rejection is then likely unless there is strong corroborating evidence.

—Joseph Paul Forgas, "Why Are Some People More Gullible Than Others?" (para. 2, p. 455)

When to use it. Use an extended definition when you want to conduct a close analysis of a word, phrase, concept, or phenomenon. In the Writing Quick Start, you might use the photo as a jumping-off point to define the term *adventure tourism*, which means traveling to participate in physically challenging outdoor activities.

Cause and Effect Uses Reasons or Results to Explain

Causes are the reasons that an event or phenomenon happens, and effects are what happen because of the event or phenomenon. Often, causes and effects are discussed together. The following excerpt explains the effects of recognizing the three types of bystanders to bullying:

> **Example**   So what do we learn if we recast the bystander in these three roles? We learn that the confederates of the bully may not be the mythical monsters we have demonized, but pupils who experience a great deal of emotional turmoil, such as feelings of self-loathing. This can lead to a series of harmful outcomes for all involved, such as an escalation in violence perpetrated against the victim (ironically to maintain a positive self-image), substance use, or truancy.
>
> —Ian Rivers, "Empower Pupils to Beat the Bullies" (para. 3, p. 440)

When to use it. Use cause and effect to show how one (or more) thing(s) leads to another or many other things. In the Writing Quick Start, you might use the photo as inspiration for writing about what motivates some people to join the polar bear club on its annual New Year's plunge.

Argument Takes and Supports a Position

Writers use arguments to persuade readers to adopt (or at least to consider) their position on an issue. In the following excerpt from an argument essay, the author tries to persuade readers that the system of tipping is flawed and offers evidence to support that claim:

> **Example**   But the system [of tipping] is flawed. Tips are paid after the service is provided, allowing opportunistic generosity of others. Society tries to stop this by imposing a strong social norm on diners—tip much less than 15–20% and either be engulfed with shame, or face disapproval from your date. But this strong social norm undermines the original rationale for tips as a way to incentivize excellent service. Studies of tipping have found that diners do part with more cash when they feel they have been better served, but not much. A study from 2000 (Lynn and McCall) found that differences in customer-service ratings accounted for only 1–5% of the variation in dining parties' tips. So much for performance-related pay. A country like Japan, where tipping is seen as rude and the service is excellent, shows that you don't need to tip to be well-looked-after.
>
> —S. K. (*The Economist*), "The Case against Tipping" (para. 4, pp. 552–53)

When to use it. Use argumentation when you are trying to convince your readers that your point of view is correct or when you want them to take action. In the Writing Quick Start, you might argue that taking a swim in freezing water in winter is a challenge more people should experience.

Combine the Patterns

Some essays use only one major pattern, but many writers combine several patterns to engage their readers and support their ideas. For example, an essay may mainly tell a story (the primary pattern), but it may also include description and illustration (secondary patterns). The following excerpt is from an essay that mainly uses cause and effect but also uses several other patterns of development:

Narration: The writer tells the story of restaurant meals.

Description: The writer helps you picture the child's behavior.

Process: The writer explains how they proceeded through a meal.

Comparison and Contrast: The writer contrasts her child's behavior with that of French children.

We ate breakfast at the hotel, but we had to eat lunch and dinner at the little seafood restaurants around the old port. We quickly discovered that having two restaurant meals a day with a toddler deserved to be its own circle of hell.

Bean would take a brief interest in the food, but within minutes she was spilling salt shakers and tearing apart sugar packets. Then she demanded to be sprung from her high chair so she could dash around the restaurant and bolt dangerously toward the docks.

Our strategy was to finish the meal quickly. We ordered while being seated, then begged the server to rush out some bread and bring us our appetizers and main courses at the same time. While my husband took a few bites of fish, I made sure Bean didn't get kicked by a waiter or lost at sea. Then we switched. We left enormous, apologetic tips to compensate for the arc of torn napkins and calamari around the table.

After a few more harrowing restaurant visits, I started noticing that the French families around us didn't look like they were sharing our mealtime agony. Weirdly, they looked like they were on vacation. French toddlers were sitting contentedly in their high chairs, waiting for their food, or eating fish and even vegetables. There was no shrieking or whining. And there was no debris around their tables.

—Pamela Druckerman, *Bringing Up Bébé*

Recognizing that many writers combine patterns, Chapters 11–20 offer readings that focus primarily on a single mode but that also show multiple patterns at work in a single essay.

PREWRITING   DRAFTING   REVISING   EDITING & PROOFREADING

A Guided Writing Assignment*

MULTIPLE PATTERNS OF DEVELOPMENT

PREWRITING

1 **Choose and narrow a topic, and select a main pattern of organization.**

Chapter 4 can help you narrow your topic. Many essays benefit from following **one dominant pattern** of organization. Select the major pattern of organization that best fits your **purpose**.

2 **Write a preliminary thesis, and generate details to support it.**

Chapter 5 can help with devising a thesis and generating details. You may also want to consult the chapter in Part 3 or 4 that corresponds to your main mode of development.

3 **Determine which secondary patterns will help you support your thesis.**

The idea-generating strategies from **Chapter 4**, especially using the modes of development, can help you flesh out your ideas with specific evidence. Be cautious about using too many patterns of organization, though, because doing so can make your essay difficult to follow.

DRAFTING

4 **Prepare a graphic organizer or an outline of your essay.**

Make sure your graphic organizer or outline

- clearly indicates the essay's **organization** and each paragraph's **relationship to the thesis statement**
- includes only details that **support your thesis**

The chapter in Part 3 or 4 that corresponds to your main mode of development can provide a model graphic organizer.

5 **Keep your purpose and audience in mind.**

Do not worry about grammar or spelling at this point. Instead, focus on the following:

- using **supporting details** that help you achieve your purpose with your readers
- making sure your **introduction** and **conclusion signal your primary pattern** of organization, so readers know what to expect or experience a satisfying sense of closure
- using **transitions** to signal that you are moving from one pattern to another, so readers can follow your train of thought

* The writing process is *recursive*; that is, you may find yourself revising as you draft or prewriting as you revise. This is especially true when writing on a computer. Your writing process may also differ from that of your classmates or may vary depending on the assignment.

6 Evaluate your draft and revise as necessary.

As you reread your essay, ask yourself questions like these:

- Have I **fully developed** my primary pattern?
- Have I **effectively used secondary patterns** to support my thesis?

Then ask a classmate or friend to read your essay and answer your questions. Refer to **Chapter 8** for help with revising, and use the **flowchart for revising essays** from **Chapters 11 to 20** that corresponds to your main pattern of development.

7 Edit the words and sentences of your essay, and then proofread carefully.

As you edit your essay, ask yourself questions like these:

- Are my sentences **concise**, **varied** (in type, length, and sentence pattern), and **parallel**?
- Do they use **strong active verbs**?
- Are my words at an appropriate **level of diction** for my readers?
- Do I use concrete language, with appropriate **connotations** and fresh **figures of speech**?

As you **proofread**, look for errors in **grammar**, **punctuation**, and **spelling**. Look for the kinds of errors you regularly make, and do not rely too heavily on spell- or grammar-checkers, which can lead you astray.

For additional help, refer to **Chapter 9**, "Editing Sentences and Words," and to the guided writing assignment in the chapter that corresponds to your main pattern of development.

In the following reading, note how the author effectively combines multiple patterns of organization.

READING

Against Forgetting: Where Have All the Animals Gone?

Derrick Jensen

Derrick Jensen writes about environmental issues for a number of publications, including *Audubon* and *The Sun Magazine*. He is the author of *Resistance against Empire* (2010), *Truths among Us: Conversations on Building a New Culture* (2011), and *The Myth of Human Supremacy* (2016). This article originally appeared in *Orion* (July/August 2013). According to the magazine's mission statement, "It is *Orion*'s fundamental conviction that humans are morally responsible for the world in which we live and that the individual comes to sense this responsibility as he or she develops a personal bond with nature."

Before Reading

1. **Preview:** Use the steps listed in Chapter 2.
2. **Connect:** Ask yourself questions, such as "Why do you think animal species are declining?"

While Reading Notice how the author uses a variety of patterns and consider why he is doing so.

After Reading To examine the author's use of multiple patterns, list the items he compares, the terms he defines, the examples he offers, the causes and effects he identifies, and the argument he makes.

Last night a host of nonhuman neighbors paid me a visit. First, two gray foxes sauntered up, including an older female who lost her tail to a leghold trap six or seven years ago. They trotted back into a thicker part of the forest, and a few minutes later a raccoon ambled forward. After he left I saw the two foxes again. Later, they went around the right side of a redwood tree as a black bear approached around the left. He sat on the porch for a while, and then walked off into the night. Then the foxes returned, hung out, and, when I looked away for a moment then looked back, they were gone. It wasn't too long before the bear returned to lie on the porch. After a brief nap, he went away. The raccoon came back and brought two friends. When they left the foxes returned, and after the foxes came the bear. The evening was like a French farce: As one character exited stage left, another entered stage right.

Although I see some of these nonhuman neighbors daily, I was entranced and delighted to see so many of them over the span of just one evening. I remained delighted until sometime the next day, when I remembered reading that, prior to conquest by the Europeans, people in this region could expect to see a grizzly bear every 15 minutes.

This phenomenon is something we all encounter daily, even if some of us rarely notice it. It happens often enough to have a name: declining baselines. The phrase describes the process of becoming accustomed to and accepting as normal worsening conditions. Along with normalization can come a forgetting that things were not always this way. And this can lead to further acceptance and further normalization, which leads to further amnesia, and so on. Meanwhile the world is killed, species by species, biome by biome. And we are happy when we see the ever-dwindling number of survivors.

I've gone on the salmon-spawning tours that local environmentalists give, and I'm not the only person who by the end is openly weeping. If we're lucky, we see 15 fish. Prior to conquest there were so many fish the rivers were described as "black and roiling." And it's not just salmon. Only five years ago, whenever I'd pick up a piece of firewood, I'd have to take off a half-dozen sowbugs. It's taken me all winter this year to see as many. And I used to go on spider patrol before I took a shower, in order to remove them to safety before the deluge. I still go on spider patrol, but now it's mostly pro forma. The spiders are gone. My mother used to put up five hummingbird feeders, and the birds would fight over those. Now she puts up two, and as often as not the sugar ferments before anyone eats it. I used to routinely see bats in the summer. Last year I saw one.

You can transpose this story to wherever you live and whatever members of   5
the nonhuman community live there with you. I was horrified a few years ago to
read that many songbird populations on the Atlantic Seaboard have collapsed by
up to 80 percent over the last 40 years. But, and this is precisely the point, I was
even more horrified when I realized that *Silent Spring* came out more than 40 years
ago, so this 80 percent decline followed an already huge decline caused by pesti-
cides, which followed another undoubtedly huge decline caused by the deforesta-
tion, conversion to agriculture, and urbanization that followed conquest.

My great-grandmother grew up in a sod house in Nebraska. When she was a   6
tiny girl—in other words, only four human generations ago—there were still
enough wild bison on the Plains that she was afraid lightning storms would spook
them and they would trample her home. Who in Nebraska today worries about
being trampled by bison? For that matter, who in Nebraska today even thinks
about bison on a monthly, much less daily, basis?

This state of affairs is problematic for many reasons, not the least of which is   7
that it's harder to fight for what you don't love than for what you do, and it's hard
to love what you don't know you're missing. *It's harder still to fight an injustice you do
not perceive as an injustice* but rather as just the way things are. How can you fight
an injustice you never think about because it never occurs to you that things have
ever been any different?

Declining baselines apply not only to the environment but to many fields.   8
Take surveillance. Back in the 1930s, there were people who freaked out at the
notion of being assigned a Social Security number, as it was "a number that will
follow you from cradle to grave." But since 9/11, according to former National Security Agency official William Binney, the U.S. government has been retaining every
email sent, in case any of us ever does anything the government doesn't like. How
many people complain about that? And it's not just the government. I received
spam birthday greetings this year from all sorts of commercial websites. How and
why does ESPN.com have my birth date? And remember the fight about GMOs?
They were perceived as scary (because they are), and now they're all over the place,
but most people don't know or don't care. The same goes for nanotechnology.

Yesterday I ate a strawberry. Or rather, I ate a strawberry-shaped object that   9
didn't have much taste. When did we stop noticing that strawberries/plums/toma-
toes no longer taste like what they resemble? In my 20s I rented a house where a
previous resident's cat had pooped all over the dirt basement, which happened to
be where the air intakes for the furnace were located. The house smelled like cat
feces. After I'd been there a few months, I wrote to a friend, "At first the smell really
got to me, but then, as with everything, I got used to the stench and it just doesn't
bother me anymore."

This is a process we need to stop. Milan Kundera famously wrote, "The   10
struggle of man against power is the struggle of memory against forgetting."
Everything in this culture is aimed at helping to distract us from—or better, help
us to forget—the injustices, the pain. And it is completely normal for us to want
to be distracted from or to forget pain. *Pain hurts.* Which is why on every level
from somatic reflex to socially constructed means of denial we have pathways
to avoid it.

But here is what I want you to do: I want you to go outside. I want you to listen 11
to the (disappearing) frogs, to watch the (disappearing) fireflies. Even if you're in a
city—especially if you're in a city—I want you to picture the land as it was before
the land was built over. I want you to research who lived there. I want you to feel
how it was then, feel how it wants to be. I want you to begin keeping a calendar of
who you see and when: the first day each year you see buttercups, the first day
frogs start singing, the last day you see robins in the fall, the first day for grasshop-
pers. In short, I want you to pay attention. If you do this, your baseline will stop
declining, because you'll have a record of what's being lost.

Do not go numb in the face of this data. Do not turn away. I want you to feel 12
the pain. Keep it like a coal inside your coat, a coal that burns and burns. I want all
of us to do this, because we should all want the pain of injustice to stop. We should
want this pain to stop not because we get used to it and it just doesn't bother us
anymore, but because we stop the injustices and destruction that are causing the
pain in the first place. I want us to feel how awful the destruction is, and then act
from this feeling.

And I promise you two things. One: Feeling this pain won't kill you. And two: 13
Not feeling this pain, continuing to go numb and avoid it, will.

11
Narration
Recounting Events

Meyrick Villarica/EyeEm/Getty Images

Writing Quick Start

ANALYZE   The photograph here shows a large group of people holding blue and white balloons.

WRITE   Working alone or with a classmate, imagine the events that occurred before and during this gathering. Who is participating, what is happening, and what did the participants do to get them to this scene shown in the photograph? Then write a brief summary of the events you imagined.

CONNECT   As you imagined the events that led up to the scene in the photograph, you probably described a series of events or turning points in the order in which they occurred. In short, you constructed a **narrative:** a chronological series of events, real or imaginary, that tells a story to make a point.

Narratives provide human interest and entertainment, spark our curiosity, and draw us close to the storyteller. They can also create a sense of shared history or provide instruction in proper behavior or conduct. In this chapter, you will read narratives; you will also write narrative essays or use narration in essays that rely on one or more of the other patterns of development.

USING NARRATION ▸ **IN COLLEGE AND THE WORKPLACE**

- Each student in your *business law course* must attend a court trial and complete the following written assignment: "Describe what happened and how the proceedings illustrate the judicial process."

- Your *sociology instructor* announces that the class session will focus on the nature and types of authority figures. She begins by asking class members to describe situations in which they found themselves in conflict with an authority figure.

- Your *job in sales* involves frequent business travel, and your company requires you to submit a report for each trip. You are expected to recount the meetings you attended, your contacts with current clients, and the new sales leads you developed.

What Are the Characteristics of a Narrative?

A narrative does not merely report events; it is *not* a transcript of a conversation or a news report. Instead, it is a story that conveys a particular meaning. It presents actions and details that build toward a *climax*, the point at which the conflict of the narrative is resolved. Most narratives also use dialogue to present portions of conversations that move the story along.

Narratives Make a Point

A narrative makes a point by telling readers about an event or a series of events. The point may be to describe the significance of the event(s), make an observation, or present new information. The writer may state the point directly, using an explicit thesis statement, or leave it unstated, using an implied thesis. Either way, the point should always be clear to the audience by the details selected and the way they are presented.

The following excerpt comes from a selection that appears later in this chapter. There, the narrator tells the story of a moment in time that was forever etched in his mind—a time that taught him things about his mother that he had never known. Through the story of a trip to a bowling alley with his mom, he recounts what he learned about her strength as a woman and her prowess as a champion bowler. Notice how he chooses vocabulary to describe the strength of character of his mother and the way she handled the rude and disrespectful man.

> My mother grabbed my hand and took one step toward the man. In that instant, I saw in her face the same resolve she had when she spanked, the same resolve when she scolded. In that instant, I thought my mother was going to hit the man. And for a moment, I thought the man saw the same thing in her eyes, and his smile disappeared from his face. Quickly, she smiled—too bright, too large—and said, "You're welcome."

Details that reinforce the main point

—Ira Sukrunguang, "Chop Suey" (para. 18)

Narratives Convey Action and Detail

Narratives present a detailed account of an event or a series of events, using *dialogue*, *physical description*, and *action verbs* to make readers feel as if they are watching the scene or experiencing the action.

Action verbs
Physical description

> I quickly learned why Doc needed a cellmate of a particular disposition. He had cancer and sometimes soiled himself. Additionally, he was in the beginning stages of dementia. He would go to the toilet but sometimes urinate all over the floor or defecate and get all the feces all over the toilet. Needless to say, this did not endear him to his less compassionate cellies. I, on the other hand, liked and respected Doc. I did not like cleaning up his mess, but one day I'll be old too, and I would hope someone would show me a modicum of kindness.

Dialogue

> The first time it happened was somewhat comical. I was asleep and awoke to a horrendous odor in the cell. I got up and turned on my lamp and there was Doc, pants half-down and feces everywhere. I said, "Damn, Doc! What did you do?"
>
> —William Peeples, "My Cellie Was the Father I Never Had" (paras. 12–13)

Narratives Present a Conflict and Create Tension

An effective narrative presents a **conflict**—such as a struggle, question, or problem—and works toward its resolution. The conflict can be between participants or between a participant and some external force, such as a law, value, tradition, or act of nature. (In the first reading, the narrator struggles to preserve Doc's dignity.) **Tension** is the suspense created as the story unfolds and the reader wonders how the conflict will be resolved. The height of the action—the point just before the resolution of the conflict—is the **climax**.

EXERCISE 11.1 ▶ BUILDING CONFLICT

Working alone or with a classmate, complete each of the following statements by setting up a conflict. Then, for one of the completed statements, write three to four sentences that build tension through action, physical description, or dialogue (or some combination of the three).

1. You are ready to leave the house when . . .
2. You have just turned in your math exam when you realize that . . .
3. Your spouse suddenly becomes seriously ill . . .
4. Your child just told you that . . .
5. Your best friend texts you in the middle of the night to . . .

Narratives Sequence Events

A narrative often presents events in **chronological order**—the order in which they happened. Some narratives use flashback and foreshadowing to add tension and drama. A **flashback** returns readers to events that took place in the past; **foreshadowing** hints at events that will occur in the future. Both techniques are used frequently in fiction and film. For example, an episode of a crime drama might open with a woman lying in a hospital bed, flash back to a scene showing the accident that put her there, and then return to the scene in the hospital. When used sparingly, flashback and foreshadowing can build interest and add variety to a narrative, especially a lengthy chronological account.

Narratives Use Dialogue

Just as people reveal much about themselves by what they say and how they say it, dialogue can reveal much about the characters in a narrative. The use of dialogue can also dramatize the action, emphasize the conflict, and reveal the personalities or motives of the key participants in a narrative. Dialogue can be strategically inserted to heighten the drama and help characterize the people depicted.

Narratives Are Told from a Particular Point of View

Most narratives use either the first-person or third-person point of view.

- The **first-person** point of view ("I first realized the problem when . . .") allows you to assume a personal tone and speak directly to your audience, permitting you to express your attitudes and feelings and offer your interpretation and commentary. A drawback to using the first person is that you cannot easily convey the inner thoughts of other participants (unless they have shared their thoughts with you). When you narrate an event that occurred in your life, the first person is probably your best choice.
- The **third-person** point of view ("The problem began when Saul Overtone . . .") gives the narrator more distance from the action and often provides a broader, more objective perspective. When you narrate an event that occurred in someone else's life, the third person is likely to be the natural choice.

EXERCISE 11.2   CHOOSING A POINT OF VIEW

Discuss the advantages and disadvantages of using the first- and third-person points of view for each of the following situations, and then decide which point of view would work better:

1. The day you and several friends played a practical joke on another friend
2. An incident of sexual or racial discrimination that happened to you or someone you know
3. An incident at work that a coworker told you about

The following readings demonstrate the techniques discussed above for writing effective narratives. The first reading is annotated to point out how William Peeples uses these techniques to help readers understand the experience of bonding with a cellmate. As you read the second essay, try to identify how the writer uses the techniques of narrative writing to help readers understand how his encounter with the police changed his life.

My Cellie Was the Father I Never Had

William Peeples

William Peeples is a convicted murderer serving a life sentence at Stateville
Correctional Center in Crest Hill, Illinois, for a crime he committed when he was
twenty-four. He was fifty-five when the autobiographical narrative below was
published in the Marshall Project, an online news outlet whose goal is to create an
audience that cares about the U.S. criminal justice system.

Before Reading

1. **Preview:** Preview the reading using the steps listed in Chapter 2.
2. **Connect:** Activate your knowledge and experience on the topic by answering the
   following questions:
   - What comes to mind when you hear the word *prison?*
   - Who do you consider to be a mentor in your life? What has that person taught
     you?

While Reading Study the annotations that accompany the reading to discover how
the essay illustrates the characteristics of narration as presented earlier in the
chapter.

Point of view: Uses first person (*I*) for this personal essay

I was born in 1964 on the South Side of Chicago. I grew up in the Robert Taylor   1
Homes, where poverty, crime, gangs, and drugs shaped my perception of life. At
the tender age of 11, I began smoking weed, drinking wine, and hanging out with
the street toughs in my neighborhood. I joined the notorious Black Gangster
Disciples, a large and violent gang in my neighborhood.

Background: Provides background to show what led him to prison

Looking back, I believe I was trying to fill the void that the absence of my   2
father left in my life. My father and mother married as teenagers. Three
months after I was born, my father was gone. I've met him, but we are virtually
strangers. The gang became my surrogate family. The leaders in the gang were
our uncles; some even treated us like their sons. Decades later I would realize
that what I mistook for love and acceptance was really just manipulation and
exploitation.

Predictably, I dropped out of school and became more involved in criminal   3
activity and drug use. By age 24, I was on death row for murder. In 2003, the
governor commuted my sentence to life without parole.

Details: Description of prison using comparison, metaphor ("hell on Earth")
Thesis: Main point

I arrived at Stateville Correctional Center in January 2003, after 16 years on   4
death row. The "Ville" is known for violence, mayhem, and degradation, yet in this
"hell on Earth," I met a kindly old man whom I came to love as a son does his
father. Charles "Doc" Smith and I met in the spring of 2005 in D House. I was
placed in the cell with him early one morning, and by 2 p.m., we were drinking
coffee and playing chess.

When I walked into the cell, Doc's first words were, "I hope you aren't gonna be a problem, young man." Doc never called me by my given name. I was either "Sonny" or "young man." I resented this initially, but in time I came to see that he used these labels affectionately.

Doc and I were cellmates for about three months, but then I got a job and wouldn't see him again for six or seven years. In just those three months, Doc developed enough of an appreciation for how I treated him that it would lead to us being cellmates again seven years later.

One morning after all those years, while I was exercising in my cell, an officer came and told me, "Pack your property. You're moving today." I was mad because I didn't request a move and was comfortable where I was. I would learn later that unbeknownst to me, Doc had pulled some strings and had me moved in with him.

When I got to my new cell and saw Doc sitting on the lower bunk, I exclaimed, "Who is this old codger in my cell?" He smiled and said, "You just try to live long enough to be an 'old codger.'"

We shook hands, and Doc explained how I came to be his cellie. "Man, I had a cellie who was crazy!" he said. "He was stealing my stuff, and when I confronted him, he threatened to beat me up. Now I ain't no chump, sonny, but I'm too old and too sick to be humbugging."

I asked Doc: "So you had them move me—why me?"

"You were one of my best cellmates," Doc replied. "You're clean. You're respectful. And I figured I'd live with you till I transfer to Dixon." (That's a medium-security prison for the aged and infirm.)

I quickly learned why Doc needed a cellmate of a particular disposition. He had cancer and sometimes soiled himself. Additionally, he was in the beginning stages of dementia. He would go to the toilet but sometimes urinate all over the floor or defecate and get all the feces all over the toilet. Needless to say, this did not endear him to his less compassionate cellies. I, on the other hand, liked and respected Doc. I did not like cleaning up his mess, but one day I'll be old too, and I would hope someone would show me a modicum of kindness.

The first time it happened was somewhat comical. I was asleep and awoke to a horrendous odor in the cell. I got up and turned on my lamp and there was Doc, pants half-down and feces everywhere. I said, "Damn, Doc! What did you do?"

He looked so embarrassed and sheepishly replied, "I'm sorry, young man. I had an accident. Don't be mad. I'll clean it up, I promise." Doc was on the verge of crying; he was so ashamed.

I looked at this man who was so pitifully not the man he'd once been, and I was determined to help salvage his dignity. "Don't trip, Doc. I got you. We'll clean this up, and nobody will even know," I told him. It took close to two and half hours to clean Doc and the cell but with bleach, soap and disinfectant. We got it done.

We had a few more episodes like that but with time and patience, we developed a system, and Doc had fewer and fewer accidents. He would also forget

---

5

Organization: Narrates events in chronological order; uses transitions of time

Background: Provides background needed to understand relationship and build tension

6

7

Dialogue: Dialogue dramatizes action, helps depict relationship, reveals character and motives

8

9

10

11

12

Details: Uses **detailed description** (*feces all over the toilet*) and **active verbs** (*urinate, defecate*) to make readers feel as if they are observing the scene

13

14

15

Dialogue: Dialogue helps depict relationship

16

to bathe, so part of my morning routine became helping him wash up, brush his teeth and shave. I think he was grateful because I never made a big deal out of it. I'd jokingly inquire each morning, "Doc, can you tell me what today is?" to which he would reply, "Yes, Sonny. Today is . . ." and then whatever day of the week it happened to be. I'd say, "No sir, Doc. Today is 'Let's wash Doc Day!,'" and we'd both laugh.

Background: Provides background readers need to further understand Doc's character

Life with Doc was far from a burden. Doc was educated, cultured, well-read and wise. He'd tell me about his dentistry practice in Oak Park before his incarceration. Doc was one of the first black men to own and live in neighboring River Forest, another prestigious suburb of Chicago. He had met the elite of black society, including Mayor Harold Washington. He'd regale me with tales of parties he attended, women he dated, and places he'd been.   17

Doc and I mutually loved chess and tennis, and boy, did Doc know a lot about the sport. His favorite female player was Chris Evert, and on the men's side, Andre Agassi. Doc knew the history of tennis and would talk to me for hours about it.   18

Organization: Transition indicates passage of time

Climax: Uses dialogue to emphasize the height of the action

In 2016, Doc finally got approved for Dixon. The night before his transfer, we stayed up all night watching tennis and playing chess. The next morning, before he left, Doc did something he never did. He hugged me real tight and told me, "Sonny, it has been an honor and a privilege to know you." I was so shocked because Doc absolutely abhorred any type of physical affection. He'd shake hands, and that was that. That morning, he hugged me, and it felt like a father hugging his beloved son.   19

Resolution: Tension is relieved as Peeples realizes impact Doc had on his life and brings story to a close

In less than a month, Dixon sent Doc back to Stateville. His cancer was terminal, and he did not have long to live. Doc died that winter, and I mourned him like we had known one another for a lifetime. When you think of bonds of love and familial cohesion, you don't think of prison—but that was where I met and grew to love one of the finest human beings I have ever known.   20

Visualize a Narrative: Create a Graphic Organizer

For more on creating a graphic organizer, see Chapter 2.

Seeing the content and structure of an essay in simplified, visual form can help you analyze a reading, recall key events as you generate ideas for an essay, and structure your own writing. Graphic Organizer 11.1 diagrams the basic structure of a narrative. You can use this graphic organizer as a basic model of a narrative, but keep in mind that narrative essays vary widely in organization and therefore may lack one or more of the elements included in the model.

GRAPHIC ORGANIZER 11.1   The Basic Structure of a Narrative Essay

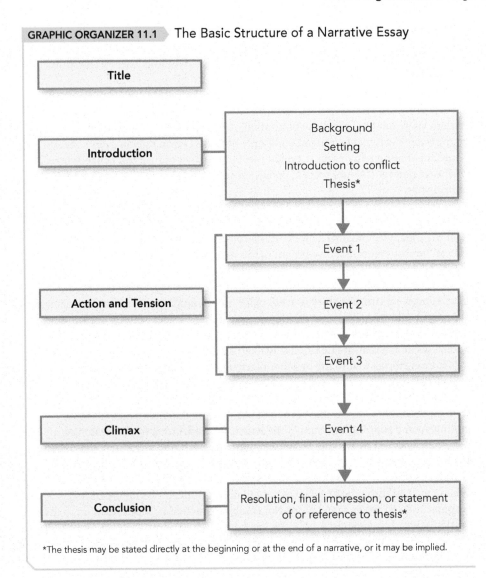

*The thesis may be stated directly at the beginning or at the end of a narrative, or it may be implied.

Right Place, Wrong Face

Alton Fitzgerald White

Alton Fitzgerald White is an actor, singer, and dancer and has appeared in several Broadway shows. He is also the author of *Uncovering the Heart Light*, a collection of poems and short stories. **Before reading**, preview the selection and make connections by thinking of incidents of racial profiling you have heard about or experienced. **While reading**, pay attention to the essay's organization. Once you have finished the selection, study Graphic Organizer 11.2 following this reading.

As the youngest of five girls and two boys growing up in Cincinnati, I was raised   1
to believe that if I worked hard, was a good person, and always told the truth, the
world would be my oyster. I was raised to be a gentleman and learned that these
qualities would bring me respect.

While one has to earn respect, consideration is something owed to every   2
human being. On Friday, June 16, 1999, when I was wrongfully arrested at my
Harlem apartment building, my perception of everything I had learned as a
young man was forever changed—not only because I wasn't given even a second
to use the manners my parents taught me, but mostly because the police, whom
I'd always naively thought were supposed to serve and protect me, were actually
hunting me.

I had planned a pleasant day. The night before was a payday, plus I had   3
received a standing ovation after portraying the starring role of Coalhouse Walker
Jr. in the Broadway musical *Ragtime*. It is a role that requires not only talent but
also an honest emotional investment of the morals and lessons I learned as a
child.

Coalhouse Walker Jr. is a victim (an often misused word, but in this case   4
true) of overt racism. His story is every black man's nightmare. He is hardworking,
successful, talented, charismatic, friendly, and polite. Perfect prey for someone
with authority and not even a fraction of those qualities. On that Friday afternoon, I became a real-life Coalhouse Walker. Nothing could have prepared me for
it. Not even stories told to me by other black men who had suffered similar
injustices.

Friday for me usually means a trip to the bank, errands, the gym, dinner, and   5
then off to the theater. On this particular day, I decided to break my pattern of
getting up and running right out of the house. Instead, I took my time, slowed my
pace, and splurged by making strawberry pancakes. Before I knew it, it was 2:45;
my bank closes at 3:30, leaving me less than 45 minutes to get to midtown Manhattan on the train. I was pressed for time but in a relaxed, blessed state of mind.
When I walked through the lobby of my building, I noticed two light-skinned
Hispanic men I'd never seen before. Not thinking much of it, I continued on to the
vestibule, which is separated from the lobby by a locked door.

As I approached the exit, I saw people in uniforms rushing toward the door. I   6
sped up to open it for them. I thought they might be paramedics, since many of
the building's occupants are elderly. It wasn't until I had opened the door and
greeted them that I recognized that they were police officers. Within seconds, I
was told to "hold it"; they had received a call about young Hispanics with guns. I
was told to get against the wall. I was searched, stripped of my backpack, put on
my knees, handcuffed, and told to be quiet when I tried to ask questions.

With me were three other innocent black men who had been on their way to   7
their U-Haul. They were moving into the apartment beneath mine, and I had just
bragged to them about how safe the building was. One of these gentlemen got off
his knees, still handcuffed, and unlocked the door for the officers to get into the
lobby where the two strangers were standing. Instead of thanking or even
acknowledging us, they led us out the door past our neighbors, who were all but
begging the police in our defense.

The four of us were put into cars with the two strangers and taken to the   8
precinct station at 165th and Amsterdam. The police automatically linked us, with
no questions and no regard for our character or our lives. No consideration was
given to where we were going or why. Suppose an ailing relative was waiting
upstairs, while I ran out for her medication? Or young children, who'd been told that
Daddy was running to the corner store for milk and would be right back? My new
neighbors weren't even allowed to lock their apartment or check on the U-Haul.

After we were lined up in the station, the younger of the two Hispanic men   9
was identified as an experienced criminal, and drug residue was found in a pocket
of the other. I now realize how naive I was to think that the police would then
uncuff me, apologize for their mistake, and let me go. Instead, they continued to
search my backpack, questioned me, and put me in jail with the criminals.

The rest of the nearly five-hour ordeal was like a horrible dream. I was hand-   10
cuffed, strip-searched, taken in and out for questioning. The officers told me that
they knew exactly who I was, knew I was in *Ragtime,* and that in fact they already
had the men they wanted.

How then could they keep me there, or have brought me there in the first   11
place? I was told it was standard procedure. As if the average law-abiding citizen
knows what that is and can dispute it. From what I now know, "standard procedure" is something that every citizen, black and white, needs to learn, and fast.

I felt completely powerless. Why, do you think? Here I was, young, pleasant,   12
and successful, in good physical shape, dressed in clean athletic attire. I was
carrying a backpack containing a substantial paycheck and a deposit slip, on my
way to the bank. Yet after hours and hours I was sitting at a desk with two officers who not only couldn't tell me why I was there but seemed determined to
find something on me, to the point of making me miss my performance.

It was because I am a black man!   13

I sat in that cell crying silent tears of disappointment and injustice with the   14
realization of how many innocent black men are convicted for no reason. When I
was handcuffed, my first instinct had been to pull away out of pure insult and
violation as a human being. Thank God I was calm enough to do what they said.
When I was thrown in jail with the criminals and strip-searched, I somehow
knew to put my pride aside, be quiet, and do exactly what I was told, hating it but
coming to terms with the fact that in this situation I was a victim. They had guns!

Before I was finally let go, exhausted, humiliated, embarrassed, and still in   15
shock, I was led to a room and given a pseudo-apology. I was told that I was at
the wrong place at the wrong time. My reply? "I was where I live."

Everything I learned growing up in Cincinnati has been shattered. Life will   16
never be the same.

| EXERCISE 11.3 | DRAWING A GRAPHIC ORGANIZER |

Using Graphic Organizer 11.1 or 11.2 as a basis, draw a graphic organizer for "My
Cellie Was the Father I Never Had."

GRAPHIC ORGANIZER 11.2   The Structure of "Right Place, Wrong Face"

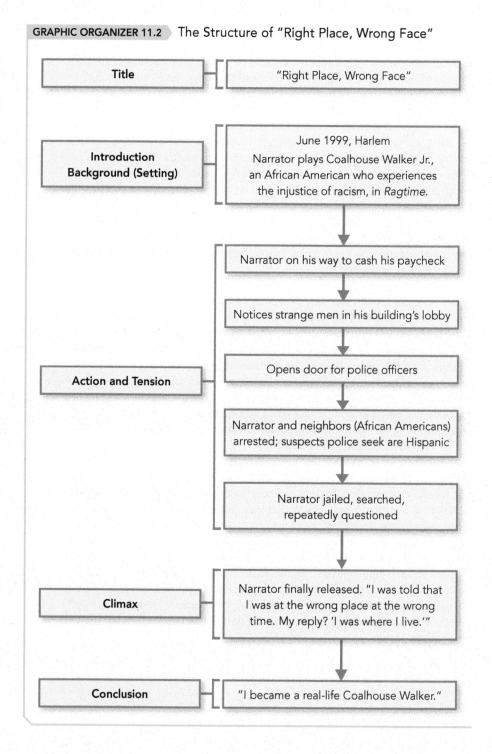

Title	"Right Place, Wrong Face"
Introduction **Background (Setting)**	June 1999, Harlem Narrator plays Coalhouse Walker Jr., an African American who experiences the injustice of racism, in *Ragtime*.
	Narrator on his way to cash his paycheck
	Notices strange men in his building's lobby
Action and Tension	Opens door for police officers
	Narrator and neighbors (African Americans) arrested; suspects police seek are Hispanic
	Narrator jailed, searched, repeatedly questioned
Climax	Narrator finally released. "I was told that I was at the wrong place at the wrong time. My reply? 'I was where I live.'"
Conclusion	"I became a real-life Coalhouse Walker."

HOW WRITERS READ ▸ NARRATION

THE READING PROCESS	STRATEGIES
BEFORE READING	**Preview** the essay to get an overview of the content and organization.
	Make connections by thinking about what the title means.
	Read the headnote (if one is provided) for background information about the author and the reading.
WHILE READING	**Identify the characteristics of a narrative.** Be sure you can answer the following questions:
	• What is the **sequence of events**? Number them in the margin.
	• What is the writer's **thesis**? Is it stated or implied?
	• Who are the **characters**, and what are their **relationships** to one another?
	• How does the **dialogue** reveal character?
	• What is the **conflict**, and how is it resolved? How does the writer create **tension**?
	• What is the author's **purpose**? Who is the intended **audience**?
AFTER READING	Draw a **graphic organizer** listing the main events of the plot. (Use your graphic organizer for review and study.)
	Analyze and evaluate the reading by answering the following questions:
	• What broader issue is the essay concerned with? That is, what is its **theme**? Express the theme in a sentence or two. Does the theme **follow logically** and **clearly** from the events in the narrative?
	• Is the **resolution** of the conflict **believable** and **well explained**?
	• What is your **reaction** (positive, negative, mixed) to the narration? Explain your reaction in detail.
	• How **objective** is the writer? How is the information in the essay influenced by the author's **beliefs** and **values**?
	• What is the writer's **tone**? Describe the tone with two or three adjectives.
	• What are the **writer's feelings** about the incident or events?
	• What does the writer **leave unspoken** or **unreported**? Are any relevant **details omitted**? If so, why?
	• What is the **lasting merit** of the essay?

EXERCISE 11.4   **THINKING CRITICALLY**

Apply the questions in the "How Writers Read" box to the selection "Right Place, Wrong Face" (pp. 243–45).

Integrate Narration into an Essay

In many of your essays, you will want to use both narration and one or more other patterns of development to support your thesis. For example, although "My Cellie Was the Father I Never Had" is primarily a narrative, it also uses description to present detailed information about the relationship that developed between the author and his prison cellmate. Similarly, "Right Place, Wrong Face" is a narrative that uses cause and effect to explain why the author was detained despite evidence that he was a respectable, law-abiding citizen. Similarly, "On the Outside: First Days of College" is a narrative that also uses cause and effect to show how the author's upbringing affected her adjustment to college life.

Although most of your college essays will not be primarily narrative, you can use stories—to illustrate a point, clarify an idea, support an argument, or capture readers' interest—in essays that rely mainly on another pattern of development or use several patterns. Here are a few suggestions for combining narration effectively with other patterns of development:

1. **Use a story.** Include a story only when it illustrates your main point (or thesis) accurately and well (not just because it's funny or interesting).
2. **Keep the narrative short.** Include only the details readers need to understand the events you are describing.
3. **Introduce the story with a transitional sentence or clause.** It should indicate that you are about to shift to a narrative and make clear the connection between the story and the point it illustrates.
4. **Use descriptive language, dialogue, and action.** These will make your narrative vivid, lively, and interesting.

> PREWRITING 〉 DRAFTING 〉 **REVISING** 〉 EDITING & PROOFREADING 〉

A Guided Writing Assignment*

NARRATION

Your Essay Assignment

Write a narrative essay about an experience that had a significant effect on you or that changed your views in some important way. You can choose an experience that

- taught you something about yourself
- revealed the true character of someone you know
- helped you discover a principle to live by
- helped you appreciate your ethnic identity
- has become a family legend (one that reveals the character of a family member or illustrates a clash of generations or cultures)
- explains the personal significance of a particular object

* The writing process is *recursive*; that is, you may find yourself revising as you draft or prewriting as you revise. This is especially true when writing on a computer. Your writing process may also differ from project to project or from that of your classmates.

1 Select a topic from the list above, or create your own.

Use one or more of the following suggestions to choose an experience to write about:

1. Alone or with another student, **list one or more broad topics**—for example, *Learn about Self, A Principle to Live By, Family Legend*—and then **brainstorm** to come up with **specific experiences** in your life for each category.
2. Flip through a **family photo album** or page through **videos and photo albums on your phone** to remind yourself of events from the past. Other prewriting strategies, like freewriting or questioning, may also help trigger memories of experiences. (Some students may be more inspired by looking at mementos.)
3. **Work backward:** Think of a principle you live by, an object you value, or a family legend. How did it become so?

After you have chosen your topic, make sure that it is **memorable and vivid** and that you can develop your main idea into a **working thesis.**

2 Consider your purpose and audience, and choose a point of view.

Ask yourself these questions:

- Will my essay's **purpose** be to **express myself, inform**, or **persuade**?
- Who is my **audience**? Will readers need any **background information** to understand my essay? Am I **comfortable writing about my experience** for this audience?
- What **point of view** best suits my purpose and audience? (In most cases, you will use **first person** to relate a personal experience.)

3 Gather details about the experience or incident.

Use idea-generating strategies to recollect as many details about the experience or incident as possible:

1. **Replay** the experience or incident in your mind's eye. Jot down what you see, hear, smell, and feel—colors, dialogue, sounds, odors, and sensations—and how these details make you feel.
2. Write down the following headings: *Scene, Key Actions, Key Participants, Key Lines of Dialogue, Feelings*. Then **brainstorm** ideas for each and list them.
3. **Describe** the incident or experience to a friend. Have your friend ask you questions as you tell the story. Jot down the details that the telling and questioning helped you recall.

As you gather details for your narrative, be sure to include those that are essential to an effective narrative:

- **Describe the scene:** Include relevant **sensory details** to allow your readers to feel as if they are there. (Looking at a photograph or video might help.) Choose details that point to or hint at the narrative's main point, and avoid those that distract readers from the main point.

- **Include key actions:** Choose actions that **create tension, build it to a climax, and resolve it.** Answer questions like these:

  Why did the experience or incident occur?

  What events led up to it, what was the turning point, and how was it resolved?

  What were its short- and long-term outcomes? What is its significance?

- **Describe key participants:** Concentrate on the **appearance** and **actions** of only those people who were directly involved, and include details that help highlight relevant character traits.

- **Quote key lines of dialogue:** Include dialogue that is **interesting, revealing,** and **related to the main point** of the narrative. To make sure the dialogue sounds natural, read the lines aloud or ask a friend to do so.

- **Capture feelings:** How did you feel during the incident, how did you reveal your feelings, and how did others react to you? How do you feel about the incident now? What have you learned from the experience?

Use at least two idea-generating strategies, and then work with a classmate to evaluate your ideas.

4 Evaluate your ideas to make sure they describe your experience or incident vividly and meaningfully.

Try these suggestions to help you evaluate your ideas:

- **Reread** everything you have written. (Sometimes reading your notes aloud is helpful.)

- **Highlight** the most relevant material, and **cross out** any material that does not directly support your main point. Then **copy** and **paste** the usable ideas to a new document to consult while drafting.

- **Collaborate** in small groups, taking turns **narrating your experience** and **stating its main point** and having classmates tell you

  1. how they react to the story
  2. what more they need to know about it
  3. how effectively the events and details support your main point

5 Focus and place your thesis effectively.

Make the main point of your narrative clear and effective by focusing your thesis. For example, a student who decided to write about a robbery at her family's home devised the following focused thesis statement for her narrative:

Example:

— focuses on 1 object — explains value —

The silver serving platter, originally owned by my great-grandmother,

— introduces experience & expresses main point —

became our most prized family heirloom after a robbery terrorized our family.

Team up with classmates to test your thesis. Is it clear? Is it interesting? Provide feedback to help your partner focus the thesis more effectively.

Consider the best placement for your thesis. A thesis statement may be placed at the beginning (as in "Right Place, Wrong Face") or at the end of a narrative, or it may be implied. (Even if you don't state your thesis explicitly in your essay, having a focused thesis written down can help you craft your narrative.)

(**Note:** Once you have a focused thesis, you may need to do some additional prewriting, or you may need to revise your thesis as you draft. Return to the steps above as needed.)

6 Choose a narrative sequence.

Organize your narrative. You may use **chronological order** from beginning to end or present some events using **flashbacks** or **foreshadowing** for dramatic effect. To help you determine the best sequence for your narrative, try the following:

1. Write a **brief description** of each event on an index card. Highlight the card that contains the climax. Experiment with various ways of arranging your details by rearranging the cards.
2. Create an **outline** or draw a **graphic organizer** of the experience or incident using Graphic Organizer 11.1 as a model.
3. Create a **list** of the events, and then cut and paste them to experiment with different sequences.

7 Write a first draft of your narrative essay.

Use the following guidelines to keep your narrative on track:

- The **introduction** should set up the sequence of events. It may also contain your **thesis**.
- The **body paragraphs** should **build tension** and follow a clear order of progression. Use **transitional words and phrases**, such as *during*, *after*, and *finally*, to guide readers. Most narratives use the past tense ("Yolanda discovered the platter . . ."), but fast-paced, short narratives may use the present ("Yolanda discovers the platter . . ."). Avoid switching between the two unless the context clearly requires it. Consider whether including a photograph (or a video or audio file if the writing project is presented online) could help engage readers by depicting the setting or a key character.
- The **conclusion** is unlikely to require a summary. Instead, try
  - **making a final observation about the experience or incident**. (Example: "Overall, I learned a lot more about getting along with people than I did about how to prepare fast food.")
  - **asking a probing question**. (Example: "Although the visit to Nepal was enlightening for me, do the native people really want or need us there?")
  - **suggesting a new but related direction of thought**. (Example: An essay on racial profiling might conclude by suggesting that police sensitivity training might have changed the outcome of the situation.)
  - **referring to the beginning of the essay** (example: "Right Place, Wrong Face," para. 16) or **restating the thesis in different words** (example: "Being Double," para. 22).

8 Evaluate your draft and revise as necessary.

Use **Figure 11.1, "Flowchart for Revising a Narrative Essay,"** to evaluate and revise your draft.

FIGURE 11.1 Flowchart for Revising a Narrative Essay

QUESTIONS

REVISION STRATEGIES

1. Highlight the sentence(s) that express the main point of your narrative. Is the main point clear?

 NO ▶

- Rework your thesis to make it more explicit.

 YES ▼

2. Summarize the conflict of your narrative in one brief sentence. Is the conflict clear? Does it relate directly to the main point?

 NO ▶

- Add events and dialogue to clarify or dramatize the conflict.
- Rework your thesis to make it better relate to the conflict.

 YES ▼

3. Place an ✗ by each important scene, person, or action. Does each clearly relate to both the main point and the *conflict*?

 NO ▶

- Delete scenes, people, or actions that don't help you make your main point or establish conflict.

 YES ▼

4. Place a checkmark ✔ by each descriptive word or phrase. Is each important scene, person, or action vividly described?

 NO ▶

- Brainstorm to discover more vivid details.
- Consider adding dialogue to bring people and events to life.

 YES ▼

5. *Number* the major events in chronological order. Is the sequence clear? If you use foreshadowing or flashbacks, is the shift from present to past or future clear?

 NO ▶

- Look for gaps in the sequence, and add any missing events.
- Consider rearranging the events.
- Use transitions to clarify the sequence of events.

 YES ▼

6. Underline the topic sentence of each paragraph. Is each paragraph focused on a separate part of the action?

 NO ▶

- Be sure each paragraph has a topic sentence and supporting details. (See Chapter 6.)
- Combine closely related paragraphs.
- Split paragraphs that cover more than one event.

 YES ▼

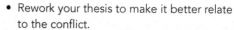

QUESTIONS		REVISION STRATEGIES

7. Highlight the dialogue. Does it sound realistic? Does it directly relate to the *conflict*?

 NO ▶

- Act out your dialogue, and record what you say.
- Cut dialogue that does not help you make your main point or add drama.

 YES ▼

8. Circle each personal pronoun and each verb. Do you use a consistent point of view and verb tense?

 NO ▶

- Revise places where your point of view shifts for no reason.
- Check for places where the tense changes for no reason, and revise to make it consistent.

YES ▼

9. Look at your introduction and conclusion. Do they address each other and the main point? Does the conclusion resolve the *conflict*?

 NO ▶

- Revise your introduction and conclusion. (See Chapter 7.)

 9 **Edit and proofread your essay.**

Refer to Chapter 9 for help with

- **editing sentences** to avoid wordiness, make your verb choices strong and active, and make your sentences clear, varied, and parallel
- **editing words** for tone and diction, connotation, and concrete and specific language

Pay particular attention to **dialogue:**

- Each quotation by a new speaker should start a **new paragraph.**
- Use **commas** to separate each quotation from the phrase that introduces it unless the quotation is integrated into your sentence. If your sentence ends with a quotation, the **period** should be inside the quotation marks.

Example: The wildlife refuge guide noted,^"American crocodiles are an endangered species

and must be protected."

Example: The wildlife refuge guide noted that/ "American crocodiles are an endangered

species and must be protected."/

Readings: Narrative in Action

Being Double

Santiago Quintana

Santiago Quintana wrote this essay for an assignment given by his first-year writing instructor. He had to describe a situation that challenged him and taught him a valuable lesson. As you read the essay, notice how Quintana's narrative creates conflict and tension and builds to a climax and resolution. Highlight the sections(s) where you think the tension is particularly intense.

Details: Exact details help readers imagine the scene.

Dialogue: Quotations sound natural and capture the relationship between mother and son.

Conflict: Description of Quintana's feelings introduces conflict and foreshadows the process he will undergo during his first year in college.

Background: Provides background about his English skills

1   A summer sun shone on the Wisconsin Indian mounds and the grass poked its little blades through my sandaled toes. "College, finally," said Mom, and her hand fell slowly on my hair. I couldn't stop the shaking. It was inside me though; outside I was as still as a statue, with a smile frozen on my lips. "Hey, should we leave some stuff in the car and come get it later, or should we all help you carry it to the building?" asked my brother as he held two crates, one with my sheets in it and the other with books. The idea of having my family parade around campus yelling in Spanish, being "those loud Mexicans" I'd seen in American movies, and carrying all my stuff with me sounded terrifying. At the same time, I thought, why not? I didn't know anyone on campus, so there was no reason for me to be concerned about what others thought of me or my family. In Mexico City, I would have been mortified to be seen walking around high school with my whole family. Then again, that was high school, that was teenage Santiago, and that was Mexico City. I was in college now, in America; it was the time to read more, stop smoking, make friends, and do all those things that I had postponed beyond the imaginary line of "when I go to college."

2   With Wisconsin as our final destination, my family and I had been traveling around the Midwest for a week. I spoke the best English, so for the whole trip, I had been translating directions and ordering food for all. In my bilingual high school, I had the top grades in English, and hours watching YouTube videos and standing in front of a mirror had made my

accent one of the least recognizable among my friends. Now, in America, all that obsession with language was paying off. My lighter skin and over rehearsed accent baffled many a waiter and cab driver when they discovered I was Mexican. My English was the reason I had chosen and been able to get into an American college. Now, here I was, my accent and lexicon ready to be put to the test.

The room was larger than I thought it would be, and my roommate quieter. My parents and I set the room up and left for coffee.

"Your roommate seems nice," said my mom.

"Yeah, a little quiet," I said, "and way younger than me."

"Everyone will be younger than you here," said my dad, "and you didn't really talk much either. You're usually so talkative."

"He's nervous dad," said my brother.

"I'm not. It's just, I don't know, weird. I don't know what to say to them," I said.

"Them? As in?" asked my dad.

"As in Americans. I don't know what to say to them, what they think is funny, and what is too much. You know my humor; I can go way overboard sometimes, and I don't want to mess up," I said.

"I see. Well, I'm sure it'll come with time. You'll get used to it," said my mom.

After my parents left I sat on my dorm bed for two or three hours and had three cups of tea. I then decided to go out for a walk and try to talk to people. I closed the door behind me and was greeted by a long, empty hallway in muted colors with doors on both sides. I walked quietly down the hallway to the stairs without meeting anyone. I went down the stairs and out the back door of the building. The air was more humid than I had ever felt, and the sun burnt my skin. I eventually found my way to the Office of International Education, where I saw a crowd of similarly terrified students standing at the door. I approached them, not sure how I would introduce myself, or what excuse I'd have for talking to them. In the end, I didn't need an excuse. One of the students recognized me from orientation and called out to me. "Hey! You're from Mexico aren't you?"

"Yeah," I answered.

3

4

5

6

7

8

9

10

11

12

13

Details: Exact **details** help readers imagine the writer's appearance and language.

Tension: Quintana anticipates the challenge of putting his English skills to work and builds tension.

Tension: Dialogue helps build tension.

Transitions: Transitions of time help sequence events.

Details: Exact details help readers visualize situation.

Tension: Dialogue reinforces Santiago's struggle and builds tension.

Transitions: Transitions of time help sequence events.

Details: Detailed description helps build tension.

"Come, I'm from El Salvador. We were just talking about how different it is to learn English in class and have to speak it all the time with other Americans and also in class. I mean, you haven't had class yet, but you'll see. It's different," he said.   14

"I've already gotten lost like three times because I couldn't understand directions," said Amy, from Japan.   15

"It's the intonation. It's all wrong," said Matej from the Czech Republic.   16

"Also, they go too fast." All of the international students had stories of struggling with English, and they all had theories for the difference.   17

Finally, the time came for my first class — Mythology. I nervously entered the classroom, took a seat, and with pen and notebook ready, prepared to take notes. As I looked around, I noticed that there were only about ten students in the class. This only added to my nervousness; I would not be able to hide. I knew college in America would be difficult, but I could not have ever imagined how difficult it would actually be. Before class, I had made myself the promise that I would ask at least one question, or participate at least once. By the end of class, I had, at the most, one sentence scribbled on the page, and I had participated much more than once. I had asked the professor to explain terms and phrases, and sometimes even to repeat himself. I knew this was annoying for the rest of the students, and I apologized profusely through my blush. The professor assured me that it was fine, that he'd rather have us know the first half of the material really well, than go through the whole of it with only a vague inkling of what we were talking about. After he let us out of class, I stopped another student, a junior, and asked him to repeat what the homework assignment was, because I hadn't understood the professor. He smiled and said I didn't need to apologize, that it was only natural I would struggle with the language for the first week or so.   18

At the end of class, I was physically, mentally, and emotionally exhausted. Wanting to be alone, I went back to my room, lay down for a bit, and then made some tea. It was early afternoon now, and I had another class after lunch. I tried to relax. My head thumped from the adrenaline, and my heart hurt from the loneliness. My roommate came in and asked if I was doing fine and if I wanted to have lunch with him and   19 his friends. "Friends, friends, how can he have friends already?" I thought, "We've been here for less than a week and you call them friends." I said yes anyway. I knew I had to get out and walk it off, so to speak. Lunch was equally stressful, but being a less formal situation, I couldn't raise my hand and ask my roommate's friends to define terms and explain phrases and repeat themselves. So I just smiled and let most of the conversation go without participating. One of my roommate's friends must have seen confusion written on my face for she took her food and sat across from me and started talking to me. I asked her to go slowly, and told her that I was just getting used to English and that I was sorry for being a nuisance. She laughed. "The first thing you need to do is stop apologizing. We are not cold, heartless people. Well, most of us aren't. We understand. I can enunciate more clearly and speak more slowly, and it won't be a problem. Tell me, you went to high school in Mexico City?"

I was hesitant at first and thought about every word and whether it was appropriate. My new friend was incredibly patient with me, and she made me feel fine about my English. I don't know when or how, but eventually I was laughing at her jokes and the others joined in on our conversation, and I stopped thinking about every word I said. The words seemed to fall effortlessly out of my mouth, already strung into phrases. I told them about Mexico City and how crazy everything is, and no it's not nearly as dangerous as reporters make it seem in the news. I learned about their home towns, their interests, and what they did for fun. I was thinking about the conversation rather than the words. I forgot myself and only then did the English that I knew finally make an appearance.

It wasn't permanent though. It still took me a while to switch from translating to talking. I still struggled in class for the rest of the month, but the moments when I forgot myself and flowed with the conversation began happening more often. They happened when I didn't apologize for my "bad English," when I didn't talk myself down, when I knew myself capable, and when I trusted the years and years of English lessons behind me, rather than searching for words like papers in a file cabinet.

20

Details: Exact details help readers understand Quintana's experience.

Climax

21

Conclusion: Transitions highlight what Quintana has learned—that he must relearn confidence each year.

Now, I am about to start my third year of college. I have increased my vocabulary and improved my style immensely. Nevertheless, there is always a week or two at the beginning of school when I have to tell myself to find that confidence again, to not apologize, and to trust my knowledge. Sometimes I still apologize and struggle when choosing words, but it has become easier and easier to find those moments when I forget it's me talking, and I just let the talking happen.

22

Analyzing the Writer's Technique

1. **Thesis** Evaluate the strength of Quintana's thesis. How clear and specific is it?
2. **Details** How effectively does Quintana use details to reinforce his main point and to help readers visualize key people and places? Did you feel more details were needed? If so, where? Which details, if any, would you suggest he add or delete?
3. **Conflict and Tension** How does Quintana establish conflict and create tension?
4. **Foreshadowing** Where does Quintana use foreshadowing? How effective is it?
5. **Title, Introduction, and Conclusion** Evaluate the title, introduction, and conclusion of the essay.

Thinking Critically about Narration

1. **Tone** Describe Quintana's tone. What words convey his attitude or perspective? Does the tone change over the course of the essay? If so, how? Does it seem appropriate for the topic?
2. **Connotation** What connotation does the phrase "those loud Mexicans" (para. 1) have in the context of the paragraph?
3. **Fact and Opinion** In paragraph 2, Quintana writes, "My English was the reason I had chosen and been able to get into an American college." Is this statement a fact or an opinion? How do you know?

Responding to the Reading

1. **Reaction** Quintana mentions one experience with other international students, but he ends up bonding with a group of Americans. Why do you think this happened?
2. **Discussion** International students have a presence on most college campuses in America. What can American colleges do to better meet the needs of these students?
3. **Journal** Write a journal entry about someone you befriended when others may have brushed him or her aside. How did you reach out to the individual, and what were the results?
4. **Essay** Quintana felt lonely and anxious as he began college in a new country with a new language. Write a narrative essay about a time when you felt like an outsider, lonely and anxious about making friends and fitting in.

Chop Suey

Ira Sukrungruang

Ira Sukrungruang, a professor at the University of South Florida, writes in many different genres: essays, stories, poetry, and memoir. His memoir *Southside Buddhist* won the 2015 American Book Award. The author calls "Chop Suey," which follows, a "flash essay" because it captures a moment in memory that he feels compelled to record in writing; it captures the first time Sukrungruang saw his mother bowl and recognized her power. **Before reading**, preview the selection and make connections by thinking of a time when you experienced or witnessed someone making an unfair assumption about you or your culture. **While reading**, consider how Sukrungruang presents the conflict and creates tension as well as how he presents his relationship with his mother.

> **JUST-IN-TIME TIP** Highlighting Revealing Details
>
> As you read, notice and highlight the words the author uses to describe his mother and his attitude toward her. When you finish reading, notice how the language changes as the essay progresses.

lkpgfoto/E+/Getty Images

My mother was a champion bowler in Thailand. This was not what I knew of her. I knew only her expectations of me to be the perfect Thai boy. I knew her distaste for blonde American women she feared would seduce her son. I knew her distrust of the world she found herself in, a world of white faces and mackerel in a can. There were many things I didn't know about my mother when I was ten. She was what she was supposed to be. My mother. 1

At El-Mar Bowling Alley, I wanted to show her what I could do with the pins. I had bowled once before, at Dan Braun's birthday party. There, I had rolled the ball off the bumpers, knocking the pins over in a thunderous crash. I liked the sound of a bowling alley. I felt in control of the weather, the rumble of the ball on the wood floor like the coming of a storm, and the hollow explosion of the pins, distant lightning. At the bowling alley, men swore and smoked and drank. 2

My mother wore a light pink polo, jeans, and a golf visor. She put on a lot of powder to cover up the acne she got at 50. She poured Vapex, a strong smelling vapor rub, into her handkerchief, and covered her nose, complaining of the haze of smoke that floated over the lanes. My mother was the only woman in the place. We were the only non-white patrons. 3

I told her to watch me. I told her I was good. I set up, took sloppy and uneven steps, and lobbed my orange ball onto the lane with a loud thud. This time there were no bumpers. My ball veered straight for the gutter. 4

My mother said to try again. I did, and for the next nine frames, not one ball hit one pin. Embarrassed, I sat next to her. I put my head on her shoulder. She patted it for a while and said bowling wasn't an easy game. 5

My mother rose from her chair and said she wanted to try. She changed her shoes. She picked a ball from the rack, one splattered with colors. When she was ready, she lined herself up to the pins, the ball at eye level. In five concise steps, she brought the ball back, dipped her knees, and released it smoothly, as if her hand was an extension of the floor. The ball started on the right side of the lane and curled into the center. Strike. 6

She bowled again and knocked down more pins. She told me about her nearly perfect game, how in Thailand she was unbeatable. 7

I listened, amazed that my mother could bowl a 200, that she was good at something beyond what mothers were supposed to be good at, like cooking and punishing and sewing. I clapped. I said she should stop being a mother and become a bowler. 8

As she changed her shoes, a man with dark hair and a mustache approached our lane. In one hand he had a cigarette and a beer. He kept looking back at his buddies a few lanes over, all huddling and whispering. I stood beside my mother, wary of any stranger. My mother's smile disappeared. She rose off the chair. 9

"Hi," said the man. 10

My mother nodded. 11

"My friends over there," he pointed behind him, "well, we would like to thank you." His mustache twitched. 12

My mother pulled me closer to her leg, hugging her purse to her chest. 13

He began to talk slower, over-enunciating his words, repeating again. "We . . . would . . . like . . . to . . . thank . . ." 14

I tugged on my mother's arm, but she stood frozen. 15

". . . you . . . for . . . making . . . a . . . good . . . chop . . . suey. You people make good food." 16

The man looked back again, toasted his beer at his friends, laughing smoke   17
from his lips.

My mother grabbed my hand and took one step toward the man. In that   18
instant, I saw in her face the same resolve she had when she spanked, the same
resolve when she scolded. In that instant, I thought my mother was going to hit
the man. And for a moment, I thought the man saw the same thing in her eyes,
and his smile disappeared from his face. Quickly, she smiled—too bright, too
large—and said, "You're welcome."

Understanding the Reading

1. **Reasons** Why did the author's mother distrust the world she lived in?
2. **Thesis** What is Sukrungruang's thesis? Is it stated or implied?
3. **Details** What detail in paragraph 1 compels the young boy to want to show his mother what he "could do with pins"?
4. **Details** Contrast the description of how the boy bowled with the description of how his mother bowled.

Analyzing the Writer's Technique

1. **Opening and Conclusion** How does the concluding paragraph connect with the opening paragraph?
2. **Description** How does Sukrungruang use description and other strategies to make his experience vivid and engaging. Cite several examples.
3. **Patterns of Organization** Identify at least two other patterns of organization Sukrungruang uses and explain the benefit of including these other patterns.
4. **Details** How well do you think Sukrungruang describes his mother? What details do you find most effective? Are there any aspects of his mother about which you would like to learn more?

Thinking Critically

1. **Tone** Describe the tone of Sukrungruang's essay. Highlight words or phrases that reveal his attitude.
2. **Inference** What can readers infer about what the American man in the bowling alley thinks of Sukrungruang's mother?
3. **Fact or Opinion** In paragraph 1, the author writes: "She was what she was supposed to be. My mother." Is this statement a fact or an opinion?
4. **Discussion** Discuss why Sukrungruang describes his mother's smile as "too bright, too large." What does this description convey about his mother's attitude toward the man?
5. **Title** Consider the title in relation to the essay as a whole. Does it effectively capture the main idea? Why or why not?

Responding to the Reading

1. **Discussion** Why does the author make such a point of the fact that his mother was what she was supposed to be? What *are* mothers supposed to be? Does this type of mindset or these expectations present problems in our society today? Why or why not?

2. **Journal** Try to put yourself in the shoes of Sukrungruang's mother. How would the encounter with the man at the bowling alley have made you feel? How do you think you would have responded? What do you learn from this encounter, and how could it possibly affect your interaction with others who are different from you? Write a journal entry in which you speculate about these questions.

3. **Essay** Sukrungruang's trip with his mom to the bowling alley was a turning point in his relationship with his mother and possibly his life. His experiences there gave him a new respect for his mother and also a taste of the rudeness and disrespect that people can have for those who are different. Write a narrative essay about an event in your life that made a lasting impression on you. Be sure to follow the basic structure of a narrative essay (see Graphic Organizer 11.1) and include dialogue, description, and action verbs.

Working Together

Ira Sukrungruang learned several things about his mom when they went to the bowling alley. Working in small groups, create a motto that captures the essence of what Sukrungruang learned that day. You may focus on one or all of the things he learned. Be prepared to share your motto and explain the significance of it to the class.

READING

On the Outside: First Days of College

Tara Westover

The daughter of survivalist Mormon parents, Tara Westover grew up in a junkyard in the mountains of Idaho and attended school for the very first time when she was seventeen years old as a college freshman. Having received no formal education as a child—the home-schooling she received was haphazard at best—she was nonetheless accepted to college, successfully completed undergraduate and graduate degrees, and wrote a memoir that almost instantly became a bestseller. This reading is an excerpt from that memoir, *Educated* (2018). **Before reading**, preview and make connections by thinking about your first day of elementary school, middle school, high school, or college. **While reading**, look for and highlight the various conflicts the author experiences.

See sections 1a, 2b, and 2c in the Just-in-Time Guide for other useful suggestions for coping with unfamiliar words and subjects.

JUST-IN-TIME TIP Working with Unfamiliar Vocabulary

In the reading itself, expect to find unfamiliar vocabulary (such as *civic humanism*, para. 10) and references to unfamiliar names, events, and concepts (such as *Hume* and *Cicero*, 9; *Scottish Enlightenment*, 10; and "*Sons of Perdition*," 11). When you encounter such unfamiliar terms, highlight them and keep reading. Research them after you finish, and then reread the paragraphs that contain them once you understand their meaning in order to gain a fuller understanding of the selection.

I got on the bus going the wrong direction. By the time I'd corrected my mistake,   1
the lecture was nearly finished. I stood awkwardly in the back until the professor, a
thin woman with delicate features, motioned for me to take the only available
seat, which was near the front. I sat down, feeling the weight of everyone's eyes.
The course was on Shakespeare, and I'd chosen it because I'd heard of Shakespeare
and thought that was a good sign. But now I was here, I realized I knew nothing
about him. It was a word I'd heard, that was all.

When the bell rang, the professor approached my desk. "You don't belong   2
here," she said.

I stared at her, confused. Of course I didn't belong, but how did she know? I   3
was on the verge of confessing the whole thing—that I'd never gone to school,
that I hadn't really met the requirements to graduate—when she added, "This
class is for seniors."

"There are classes for seniors?" I said.   4

She rolled her eyes as if I were trying to be funny. "This is 382. You should be   5
in 110."

It took most of the walk across campus before I understood what she'd said,   6
then I checked my course schedule and, for the first time, noticed the numbers
next to the course names.

I went to the registrar's office, where I was told that every freshman-level   7
course was full. What I should do, they said, was check online every few hours and
join if someone dropped. By the end of the week, I'd managed to squeeze into
introductory courses in English, American history, music, and religion, but I was
stuck in a junior-level course on art in Western Civilization.

Freshman English was taught by a cheerful woman in her late twenties who   8
kept talking about something called the "essay form," which, she assured us, we
had learned in high school.

My next class, American history, was held in an auditorium named for the   9
prophet Joseph Smith. I'd thought American history would be easy because Dad
had taught us about the Founding Fathers—I knew all about Washington,
Jefferson, Madison. But the professor barely mentioned them at all, and instead
talked about "philosophical underpinnings" and the writings of Cicero and Hume,
names I'd never heard.

In the first lecture, we were told that the next class would begin with a quiz on   10
the readings. For two days I tried to wrestle meaning form the textbook's dense
passages, but terms like "civic humanism" and "the Scottish Enlightenment" dot-
ted the page like black holes, sucking all the other words into them. I took the quiz
and missed every question.

That failure sat uneasily in my mind. It was the first indication of whether I   11
would be okay, whether whatever I had in my head by way of *education* was
enough. After the quiz, the answer seemed clear: it was not enough. On realizing
this, I might have resented my upbringing but I didn't. My loyalty to my father had
increased in proportion to the miles between us. On the mountain, I could rebel.
But here, in this loud, bright place, surrounded by gentiles disguised as saints, I
clung to every truth, every doctrine he had given me. Doctors were Sons of Perdition. Homeschooling was a commandment from the Lord.

Failing a quiz did nothing to undermine my new devotion to an old creed, but 12
a lecture on Western art did.

The classroom was bright when I arrived, the morning sun pouring in warmly 13
through a high wall of windows. I chose a seat next to a girl in a high-necked
blouse. Her name was Vanessa. "We should stick together," she said. "I think we're
the only freshmen in the whole class."

The lecture began when an old man with small eyes and a sharp nose shut- 14
tered the windows. He flipped a switch and a slide projector filled the room with
white light. The image was of a painting. The professor discussed the composition,
the brushstrokes, the history. Then he moved to the next painting, and the next
and the next.

Then the projector showed a peculiar image, of a man in a faded hat and over- 15
coat. Behind him loomed a concrete wall. He held a small paper near his face but
he wasn't looking at it. He was looking at us.

I opened the picture book I'd purchased for the class so I could take a closer 16
look. Something was written under the image in italics but I couldn't understand
it. It had one of those black-hole words, right in the middle, devouring the rest. I'd
seen other students ask questions, so I raised my hand.

The professor called on me, and I read the sentence aloud. When I came to the 17
word, I paused. "I don't know this word," I said. "What does it mean?"

There was silence. Not a hush, not a muting of the noise, but utter, almost vio- 18
lent silence. No papers shuffled, no pencils scratched.

The professor's lips tightened. "Thanks for *that*," he said, then returned to his 19
notes.

I scarcely moved for the rest of the lecture. I stared at my shoes, wondering 20
what had happened, and why, whenever I looked up, there was always someone
staring at me as if I was a freak. Of course I was a freak, and I knew it, but I didn't
understand how *they* knew it.

When the bell rang, Vanessa shoved her notebook into her pack. Then she 21
paused and said, "You shouldn't make fun of that. It's not a joke." She walked away
before I could reply.

I stayed in my seat until everyone had gone, pretending the zipper on my coat 22
was stuck so I could avoid looking anyone in the eye. Then I went straight to the
computer lab to look up the word "Holocaust."

I don't know how long I sat there reading about it, but at some point I'd read 23
enough. I leaned back and stared at the ceiling. I suppose I was in shock, but
whether it was the shock of learning about something horrific, or the shock of
learning about my own ignorance, I'm not sure. I do remember imagining for a
moment, not the camps, not the pits or chambers of gas, but my mother's face. A
wave of emotion took me, a feeling so intense, so unfamiliar, I wasn't sure what it
was. It made me want to shout at her, at my own mother, and that frightened me.

I searched my memories. In some ways the word "Holocaust" wasn't wholly 24
unfamiliar. Perhaps Mother *had* taught me about it, when we were picking rosehips
or tincturing hawthorn. I did seem to have a vague knowledge that Jews had been
killed somewhere, long ago. But I'd thought it was a small conflict, like the Boston
Massacre, which Dad talked about a lot, in which half a dozen people had been

martyred by a tyrannical government. To have misunderstood it on this scale—five versus six million—seemed impossible.

I found Vanessa before the next lecture and apologized for the joke. I didn't   25
explain, because I couldn't explain. I just said I was sorry and that I wouldn't do it again. To keep that promise, I didn't raise my hand for the rest of the semester.

Understanding the Reading

1. **Reasons** What one event confirmed Westover's belief that her education prior to college was not enough to enable her to be successful?
2. **Thesis** What is Westover's thesis?
3. **Detail** In paragraph 11, what do you find out about Westover's relationship to her father?
4. **Vocabulary** Explain the meaning of each of the following words as it is used in the reading: *verge* (para. 3), *underpinnings* (9), *gentiles* (11), *tyrannical* (24). Refer to your dictionary as needed.

Analyzing the Writer's Technique

1. **Language** In paragraph 10, Westover describes "civic humanism" and "the Scottish Enlightenment" as "black holes, sucking all the other words into them." What does she mean by this description?
2. **Patterns of Organization** Identify at least two other patterns of organization Westover uses and explain the benefit of including these other patterns.
3. **Climax** What is the climax of the story, and when and how is tension resolved?
4. **Conclusion** Is Westover's final paragraph an effective conclusion? Why or why not?

Thinking Critically

1. **Tone** Based on the language the author uses and the style of her writing, what do you think the tone of the essay is? Explain your answer.
2. **Inference** What can you infer about the religious beliefs of the father that had been passed down to the children (para. 11)?
3. **Fact or Opinion** In paragraph 20, Westover writes, "Of course I was a freak, and I knew it, but I didn't understand how *they* knew it." Is this statement fact or opinion?
4. **Visual** Westover did not include a photograph with her essay. If you were choosing a photograph for this reading, what would it look like? How would it contribute to the overall impression of the narrative?

Responding to the Reading

1. **Discussion** Why do you think that Westover paints such an unflattering picture of her mother as her teacher (para. 23)? Do you think Westover was justified in being mad at her? Why do you think she was frightened when she had intense feelings toward her mother?

2. **Journal** Westover's first day of school definitely went badly wrong. Write a journal entry in which you discuss a memorable first day of school, and be sure to explain why you remember it so well.

3. **Essay** Have you ever been in a place where you felt that you did not belong or where you felt so different that people stared at you "as if you were a freak"? Brainstorm to recollect the details of this incident, and then write a narrative essay about this memorable but uncomfortable time in your life. Be sure to follow the basic structure of a narrative essay (see Graphic Organizer 11.1) and include dialogue, description, and action verbs as Westover does.

Working Together

Working in small groups, discuss the challenges freshmen typically face when they set foot on their college campus for freshman orientation or their first days of classes. Write a tip sheet entitled "What You Need to Know for the First Day of College."

Apply Your Skills: Additional Essay Assignments

Write a narrative on one of the topics listed below, using the elements and techniques of narration you learned in this chapter. Depending on the topic you choose, you may need to do research to gather support for your ideas.

To Express Your Ideas

1. Write a narrative about an incident or experience that you see differently now than you did when it happened.

2. In "Right Place, Wrong Face," Alton Fitzgerald White says he always believed that the police "were supposed to serve and protect" him (para. 2). After the incident he describes in the essay, he feels otherwise. Write a narrative describing an incident involving police officers or law enforcement agents that you may have experienced, observed, or read about. Did the incident change your attitude about police or law enforcement or confirm opinions you already held?

To Inform Your Reader

3. In "On the Outside: First Days of College," Westover suffers because she is unprepared for her new collegiate environment. Write an essay informing your reader about ways to learn about what is expected of students in college.

To Persuade Your Reader

4. At one time, America was described as a melting pot, where newcomers shed their cultural identity in favor of becoming an American. Critics of this loss of cultural identity would prefer to think of America as a tossed salad in which all the

"ingredients" retain their distinctive identities. Write an essay taking a position on whether immigrants to the United States should attempt to blend in or strive to retain their culture, language, and other unique cultural characteristics. Support your position, drawing on your own experiences, the experiences of friends and family members, or the experience of the mother and son in "Chop Suey."

5. In "Right Place, Wrong Face," White takes a position on racial profiling. Write an essay persuading your reader to take a particular stand on an issue of your choice. Use a story from your experience to support your position or tell how you arrived at it.

Cases Using Narration

6. Write a paper for a sociology course on the advantages of an urban, suburban, or rural lifestyle. Support some of your main points with events and examples from your own experiences.

7. Write a draft of the presentation you will give as the new human resource director of a nursing care facility in charge of training new employees. You plan to hold your first orientation session next week, and you want to emphasize the importance of teamwork and communication by telling related stories from your previous job experiences.

SYNTHESIZING IDEAS   **HARSH TREATMENT OF OUTCASTS**

Both "Right Place, Wrong Face" (pp. 243–45) and "Chop Suey" (pp. 259–61) describe the harsh treatment of someone seen as an outcast—a person who does not deserve respect or courtesy.

Analyzing the Readings

1. Compare the situations of each disrespected person. Then consider how each one responded to those who treated him harshly.

2. Compare the social issues that each author addresses in the narrative of his experience.

Essay Idea

Write an essay describing a situation in which you feel you or someone you know was treated as an outcast. Describe the background to the situation, the treatment received, and the response to the treatment.

12
Description
Portraying People, Places, and Things

Barry Winiker/Getty Images

Writing Quick Start

ANALYZE Suppose the owner of a local restaurant that you go to often asks you to increase the restaurant's presence on social media by praising the restaurant in an Instagram post or giving the restaurant a positive review on Yelp. You decide to include several photos of menu items, including the one shown here.

WRITE Create an appealing description to accompany this photograph. Use words that will appeal to the readers' senses of sight and smell, but also their senses of sound and even touch. You may even want to include a comparison that will help readers understand the dining experience.

CONNECT As you wrote your post or review, you probably included lots of details that will make readers' mouths water, such as details about how scrumptious the dish looks, its delicious aroma, the creamy texture of the dish's sauce, and its delectable taste. You may also have chosen to include details about how the dining room looks, feels, and smells; how the waitstaff behaves with customers; and how customers react to the food, the service, and the ambience.

The review or post you wrote is a good example of descriptive writing. It includes details that appeal to the readers' senses, enabling them to imagine tasting the food or visualizing the restaurant you described. In this chapter you will learn to use description to make your writing vivid and lively.

Description presents information in a way that appeals to one or more of the five senses (sight, sound, smell, taste, and touch) by creating an overall (dominant) impression or feeling. If you included concrete details and maybe an effective comparison in your Writing Quick Start, you wrote a successful **description.**

You use description every day—to describe a pair of shoes you bought, a flavor of ice cream you tasted, or a concert you attended recently. If you were an eyewitness to a car theft, the detective investigating the crime would ask you to describe what you saw.

Writers rely on description to present detailed information about people, places, and things and to grab and sustain their readers' interest. When you write vivid descriptions, you not only make your writing livelier and more interesting but also indicate your attitude toward the subject through your choice of concrete words and specific details.

USING DESCRIPTION   **IN COLLEGE AND THE WORKPLACE**

- In a *chemistry lab report*, you describe the odor and appearance of a substance made by combining two chemicals.

- In an *art history class*, you visit a local gallery, choose a painting, and describe in a two-page paper the artist's use of line or color.

- As a *nurse* at a local treatment center for burn victims, you record on each patient's medical chart the overall appearance of and change in second- and third-degree burns.

What Are the Characteristics of a Description?

Successful descriptions offer readers more than just a list of sensory details or a catalog of characteristics. In a good description, the details work together to create a dominant effect or impression.

Description Uses Sensory Details

Sensory details appeal to one or more of the five senses—sight, sound, smell, taste, and touch—and help your readers experience the object, sensation, event, or person you are describing.

Sight. When you describe what something looks like, you help your reader create a mental picture of the subject. In the following excerpt, notice how Loren Eiseley uses visual detail—shape, color, action—and specific nouns and noun phrases to describe what he comes across in a field.

Noun and noun phrases

Descriptive adjectives of shape and color

Active verbs and adverbs used to depict motion

                                                                    noun   adjective
I found a giant slug feeding from a funnel of pink ice cream in an abandoned
noun phrase   active verbs
Dixie cup. I could see his eyes telescope and protrude in a kind of dim, uncertain
     noun   adjective   active verbs   adjective
ecstasy as his dark body bunched and elongated in the curve of the cup.

—Loren Eiseley, "The Brown Wasps"

This description allows the reader to imagine the slug eating the ice cream in a way that a bare statement of the facts—"I saw a slug in a paper cup"—would not.

Sound. Sound can also be a powerful descriptive tool. Can you "hear" the engines in the following description?

Descriptive adjectives

Active verbs used to evoke specific sounds; some are *onomatopoetic*—they sound like what they describe.

                   adjective   adjective   adjective
They were one-cylinder and two-cylinder engines, and some were make-and-break
                    adjective   adjective
and some were jump-spark, but they all made a sleepy sound across the lake. The
               active verbs   adjective   active verb
one-lungers throbbed and fluttered, and the twin-cylinder ones *purred* and *purred*,

and that was a quiet sound too.

—E. B. White, "Once More to the Lake"

Smell. Smells are sometimes difficult to describe, partly because the English language does not have as many adjectives for smells as it does for sights and sounds. Smell can be an effective descriptive device, however, as shown here:

Driving through farm country at summer sunset provides a cavalcade of smells:

Nouns used to evoke distinct odors

                       nouns
manure, cut grass, honeysuckle, spearmint, wheat chaff, scallions, chicory, tar

from the macadam road.

—Diane Ackerman, *A Natural History of the Senses*

Notice how Diane Ackerman lists nouns that evoke distinct odors and leaves it to the reader to imagine how they smell.

Taste.   Words that evoke the sense of taste can make descriptions lively. Consider this restaurant critic's description of Vietnamese cuisine:

adjectives

In addition to balancing the primary flavors—the sweet, sour, bitter, salty and

peppery tastes . . .—medicinal herbs were used in most dishes. . . . For instance,

the orange-red annatto seed is used for its "cooling" effect as well as for the

adjective

mildly tangy flavor it lends.

—Molly O'Neill, "Vietnam's Cuisine: Echoes of Empires"

Descriptive **adjectives** of taste

Touch.   Annie Dillard's descriptions of texture, temperature, and weight allow a reader not only to visualize but also to experience what it feels like to hold a Polyphemus moth cocoon:

active verb & adverb   adjective

We passed the cocoon around. . . . The pupa began to jerk violently, in heart-

noun   noun   adjective

stopping knocks. Who's there? I can still feel those thumps, urgent through a

nouns and noun phrases   noun

muffling of spun silk and leaf, urgent through the swaddling of many years,

noun

against the curve of my palm.

—Annie Dillard, *Pilgrim at Tinker Creek*

Active verbs conveying temperature and motion

Descriptive **adjectives** of weight and texture

Nouns and noun phrases

Description Uses Active Verbs and Varied Sentences

Sensory details are often best presented through active, vivid verbs. In fact, active verbs are often more effective than adverbs in creating striking and lasting impressions, as the following example demonstrates:

adverb

Original   The team captain *proudly* accepted the award.

verb   verb

Revised   The team captain marched to the podium, grasped the trophy, and

verb

saluted his teammates.

Using varied sentences also contributes to the effective expression of sensory details. Be sure to use different types and patterns of sentences and to vary their lengths.

For more on using active verbs and varying sentence types, patterns, and length, see Chapter 9.

EXERCISE 12.1 **USING SENSORY DETAILS, ACTIVE VERBS, AND VARIED SENTENCES**

Using sensory details, active verbs, and varied sentences, describe one of the common objects in the following list or one of your own choosing. Do not name the object in your description. Exchange papers with a classmate. Your reader should be able to guess the item you are describing from the details you provide.

1. A piece of clothing
2. A food item
3. An appliance
4. A plant
5. An animal

Description Creates a Dominant Impression

For more on thesis statements, see Chapter 5.

An effective description leaves the reader with a **dominant impression**—an overall attitude, mood, or feeling about the subject. The impression may be awe, inspiration, anger, or distaste, for example.

Let's suppose that you are writing about an old storage box you found in your parents' attic. The aspect of the box you want to emphasize (your *slant, angle,* or *perspective*) is memories of childhood. Given this slant, you might describe the box in several ways, each of which would convey a different dominant impression.

- "A box filled with treasures from my childhood brought back memories of long, sunny afternoons playing in our backyard."
- "Opening the box was like lifting the lid of a time machine, revealing toys and games from another era."
- "When I opened the box, I was eight years old again, fighting over my favorite doll with my twin sister, Erica."

Notice that each example provides a different impression of the box's contents and would require a different type of support. That is, only selected objects from within the box would be relevant to each impression. Note, too, that in all of these examples, the dominant impression is stated directly in a thesis statement rather than implied.

To write an effective description, select details carefully, including only those that contribute to the dominant impression you are trying to create. Notice that Dillard, in the paragraph above, does not clutter her description by describing the physical appearance of the cocoon. Instead, she focuses on its movement and how it feels in her hand.

EXERCISE 12.2 ▶ **FOCUSING THE DOMINANT IMPRESSION**

As you read the following paragraph, cross out details that do not contribute to the dominant impression:

> All morning I had had a vague sense that bad news was on its way. As I stepped outside, the heat of the summer sun, unusually oppressive for ten o'clock, seemed to sear right through me. In fact, now that I think about it, everything seemed slightly out of kilter that morning. The car, which had been newly painted the week before, had stalled several times. The flowers in the garden, planted for me by my husband, purchased from a nursery down the road, were drooping. It was as though they were wilting before they even had a chance to grow. Even my two cats, who look like furry puffballs, moved listlessly across the room, ignoring my invitation to play. It was then that I received the phone call from the emergency room telling me about my son's accident.

Description Uses Connotative Language Effectively

Most words have two levels of meaning: denotative and connotative. The *denotation* of a word is its precise dictionary meaning. Often, however, feelings and attitudes—emotional colorings or shades of meaning—are also associated with a word. These are the word's *connotations*.

For more on connotation versus denotation, see Chapter 3.

Word	Denotation	Connotations
Flag	A piece of cloth used as a national emblem	Patriotism, love, and respect for one's country

As you write, be careful to select words with connotations that strengthen the dominant impression you are creating.

Description Uses Comparisons

Comparing the person or object you are describing to something your readers are familiar with can help them visualize your subject. Several types of comparisons are used in descriptive writing: similes, metaphors, and personification.

For more on simile, metaphor and personification, see Chapter 3.

Figure of Speech	Definition	Example
Simile	A direct comparison introduced by words such as *like* or *as*	*His lips were as soft as a rosebud's petals.*
Metaphor	An indirect comparison describing one thing as if it were another	*. . . his rosebud lips . . .*
Personification	A comparison that gives human qualities or characteristics to an inanimate object	*The television screen stared back at me.*

| EXERCISE 12.3 | **APPEALING TO THE SENSES** |

Write a paragraph describing an animal or pet. Focus on one sense or appeal to several. If possible, include a simile or a metaphor.

For more on methods of organization, see Chapter 7.

Description Follows a Method of Organization

Effective descriptions must follow a clear method of organization. Three common methods of organization used in descriptive writing are spatial order, chronological order, and most-to-least or least-to-most order.

- When you use **spatial order**, you describe a subject from top to bottom, from left to right, from near to far away, or from a central point outward. For example, if you are describing a college campus, you might start by describing a building at the center of the campus—the library, perhaps—and then move to surrounding buildings.

  In writing a description using spatial order, you can use either a fixed or a moving **vantage point**. With a fixed vantage point, you describe what you see from a particular position. With a moving vantage point, you describe your subject from different positions. A fixed vantage point is like a stationary camera trained on a subject from one direction. A moving vantage point is like a handheld camera that captures the subject from many directions.

- **Chronological order** works well when you need to describe events or changes that occur over a period of time. You might use chronological order to describe the changes in a puppy's behavior as it grows or to relate changing patterns of light and shadow as the sun sets.

- You might use either **most-to-least** or **least-to-most order** to describe the smells in a flower garden or the sounds of an orchestra tuning up for a concert.

- Clustering details by the **five senses**—how your subject looks, sounds, smells, tastes, and feels—might make sense for a topic such as a hot fudge sundae or a delicious meal at a restaurant.

The following readings demonstrate the techniques discussed above for writing effective descriptive essays. The first reading is annotated to point out how Joan Didion uses these techniques to make the Santa Ana winds and the resulting human behavior come alive. As you read the second essay, try to identify for yourself how the writer uses the techniques of descriptive writing to help readers imagine the Dreamland pool as it was to residents of Portsmouth, Ohio, in its prosperous past.

READING

The Santa Ana

Joan Didion

Joan Didion, a native Californian, is an award-winning American essayist and novelist, best known for her coverage of social and political issues in works like *Slouching toward Bethlehem* (1968), in which this selection appeared; *The White Album* (1979); and *Political Fictions* (2001). She is also the author of numerous novels (such as *Play It as*

It Lays, 1970; A Book of Common Prayer, 1977; and The Last Thing He Wanted, 1996) and screenplays (such as A Star Is Born, 1976; True Confessions, 1981; and Up Close & Personal, 1996). The Year of Magical Thinking (2005), her memoir about the death of her husband and writing partner, John Gregory Dunne, won the National Book Award. More recently, she has published Blue Nights (2011), a memoir about the death of her daughter, and South and West (2017), which includes a description of a road trip she took through the South in 1970 and excerpts from her notebooks. She was awarded the National Humanities Medal in 2013 for her lifetime contribution to American letters.

Before Reading

1. **Preview:** Use the steps listed in Chapter 2.
2. **Connect:** Have you ever experienced a tornado, hurricane, or other extreme weather event? If not, do you know anyone who has, or have you read about or seen coverage of such a weather event on television? What emotions did you experience before, during, and after the event?

While Reading Pay close attention to how the writer appeals to the senses in her description of Los Angeles and its people when the Santa Ana wind blows in.

There is something uneasy in the Los Angeles air this afternoon, some unnatural stillness, some tension. What it means is that tonight a Santa Ana will begin to blow, a hot wind from the northeast whining down through the Cajon and San Gorgonio Passes, blowing up sandstorms out along Route 66, drying the hills and the nerves to the flash point. For a few days now we will see smoke back in the canyons, and hear sirens in the night. I have neither heard nor read that a Santa Ana is due, but I know it, and almost everyone I have seen today knows it too. We know it because we feel it. The baby frets. The maid sulks. I rekindle a waning argument with the telephone company, then cut my losses and lie down, given over to whatever it is in the air. To live with the Santa Ana is to accept, consciously or unconsciously, a deeply mechanistic view of human behavior.

I recall being told, when I first moved to Los Angeles and was living on an isolated beach, that the Indians would throw themselves into the sea when the bad wind blew. I could see why. The Pacific turned ominously glossy during a Santa Ana period, and one woke in the night troubled not only by the peacocks screaming in the olive trees but by the eerie absence of surf. The heat was surreal. The sky had a yellow cast, the kind of light sometimes called "earthquake weather." My only neighbor would not come out of her house for days, and there were no lights at night, and her husband roamed the place with a machete. One day he would tell me that he had heard a trespasser, the next a rattlesnake.

"On nights like that," Raymond Chandler once wrote about the Santa Ana, "every booze party ends in a fight. Meek little wives feel the edge of the carving knife and study their husbands' necks. Anything can happen." That was the kind of wind it was. I did not know then that there was any basis for the effect it had on all of us, but it turns out to be another of those cases in which science bears out folk wisdom. The Santa Ana, which is named for one of the canyons it rushes through, is a *foehn* wind, like the *foehn* of Austria and Switzerland and the *hamsin* of Israel. There are a number of persistent malevolent winds, perhaps the best known of which are

1

2

3

Details: Uses striking verbs and sensory details (appeals to the reader's senses of sight and sound)

Dominant impression: <u>Thesis</u> identifies topic of description

Details: Chooses words with powerful connotations and appeals to reader's senses of sight (*yellow*), sound (*screaming*), touch (*glossy*)

Dominant impression: Uses anecdote to reinforce main idea

Dominant impression: Examples (*meek little wives*; *nausea*; *suicide*) support dominant impression

Robert Landau/Getty Images

the mistral of France and the Mediterranean sirocco, but a *foehn* wind has distinct characteristics: it occurs on the leeward slope of a mountain range and, although the air begins as a cold mass, it is warmed as it comes down the mountain and appears finally as a hot dry wind. Whenever and wherever a *foehn* blows, doctors hear about headaches and nausea and allergies, about "nervousness," about "depression." In Los Angeles some teachers do not attempt to conduct formal classes during Santa Ana, because the children become unmanageable. In Switzerland the suicide rate goes up during the *foehn,* and in the courts of some Swiss cantons the wind is considered a mitigating circumstance for crime. Surgeons are said to watch the wind, because blood does not clot normally during a *foehn.* A few years ago an Israeli physicist discovered that not only during such winds, but for the ten or twelve hours which precede them, the air carries an unusually high ratio of positive to negative ions. No one seems to know exactly why that should be; some talk about friction and others suggest solar disturbances. In any case the positive ions are there, and what an excess of positive ions does, in the simplest terms, is make people unhappy. One cannot get much more mechanistic than that.

Easterners commonly complain that there is no "weather" at all in Southern   4
California, that the days and the seasons slip by relentlessly, numbingly bland. That is quite misleading. In fact the climate is characterized by infrequent but violent extremes: two periods of torrential subtropical rains which continue for weeks and wash out the hills and send subdivisions sliding toward the sea; about twenty scattered days a year of the Santa Ana, which, with its incendiary dryness, invariably means fire. At the first prediction of a Santa Ana, the Forest Service flies men and equipment from northern California into the southern forests, and the Los Angeles Fire Department cancels its ordinary non-firefighting routines. The Santa Ana

Comparison: Uses contrast to highlight weather extremes; transition signals contrast

Details: Appeals to reader's senses

Organization: Uses transitions to convey chronological order

caused Malibu to burn the way it did in 1956, and Bel Air in 1961, and Santa Barbara in 1964. In the winter of 1966–67 eleven men were killed fighting a Santa Ana fire that spread through the San Gabriel Mountains. Just to watch the front-page news out of Los Angeles during a Santa Ana is to get very close to what it is about the place. The longest single Santa Ana period in recent years was in 1957, and it lasted not the usual three or four days but fourteen days, from November 21 until December 4. On the first day 25,000 acres of the San Gabriel Mountains were burning, with gusts reaching 100 miles an hour. In town, the wind reached Force 12, or hurricane force, on the Beaufort Scale; oil derricks were toppled and people ordered off the downtown streets to avoid injury from flying objects. On November 22 the fire in the San Gabriels was out of control. On November 24 six people were killed in automobile accidents, and by the end of the week the Los Angeles *Times* was keeping a box score of traffic deaths. On November 26 a prominent Pasadena attorney, depressed about money, shot and killed his wife, their two sons, and himself. On November 27 a South Gate divorcee, twenty-two, was murdered and thrown from a moving car. On November 30 the San Gabriel fire was still out of control, and the wind in town was blowing eighty miles an hour. On the first day of December four people died violently, and on the third the wind began to break.

It is hard for people who have not lived in Los Angeles to realize how radically the Santa Ana figures in the local imagination. The city burning is Los Angeles's deepest image of itself: Nathanael West perceived that, in *The Day of the Locust*; and at the time of the 1965 Watts riots what struck the imagination most indelibly were the fires. For days one could drive the Harbor Freeway and see the city on fire, just as we had always known it would be in the end. Los Angeles weather is the weather of catastrophe, of apocalypse, and, just as the reliably long and bitter winters of New England determine the way life is lived there, so the violence and the unpredictability of the Santa Ana affect the entire quality of life in Los Angeles, accentuate its impermanence, its unreliability. The wind shows us how close to the edge we are.

5   **Conclusion:** Makes a final statement about how the Santa Ana affects life in Los Angeles

Comparison: Uses comparison to highlight the effect of the wind on people's lives

Visualize a Description: Create a Graphic Organizer

Seeing the content and structure of an essay in simplified, visual form can help you analyze a reading, recall key images as you generate ideas for an essay, and structure your own writing. Graphic Organizer 12.1 diagrams the basic structure of a descriptive essay. When you write an essay in which your primary purpose is to describe something, you will need to follow the standard essay format—title, introduction, body, and conclusion—with slight adaptations and adjustments.

For more on creating a graphic organizer, see Chapter 2.

- The **introduction** should provide a context for the description and present the thesis statement, which states or suggests the dominant impression.

- The **body** of the essay should present sensory details that support the dominant impression.
- The **conclusion** draws the description to a close and makes a reference to the dominant impression. It may offer a final detail or make a closing statement.

When you incorporate a description into an essay in which you also use other patterns of development, you will probably need to condense or eliminate one or more of the elements of your descriptive essay.

GRAPHIC ORGANIZER 12.1 The Basic Structure of a Descriptive Essay

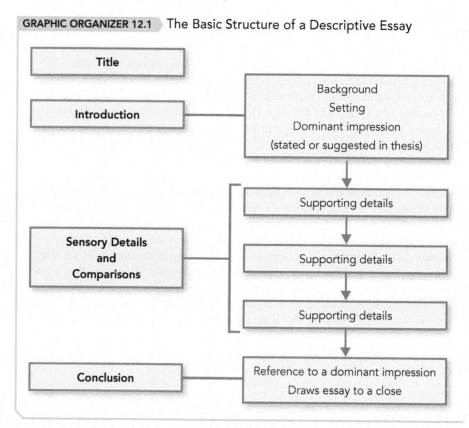

Title

| Introduction | | Background
Setting
Dominant impression
(stated or suggested in thesis) |

	Supporting details
Sensory Details and Comparisons	Supporting details
	Supporting details

| Conclusion | | Reference to a dominant impression
Draws essay to a close |

READING

Dreamland, Portsmouth, Ohio

Sam Quinones

Sam Quinones is a freelance journalist, a former *Los Angeles Times* reporter, and a storyteller. He is the author of *Dreamland: The True Tale of America's Opiate Epidemic* (2015), from which this selection was taken, as well as *The Virgin of the American Dream: Guadalupe on the Walls of Los Angeles* (2019). **Before reading**, preview and make connections by thinking of a special place or experience that lives within your memory. What makes it so special? **While reading**, highlight the details that help you visualize Dreamland.

In 1929, three decades into what were the great years for the blue-collar town of   1
Portsmouth, on the Ohio River, a private swimming pool opened and they called it
Dreamland. The pool was the size of a football field. Over the decades, generations
of the town grew up at the edge of its crystal-blue water.

Dreamland was the summer babysitter. Parents left their children at the pool every   2
day. Townsfolk found respite from the thick humidity at Dreamland and then went
across the street to the A&W stand for hot dogs and root beer. The pool's french fries
were the best around. Kids took the bus to the pool in the morning, and back home in
the afternoon. They came from schools all over Scioto County and met each other and
learned to swim. Some of them competed on the Dreamland Dolphins swim team,
which practiced every morning and evening. WIOI, the local radio station, knowing so
many of its listeners were sunbathing next to their transistor radios at Dreamland,
would broadcast a jingle—"Time to turn so you won't burn"—every half hour.

The vast pool had room in the middle for two concrete platforms, from   3
which kids sunned themselves then dove back in. Poles topped with floodlights
rose from the platforms for swimming at night. On one side of the pool was an
immense lawn where families set their towels. On the opposite side were locker
rooms and a restaurant.

Dreamland could fit hundreds of people, and yet, magically, the space   4
around it kept growing and there was always room for more. Jaime Williams, the
city treasurer, owned the pool for years. Williams was part owner of one of the
shoe factories that were at the core of Portsmouth's industrial might. He bought
more and more land, and for years Dreamland seemed to just get better. A large
picnic area was added, and playgrounds for young children. Then fields for softball
and football, and courts for basketball and shuffleboard, and a video arcade.

For a while, to remain white only, the pool became a private club and the   5
name changed to the Terrace Club. But Portsmouth was a largely integrated town.
Its chief of police was black. Black and white kids went to the same schools. Only
the pool remained segregated. Then, in the summer of 1961, a black boy named
Eugene McKinley drowned in the Scioto River, where he was swimming because
he was kept out of the pool. The Portsmouth NAACP pushed back, held a wade-in,
and quietly they integrated the pool. With integration, the pool was rechristened
Dreamland, though blacks were never made to feel particularly comfortable there.

Dreamland did wash away class distinctions, though. In a swimming suit, a   6
factory worker looked no different from the factory manager or clothing-shop owner.
Wealthy families on Portsmouth's hilltop donated money to a fund that would go to
pay for summer passes for families from the town's East End, down between the tracks
and the Ohio River. East End river rats and upscale hilltoppers all met at Dreamland.

California had its beaches. Heartland America spent its summers at   7
swimming pools, and, down at a far end of Ohio, Dreamland took on an outsized
importance to the town of Portsmouth. A family's season pass was only
twenty-five dollars, and this was a prized possession often given as a Christmas
present. Kids whose families couldn't afford that could cut a neighbor's grass for
the fifteen cents that a daily pool pass cost.

Friday swim dances began at midnight. They hauled out a jukebox and kids   8
spent the night twisting by the pool. Couples announced new romances by walking
hand in hand around Dreamland. Girls walked home from those dances and

families left their doors unlocked. "The heat of the evening combined with the cool water was wonderful," one woman remembered. "It was my entire world. I did nothing else. As I grew up and had my own children, I took them, too."

In fact, the cycle of life in Portsmouth was repeated over and over at Dreamland. A toddler spent her first years at the shallow end watched by her parents, particularly her mother, who sat on a towel on the concrete near the water with other young moms. When the child left elementary school, she migrated out to the middle section of Dreamland as her parents retreated to the grass. By high school, she was hanging out on the grass around the pool's ten-foot deep end, near the high dive and the head lifeguard's chair, and her parents were far away. When she married and had children, she returned to the shallow end of Dreamland to watch over her own children, and the whole thing began again. 9

"My father, a Navy Vet from World War II, insisted that his four children learn not only how to swim but how not to be afraid of water," one man wrote. "My younger sister jumped off the fifteen-foot high diving board at age three. Yes, my father, myself and brother were in the water just in case. Sister pops up out of the water and screams . . . 'Again!'" 10

For many years, Dreamland's manager, Chuck Lorentz, a Portsmouth High School coach and strict disciplinarian, walked the grounds with a yardstick, making sure teenagers minded his "three-foot rule" and stayed that far apart. He wasn't that successful. It seems half the town got their first kiss at the pool, and plenty lost their virginity in Dreamland's endless grass. 11

Lorentz's son, meanwhile, learned to swim before he could walk and became a Dreamland lifeguard in high school. "To be the lifeguard in that chair, you were right in the center of all the action, all the strutting, all the flirting," said John Lorentz, now a retired history professor. "You were like a king on a throne." 12

sbk_20d pictures/Moment Select/Getty Images

Memories of Dreamland, drenched in the smell of chlorine, Coppertone, and french fries, were what almost everyone who grew up in Portsmouth took with them as the town declined. 13

Two Portsmouths exist today. One is a town of abandoned buildings at the edge of the Ohio River. The other resides in the memories of thousands in the town's diaspora who grew up during its better years and return to the actual Portsmouth rarely, if at all. When you ask them what the town was back then, it was Dreamland. 14

EXERCISE 12.4 ▸ DRAWING A GRAPHIC ORGANIZER

Using Graphic Organizer 12.1 or 12.2 as a basis, draw a graphic organizer for "The Santa Ana."

GRAPHIC ORGANIZER 12.2 The Structure of "Dreamland, Portsmouth, Ohio"

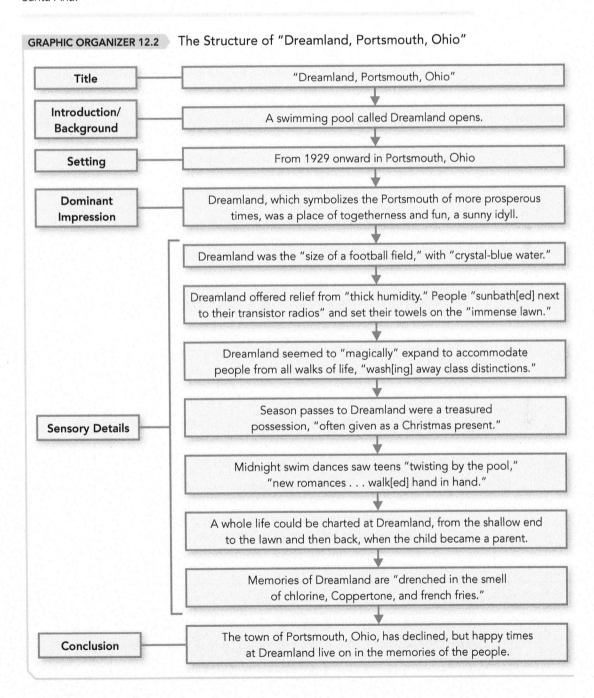

Title	"Dreamland, Portsmouth, Ohio"
Introduction/ Background	A swimming pool called Dreamland opens.
Setting	From 1929 onward in Portsmouth, Ohio
Dominant Impression	Dreamland, which symbolizes the Portsmouth of more prosperous times, was a place of togetherness and fun, a sunny idyll.
Sensory Details	Dreamland was the "size of a football field," with "crystal-blue water."
	Dreamland offered relief from "thick humidity." People "sunbath[ed] next to their transistor radios" and set their towels on the "immense lawn."
	Dreamland seemed to "magically" expand to accommodate people from all walks of life, "wash[ing] away class distinctions."
	Season passes to Dreamland were a treasured possession, "often given as a Christmas present."
	Midnight swim dances saw teens "twisting by the pool," "new romances . . . walk[ed] hand in hand."
	A whole life could be charted at Dreamland, from the shallow end to the lawn and then back, when the child became a parent.
	Memories of Dreamland are "drenched in the smell of chlorine, Coppertone, and french fries."
Conclusion	The town of Portsmouth, Ohio, has declined, but happy times at Dreamland live on in the memories of the people.

HOW WRITERS READ   DESCRIPTION

THE READING PROCESS	STRATEGIES
BEFORE READING	**Preview** the essay to get an overview of the content and organization. **Make connections** by thinking about what the subject of the essay would look, sound, taste, smell, or feel like. **Read the headnote** (if one is provided) for background information about the author and the reading.
WHILE READING	**Identify the characteristics of description** (pp. 269–74). Be sure you can answer the following questions: • What is the **subject**, and on what **aspect(s)** of the subject does the essay focus? • What is the **dominant impression**? How do individual **sensory details** contribute to the dominant impression? Highlight key details. • How does the writer use **language** to achieve the desired effect? Circle powerful word choices or place a checkmark in the margin. • What is the author's **vantage point**? How does the vantage point affect the description? • What is the writer's **thesis**? Is it stated or implied? • What is the author's **purpose**? Who is the intended **audience**?
AFTER READING	Draw a **graphic organizer** listing the key elements of the description. (Use your graphic organizer for review and study.) **Analyze and evaluate** the reading by answering the following questions: • How do the **title**, **introduction**, and **conclusion** hint at the dominant impression? • What is the **writer's attitude** toward the subject? Highlight words with strong connotations that reveal the writer's feelings. • What is the **writer's purpose**, and how does the description help the writer achieve this goal? • What does the writer leave undescribed? Are any relevant **details omitted**, and if so, why? • What **overall impression** is the author trying to leave readers with? • Is the description **objective**, or is it **slanted** (or even biased)? • What **thoughts and feelings** did the essay evoke in you? Explain your reaction in detail.

EXERCISE 12.5   **READING CRITICALLY**

Apply the questions in the "How Writers Read" box above to "Dreamland, Portsmouth, Ohio."

Integrate Description into an Essay

Sometimes description alone fulfills the purpose of an essay. In most cases, however, you will use description in essays that mainly rely on a different mode. For instance, in a narrative essay, description helps readers experience events, reconstruct scenes, and visualize action. Although most of your college essays will not be primarily descriptive, you can use description in essays that explain the causes or effects of a phenomenon, compare or contrast animal species, or illustrate defensive behavior in children, for example.

Here are a few suggestions for combining description effectively with other patterns of development:

1. **Include only relevant details.** Whether you describe an event, a person, or a scene, the sensory details you choose should enhance the reader's understanding of your subject.
2. **Keep the description focused.** Select enough details to make your essential points and dominant impression clear. Readers may become impatient if you include too many descriptive details.
3. **Make sure the description fits the essay's tone and point of view.** A personal description, for example, is not appropriate in an essay explaining a technical process.

PREWRITING	DRAFTING	REVISING	EDITING & PROOFREADING

A Guided Writing Assignment*

DESCRIPTION

Your Essay Assignment

Write a descriptive essay about something you can picture clearly or that you can readily observe. Choose one of the following to describe in detail:

- an unusual, striking, or surprising object
- a place that has significance to you, your family, or your cultural group
- a person who influenced you (for good or ill)

Examples: A robot you built from a kit; a playground you hung around in as a child; a teacher who changed your expectations about school or learning.

---

* The writing process is *recursive*; that is, you may find yourself revising as you draft or prewriting as you revise. This is especially true when writing on a computer. Your writing process may also differ from project to project or from that of your classmates.

1 Select a topic from the list on the previous page, or create your own.

Use one or more of the following suggestions to choose a subject to describe:

1. **List one or more broad topics**, such as *An Unusual Object, A Place with Personal Significance,* or *An Influential Person.* Then alone or with another student, **brainstorm a list of objects**, **activities**, or **people** that fit the assignment. Other prewriting strategies, like freewriting or questioning, may also help you generate topic ideas.

2. **Picture the objects in your room** or on your desk and ask yourself questions, such as "Who gave me that object?" or "Why did I buy [or make] it?"

3. **Work backward:** Think about the most influential people or most important values in your life, and then think about a place or object that represents them in your mind.

2 Consider your purpose and audience, and choose a perspective and point of view.

Ask yourself these questions:

- Will my essay's **purpose** be to **express myself**, **inform**, or **persuade**?

- Who is my **audience**? Will readers need any **background information** to understand my essay? Have I chosen a person, place, or thing that I can write about honestly for this audience?

- What **point of view** best suits my purpose and audience? The first person (*I, we*) will work best if describing an object with personal significance or if your purpose is expressive; third person (*it, they, he/she*) will be most appropriate if describing something objectively, of if your purpose is informative.

3 Choose an aspect of your subject to emphasize, and collect sensory details.

Choose one trait or aspect of your subject to focus on.

If it's a . . .	try focusing on . . .
person	a character trait
thing	its usefulness, value, or beauty

Then record details that support the slant you have chosen.

1. **Describe your subject to a friend**, concentrating on the slant you have chosen, and make notes on your comments and your friend's response.

2. **Draw a quick sketch** of your subject and label the parts.

3. **Make a table** and label each section with one of the senses. Then list the sensory details associated with your subject.

Generate comparisons. Think of appropriate comparisons—**similes, metaphors, personifications**—for as many details in your list as possible. Then select the one or two strongest comparisons and try to use them in your essay. Use at least two prewriting strategies to generate details. (More prewriting strategies appear in Chapter 4.)

4 Evaluate your details.

Reread your notes, highlighting the **vivid, concrete details** that will create pictures in your reader's mind. Cross out the following:

- vague details
- irrelevant details
- details that do not support your slant

Then copy and paste the remaining details into a new document for easy access when drafting.

In small groups, share your ideas and details.

1. Have each writer **explain her or his slant** on the subject and **provide a list of details.**
2. As a group, **evaluate each writer's details** in terms of her or his slant and suggest improvements.

5 Create a dominant impression.

Your **dominant impression** should

- appeal to **your audience**
- offer an **unusual perspective**
- provide **new insights** on your subject

Description often includes an element of surprise; a description with an unexpected slant and new insights is more likely to engage the readers' imagination.

Think of the dominant impression as

1. **a thesis** that conveys your main point and pulls your details together
2. **a mood or feeling about the subject**, which all the details in your essay explain or support

Team up with a classmate to evaluate each other's dominant impression. Underline or highlight any problematic wording and give feedback.

6 Choose a method of organization.

Select the **method of organization** that will best support your dominant impression:

- If you are focusing on a person's slovenly appearance, then a **spatial** (top to bottom, left to right) organization may be effective. If using spatial organization, also consider what **vantage point(s)** will provide the most useful information or from which vantage point(s) you can provide the most revealing or striking details.
- If you are describing a visit to a wildlife preserve, **chronological** order might be a useful method of organization (what you saw or experienced first, next, last).
- A **most-to-least** or **least-to-most** arrangement might work best for a description of the symptoms of pneumonia.
- If you are describing a chocolate chip cookie, you may want to organize by the **five senses**, clustering details about how it looks, smells, tastes, and feels in your mouth.

7 Write a first draft of your descriptive essay.

Use the following guidelines to keep your narrative on track:

- The **introduction** should set up your **dominant impression**, which you may choose to state in a thesis.
- The **body paragraphs** should include **striking sensory details** that support your **dominant impression**. Be sure to include **enough details** that readers can picture your subject but not so many that readers will get bored. Try to work your one or two strongest comparisons into your draft. Organize each body paragraph so that it focuses on a **single topic**, and use **transitions** (*first, next, above, below, before, after*) to make relationships among details clear. You may want to include a **photograph** (or video or audio file if presenting your description online), but remember that an illustration cannot substitute for a detailed, sensory description.
- The **conclusion** should **revisit your dominant impression**. You may also want to refer to the beginning of your essay or make a final observation about the significance of your subject.

8 Evaluate your draft and revise as necessary.

Use **Figure 12.1, "Flowchart for Revising a Descriptive Essay,"** to help you discover the strengths and weaknesses of your descriptive essay.

FIGURE 12.1 Flowchart for Revising a Descriptive Essay

QUESTIONS   REVISION STRATEGIES

1. Without looking at your essay, *state* the dominant impression in a sentence. Then highlight the sentences that express the *dominant impression*. Do they successfully convey the impression?

 NO ▶

- Reread your essay. Make a list of the different impressions it conveys.
- Choose one impression that you have the most to say about, and brainstorm to develop additional details that support it.

 YES ▼

2. Place a ✔ by each sensory detail. Does each detail support your *dominant impression*?

 NO ▶

- Eliminate irrelevant sensory details.

 YES ▼

3. Highlight your sensory details. Is your language vivid enough to help readers visualize the topic? Are the connotations of your language appropriate?

 NO ▶

- Brainstorm additional sensory details.
- Replace passive verbs with active ones.
- Vary your sentences.
- Replace vague or inappropriate words with words that better support your dominant impression.

 YES ▼

4. [Bracket] each comparison—simile, metaphor, and analogy. Is each fresh and effective?

 NO ▶

- Eliminate clichés.
- Brainstorm fresh comparisons or discuss with a friend.

 YES
▼

5. Outline your details and examine your organization. Is it clear from your essay how the details are organized?

 NO ▶

- Rearrange your details. Experiment to see which order works best.
- Add transitions to connect your ideas.

 YES
▼

6. Underline each paragraph's topic sentence. Check (✔) the sensory details against the topic sentence. Does the topic sentence make clear what the paragraph is describing?

 NO ▶

- Revise so that each paragraph has a clear topic sentence and supporting details clearly relate to the topic sentence.

 YES
▼

7. Reread your introduction and conclusion. Is each effective?

NO ▶

- Revise your introduction and conclusion so that they meet the guidelines in Chapter 7.

 9 Edit and proofread your essay.

Refer to Chapter 9 for help with

- **editing sentences** to avoid wordiness, making your verb choices strong and active, and making your sentences clear, varied, and parallel
- **editing words** for tone and diction, connotation, and concrete and specific language

Pay particular attention to the **punctuation of adjectives**.

1. Use a comma between **coordinate adjectives** that are not joined by *and*.

- **Singh was a *confident, skilled* pianist.**

Coordinate adjectives are a series of adjectives whose order can be changed (*skilled, confident* pianist or *confident, skilled* pianist).

2. Do not use commas between **cumulative adjectives** whose order cannot be changed.

- ***Two frightened brown* eyes peered at us from under the sofa.**

You would not write *frightened two brown* eyes.

3. Use a hyphen to connect two words that work together as an adjective before a noun *unless* the first word is an adverb ending in *-ly*.

- *well-used* book
- *foil-wrapped* pizza
- **perfectly thrown pass**

Readings: Description in Action

Sometimes, We Give

Maia Nault

Maia Nault wrote the following essay in response to an assignment that asked her to describe an encounter with someone who had made a lasting impression on her life. As you read, study the annotations that accompany the reading to discover how the essay illustrates the characteristics of effective descriptive writing as presented earlier in the chapter.

Introduction: Nault builds toward her dominant impression by describing her reaction to a homeless man on the sidewalk.

A grimy, bearded man sat and squirmed between a heap of blankets and cardboard mats across the street, baking on the sidewalk, while the sun glared down mercilessly during one of summer's hottest days. Heavy, lunchtime foot traffic bustled through one of the city's busiest plazas as everyone hurried from their offices to the chilled, air-conditioned relief of their destinations. The air was thick and uncomfortable, full of car exhaust and the smell of sweat, but I stood unmoving in the middle of the plaza. I ignored the people shoving past me, and stared worriedly at the homeless man across the street. No one was stopping to help him. I had never interacted with a homeless person before—what was the right thing to do? My options swam in panicked circles through my mind, and my eyes darted nervously from the homeless man to the passing crowds. That day, I was called upon to make decisions that would test my character.

Dominant impression: Thesis identifies the topic of the description.

1

From the minute I clambered out of bed, I knew that it was going to be a difficult day. I slept through my alarm, didn't have time for breakfast, and forgot to pack my lunch the night before. On top of that, I managed to set myself up for a wardrobe malfunction. My pencil skirt was wrinkled, a hole the size of my dog's face had somehow materialized in the armpit of my blouse, and I donned my go-to black flats without putting on a pair of socks to help my feet breathe. It was the fourth day of my internship, and I was desperate to make a good impression, though I seemed to be failing miserably. My sweaty toes squelched together in my

Details: Appeals to the reader's sense of sight and touch

Comparison: Uses comparison and simile to add humor and realism to visual details

2

flats, which were more like swimming pools by the time I got to work that morning. I could feel the makeup melting on my face, and my hair felt like a frizzy rat's nest on top of my head. I was a disheveled mess.

I left the office around noon to buy lunch and spotted the homeless man a block away. One look at this crumpled soul in his threadbare, filthy clothes halted my pity party and put things into perspective; I looked and felt like a wreck, but the sunburnt man across the street was surely having a worse day than I was.

Person after person walked past the homeless man, ignoring him completely. I pleaded with myself to do something, but the best I could manage was to drag my slippery feet around the block three times just to end up in the same spot again. I was nervous, stalling for time, and I couldn't figure out why. A different kind of sweat broke out across the nape of my neck and slid down my back as I chewed my nail anxiously. Was I scared of standing out from the crowd? Would people judge me? Did any of that even matter?

Then suddenly a wave of calmness washed over me. I took a slow, steady breath. *No,* I told myself. *None of that matters.* As my jittery mind became still, my legs mobilized. I wanted to do the right thing; I knew what that was because I knew myself.

I am kind. I walked into a nearby grocery store and hoisted a plastic basket onto my shoulder. *I am generous.* I filled my basket with water bottles, bananas, peanut butter, bagels, vitamins, and sunscreen. *I am resolute.* I paid, marched out of the store, clenched my fists tightly around my shopping bags, turned on my sweaty heel, and didn't stop until I was standing half a block from the homeless man. He sat on the sidewalk, leaning with his back against the side of a brick building, wearing a filthy, gray tank-top and dingy cargo pants with rips in the knees. His hair was dirty and wild, barely restrained by a flimsy elastic tie. He wasn't begging; his exposed knees were pulled up to his chest and his head was cradled in his arms, hidden from view. His shoulders shook slightly from quiet sobs but he didn't bother anyone passing him on the sidewalk.

I glanced up and down the sidewalk, assuring myself that there weren't any creeps around and that this wasn't going to turn into an ambush. My

3

4

5

6

7

Comparison: Uses metaphor and contrast to highlight author's connection with the homeless man

Details: Appeals to reader's touch

Dominant impression: Uses questions to support main idea

Comparison: Uses metaphor

Details: Uses striking verbs to present details

Dominant impression: Uses striking verbs and specific adjectives that appeal to the senses to support main idea.

Details: Chooses words with powerful connotations

Comparison: Uses personification

Details: Appeals to reader's sense of touch, sight, and sound

strategy was a simple one: approach target, complete a quick drop-off, leave target. No chit-chat, no surprises, no wasting time. Unfortunately, that plan dissolved as soon as he dragged his face up from his arms, scrubbed his dusty knuckles across his eyes, and fixed me with a watery gaze. His tears had cut paths through the grime on his face, leaving dark smudges on his cheeks. I imagined that, at some point, he may have had an attractive face. His eyes were tired but a pretty light green color, his long hair was greasy but blonde, and if it weren't for the red, splotchy sunburn, he would have had clear, fair skin.

I took a moment to process his features as we looked at one another, when an odd realization struck me. "You're so young," I blurted. I could feel my melting face light up with embarrassment, and he cracked a dry-lipped smile that revealed perfectly straight teeth. "Hello to you, too," he responded. "My name is Michael." His voice sounded a little congested from crying but was mellow and warm, with a pleasant tone that made me believe he enjoyed talking to people. From far away he looked old, grizzly, and emaciated, clinging to the ragged clothes that he must have filled out before hunger took its toll. I realized now that those assumptions were only based on a stereotype. Up close, he looked so different—not quite what I expected a homeless man to look like. He had no wrinkles, and he wasn't skin-and-bones skinny. His face was youthful, though his unkempt beard covered quite a bit of it, and while he was a little on the thin side, he looked healthy and lean. There were no hard lines around his eyes or mouth, and he had big, bright eyes that shone through the sweat and caked-on dirt with a depth of intelligence and curiosity that I didn't expect to see.

I learned a little more about Michael each time I visited, every couple of weeks, to drop off more essentials. He was pleasant, with an easygoing disposition and a genuine smile. Our conversations were brief, as I was reluctant to delve too deeply into his life and even more reluctant to give away anything about myself, but he expressed his gratitude for the visits nonetheless. On my third visit, as I was leaving, I learned that Michael was a student about a year ago. His voice quavered as he told me about his studies; he used to be a history student, a junior in college, and he really loved to read. I remember watching his nose turn red and his eyes well up

8

9

as he told me these things, and I was reminded of the first time I saw him, crying with his knees curled up to his chest. I walked away from him that day realizing that I could have been talking to one of my friends from school. He was my age—a college student—and in another life, he could have been just a regular guy on campus that I bumped into now and then. The thought made my chest tighten and my eyes sting; I couldn't comprehend how this could happen to somebody so young and full of potential.

On my fourth visit, I brought with me a couple of novels from the giveaway pile in our office's kitchen. Michael's smile stretched across his face when I presented him with the books, along with another bag of food, and he reached for them eagerly. His happiness was palpable; tears sprang to his green eyes again and this time, I couldn't help but to cry with him a little bit. He thanked me, so many times, and I waved goodbye as I turned to walk away. My heart felt light and happy, and I was proud of myself for being brave enough to help somebody.

I was a few steps away from Michael when a strong grip on my upper arm and a rough, gravelly voice stopped me. "What about me? Where's my bag?" I craned my head back and stared wide-eyed into the wild, bloodshot eyes of another homeless man. This man was older, more wrinkled and worn down than Michael. He was wearing layer upon layer of ripped, dusty clothes the color of wet cement, and the strong smell of body odor sprung to my nose. I always checked before approaching Michael. How did I not see him? What did I miss? What should I do now?

Before I knew it, I was being pushed aside and shielded from the intruder. In one quick movement, Michael had managed to wedge himself between me and the other man, breaking his hold on my arm. "Leave her alone," he warned firmly.

At least, I think it was a firm warning.

When I think about it now, I try very hard not to romanticize this encounter. Michael was certainly brave to put himself in harm's way for me, but his voice trembled and his eyes and posture lacked the strength and durability that we expect from strong, heroic characters. Michael's voice shook and broke as he told me to leave, to find a cop, and to not come back to this spot for a while. In truth, he didn't seem at all confident in his decision to jump up and rescue me. Michael was not sure how to handle himself, and

---

Details: Appeals to the reader's sense of sight

10 **Organization:** Uses transition to suggest chronological order

Dominant impression: Uses description of feeling to support main idea

11 **Active verbs:** Uses striking verbs to present details

Details: Appeals to reader's sense of sight, smell, and touch

12 **Connotation:** Chooses words with powerful connotations

13

14 **Dominant impression:** Topic sentence focuses on author's feelings about the encounter.

neither of these men were prepared to fight each other; the intruder had the same scared look on his face that Michael had. In the end, I was protected from one hungry, frightened man by another, equally hungry, frightened man. This wasn't a climactic scene between a hero, villain, and innocent; we were three ordinary people caught in a very sad, confusing situation.

I never saw Michael again. I waited a couple of weeks before one day returning to his spot at lunchtime, but he wasn't there. I left a bag of water bottles and bread on the spot where his cardboard mats and blankets used to be; I came back the following day to see that the bag was gone, but I have no way of knowing whether or not he found it. I think about Michael whenever I pass through that part of town, and I think about all the choices I made that led to that last encounter. We are sometimes called upon to make decisions, and in those weeks, I decided to be so many things: kind, generous, unwavering, frightened, flawed, and brave. I chose to be true to my character and in the end my decision to give, when others wouldn't, helped me, too.

15

Dominant impression: Uses adjectives to reinforce main idea

Analyzing the Writer's Technique

1. **Dominant Impression** Describe Nault's dominant impression. Is it stated or implied?
2. **Sensory Language** Which examples of sensory language did you find particularly strong and engaging? What makes them effective? Which, if any, are weak, and how can they be improved?
3. **Comparisons** The annotations point out some of the comparisons Nault uses to explain her topic. Identify several others. Which ones are particularly effective? Do any seem ineffective? If so, why?
4. **Patterns** In addition to description, what other patterns of development does the writer use? How do these patterns make the description more effective?

Thinking Critically about Description

1. **Omissions** Nault leaves out the name of the place where she works. What other information is omitted that might have given you a fuller understanding of her encounters with the homeless man?
2. **Tone** What is Nault's tone? How does it affect your attitude toward the information that is contained in the essay?
3. **Connotation** One of the annotations (para. 7) points out a couple of Nault's word choices with particularly rich connotations. What connotation does the phrase "drag my slippery feet" have in the context of paragraph 4?

4. **Metaphor** The phrase "crumpled soul" (para. 3) offers a vivid metaphor. What does Nault seem to be comparing? What would it lose if you were to translate the metaphor into less figurative language?

Responding to the Reading

1. **Reaction** In paragraph 4, Nault wonders why she was nervous when she first noticed the homeless man and ignored him by walking around the block. How do you react when you come face to face with a homeless person? Why do you think you respond as you do?

2. **Discussion** Nault notes that Michael did not look like the stereotypical homeless person to her. What other groups of people do you stereotype? Have you ever had your stereotype exploded by getting to know a member of the group?

3. **Journal** Write a journal entry about someone you befriended when others ignored him or her. How did you reach out to the individual, and what were the results?

4. **Essay** Nault's personal encounter with Michael tested her character. Write an essay describing a time when you were called upon to make a decision that tested your character.

I'm Not Leaving until I Eat This Thing

John T. Edge

Edge is the director of the Southern Foodways Symposium at the University of Mississippi and the editor of the *Encyclopedia of Southern Culture*. A James Beard Foundation award winner, Edge has written several books, including the *Truck Food Cookbook* (2012) and *The Potlikker Papers: A Food History of the Modern South* (2017). Edge has also written for numerous newspapers and magazines, including the *Oxford American*, a literary magazine featuring southern writers. **Before reading**, preview and make connections by thinking about the most unusual food you have ever eaten. **While reading**, highlight particularly vivid descriptive words and phrases that convey the experience of eating pickled pig lips.

> **JUST-IN-TIME TIP**   Interpreting Details
>
> Edge conveys many of the details about eating pickled pig lips through the people he includes in his essay. Through Lionel, in particular, he is able to present useful information and vivid sensory details. As you read, it is easy to focus on the people, rather than on the details they reveal about the subject of the essay. Try making marginal notes indicating the qualities or characteristics being revealed. For example, in paragraph 6, you could note that Lionel provides the historical background about pig lips.

It's just past 4:00 on a Thursday afternoon in June at Jesse's Place, a country juke   1
17 miles south of the Mississippi line and three miles west of Amite, Louisiana. The
air conditioner hacks and spits forth torrents of Arctic air, but the heat of summer
can't be kept at bay. It seeps around the splintered doorjambs and settles in, trans-
forming the squat particleboard-plastered roadhouse into a sauna. Slowly, the
dank barroom fills with grease-smeared mechanics from the truck stop up the
road and farmers straight from the fields, the soles of their brogans thick with dirt
clods. A few weary souls make their way over from the nearby sawmill. I sit alone
at the bar, one empty bottle of Bud in front of me, a second in my hand. I drain the
beer, order a third, and stare down at the pink juice spreading outward from a
crumpled foil pouch and onto the bar.

I'm not leaving until I eat this thing, I tell myself.   2

Half a mile down the road, behind a fence coiled with razor wire, Lionel   3
Dufour, proprietor of Farm Fresh Food Supplier, is loading up the last truck of the
day, wheeling case after case of pickled pork offal out of his cinder-block processing plant and into a semitrailer bound for Hattiesburg, Mississippi.

His crew packed lips today. Yesterday, it was pickled sausage; the day before   4
that, pig feet. Tomorrow, it's pickled pig lips again. Lionel has been on the job since
2:45 in the morning, when he came in to light the boilers. Damon Landry, chief
cook and maintenance man, came in at 4:30. By 7:30, the production line was at
full tilt: six women in white smocks and blue bouffant caps, slicing ragged white
fat from the lips, tossing the good parts in glass jars, the bad parts in barrels bound
for the rendering plant. Across the aisle, filled jars clatter by on a conveyor belt as
a worker tops them off with a Kool-Aid-red slurry of hot sauce, vinegar, salt, and
food coloring. Around the corner, the jars are capped, affixed with a label, and
stored in pasteboard boxes to await shipping.

Unlike most offal—euphemistically called "variety meats"—lips belie their   5
provenance. Brains, milky white and globular, look like brains. Feet, the ghosts of
their cloven hoofs protruding, look like feet. Testicles look like, well, testicles. But
lips are different. Loosed from the snout, trimmed of their fat, and dyed a preter-
natural pink, they look more like candy than like carrion.

At Farm Fresh, no swine root in an adjacent feedlot. No viscera-strewn killing   6
floor lurks just out of sight, down a darkened hallway. These pigs died long ago at
some Midwestern abattoir. By the time the lips arrive in Amite, they are, in
essence, pig Popsicles, 50-pound blocks of offal and ice.

"Lips are all meat," Lionel told me earlier in the day. "No gristle, no bone, no   7
nothing. They're bar food, hot and vinegary, great with a beer. Used to be the lips
ended up in sausages, headcheese, those sorts of things. A lot of them still do."

Lionel, a 50-year-old father of three with quick, intelligent eyes set deep in a   8
face the color of cordovan, is a veteran of nearly 40 years in the pickled pig lips
business. "I started out with my daddy when I wasn't much more than 10," Lionel
told me, his shy smile framed by a coarse black mustache flecked with whispers of
gray. "The meatpacking business he owned had gone broke back when I was 6, and
he was peddling out of the back of his car, selling dried shrimp, napkins, straws,
tubes of plastic cups, pig feet, pig lips, whatever the bar owners needed. He sold to
black bars, white bars, sweet shops, snowball stands, you name it. We made the

rounds together after I got out of school, sometimes staying out till two or three in the morning. I remember bringing my toy cars to this one joint and racing them around the floor with the bar owner's son while my daddy and his father did business."

For years after the demise of that first meatpacking company, the Dufour family sold someone else's product. "We used to buy lips from Dennis Di Salvo's company down in Belle Chasse," recalled Lionel. "As far as I can tell, his mother was the one who came up with the idea to pickle and pack lips back in the '50s, back when she was working for a company called Three Little Pigs over in Houma. But pretty soon, we were selling so many lips that we had to almost beg Di Salvo's for product. That's when we started cooking up our own," he told me, gesturing toward the castiron kettle that hangs from the rafters by the front door of the plant. "My daddy started cooking lips in that very pot."

Lionel now cooks lips in 11 retrofitted milk tanks, dull stainless-steel cauldrons shaped like oversized cradles. But little else has changed. Though Lionel's father has passed away, Farm Fresh remains a family-focused company. His wife, Kathy, keeps the books. His daughter, Dana, a button-cute college student who has won numerous beauty titles, takes to the road in the summer, selling lips to convenience stores and wholesalers. Soon, after he graduates from business school, Lionel's younger son, Matt, will take over operations at the plant. And his older son, a veterinarian, lent his name to one of Farm Fresh's top sellers, Jason's Pickled Pig Lips.

"We do our best to corner the market on lips," Lionel told me, his voice tinged with bravado. "Sometimes they're hard to get from the packing houses. You gotta kill a lot of pigs to get enough lips to keep us going. I've got new customers calling every day; it's all I can do to keep up with demand, but I bust my ass to keep up. I do what I can for my family—and for my customers.

"When my customers tell me something," he continued, "just like when my daddy told me something, I listen. If my customers wanted me to dye the lips green, I'd ask, 'What shade?' As it is, every few years we'll do some red and some blue for the Fourth of July. This year we did jars full of Mardi Gras lips—half purple, half gold," Lionel recalled with a chuckle. "I guess we'd had a few beers when we came up with that one."

Meanwhile, back at Jesse's Place, I finish my third Bud, order my fourth. *Now, I tell myself, my courage bolstered by booze, I'm ready to eat a lip.*

They may have looked like candy in the plant, but in the barroom they're carrion once again. I poke and prod the six-inch arc of pink flesh, peering up from my reverie just in time to catch the barkeep's wife, Audrey, staring straight at me. She fixes me with a look just this side of pity and asks, "You gonna eat that thing or make love to it?"

Her nephew, Jerry, sidles up to a bar stool on my left. "A lot of people like 'em with chips," he says with a nod toward the pink juice pooling on the bar in front of me. I offer to buy him a lip, and Audrey fishes one from a jar behind the counter, wraps it in tinfoil, and places the whole affair on a paper towel in front of him.

I take stock of my own cowardice, and, following Jerry's lead, reach for a bag of potato chips, tear open the top with my teeth, and toss the quivering hunk of hog flesh into the shiny interior of the bag, slick with grease and dusted with salt. Vinegar vapors tickle my nostrils. I stifle a gag that rolls from the back of my throat, swallow hard, and pray that the urge to vomit passes.

With a smash of my hand, the potato chips are reduced to a pulp, and I feel   17
the cold lump of the lip beneath my fist. I clasp the bag shut and shake it hard in an effort to ensure chip coverage in all the nooks and crannies of the lip. The technique that Jerry uses—and I mimic—is not unlike that employed by home cooks mixing up a mess of Shake 'n Bake chicken.

I pull from the bag a coral crescent of meat now crusted with blond bits of   18
potato chips. When I chomp down, the soft flesh dissolves between my teeth. It tastes like a flaccid cracklin', unmistakably porcine, and not altogether bad. The chips help, providing texture where there was none. Slowly, my brow unfurrows, my stomach ceases its fluttering.

Sensing my relief, Jerry leans over and peers into my bag. "Kind of look like   19
Frosted Flakes, don't they?" he says, by way of describing the chips rapidly turning to mush in the pickling juice. I offer the bag to Jerry, order yet another beer, and turn to eye the pig feet floating in a murky jar by the cash register, their blunt tips bobbing up through a pasty white film.

Understanding the Reading

1. **Reasons** According to the author, why are there no live pigs at Farm Fresh Food Supplier?
2. **Details** What are the ingredients in the "Kool-Aid-red slurry"?
3. **Explanation** How are pig lips different from pork brains, feet, and testicles?
4. **Thesis** What is the author's thesis? Is it stated or implied?
5. **Vocabulary** Explain the meaning of each of the following words as it is used in the reading: *carrion* (para. 5), *demise* (9), *cauldrons* (10), *bravado* (11), and *flaccid* (18).

Analyzing the Writer's Technique

1. **Dominant Impression** Express the essay's dominant impression in your own words.
2. **Comparison** Explain the comparison between the contents of the potato chip bag and Frosted Flakes.
3. **Conclusion** Evaluate the essay's conclusion. If the essay had ended with paragraph 12 instead of paragraph 19, would the conclusion have been more effective or less so? Why?
4. **Audience** What audience is the author addressing? What details help you determine the audience?
5. **Title** The title of Edge's essay is very vague. Why do you think the author chose this title? If you had to create a clever title for this essay, what would it be?

Thinking Critically about Description

1. **Omitted Details** What details are omitted from this essay that might have been included?
2. **Connotation** What is the connotation of the phrase "quivering hunk of hog flesh" (para. 16)?
3. **Details** How does the way in which the author describes eating a pig lip affect the way that you might view eating one?
4. **Sensory Detail** Which examples of sensory language did you find particularly powerful and engaging? What makes them effective?
5. **Attitude** What is the author's attitude toward those who eat at Jesse's Place?

Responding to the Reading

1. **Reaction** How would you react if a waiter accidentally served you the wrong dish—a plate of pig lips—and you unsuspectingly took a big bite?
2. **Journal** Do you have a favorite food? Write a journal entry that describes the food in vivid detail.
3. **Discussion** In small groups, discuss the nastiest, most disgusting foods that you have ever eaten and your reaction.
4. **Essay** Lionel Dufour's daughter spends her summers selling pig lips to convenience stores and wholesalers. Suppose you were asked to spend next summer selling a food product that many people might find distasteful or repulsive. Write an essay in which you describe the three most important selling features of this food. Be sure to use words that appeal to the senses.

Working Together

Collaboration Suppose you were to open a restaurant that specialized in dishes featuring beef tongue, chitlins (hog intestines), brains, chicken feet, or mountain oysters (pork testicles). Working with a partner, create a name for the restaurant and a thirty-second radio advertisement for its grand opening.

> READING

Underground Lair: Inside a Chicken Processing Plant

Gabriel Thompson

This selection is from the book *Working in the Shadows: A Year of Doing the Jobs (Most) Americans Won't Do* (2010). The book (and this excerpt from it) describes Thompson's experiences working undercover at jobs staffed mostly by undocumented immigrants. Thompson has also published several other books—*There's No José Here* (2006), *Calling All Radicals* (2007), *America's Social Arsonist* (2016), and *Chasing the Harvest* (2017)—as well as numerous articles in publications including *New York* magazine, *The Nation*, and *The New York Times*. **Before reading**, preview and make connections by thinking about your experiences, or those of a friend or family member, working a low-paying job. **While reading**, identify the dominant impressions Thompson creates and the strategies he uses to reinforce it.

JUST-IN-TIME TIP   Focusing on Sensory Details

Thompson conveys information about his job and surroundings by using many of the characteristics of descriptive essays. Use the following chart to analyze and evaluate Thompson's use of sensory details. Highlight the descriptive nouns, noun phrases, and adjectives as well as the active verbs and adverbs that Thompson uses to convey the experience of working in a chicken processing plant. After reading, analyze his use of these characteristics to create a dominant impression.

Descriptive Characteristic	Examples
Active verbs	1. "workers scurry about" (para. 2)
Sensory details (sound, smell, touch, sight, taste)	
Varied sentences	
Comparisons	
Connotative language	

Give several examples for each type of characteristic used, including the paragraph numbers for reference. The first one has been done for you.

Superhero comics aren't complete without an evil genius. Often he seeks to construct the ultimate weapon to hold the world hostage; if he's really deranged he simply wants to use it to end human civilization. Since the construction of the weapon must be clandestine, work goes on belowground or behind hidden doors. Walk through the door and an immense world of nameless and undoubtedly evil scientists are at work, tinkering with mysterious equipment while wearing smocks and continuously checking devices.   1

That's the image that immediately comes to mind when I push through the double doors that separate the break room from the plant floor. This isn't a workplace: This is an underground lair. In the first room, workers scurry around in plastic blue smocks akin to a surgeon's, carrying buckets of chicken pieces. Others lean over a long conveyor belt that moves a continuous stream of meat, their feet planted as they arrange the pieces in a line. We weave our way around large metal machinery and step through a frothy puddle of foam that spews from a thick hose on the cement floor. The smell is a mixture of strong industrial cleaner and fresh meat. To my left is a chest-high cylinder filled to the brim with chicken bits; while   2 it captures my attention, I step on what feels like a sponge and lift my foot to find a piece of pink meat, now flattened. Up ahead, I can see from the puffs of condensation coming from his mouth that Lonnie is saying something to our group—the temperature is frigid, probably in the low forties—but I can't hear anything. I remove my earplugs and am greeted by the roar of machinery. It's not a piercing noise, more of a loud, all-encompassing rumble: Think of the sound you hear when putting your ear to a seashell and multiply by a hundred. I put my earplugs back in.

We walk beneath a doorway and the full scale of the processing floor is revealed. I see no walls in front of me, just open space filled with workers standing in various areas without moving their feet. Hundreds of dead and featherless chickens are hanging upside down from stainless steel hooks, moving rapidly across my field of vision. I hear a beeping sound and step aside from a man driving a scooter-like contraption, which is carrying a container of steaming chicken meat (the contraption turns out to be a pallet truck, and the steam is actually from dry ice). As we cross the plant floor we pass beneath a line of chickens, whirling along more steel hooks; liquid falls from their carcasses and lands with chilly plops on my scalp. Hopefully water. In front of us dozens of workers are slicing up chickens—the debone department—but we proceed further, until we're standing aside a blond-haired woman in her forties who, like Lonnie, is wearing a hard hat. 3

"This is your supervisor, Barbara," Lonnie tells us, "but she won't be needing you tonight." He tells Ben and Diane to follow him and motions me to stay put. When he returns he leads me through another doorway. "You're going to work in a different department today, but check in with DSI tomorrow," he says. Lonnie deposits me at the end of a line where boxes are being stacked. 4

The nearest person is a skinny white man with the hood of his Alabama football sweatshirt pulled tight over his head. I stay quiet, feeling slightly intimidated by my new coworker, who has deep lines cutting across his gaunt face and is missing a few front teeth. But when he turns to me he flashes a friendly smile. "How long you been here?" he asks. 5

"About five minutes." 6

He lets loose a squeaking chuckle, his shoulders bouncing up and down. "I've only been here two weeks." Kyle, it turns out, is my neighbor. He lives in a trailer with his wife and two kids about half a mile from where I'm staying. "Been right at that trailer for eighteen years, on land that was my granddaddy's. I worked in the plant four years, then quit. Now I'm back . . . don't know exactly why."* 7

Kyle normally works in DSI, but he says that today they're short people in the IQF department, another mysterious trio of initials. In IQF, bags of chicken wings 8

---

* A note here on accents. Kyle, like many native Alabamans at the plant, speaks in a very heavy and melodic drawl. It was beautiful to hear, but that beauty soon becomes distracting when I attempt to render it accurately on the page. For example, when he told me he had been at the trailer for eighteen years, it sounded to my ears like: "Been rahht at tha-yat trawla' for eightee-yin years." For the sake of readability, I will not try to capture every nuance of the local dialect. One final point to illustrate the strength of the country accent: It took me a week of hanging out with Kyle before I finally realized that his name wasn't, in fact, Kyle. It was Gil. Later, when I listened repeatedly to a message he left on my cell phone, I realized that it wasn't Gil, but another name entirely. Here, he will remain Kyle. [Thompson's note.]

are stuffed into boxes, taped, and shoved down on rollers to us. Our task is to stack the forty-pound boxes onto pallets. Once a pallet is stacked with forty-nine boxes—seven boxes to a row, seven rows high—a pallet driver whisks it away and we start loading up another. This is almost identical to the stacking of lettuce boxes completed by loaders on the machine, except that the pace here is much slower. I help Kyle do this for twenty minutes, until the machine at the front of the line breaks. A black woman with short blond hair, who has been taping the boxes shut, lets out a good-natured curse. It takes several minutes for a group of men to fix the machine; several minutes later it breaks down again. Over the coming month, I'll occasionally be asked to help out in IQF, and during almost every shift the machine breaks down—hourly. For this reason alone, it's considered a good place to work (as one of the "good" jobs, it also doesn't have a single immigrant working in the department).

With nothing to do, Kyle and I take a seat on the rollers. "You ever work in debone?" I ask him. 9

"Way back when I started, they tried to get me on there. Stayed a month. They told me I couldn't work fast enough so they shifted me out. I made sure I wasn't working fast enough too. Run you like slaves over there. I already knew how they did, though, 'cause my old lady was on the debone line for years." Now, he tells me, she's working at Wal-Mart. 10

The machine is finally fixed and we return to stacking boxes. After thirty minutes the black woman who was cursing the contraption asks me to come up and tape boxes. I'm happy for the change in scenery, but this task soon becomes tedious. My job is to shake the box so that the bags lie flat, then pull the two top flaps together and shove it through a machine that tapes it shut. Cutting lettuce confirmed in my mind that much of what we call "low-skilled labor" is in fact quite difficult. But at the chicken plant, I'm already learning, many of the jobs are designed so that a person off the street, with minimal instruction, can do them correctly the very first time. I'm sure this is considered a "breakthrough" by the managerial class, but all it does is leave me bored within fifteen minutes. 11

Sometime after 2:00 a.m., I'm told to take a break. I hang up my gloves and white smock on a hook and walk away from IQF. A minute later I've pushed through one swinging door and walked beneath two other doorways, and I'm watching an endless line of carved-up carcasses fall into a large container. I have no idea where I am. To my left, dozens of immigrant men and women are cutting up chickens with knives and scissors. I approach one woman who can't be much taller than four feet, and ask her in Spanish if she can tell me how to get to the break room. She looks at me and shakes her head. 12

"She doesn't speak Spanish," another woman says, in Spanish. "You go straight down that row and make a left." I hear the two speak in what sounds like an Indian dialect, thank them both, and follow her directions. 13

The break room is mostly empty, but I notice Ben sitting alone in a corner booth. We're both struck by how disorganized everything seems to be. Like me, Ben has been hired for one department (debone), transferred to another (DSI), and then relocated once more, with unclear instructions along they way. He doesn't even 14 know the name of the department that he's in. "Whatever it is, they have me standing and watching chickens go by."

"That's it?" I ask. "Are you supposed to *do* anything?" 15

"Uh, I think like maybe they said to look for mold." 16

"Mold? The chickens have mold?" 17

"Not yet anyway. I haven't seen any. I'm looking for green stuff." 18

"And if they have mold, what do you do?" 19

"I dunno." Ben pushes his sliding glasses up, beginning to look concerned. "I 20
hope that's what I heard. I'm pretty sure somebody said something about mold."
He looks at his watch and stands up. "I gotto go."

By now there are perhaps fifty people sitting in nearby booths, with about 21
an equal number of whites, blacks, and Latinos, who are mostly gathered in
self-segregated groups. One wall is plastered with what are meant to be inspiring
corporate messages in Spanish and English, illustrated with geometric shapes and
arrows. The "Cornerstones of Continuous Improvement" are written at each point
of a large triangle: "Quality, Process Improvement, Teamwork." Next to this
diagram is a more detailed "14 Points of Continuous Improvement," which include
quizzical tips like "Drive Out Fear." Workers pass these grand pronouncements
without pause, but they take note of a yellow flyer taped to the wall that reads
"Taco Soup Wednesday Night."

I'm joined a few minutes later by a white man in a flannel coat who tells me 22
that he's been on the debone line for five months. He snorts when I tell him that
I'm impressed he's lasting so long.

"It's work release," he says. "The only reason I'm here is 'cause they locked 23
my ass up." I don't ask what landed him in prison, but he does reveal that after the
death of his father, he went on a number of epic alcohol binges. "Can't do that anymore 'cause I'm locked up and got myself a bleeding ulcer. But I'll tell you one
thing," he says before I depart, "once I'm free you ain't never gonna see me step
foot inside a chicken plant again."

I use the bathroom and manage to find my way back to Kyle and the boxes. 24
He is seated on the rollers, hood pulled even lower on his head to ward off the
cold, while a mechanic tries to get the machine back up and working.

For reasons that aren't explained, IQF is released earlier than other departments. 25
As I walk toward the break room at 7:40 a.m., I meet a stream of men and women
heading in the other direction, getting ready to begin the day shift. I swipe my ID
card to sign out, am hit by the bright sunshine of another scorching day, hop on
my bike, and pedal home. Kyle has agreed to pick me up tonight, so I don't have to
worry about getting run over by a chicken truck. Back in my trailer I eat a quick
breakfast of cereal and a peanut butter and jelly sandwich, type up my notes, and
lay down. The sun is streaming through the window, my trailer shakes each time a
truck loaded with live chickens passes, and my neighbor's roosters are engaged
with a dog in some sort of noise competition. I can't be bothered; I fall asleep
instantly.

Understanding the Reading

1. **Reasons** Why does Thompson mention and describe the two posters in paragraph 21? What is the significance of the poster describing the food?
2. **Details** In paragraph 8, Thompson mentions stacking lettuce boxes. How would he know about this job?
3. **Reasons** Why is the IQF a good place to work?
4. **Details** What erroneous assumption does the author make about the woman of whom he asks directions to the break room (para. 12)? Why did he assume this about her?
5. **Vocabulary** Explain the meaning of each of the following words or phrases as it is used in the reading: *deranged* (para. 1), *clandestine* (1), *lair* (2), *gaunt* (5), and *pronouncement* (21). Refer to a dictionary as needed.

Analyzing the Writer's Technique

1. **Dominant Impression** What dominant impression does Thompson convey in this essay? Is it stated or implied? Explain your answers.
2. **Title** What is the significance of the essay's title?
3. **Descriptive Language** How does Thompson's descriptive language allow you to understand and picture the processing floor (para. 3)? What words and phrases are most descriptive in this section?
4. **Patterns** What patterns other than description does Thompson use in this essay? What purposes do they serve?

Thinking Critically about Description

1. **Connotation** What connotation does the word *lair* suggest (para. 2)?
2. **Detail** Why does the author make a point to say that Kyle's wife left the plant and went to work for Walmart?
3. **Connotation** Why does the author put the word *breakthrough* (para. 11) in quotations?
4. **Objective/Subjective** Is the essay objective, subjective, or a mixture of both? Explain your answer.
5. **Tone** Describe Thompson's tone in this essay. What information does his tone convey that is not directly stated?

Responding to the Reading

1. **Reaction** The author attempts to blend in with the other workers at the plant. Do you think that he is successful in doing so? Why or why not? Give examples from his behavior or his words that support your answer.
2. **Discussion** What do you think Thompson learned as a result of his undercover experience in the chicken processing plant?
3. **Journal** Thompson writes that much of what we call "low-skilled labor" is actually very difficult. Discuss some low-skilled jobs that you know about and explain what makes them so difficult.
4. **Essay** Write an essay in which you describe the worst job you or someone you know has ever had. In addition to describing the job, explain why the job was so bad.

Working Together

1. The poster in the break room of the chicken plant was entitled "14 Points of Continuous Improvement." Working with a small group of your peers, list fourteen changes that could be implemented in that plant in order to create a better work environment.

2. Many businesses have a catchy advertising slogan that draws the public's attention to their company. Working with a small group of your peers, brainstorm slogans that you hear on TV or radio. Then assume that you are Gabriel Thompson, and you want to create a slogan for the chicken plant that will "tell it like it is." Make sure your slogan is simple, catchy, and honest. Be prepared to share your slogan with the class and explain its significance.

Apply Your Skills: Additional Essay Assignments

Using what you learned about description in this chapter, write a descriptive essay on one of the topics listed below. Depending on the topic you choose, you may need to conduct research.

For more about locating and documenting sources, see Part 5.

To Express Your Ideas

1. Suppose a famous person, living or dead, visited your house for dinner. Write an essay describing the person and the evening and expressing your feelings about the occasion.

2. In "Dreamland, Portsmouth, Ohio," the author describes a place and what it meant to the townspeople of Portsmouth. Write an essay for your classmates describing a place that you visited as a child that still evokes fond memories.

To Inform Your Reader

3. Write a report for your local newspaper on a local sporting event you observed or participated in.

4. Write an essay describing one aspect of your life or that of your community that changed as a result of the Covid-19 virus.

To Persuade Your Reader

5. Write a letter to persuade your parents to lend you money. The loan may be to purchase a used car or to rent a more expensive apartment, for example. Include a description of your current car or apartment.

6. "Sometimes, We Give" describes a homeless man and one woman's response to him. Write a persuasive essay taking a position on the responsibility Americans (or their government) have toward the homeless.

Cases Using Description

7. Imagine that you are a product buyer for a cosmetics distributor, a food company, or a furniture dealership. Write a descriptive review of a product recommending to the board of directors whether to distribute it. Use something that you are familiar with or come up with your own product (such as a new cosmetic, an advice book on nutrition, or an electronic gadget for the home). Describe the product in a way that will help convince the company to accept your recommendation.

8. Write a brief description of your ideal internship. Then write an essay to accompany your application for your ideal summer internship. The sponsoring agency requires every applicant to submit an essay that describes the knowledge and experience the applicant can bring to the internship and the ways that the position would benefit the applicant personally and professionally.

SYNTHESIZING IDEAS   WORKING LOW-PAYING JOBS

Both "Underground Lair: Inside a Chicken Processing Plant" (pp. 297–301) and "I'm Not Leaving until I Eat This Thing" (pp. 293–96) describe food-processing plants. Thompson works in a chicken processing plant, and Edge reports on a plant producing pickled meat products.

Analyzing the Readings

1. Compare how Thompson and Edge feel about the processing plants. How does each author reveal his or her attitudes? How are they the same, and how do they differ?

2. As a writer who is researching jobs that most Americans won't do, Thompson works "undercover," but Edge merely visits the plant. How do you think these differences affect the essays and the authors' reported experiences?

Essay Idea

Write an essay describing a workplace you know well, and describe it to create a dominant impression. Then explain whether your experiences were more similar to those of Thompson or Edge—or why they did not resemble those of either.

Ben Osborne/Getty Images

Writing Quick Start

ANALYZE   In an environmental science class, the instructor presents the photograph on this page showing an oil spill cleanup and says, "This is an example, a specific situation that illustrates the larger concept or idea of environmental pollution." Next she asks the class to think of other examples that also illustrate the idea of environmental pollution.

WRITE   Choose one form of pollution and draft a paragraph that presents examples illustrating it. You might choose a common form of pollution such as water, soil, or air pollution, or you might consider less well-known ones such as noise, light, visual, or outer space pollution. Begin with a topic sentence similar to the instructor's opening statement. Then select situations that you have observed or read about that illustrate it.

CONNECT   The paragraph you just wrote could be part of an illustration essay. An illustration essay uses examples to reveal a topic's essential characteristics and reinforce the thesis statement. In this chapter you will learn to use specific examples that make abstract ideas more understandable.

In this chapter you will learn to

- understand the purpose and function of illustration essays
- use graphic organizers to visualize illustration essays
- integrate illustration into an essay
- read and think critically about illustration
- plan, organize, draft, revise, and edit essays using illustration

Explaining a concept through examples is an effective way to enable your reader to understand difficult or unfamiliar ideas by connecting them to real-life situations with which they are familiar. Examples help readers move from general ideas (which tend to be theoretical and abstract) to specific ones (which tend to be practical and realistic).

USING ILLUSTRATION   **IN COLLEGE AND THE WORKPLACE**

- Your *literature instructor* assigns an analysis of metaphor and simile in the poems of Emily Dickinson. To explain your point about Dickinson's use of animal metaphors, you provide specific examples from several of her poems.

- You are studying sexual dimorphism (differences in appearance between the sexes) in a *biology course*. The following question appears on an exam: "Define sexual dimorphism and illustrate its occurrence in several different species." In your answer, you give examples of peacocks, geese, and chickens, explaining how the males and females in each species differ in physical appearance.

- As an *elementary school reading teacher,* you are writing a letter to the school board justifying the cost of the new computer software you have requested. In your letter, you provide several examples of the software's benefits to students.

What Are the Characteristics of Illustration Essays?

Effective illustration essays support a generalization, explain, and clarify by providing examples that maintain readers' interest and achieve the author's purpose. Because a good illustration essay is more than a list of examples, a well-thought-out organization is essential.

Illustration Supports Generalizations

Examples are an effective way to support a **generalization**—a broad statement about a topic. Thesis statements often contain a generalization, and the body of an illustration essay contains examples that support it.

The following statements are generalizations because they make assertions about an entire group or category:

- Most college students are energetic, ambitious, and eager to get ahead in life.
- Gestures play an important role in nonverbal communication.
- Boys are more willing to participate in class discussions than girls are.

To explain and support any of these generalizations, you could provide specific examples, along with other types of evidence (facts, statistics, expert opinions), to show how or why the statement is accurate. For instance, in addition to providing

relevant facts and statistics, you could also support the first generalization by providing examples of several college students who demonstrate energy and ambition.

For more about idea-
generating strategies, see
Chapter 4.

EXERCISE 13.1 **DEVELOPING EXAMPLES TO SUPPORT GENERALIZATIONS**

Using one or more prewriting strategies for generating ideas, provide at least two
examples that support each of the following general statements:

1. Television offers some programs with educational or social value.
2. Today's parents are not strict enough with their children.
3. The favorite pastime of most men is watching sports on television.

Illustration Explains or Clarifies

Examples are useful when you need to explain an unfamiliar topic, a difficult concept,
or an abstract term.

Unfamiliar topics. Use examples to help readers understand a topic about which
they know little or nothing. An instructor of abnormal psychology, for example, might
provide case studies of patients with schizophrenia and other disorders to help make
the characteristics of each disorder easier to understand and remember.

Difficult concepts. Many concepts are difficult to grasp by definition alone. For
instance, a reader might guess that the term *urbanization*, a key concept in sociology, has
something to do with cities. Defining the concept as "the process by which an area
becomes part of a city" gives readers a place to begin. Providing examples of formerly
suburban areas that have become urban makes the concept even more understandable.

Abstract terms. Abstract terms refer to ideas rather than to concrete things you
can see and touch. Terms such as *truth* and *justice* are abstract. Because abstractions
are difficult to understand, examples help clarify them. In many cases, however,
abstract terms mean different things to different people. By providing examples, you
can clarify what *you* mean by an abstract term. Suppose you use the term *unfair* to
describe your employer's treatment of workers. Readers might have different ideas of
fairness. Providing examples of the employer's unfair treatment would make your
meaning clear.

EXERCISE 13.2 **PROVIDING EXAMPLES TO EXPLAIN AND CLARIFY**

The following list contains a mix of unfamiliar topics, difficult concepts, and abstract
terms. Choose three items from the list, and provide at least two examples of each
that illustrate their meanings.

1. Phobia
2. Conformity
3. Gender role
4. Self-fulfilling prophecy
5. Sexual harassment

Illustration Considers Purpose and Audience

The number of examples a writer should include depends on his or her purpose and audience. For example, in an essay arguing that one car is a better buy than another, a series of examples explaining the various models, years, and options available to potential car buyers might be most persuasive. But if you are writing an essay for an audience of high school students about the consequences of dropping out of school, a single poignant example might be more compelling.

A careful analysis of your audience should play a key role in deciding what types of examples to include in your essay. For an expert audience, technical examples might be more appropriate; for novice readers, personal or everyday examples might be more effective. For instance, suppose you want to persuade readers that the Food and Drug Administration should approve a new cancer drug. If your audience is composed of doctors, your examples would likely include the results of scientific studies regarding the drug's effectiveness. But if your audience is the general public, your examples might focus on personal anecdotes about lives being saved.

It can be useful to provide examples that represent different aspects of or viewpoints on your topic. In writing about the new drug, for instance, you might include expert opinion from researchers as well as the opinions of doctors, patients, and a representative of the company that manufactures the drug.

EXERCISE 13.3 **DEVELOPING EXAMPLES FOR A SPECIFIC AUDIENCE**

For one of the following topics, suggest examples that would suit the different audiences listed:

1. Your college's policy on student on-campus employment
   a. First-year students attending a college orientation session
   b. Students already working on campus
   c. Parents or spouses of students who work on campus
2. A proposal recommending that drivers over age sixty-five undergo periodic assessment of their ability to operate a motor vehicle safely
   a. Senior citizens
   b. State senators
   c. Adult children of elderly drivers

Illustration Uses Carefully Selected Examples

Examples must be relevant, representative, accurate, and striking.

- *Relevant* examples have a direct and clear relationship to your thesis. If your essay advocates publicly funded preschool programs, support your case with examples of successful publicly funded programs, not privately operated programs.
- *Representative* examples show a typical or real-life situation, not a rare or unusual one. In an essay arguing that preschool programs advance children's reading skills, one example of an all-day, year-round preschool would not be representative of all or most other programs.

- *Accurate* and *specific* examples provide readers with enough information to evaluate their reliability. Notice how the second example below provides better (more specific) detail for the reader.

Overly General	Most students in preschool programs have better language skills than children who don't attend such programs.
Specific, Detailed	According to an independent evaluator, 73 percent of children who attended the Head Start program in Clearwater had better language skills after one year of attendance than students who did not attend the program.

Striking and dramatic examples make a strong, lasting impression on readers. For example, in an essay about identity theft, a writer might relate shocking incidents of how victims' lives are drastically changed with the swipe of a credit card.

Sometimes it is necessary to conduct research to find examples outside your knowledge and experience. For the essay on preschool programs, you would need to do research to obtain statistical information. You might also interview a preschool administrator or teacher to gather firsthand anecdotes and opinions or visit a preschool classroom to observe the program in action.

Illustration Uses Subexamples to Add Detail

When providing examples that are broad general categories, you will often find it helpful to include **subexamples**—specific examples that help explain the general examples. Suppose you are writing an essay about the problems that new immigrants to America face and you use three examples: problems with the language, with the culture, and with technology. For the broad culture example, you might give subexamples of how some immigrants do not understand certain American holidays, ways of socializing, and methods of doing business.

Illustration Organizes Details Effectively

When supporting a thesis with examples, organize the examples and the details that accompany them so readers can follow them easily. Often one of the methods of organization discussed in Chapter 6 will be useful:

- spatial order
- chronological order
- most-to-least or least-to-most order

For example, in an essay explaining why people wear unconventional dress, you might arrange the examples spatially, starting with outlandish footwear and continuing upward to headgear. For other writing assignments, you may want to organize your examples according to another pattern of development, such as comparison and contrast or cause and effect. For example, to support the thesis that a local department store needs to improve its customer service, you might begin by contrasting the department store with several other retailers that provide better service, offering examples of the services that each provides.

The following readings demonstrate the techniques for writing effective illustration essays. The first is annotated to point out how Deborah Tannen uses these techniques to help readers understand how families communicate. As you read the second essay, try to identify how the writer uses the techniques of illustration to help readers understand road rage.

READING

What's That Supposed to Mean?

Deborah Tannen

Deborah Tannen, a professor of linguistics at Georgetown University, has published numerous scholarly articles and several popular books about interpersonal communication, including *You Were Always Mom's Favorite, You're Wearing That?*, and *I Only Say This Because I Love You*, from which this excerpt was taken.

Before Reading

1. **Preview:** Use the steps listed in Chapter 2.
2. **Connect:** Think of a conversation between members of your own family in which a conflict or misunderstanding occurred. Why do you think it occurred? Could it have been avoided?

While Reading Study the examples Tannen offers and read the annotations provided.

Introduction: Uses a familiar situation to engage readers; introduces first extended example illustrating *metamessage*

Elizabeth, a college professor in her thirties, is making Thanksgiving dinner for her extended family in her own home. Her mother, who is visiting, is helping out in the kitchen. As Elizabeth prepares the turkey, her mother remarks, "Oh, you put onions in the stuffing?" 1

Feeling suddenly as if she were sixteen years old again, Elizabeth turns on her mother. "Why do you have to criticize everything I do?" 2

"I didn't criticize," her mother replies. "I just asked a question. What's got into you? I can't even open my mouth!" 3

Transition: Moves readers from example to explanation

Because family members have a shared history, everything we say echoes with meanings from the past. We develop a sixth sense for sniffing out criticism in almost anything a loved one says—even an innocent question about the ingredients in holiday stuffing. 4

Topic sentence

When family members talk to one another, there are often two meanings to what they say. The *message* is the meaning of the words and sentences spoken, what anyone with a dictionary and a grammar book could figure out. Two people in a conversation usually agree on what the message is. The *metamessage* (the prefix *meta* means, among other things, going beyond or higher) is meaning that is not stated—at least not in so many words—but that is gleaned from every aspect of context; the way something is said, who is saying it, or the fact that it is said at all. You might say that the message is the "word meaning," while the metamessage is the "heart meaning"—the meaning we react to most strongly, that triggers emotion. 5

Concept to be explained through examples

As in the case of Elizabeth and her mother, grown children often seem to take every remark of a parent as criticism. They become attuned to any hint—any metamessage—of disapproval. Understanding this, Elizabeth's mother might refrain from offering advice or even making helpful suggestions unless asked. Sometimes, smoother family talk is a simple matter of tongue-biting.

6

First hypothetical example of ways to improve family communication

Sometimes, however, it's more complex. The following situations show ways to stop your nearest and dearest from pushing your buttons in conversation, as well as ways to avoid pushing theirs.

7

Thesis: There are ways to improve the communication that occurs in families.

Diet Police

Irene and David, a married couple from Vermont, are looking over menus in a restaurant. David says he will order a steak.

8

Relevant and representative example to illustrate *metamessage*

"Did you notice they also have salmon?" Irene asks.

9

"Will you please stop criticizing what I eat?" David protests.

10

"I didn't criticize," says Irene. "I just pointed out something I thought you might like."

11

David was reacting to what he saw as Irene's metamessage: that he eats too much red meat. It's possible that Irene really was not feeling disapproval when she pointed out the salmon on the menu. But most likely she was, and preferred to raise her concern as a question to avoid a fight.

12

Topic sentence: Moves readers from example to explanation

When David reacted with annoyance, Irene cried literal meaning. Every one of us does that when we want to avoid discord. As a result, the deeper meanings of the conversation often are left unaddressed.

13

It might help to "metacommunicate"—that is, to talk about ways of talking. David might explain that Irene's suggestion made him feel like he was living with the diet police. If Irene actually did mean to express concern about David's health, she should admit that. By clarifying the meaning each person intended and perceived, the couple could build a bridge of understanding.

14

Topic sentence: Second way to improve family communication

"Don't Call Us . . ."

There is another aspect of communication complicating everything we say to each other, and it's especially powerful in families. That is our simultaneous but conflicting desires for connection and control. We all seek connection: it makes us feel safe and loved. But being close gives family members a kind of power to control our actions that can limit our freedom and make us feel hemmed in. "Don't tell me what to do. Don't try to control me," are frequent protests within families. It is automatic for many of us to see others' incursions on our freedom as control maneuvers. We are less likely to think of them as connection maneuvers, but they often are that too.

15

Second concept to be explained through example

Transition: Transitional sentence moves readers from explanation to example.

Nathan and Joan, a couple in their late twenties, were leaving Joan's parents after a family visit. Holding the hand of her three-year-old daughter, Joan wobbled under the weight of a pregnancy nearing its term. As everyone said their good-byes, Joan's mother, Nora, said, "I'll see you when you give birth. I can't wait to get that call when you go into labor!"

16

Relevant and representative example to illustrate *conflicting desire for connection and control*

Joan and Nathan stiffened. When Joan was about to give birth to their first   17
child, Nora and her husband drove to the couple's town so they would be close to
the hospital. This had annoyed Nathan, who had expected his in-laws to wait until
they were asked to come.

"We're not going to call you when she goes into labor," Nathan said to his   18
mother-in-law. "I'll call to tell you when the baby is born."

Nora instantly protested that he had no right to keep such crucial knowledge   19
from her. He retorted that they had a right to keep the birth private and quiet, as
their daughter's birth had *not* been—because of Nora's showing up.

Nora defended herself: it had not been her idea to come ahead in that case,   20
but her husband's. She promised to abide by any rules they set, insisting that not
telling her when her daughter went into labor was too cruel an exclusion.

<u>Nathan and Nora were both struggling to find their footing on the connection/   21
control continuum.</u> He was feeling an assault on his sense of control over his
family, and she was feeling an assault on her sense of connection with her
daughter. But Nora was also feeling a loss of control, as if her hands would be
tied at a crucial moment—and Nathan was also feeling a loss of connection,
with his wife.

<u>There are a few communication keys that would have helped them.</u> Timing   22
is one. Nora could have avoided putting Nathan on the defensive by making her
case to be present at the birth in a calmer setting—by letter, or in a carefully
thought-out conversation about how she felt and what she would be willing to
promise. It probably also would have helped to say she was sorry she had come
uninvited the first time. Nathan could have avoided committing himself one way or the
other about calling Nora when Joan went into labor. Then later he could just not have
done it, and soothed hurt feelings by explaining, "Things happened so fast I wasn't
able to call."

"Didn't I Tell You?"

Even though you're related, it's easy to feel at times like you're talking to a   23
stranger. <u>Age and gender differences are among the obstacles that can get in the
way.</u> Cindy, a small-business owner, was increasingly distressed because her grown
son continued living at home after graduating from college and beginning a full-
time job. His upkeep was straining her tight budget. After about three months, she
said to him, "I think it would be fair for you to pay rent."

He replied, "I'm leaving soon."   24

Cindy was relieved that she had finally spoken up and settled the matter. But   25
time passed and no rent appeared. After several more months, her anger erupted.
During this quarrel it emerged that her son had felt that the issue of paying rent,
though raised, had been left in abeyance for a little while longer. Cindy, on the
other hand, had assumed that expressing her opinion implied a request for action,
that all she had to do was make her wishes known and her son would feel obligated to honor them.

Her son's interpretation was similar to the way many men react to women's   26
indirect requests. Since he himself would ask directly, he did not recognize Cindy's
statement of preferences as a request for action. <u>Because</u> men often honestly miss

---

Left margin annotations:

Topic sentence: Moves readers from example to explanation

Topic sentence: Prepares readers for list of ways to improve communication

Second hypothetical example of ways to improve family communication

Topic sentence: Third issue in family communication

Transition: Highlights that explanation of example is coming

indirect requests, Cindy would have done better to end her first talk with a direct statement, such as, "Then we agree you'll start paying rent next month." Or she could have finished with a question like, "When can I expect a check?"

Third hypothetical example of ways to improve family communication

Conversation with our family is an ongoing balancing act as we try to clarify meanings that did not get across or dispel misunderstandings—and at the same time interpret what is being said to us. Staying aware of all the subtleties of family talk can give us the power to improve the most important relationships in our lives.　　27

Conclusion: Restates thesis in different words

Visualize an Illustration Essay: Create a Graphic Organizer

Graphic Organizer 13.1 will help you visualize the components of an illustration essay. The structure is straightforward:

For more on creating a graphic organizer, see Chapter 2.

- The introduction contains background information and usually includes the thesis.

GRAPHIC ORGANIZER 13.1　The Basic Structure of an Illustration Essay

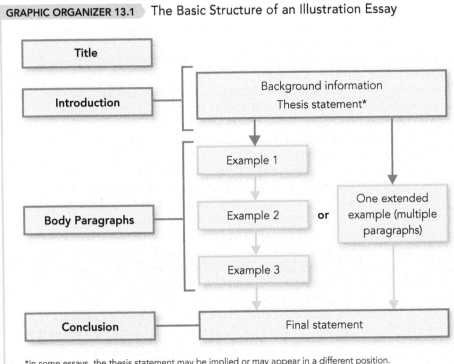

*In some essays, the thesis statement may be implied or may appear in a different position.

- The body paragraphs provide one or more related examples. For an essay using one extended example, such as a highly descriptive account of an auto accident intended to persuade readers to wear seat belts, the body of the essay will focus on the details of that one example.
- The conclusion presents a final statement.

READING

Rambos of the Road

Martin Gottfried

Martin Gottfried has been a drama critic for such publications as the *New York Post* and *New York* magazine. He has also written several books, including biographies of Stephen Sondheim, Arthur Miller, and Angela Lansbury. This essay was first published in *Newsweek,* the weekly news magazine, in 1986. **Before reading,** preview the reading and make connections by thinking of overly aggressive drivers you have encountered. **While reading,** notice where Gottfried employs compelling examples to support his thesis, and highlight those you find particularly striking. Read the illustration essay first, and then study Graphic Organizer 13.2. What parts of the reading are included in the graphic organizer and why?

The car pulled up and its driver glared at us with such sullen intensity, such hatred, that I was truly afraid for our lives. Except for the Mohawk haircut he didn't have, he looked like Robert De Niro in *Taxi Driver,* the sort of young man who, delirious for notoriety, might kill a president. 1

He was glaring because we had passed him and for that affront he pursued us to the next stoplight so as to express his indignation and affirm his masculinity. I was with two women and, believe it, was afraid for all three of us. It was nearly midnight and we were in a small, sleeping town with no other cars on the road. 2

When the light turned green, I raced ahead, knowing it was foolish and that I was not in a movie. He didn't merely follow, he chased, and with his headlights turned off. No matter what sudden turn I took, he followed. My passengers were silent. I knew they were alarmed, and I prayed that I wouldn't be called upon to protect them. In that cheerful frame of mind, I turned off my own lights so I couldn't be followed. It was lunacy. I was responding to a crazy *as* a crazy. 3

"I'll just drive to the police station," I finally said, and as if those were the magic words, he disappeared. 4

It seems to me that there has recently been an epidemic of auto macho—a competition perceived and expressed in driving. People fight it out over parking spaces. They bully into line at the gas pump. A toll booth becomes a signal for elbowing fenders. And beetle-eyed drivers hunch over their steering wheels, squeezing the rims, glowering, preparing the excuse of not having seen you as they muscle you off the road. Approaching a highway on an entrance ramp recently, I was strong-armed by a trailer truck, so immense that its driver all but blew me 5 away by blasting his horn. The behemoth was just inches from my hopelessly mismatched coupe when I fled for the safety of the shoulder.

And this is happening on city streets, too. A New York taxi driver told me that   6 "intimidation is the name of the game. Drive as if you're deaf and blind. You don't hear the other guy's horn and you sure as hell don't see him."

The odd thing is that long before I was even able to drive, it seemed to me that   7 people were at their finest and most civilized when in their cars. They seemed so orderly and considerate, so reasonable, staying in the right-hand lane unless passing, signaling all intentions. In those days you really eased into highway traffic, and the long, neat rows of cars seemed mobile testimony to the sanity of most people. Perhaps memory fails, perhaps there were always testy drivers, perhaps—but everyone didn't give you the finger.

A most amazing example of driver rage occurred recently at the Manhattan   8 end of the Lincoln Tunnel. We were four cars abreast, stopped at a traffic light. And there was no moving even when the light had changed. A bus had stopped in the cross traffic, blocking our paths: it was a normal-for-New-York-City gridlock. Perhaps impatient, perhaps late for important appointments, three of us nonetheless accepted what, after all, we could not alter. One, however, would not. He would not be helpless. He would go where he was going even if he couldn't get there. A Wall Street type in suit and tie, he got out of his car and strode toward the bus, rapping smartly on its doors. When they opened, he exchanged words with the driver. The doors folded shut. He then stepped in front of the bus, took hold of one of its large windshield wipers and broke it.

The bus doors reopened and the driver appeared, apparently giving the fellow   9 a good piece of his mind. If so, the lecture was wasted, for the man started his car and proceeded to drive directly *into the bus*. He rammed it. Even though the point at which he struck the bus, the folding doors, was its most vulnerable point, ramming the side of a bus with your car has to rank very high on a futility index. My first thought was that it had to be a rental car.

To tell the truth, I could not believe my eyes. The bus driver opened his   10 doors as much as they could be opened and he stepped directly onto the hood of the attacking car, jumping up and down with both his feet. He then retreated into the bus, closing the doors behind him. Obviously a man of action, the car driver backed up and rammed the bus again. How this exercise in absurdity would have been resolved none of us will ever know for at that point the traffic unclogged and the bus moved on. And the rest of us, we passives of the world, proceeded, our cars crossing a field of battle as if nothing untoward had happened.

It is tempting to blame such belligerent, uncivil and even neurotic behavior on   11 the nuts of the world, but in our cars we all become a little crazy. How many of us speed up when a driver signals his intention of pulling in front of us? Are we resentful and anxious to pass him? How many of us try to squeeze in, or race along the shoulder of a lane merger? We may not jump on hoods, but driving the gantlet, we seethe, cursing not so silently in the safety of our steel bodies on wheels—fortresses for cowards.

What is it within us that gives birth to such antisocial behavior and why, all of a sudden, have so many drivers gone around the bend? My friend Joel Katz, a Manhattan psychiatrist, calls it "a Rambo pattern. People are running around thinking the American way is to take the law into your own hands when anyone does anything wrong. And what constitutes 'wrong'? Anything that cramps your style."   12

It seems to me that it is a new America we see on the road now. It has the mentality of a hoodlum and the backbone of a coward. The car is its weapon and hiding place, and it is still a symbol even in this. Road Rambos no longer bespeak a self-reliant, civil people tooling around in family cruisers. In fact, there aren't families in these machines that charge headlong with their brights on in broad daylight, demanding we get out of their way. Bullies are loners, and they have perverted our liberty of the open road into drivers' license. They represent an America that derides the values of decency and good manners, then roam the highways riding shotgun and shrieking freedom. By allowing this to happen, the rest of us approve.   13

> **EXERCISE 13.4**   **DRAWING A GRAPHIC ORGANIZER**

Using Graphic Organizer 13.1 or 13.2 as a basis, draw a graphic organizer for "What's That Supposed to Mean?"

> **HOW WRITERS READ**   **ILLUSTRATION**

THE READING PROCESS	STRATEGIES
BEFORE READING	**Preview** the essay to get an overview of the content and organization.
	Make connections by thinking about what the title means and considering what examples from your personal experience would be relevant.
	Read the headnote (if one is provided) for background information about the author and the reading.
WHILE READING	**Identify the characteristics of illustration.** Be sure you can answer the following questions:
	• What is the writer's **thesis**? Is it stated or implied? If the thesis is unstated, ask yourself what one major point all of the examples illustrate.
	• What are the **main points**, and how does each example illustrate them? Make notes in the margin.
	• How are the examples **organized**—chronologically, spatially, or in some other way?
	• What is the author's **purpose**? Who is the intended **audience**?
	• How does the writer use **language** to achieve the desired effect? Circle strong word choices or place a checkmark in the margin.

AFTER READING

Draw a **graphic organizer** showing the key examples and identifying how they are organized. (Use your graphic organizer for review and study.)

Analyze and evaluate the reading by answering the following questions:

- How well do the examples **explain or clarify the thesis**?
- After reading the essay, are you **convinced by the writer's thesis**? How could the author have done a better job of convincing you?
- What is the **emotional impact** of the examples and any **visual aids**? Explain your reaction in detail.
- Are the examples **fair, accurate, representative**, and **relevant**? Would **other types of evidence** have strengthened the essay?
- What is the **writer's attitude** toward the subject? Highlight words with strong connotations that reveal the writer's feelings.
- What is the writer's **tone**? Describe the tone with two or three adjectives.
- What **types of evidence**, other than examples, does the author offer to support the thesis?
- Does the author **omit** examples that would contradict or weaken the thesis?

EXERCISE 13.5   READING CRITICALLY

Apply the questions in the "How Writers Read" box to the selection "Rambos of the Road."

Integrate Illustration into an Essay

Examples are an effective way to support a thesis that relies on one or more other patterns of development. For instance, you might use examples in the following ways:

- to *define* a particular advertising ploy
- to *compare* two types of small businesses
- to *classify* types of movies
- to *show the effects* of aerobic exercise
- to *argue* that junk food is unhealthy because of its high fat and salt content

When using examples in an essay where illustration is not the main pattern of development, keep the following tips in mind:

1. **Choose effective examples.** They should be relevant, representative, accurate, specific, and striking.
2. **Use transitions such as "for instance" or "for example."** They make it obvious that an example follows.
3. **Provide enough details to help your readers understand how an example supports your point.** Do not overwhelm your readers with too many details.

GRAPHIC ORGANIZER 13.2   The Structure of "Rambos of the Road"

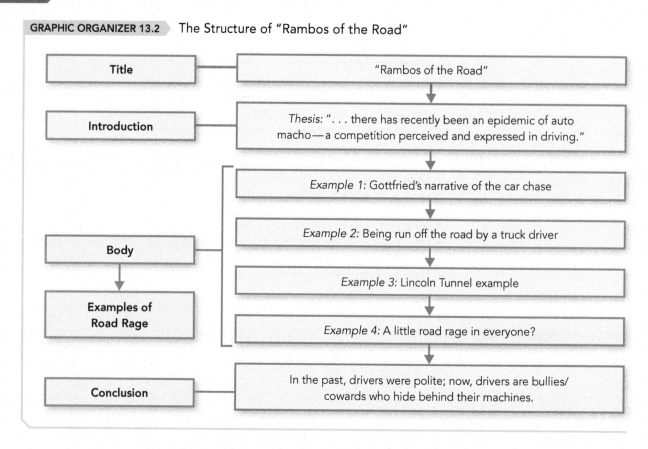

Title	"Rambos of the Road"
Introduction	*Thesis:* ". . . there has recently been an epidemic of auto macho—a competition perceived and expressed in driving."
Body / **Examples of Road Rage**	*Example 1:* Gottfried's narrative of the car chase
	Example 2: Being run off the road by a truck driver
	Example 3: Lincoln Tunnel example
	Example 4: A little road rage in everyone?
Conclusion	In the past, drivers were polite; now, drivers are bullies/cowards who hide behind their machines.

PREWRITING   DRAFTING   **REVISING**   EDITING & PROOFREADING

A Guided Writing Assignment*

ILLUSTRATION

Your Essay Assignment

Write an illustration essay explaining a topic your readers might find unfamiliar or challenging and that you can illustrate effectively with examples. Imagine you are writing for your campus newspaper, and choose a topic that you think might interest your readers. The following are some options:

- the popularity of a certain type of sport, television show, or hobby
- the connection between clothing and personality

* The writing process is *recursive*; that is, you may find yourself revising as you draft or prewriting as you revise. This is especially true when writing on a computer. Your writing process may also differ from essay to essay or from that of your classmates.

- the problems of balancing school, work, and family
- effective (or ineffective) parenting, teaching, or managing employees
- a concept from one of your courses, such as stress management or ergonomic design

1 Select a topic from the list, or create your own.

Use one or more of the following suggestions to generate topic ideas:

1. **Peruse your textbooks**, looking for boldfaced terms that you find interesting or want to learn about. List several and then, alone or with another student, brainstorm examples that would help to illustrate or explain the concept. You may need to read your textbook to understand the meaning of the term.

2. **Work backward.** Make a list of the things you do for fun or find challenging and then consider what they have in common. Use that common thread as your topic.

After you have chosen your topic, make sure that you can **develop your main idea into a well-focused working thesis**.

2 Consider your purpose, audience, and point of view.

Ask yourself these questions:

- Will my essay's **purpose** be to **express myself, inform**, or **persuade**? Several examples may be needed to persuade. One extended example may be sufficient to inform readers about a very narrow topic (for example, how to select an educational toy for a child).

- Who is my **audience**? Will readers need any **background information** to understand my essay? **What types of examples** will be most effective with these readers? Straightforward examples, based on everyday experience, may be appropriate for an audience unfamiliar with your topic; more technical examples may be appropriate for an expert audience.

- What **other evidence** (such as facts and statistics, expert opinion) will I need to make my case with my audience? Do I have enough information to write about this topic, or must I consult additional sources? How might I use **additional patterns of development** within my illustration essay? (For example, you might use narration to present an extended example from your own life.)

- What **point of view** best suits my purpose and audience? (Unless the examples you use are all drawn from your personal experience, you will probably use the **third person** when using examples to explain.)

3 Narrow your topic and generate examples:

Narrow your topic. Use prewriting to make your topic manageable. Be sure you can support your topic with one or more examples.

Use idea-generating strategies to come up with a wide variety of examples:

1. Write down the generalizations your essay will make, and then **brainstorm** examples that support them.

2. **Freewrite** to bring to mind relevant personal experiences or stories told by friends and relatives.

3. **Conduct research** to find examples used by experts and relevant news reports and to locate other supporting information, like facts and statistics.

4. **Review textbooks** for examples used there.

Hint: Keep track of where you found each example so that you can cite your sources accurately.

4 Evaluate your examples.

Try these suggestions to help you evaluate your examples:

- **Reread everything you have written.** (Sometimes reading your notes aloud is helpful.)

- **Highlight examples** that are **representative** (or typical) yet **striking**. Make sure they are **relevant** (they clearly illustrate your point). Unless you are using just one extended example, make sure your examples are **varied**. Then **copy and paste** the usable ideas to a new document to consult while drafting.

- **Collaborate.** In small groups, take turns **giving examples** and having classmates tell you

    1. what they think your **main idea** is. (If they don't get it, rethink your examples.)

    2. what **additional information** they need to find your main idea convincing.

Classmates can also help narrow your topic or think of more effective examples.

5 Draft your thesis statement.

Try one or more of the following strategies to **develop a generalization** that your examples support. (Your generalization will become your working thesis.)

1. Systematically **review your examples** asking yourself what they have in common.

2. **Discuss your thesis with a classmate.** Do the examples support the thesis? If not, try to improve on each other's examples or revise the thesis.

3. In a **two-column list**, write words in the left column describing how you feel about your narrowed topic. (For example, the topic *cheating on college exams* might generate such feelings as anger, surprise, and confusion.) In the right column, add details about specific situations in which these feelings arose. (For example, your thesis might focus on your surprise on discovering that a good friend cheated on an exam.)

4. **Research** your topic in the library or on the Internet to uncover examples outside your own experience. Then ask yourself what the examples from your experience and your research have in common.

Note: As you draft, you may think of situations or examples that illustrate a different or more interesting thesis. Don't hesitate to revise your thesis as you discover more about your topic.

Collaborate with classmates to make sure your examples support your thesis statement.

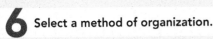 **Select a method of organization.**

- If you are using a **single, extended example**, you are most likely to use **chronological order** to relate events in the sequence in which they happened.
- If you are using **several examples**, you are most likely to organize the examples from most to least or least to most important.
- If you are using **many examples**, you may want to **group them into categories**. For instance, in an essay about the use of slang, you might classify examples according to regions or age groups in which they are used.

Hint: An outline or graphic organizer will allow you to experiment to find the best order for supporting paragraphs.

7 **Write a first draft of your illustration essay.**

Use the following guidelines to keep your illustration essay on track:

- The **introduction** should spark readers' interest and include background information (if needed by readers). Most illustration essays include a **thesis** near the beginning to help readers understand the point of upcoming examples.
- The **body paragraphs** should include **topic sentences** to focus each paragraph (or paragraph cluster) on one key idea. Craft **one or more examples** for each paragraph (or cluster) to illustrate that key idea. Use **vivid descriptive language** to make readers feel as if they are experiencing or observing the situation. Include **transitions**, such as *for example* or *in particular*, to guide readers from one example to another. (Consult Chapter 8 for help with crafting effective descriptions.)
- The **conclusion** should **include a final statement** that pulls together your ideas and reminds readers of your thesis.

8 **Evaluate your draft, and revise as necessary.**

Use **Figure 13.1, "Flowchart for Revising an Illustration Essay,"** to evaluate and revise your draft.

FIGURE 13.1 Flowchart for Revising an Illustration Essay

QUESTIONS   REVISION STRATEGIES

1. Highlight your thesis statement. Place a ✔ by each example. Do your examples clearly support the generalization your thesis makes?

 NO ▶

- Revise your thesis, changing your generalization so that it fits your examples.

 YES
▼

(continued on next page) ▶

(Figure 13.1 continued)

QUESTIONS REVISION STRATEGIES

2. *Write* a sentence describing your readers. ~~Cross out~~ any examples that won't appeal to them. Do you have enough examples left?

NO ▶
- Brainstorm more appealing examples.
- Add examples that represent different aspects of or viewpoints on your topic.

YES ▼

3. Write a sentence stating the purpose of your essay. ~~Cross out~~ any examples that don't fulfill your purpose. Do you have enough examples left?

NO ▶
- Brainstorm examples more appropriate to your purpose.
- Add some of these examples or consider cutting back and using one extended example.

YES ▼

4. Reread your examples. Is each one accurate, relevant, striking, representative, and specific? Are the examples varied?

NO ▶
- Brainstorm to replace dull, irrelevant, or misleading examples.
- Conduct research to discover facts, expert opinion, or statistics.

YES ▼

5. Reread your supporting paragraphs. Does each one have a topic sentence? Does each topic sentence clearly make a point that the example(s) in that paragraph illustrate?

NO ▶
- Add or revise the topic sentence to clearly indicate the point each example or group of examples illustrates.
- Reorganize your essay, grouping examples according to the idea they illustrate.

YES ▼

6. Outline your essay. [Bracket] each transition. Is your organization clear and effective?

NO ▶
- Add transitions or use a different organizing strategy. (See Chapter 6.)

YES ▼

7. Reread your introduction and conclusion. Is each effective?

NO ▶
- Revise your introduction to engage readers and provide background.
- Revise your conclusion to remind readers of your thesis and create a satisfying ending.

REVISING

9 Edit and proofread your essay.

Refer to Chapter 9 for help with

- **editing sentences** to avoid wordiness, making your verb choices strong and active, and making your sentences clear, varied, and parallel
- **editing words** for tone and diction, connotation, and concrete and specific language

Pay particular attention to the following:

1. Keep **verb tenses** consistent in your extended examples. When using an event from the past as an example, however, always use the past tense to describe it.

   Example: Special events *are* an important part of children's lives. Parent visitation day at school *was* an event my daughter *talked* about for an entire week. Children *are* also excited by . . .

2. Use **first person** (*I, me, we, us*), **second person** (*you*), or **third person** (*he, she, it, him, her, they, them*) consistently.

   Example: I visited my daughter's first-grade classroom during parents' week last month. Each parent was invited to read a story to the class, and ~~you~~ ^{we} were encouraged to ask the children questions afterward.

3. Avoid **sentence fragments** when introducing examples. Each sentence must have both a subject and a verb.

   Example: Technology has become part of teenagers' daily lives. ~~For example, high~~ ^{High} school students who carry iPhones_{are one example.}

EDITING & PROOFREADING

Readings: Illustration in Action

STUDENTS WRITE

Conforming to Stand Out: A Look at American Beauty

Nick Ruggia

Nick Ruggia, a student at the University of Maryland at College Park, wrote this essay in response to an assignment in which he was asked to examine an American

Title: Ruggia identifies his topic and suggests his thesis.

obsession. He chose to write about Americans' obsession with physical appearance. As you read his illustration essay, notice how he supports his thesis with a variety of examples.

Introduction: Ruggia offers a biological reason for focusing on women. In his thesis statement, he makes a generalization about American women and previews his organization by presenting his three examples in the order in which he will discuss them.

In nature, two factors largely determine survival of the species: access to resources and physical attraction (necessary for the ability to mate). Humans function under the same basic rules. In modern America, where almost everyone can acquire the basic resources to live, humans are striving harder than ever to be physically attractive. Although men are increasingly caught up in its grip, the pressure to be beautiful falls most intensely on women. The thin craze, the plastic surgery craze, and the body art craze represent some of the increasingly drastic lengths American women are being driven to in their quest for physical perfection.

1

Organization: A topic sentence introduces example 1, the thin craze. In this paragraph and the next two, Ruggia uses specific celebrities to support his claims.

Supporting evidence: Ruggia cites the sources for his subexamples using MLA style. The statistics suggest that the celebrities are representative of Americans in general.

Since Kate Moss's wafer-thin frame took the modeling industry by storm, skinny has driven America's aesthetics. Hollywood is a mirror for our desires, and our stars are shrinking. Nicole Ritchie and Angelina Jolie, among others, have publicly struggled with eating disorders. Jennifer Anniston and Reese Witherspoon are rumored to be following a diet of baby food to keep weight off (Crawford A1). And the stars aren't alone. According to the United States National Institutes of Mental Health, about 0.9 percent of American women will suffer from anorexia in their lifetimes, while another 1.5 percent will be bulimic and 3.5 percent will binge. These numbers exclude the disordered eaters who do not meet all the criteria necessary for diagnosis or do not accurately self-report. In a population of 300 million, these statistics represent millions of women struggling with eating disorders. Men are not immune either, with 0.2 to 0.3 percent of men diagnosed with bulimia or anorexia and 2 percent diagnosed with binge eating (*The Numbers*).

2

Organization: A transitional sentence leads into the topic sentence for example 2, the plastic surgery craze, supported by detailed statistics from reliable sources.

But for every Kate Moss idolizer, there's a would-be Pamela Anderson. This ideal, fed by porn and Hollywood, is plastic perfection: instead of anorexically denying their curves, many women choose to enhance their features through surgery. The American Society of Aesthetic Plastic Surgery (ASAPS) reported that in 2015, cosmetic surgeries were up 7 percent, with an overall increase of nearly 40 percent since 2011. While

3

it must be remembered that some people have more than one surgery, still, the scope of this practice is staggering nonetheless. Further evidence is provided by the surgically enhanced lips, stomachs, buttocks, and breasts that cover the pages of men's magazines all over the country. Strippers, porn stars like Jenna Jameson, and *Playboy* models like Anderson and the late Anna Nicole Smith flaunt enormous fake breasts. Clearly there is a disconnect between the sexless anorexic standard that so many women strive for and the bottle blonde bombshell that so many men favor. What everyone seems to agree on, though, is that plastic surgery is a response to the fear of aging. And in this way as well, men too are increasingly vulnerable to the superficial, with the ASAPS reporting that they accounted for 9.5 percent of plastic surgeries in 2015.

Body art, in the form of piercing and tattoos, also illustrates (literally) Americans' obsession with physical appearance. The pierced and tattooed once jarred on public sensibilities, but now these body modifications have gone mainstream. Even "alternative" piercings are now accepted: the late Amy Winehouse, a heavily tattooed popular musician, has added to the popularity of the "Monroe" piercing, located above the lip where Marilyn Monroe had a mole. About 40 percent of the millennial generation has at least one tattoo, and nearly a quarter have pierced something other than their ears (*Millennials*). Once largely limited to sailors, criminals, and punk rockers—and to men—body art has become big business, drawing in more women as it spreads.

Maybe Americans have gone too far in basing their self-worth on physical appearance. Every visible part of the human body has been marketed as a fixable flaw or an opportunity for more adornment. Of course, Americans have always cared about their looks and made great efforts to improve them, but once most people kept the issue in perspective. Today, appearance rules. And men increasingly are joining women in obedience to its commands. Both sexes, though, will find that basing self-esteem on physical appearance, a fleeting commodity at best, is a recipe for misery.

Supporting evidence: Ruggia cites striking subexamples.

4   **Organization:** A topic sentence introduces example 3, the body art craze.

5   **Conclusion:** Ruggia acknowledges that attention to appearance is nothing new, but suggests that Americans today place too much emphasis on it.

Sources: Ruggia lists his sources in MLA style, with the entries in alphabetical order. Notice the style for listing documents from Web sites sponsored by organizations and government agencies.

Works Cited

Crawford, Trish. "Celebrity 'Baby Food Diet' Recipe for Eating Disorder."
    Toronto Star, 18 May 2010, p. A1.

Millennials: Confident, Connected, Open to Change. Pew Research Center
    for the People and the Press, 24 Feb. 2010, www.pewsocialtrends
    .org/2010/02/24/millennials-confident-connected-open-to-change/
    #the-millennial-identity.

"2015 Quick Facts." American Society of Aesthetic Plastic Surgery, 2016,
    www.surgery.org/sites/default/files/2015-quick-facts.pdf.

The Numbers Count: Mental Disorders in America. United States, Department
    of Health and Human Services, National Institutes of Mental Health. 2013,
    www.lb7.uscourts.gov/documents/12-cv-1072url2.pdf.

Analyzing the Writer's Technique

1. **Examples** Evaluate the three main examples Ruggia provides. How well do they illustrate his thesis? What other examples could he have used?
2. **Sources** Ruggia used four sources in writing the essay. What kinds of sources are they? How does his use of these sources strengthen his essay?
3. **Evidence** Ruggia uses celebrities and statistics as evidence to support each of the topic sentences about his three main examples. What other types of evidence could he have used?

Thinking Critically about Illustration

1. **Emotional Response** Do any of Ruggia's examples or pieces of evidence create an emotional impact? If so, choose several and explain their effects.
2. **Connotation** What are the connotations of "bottle blonde bombshell" (para. 3)?
3. **Alternative Viewpoints** What other types of sources could Ruggia have consulted to research and discuss alternative viewpoints?
4. **Generalization** Is the generalization in the essay's last sentence well-supported and well-explained in the essay?

Responding to the Essay

1. **Discussion** Discuss the meaning and effectiveness of Ruggia's title.
2. **Journal** In your journal, respond to the following question: To what extent do you agree that piercings and tattoos are widely accepted?
3. **Thinking Critically** What do you think is the reason for the "disconnect" that Ruggia mentions in paragraph 3? Is the problem that women don't understand what men want? That men don't understand what women want? Both? Something else?
4. **Essay** Are Americans obsessed with appearances in other ways? Write an essay explaining another American obsession. Use examples to support your thesis.

Using Emoji for Digital-Age Language Learning

Gretchen McCullough

Gretchen McCullough writes the Resident Linguist column for *Wired* magazine and has written for a number of other publications, including *The Wall Street Journal*, *Mental Floss*, and *Slate*. She is especially interested in writing about what she calls the "language of the internet." A podcaster and blogger, McCullough also publishes a monthly newsletter and has published the book *Because Internet: Understanding the Rules of Language* (2019). In the following piece, she explores how children use emoji to learn language and communicate. **Before reading**, preview and make connections by thinking about the emoji you use most often and how they help you communicate. **While reading**, observe and highlight how the author uses examples to illustrate various stages of emoji use.

> **JUST-IN-TIME TIP**   Organizing Information to Promote Recall
>
> To explain emoji use, the author tracks how it progresses and changes among children and draws comparisons between children and adults. To make review and recall easier, create a two-column list of ages and the characteristics of emoji use. Also highlight how emoji use differs between adults and children.

A couple of months ago, NPR reporter Lulu Miller tweeted a question. She knew a   1
five-year-old who was texting exclusively in emoji, and wondered if [there were] any studies about kids, too young to read, who used emoji to communicate. People wouldn't stop tagging me in the thread, but we couldn't find any existing studies, so I decided to run a survey and make a small corpus of my own (McCullough).

I wanted to find out not only whether kids were texting emoji but which   2
emoji, and why? How do they organize emoji into sequences and ideas, and how do these early ramblings shift as kids learn to read? So I asked parents and other people with young children in their life to copy-paste in a few examples of their kids' electronic communication, with names and other identifying details removed. The results are charming and linguistically interesting (Pardes).

When kids use emoji it may seem random—a bunch of silly pictures on a screen.   3
But kids start out learning spoken and signed languages in a similar way: by babbling nonsense syllables, which teaches them the rhythm of conversation and trains them to make fine articulatory movements. The silly strings of emoji that young kids send could serve a similar purpose. By exposing kids to the rhythm of electronic conversations, emoji may be a useful precursor to reading—a way of acclimating kids to the digital reality of using symbols to communicate with people they care about.

But let's start with the survey results. Yes, many preliterate kids send   4
emoji-only text messages, and ages three to five seems to be the peak time for them. They're often quite elaborate. One five-year-old favored "any animal that pinches," such as the following string:

A five-and-a-half-year-old's go-to emoji were "Animals, poo, unicorns, hearts." 5
A third kid of the same age was similar: "Unicorn. Poo. Lightning. Dinosaurs."
Younger kids didn't have as clear preferences, but they were still emoji fans. Here's
a string of animals and hearts from a three-year-old:

These emoji texts are adorable, but as a linguist, I'm interested in what kids are 6
trying to communicate. Many kids seem to be working their way through the emoji
keyboard systematically. For example, several kids put the blue heart right before the
green heart, which is also the order that they appear in many emoji keyboard apps.
However, kids are also willing to combine emoji from different sections, especially
animals, foods, and hearts, which all appear in different screens of an emoji keyboard.

One thing is very clear: The kids don't use emoji like adults or teens do. 7
Overall, the most popular emoji are the face, hand, and heart emoji (Medlock and
McCullough). While the kids use faces and hearts, hand shapes—like thumbs
up 👍 and prayer hands 🙏—are not at all common for the younger set.
Conversely, the kids use object emoji, like food and animals, far more than adults
or teens do. Both kids and adults like happy faces, but their other face preferences
are different: Kids don't use the faces that convey a note of irony, such as the
otherwise-popular tears of joy 😂, loudly sobbing face 😭, or thinking face 🤔.
Instead, kids prefer faces with the tongue stuck out 😛 or blowing a kiss 😘.

Kids also use emoji sequences differently. When mature emoji users use 8
strings of emoji, they're generally in groups of two to five, after a sequence of
words, such as "I LITERALLY CAN'T HANDLE THIS 😊😊😊" or "omg i love you
💛💚". When adults or teens create extended emoji-only sequences, they
typically impose some rules on themselves: Either they try to recount a story for
someone else to guess—a kind of emoji charades—or they try to create something
aesthetically pleasing, as emoji art.

The kids, on the other hand, are less structured: The emoji take the form of a 9
drawing, or a selection of stickers. The kids also tended to send longer messages,
and were more likely to send the same emoji three or five or 20 times in a row.

As the kids got older and learned how to read and write, their emoji messages 10
grew more sophisticated. A six-year-old and a nearly-seven-year-old, both fluent
readers, sent messages containing both semantically appropriate words and
slightly less-random strings of emoji, such as:

A few years later, kids seem to age out of the "strings of random emoji" phase 11
entirely: a 10-year-old sent full English sentences, and her emoji-only messages

used line breaks and spacing, to make sequences into borders and larger shapes, like a large face made out of face emoji. Several adults noted that their kids had simply stopped sending long emoji-filled messages once they learned how to read—surely reassuring for anyone who's wondering about the future of the English language.

What can we make of the long-term effect on children of sending emoji? The true effect of these texts may be bigger than any single message. Studies show that kids don't acquire a language just from media exposure—they need a person to interact with, at least to start.

In one study (Kuhl et al.), researchers had nine-month-olds from monolingual English-speaking households interact over four weeks with research assistants speaking Mandarin. The research assistants would speak normal child-directed Mandarin to the babies, reading them picture books in Mandarin and playing with a few toys. Sure enough, those kids showed better recognition of Mandarin sounds than a control group who had come in and played with an English speaker. But then, the researchers played a second set of babies video of the same research assistants reading the same books and playing with the same toys in Mandarin. Despite the fact that this group had received identical input to the first babies, the babies who'd listened to the recordings didn't show any improvement on their ability to recognize Mandarin sounds.

While kids who already speak a given language can learn words from watching children's television programs, like *Sesame Street* and *Mister Rogers' Neighborhood*, they don't learn grammar or sounds from TV (Naigles and Mayeux 136, 141). And kids don't learn much at all from children's programming in a language they don't already have real-life exposure to. There's something really important about social interaction, and this carries over into emoji messages.

Sending long strings of emoji could be like digital babbling: the nonsense strings that get us used to how our bodies work and how to take turns in a conversation. The adults texting the kids back sometimes replied with emoji, but many times they also replied with words ("Hahahaha. Dinos and dino food!") or a mix of words and emoji—even when the child didn't know how to read yet. Presumably, the other adult whose phone the kid was using would read the words aloud.

Think what this is teaching kids about reading and writing. When I was a kid, the written word was a thing of picture books and stop signs and cereal boxes and ABC fridge magnets. Writing often came with colorful, child-friendly illustrations, but it wasn't often created specifically for me. Writing was created by professionals or incorporated into a literacy lesson: Here's a story about talking animals; here's how you write your name. Writing wasn't used to communicate with me—after all, why would my parents leave me a note before I could read it?

Kids still get picture books read to them. But now that we all communicate in writing so much more often, kids also are read text messages. For a kid to get a text message written directly for them, and read directly to them, which they can reply to in some fashion, it teaches them something powerful about the written word—that it can be used to connect with people you care about.

Links

Kuhl, Patricia K., et al. "Foreign-Language Experience in Infancy: Effects of Short-Term Exposure and Social Interaction on Phonetic Learning." *Proceedings of the National Academy of Sciences of the United States*, vol. 100, no. 15 (July 2003), pp. 9096–101, doi.org/10.1073/pnas.1532872100.

McCullough, Gretchen. "By popular demand, I've rustled us up a quick CHILD EMOJI AND ELECTRONIC COMMUNICATION survey!" *Twitter*, 25 Oct. 2018, 4:25 p.m., twitter.com/GretchenAMcC.

Medlock, Ben, and Gretchen McCullough. "The Linguistic Secrets Found in Billions of Emoji—SXSW Interactive 2016." South by Southwest Festival, 12 Mar. 2016, Austin Convention Center. Soundcloud, 2016, soundcloud.com/officialsxsw/the-linguistic-secrets-found-in-billions-of-emoji-sxsw-interactive-2016. Conference presentation.

Miller, Lulu. "Guys, Guys, Guys. the 10 year old girl on my block just informed me that she texts with a 5 YEAR OLD, who is preliterate, + exclusively uses emojies to communicate. WTF? Have any linguists studied this phenomena + written weighty treatises about it? i want to know everything." *Twitter*, 25 Oct. 2018, 3:15 p.m., twitter.com/lmillernpr/status/1055583571317022720.

Naigles, Leticia R., and Lara Mayeux. "Television as Incidental Language Teacher." In Singer, Dorothy G., and Jerome L. Singer. *Handbook of Children and the Media*, Sage Publications, 2001, pp. 135-52.

Pardes, Arielle. "Academics Gathered to Share Emoji Research, and It Was 💧." *Wired*, 27 June 2018, www.wired.com/story/academic-emoji-conference/.

Understanding the Reading

1. **Summarizing** What are the main differences McCullough presents in emoji use of children versus that of adults?
2. **Details** What types of face emoji do children prefer?
3. **Details** Explain what the author means by "emoji charades" (para. 7).
4. **Vocabulary** Explain the meaning of each of the following words as it is used in the reading: *corpus* (para. 1), *articulatory* (3), *precursor* (3), *linguist* (5), and *aesthetically* (7).

Analyzing the Writer's Technique

1. **Introduction** The essay begins with a tweet and an explanation of how that tweet prompted McCullough to conduct a study on how young children use emoji while texting. Why is this an effective introduction?
2. **Audience** What audience do you think McCullough is addressing in this selection? How do her examples address or appeal to this audience?
3. **Conclusion** McCullough's poignant conclusion seems somewhat at odds with the playful tone of the rest of the essay. Is this change in tone appropriate, given what she says at the end of the essay?

Thinking Critically about Illustration

1. **Inference** What advice might McCullough give to parents about helping their children learn to communicate effectively?
2. **Use of Visuals** Many of the examples that the author includes are emoji themselves, often in strings. Evaluate how helpful such examples are in helping you understand emoji use.

3. **Connotation** In paragraph 2, the author uses the words *charming and linguistically interesting*, and in paragraph 5, she includes the phrase *emoji texts are adorable, but as a linguist. . . .* What impression does the author create through her choice of words in these paragraphs?

4. **Alternative Examples** McCullough uses mostly scientific research and examples from children to support her thesis. What other types of evidence might she have included?

Responding to the Reading

1. **Discussion** What do you think about children ages three to five texting emoji? Who do you think they text? What do you think they text about? Is there any benefit to this activity or is it just child's play? Could it possibly be harmful? What does the author think about this practice? Do you know any very young children who text?

2. **Journal** If you had to summarize this reading using only emoji, what emoji would you use? Create a string of ten emoji related to this reading and explain the meaning of each.

3. **Essay** Write an essay in which you discuss both the benefits and the drawbacks of using emoji in your written communication.

Working Together

Although the title of this essay, "Using Emoji for Digital-Age Language Learning," accurately reflects the content, a different title could do more to spark readers' interest. In small groups, come up with a list of at least three alternative titles for this selection. (**Hint:** Recall the suggestions for writing a good title in Chapter 7, such as asking a question that the essay answers, using alliteration, and creating a play on words.)

EXPLORE, RESEARCH, WRITE

In "Using Emoji for Digital-Age Language Learning," McCullough uses research to explain how emojis may allow young children to communicate in writing with those with whom they have relationships. Other researchers have also studied this phenomenon. Some reports about this research include the following:

- "Why I Use Emoji in Research and Teaching" by Jennifer Fane, a lecturer in health and early childhood education at Flinders University in Australia (*The Conversation*, 2017)

- "Talking to Children about Technology" by Playful Learning, a studio offering educational enrichment to preschool and elementary school children (2019)

- "We Wouldn't Feed Our Kids Junk Food. So Why Let Them Use Emojis?" by Laura Freeman (*The Spectator*, 12 May 2018)

Using your own ideas and one or more of the selections listed here, write a thoughtful illustration essay that goes beyond "Using Emoji for Digital-Age Language Learning." Be sure to include at least one quotation from one of the readings and to cite it correctly at the end of the essay.

The Guided Writing Assignment in this chapter can walk you through the process of writing an illustration essay; for help with evaluating sources, see Chapter 21; for help choosing and synthesizing ideas from sources, see Chapter 22; for help with documenting sources, see Chapter 23.

Why Walking Helps Us Think

Ferris Jabr

Ferris Jabr is a writer based in Portland, Oregon. His work has been anthologized in *The Best American Science and Nature Writing* series, and he has worked as a staff editor at *Scientific American*, where he is now a contributing writer. He has also written for publications including *The New York Times Magazine*, *Outside*, *Slate*, and *The New Yorker*, where this essay originally appeared. **Before reading**, preview the essay and make connections by thinking about benefits you notice when you go for a walk. **While reading**, identify the examples Jabr uses to support his thesis and consider how effectively they support his generalization.

JUST-IN-TIME TIP   Organizing Cause-and-Effect Relationships

Although this is an illustration essay, Jabr also uses cause and effect to explain how walking helps us. To comprehend and clarify these relationships, make marginal notes identifying the causes and effects discussed in paragraphs 2, 3, 7, and 9. (The first one for para. 2 has been done for you; it contains numerous cause-and-effect relationships.)

Paragraph	Causes or Effects
2	Walking changes our body rhythms (heart rate, circulation, etc.), improves memory and attention, promotes connections among brain cells, increases hippocampus volume, and stimulates neuron growth.
3	
7	
9	

Since at least the time of peripatetic Greek philosophers, many other writers have   1
discovered a deep, intuitive connection between walking, thinking, and writing. "How vain it is to sit down to write when you have not stood up to live!" Henry David Thoreau penned in his journal. "Methinks that the moment my legs begin to move, my thoughts begin to flow." Thomas DeQuincey has calculated that William Wordsworth—whose poetry is filled with tramps up mountains, through forests, and along public roads—walked as many as a hundred and eighty thousand miles in his lifetime, which comes to an average of six and a half miles a day starting from age five.

What is it about walking, in particular, that makes it so amenable to thinking   2
and writing? The answer begins with changes to our chemistry. When we go for a
walk, the heart pumps faster, circulating more blood and oxygen not just to the
muscles but to all the organs—including the brain. Many experiments have shown
that after or during exercise, even very mild exertion, people perform better on
tests of memory and attention (Voss et al.). Walking on a regular basis also promotes new connections (Erickson, Mark I., et al.) between brain cells, staves off the
usual withering of brain tissue that comes with age (Erickson, K. I., et al.), increases
the volume of the hippocampus (a brain region crucial for memory), and elevates
levels of molecules that both stimulate the growth of new neurons and transmit
messages between them (Segal, S. K., et al.).

The way we move our bodies further changes the nature of our thoughts, and   3
vice versa. Psychologists who specialize in exercise music have quantified what
many of us already know (Karageorghis and Priest): listening to songs with high
tempos motivates us to run faster, and the swifter we move, the quicker we prefer
our music (Barney et al.). Likewise, when drivers hear loud, fast music, they unconsciously step a bit harder on the gas pedal (Warren). Walking at our own pace creates an unadulterated feedback loop between the rhythm of our bodies and our
mental state that we cannot experience as easily when we're jogging at the gym,
steering a car, biking, or during any other kind of locomotion. When we stroll, the
pace of our feet naturally vacillates with our moods and the cadence of our inner
speech; at the same time, we can actively change the pace of our thoughts by
deliberately walking more briskly or by slowing down.

Because we don't have to devote much conscious effort to the act of walking,   4
our attention is free to wander—to overlay the world before us with a parade of
images from the mind's theatre. This is precisely the kind of mental state that
studies have linked to innovative ideas and strokes of insight. Earlier this year,
Marily Oppezzo and Daniel Schwartz of Stanford published what is likely the first
set of studies that directly measure the way walking changes creativity in the
moment. They got the idea for the studies while on a walk. "My doctoral advisor
had the habit of going for walks with his students to brainstorm," Oppezzo says of
Schwartz. "One day we got kind of meta."

In a series of four experiments, Oppezzo and Schwartz asked a hundred and   5
seventy-six college students to complete different tests of creative thinking while
either sitting, walking on a treadmill, or sauntering through Stanford's campus. In
one test, for example, volunteers had to come up with atypical uses for everyday
objects, such as a button or a tire. On average, the students thought of between
four and six more novel uses for the objects while they were walking than when
they were seated. Another experiment required volunteers to contemplate a metaphor, such as "a budding cocoon," and generate a unique but equivalent metaphor,
such as "an egg hatching." Ninety-five percent of students who went for a walk
were able to do so, compared to only fifty percent of those who never stood up. But
walking actually worsened people's performance on a different type of test, in
which students had to find the one word that united a set of three, like "cheese"
for "cottage, cream, and cake." Oppezzo speculates that, by setting the mind adrift
on a frothing sea of thought, walking is counterproductive to such laser-focused

thinking: "If you're looking for a single correct answer to a question, you probably don't want all of these different ideas bubbling up."

Where we walk matters as well. In a study led by Marc Berman of the University of South Carolina, students who ambled through an arboretum improved their performance on a memory test more than students who walked along city streets. A small but growing collection of studies suggests that spending time in green spaces—gardens, parks, forests—can rejuvenate the mental resources that man-made environments deplete. 6

Psychologists have learned that attention is a limited resource that continually drains throughout the day. A crowded intersection—rife with pedestrians, cars, and billboards—bats our attention around. In contrast, walking past a pond in a park allows our mind to drift casually from one sensory experience to another, from wrinkling water to rustling reeds. 7

Still, urban and pastoral walks likely offer unique advantages for the mind. A walk through a city provides more immediate stimulation—a greater variety of sensations for the mind to play with. But, if we are already at the brink of over-stimulation, we can turn to nature instead. Virginia Woolf relished the creative energy of London's streets, describing it in her diary as "being on the highest crest of the biggest wave, right in the centre & swim of things." But she also depended on her walks through England's South Downs to "have space to spread my mind out in" (Dobbs). And, in her youth, she often travelled to Cornwall for the summer, where she loved to "spend my afternoons in solitary trampling" through the countryside (Dobbs). 8

Perhaps the most profound relationship between walking, thinking, and writing reveals itself at the end of a stroll, back at the desk. There, it becomes apparent that writing and walking are extremely similar feats, equal parts physical and mental. When we choose a path through a city or forest, our brain must survey the surrounding environment, construct a mental map of the world, settle on a way forward, and translate that plan into a series of footsteps. Likewise, writing forces the brain to review its own landscape, plot a course through that mental terrain, and transcribe the resulting trail of thoughts by guiding the hands. Walking organizes the world around us; writing organizes our thoughts. 9

Links

Barney, David, et al. "College Students' Usage of Personal Music Players (PMP) during Exercise." *ICHPER-SD Journal of Research*, vol. 7, no. 1 (2012), pp. 23–26, eric.ed.gov/?id=EJ973952.

Berman, Marc G., et al. "The Cognitive Benefits of Interacting with Nature." *Psychological Science*, vol. 19, no. 12 (Dec. 2008), pp. 1207–12, doi:10.1111/j.1467-9280.2008.02225.x.

Dobbs, David. "Virginia Woolf Takes a Walk, Finds a Novel." *Neuron Culture*, 4 June 2014, daviddobb .net/smoothpebbles/virginia-woolf-takes-a-walk-finds-a-novel.

Erickson, K. I., et al. "Physical Activity Predicts Gray Matter Volume in Late Adulthood." *Neurology*, vol. 75, no. 16 (2010), pp. 1415–22, doi:10.1212/WNL.0b013e3181f88359.

Erickson, Mark I., et al. "Exercise Training Increases Size of Hippocampus and Improves Memory." *Proceedings of the National Academy of Sciences of the United States of America*, vol. 108, no. 7, pp. 3017–22, doi:10.1073/pnas.1015950108.

Karageorghis, Costas I., and David-Lee Priest. "Music in the Exercise Domain: A Review and Synthesis." *International Review of Sport Exercise Psychology*, vol. 5, no. 1, pp. 67–84, doi:10.1080/ 1750984X.2011.631027.

Oppezzo, Marily, and Daniel L. Schwartz. "Give Your Ideas Some Legs: The Positive Effect of Walking on Creative Thinking." *Journal of Experimental Psychology: Learning, Memory, and Cognition*, vol. 40, no. 4 (2014), pp. 1142–52, doi: 10.1037/a0036577.

Segal, S. K., et al. "Exercise-Induced Noradrenergic Activation Enhances Memory Consolidation in Both Normal Aging Patients with Amnestic Mild Cognitive Impairment." *Journal of Alzheimers Disease*, vol. 32, no. 4 (2012), pp. 1011–18, doi:10.3233/JAD-2012-121078.

Voss, M. W., et al. "Plasticity of Brain Networks in a Randomized Intervention Trial of Exercise Training in Older Adults." *Front Aging Neuroscience*, vol. 32 (2010), doi:10.3389/fnagi.2010.00032.

Warren, Brodsky. "The Effects of Music Tempo on Simulated Driving Performance and Vehicular Control." *Transportation Research Part F: Traffic Psychology and Behaviour*, vol. 4, no. 4 (2001), pp. 219–41, doi:10.1016/S1369-8478(01)00025-0.

Woolf, Virginia. "[Sunday 5 September 1926.]" *Woolf Online*, edited by Pamela L. Caughie, et al., 2016, www.woolfonline.com.

Understanding the Reading

1. **Summarizing** Briefly explain the changes to our body chemistry that result from walking.
2. **Detail** What have psychologists discovered about the effects of music?
3. **Detail** How does location affect our thinking when we walk?
4. **Vocabulary** Explain the meaning of each of the following words as it is used in the reading: *peripatetic* (para. 1), *amenable* (2), *vacillates* (3), *cadence* (3), and *rejuvenate* (6).

Analyzing the Writer's Technique

1. **Introduction** Why does the author mention Thoreau and Wordsworth in the introduction?
2. **Thesis** Express Jabr's thesis in your own words. Is it stated directly in the essay or only implied?
3. **Audience** What audience do you think Jabr is addressing in this selection? How do his examples address or appeal to this audience?

Thinking Critically about Illustration

1. **Connotation** What is the connotation of *ambled* (para. 6)? Is Jabr using it to mean something positive or negative?
2. **Sources** Jabr's examples are drawn primarily from university studies. How trustworthy do you consider these sources of information? What other source types could Jabr have used to give alternative viewpoints?
3. **Examples** Evaluate the effectiveness of the examples in this selection. Does Jabr provide a variety of relevant and useful examples to support his thesis?
4. **Meaning** What does the author mean when he says that walking "creates an unadulterated feedback loop between the rhythm of our bodies and our mental state"? How is it possible to change the pace of our thoughts?

Responding to the Reading

1. **Reaction** Jabr quotes the writer Virginia Woolf (para. 8) as relishing the "creative energy" of the city while depending on walks in the countryside for "space to spread my mind out in." Where do you go to find creative energy or mental stimulation? Where do you go to rejuvenate your mental resources?

2. **Journal** Aside from the physical effects of walking described in the selection, how does walking affect you? If you typically do not walk, how do other forms of exercise affect your mental state? Write a journal entry describing the effects of walking or exercise on your thinking and your writing.

3. **Essay** Jabr compares writing and walking as "equal parts physical and mental." Consider the mental map you create when you walk from class to home, then write an essay giving examples of that landscape. Describe your path from your starting point to your destination, and give examples of landmarks and points of interest along the way.

Working Together

Imagine that you have been asked to help promote a walking trail system that goes around and through your campus or your town. Working with a partner, create a list of "talking points" to highlight the benefits of walking in both green spaces and urban environments. If you know the area well enough, suggest pathways that would offer stimulation and/or rejuvenation for people walking along the trail. Be prepared to share your work with the class.

> ### EXPLORE, RESEARCH, WRITE
>
> In "Why Walking Helps Us Think," Jabr uses research to explain the connection among walking, thinking, and creativity. Other researchers have also studied the benefits of walking and other types of exercise. Reports about the emotional, physical, and psychological benefits of exercise include the following:
>
> - "This Is the One Simple Act That Helps Me Be More Creative" by Samantha Radocchia (*Fast Company*, 2019)
>
> - "The Mental Health Benefits of Exercise" by Lawrence Robinson, Jeanne Segal, PhD, and Melinda Smith, MA (*Help Guide*, June 2019)
>
> - "Walking and Moderate Exercise Boost Your Mental and Physical Health" by Suzanne Kane (*Psych Central*, 14 February 2019)
>
> Using your own ideas and one or more of the selections listed here, write a thoughtful illustration essay that goes beyond what the article tells and presents other information and examples of the relationship between exercise and healthy living. Be sure to include at least one quotation from one of the readings and to cite it correctly at the end of the essay.

The Guided Writing Assignment in this chapter can walk you through the process of writing an illustration essay. For help with evaluating sources, see Chapter 21; for help choosing and synthesizing ideas from sources, see Chapter 22; for help with documenting sources, see Chapter 23.

Apply Your Skills: Additional Essay Assignments

Using what you learned about illustration in this chapter, write an illustration essay on one of the topics below. Depending on the topic you choose, you may need to conduct library or Internet research.

For more on locating and documenting sources, see Part 5.

To Express Your Ideas

1. In an article for the campus newspaper, explain what you consider to be the three most important qualities of a college instructor. Support your opinion with vivid examples from your experience.
2. Explain to a general audience the role played by grandparents within a family, citing examples from your own family or other families you know well.
3. Write an essay discussing how one aspect of your life has changed (or how some aspect of life in your community has changed) as a result of a natural disaster (such as a flood), political event (an election), or health crisis (a pandemic). Support your ideas with examples that illustrate the changes you experienced or observed.

To Inform Your Reader

4. In "Rambos of the Road," Martin Gottfried explains the concept of "auto macho," also known as "road rage," using examples from his own experience. Explain the concept of *peer pressure*, using examples from your experience.
5. Describe to an audience of college students the qualities or achievements you think should be emphasized during job interviews. Give examples that show why the qualities or achievements you choose are important to potential employers.

To Persuade Your Reader

6. Argue for or against an increased emphasis on physical education in public schools. Your audience is your local school committee.
7. In a letter to the editor of a local newspaper, argue for or against the establishment of a neighborhood watch group.

Cases Using Illustration

8. Prepare an oral presentation you will give to your local town board to convince board members to lower the speed limit on your street. Use examples as well as other types of evidence.
9. Write a letter to the parents of three-year-old children who will begin attending your day care center this year, explaining how they can prepare their children for the day care experience. Support your advice with brief but relevant examples.

SYNTHESIZING IDEAS   CIVILITY

Both "American Jerk: Be Civil, or I'll Beat You to a Pulp" (pp. 23–24) and "Rambos of the Road" (pp. 314–16) deal with bad behavior and incivility.

Analyzing the Readings

1. What types of behaviors does each reading address? Compare the authors' attitudes toward these behaviors.

2. Write a journal entry comparing the techniques that each author uses to support his thesis, especially considering the tone of each. Which is more effective? Explain your choice.

Essay Idea

Choose a public setting or forum in which selfish behavior and a lack of civility are evident to you. Write an essay illustrating the behavior.

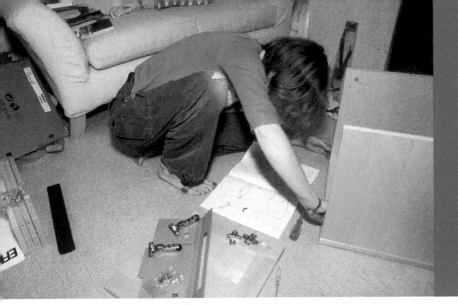

14
Process Analysis
Explaining How Something Works or Is Done

In this chapter you will learn to

- understand the purpose and function of process analysis essays
- use graphic organizers to visualize process analysis essays
- integrate process analysis into an essay
- read and think critically about process analysis
- plan, organize, draft, revise, and edit essays using process analysis

Writing Quick Start

ANALYZE The photograph above shows a person assembling a piece of furniture. Assembling furniture, equipment, or even toys can be a frustrating, time-consuming task. Instructions are often unclear or poorly written, and diagrams are often confusing. Customers may have to resort to online help or hope that an instructional video has been posted to YouTube.

WRITE Write a brief paragraph describing how to assemble something (like a bookshelf or a Lego kit) or set something up (like a new DVR or scanner). Your readers are not particularly handy and have little experience with assembly, so be sure to let them know what to expect by informing them if they will need any special tools or equipment and by warning them of common pitfalls and frustrations. (No one wants to end up with extra parts or an object that simply does not work.)

CONNECT You probably guided your readers step by step, starting with unpacking the box, then addressing how to use the instructions, and ending up with testing out the object (Is the table wobbly? Does the printer work?). If you did, then your paragraph is probably a good example of a **process analysis**: a step-by-step discussion of how something works, is done, or is made.

Process analysis provides clear, direct, and practical information. A process essay might explain how to register for classes or how a medication works, how to make a pizza, or how a college or university assesses applicants. Its purpose is always to inform. In order for a process essay to be helpful, it must be well organized and written specifically for the intended audience. In this chapter, you will read process analyses; you will also write a process analysis essay or use process analysis in essays that rely on one or more of the other patterns of development.

USING PROCESS ANALYSIS   **IN COLLEGE AND THE WORKPLACE**

- For a *child development course*, your assignment is to visit a day care center, observe one confrontation between a child and a teacher, and explain how the teacher resolved the conflict.

- As part of a *chemistry lab report*, you need to summarize the procedure you followed in preparing a solution or conducting an experiment.

- While working as an *engineer* at a water treatment plant, you are asked to describe how the city's drinking water is tested and treated for contamination.

What Are the Characteristics of a Process Analysis Essay?

Most process analysis essays fall into two categories:

- A **how-to essay** explains how to do something to readers who want or need to perform the process. It may explain how to teach a child the alphabet, for instance. Your primary purpose in writing a how-to essay is to present the steps in the process clearly and completely so that your readers can perform the task you describe.

- A **how-it-works essay** explains how something works to readers who want to understand the process but not actually perform it. For example, you might explain how a popular radio talk show screens its callers. Your primary purpose in writing a how-it-works essay is to present the steps in the process clearly enough so that your readers can fully understand it.

Some essays contain elements of both types of process analysis. In writing about how a car alarm system works, for example, you might find it necessary to explain how to activate and deactivate the system as well as how it works.

A process analysis essay should include everything your reader needs to know to understand or perform the process. This usually means providing

- an explicit thesis statement
- a clear, step-by-step description of the process in chronological order

- definitions of key terms, descriptions of needed equipment, and any other important background information
- enough detail for readers to follow the process
- help with avoiding potential problems

Process Analyses Usually Include an Explicit Thesis Statement

A process analysis usually contains a clear thesis that identifies the process to be discussed and suggests why the process is important or useful to the reader.

How To   By carefully preparing for a vacation in a foreign country,

process

why it's useful

you can save time and prevent hassles.

How It Works   Although understanding the grieving process will not lessen the

process

grief that you experience after the death of a loved one, knowing

why it's useful

that your experiences are normal does provide some comfort.

Process Analysis Is Organized Chronologically

The steps or events in a process analysis are usually organized in chronological order — that is, the order in which the steps are normally completed. For essays that explain lengthy processes, the steps may be grouped into categories or divided into substeps, with headings such as *Preparing for the Interview, During the Interview,* and *After the Interview.* Transitions, such as *Before you are called for an interview* or *Once the interview is over,* are often used to make the order of steps and substeps clear.

Sometimes the steps of a process do not have to occur in any particular order. For example, in an essay on how to resolve a dispute between two coworkers, the order of the recommended actions may depend on the nature of the dispute. In this situation, some logical progression of recommended actions should be used, such as starting with informal or simple steps and progressing to more formal or complex ones.

EXERCISE 14.1   **WRITING A THESIS STATEMENT FOR PROCESS ANALYSIS**

Choose one of the following processes. The process should be one you are familiar with and can explain to others. Draft a working thesis statement and a chronological list of the steps or stages of the process.

1. How to study for an exam
2. How to use online dating services
3. How to end a relationship with a friend or partner
4. How to get an A in your writing class
5. How to complete an application (for college, a job, a credit card)

Process Analysis Provides Background Information Helpful to Readers

For more on defining terms, see Chapter 17.

In some process analysis essays, readers may need additional information to understand the process. For example, in an essay explaining how scuba diving works to readers who are unfamiliar with the topic, you might need to define unfamiliar terms, such as *oxygen toxicity* or *decompression sickness*; you might need to provide background information about risks of injury or a history of the sport; and you would need to describe equipment such as dive masks, buoyancy compensators, and dive gauges. In a how-to essay, you might also need to explain where to obtain the equipment or training.

EXERCISE 14.2   **PROVIDING BACKGROUND INFORMATION IN A PROCESS ESSAY**

For one of the following processes, list (a) the technical terms that you need to define in order to explain the process, (b) useful background information you might include in the essay, and (c) the types of equipment needed to perform the task.

1. How to perform a task at home or at work (such as changing the oil in a car or taking notes during a court hearing)
2. How a piece of equipment or a machine works (such as a treadmill or a lawn mower)
3. How to repair an object (such as a leaky faucet or a ripped piece of clothing)

Process Analysis Provides an Appropriate Level of Detail

In deciding what to include in a process analysis essay, be careful not to overwhelm your readers with too many details. An explanation of how to perform CPR written by and for physicians could be highly technical, but the same description should be much simpler when written for volunteers in the local ambulance corps.

For a process involving many complex steps or highly specialized equipment, consider including a drawing or diagram to help your readers visualize the steps they need to follow or understand. For example, in an essay explaining how to detect a wiring problem in an electric stove, you might include a diagram of the stove's circuitry.

To keep your writing lively and interesting when explaining technical or scientific processes, use sensory details and figures of speech. Rather than giving dry technical details, try using descriptive language.

Process Analysis Anticipates Difficulties and Offers Solutions

A how-to essay should anticipate potential trouble spots or areas of confusion and offer advice on how to avoid or resolve problems. It should also warn readers of any difficult, complicated, or critical steps, encouraging them to pay special attention or take extra care. For instance, in a how-to essay on hanging wallpaper, you would warn readers about the difficulties of handling sheets of wallpaper and suggest folding the sheets to make them easier to work with.

EXERCISE 14.3   **IDENTIFYING POTENTIAL DIFFICULTIES IN A PROCESS**

For one of the processes listed in Exercise 14.1 or Exercise 14.2, identify potential trouble spots in the process and describe how to avoid or resolve them.

The following readings demonstrate the techniques for writing effective process analyses as discussed above. The first reading is annotated to point out how Susan Silk and Barry Goldman use these techniques to help readers avoid saying the wrong thing to a suffering friend or relative. As you read the second essay, try to identify for yourself how the writer uses the techniques of process analysis to help readers understand how to transform a "shitty first draft" into a compelling piece of writing.

HOW-TO ESSAY   **READING**

How Not to Say the Wrong Thing

Susan Silk and Barry Goldman

Susan Silk is the founder and CEO of MSI Strategic Communication, a company that provides communication consulting services. Barry Goldman is an arbitrator, mediator, and author. Using their experience, they have written an essay to help readers avoid saying the wrong thing when trying to provide comfort to someone who needs it.

Before Reading

1. **Preview:** Use the steps listed in Chapter 2.
2. **Connect:** Think about a time you (or someone you know) said the wrong thing. How did you (or the other person) try to repair the relationship?

While Reading Study the annotations to identify the characteristics of process analysis.

When Susan had breast cancer, we heard a lot of lame remarks, but our favorite came from one of Susan's colleagues. She wanted, she needed, to visit Susan after the surgery, but Susan didn't feel like having visitors, and she said so. Her colleague's response? "This isn't just about you."   1

> **Introduction:** Presents an anecdote to help readers identify with the situation

"It's not?" Susan wondered. "My breast cancer is not about me? It's about you?"   2

The same theme came up again when our friend Katie had a brain aneurysm. She was in intensive care for a long time and finally got out and into a step-down unit. She was no longer covered with tubes and lines and monitors, but she was still in rough shape. A friend came and saw her and then stepped into the hall with Katie's husband, Pat. "I wasn't prepared for this," she told him. "I don't know if I can handle it."   3

> **Background:** Provides another anecdote to show problem is widespread

This woman loves Katie, and she said what she did because the sight of Katie in this condition moved her so deeply. But it was the wrong thing to say. And it was wrong in the same way Susan's colleague's remark was wrong.   4

Susan has since developed a simple technique to help people avoid this mistake. It works for all kinds of crises: medical, legal, financial, romantic, even existential. She calls it the Ring Theory.   5

> **Thesis:** Thesis identifies process and indicates why it is important to learn.

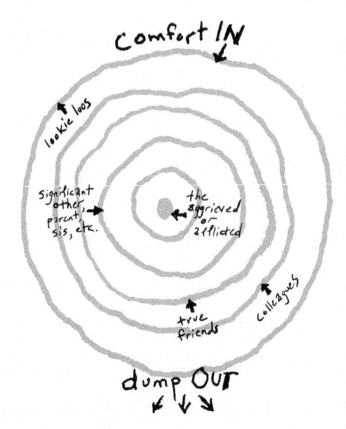

comfort IN

lookie loos

significant other, parent, sis, etc.

the aggrieved or afflicted

true friends

colleagues

dump OUT

Copyright Wes Bausmith, Los Angeles Times, April 7, 2013

Organization: Transitional words and phrases signal chronological stages of process.

Draw a circle. This is the center ring. In it, put the name of the person at the center of the current trauma. For Katie's aneurysm, that's Katie. Now draw a larger circle around the first one. In that ring put the name of the person next closest to the trauma. In the case of Katie's aneurysm, that was Katie's husband, Pat. Repeat the process as many times as you need to. In each larger ring put the next closest people. Parents and children before more distant relatives. Intimate friends in smaller rings, less intimate friends in larger ones. When you are done you have a Kvetching Order. One of Susan's patients found it useful to tape it to her refrigerator. 6

Here are the rules. The person in the center ring can say anything she wants to anyone, anywhere. She can kvetch and complain and whine and moan and curse the heavens and say, "Life is unfair" and "Why me?" That's the one payoff for being in the center ring. 7

Everyone else can say those things too, but only to people in larger rings. 8

When you are talking to a person in a ring smaller than yours, someone closer to the center of the crisis, the goal is to help. Listening is often more helpful than 9 talking. But if you're going to open your mouth, ask yourself if what you are about to say is likely to provide comfort and support. If it isn't, don't say it. Don't, for example, give advice. People who are suffering from trauma don't need advice. They need comfort and support. So say, "I'm sorry" or "This must really be hard for you" or "Can I bring you a pot roast?" Don't say, "You should hear what happened to me" or "Here's what I would do if I were you." And don't say, "This is really bringing me down."

Anticipation of difficulties and solutions: Identifies trouble spots and offers advice.

If you want to scream or cry or complain, if you want to tell someone how shocked you are or how icky you feel, or whine about how it reminds you of all the terrible things that have happened to you lately, that's fine. It's a perfectly normal response. Just do it to someone in a bigger ring.   10

Point of view: Second person (you) is commonly used in how-to essays, though it may be frowned on in academic writing.

Comfort IN, dump OUT.   11

There was nothing wrong with Katie's friend saying she was not prepared for how horrible Katie looked, or even that she didn't think she could handle it. The mistake was that she said those things to Pat. She dumped IN.   12

Complaining to someone in a smaller ring than yours doesn't do either of you any good. On the other hand, being supportive to her principal caregiver may be the best thing you can do for the patient.   13

Most of us know this. Almost nobody would complain to the patient about how rotten she looks. Almost no one would say that looking at her makes them think of the fragility of life and their own closeness to death. In other words, we know enough not to dump into the center ring. Ring Theory merely expands that intuition and makes it more concrete: Don't just avoid dumping into the center ring, avoid dumping into any ring smaller than your own.   14

Remember, you can say whatever you want if you just wait until you're talking to someone in a larger ring than yours.   15

Conclusion: Final paragraph cleverly connects to the introduction and speaks directly to the reader.

And don't worry. You'll get your turn in the center ring. You can count on that.   16

Visualize a Process Analysis Essay: Create a Graphic Organizer

Seeing the content and structure of an essay in simplified, visual form can help you analyze a reading, recall key steps as you generate ideas for an essay, and structure your own writing. Graphic Organizer 14.1 shows the basic structure of a process analysis essay. When your main purpose is to explain a process, follow this standard format. When you incorporate process analysis into an essay using one or more other patterns of development, briefly introduce the process and then move directly to the steps involved. If the process is complex, you may want to add a brief summary of it before the transition back to the main topic of the essay.

For more on creating a graphic organizer, see Chapter 2.

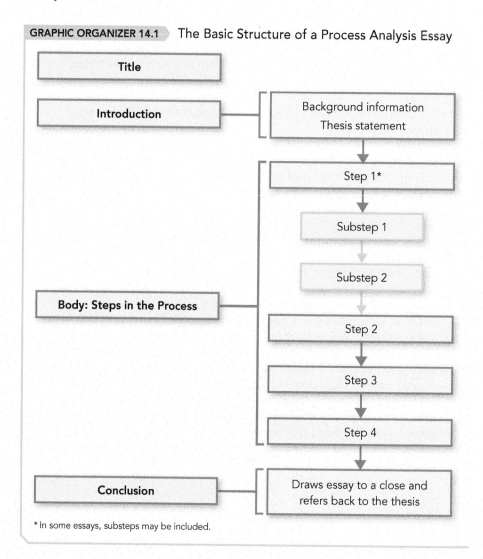

GRAPHIC ORGANIZER 14.1   The Basic Structure of a Process Analysis Essay

Title

Introduction → Background information / Thesis statement

Step 1*

Substep 1

Substep 2

Body: Steps in the Process

Step 2

Step 3

Step 4

Conclusion → Draws essay to a close and refers back to the thesis

* In some essays, substeps may be included.

READING HOW-IT-WORKS ESSAY

Shitty First Drafts

Anne Lamott

Anne Lamott has published several nonfiction works, including *Bird by Bird: Instructions on Writing and Life* (1995), from which this essay is taken; *Small Victories: Spotting Improbable Moments of Grace* (2014); *Hallelujah Anyway: Rediscovering Mercy* (2017); and *Almost Everything: Notes on Hope* (2018). She is also the author of several novels, including *Blue Shoe* (2002) and *Imperfect Birds* (2010). **Before reading**, preview the selection and make connections by thinking about first drafts you have written. Were you satisfied with them? Why or why not? **While reading**, paraphrase each step of the process, and think about how Lamott reveals her attitude toward writing. Read the essay first, and then compare it to Graphic Organizer 14.2. What was omitted and why?

Now, practically even better news than that of short assignments is the idea of shitty first drafts. All good writers write them. This is how they end up with good second drafts and terrific third drafts. People tend to look at successful writers who are getting their books published and maybe even doing well financially and think that they sit down at their desks every morning feeling like a million dollars, feeling great about who they are and how much talent they have and what a great story they have to tell; that they take in a few deep breaths, push back their sleeves, roll their necks a few times to get all the cricks out, and dive in, typing fully formed passages as fast as a court reporter. But this is just the fantasy of the uninitiated. I know some very great writers, writers you love who write beautifully and have made a great deal of money, and not one of them sits down routinely feeling wildly enthusiastic and confident. Not one of them writes elegant first drafts. All right, one of them does, but we do not like her very much. We do not think that she has a rich inner life or that God likes her or can even stand her. (Although when I mentioned this to my priest friend Tom, he said you can safely assume you've created God in your own image when it turns out that God hates all the same people you do.)

Very few writers really know what they are doing until they've done it. Nor do they go about their business feeling dewy and thrilled. They do not type a few stiff warm-up sentences and then find themselves bounding along like huskies across the snow. One writer I know tells me that he sits down every morning and says to himself nicely, "It's not like you don't have a choice, because you do—you can either type, or kill yourself." We all often feel like we are pulling teeth, even those writers whose prose ends up being the most natural and fluid. The right words and sentences just do not come pouring out like ticker tape most of the time. Now, Muriel Spark is said to have felt that she was taking dictation from God every morning—sitting there, one supposes, plugged into a Dictaphone, typing away, humming. But this is a very hostile and aggressive position. One might hope for bad things to rain down on a person like this.

For me and most of the other writers I know, writing is not rapturous. In fact, the only way I can get anything written at all is to write really, really shitty first drafts.

The first draft is the child's draft, where you let it all pour out and then let it romp all over the place, knowing that no one is going to see it and that you can shape it later. You just let this childlike part of you channel whatever voices and visions come through and onto the page. If one of the characters wants to say, "Well, so what, Mr. Poopy Pants?" you let her. No one is going to see it. If the kid wants to get into really sentimental, weepy, emotional territory, you let him. Just get it all down on paper because there may be something great in those six crazy pages that you would never have gotten to by more rational, grown-up means. There may be something in the very last line of the very last paragraph on page six that you just love, that is so beautiful or wild that you now know what you're supposed to be writing about, more or less, or in what direction you might go—but there was no way to get to this without first getting through the first five and a half pages.

I used to write food reviews for *California* magazine before it folded. (My writing food reviews had nothing to do with the magazine folding, although every single review did cause a couple of canceled subscriptions. Some readers took umbrage at my comparing mounds of vegetable puree with various ex-presidents' brains.) These reviews always took two days to write. First I'd go to a restaurant several times with a few opinionated, articulate friends in tow. I'd sit there writing down everything anyone said that was at all interesting or funny. Then on the following Monday I'd sit down at my desk with my notes and try to write the review. Even after I'd been doing this for years, panic would set in. I'd try to write a lead, but instead I'd write a couple of dreadful sentences, XX them out, try again, XX everything out, and then feel despair and worry settle on my chest like an x-ray apron. It's over, I'd think calmly. I'm not going to be able to get the magic to work this time. I'm ruined. I'm through. I'm toast. Maybe, I'd think, I can get my old job back as a clerk-typist. But probably not. I'd get up and study my teeth in the mirror for a while. Then I'd stop, remember to breathe, make a few phone calls, hit the kitchen and chow down. Eventually I'd go back and sit down at my desk, and sigh for the next ten minutes. Finally I would pick up my one-inch picture frame, stare into it as if for the answer, and every time the answer would come: all I had to do was to write a really shitty first draft of, say, the opening paragraph. And no one was going to see it.

So I'd start writing without reining myself in. It was almost just typing, just making my fingers move. And the writing would be terrible. I'd write a lead paragraph that was a whole page, even though the entire review could only be three pages long, and then I'd start writing up descriptions of the food, one dish at a time, bird by bird, and the critics would be sitting on my shoulders, commenting like cartoon characters. They'd be pretending to snore, or rolling their eyes at my overwrought descriptions, no matter how hard I tried to tone those descriptions down, no matter how conscious I was of what a friend said to me gently in my early days of restaurant reviewing. "Annie," she said, "it is just a piece of *chicken*. It is just a bit of *cake*."

But because by then I had been writing for so long, I would eventually let myself trust the process—sort of, more or less. I'd write a first draft that was maybe twice as long as it should be, with a self-indulgent and boring beginning, stupefying descriptions of the meal, lots of quotes from my black-humored friends that made them sound more like the Manson girls than food lovers, and no ending to speak of. The whole thing would be so long and incoherent and hideous that for the rest of the day I'd obsess about getting creamed by a car before I could write a decent second draft. I'd worry that people would read what I'd written and believe that the accident had really been a suicide, that I had panicked because my talent was waning and my mind was shot.

5

6

7

The next day, I'd sit down, go through it all with a colored pen, take out 8
everything I possibly could, find a new lead somewhere on the second page, figure
out a kicky place to end it, and then write a second draft. It always turned out fine,
sometimes even funny and weird and helpful. I'd go over it one more time and
mail it in.

Then, a month later, when it was time for another review, the whole process 9
would start again, complete with the fears that people would find my first draft
before I could rewrite it.

Almost all good writing begins with terrible first efforts. You need to start 10
somewhere. Start by getting something—anything—down on paper. A friend of
mine says that the first draft is the down draft—you just get it down. The second
draft is the up draft—you fix it up. You try to say what you have to say more accurately. And the third draft is the dental draft, where you check every tooth, to see if
it's loose or cramped or decayed, or even, God help us, healthy.

EXERCISE 14.4 DRAWING A GRAPHIC ORGANIZER

Using Graphic Organizer 14.1 or 14.2 as a basis, draw a graphic organizer for "How
Not to Say the Wrong Thing."

HOW WRITERS READ   PROCESS ANALYSIS

THE READING PROCESS   STRATEGIES

BEFORE READING

Preview the essay to get an overview of its content and organization.
Make connections by thinking about any experience you might have with this
or a similar process.

AFTER READING

Analyze and evaluate the reading by answering the following questions:

- Is the author **experienced and knowledgeable** about the process? Check the writer's credentials.
- Are the steps in the process **clear, sequential, distinct,** and **sufficiently detailed**? Can you visualize them or explain them in your own words? Have any steps been left out?
- Are there **other, similar processes**? If so, how are they similar to or different from the process explained in the essay?
- Can you **apply** this information to your own life?
- What was the **author's purpose** for writing the essay? Is it overt, or are the motives hidden?
- Can the steps be **grouped into larger categories** to help you remember how to carry out the process correctly or effectively?
- Does the essay provide **warnings about troublesome steps**? Should it?

READING CRITICALLY

Apply the questions in the "How Writers Read" box to the selection "Shitty First Drafts."

GRAPHIC ORGANIZER 14.2   The Structure of "Shitty First Drafts"

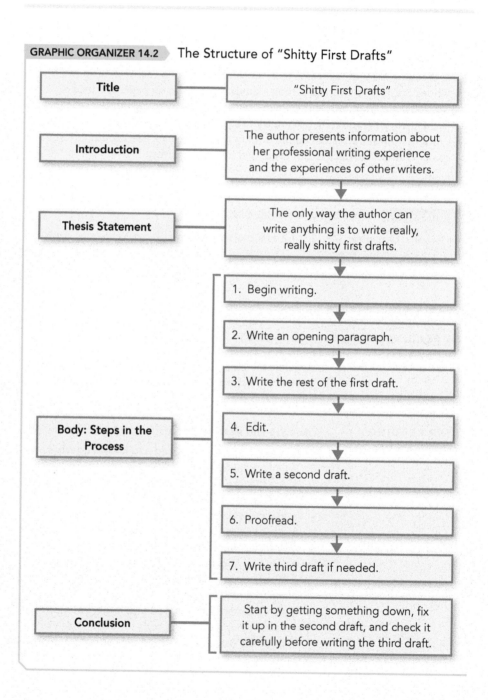

Integrate Process Analysis into an Essay

You may find it helpful to incorporate a process analysis into a discussion that relies on a different pattern of development. For instance, in a descriptive essay about an alcohol abuse program for high school students, you might decide to include a brief process analysis of how alcohol impairs mental functioning. Lamott incorporates illustration and description to make her process analysis engaging. Here are a few suggestions for incorporating process analysis effectively into essays based on other patterns of development:

1. **Explain only the major steps in the process.** Don't go over every step in detail, to avoid diverting your readers from the primary focus of your essay.
2. **Introduce the process analysis with a transitional sentence that alerts readers that a process analysis will follow.** For example, here is how you might introduce a brief summary of the process by which AIDS spreads through HIV (human immunodeficiency virus):

    > Before you explain to teenagers *how* to avoid contracting HIV, you need to let them know *what* they are avoiding. Teenagers need to know that HIV is transmitted by . . .

3. **It is sometimes helpful to use the word** *process* **or** *procedure* **to let readers know that a process analysis is to follow.** In the preceding example, the final sentence might be revised to read as follows:

    > Teenagers need to know that HIV is transmitted by the following process.

4. **Once you have completed the process analysis, alert readers that you are about to return to the main topic.** You might conclude the process with a summary statement like this:

    > Above all, teenagers need to know that HIV is transmitted through an exchange of bodily fluids.

PREWRITING ▷ DRAFTING ▷ **REVISING** ▷ EDITING & PROOFREADING

A Guided Writing Assignment[*]

> ## PROCESS ANALYSIS

Your Essay Assignment

Write a process analysis essay explaining how something works or is done. Choose a topic you are familiar with or that you can learn about through observation or research. Try to select a topic that your readers—your instructor and your fellow students—will find interesting or useful. Below are some options to help you get started.

[*] The writing process is *recursive;* that is, you may find yourself revising as you draft or prewriting as you revise. This is especially true when writing on a computer. Your writing process may also differ from project to project or from that of your classmates.

How-To Essay Topics

- How to improve your _____ (study habits, wardrobe, batting average)
- How to be a successful _____ (diver, parent, gardener)
- How to make or buy _____ (an object for personal use or enjoyment)

How-It-Works Essay Topics

- How a decision is made to _____ (accept a student at a college, add or eliminate a state agency)
- How _____ (a quilt, a news broadcast, a Web site, a football team) is put together
- How your college _____ (spends tuition revenues, hires professors, raises money)

PREWRITING

1 Select a topic from the list above, or create one of your own.

Use the following tips to select a process to write about:

- For a **how-to essay**, choose a process that you can **visualize or perform** as you write. Keep the equipment nearby for easy reference. For example, if you are writing an essay about how to scuba dive, it may be helpful to have your scuba equipment in front of you.
- For a **how-it-works essay**, choose a topic about which you **have background knowledge** or for which you can **find reliable information readily**.
- Choose a topic that is **useful** and **interesting** to your readers. Unless you can find a way to make an essay about how to do laundry interesting, do not write about it.

2 Consider your purpose, audience, and point of view.

Ask yourself these questions:

- Will my **purpose** be to **express myself, inform,** or **persuade**? (Process analyses tend to be informative.)
- Who is my **audience**? Will readers need any **background information** to understand my essay? Will they need me to **define terms** or **describe** (or **diagram**) **equipment**? How much **detail** do I need to go into for them to follow the steps or understand the process? Where will they need **special help** or **warnings**? (Check whether your readers will need background, definitions, or warnings by asking one or two classmates to tell you how they would explain key terms to a novice.)
- What **point of view** best suits my purpose and audience? **How-to** essays commonly use the **second person**, addressing the reader directly as *you*. (Hint: Second person is often considered inappropriate in college writing.) **How-it-works** essays commonly use the **third person** (*he, she, it*).

3 Explore your subject and generate details.

Use idea-generating strategies to come up with the details your process analysis essay will use.

1. **List the steps** or **diagram the process**, keeping these questions in mind:
   - What separate actions are involved?
   - What steps are obvious to me but may not be obvious to someone unfamiliar with the process?
   - What steps, if omitted, will lead to problems or failure?
2. Ask a friend or classmate to **act out your process**. What problems did this person encounter? What additional details did you need to add?
3. Do some research to see **how others have described the process**. What details do other writers include? Do they generally add steps you've omitted or omit steps you've included? Be sure to keep track of any information you borrow from sources.
4. Alone or in pairs, list the words *looks like, sounds like, smells like,* and *feels like* across the top of a page and then **list as many words or comparisons** below as you can think of in ten or fifteen minutes.

4 Draft your thesis statement.

Tell readers why the process is **important**, **beneficial**, or **relevant** to them:

_____ is important/beneficial/relevant because _____.
Name process   State reasons audience can relate to

Be sure to consider what *your* audience will find compelling.

5 Organize your essay.

Organize your ideas logically.

- For a process with **fewer than ten steps**, you can usually arrange the steps **chronologically**, devoting **one paragraph per step**.
- For a **more complicated process, group the steps** into three or four categories; use **one paragraph per group**, including **a topic sentence** to introduce the group and the **rest of the paragraph** to explain the individual steps involved. For an essay on how to run a garage sale, the steps might be grouped as follows:

  Group 1: Locating and collecting merchandise
  Group 2: Advertising
  Group 3: Pricing and setting up
  Group 4: Conducting the sale

Hint: An outline or graphic organizer will allow you to experiment to find the best order for supporting paragraphs.

To determine how usable your instructions are, ask a classmate to try them out.

Write a first draft of your process analysis essay.

Use the following guidelines to keep your process analysis on track:

- The **introduction** should present your **thesis statement**, include necessary **background information**, and convince readers the process is **relevant** to them. For lengthy or complex processes, consider including an **overview** of the steps.
- The **body paragraphs** should **identify each step** and make clear why it is important to the process. If the process is complex, including **a drawing or diagram** to outline steps can be helpful. (If including a graphic, introduce it in your essay and refer to it by its title.)
  - Use **headings** that name your main topics and signal changes in topic, whether your essay is brief or lengthy.
  - Use **transitions**, such as *before*, *next*, and *finally*, to signal steps in the process.
  - Make sure your **tone** is appropriate to your audience and purpose. In some situations, a matter-of-fact tone is appropriate; in others, an emotional or humorous tone may be suitable.
- The **conclusion** might emphasize the **value** or **importance** of the process, describe **particular situations** in which it is useful, or offer **a final amusing** or **emphatic comment** or **anecdote**. An essay that ends with the final step in the process may sound incomplete.

 Evaluate your draft, and revise as necessary.

Use **Figure 14.1, "Flowchart for Revising a Process Analysis Essay,"** to evaluate and revise your draft.

FIGURE 14.1 Flowchart for Revising a Process Analysis

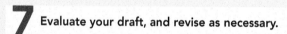

QUESTIONS | REVISION STRATEGIES

1. Highlight your thesis statement. Does it make clear the importance of your process?

 NO ▶

- Ask yourself: Why would readers want or need to know this process? Incorporate the answers into your thesis statement.

YES ▼

2. *Number* the steps of your process. Are they in chronological order (or some other logical progression)? Is the order clear?

 NO ▶

- Create a graphic organizer or outline to determine the best order.
- Visualize or carry out the process to determine if steps are missing.
- Rearrange steps and add transitions.

YES ▼

QUESTIONS		REVISION STRATEGIES

3. [Bracket] any background information in your introduction. Is it sufficient? Have you provided an overview or shown the importance of the process?

 NO ▶

- Add an overview, if necessary.
- Give an example of a situation in which the process might be used.
- Explain that related processes and ideas depend on the process you are describing.

 YES ▼

4. Place an ✗ beside any technical terms you have used. Have you defined them? Are your definitions clear?

 NO ▶

- Ask a classmate to read your draft and identify any other terms that need to be defined or clarified.
- Add or revise definitions as needed.

 YES ▼

5. 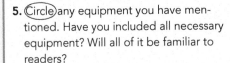Circle any equipment you have mentioned. Have you included all necessary equipment? Will all of it be familiar to readers?

 NO ▶

- Add equipment you have overlooked.
- Describe equipment that might be unfamiliar to readers.

 YES ▼

6. Place ✔s beside key details of the process. Have you included an appropriate level of detail for your readers?

 NO ▶

- Add or delete background information.
- Add or delete definitions of technical terms.
- Add or delete other detail.

 YES ▼

7. For a how-to essay, underline sections where you have anticipated potential difficulties for your readers. Have you anticipated all likely trouble spots? Are these sections clear and reassuring?

 NO ▶

- Add more detail about critical steps.
- Add warnings about confusing or difficult steps.
- Offer advice on what to do if things go wrong.

 YES ▼

8. Reread your introduction and conclusion. Is each effective?

 NO ▶

- Revise your introduction and conclusion so that they meet the guidelines in Chapter 7.

REVISING

355

8 Edit and proofread your essay.

Refer to Chapter 9 for help with

- **editing sentences** to avoid wordiness, making your verb choices strong and active, and making your sentences clear, varied, and parallel
- **editing words** for tone and diction, connotation, and concrete and specific language

Look out especially for **comma splices.** A **comma splice** occurs when two independent clauses are joined only by a comma. To correct a comma splice

- add a coordinating conjunction (*and, but, for, nor, or, so,* or *yet*)

   Example: The first step in creating a flower arrangement is to choose an attractive container, ~~the~~ *but* the container should not be the focal point of the arrangement.

- change the comma to a semicolon

   Example: Following signs is one way to navigate a busy airport*;* looking for a map is another.

- divide the sentence into two sentences

   Example: To lower fat consumption in your diet, first learn to read food product labels*. Next* ~~next~~ eliminate those products that contain trans fats or unsaturated fats.

- subordinate one clause to the other

   Example: *After you have placed* ~~Place~~ the pill on the cat's tongue, hold its mouth closed, rubbing its chin until it swallows the pill.

Readings: Process Analysis in Action

Going Vegan: How to Have Your Eggless Cake, and Eat It, Too!

Justine Appel

Justine Appel wrote the following essay in response to an assignment that asked her to explain a process that she had mastered. As you read the essay, consider whether the steps described in the essay clearly explain the process of adopting a vegan lifestyle.

As America's vast and varied food culture continues to change shape over the years, dietary advice runs rampant, experts relentlessly recommend and disagree, and restaurants strive to make room for all restrictions from low-carb to gluten-free. Many people use the way they eat not only to address their health, but also to express their values. One such diet that continues to draw attention is veganism.

Although the vegetarian diet, which excludes meat, fish, and poultry, is widely accepted in many parts of the world, the idea of avoiding all foods, fabrics, and substances derived from animals often seems difficult or even extreme in the United States today. Nonetheless, for those who feel passionately about animal welfare and environmental health, adopting a vegan lifestyle does not have to be complicated; with some research, preparation, and the right attitude, adopting veganism can become second nature.

As with all major lifestyle changes, the very first step is to evaluate the reasons for making a change. While there is a standard concept of veganism, all vegans have their own reasons for abstaining from animal products, which govern their individual choices. Some people are vegan for health reasons, and thus probably would not turn down a pair of wool socks. Some are only opposed to industrial farming, and would feel comfortable eating eggs from a small, local farm. Still others do not believe in using animals for human consumption at all, and avoid honey, glue, silk, and refined sugar (which is sometimes processed with animal bone char) on top of the usual list of animal-based food (Bratskeir).

After considering the grounds for choosing a vegan diet, it is important to maintain a critical mindset towards these issues. Being vegan is a deliberate ethical choice, but that does not mean one's ethics as a vegan cannot evolve. Staying conscious about the effects of such a lifestyle is a process, so consider this step "repeat as needed." For example, replacing dairy milk and eggs with coconut milk and tropical fruit for someone living in New England might not align with their desire to reduce their ecological footprint. Eating vegan is a process, not a destination, and critical engagement is an important part of maintaining such a diet.

1

2

Background: Defines *veganism*

Thesis: Thesis reveals relevance of topic for readers who might be considering "going vegan"

3

Organization: Topic sentence identifies step 1: think about the reasons for making a change; uses a transition to keep readers on track

4

Organization: Transition provides segue to step 2: remain critical about the reasons for choosing veganism.

Support: Offers an example to make the concept of the "critical mindset" concrete

Organization: Transition sentence introduces step 3: learn to identify animal products.

Support: Identifies animal ingredients that may be unfamiliar to readers

Organization: Transition sentence introduces step 4: learn what foods to eat for a healthful diet.

Support: Offers specific details to help readers maintain healthy protein and iron levels

Organization: Another transitional sentence introduces step 5: go food shopping.

Support: Lists familiar and unfamiliar foods (lentils, nut butters, and so forth) that can support a healthy vegan diet

The next step is a little easier, though it requires some investigation. Start to become familiar with the many forms of animal products and learn how to distinguish them on ingredient labels. While some animal ingredients are obvious (butter, milk, eggs), others are disguised by unfamiliar vocabulary. Gelatin, a substance used in marshmallows, Jello, and gummy candy, usually comes from animal bones and cartilage. Lecithin is a common food additive that can come from animal tissue. A quick online search will procure several lists of hidden animal products. Fortunately, milk and eggs are common allergens, and will usually be listed in bold in the allergy warning below the ingredients list, which is much faster to find.   5

Practicing veganism is not just about avoidance. It is important for vegans to know what to seek out, too. Since animal-based foods are good sources of several important nutrients, take the time to research some adequate substitutes and alternatives. It is especially important to find good sources of protein, iron, and vitamin B12, since these nutrients are most easily available in animal products. Foods made from nuts, beans, or soy have high levels of protein and are usually quite filling (Shubrook). Meanwhile, lentils, beans, and spinach are good vegan sources of iron (Leonard). Many fruits and vegetables are rich in other important dietary nutrients, and it is important to eat both and not just refined grains and heavily processed food ("The Right Plant-Based Diet"). All bodies have different needs, so consult a doctor or nutritionist about how to get a healthy amount of vitamins, minerals, and other nutrients. In the meantime, eating a diverse array of foods is always a good measure.   6

Knowing how to shop for all these vegan ingredients is a critical part of maintaining a healthy vegan diet. Vegan staples can be found all over an average grocery store, and one of the many exciting aspects of going vegan is discovering new ingredients and dishes. Lentils, seeds, nut butters, and whole grains are standard grocery items that vegans can eat, while tempeh, nutritional yeast, and chia seeds are more adventurous purchases. Health food stores, with their bulk sections and plant-based protein brands, provide a wide range of choices for vegans that often elude them in big grocery chains. There are countless vegan meals and   7 snacks out there, so do not waste time and energy buying or preparing food that is unappetizing.

Knowing how to cook goes hand in hand with knowing how to shop and is an empowering tool for vegans, since it allows them to make dishes they will love and can share with friends and family. The Internet has tons of great cooking tutorials and blogs, which are often more personal and helpful than standard recipes. Use the Internet as a resource for tips on vegan cooking, and supplement with a few vegan cookbooks or favorite recipes from friends and family members. Sometimes the best recipes are the simplest ones — think stir-fries, veggie sandwiches, and easy soups. A major advantage to cooking plant-based meals is that mistakes never pose the same level of risk as undercooking meat. Finding one night a week to cook meals in bulk will mean less cooking down the road. Leftovers are a vegan's best friend.

8   **Organization:** Transition introduces step 6: polish cooking skills.

As useful as it is to know how to cook, going vegan should not mean the end of going out to eat. Become familiar with the good restaurants in town that have vegan options and recommend them when a group of friends is going out for lunch or dinner. Once there, do not be afraid to ask the waiter about the ingredients. It is easy for them to find out, and vegans eventually develop a shrewd sense of what aligns with their diet and what does not. For example, naan, a type of Indian bread, usually comes with butter, whereas roti, another type, does not. When in an unfamiliar city, look for Thai, Chinese, Indian, or Middle Eastern restaurants, as they are usually the most accommodating to vegan diets.

9   **Organization:** Transitional sentence prepares readers for step 7: learn about restaurants with vegan options

Support: Identifies a potential trouble spot (eating out) and offers several restaurant types from which the reader may choose

Unfortunately, it is not uncommon for vegans to get stuck somewhere without enough food to satisfy their hunger, particularly when traveling in regions farther away from big cities. While American cities and coastal regions usually contain a wider diversity of vegan food, some areas are not as amenable to plant-based diets. Make sure to carry high-protein snacks when traveling to avoid feeling starved. Being prepared with trail mix and other travel-hardy food can save the day when the only restaurants around are steakhouses or seafood joints.

10   **Organization:** Transitional sentence introduces step 8, with a topic sentence on satisfying your hunger

Support: Identifies trouble spot (traveling while vegan) and advice for avoiding the problem

Organization: Transitional sentence prepares readers for step 9: be prepared for awkward situations.

Establishing a vegan diet as an individual is one thing; social gatherings as a vegan are another. Eating with a crowd takes a level of etiquette and preparedness that omnivores rarely have to think about. Declining to eat meat and dairy can bring up a surprising amount of awkwardness in social settings. Hosts offering their guests food is a matter of hospitality, and turning down certain foods, especially on ethical grounds, can feel uncomfortable and even rude. While it can be upsetting to refuse generous offers of animal-derived food, there are ways to pre-empt those situations. A smart vegan tells the host of their dietary restrictions in advance, and a thoughtful one asks if they can contribute a vegan dish to the meal. Vegans should communicate openly with their friends and relatives so they will not receive non-vegan gifts or surprise anyone with their food choices. Friends and family may forget or make mistakes, which is okay. If anything, take it as an opportunity to share opinions and knowledge and to learn about why others make the food choices they make. Although preaching about the moral superiority of one's diet will most certainly be unwelcome, an earnest description of veganism might make for interesting, friendly dialogue.   11

Support: Identifies possible **trouble spot** (awkward social situations) and offers **practical advice** for avoiding pitfalls

Organization: Transitional phrase prepares readers for final step: be prepared to answer questions about the vegan lifestyle.

To that end, be prepared to answer many questions. Some of them may seem silly ("Is goat cheese vegan?"), but it is necessary to remember that everyone comes from a different background and therefore will have a unique set of values and beliefs. Recognize that food and clothing are political, but they also can be deeply personal or important in different cultural atmospheres. Vegans who remain open to new thoughts and ideas and refrain from passing moral judgment on other peoples' lifestyle choices have an easier time moving through the world.   12

Conclusion: Transition emphasizes reason to go vegan: it's an ethical choice for today; emphasizes value of process

As the twenty-first century progresses, the political, social, and environmental effects of our day-to-day decisions are becoming more evident. There is no single issue that takes precedence over another, and being vegan is just one way to live consciously in an imperfect world. However, overcoming the doubts and suspicions surrounding veganism is an important first step in challenging norms and recognizing the connections between people, animals, and the earth. Finding veganism achievable makes other positive changes seem achievable, too.   13

Works Cited

Bratskeir, Kate. "Not All Sugar Is Vegan. Surprise!" *HuffPost*, 7 Dec. 2017,
www.huffpost.com/entry/sugar-vegan-bone-char-yikes_n_6391496.

Leonard, Jayne. "The Best Iron-Rich Vegetarian Foods." *Medical News
Today*, 5 Dec. 2018, www.medicalnewstoday.com/articles/323902.php.

"The Right Plant-Based Diet for You." *Harvard Health*, Jan. 2018, www
.health.harvard.edu/staying-healthy/the-right-plant-based-diet-for-you.

Shubrook, Nicola. "The Best Vegan Protein Sources." *BBC Good Food*, 5
Dec. 2018, www.bbcgoodfood.com/howto/guide/best-sources
-protein-vegan.

Analyzing the Writer's Technique

1. **Introduction** How successful are the first two paragraphs at providing a reason for learning the process?
2. **Title** Evaluate Appel's choice of title. What are its strengths?
3. **Organization** Explain how Appel has organized the steps in the process.
4. **Conclusion** Does Appel's conclusion bring the essay to a satisfying close? Why or why not?
5. **Opinion** Appel says that going vegan is an ethical choice. How does she convey her opinion? What reasons does she give?

Thinking Critically about Process Analysis

1. **Response** How does Appel's use of phrases such as "gelatin . . . usually comes from animal bones" (para. 5) and "lecithin . . . can come from animal tissue" (5) affect you as a reader? Do they increase or decrease the essay's effectiveness?
2. **Tone** How would you describe Appel's tone? What words or ideas help establish the tone?
3. **Audience** Who is the intended audience for this essay? How do you know? Is the essay appropriate for this audience? Why or why not?
4. **Omissions** What has Appel omitted from her process analysis, if anything? What additional information or advice might someone who is totally ignorant about the vegan lifestyle need? Would you need any additional information?

Responding to the Essay

1. **Reaction** Appel made a major change when she chose to adhere to a vegan life-style. Do you think you could make the same lifestyle change? Why or why not? What would be the most difficult food for you to give up? How do you think your

family and friends would respond to your lifestyle change? What would be your primary reason for making the change?

2. **Discussion** How important is it to follow the steps in the order Appel presents them? What are some other processes in which following the steps in order is especially important? List two or three.

3. **Essay** Appel sees the choice of a vegan lifestyle as a positive one. Write an essay explaining a change you have made or would like to make in your life that would change some facet of your life (your health, your sense of accomplishment) for the better. Describe the process that you would have to follow in order to make the change.

The Psychology of Stuff and Things

Christian Jarrett

Dr. Christian Jarrett is a neuroscientist and a senior editor for *Aeon* magazine. He is the founding editor of the British Psychological Society's *Research Digest* blog. He also blogs for both the British Psychological Society and *Psychology Today*. He has published essays in numerous magazines such as *The Times* (London), *Psychology Today*, *The Guardian*, and *Outdoor Fitness*. He has also published several books, including *This Book Has Issues* (2008), *The Rough Guide to Psychology* (2010), and *Great Myths of the Brain* (2015). At the end of his essay, Jarrett includes a list of references. Because he is writing in a journal for and by psychologists, he uses the citation style of the American Psychological Association (or APA). **Before reading**, preview and make connections by thinking about which possessions you are most attached to. **While reading**, highlight each step in the process. Because the process he describes occurs over a lifetime, underline transitions that signal chronological order or the next step in the process.

See the Just-in-Time Guide (section 5c) following Chapter 3.

JUST-IN-TIME TIP Testing Your Understanding

This article offers detailed, research-based explanations of how our relationship to our belongings changes over our lifetimes. The headings divide this reading by life stages, and the first sentence under each heading states concisely what happens during that stage. As you read, pay attention to the headings and topic sentences. Then test your understanding and recall by describing in your own words what happens at each stage. If you cannot, then you know you need to reread that section.

A man's Self is the sum total of all that he can call his.

—William James, *The Principles of Psychology* (1890)

Stuff everywhere. Bags, books, clothes, cars, toys, jewelry, furniture, iPads. If we're relatively affluent, we'll consider a lot of it ours. More than mere tools, luxuries or junk, our possessions become extensions of the self. We use them to signal to ourselves, and others, who we want to be and where we want to belong. And long

1

after we're gone, they become our legacy. Some might even say our essence lives on in what once we made or owned.

Childhood and Adolescence

Our relationship with stuff starts early. The idea that we can own something, possess it as if a part of ourselves, is one that children grasp by the age of two. And by six, they exhibit the "endowment effect," placing extra value on an object simply by virtue of it being, or having been, theirs. Although children understand ownership from a very young age, they think about it in a more simplistic way than adults. A study by Ori Friedman and Karen Neary in 2008 showed that aged between two and four, kids make the assumption that whoever is first in possession of the object is the owner, regardless of whether they later give it away. 2

With ownership comes envy. When youngsters play with friends, they soon discover other people's toys they'd like to get their hands on. Or they experience the injustice of being forced to share what they had assumed was theirs alone. In his 1932 book *The Moral Judgment of the Child*, Jean Piaget observed that even babies express jealousy over objects, giving signs of "violent rage" when a toy is taken from them and given to another. When Batya Licht and her colleagues in 2008 filmed 22-month-olds playing with their peers in day-care, nearly a quarter of all sources of conflict were over possessions—where the "child either defended his or her objects from another child, or wanted to take an object from another child." 3

Most children have an unusually intense relationship with a specific "attachment object," usually a favorite blanket or a soft toy. In an intriguing study by Bruce Hood and Paul Bloom, the majority of three- to six-year-old children preferred to take home their original attachment object, as opposed to a duplicate made by a "copying machine." To the prospect of taking a copy, "the most common response was horror," says Nathalia Gjersoe, who helped run the studies. "A few 4

"When youngsters play with friends, . . . they experience the injustice of being forced to share what they had assumed was theirs alone."
H. Armstrong Roberts/ClassicStock/Getty Images

very sweet and obedient children said okay but then burst into tears." Four of the children even refused for their attachment toy or object to be copied in the first place. That's despite the fact they were happy enough to take a copy of an experimenter's toy. It's as if the children believed their special object had a unique essence, a form of magical thinking that re-appears in adulthood in our treatment of heirlooms, celebrity memorabilia and artwork.

As children mature into teens, we see possessions starting to act as a crutch for the self. In 2007, Lan Chaplin and her colleagues interviewed participants aged between eight and 18 and found that "materialism" (identified by choosing material goods in answer to "What makes me happy?") peaked at middle adolescence, just when self-esteem tended to be lowest. In a follow-up, materialism was reduced in teens who were given flattering feedback from peers to boost their self-esteem.   5

Through adolescence, possessions increasingly reflect who people are, or at least how they would like to see themselves. In his seminal paper "Possessions and the Extended Self" Russell Belk quotes from novelist Alison Lurie's book *The Language of Clothes*, in which she observes: ". . . when adolescent girls exchange clothing they share not only friendship, but also identities—they become soulmates." Similarly, in interviews with teens, Ruthie Segev at Jerusalem College of Technology found evidence that selecting and buying gifts for their friends helps adolescents achieve a sense of identity independent from their parents, and that the mutual exchange of the same or similar gifts between friends helps them to create a feeling of overlapping identities.   6

In the transition from adolescence to adulthood, it's the first car that often becomes the ultimate symbol of a person's emerging identity. Interviews with car owners conducted by Graham Fraine and colleagues in 2007 found that young drivers, aged 18 to 25, were particularly likely to make the effort to personalize their cars with stickers, unusual number plates and seat covers, as if marking out their territory.   7

Adulthood

As our lives unfold, our things embody our sense of self-hood and identity still further, becoming external receptacles for our memories, relationships and travels. "My house is not 'just a thing,'" wrote Karen Lollar in 2010. "The house is not merely a possession or a structure of unfeeling walls. It is an extension of my physical body and my sense of self that reflects who I was, am, and want to be."   8

As our belongings accumulate, becoming more infused with our identities, so their preciousness increases. People whose things are destroyed in a disaster are traumatized, almost as if grieving the loss of their identities. Photographs from the aftermath of Hurricane Sandy, which struck the US East coast in 2012, show people standing bereft, staring in shock and bewilderment at all they've lost. Reflecting on the fire that took her home, Lollar says it was like "a form of death." Alexandra Kovach, who also lost her home in a fire, wrote in *The Washington Post* in 2007: "It isn't just a house. It's not the contents, or the walls, but the true feeling of that home—and all that it represents."   9

Later Life and Beyond

Older people don't just form bonds with their specific belongings, they seem to have an affection for brands from their youth too. Usually this manifests in a taste   10 for music, books, films and other entertainment from yesteryear, but the same has been shown for fashions and hairstyles, it has been hinted at for perfumes, and in a study published in 2003 by Robert Schindler and Morris Holbrook, it was found that it also extends to the car.

How Mercury's new 161-horsepower engine makes <u>any</u> driving easy

PASSING—Extra power is provided instantly, when-ever needed, by unique new 4-barrel carburetor.

GET IN AND TRY IT—You'll find Mercury's entirely new V-161 engine *smoother, quieter.* And with new ball-joint suspension, you'll enjoy greater handling ease.

HILL CLIMBING—V-161 power is *eager* power. And there's plenty in reserve to do the job effortlessly.

MAKE DRIVING AS EASY AS YOU WISH with optional 4-way power seat, power steering, power brakes, power windows, Merc-O-Matic Drive.

How often have you wished for more "go" from the car you now drive—especially when passing or hill climbing? How often have you been annoyed by sluggishness in traffic, stiff handling when parking, or wheel tug on curves? Now—you can solve driving problems like these with Mercury's completely new V-161 engine teamed with new ball-joint front wheel suspension. The combination gives you a new feeling of safety in driving—smoother, easier power, unique in a popular-priced car. Road test a 1954 Mercury.

THE CAR THAT MAKES <u>ANY</u> DRIVING EASY

New 1954 MERCURY

MERCURY DIVISION · FORD MOTOR COMPANY

"Older people don't just form bonds with their specific belongings, they seem to have an affection for brands from their youth too." Jeff Morgan 11/Alamy

Dozens of participants aged 16 to 92 rated their preference for the appearance   11
of 80 cars, ranging from the 1915 Dodge Model 30-35 to the 1994 Chrysler
Concorde. Among men, but not women, there was a clear preference for cars that
dated from the participants' youth (peaking around age 26). This was particularly
the case for men who were more nostalgic and who believed that things were
better in the old days. What other examples might there be? "Children of both
sexes tend to have strong feelings about foods they like as they grow up," says
Schindler. "Although we haven't studied food, I would expect both men and
women to have a lifetime fondness for foods they enjoyed during their youth."

As with human relationships, the attachments to our things deepen with the   12
passage of time. Elderly people are often surrounded by possessions that have
followed them through good times and bad, across continents and back. In 2000,
Linda Price at the University of Arizona and her colleagues interviewed 80 older
people about their decisions regarding these "special possessions." A common
theme was the way cherished objects come to represent particular memories. "I
can look at anything [in this house] and remember special occasions," recalled
Diane, aged 70. "It's almost like a history of our life."

After a person dies, many of their most meaningful possessions become family   13
heirlooms, seen by those left behind as forever containing the lost person's essence.
This idea is also seen in the behaviors that follow the death of a celebrity. In a
process that Belk calls "sacralization," possessions owned by a deceased star can
acquire astonishing value overnight, both sentimental and monetary. This is often
true even for exceedingly mundane items such as President Kennedy's tape
measure, auctioned for $48,875 in 1996. A study by George Newman and colleagues
in 2011 provided a clue about the beliefs underlying these effects. They showed that
people place more value on celebrity-owned items, the more physical contact the
celebrity had with the object, as if their essence somehow contaminated the item
through use.

The Future

Our relationship with our stuff is in the midst of great change. Dusty music and   14
literary collections are being rehoused in the digital cloud. Where once we expressed
our identity through fashion preferences and props, today we can cultivate an online
identity with a carefully constructed homepage. We no longer have to purchase an
item to associate ourselves with it, we can simply tell the world via Twitter or
Facebook about our preferences. The self has become extended, almost literally, into
technology, with Google acting like a memory prosthetic. In short, our relationship
with our things, possessions and brands remains as important as ever, it's just the
nature of the relationship is changing. Researchers and people in general are gradually
adjusting. The psychology of our stuff is becoming more interdisciplinary, with new
generations building on the established research conducted by consumer
psychologists.

Twenty-five years after he published his seminal work on objects and the   15
"extended self," Russell Belk has composed an update: "The extended self in a digital world," currently under review. "The possibilities for self extensions have never
been so extensive," he says.

Bibliography

Belk, R. W. (1988). Possessions and the extended self. *Journal of Consumer Research, 15,* 139–168.

Belk, R. W. (2013). The extended self in a digital world. *Journal of Consumer Research, 40*(3), 477–500.

Chaplin, L. N. & John, D. R. (2007). Growing up in a material world: Age differences in materialism in children and adolescents. *Journal of Consumer Research, 34*(4), 480–493.

Fraine, G., Smith, S. G., Zinkiewicz, L., Chapman, R. & Sheehan, M. (2007). At home on the road? Can drivers' relationships with their cars be associated with territoriality? *Journal of Environmental Psychology, 27*(3), 204–214.

Friedman, O. & Neary, K. R. (2008). Determining who owns what: Do children infer ownership from first possession? *Cognition, 107*(3), 829–849.

Hood, B. M. & Bloom, P. (2008). Children prefer certain individuals over perfect duplicates. *Cognition, 106*(1), 455–462.

Kovach, A. (2007, 27 October). What fire couldn't destroy. *Washington Post.* Retrieved 4 June 2013 from: www.washingtonpost.com/wp-dyn/content/article/2007/10/26/AR2007102601774 .html

Licht, B., Simoni, H. & Perrig-Chiello, P. (2008). Conflict between peers in infancy and toddler age: What do they fight about? *Early Years, 28*(3), 235–249.

Lollar, K. (2010). The liminal experience: Loss of extended self after the fire. *Qualitative Inquiry, 16*(4), 262–270.

Newman, G. E., Diesendruck, G. & Bloom, P. (2011). Celebrity contagion and the value of objects. *Journal of Consumer Research, 38*(2), 215–228.

Piaget, J. (1965). *The moral judgment of the child.* New York: The Free Press. (Original work published 1932).

Price, L. L., Arnould, E. J. & Curasi, C. F. (2000). Older consumers' disposition of special possessions. *Journal of Consumer Research, 27*(2), 179–201.

Schindler, R. M. & Holbrook, M. B. (2003). Nostalgia for early experience as a determinant of consumer preferences. *Psychology and Marketing, 20*(4), 275–302.

Segev, R., Shoham, A. & Ruvio, A. (2012). What does this gift say about me, you, and us? The role of adolescents' gift giving in managing their impressions among their peers. *Psychology & Marketing, 29*(10), 752–764.

Understanding the Reading

1. **Summarizing** What are the steps in the process that Jarrett describes?
2. **Meaning** What does the author mean when he says that "our essence lives on in what once we made or owned" (para. 1)?
3. **Details** Explain the importance to sports fans of collecting paraphernalia and wearing team colors. To what part of the process does this relate?
4. **Vocabulary** Explain the meaning of each of the following words as it is used in the reading: *essence* (para. 1), *memorabilia* (4), *materialism* (5), *seminal* (6), *receptacles* (8), and *prosthetic* (14).

Analyzing the Writer's Technique

1. **Thesis** Identify Jarrett's thesis statement. What background information does he provide to support it?

2. **Conclusion** Does Jarrett's conclusion bring the essay to a satisfying close? Why or why not?
3. **Purpose** Explain how Jarrett's citation of research supports his purpose in writing the essay.
4. **Audience** Who is Jarrett's audience? Does his advice apply to others outside this group?
5. **Patterns** What methods of development, in addition to process, does Jarrett use in this essay? What does each add to your understanding of Jarrett's explanation of how our possessions become an extension of our selves?

Thinking Critically about Text and Images

1. **Tone** How would you describe Jarrett's tone? The essay appears to have been written for students of psychology and other psychologists. How could Jarrett have made the essay easier to read for a more general audience?
2. **Conclusion** What is Jarrett suggesting about how we will identify with our possessions in the digital age?
3. **Visuals** What concept does each of the photographs in this reading illustrate?
4. **Additional Evidence** What additional evidence could Jarrett have included to make his claim about our relationship with our possessions more convincing?

Responding to the Reading

1. **Discussion** Do you believe that your essence lives on in what you once made or owned? Why or why not? What do you believe your possessions say about you?
2. **Journal** How does this essay make you feel about the possessions you have accumulated? Will it make any difference in what you do with your accumulated possessions in the future?
3. **Essay** Jarrett says that "most children have an unusually intense relationship with a specific 'attachment object,' usually a favorite blanket or soft toy." Reflect on your childhood and try to remember what your favorite toy or "attachment object" was. Write an essay in which you describe this object, explain how your attachment to it developed, and include a story or two about it.

Working Together

If Christian Jarrett were to design a bumper sticker based on the information in this essay, what would it say? In small groups, devise a brief motto that captures the essence of this essay.

EXPLORE, RESEARCH, WRITE

In "The Psychology of Stuff and Things," Christian Jarrett describes how people come to view their possessions as "extensions of the self." Other researchers have also studied this phenomenon. Reports about such research include the following:

- "A History of Humans Loving Inanimate Objects" by Paul Hibert (*Pacific Standard*, 14 June 2017)
- "Why Children Become So Attached to Toys and Comfort Blankets" by Steven Morris (*The Guardian*, 9 March 2007)
- "More Than Just Teddy Bears" by Colleen Goddard (*Psychology Today*, 15 July 2014)

Using your own ideas and information or ideas from one or more of the selections listed here, write a thoughtful process analysis essay that goes beyond what "The Psychology of Stuff and Things" tells us about the childhood stage of "stuff" possession (paras. 2–4) to explain how this stage develops. Be sure to incorporate at least one quotation from a reading and cite it correctly at the end of the essay.

The Guided Writing Assignment in this chapter can walk you through the process of writing a process analysis essay; for help with evaluating sources, see Chapter 21; for help choosing and synthesizing ideas from sources, see Chapter 22; for help with documenting sources, see Chapter 23.

READING

How to Spot Fake News

Eugene Kiely and Lori Robertson

Eugene Kiely is a journalist who reports on government and politics and is also the director of FactCheck.org, an organization dedicated to monitoring political news for accuracy. He was formerly an editor at *USA Today* and the state editor for *The Philadelphia Inquirer*. Lori Robertson is the managing editor at FactCheck.org; previously, she was an editor and writer for *American Journalism Review*, a media watchdog publication. **Before reading**, preview and make connections by thinking about the fake news that you have encountered on traditional news or social media sites. **While reading**, identify patterns other than process analysis that are used in this essay.

JUST-IN-TIME TIP   Using Summary Statements

Summary statements, often using key words and phrases from the reading, can help you keep track of steps in a process and what each step involves. This technique is especially useful when reading a process analysis essay full of detailed examples. Highlight these key words as you read, or create a chart listing each step and the key words and phrases that summarize it. The start of a summary chart for "How to Spot Fake News" is shown on page 370.

Steps	Summary Statements
Consider the source.	Check bogus URL, "about" page, contact information

Fake news is nothing new. But bogus stories can reach more people more quickly   1
via social media than what good old-fashioned viral emails could accomplish in
years past. Concern about the phenomenon led Facebook and Google to announce
that they will crack down on fake news sites, restricting their ability to garner ad
revenue (Wingfield et al.). Perhaps that could dissipate the amount of malarkey
online, though news consumers themselves are the best defense against the
spread of misinformation.

Not all of the misinformation being passed along online is complete fiction,   2
though some of it is. Snopes.com has been exposing false viral claims since the
mid-1990s, whether that is fabricated messages, distortions containing bits of
truth and everything in between. Founder David Mikkelson warned in a
November 17 article not to lump everything into the "fake news" category. "The
fictions and fabrications that comprise fake news are but a subset of the larger
bad news phenomenon, which also encompasses many forms of shoddy,
unresearched, error-filled, and deliberately misleading reporting that do a
disservice to everyone," he wrote. A lot of these viral claims are not "news" at all,
but fiction, satire and efforts to fool readers into thinking they are for real.

We have long encouraged readers to be skeptical of viral claims, and make   3
good use of the delete key when a chain email hits their inboxes. In December
2007, we launched our Ask FactCheck feature, where we answer readers' questions,
the vast majority of which concern viral emails, social media memes and the like.
Our first story was about a made-up email that claimed then-House Speaker
Nancy Pelosi wanted to put a "windfall" tax on all stock profits of 100 percent and
give the money to, the email claimed, "the 12 Million Illegal Immigrants and other
unemployed minorities." We called it "a malicious fabrication"—that is "fake news"
in today's parlance.

In 2008, we tried to get readers to rid their inboxes of this kind of garbage. We   4
described a list of red flags—we called them Key Characteristics of Bogusness—
that were clear tip-offs that a chain email wasn't legitimate. Among them are an
anonymous author; excessive exclamation points, capital letters and misspellings;
entreaties that "This is NOT a hoax!"; and links to sourcing that does not support
or completely contradicts the claims being made.

Those all still hold true, but fake stories—as in, completely made-up   5
"news"—has grown more sophisticated, often presented on a site designed to
look (sort of) like a legitimate news organization. Still, we find it is easy to

figure out what is real and what is imaginary if you are armed with some criti-cal thinking and fact-checking tools of the trade. Here is our advice on how to spot a fake.

Consider the source. In recent months, we have fact-checked fake news from   6
abcnews.com.co (not the actual URL for ABC News), WTOE 5 News (whose "about" page says it is "a fantasy news website"), and the *Boston Tribune* (whose "contact us" page lists only a gmail address). Earlier this year, we debunked the claim that the Obamas were buying a vacation home in Dubai, a made-up missive that came from WhatDoesItMean.com, which describes itself as "One of the Top Ranked Websites in the World for New World Order, Conspiracy Theories and Alternative News" and further says on its site that most of what it publishes is fiction.

Clearly, some of these sites do provide a "fantasy news" or satire warning, like   7
WTOE 5, which published the bogus headline, "Pope Francis Shocks World, Endorses Donald Trump for President, Releases Statement." Others are not so upfront, like the *Boston Tribune*, which does not provide any information on its mis-sion, staff members or physical location—further signs that maybe this site is not a legitimate news organization. The site, in fact, changed its name from Associated Media Coverage, after its work had been debunked by fact-checking organizations (Cave). Snopes.com, which has been writing about viral claims and online rumors since the mid-1990s, maintains a list of known fake news websites, several of which have emerged in the past two years.

Read beyond the headline. If a provocative headline drew your attention, read   8
a little further before you decide to pass along the shocking information. Even in legitimate news stories, the headline does not always tell the whole story. But fake news, particularly efforts to be satirical, can include several revealing signs in the text. That abcnews.com.co story that we checked, headlined "Obama Signs Executive Order Banning The Pledge of Allegiance in Schools Nationwide," went on to quote "Fappy the Anti-Masturbation Dolphin." We have to assume that the many readers who asked us whether this viral rumor was true had not read the full story.

Check the author. Another tell-tale sign of a fake story is often the byline. The   9
pledge of allegiance story on abcnews.com.co was supposedly written by "Jimmy Rustling." Who is he? Well, his author page claims he is a "doctor" who won "four-teen Peabody awards and a handful of Pulitzer Prizes." That is pretty impressive, if true, but it is not. No one by the name of "Rustling" has won a Pulitzer or Peabody award. The photo accompanying Rustling's bio is also displayed on another bogus story on a different site, but this time under the byline "Darius Rubics." The Dubai story was written by "Sorcha Faal, and as reported to her Western Subscribers." The Pope Francis story has no byline at all.

Examine the support. Many times these bogus stories will cite official—or   10
official-sounding—sources, but once you look into it, the source does not back up the claim. For instance, the *Boston Tribune* site wrongly claimed that President Obama's mother-in-law was going to get a lifetime government pension for having babysat her granddaughters in the White House, citing "the Civil Service Retirement Act"

and providing a link, but the link to a government benefits website does not support the claim at all.

The banning-the-pledge story cites the number of an actual executive order—you can look it up. It does not have anything to do with the Pledge of Allegiance. Another viral claim we checked a year ago was a graphic purporting to show crime statistics on the percentage of whites killed by blacks and other murder statistics by race. Then-presidential candidate Donald Trump retweeted it, telling Fox News commentator Bill O'Reilly that it came "from sources that are very credible." But almost every figure in the image was wrong—FBI crime data is publicly available—and the supposed source given for the data, "Crime Statistics Bureau—San Francisco," doesn't exist.

Recently, we have received several questions about a fake news story on the admittedly satirical site Nevada County Scooper, which wrote that Vice President-elect Mike Pence, in a "surprise announcement," credited gay conversion therapy for saving his marriage. Clearly such a "surprise announcement" would garner media coverage beyond a website you are never heard of. In fact, if you Google this, the first link that comes up is a Snopes.com article revealing that this is fake news.

Check the date. Some false stories are not completely fake, but rather distortions of real events. These mendacious claims can take a legitimate news story and twist what it says—or even claim that something that happened long ago is related to current events. Since Trump was elected president, we have received many inquiries from readers wanting to know whether Ford had moved car production from Mexico to Ohio, because of Trump's election. Readers cited various blog items that quoted from and linked to a CNN Money article titled "Ford shifts truck production from Mexico to Ohio." But that story is from August 2015, clearly not evidence of Ford making any move due to the outcome of the election. (A reminder again to check the support for these claims.)

One deceptive website did not credit CNN, but instead took CNN's 2015 story and slapped a new headline and publication date on it, claiming, "Since Donald Trump Won The Presidency . . . Ford Shifts Truck Production From Mexico To Ohio." Not only is that a bogus headline, but the deception involves copyright infringement.

If this Ford story sounds familiar, that is because the CNN article has been distorted before. In October 2015, Trump wrongly boasted that Ford had changed its plans to build new plants in Mexico, and instead would build a plant in Ohio. Trump took credit for Ford's alleged change of heart and tweeted a link to a story on a blog called Prntly.com, which cited the CNN Money story, but Ford had not changed its plans at all, and Trump deserved no credit.

In fact, the CNN article was about the transfer of some pickup assembly work from Mexico to Ohio, a move that was announced by Ford in March 2014. The plans for new plants in Mexico were still on, Ford said. "Ford has not spoken with Mr. Trump, nor have we made any changes to our plans," Ford said in a statement.

Determine if it is a joke. Remember, there is such thing as satire. Normally, it is clearly labeled as such, and sometimes it is even funny. Andy Borowitz has been writing a satirical news column, the Borowitz Report, since 2001, and it has appeared in the *New Yorker* since 2012, but not everyone gets the jokes. We have fielded several questions on whether Borowitz's work is true. Among the headlines our readers have flagged: "Putin Appears with Trump in Flurry of Swing-State Rallies" and "Trump Threatens to Skip Remaining Debates If Hillary Is There." When we told readers these were satirical columns, some indicated that they suspected the details were far-fetched but wanted to be sure.

And then there are the more debatable forms of satire, designed to pull one   18
over on the reader. That "Fappy the Anti-Masturbation Dolphin" story is the work of online hoaxer Paul Horner, whose "greatest coup," as described by the *Washington Post* in 2014 (Dewey "This"), was when Fox News mentioned, as fact, a fake piece titled, "Obama uses own money to open Muslim museum amid government shutdown." Horner told the *Post* after the election that he was concerned his hoaxes aimed at Trump supporters may have helped the campaign (Dewey "Facebook").

The posts by Horner and others—whether termed satire or simply "fake   19
news"—are designed to encourage clicks and generate money for the creator through ad revenue. Horner told the *Washington Post* he makes a living off his posts. Asked why his material gets so many views, Horner responded, "They just keep passing stuff around. Nobody fact-checks anything anymore."

Check your biases. We know this is difficult. Confirmation bias leads peo-   20
ple to put more stock in information that confirms their beliefs and discount information that does not. But the next time you are automatically appalled at some Facebook post concerning, say, a politician you oppose, take a moment to check it out.

Try this simple test: What other stories have been posted to the "news"   21
website that is the source of the story that just popped up in your Facebook feed? You may be predisposed to believe that Obama bought a house in Dubai, but how about a story on the same site that carries this headline: "Antarctica 'Guardians' Retaliate Against America With Massive New Zealand Earthquake." That, too, was written by the prolific "Sorcha Faal, and as reported to her Western Subscribers."

We are encouraged by some of the responses we get from readers, who—like   22
the ones uncertain of Borowitz's columns—express doubt in the outrageous and just want to be sure their skepticism is justified. We are equally discouraged when we see debunked claims gain new life.

We have seen the resurgence of a fake quote from Donald Trump since the   23
election—a viral image that circulated last year claims Trump told *People* magazine in 1998: "If I were to run, I'd run as a Republican. They're the dumbest group of voters in the country. They believe anything on Fox News. I could lie and they'd still eat it up. I bet my numbers would be terrific." We found no such quote in *People*'s archives from 1998, or any other year. A public relations representative for the magazine confirmed that. *People*'s Julie Farin told us in an email last year, "We combed through every Trump story in our archive. We couldn't find anything remotely like this quote—and no interview at all in 1998." Comedian Amy Schumer may have contributed to the revival of this fake meme. She put it on

Instagram, adding at the end of a lengthy message, "Yes this quote is fake but it doesn't matter."

Consult the experts. We know you are busy, and some of this debunking   24
takes time, but we get paid to do this kind of work. Between FactCheck.org, Snopes.com, the *Washington Post* Fact Checker and PolitiFact.com, it is likely at least one has already fact-checked the latest viral claim to pop up in your news feed.

FactCheck.org was among a network of independent fact-checkers who signed   25
an open letter to Facebook's Mark Zuckerberg suggesting that Facebook "start an open conversation on the principles that could underpin a more accurate news ecosystem on its News Feed." We hope that conversation happens, but news readers themselves remain the first line of defense against fake news ("Open Letter").

Links

Cave, Anthony. "Popular Internet Story Claims Arizona, Missouri, and Texas Enacted Two-Pet Limit." *Politifact*, Arizona Edition blog, 13 Mar. 2016, 2:04 p.m., www.politifact.com/arizona/statements/2016/may/13/blog-posting/popular-internet-story-claims-arizona-missouri-and.

Dewey, Caitlin. "Facebook Fake-News Writer: 'I Think Donald Trump Is in the White House Because of Me.'" *The Washington Post*, 17 Nov. 2016, www.washingtonpost.com/news/the-intersect/wp/2016/11/17/facebook-fake-news-writer-i-think-donald-trump-is-in-the-white-house-because-of-me/?noredirect=on.

Dewey, Caitlin. "This Is Not an Interview with Banksy." *The Washington Post*, 22 Oct. 2014, www.washingtonpost.com/news/the-intersect/wp/2014/10/21/this-is-not-an-interview-with-banksy/?noredirect=on.

Mikkelson, David. "We Have a Bad News Problem, Not a Fake New Problem." *Snopes*, 17 Nov. 2016, www.snopes.com/news/2016/11/17/we-have-a-bad-news-problem-not-a-fake-news-problem.

"Open Letter to Mark Zuckerberg from the World's Fact Checkers." *Poynter*, 17 Nov. 2016, www.poynter.org/fact-checking/2016/an-open-letter-to-mark-zuckerberg-from-the-worlds-fact-checkers.

"Pope Francis Shocks World, Endorses Donald Trump for President, Releases Statement." *WTOE 5 News*, web.archive.org/web/20161115024211/http:/wtoe5news.com/us-election/pope-francis-shocks-world-endorses-donald-trump-for-president-releases-statement.

Wingfield, Nick, et al. "Google and Facebook Take Aim at Fake News Sites." *The New York Times*, 14 Nov. 2016, www.nytimes.com/2016/11/15/technology/google-will-ban-websites-that-host-fake-news-from-using-its-ad-service.html.

Understanding the Reading

1. **Detail** What are the "Key Characteristics of Bogusness" (para. 4)?
2. **Thesis** What is the reading's thesis. Is it implied or stated?
3. **Summarizing** According to Kiely and Robertson, why should people read more than a provocative headline to verify the accuracy of a piece of news (para. 8)?
4. **Vocabulary** Explain the meaning of each of the following words as it is used in the reading: *dissipate* (para. 1), *malicious* (3), *missive* (6), *provocative* (8), and *mendacious* (13).

Analyzing the Writer's Technique

1. **Organization** How do Kiely and Robertson order the steps in their process analysis? Is their organization effective? Why or why not?
2. **Level of Detail** Is there enough detail for the selection to be of practical use?
3. **Audience** Who is the intended audience of this essay? Does the authors' advice apply to others outside this group?
4. **Patterns** What method of development, in addition to process, do the authors use extensively in the essay?

Thinking Critically about Process Analysis

1. **Tone** How would you describe Kiely and Robertson's tone? Use examples from the text to support your answer.
2. **Assumptions** What assumptions do the authors make about their readers?
3. **Purpose** Why do you think the authors wrote this essay?
4. **Credibility** Are Kiely and Robertson qualified to offer advice on how to spot fake news? Why or why not?

Responding to the Reading

1. **Discussion** Brainstorm and discuss possible motives people have for creating fake news other than for profit.
2. **Journal** The authors use words like *defense*, *malicious*, *distortion*, and *deception* when referring to fake news. All of these words connote danger. Do you think that fake news is a dangerous trend? Write a journal entry in which you address the question and explain your answer.
3. **Essay** Kiely and Robertson present "fact-checking tools of the trade" and describe how people can use them to verify the accuracy of news they read. Using one of the fake news articles below, write an essay in which you apply the steps the authors suggest to the reading:
   - "Colorado Pot Shop Accepting Food Stamps—Taxpayer-Funded Marijuana for Welfare Recipients" (*National Report*, web.archive.org/web/20170228020952/http://nationalreport.net/colorado-pot-shop-accept-food-stamps-taxpayer-funded-marijuana/)
   - "Pope Francis Shocks World, Endorses Donald Trump for President, Releases Statement" (WTOE 5 News, web.archive.org/web/20161115024211/http://wtoe5news.com/us-election/pope-francis-shocks-world-endorses-donald-trump-for-president-releases-statement/)

Working Together

Working with a group of your peers, create a public service announcement (PSA) that raises awareness of the pervasiveness of fake news. Assume that the announcement will appear on Facebook as text, but you may include a visual with your announcement if doing so enhances your message. Be prepared to share your group's PSA with the class and explain its relevance.

The Guided Writing Assignment in this chapter can walk you through the process of writing a process analysis essay; for help with evaluating sources, see Chapter 21; for help choosing and synthesizing ideas from sources, see Chapter 22; for help with documenting sources, see Chapter 23.

EXPLORE, RESEARCH, WRITE

In "How to Spot Fake News," Eugene Kiely and Lori Robertson describe how people can use "fact-checking tools of the trade" to "figure out what is real and what is imaginary." Other researchers have also studied the phenomenon of fake news that is now "reaching more people more quickly via social media." Facebook is one of the social media sites that has contributed to the spread of fake news. Some reports about Facebook and its efforts to combat fake news include the following:

- "How Facebook Plans to Crack Down on Fake News" by Ashley May (*USA Today*, 19 November 2016)

- "Working to Stop Misinformation and False News" by Adam Mosseri (*Facebook for Media*, 7 April 2017)

- "Facebook Is Changing News Feed (Again) to Stop Fake News" by Emily Dreyfuss and Issie Lapowsky (*Wired*, 18 April 2019)

Using your own ideas and one or more of the selections listed here, write a thoughtful process analysis essay that goes beyond what "How to Spot Fake News" tells us about the steps Facebook is taking or should take to address the spread of fake news. Be sure to incorporate at least one quotation from a reading and cite it correctly at the end of the essay.

Apply Your Skills: Additional Essay Assignments

For more on locating and documenting sources, see Part 5.

Write a process analysis essay on one of the following topics. Depending on the topic you choose, you may need to conduct research.

To Express Your Ideas

1. How children manage their parents
2. How to relax and do nothing
3. How to find enough time for your children or girlfriend/boyfriend/spouse

To Inform Your Reader

4. How to avoid or speed up red-tape procedures
5. How a particular type of sports equipment protects an athlete
6. How to remain calm while giving a speech

To Persuade Your Reader

7. How important it is to vote in a presidential election
8. How important it is to select the right courses in order to graduate on time
9. How important it is to exercise every day

Cases Using Process Analysis

10. In your communication course, you are studying how friendships develop and the strategies that people use to meet others. Write an essay describing the strategies people use to make new friends.
11. You are employed by a toy manufacturer and have been asked to write a brochure that encourages children to use toys safely. Prepare a brochure that describes at least three steps children can follow to avoid injury.

SYNTHESIZING IDEAS   INTERPERSONAL RELATIONSHIPS

Both "How Not to Say the Wrong Thing" (pp. 343–45) and "Going Vegan: How to Have Your Eggless Cake and Eat It, Too!" (pp. 356–61) discuss, in part, how to deal with others. "Going Vegan" discusses how to handle potentially difficult family meals, and "How Not to Say the Wrong Thing" focuses on how to interact with others who are going through a difficult time.

Analyzing the Readings

1. Evaluate the level of detail in each essay. Which essay is more helpful?
2. Write a journal entry in which you discuss ways in which you or someone close to you could use the information from each of the essays to communicate with friends and family more effectively.

Essay Idea

Think of other situations in which interpersonal communication is important. Write a process essay explaining the steps in creating a positive interaction. For example, you might write about how to communicate with an instructor, the parents of your boyfriend or girlfriend, or an elderly neighbor or relative.

15

Comparison and Contrast

Showing Similarities and Differences

Luca Tettoni/Robert Harding World Imagery/Getty Images; Jesper Mattias/
Getty Images

Writing Quick Start

ANALYZE   Carefully examine the photographs on this page, noting any details that would help someone who cannot see the images understand the differences and similarities between the two types of dancing. Consider how to describe each style of dancing and how each is performed.

WRITE   Draft a paragraph describing how the two dances shown are the same and how they are different. Consider who the dancers are and where the dances seem to be taking place. How would you describe them? What type of dance does each illustrate? What mood or feeling does each dance convey?

CONNECT   The paragraph you drafted is an example of comparison and contrast. You probably organized your paragraph in one of two ways:

1. You might have written about one set of dancers and then the other.
2. You might have talked first about the dancers in both photographs, then the setting for each dance, and so forth.

In this chapter you will learn to write effective comparison and contrast paragraphs and essays and examine two methods of organizing your writing.

Using **comparison and contrast** involves looking at similarities (**comparison**), differences (**contrast**), or both. Regardless of how a comparison and contrast essay is organized, the essence of the analysis is to identify shared characteristics between the items being examined and to determine how these shared characteristics are the same or different.

USING COMPARISON AND CONTRAST   IN COLLEGE AND THE WORKPLACE

- For a course in *criminal justice*, your instructor asks you to participate in a panel discussion comparing organized crime in Italy, Japan, and Russia.

- For a *journalism course*, you are asked to interview two local television news reporters and write a paper contrasting their views on journalistic responsibility.

- As a *computer technician* for a pharmaceutical firm, you are asked to compare and contrast several models of tablet computers and recommend the one the company should purchase for its salespeople.

What Are the Characteristics of Comparison and Contrast Essays?

Whether used as the primary pattern of development or alongside other patterns, successful comparison and contrast writing generally meets several criteria.

Comparison and Contrast Has a Clear Purpose and Is Written for a Specific Audience

A comparison and contrast essay usually has one of three purposes:

- **To express ideas:** The purpose of an essay about dancing could be to express the writer's love of both traditional and street dancing, comparing how each improves mood while also lowering stress and anxiety. The audience might be readers of a blog for dancers.
- **To inform:** The purpose of an essay about dancing could be to inform readers about types of dancing classes, comparing private and group lessons. The audience might be adults who are interested in learning new dance styles.
- **To persuade:** The purpose of an essay about dancing could be to persuade readers that dancing has more mental and physical benefits than gym workouts. The audience might be students who are looking for new forms of fitness.

Comparison and Contrast Considers Shared Characteristics

You cannot compare or contrast two things unless they have something in common. When making a comparison, a writer needs to choose a **basis of comparison**—a fairly broad common characteristic on which to base the essay. The paragraph you wrote comparing styles of dancing may have focused on the similarities and differences in settings, skills needed, and so forth. For another essay comparing baseball and football, for example, a basis of comparison might be the athletic skills required or the rules and logistics of each sport.

To develop a comparison and contrast essay, the writer examines two subjects using **points of comparison**—characteristics relating to the basis of comparison. In an essay using athletic skills as a basis of comparison, for example, points of comparison might be height and weight requirements, running skills, and hand-eye coordination. In an essay based on rules and logistics, points of comparison might include scoring, equipment, and playing fields.

EXERCISE 15.1 **IDENTIFYING BASES OF COMPARISON**

For three items in the following list, identify two possible bases of comparison:

1. Two means of travel or transportation
2. Two means of communication (emails, telephone calls, video chats, letters, texts)
3. Two pieces of equipment
4. Two magazines or books
5. Two types of television programming

Comparison and Contrast Is Organized Point by Point or Subject by Subject

You probably organized your paragraph comparing or contrasting two styles of dancing in one of two ways:

1. You wrote, first, about formal, traditional dancing and then about casual, contemporary dance styles (or vice versa)
2. You discussed each point of similarity or difference with examples from traditional and contemporary dance styles.

Most comparison and contrast essays use one of these two primary methods of organization:

- **Subject-by-subject organization.** The author describes the key points or characteristics of one subject before moving on to those aspects of a second subject.
- **Point-by-point organization.** The writer moves back and forth between two or more subjects, comparing them on the basis of several key points or characteristics.

Comparison and Contrast Fairly Examines Similarities, Differences, or Both

Depending on their purpose and audience, writers using comparison and contrast may focus on similarities, differences, or both. In an essay intended to *persuade* readers that performers Beyoncé Knowles and Taylor Swift have much in common in terms of talent and cultural influence, the writer would focus on similarities: hit records, millions of fans, and parts in movies. An essay intended to *inform* readers about the singers would probably cover both similarities and differences, discussing the singers' different childhoods or singing styles.

An essay focusing on similarities often mentions a few differences, usually in the introduction, to let readers know the writer is aware of the differences. Conversely, an essay that focuses on differences might mention a few similarities.

Whether you cover similarities, differences, or both in an essay, you should strive to treat your subjects fairly. Relevant information should not be purposely omitted to show one subject in a more favorable light. In an essay about Knowles and Swift, for instance, you should not leave out information about Swift's charitable contributions while mentioning Knowles's charitable causes in an effort to make Knowles appear to be the more charitable person.

Comparison and Contrast Makes a Point

A successful comparison and contrast essay has a main point that sparks readers' interest in the subjects rather than boring them with a mechanical listing of similarities or differences. This main point can serve as the **thesis** for the essay, or the thesis can be implied in the writer's choice of details.

An explicit thesis has three functions:

1. To identify the *subjects* being compared or contrasted
2. To suggest whether the focus is on *similarities, differences,* or *both*
3. To state the *main point* of the comparison or contrast

The following two sample theses meet all three criteria. Note, too, that each thesis suggests why the comparison or contrast is meaningful and worth reading about.

> ┌────── similarities ──────┐ ┌────── subjects ──────┐
> Similar appeals in commercials for three popular breakfast cereals
> ┌────────── main point ──────────┐
> reveal America's obsession with fitness and health.

> ┌────────── subjects ──────────┐
> The two cities Niagara Falls, Ontario, and Niagara Falls, New York,
> ┌────── differences ──────┐ ┌────── main points ──────┐
> demonstrate two different approaches to appreciating nature and
> ┌──────────────────────────┐
> preserving the environment.

EXERCISE 15.2   **WRITING AN EFFECTIVE THESIS STATEMENT**

For one of the topic pairs you chose in Exercise 15.1, select the basis of comparison that seems most promising. Then write a thesis statement that identifies the subjects, the focus (similarities, differences, or both), and the main point.

Comparison and Contrast Considers Significant and Relevant Shared Characteristics

A comparison and contrast essay considers characteristics that readers will find significant as well as relevant to the essay's purpose and thesis. In general, college writers should discuss at least three or four significant characteristics to support the thesis, describing or explaining each characteristic in detail so that readers can grasp the main point of the comparison or contrast. Writers often use sensory details, dialogue, examples, expert testimony, and other kinds of evidence to convince readers that the items being compared (or contrasted) are, in fact, similar (or dissimilar).

The following readings demonstrate the techniques discussed above for writing effective comparison and contrast essays. The first reading is annotated to show how Jan Diehm and Amber Thomas use these techniques to compare women's pockets to men's. As you read the second essay, try to identify how Jean Eshelman applies the techniques to compare a Hollywood and a Bollywood film.

READING ▸ POINT-BY-POINT ORGANIZATION

Pockets

Jan Diehm and Amber Thomas

Jan Diehm is a journalist-engineer at *The Pudding*, an online publication that "explains ideas debated in culture with visual essays." She has extensive experience in graphic design and has worked at a number of media outlets, including CNN, *The Guardian*, *ABC News*, and *The Huffington Post*. Amber Thomas, who describes herself as "a data-lover and professional question asker," also works at *The Pudding*, where she is a senior journalist-engineer. In the selection below, they use visuals to compare women's pockets to men's.

Before Reading

1. **Preview:** Use the steps listed in Chapter 2.
2. **Connect:** Consider men's and women's fashions. Do most of them feature pockets? What should designers consider when they create clothing with pockets? Should pockets on women's and men's clothing have a similar design and function?

While Reading Study the annotations that accompany the reading to discover how the essay illustrates the characteristics of comparison and contrast.

Background: Introduces topic

There are few things more frustrating than collecting your belongings only to realize that the pockets in your pants are too small to hold them. Or worse, the fabric designed to look like a pocket is merely for decoration and doesn't open at all. For wearers of women's clothes, this struggle is real. You don't have to look far to find Twitter rants, articles, and videos in which people are either

1

complaining about not having pockets or rejoicing over that rare gem that is the "dress with pockets." And sure, we could all carry handbags, which is likely what the 8 billion dollar purse industry hopes we'll do (O'Connell), but not everyone wants to carry a bag. <u>After all, men's pants pockets are basically the pockets of our dreams.</u>

[L]ike so many things on the internet, we could find complaints and anecdotes galore but little data illustrating just how inferior women's pockets really are to men's. So, we went there.

How Do Measurements Differ?

We measured the pockets in both men's and women's pants in 20 of the US' most popular blue jeans brands. **Take a look at what we found.**

On average, the pockets in women's jeans are 48% shorter and 6.5% narrower than men's pockets.

6.4"
6"
5.6"
9.1"

Fashion over Function: What Can Actually Fit?

<u>Beyond the obvious measurement differences,</u> we wanted to see just how functional all these pockets were. After all, a pocket is only as good as what you can fit in it. Here, we programmatically determined whether various everyday items could fit in an otherwise empty pocket in jeans that aren't being worn. (If an object won't fit in the pocket of a pair of jeans on the hanger, it certainly won't fit when you're

Thesis: <u>Thesis</u> indicates subjects being contrasted (men's and women's pockets) and suggests purpose (to persuade)

Purpose: Provide data to support claim of inferiority of women's pockets

Point of comparison 1: Measurements

Evidence: Visual gives measurements of women's and men's pockets

Point of comparison 2: Functionality

Organization: <u>Transition provides link between points of comparison 1 and 2</u>

wearing them.) Only 40 percent of women's front pockets can completely fit one of the three leading smartphone brands. Less than half of women's front pockets can fit a wallet *specifically* designed to fit in front pockets. And you can't even cram an average woman's hand beyond the knuckles into the majority of women's front pockets.

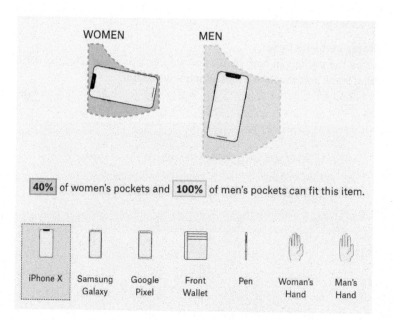

Evidence: Visuals show what will fit in women's and men's pockets

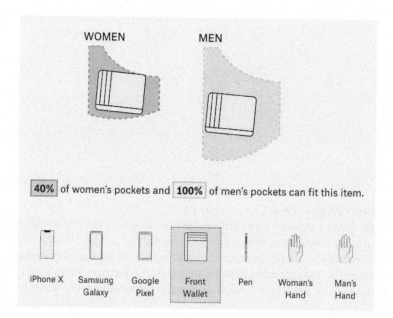

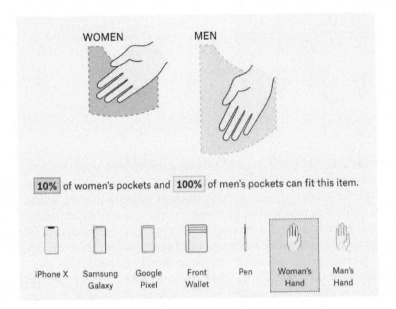

10% of women's pockets and 100% of men's pockets can fit this item.

| iPhone X | Samsung Galaxy | Google Pixel | Front Wallet | Pen | Woman's Hand | Man's Hand |

Here are a few other questions that you may be asking.   5

What about **Different Styles?**

Predictably, skinny jeans, which more closely hug the hips, have smaller front pockets   6
for both men and women, but the gap between women's and men's jeans is still noticeable in both skinny and straight styles. On average, women's skinny jean pockets were
3.5 inches (48%) shorter and 0.3 inches (6%) narrower than men's skinny jeans. Women's
straight jean pockets were 3.4 inches (46%) shorter and 0.6 inches (10%) narrower.

Point of comparison 3: Style differences

Evidence: Provides **exact measurements** to support difference in size of front pockets, organizing data by alternating between women's/men's pockets

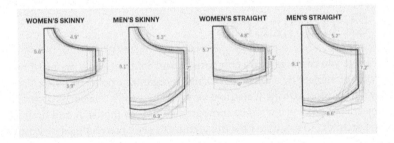

What about **Back Pockets?**

The gap between women's and men's back pockets was less egregious. Women's   7
pockets were still smaller, but not by much: women's skinny jean pockets were
0.3 inches (5%) shorter and 0.1 inches (2%) narrower, and women's straight jean
pockets were 0.4 inches (7%) shorter and 0.1 inches (2%) narrower. Ultimately,
men's back pockets were a bit deeper but just about the same width as women's.

Point of comparison 4: Back pockets

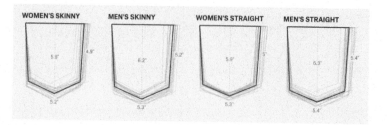

Conclusion: Reinforces the thesis

While the sheer inconvenience of not being able to keep your belongings in your pocket may seem like a small issue, it is one that women have faced for centuries. For women, it was (and still is) about equality. Pockets, unlike purses, are hidden, private spaces. By restricting the space in which women can keep things safe and retain mobility of both hands, we are also restricting their ability to "navigate public spaces, to carry seditious (or merely amorous) writing, or to travel unaccompanied" (chelseagsummers). If you think this idea is outdated, think about the last time a woman asked her boyfriend/male friend/anyone in men's pants to carry her phone/wallet/keys on an outing.

8

Links

chelseagsummers. "The Politics of Pockets." *Vox,* 19 Sept. 2016, www.vox.com/2016/9/19/12865560/
    politics-of-pockets-suffragettes-women.

O'Connell, Liam. "Retails Sales of Handbags in the United States from 2010 to 2018 (in Dollars)."
    Statista, 18 July 2019 (last updated), https://www.statista.com/statistics/316526/retail
    -sales-value-of-women-s-handbags-in-the-us/.

Visualize a Comparison and Contrast Essay: Create Graphic Organizers

For more on creating a graphic organizer, see Chapter 2.

As noted earlier, you can organize a comparison and contrast essay in one of two ways: point by point or subject by subject. ("Pockets" is organized point by point; "How to Be 'Somebody': Hollywood's *On the Waterfront* versus Bollywood's *Ghulam*" is organized subject by subject.) Suppose you want to compare two houses (house A and house B) built by the same architect to evaluate how the architect's style has changed over time. After brainstorming, you decide to base your essay on these points of comparison:

- layout
- size
- building materials
- landscaping

Point-by-Point Organization

Graphic Organizer 15.1 shows the basic structure of an essay using *point-by-point organization*, in which you go back and forth between the subjects (in this case, two houses), noting similarities and differences between them on each of the points of comparison.

GRAPHIC ORGANIZER 15.1 The Basic Structure of a Point-by-Point Comparison and Contrast Essay*

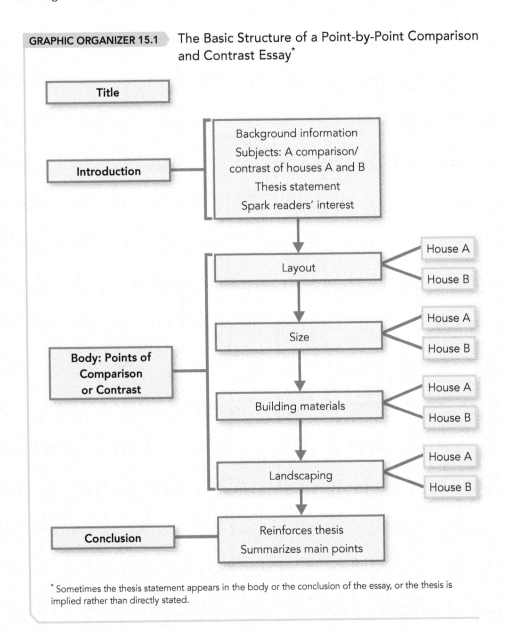

* Sometimes the thesis statement appears in the body or the conclusion of the essay, or the thesis is implied rather than directly stated.

Subject-by-Subject Organization

Graphic Organizer 15.2 shows the basic structure of an essay using *subject-by-subject organization*, in which you first discuss all the points of comparison—in this case, layout, size, building materials, and landscaping for the first subject (house A) before doing the same for the second subject (house B).

GRAPHIC ORGANIZER 15.2   The Basic Structure of a Subject-by-Subject Comparison and Contrast Essay*

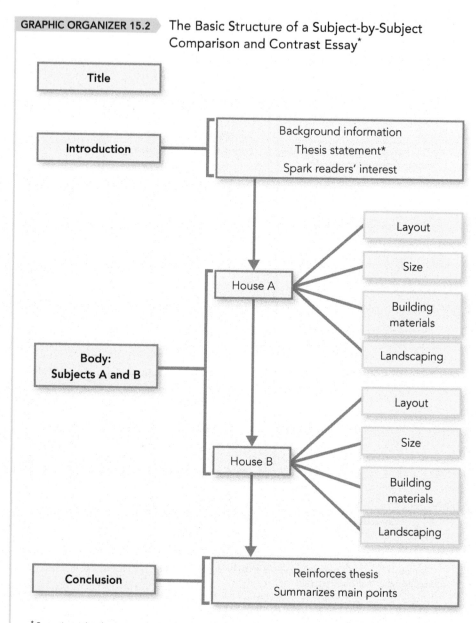

* Sometimes the thesis statement appears in the body or the conclusion of the essay, or the thesis is implied rather than directly stated.

How to Be "Somebody": Hollywood's *On the Waterfront* versus Bollywood's *Ghulam*

Jean Eshelman

Jean Eshelman lives in New York City, where she works as a content analyst for Netflix, specializing in Indian film and television. She is a fan of films old and new from all over the world, but she has a particular fondness for Bollywood song and dance and for films from the "Golden Age" of Hindi cinema (1940s–1960s). **Before reading**, think about a time when you struggled with a decision that involved mixed loyalties. **While reading**, highlight the subjects that Eshelman addresses. Then compare your notes with Graphic Organizer 15.3.

Many U.S. movie fans instantly know the line "I could have been a contender" from Elia Kazan's 1954 *On the Waterfront*. However, they may not be aware that a 1998 Indian hit, Vikram Bhatt's *Ghulam* ("Slave"), was inspired by Kazan's film. The two movies share storylines and themes but approach the content quite differently. Analyzing these differences illustrates important differences between Hollywood films and India's popular Hindi-language cinema, often called "Bollywood." Some of the most revealing differences are apparent in the cinematic presentation, characterization of the protagonist, portrayal of the relationship between the brothers, and the climax of each film.   1

Set in New Jersey in the 1950s, *On the Waterfront* follows the life of Terry Malloy (Marlon Brando), a young dock worker who once had a promising boxing career. The corrupt union boss, Johnny Friendly, controls the longshoremen's union, and Johnny's right-hand man is Terry's older brother, Charley. The film was nominated for twelve Academy Awards and won eight, including the coveted Best Picture and Best Director awards.   2

On the Waterfront's cinematic presentation is serious and restrained. Kazan's film is a classic, and classy, black-and-white Hollywood drama that was filmed on location near the docks of Hoboken, New Jersey. Although violence erupts now and then, the story is told largely through conversations that fill in the characters' histories.   3

The restraint carries over into *On the Waterfront*'s characterization of Terry, the protagonist. Terry bottles up his emotions—typical behavior for a U.S. tough guy in a 1950s film. He often appears to have little or no outward reaction to shocking events. The film begins with Terry lying to fellow longshoreman Joey Doyle to lure him to the roof of his apartment building, where gangsters are waiting. To Terry's shock, the gangsters throw Joey to his death. Terry may be appalled at the murder and at his own role in it, but he merely says quietly, "He wasn't a bad kid, that Joey" (see fig. 1). Terry represses his conscience out of loyalty to the waterfront code of pretending to be "deaf and dumb" rather than talking to authorities. For most of the film, he cannot decide whether or not he should testify against Johnny Friendly. Terry's brother Charley finally pulls a gun on Terry and demands that he not testify. Shaking his head sadly, Terry gently pushes the gun aside, saying only   4

Fig. 1. Terry (right) reacts to Joey's murder.

"Charley, oh, Charley. Wow." Sorrow, not anger or fear, is his reaction when he finally accepts that his loyalty to his brother and Johnny has been misplaced.

The relationship between older brother Charley and younger brother Terry is   5
realistically drawn. Charley cares about Terry, but he too keeps his feelings mostly hidden. He communicates brotherly love mainly through actions, helping his little brother get easy jobs and easy money and protecting him by keeping him in Johnny Friendly's good graces. But the film suggests that Charley has always expected Terry to do occasional "favors" for Johnny, including throwing a boxing match that Terry could have won. Charley sees Terry's sense of right and wrong as a liability, both to Terry's safety and to Charley's job. In the film's most famous scene (see fig. 2), Terry finally speaks up to explain how much Charley's interference has hurt: "You was my brother. You should have looked out for me just a little

Fig. 2. Charley and Terry reconcile.

bit. . . . I could have been a contender. I could have been somebody, instead of a bum, which is what I am, let's face it." To his credit, Charley does not argue; instead, he seems to regret the way he has treated Terry.

The climax of *On the Waterfront* is a "Hollywood ending" that shows a lone 6 individual standing up for what is morally right, facing hostility from all sides but still emerging victorious. When Terry testifies against Johnny Friendly, the other longshoremen react with disgust that he has become "a stool pigeon." Terry stands on the waterfront shouting that Johnny has betrayed the union workers and that he is "glad what I done." Johnny's men beat him nearly unconscious. Inspired by Terry's courage, the longshoremen all refuse to work unless Terry leads them. He staggers to his feet, and the whole crowd follows him to the pier. In the end, he does become "somebody," a leader rather than "a bum."

Despite the similarities to *On the Waterfront*, the cinematic presentation, char- 7 acterization of the main character, the relationship between the brothers, and the climax are all very different in the Indian film *Ghulam*, which takes place in Mumbai in the 1990s. Bhatt's film borrows heavily from the storyline of *On the Waterfront*, but he adapts it, doing what he needs to do to make a box-office hit in India. Like *On the Waterfront*, *Ghulam* focuses on a young boxer whose conscience awakens during the film, but in the Indian film, the main character is not a worker but a layabout and petty thief named Siddharth Marathe, called "Siddhu." Strongman Ronnie Singh (the Johnny Friendly–like character) controls a neighborhood full of poor shopkeepers from whom Ronnie demands protection money. Siddhu's brother Jai (like Charley) works for Ronnie, helping his boss's extortion business seem legitimate.

The cinematic presentation of *Ghulam* is full-color, elaborate, and unre- 8 strained. The film is packed with not just drama and romance, but action, comedy, and hit musical numbers. *Ghulam*'s success shows that Indian audiences did not want subtlety and restraint in Bollywood films of the period. Events are not merely talked about, but shown in dramatic detail. Climactic moments, such as the murder of Hari (the Joey Doyle character), are shot from multiple angles, all edited together with emphatic music.

Ghulam's characterization of its hero, Siddhu, shows a preference for clear-cut 9 black-and-white characters over shades of gray. At the beginning of the film, Siddhu is portrayed as a bad boy—he steals from his lawyer's purse as she defends him in court—but it's soon clear he is not a bad human being. He readily shows his deep-seated sense of right and wrong. When he realizes that he has been duped into luring Hari to his death, Siddhu reacts with outrage and horror (see fig. 3). Siddhu may at first seem extremely naive about Ronnie's evil behavior, but when he finally recognizes it, he never questions the need to fight back bravely. Being realistic, ambivalent, and morally gray is not for a Bollywood hero; being larger than life and stronger than evil is essential.

The brotherly relationship between Jai and Siddhu depicts more big emotional 10 moments, and a greater expectation that the younger brother show respect to the older one, than Western audiences typically see. Jai behaves like an indulgent parent toward Siddhu, calling him a "kid," and Siddhu displays an almost childlike trust of his brother. When Siddhu first learns how involved Jai is in Ronnie's illegal activities, Siddhu hesitates to file a legal case out of the respect he owes to his older

Fig. 3. Siddhu reacts to Hari's murder

brother, but after Jai insists he throw a boxing match to win money for Ronnie, Siddhu's mind is made up. "From now on, I'll only do what's right," he tells Jai. "It's your job to cover Ronnie's evil deeds and mine to expose them." When Jai pulls a gun, Siddhu reminds him of his duty as an older brother. "All your life you've walked an evil path. When I came after you, why didn't you show me the right path? You were my older brother. Why didn't you think of me?" Siddhu tries to convince Jai to join him in the fight against Ronnie, but Jai lacks his little brother's courage.

The climax of *Ghulam* provides an extended fight sequence between Siddhu   11
and Ronnie, but it is not enough to satisfy a Bollywood audience's wish for an over-the-top climax. Ronnie gets up and commands his men to kill Siddhu—but the locals roar back, "Kill them all!" The overwhelming crowd, made up of men, women, and children of all ages and religions, sends Ronnie and his thugs fleeing the area, never to return. Unlike Terry in *Waterfront,* who leads the crowd of longshoremen, Siddhu has already left, having fulfilled his new older-brother role of showing the crowd "the right path."

Ghulam's use of *On the Waterfront*'s same-but-different storyline suggests that   12
the Hollywood classic was repurposed to give local Indian audiences the Bollywood flair and emotional resonance they expected. The understated and realistic black-and-white American Oscar winner gives way to a full-color Bollywood film filled with song and dance, stunts, family drama, fistfights, and tears. Brando's reserved Terry Malloy, slowly accepting his guilt and his brother's complicity, becomes "somebody"; Aamir Khan's open-hearted Siddharth Marathe, an outraged innocent finally ready to do the right thing, shows "the right path." And local audiences in the United States and in India cheered a story that seemed tailor-made for them.

Works Cited

Ghulam. Directed by Vikram Bhatt, performances by Aamir Khan, Rajit Kapur, and Sharat Saxena, NH Studioz, 1998.

On the Waterfront. Directed by Elia Kazan, performances by Marlon Brando, Rod Steiger, and Lee J. Cobb, Horizon Pictures, 1954.

EXERCISE 15.3 DRAWING A GRAPHIC ORGANIZER

Using Graphic Organizer 15.1 as a basis, draw a graphic organizer for "Pockets."

GRAPHIC ORGANIZER 15.3 The Structure of "How to Be 'Somebody': Hollywood's *On the Waterfront* versus Bollywood's *Ghulam*"

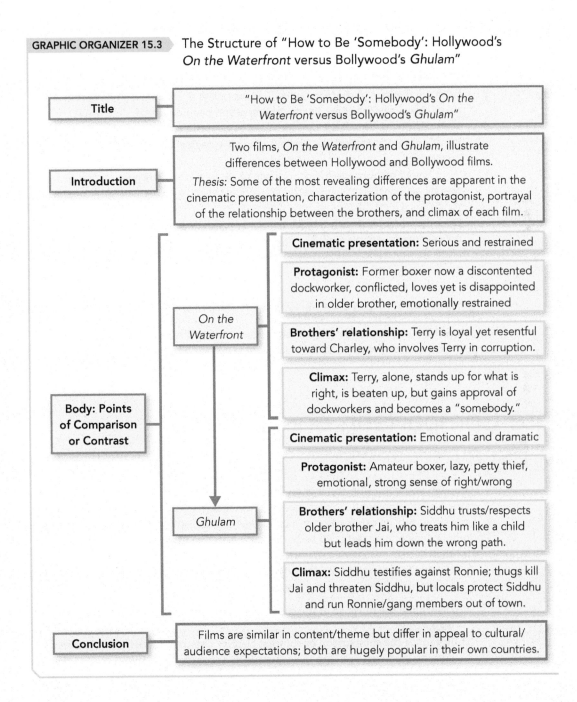

HOW WRITERS READ   **COMPARISON AND CONTRAST**

THE READING PROCESS	STRATEGIES
BEFORE READING	**Preview** the essay to get an overview of its content and organization.
	Make connections by comparing your knowledge and experience with the topic discussed in the selection.
AFTER READING	**Analyze and evaluate** the reading by answering the following questions:
	• What are the **shared characteristics**? Are the points of comparison **relevant** to the thesis? Have any important points of comparison been **omitted**?
	• How well do the **details** support these main points of the comparison or contrast? Would **more or different details** have made the comparison or contrast more convincing?
	• What is your **response** to the comparison or contrast? Do you agree or disagree with the author? Did the comparison or contrast change your **perspective** on the topic?
	• Does the writer treat each subject fairly and provide **balanced coverage**? Or does the coverage seem biased?

EXERCISE 15.4 ▸ **READING CRITICALLY**

Apply the questions in the "How Writers Read" box to the selection "How to Be 'Somebody': Hollywood's *On the Waterfront* versus Bollywood's *Ghulam*."

Integrate Comparison and Contrast into an Essay

Although you will write some essays using comparison and contrast as the primary pattern of development, in most cases you will integrate comparisons or contrasts into essays that rely on other patterns, such as description, process analysis, or argument. Comparisons or contrasts can be particularly effective in persuasive essays, as "Pockets" shows.

Use the following tips to incorporate comparison or contrast into essays based on other patterns of development:

1. **Determine the purpose of the comparison or contrast.** What will it contribute to your essay?
2. **Introduce the comparison or contrast clearly.** Use transitional words and expressions to guide readers into the comparison or contrast and then back to the

essay's primary pattern of development, and tell readers how the comparison or contrast supports your main point. Do not leave it to your audience to figure out why you have included the comparison.

3. **Keep the comparison or contrast short and to the point.** Avoid distracting readers from your main message.

4. **Organize the points of the comparison or contrast appropriately.** Use point-by-point or subject-by-subject organization, even though the comparison or contrast is part of a larger essay.

PREWRITING	DRAFTING	REVISING	EDITING & PROOFREADING

A Guided Writing Assignment*

COMPARISON AND CONTRAST

Your Essay Assignment

Write an essay comparing or contrasting a pair of subjects. Choose subjects to compare or contrast that your readers might find surprising or enlightening. The following are some options to help you get started:

- two or more forms of entertainment (movies, concerts, radio, music videos)
- two or more styles of communication, dress, or teaching
- two or more public figures
- the right and wrong ways of doing something
- two or more different cultures' views on the roles that men and women should play

1 **Select an essay topic from the list above, or create one of your own.**

Consider your interests and experiences: Choose subjects that you **already know about, want to learn more about, want to write about,** or **have experience with.**

Brainstorm, alone or in groups, a list of subjects you would like to write about. Since comparison and contrast can work with any two comparable subjects, you should be able to find a subject you and your reader will find engaging.

*The writing process is *recursive*; that is, you may find yourself revising as you draft or prewriting as you revise. This is especially true when writing on a computer. Your writing process may also differ from project to project or from that of your classmates.

2 Consider your purpose and audience, and choose a basis for comparison.

Ask yourself these questions:

- Will my essay's **purpose** be to **express myself**, **inform**, or **persuade**? What **basis of comparison** will work best, given my purpose? To **inform** readers about two football positions, you could compare the height, weight, skills, and training of players at each position. To **persuade** readers that one quarterback was better than another, you could compare the number of interceptions, completions, and passing yards of each.

- Who is my **audience**? How much do my readers **already know** about the topic? What kind of **supporting details** will they find **convincing** and **engaging**? Readers who are football fans will need different information from those who do not watch the sport.

3 Explore your subjects and develop points of comparison.

Keeping your learning style in mind, **explore how your two subjects are similar**, **how they are different**, **or both**.

- Create a **two-column list** of similarities and differences. Jot down ideas in the appropriate column.
- Ask a classmate to help you **brainstorm** by mentioning only similarities. For each similarity, generate a difference.
- **Use visualization.** Draw a sketch of your subjects.
- **Create a scenario** in which your subjects interact. For example, if your topic is the cars of today and the cars of 1950, imagine asking your great-grandfather to drive a 2018 luxury car. How would he react? What would he say?

4 Draft your thesis statement.

Your thesis statement **should**

- identify the subjects
- suggest whether you will focus on similarities, differences, or both
- state your main point

An effective thesis will also **engage your readers**, telling them why your comparison or contrast is important, surprising, or useful.

Example:

— subjects —

The mystery novels of both Robert B. Parker and Sue Grafton are popular because

main point: focus on similarities

readers are fascinated by the intrigues of witty, independent private detectives.

Team up with a classmate to review each other's thesis statement. Try to identify the subjects for comparison, the focus (similarities, differences, or both), and the main point. If these are unclear or ineffective, offer suggestions for improvement.

5 Choose a method of organization.

Decide whether you will use **point-by-point (Graphic Organizer 15.1)** or **subject-by-subject (Graphic Organizer 15.2)** organization.

- **Point-by-point** often works better for lengthy essays (because it keeps both subjects current in the reader's mind) and for complicated or technical subjects.
- **Subject-by-subject** organization tends to emphasize the larger picture.

If you are not sure which will be most effective, **create an outline or graphic organizer** for both patterns to see which works better.

6 Write a first draft of your comparison or contrast essay.

- The **introduction** should **spark your readers' interest**, **introduce your subjects**, provide any necessary **background information**, and include your **thesis**.
- The **body paragraphs** should include **topic sentences** that focus on **a point of comparison**.
  - For **point-by-point** organization, **discuss the subjects in the same order for each point**, and **arrange your points of comparison logically**, from simplest to most complex, for example.
  - For **subject-by-subject** organization, **cover the same points** for both subjects **in the same order** in both halves of your essay, and use **transitions** such as *similarly*, *in contrast*, *on the one hand*, *on the other hand*, and *not only . . . but also* to alert readers as you **switch from one subject to the other**.
- The **conclusion** should remind readers of your **thesis** and offer a **final comment** on your comparison or contrast. If your essay is lengthy or complex, consider **summarizing** your main points in the conclusion.

7 Evaluate your draft, and revise as necessary.

Use **Figure 15.1, "Flowchart for Revising a Comparison or Contrast Essay,"** to evaluate and revise your draft.

FIGURE 15.1 Flowchart for Revising a Comparison or Contrast Essay

QUESTIONS

REVISION STRATEGIES

1. Highlight your thesis statement. Does it identify the subjects being compared; indicate whether you will compare, contrast, or both; and state your main point? Does it suggest why your comparison or contrast is meaningful?

NO

- Consider your audience: What would make the comparison or contrast meaningful to your readers?
- Brainstorm reasons for making the comparison, or work backward from your reasons to revise your thesis.

 YES

(continued on next page) ▶

(Figure 15.1 continued)

QUESTIONS   REVISION STRATEGIES

2. Write the basis of comparison at the top of the page. Is your basis of comparison clear? Does it clearly relate to your thesis?

 ▶

- Talk with a friend or classmate about your basis of comparison while he or she helps you think of a better basis for comparison.
- Review your points of similarity or difference and work backward to derive your basis of comparison.

3. Place a ✔ next to the sentences that focus on similarities or mark an ✘ next to sentences that focus on differences. Have you included all significant points of comparison? Do you fairly examine similarities and differences? Is each similarity or difference significant, and does each support your thesis?

 ▶

- Delete insignificant or irrelevant similarities or differences.
- Review your prewriting to identify any significant points of comparison you overlooked.
- Conduct research or ask a classmate to suggest ideas.

4. Reread your supporting paragraphs. Does each one have a clear topic sentence that relates to your point of comparison or contrast?

 ▶

- Add or revise the topic sentence to focus on the point of comparison.
- Consider splitting paragraphs that focus on more than one point or characteristic and combining paragraphs that focus on the same one.

5. Draw a **wavy underline** under the concrete details in each paragraph. Do you include enough details to make your comparisons vivid and interesting? Have you provided roughly the same amount of detail for both subjects?

 ▶

- Add or delete details as necessary.
- Review your prewriting to see if you overlooked any significant details.
- Brainstorm or research your subjects to come up with additional details.

REVISING

398

QUESTIONS	REVISION STRATEGIES

6. Draw a graphic organizer. Did you use either point-by-point or subject-by-subject organization consistently? Will your organization be clear to your reader?

 NO ▶

- Study your graphic organizer to find inconsistencies or gaps.
- Reorganize your essay using one method of organization consistently.
- Add transitions to make the shift to a new subject or point of comparison clearer.

YES
▼

7. Reread your introduction and conclusion. Does your introduction convey why your comparison is meaningful? Is your conclusion relevant and satisfying?

 NO ▶

- Revise your introduction to engage readers and emphasize the importance of your comparison.
- Consider concluding with an action or way of thinking that is appropriate given your comparison.

---

8 Edit and proofread your essay.

Refer to Chapter 9 for help with

- **editing sentences** to avoid wordiness, use strong and active verbs, and make your sentences clear, varied, and parallel
- **editing words** for tone and diction, connotation, and concrete and specific language

When proofreading, make sure

- you use the **correct form of adjectives** and **adverbs** when **comparing two items** (comparative) or **three or more items** (superlative)

	Positive	Comparative	Superlative
Adjectives	sharp	sharper	sharpest
Adverbs	early	earlier	earliest

Example: Both *No Country for Old Men* and *True Grit* were suspenseful,

but I liked *True Grit* ~~best.~~ better.

Example: George, Casey, and Bob are all bad at basketball, but Bob's game

is ~~worse.~~ worst.

- items linked by **correlative conjunctions** (*either . . . or, neither . . . nor, not only . . . but also*) are in the **same grammatical form**

Example: The Grand Canyon is not only a spectacular tourist attraction but also

~~scientists consider it~~ a useful geological record / for scientists.

Readings: Comparison and Contrast in Action

Border Bites

Heather Gianakos

Heather Gianakos was a first-year student when she wrote the following comparison and contrast essay for her composition course. Although she has always enjoyed both styles of cooking that she discusses, she needed to do some research to learn more about their history. As you read the essay, consider the writer's thesis and points of comparison.

Introduction: Indicates Gianakos will examine both similarities and differences but will focus on differences. Her thesis statement gives a basis of comparison of her two subjects, Mexican and southwestern cooking: the traditions and geographic locations of the people who developed them. It also makes a point: that these differences have led to the differences in the food.

Chili peppers, tortillas, tacos: All these foods belong to the styles of cooking known as Mexican, Tex-Mex, and southwestern. These internationally popular styles often overlap; sometimes it can be hard to tell which style a particular dish belongs to. Two particular traditions of cooking, however, play an especially important role in the kitchens of Mexico and the American Southwest — native-derived Mexican cooking ("Mexican") and Anglo-influenced southwestern cooking, particularly from Texas ("southwestern"). The different traditions and geographic locations of the inhabitants of Mexico and of the Anglo-American settlers in the Southwest have resulted in subtle, flavorful differences between the foods featured in Mexican and southwestern cuisine.

Subject A: southwestern

Subject B: Mexican

Point of comparison 1: The physical conditions in which the two styles developed. Notice that Gianakos uses point-by-point comparison, discussing both subjects in each paragraph and often using transitions between them.

Evidence: Notice that Gianakos cites sources in the text and includes a list of works cited at the end.

Many of the traditions of southwestern cooking grew out of difficult situations — cowboys and ranchers cooking over open fires, for example. Chili, which can contain beans, beef, tomatoes, corn, and many other ingredients, was a good dish to cook over a campfire because everything could be combined in one pot. Dry foods, such as beef jerky, were a convenient way to solve food storage problems and could be easily tucked into saddlebags. In Mexico, by contrast, fresh fruits and vegetables such as avocados and tomatoes were widely available and did not need to be dried or stored. They could be made into spicy salsa and guacamole. Mexicans living in coastal areas could also enjoy fish and lobster dishes (Jamison and Jamison 5).

Corn has been a staple in the American Southwest and Mexico since the time of the Aztecs, who made tortillas (flat, unleavened bread, originally made from stone-ground corn and water) similar to the ones served in Mexico today (Jamison and Jamison 5). Southwesterners, often of European descent, adopted the tortilla but often prepared it with wheat flour, which was easily available to them. Wheat-flour tortillas can now be found in both Mexican and southwestern cooking, but corn is usually the primary grain in dishes with precolonial origins. Tamales (whose name derives from a word in Nahuatl, the Aztec group of languages) are a delicious example: A hunk of cornmeal dough, sometimes combined with ground meat, is wrapped in corn husks and steamed. In southwestern cooking, corn is often used for leavened corn bread, which is made with corn flour rather than cornmeal and can be flavored with jalapeños or back bacon.

Meat of various kinds is often the centerpiece of both Mexican and southwestern tables. However, although chicken, beef, and pork are staples in both traditions, they are often prepared quite differently. Fried chicken rolled in flour and dunked into sizzling oil or fat is a popular dish throughout the American southwest. In traditional Mexican cooking, however, chicken is often cooked more slowly, in stews or baked dishes, with a variety of seasonings, including ancho chiles, garlic, and onions.

Ever since cattle farming began in Texas with the early Spanish missions, beef has been eaten both north and south of the border. In southwestern cooking, steak—flank, rib eye, or sirloin—grilled quickly and served rare is often a chef's crowning glory. In Mexican cooking, beef may be combined with vegetables and spices and rolled into a fajita or served ground in a taco. For a Mexican food purist, in fact, the only true fajita is made from skirt steak, although Mexican food as it is served in the United States often features chicken fajitas.

In Texas and the Southwest United States, barbecued pork ribs are often prepared in barbecue cook-offs, similar to chili-cooking competitions. Such competitions have strict rules for the preparation and presentation of the food and for sanitation (Central Texas). However, while the BBQ is seen as a southwestern specialty, barbecue ribs as they are served in southwestern-themed restaurants today

---

3 **Point of comparison 2:** The use of corn and wheat

4 **Point of comparison 3:** The use of chicken

Subject A: Southwestern

Subject B: Mexican

5 **Point of comparison 4:** The use of beef

Subject A: Southwestern

Subject B: Mexican

6 **Point of comparison 5:** The use of pork

Subject A: Southwestern

Subject B: Mexican

actually come from a Hispanic and Southwest Mexican tradition dating from the days before refrigeration: Since pork fat, unlike beef fat, has a tendency to become rancid, pork ribs were often marinated in vinegar and spices and then hung to dry. Later the ribs were basted with the same sauce and grilled (Campa 278). The resulting dish has become a favorite both north and south of the border, although in Mexican cooking, where beef is somewhat less important than in southwestern cooking, pork is equally popular in many other forms, such as chorizo sausage.

Conclusion: Gianakos returns to the idea of overlap mentioned in the introduction and makes clear her purpose—to inform readers about the differences between the two cuisines.

Cooks in San Antonio or Albuquerque would probably tell you that the food they cook is as much Mexican as it is southwestern. Regional cuisines in such areas of the Southwest as New Mexico, Southern California, and Arizona feature elements of both traditions; chimichangas—deep-fried burritos—actually originated in Arizona (Jamison and Jamison 11). Food lovers who sample regional specialties, however, will note—and savor—the contrast between the spicy, fried or grilled, beef-heavy style of southwestern food and the richly seasoned, corn- and tomato-heavy style of Mexican food.

7

Gianakos lists her sources at the end of her paper, following MLA style.

Works Cited

Campa, Arthur L. *Hispanic Culture in the Southwest*. U of Oklahoma P, 1979.

Central Texas Barbecue Association. 16 Aug. 2004, www.ctbabbq.com/rules/.

Jamison, Cheryl Alters, and Bill Jamison. *The Border Cookbook*. Harvard Common, 1995.

Analyzing the Writer's Technique

1. **Background** Evaluate Gianakos's title and introduction. Do they provide the reader with enough background on her topic?
2. **Organization** Using a point-by-point organization, Gianakos presents her two subjects in the same order—first southwestern cuisine, then Mexican cuisine—for each point of comparison except in paragraph 3. Why do you think she discusses the two cuisines together in this paragraph?
3. **Sources** How does Gianakos's use of sources contribute to her essay?

Thinking Critically about Comparison and Contrast

1. **Response** Reread the first sentence of the essay. What type of cooking is mentioned here and never discussed again in the essay? How does this decision by Gianakos affect your response to the first paragraph and to the essay as a whole?
2. **Tone** Describe Gianakos's tone. Is it effective in this essay?
3. **Language** What do phrases such as "subtle, flavorful differences" (para. 1), "Food lovers" (7), and "richly seasoned" (7) contribute to the essay? If Gianakos had included more phrases like these, how would the essay be changed?
4. **Omissions** What comparisons did Gianakos not make that she could have made?

Responding to the Essay

1. **Discussion** In groups of two or three, discuss other regional cuisines that might make effective topics for a comparison and contrast essay. What traits do they share? What distinguishes them?
2. **Journal** Gianakos compares the cuisines of the American Southwest and Mexico using the traditions and geographic locations of the people who lived there as the basis of comparison. In your journal, explore several other possible bases of comparison that could be used to compare these cuisines.
3. **Essay** Write an essay comparing foods of two other regional cuisines.

READING

His Marriage and Hers: Childhood Roots

Daniel Goleman

Daniel Goleman holds a Ph.D. in behavioral and brain sciences and has published a number of books on psychology, including *The Brain and Emotional Intelligence: New Insights* (2011) and *Leadership: The Power of Emotional Intelligence* (2011). Goleman reported on the brain and behavioral sciences for *The New York Times* for many years and was elected a fellow of the American Association for the Advancement of Science for his efforts to bring psychology to the public. In his book *Emotional Intelligence* (1995), from which the following selection was taken, Goleman describes the emotional skills required for daily living and explains how to develop those skills. **Before reading**, preview the selection and make connections by thinking about the ways communication between men and women differs. **While reading**, notice how Goleman uses comparison and contrast to explore differences between the sexes and highlight his key points of comparison.

JUST-IN-TIME **TIP** Reading Comparison and Contrast

"His Marriage and Hers: Childhood Roots" offers a lot of information about differences in men's and women's communication styles. To retain more of what you read, create a two-column chart with differences in conversational style on the left and reasons for these differences on the right. (The list of differences and the first reason have been done for you.)

Differences	Reasons for Differences
"Emotional realities" (para. 2)	Partly biological, partly differences in social experience
"Lessons about handling emotions" (para. 3)	
Language acquisition (para. 4)	
Levels of aggression (para. 5)	
Styles of play (para. 6)	
Communication skills (para. 7)	
Roles in marriage (para. 8)	
Attitudes about relationship (para. 9)	
Reading facial expressions (para. 10)	

As I was entering a restaurant on a recent evening, a young man stalked out the door, his face set in an expression both stony and sullen. Close on his heels a young woman came running, her fists desperately pummeling his back while she yelled, "Goddamn you! Come back here and be nice to me!" That poignant, impossibly self-contradictory plea aimed at a retreating back epitomizes the pattern most commonly seen in couples whose relationship is distressed: She seeks to engage, he withdraws. Marital therapists have long noted that by the time a couple finds their way to the therapy office, they are in this pattern of engage-withdraw, with his complaint about her "unreasonable" demands and outbursts, and her lamenting his indifference to what she is saying.

This marital endgame reflects the fact that there are, in effect, two emotional realities in a couple, his and hers. The roots of these emotional differences, while they may be partly biological, also can be traced back to childhood and to the separate emotional worlds boys and girls inhabit while growing up. There is a vast amount of research on these separate worlds, their barriers reinforced not just by the different games boys and girls prefer but by young children's fear of being teased for having a "girlfriend" or "boyfriend" (Maccoby and Jacklin). One study of children's friendships found that three-year-olds say about half their friends are of the opposite sex; for five-year-olds it's about 20 percent, and by age seven almost no boys or girls say they have a best friend of the opposite sex (Gottman). These separate social universes intersect little until teenagers start dating.

Meanwhile, boys and girls are taught very different lessons about handling   3
emotions. Parents, in general, discuss emotions—with the exception of anger— more with their daughters than their sons (Brody and Hall). Girls are exposed to more information about emotions than are boys: when parents make up stories to tell their preschool children, they use more emotion words when talking to daughters than to sons; when mothers play with their infants, they display a wider range of emotions to daughters than to sons; when mothers talk to daughters about feelings, they discuss in more detail the emotional state itself than they do with their sons—though with the sons they go into more detail about the causes and consequences of emotions like anger (probably as a cautionary tale).

Leslie Brody and Judith Hall, who have summarized the research on differences   4
in emotions between the sexes, propose that because girls develop facility with language more quickly than do boys, this leads them to be more experienced at articulating their feelings and more skilled than boys at using words to explore and substitute for emotional reactions such as physical fights; in contrast, they note, "boys, for whom the verbalization of affects is de-emphasized, may become largely unconscious of their emotional states, both in themselves and others" (p. 454).

At age ten, roughly the same percent of girls as boys are overtly aggressive,   5
given to open confrontation when angered. But by age thirteen, a telling difference between the sexes emerges: Girls become more adept than boys at artful aggressive tactics like ostracism, vicious gossip, and indirect vendettas. Boys, by and large, simply continue being confrontational when angered, oblivious to these more covert strategies (Cairns and Cairns). This is just one of many ways that boys—and later, men—are less sophisticated than the opposite sex in the byways of emotional life.

When girls play together, they do so in small, intimate groups, with an   6
emphasis on minimizing hostility and maximizing cooperation, while boys' games are in larger groups, with an emphasis on competition. One key difference can be seen in what happens when games boys or girls are playing get disrupted by someone getting hurt. If a boy who has gotten hurt gets upset, he is expected to get out of the way and stop crying so the game can go on. If the same happens among a group of girls who are playing, the game stops while everyone gathers around to help the girl who is crying. This difference between boys and girls at play epitomizes what Harvard's Carol Gilligan points to as a key disparity between the sexes: boys take pride in a lone, tough-minded independence and autonomy, while girls see themselves as part of a web of connectedness. Thus boys are threatened by anything that might challenge their independence, while girls are

more threatened by a rupture in their relationships. And, as Deborah Tannen has pointed out in her book *You Just Don't Understand*, these differing perspectives mean that men and women want and expect very different things out of a conversation, with men content to talk about "things," while women seek emotional connection.

Sally and Richard Greenhill/Alamy

Hera foto/Alamy

In short, these contrasts in schooling in the emotions foster very different   7
skills, with girls becoming "adept at reading both verbal and nonverbal emotional
signals, at expressing and communicating their feelings," and boys becoming
adept at "minimizing emotions having to do with vulnerability, guilt, fear, and
hurt" (Brody and Hall 454). Evidence for these different stances is very strong in the
scientific literature. Hundreds of studies have found, for example, that on average
women are more empathic than men, at least as measured by the ability to read
someone else's unstated feelings from facial expression, tone of voice, and other
nonverbal cues. Likewise, it is generally easier to read feelings from a woman's
face than a man's; while there is no difference in facial expressiveness among very
young boys and girls, as they go through the elementary-school grades boys
become less expressive, girls more so. This may partly reflect another key difference: women, on average, experience the entire range of emotions with greater
intensity and more volatility than men—in this sense, women are more "emotional" than men (Brody and Hall).

All of this means that, in general, women come into a marriage groomed   8
for the role of emotional manager, while men arrive with much less appreciation of the importance of this task for helping a relationship survive. Indeed,
the most important element for women—but not for men—in satisfaction
with their relationship reported in a study of 264 couples was the sense that
the couple has "good communication" (Davis and Oathout). Ted Huston, a psychologist at the University of Texas who has studied couples in depth, observes,
"For the wives, intimacy means talking things over, especially talking about the
relationship itself. The men, by and large, don't understand what the wives
want from them. They say, 'I want to do things with her, and all she wants to do
is talk.'" During courtship, Huston found, men were much more willing to spend
time talking in ways that suited the wish for intimacy of their wives-to-be. But
once married, as time went on the men—especially in more traditional couples—spent less and less time talking in this way with their wives, finding a
sense of closeness simply in doing things like gardening together rather than
talking things over.

This growing silence on the part of husbands may be partly due to the fact   9
that, if anything, men are a bit Pollyannaish about the state of their marriage,
while their wives are attuned to the trouble spots: in one study of marriages, men
had a rosier view than their wives of just about everything in their relationship—lovemaking, finances, ties with in-laws, how well they listened to each
other, how much their flaws mattered (Sternberg). Wives, in general, are more
vocal about their complaints than are their husbands, particularly among
unhappy couples. Combine men's rosy view of marriage with their aversion to
emotional confrontations, and it is clear why wives so often complain that their
husbands try to wiggle out of discussing the troubling things about their relationship. (Of course this gender difference is a generalization and is not true in every
case; a psychiatrist friend complained that in his marriage his wife is reluctant to
discuss emotional matters between them and he is the one who is left to bring
them up.)

The slowness of men to bring up problems in a relationship is no doubt   10
compounded by their relative lack of skill when it comes to reading facial
expressions of emotions. Women, for example, are more sensitive to a sad
expression on a man's face than are men in detecting sadness from a woman's
expression.[1] Thus a woman has to be all the sadder for a man to notice her
feelings in the first place, let alone for him to raise the question of what is
making her so sad.

Consider the implications of this emotional gender gap for how couples   11
handle the grievances and disagreements that any intimate relationship inevitably
spawns. In fact, specific issues such as how often a couple has sex, how to discipline the children, or how much debt and savings a couple feels comfortable with
are not what make or break a marriage. Rather, it is how a couple discusses such
sore points that matters more for the fate of their marriage. Simply having reached
an agreement about how to disagree is key to marital survival; men and women
have to overcome the innate gender differences in approaching rocky emotions.
Failing this, couples are vulnerable to emotional rifts that eventually can tear their
relationship apart. . . . [T]hese rifts are far more likely to develop if one or both
partners have certain deficits in emotional intelligence.

Note

1. The research is by Dr. Ruben C. Gur at the University of Pennsylvania School of Medicine.

Works Cited

Brody, Leslie R., and Judith A. Hall. "Gender and Emotion." *Handbook of Emotions,* edited by
    Michael Lewis and Jeannette Haviland, Guilford Press, 1993.
Cairns, Robert B., and Beverley D. Cairns. *Lifelines and Risks.* Cambridge UP, 1994.
Davis, Mark H., and H. Alan Oathout. "Maintenance of Satisfaction in Romantic Relationships:
    Empathy and Relational Competence." *Journal of Personality and Social Psychology,* vol. 53,
    no. 2 (1987), pp. 397–410.
Gottman, John. "Same- and Cross-Sex Friendship in Young Children." *Conversation of Friends,*
    edited by J. Gottman and J. Parker, Cambridge UP, 1986.
Maccoby, Eleanor, and C. N. Jacklin. "Gender Segregation in Childhood." *Advances in Child
    Development and Behavior,* edited by H. Reese, Academic Press, 1987.
Sternberg, Robert J. "Triangulating Love." *The Psychology of Love,* edited by Robert Sternberg and
    Michael Barnes, Yale UP, 1988.

Understanding the Reading

1. **Summarizing** In one or two sentences, explain the differences that Goleman
   claims exist between men's and women's ways of expressing emotion.
2. **Causes** According to Goleman, what are the root causes of the differences between
   how men and women express emotion?
3. **Details** How can the emotional differences between spouses cause marital difficulties, according to the writer?

4. **Differences** Explain how boys and girls play differently, according to Goleman.
5. **Vocabulary** Explain the meaning of each of the following words as it is used in the reading: *epitomizes* (para. 1), *articulating* (4), *ostracism* (5), *vendettas* (5), *disparity* (6), and *empathic* (7).

Analyzing the Writer's Technique

1. **Thesis** What is Goleman's thesis?
2. **Audience and Purpose** Identify the purpose of and intended audience for the essay.
3. **Objectivity** Do you think Goleman maintains an objective stance on the issue, despite his gender? Explain your answer.

Thinking Critically about Text and Visuals

1. **Organization** Discuss the type of organization the author used (point by point, subject by subject, or mixed). Does the organization seem to affect the author's fairness? Do you detect any bias? If so, explain.
2. **Language** How does the use of quotation marks around the word *unreasonable* (para. 1) affect its connotation?
3. **Tone** How does the real-life example in paragraph 1 affect the essay, especially its tone?
4. **Fact/Opinion** Do you consider the essay to be primarily fact, opinion, or informed opinion? Justify your answer.
5. **Visual** What key ideas from the essay do the photographs on page 406 illustrate?

Responding to the Reading

1. **Discussion** In groups of two or three, discuss Goleman's generalizations about men and women. Do any seem inaccurate and, if so, which one(s)? Discuss the evidence, if any, that would prove Goleman wrong.
2. **Journal** In your journal, describe a situation from your experience that either confirms or contradicts one of Goleman's generalizations.
3. **Essay** Make a list of the emotional differences and resulting behavioral conflicts between men and women that you have observed. Decide which differences Goleman explains. Write an essay reporting your findings.

Working Together

In small groups of three or four students, brainstorm a list of emotional differences between the sexes. Using that list as a springboard, work independently to compose a one-paragraph letter to an advice columnist describing a conflict that has arisen between a man and a woman. Trade letters with a member of your group. Then, taking on the role of the columnist, respond to your group member's letter, explaining the root of the problem—emotional differences—and offering a solution. Be creative with the name of the letter writer and the advice columnist. If your class has a blog or a discussion board, you may post these letters so that all members of the class can read them.

The Guided Writing Assignment in this chapter can walk you through the process of writing an illustration essay; for help with evaluating sources, see Chapter 21; for help choosing and synthesizing ideas from sources, see Chapter 22; for help with documenting sources, see Chapter 23.

EXPLORE, RESEARCH, WRITE

In "His Marriage and Hers," Daniel Goleman uses research to explain how "the marital endgame" reflects the emotional differences between men and women. Many researchers have also studied how and why men and women experience emotional life differently. Reports about this research include the following:

- "Are Women More Emotional Than Men?" by David Schmitt, PhD, Brunel University, London (*Psychology Today*, 10 April 2015)
- "Are Women More Emotionally Expressive Than Men?" by Cynthia May, PhD, College of Charleston (*Scientific American*, 30 August 2017)
- "Gender Differences in Intimacy, Emotional Expressivity, and Relationship Satisfaction" by Melissa Ubando, a student at Pepperdine University (*Pepperdine Journal of Communication Research*, vol. 1, article 13, 2016)

Using your own ideas and one or more of the selections listed here, write a thoughtful comparison and contrast essay that goes beyond "His Marriage and Hers: Childhood Roots." Be sure to include at least two quotes from the readings and cite them correctly at the end of the essay.

READING

On a Plate

Toby Morris

Toby Morris is an illustrator and a comic artist from Auckland, New Zealand, who created the popular comic series *The Pencilsword*. In addition, he has published a graphic memoir entitled *Don't Puke on Your Dad: A Year in the Life of a New Father* (2013). The comic strip below appeared in *The Pencilsword*. **Before reading**, preview the selection and make connections by thinking of the different ways one might define success. **While reading**, notice how the author uses both words and visuals to explore differences in the life experiences of the two characters.

JUST-IN-TIME TIP Reading Graphic Essays

Although "On a Plate" appears in a nontraditional, graphic (or comic-like) format, it addresses a serious issue and has a thesis. It uses graphics to illustrate the points of comparison and to provide supporting details. Here are a few hints for reading this kind of selection:

1. **Study the organization.** Because it is not written in traditional paragraph form, you may need to read it differently. Begin by determining how this graphic is organized. What do the double columns stand for? Whose words are conveyed in the three kinds of speech text—the text in the orange boxes, the white speech bubbles, and the white cloud (or thought) bubbles?

2. **Pay attention to dialogue.** The dialogue is important to understanding this graphic. Ask yourself, "What do the comments reveal about Richard and Paula, their families, and their contacts?" You may have to infer (reason out) this; the revelations are not directly stated.

3. **Analyze and interpret the author's commentary.** Here you will find the author's message. Determine what the author wants you to know about the situations depicted in the graphic.

Toby Morris. "On a Plate," *The Wireless*, 2015. Copyright © 2015 by Toby Morris. Used with permission.

Toby Morris. "On a Plate," *The Wireless*, 2015. Copyright © 2015 by Toby Morris. Used with permission.

Toby Morris. "On a Plate," *The Wireless*, 2015. Copyright © 2015 by Toby Morris. Used with permission.

Toby Morris. "On a Plate," *The Wireless*, 2015. Copyright © 2015 by Toby Morris. Used with permission.

Understanding the Reading

1. **Topic** What groups in society do Richard and Paula represent?
2. **Thesis** What is the thesis of "On a Plate"? Is the thesis stated or implied?
3. **Details** Contrast Paula's living conditions with Richard's (frames 3–4).
4. **Differences** Compare Richard and Paula's approach to homework (frames 5–6, 11–12).

Analyzing the Writer's Technique

1. **Points of Comparison** Identify the points of comparison on which the visual story is based.
2. **Title** What is the meaning of the title?
3. **Organization** Evaluate the effectiveness of the point-by-point organization in the essay. How would the essay differ if it had been written using a subject-by-subject organization?
4. **Conclusion** Evaluate the story's conclusion. How does it reflect the thesis and organization of the visual story?

Thinking Critically about Text and Visuals

1. **Assumptions** What assumptions does the author make?
2. **Visual Details** What differences do you notice in the way that the author depicts the two fathers? What details in frame 11 of Richard's dorm room catch your eye?
3. **Graphics** What information and feelings are presented visually that would be difficult to express if only words were used?
4. **Bias** Do you think Toby Morris appears to favor one side of the comparison? What details make you think so?

Responding to the Reading

1. **Discussion** In small groups, discuss which values each member of the group holds dear. Be prepared to share your lists with the class and to defend your positions.
2. **Journal** Translate one pair of frames from "On a Plate" into writing. Try to convey all the details included in the frames, as well as the implied meaning of the frames. Then compare your "translation" with the frames themselves. What advantages and disadvantages does each method of communication have?
3. **Essay** Choose one life stage (infancy, childhood, teen years, young adulthood, old age) and write an essay exploring fully the advantages and disadvantages of the privileged and underprivileged in that life stage.

Working Together

In small groups, brainstorm an alternate ending to the story. Then add a final frame for both Richard and Paula. Sketch out the frames and include a caption for each. Be prepared to share your sketches and captions with the class.

The Guided Writing Assignment in this chapter can walk
you through the process of
writing an illustration essay; for
help with evaluating sources,
see Chapter 21; for help
choosing and synthesizing
ideas from sources, see Chapter 22; for help with documenting sources, see Chapter 23.

> **EXPLORE, RESEARCH, WRITE**
>
> In "On a Plate," Toby Morris examines the topic of income inequality. Other
> researchers have also studied income inequality, and some research reports are
> listed below. The first two articles favor reducing or overcoming income inequality,
> and the third supports an opposing view.
>
> - "What America Can Do to Stop Income Inequality" by Robert Reich, PhD
>   and former labor secretary under President Bill Clinton (*The Christian
>   Science Monitor*, 13 May 2014)
> - "How to Solve Income Inequity" by John Divine, senior investing reporter
>   for *US News and World Report* (*US News and World Report*, 14 February
>   2017, https://money.usnews.com/investing/articles/2017-02-14/
>   how-to-solve-income-inequality)
> - "Stop Caring about Income Inequity" by Louis Sarkozy, student of religion
>   and philosophy at New York University, contributor to the "Beltway
>   Confidential" blog, and son of former French President Nikolas Sarkozy
>   (*Washington Examiner*, 6 June 2018)
>
> Using your own ideas and one or more of the selections listed here, write an essay in
> which you compare two viewpoints on overcoming income inequality. Be sure to
> include at least one quote per viewpoint from the readings and cite them correctly
> at the end of the essay.

Apply Your Skills: Additional Essay Assignments

For more on locating and documenting sources, see Part 5.

Using what you have learned in this chapter, write a comparison or contrast essay on one
of the topics below. Depending on the topic you choose, you may need to conduct research.

To Express Your Ideas

1. Compare two families that you know or are part of. Include points of comparison
   that reveal what is valuable and important in family life.
2. Compare your lifestyle today with the lifestyle you intend to follow after you graduate from college.

To Inform Your Reader

3. Write an essay comparing your life or life in your community before and after a
   major event. The event may be positive (such as a graduation or a new software company moving to town) or negative (such as an act of terrorism or a pandemic). Be sure
   to identify a basis of comparison and specific, consistent points of comparison

(interpersonal relationships or access to medical care, for example). You may use current online sources to document the changes you observed.

4. Compare two types of social media, such as Snapchat and Instagram or Pinterest.

To Persuade Your Reader

5. Choose a technological change that has occurred in recent years, and argue either that it is beneficial or that its drawbacks outweigh its usefulness.

6. Compare two views on a controversial issue, arguing in favor of one of them.

Cases Using Comparison and Contrast

7. Imagine that you are taking a course in photography. Write a paper comparing and contrasting the advantages of black-and-white versus color images. Your instructor is your audience.

8. Imagine that you are working in the advertising department of a company that manufactures skateboards. Write a memo evaluating two periodicals and recommending which one the company should use to run its advertisements. Your manager is your audience.

Working Together

Form a small group of three or four students. Choose two restaurants that are familiar to all of you, and brainstorm a list of similarities and differences in the two restaurants. Then decide which restaurant you will recommend. Using this information, write a creative and entertaining thirty-second radio advertisement that will persuade listeners to choose Restaurant A over Restaurant B. Choose a member of your group to present the ad to the class.

SYNTHESIZING IDEAS   **ATTITUDES TOWARD CLASS**

Both "Underground Lair: Inside a Chicken Processing Plant" (pp. 297–301) and "On a Plate" (pp. 411–14) explore attitudes toward class.

Analyzing the Readings

1. What attitudes toward class do the readings present?

2. Watch a television program, and then write a journal entry analyzing the attitudes toward class that the characters exhibit. How closely do the characters' attitudes match the attitudes presented in either reading?

Essay Idea

Write an essay explaining your attitude toward class and comparing or contrasting it to the attitude presented in either of the readings.

16

Classification and Division

Explaining Categories and Parts

Images Etc Ltd./Alamy

In this chapter you will learn to

- understand the purpose and function of classification and division essays

- use graphic organizers to visualize classification and division essays

- integrate division and classification into an essay

- read and think critically about division and classification

- plan, organize, draft, revise, and edit essays using division and classification

Writing Quick Start

ANALYZE   The photograph on this page shows fruits and vegetables on display at a farmers' market. Notice that they are arranged by produce type. Can you imagine how difficult it would be to find what you need if all produce were randomly piled onto a table or shelf, with broccoli, pears, peppers, and bananas all mixed together? Most stores and markets group their products for the convenience of their customers.

WRITE   Take a few minutes to brainstorm other ways a favorite store or Web site could group its products for customer convenience. You may propose a serious method or a humorous one. Then draft a paragraph describing your system. List the characteristics of each product group, describe the products that belong in each group, and give each group a title.

CONNECT   To draft your paragraph, you chose a particular store or Web site and then decided upon categories or groups by which to organize the products, describing each group. Your paragraph is a good example of **classification**, a method of organization that sorts or groups people, things, or ideas into categories to make them more understandable. In this chapter, you will also learn about **division**, which breaks an item down into its component parts. Both of these methods of organization will be useful as you write effective paragraphs and essays.

Classification is used in daily life as well as in writing. Your dresser drawers are probably organized by categories, with socks and sweaters in different drawers. Supermarkets, shopping Web sites, libraries, and even restaurant menus arrange items into groups according to similar characteristics. The same holds true for division. The humanities department at your college, for example, may be divided into English, modern languages, and philosophy; and modern languages might be divided into Spanish, French, Italian, Chinese, and Russian.

USING CLASSIFICATION AND DIVISION ▷ IN COLLEGE AND THE WORKPLACE

- In a *human physiology course*, you study the structure and parts of the human ear by identifying the function of each part.

- In preparing a *business management report*, you consider how debt liability differs for three types of businesses: a sole proprietorship, a partnership, and a corporation.

- While working as a *facilities planner*, your supervisor asks you to conduct a feasibility study of several new sites. You begin by sorting the sites into three categories: in-state, out-of-state, and international.

What Are the Characteristics of Classification and Division Essays?

A successful classification or division essay uses one principle of classification or division to create meaningful categories or parts that are broad enough to include all of the members of the group.

Classification Groups and Division Divides Ideas According to One Principle

Developing an effective set of categories or parts requires you to do two things:

- Choose **one principle of classification or division** and use it. An essay classifying fish could choose size or diet as a classification principle, not both. An essay about an aquarium could divide the topic according to either the type of fish displayed or the quality of the exhibits.
- Identify **a manageable number of categories or parts**. An essay classifying birds according to diet, for example, might use five or six types of diet, not twenty.

EXERCISE 16.1 ▷ IDENTIFYING PRINCIPLES OF CLASSIFICATION OR DIVISION

Brainstorm three different principles of classification or division for each of the following topics:

1. Sports teams
2. Fast-food restaurants
3. Television shows

4. Academic subjects
5. Novels

Purpose and Audience Drive the Writer's Choice of a Principle

Several different principles can be used to categorize groups or divide an item into parts, so writers should choose a principle of classification or division that is appropriate to their purpose and audience. For instance, to inform parents about the types of day-care facilities on or near campus, you might classify day-care centers according to the services they offer because your readers would likely be looking for that information. If you were writing to persuade readers to take their children to a new museum, you might divide the exhibits according to their suitability for children of different ages.

Categories and Parts Are Exclusive and Comprehensive

Choose categories (for classification) or parts (for division) that do not overlap. In other words, each item that you discuss should fit in no more than one category. A familiar example is age: The categories 25 to 30 and 30 to 35 are not mutually exclusive because someone who is 30 years old would fit into both. In an essay about the nutritional value of pizza, you could divide your topic into the nutritional attributes of carbohydrates, proteins, and fats, but you should not add a separate category for saturated fat because it is already contained in the fats category.

The categories or parts you choose should also be comprehensive. In a division essay, all the major parts of an item should be included. In a classification essay, each member of the group should fit into one category or another. For example, an essay categorizing fast-food restaurants according to the type of food they serve would have to include categories for pizza, hamburgers, hot dogs, tacos, and fried chicken.

EXERCISE 16.2   **CLASSIFYING AND DIVIDING BY CATEGORY**

Choose a principle of classification or division for two of the topics listed in Exercise 16.1. Then make a list of categories in which each item could be included or parts into which each item could be divided.

Classification or Division Fully Explains Each Category or Part

A classification or division essay should contain enough detail for readers to understand each category or part easily. Use facts, descriptions, quotations, comparisons, or examples to help readers "see" your categories or parts.

Classification or Division Includes a Thesis

The thesis statement of a classification or division essay should identify the topic. It may also reveal the principle used to classify or divide the topic. In most cases it also should suggest why the classification or division is relevant or important.

Here are two examples of effective thesis statements:

Most people consider videos a form of entertainment; however, videos can also serve educational, commercial, and political functions.

Importance (implied)
Topic
Principle
Categories

The Grand Canyon is divided into two distinct geographical areas—the North Rim and the South Rim—each offering different views, activities, and climatic conditions.

The following readings demonstrate the techniques for writing effective classification or division essays discussed above. The first reading is annotated to point out how Johanna Blakley classifies TV shows in terms of their appeal to liberals, conservatives, and those in the middle. As you read the second essay, try to identify for yourself how Michael Moss uses the techniques of division to show what makes potato chips nearly irresistible.

CLASSIFICATION READING

Reds, Blues, and Purples: Which Five TV Shows Bring Them All Together?

Title: Indicates categories and principle

Johanna Blakley

Johanna Blakley is the director of research and managing director of the Norman Lear Center, a nonpartisan research center based in Los Angeles and housed within the Annenberg School for Journalism and Communication at the University of Southern California. Blakley conducts research on a wide range of topics, including global entertainment and entertainment education. She is an expert in the media habits of liberals and conservatives. This selection was published by *The Conversation* (2019), a Web site that gives academics and researchers from a wide array of disciplines a platform for sharing their knowledge with a wider public.

Before Reading

1. **Preview:** Use the steps listed in Chapter 2.
2. **Connect:** How do the television programs you watch compare to those of your friends and relatives? What do you think influences viewing preferences?

While Reading Study the annotations and highlight the facts, descriptions, and examples that are especially effective in helping you understand how the author classifies the viewers by type.

1   There has been a lot of concern about how conservatives and liberals consume their news from sources that merely confirm their preexisting beliefs (Garrett). The result, supposedly, has been a disintegration of a shared reality and a fracturing of the nation's political life. But does this trend extend to the shows we choose to watch on TV to relax and unwind?

Relevance: Mentions public's concern about fracturing of nation's political life

Introduction: Identifies topic, principle of classification, and purpose (to inform readers about research results)

Thesis

Since 2007, the Norman Lear Center at the University of Southern California has been tracking how Americans' favorite TV shows are connected to their attitudes on a host of hot-button political issues (Baker and Blakley). In each of these studies—including our most recent one (Blakley et al.)—we found that people with different political beliefs seem to be drawn to different types of TV entertainment, but in the most recent study, there was also a distinct overlap: certain shows that appealed to everyone across the political spectrum. These programs, we found, tend to have a quality that, at the very least, hints at some shared values in a polarizing age.

2

Organization: Names categories

Preferences of "Blues," "Purples" and "Reds"

For the study, we surveyed more than 3,000 people using a national sample designed to represent the U.S. population. Respondents were asked about their entertainment preferences, viewing behaviors and their feelings about specific television shows. They were also asked about their happiness, political beliefs, voting history and personal traits. Using a statistical clustering analysis, we identified three ideological groups in the United States that share common attitudes and values, regardless of voting history or political party preferences:

3

Organization: Categories delineated in numbered list

Support: Uses description, implied contrast ("most women . . . largest number of African Americans"), and statistics to delineate **Category 1**

1. **Blues**, who have liberal attitudes toward abortion, the environment, guns, marriage and immigration, make up 47% of the population. This group has the most women and the largest number of African Americans. They are also the least satisfied with their lives.

Support: Uses description, implied contrast ("largest share of Asians and Hispanic . . . most religious and satisfied") and statistics to delineate **Category 2**

2. **Purples**, a swing group comprising 18% of the population, hold positions across the political spectrum. This group has the largest share of Asians and Hispanics, and those in it are the most religious and the most satisfied with their lives.

Support: Uses description, implied contrast ("highest proportion of senior citizens") and statistics to delineate **Category 3**

3. **Reds** make up 35% of the country and hold conservative views on most issues. They are sympathetic toward the police and skeptical about affirmative action, immigrants and Islam. Reds have the highest proportion of senior citizens.

Each group demonstrated its own particular taste in media and entertainment.

Support: Uses examples of **Blues'** viewing habits to categorize

Blues like many more TV shows than Reds and are open to viewing foreign films and TV series, as well as content that does not reflect their values. Many Blues enjoy watching "Modern Family," "The Big Bang Theory," "The Simpsons," "South Park" and "Law & Order: SVU."

4

Support: Uses examples of **Purples'** viewing habits to categorize, including overlap of preferred shows with Blues and Reds

Purples are the most voracious TV viewers and enjoy more about the viewing experience than other groups. They appreciate the educational value of TV programming and are the most likely to say they take action based on what they learn about politics and social issues from fictional movies and TV shows. Their favorite shows include "The Voice" and "Dancing with the Stars," but they also like "Saturday Night Live"—a favorite among Blues as well—and "Duck Dynasty," which is preferred by Reds.

5

Support: Uses examples of **Reds'** viewing habits to categorize

Reds say they seldom watch entertainment TV, but when they do, many claim they watch for an adrenaline boost. They prefer the Hallmark, History and Ion channels far more than others, while their favorite show is "NCIS."

6

Support: Names shows that demonstrate overlap among groups

The Shows That Bring Everyone Together

And yet there was some significant overlap. Five shows that all three ideological groups watched include "America's Funniest Home Videos," "Bones," "Criminal

7

Minds," "MythBusters" and "Pawn Stars." Four of these shows were well-liked, but "Pawn Stars" was actually one of the least-liked shows in our sample of 50. (We concluded that "Pawn Stars" had the dubious distinction of being the most hate-watched show in America.)

But what about those four shows that everyone seems to like? What common elements might they share? My suspicion, one that we will explore in the next iteration of this study, is that all four of these shows—and even "Pawn Stars," to an extent—value truth. "Bones" and "Criminal Minds" are classic police procedurals: whodunits that follow a string of clues to arrive at a fact-based conclusion. "MythBusters" is entirely about the delights of scientific skepticism and the quest for truth. And I would argue that the clips seen on "America's Funniest Home Videos" remain appealing after all these years precisely because they are so raw and unscripted; we all delight in real human foibles, the stuff that we think we could not make up if we tried. Even in "Pawn Stars," customers discover the true market value of their treasured items.

In a cultural moment defined by moral panic around fake news and alternative facts (Carlson), perhaps it should not come as a surprise that the neutral ground Americans of all political stripes have chosen is storytelling devoted to finding the bad guy, debunking the myth and exposing how silly humans can really be.

8   **Support:** Analyzes common favorites to identify shared value: the appeal of truth

9   **Conclusion:** Reinforces thesis and offers a light-hearted perspective on TV shows all Americans enjoy

Links

Baker, Tessa, and Johanna Blakley. "You Are What You Watch (and Listen To, and Read): How Americans' Entertainment Habits Track Their Political Values." *The Norman Lear Center* and *Zogby International*, April 2008.

Blakley, Johanna, et al. "Are You What You Watch? Tracking the Political Divide through TV Preferences." *Media Impact Project, USC Lear Center*, May 2019, learcenter.org/wp-content/uploads/2019/05/are_you_what_you_watch.pdf.

Carlson, Matt. "Fake News as an Informational Moral Panic: The Symbolic Deviancy of Social Media during the 2016 U.S. Presidential Election." *Information, Communication, and Society*, vol. 21, no. 1 (2018), doi: 10.1080/1369118X.2018.1505934.

Garrett, R. Kelly. "Facebook's Problem Is More Complicated Than Fake News." *The Conversation*, 16 Nov. 2016, theconversation.com/facebooks-problem-is-more-complicated-than-fake-news-68886.

Visualize a Classification or Division Essay: Create a Graphic Organizer

Graphic Organizer 16.1 outlines the basic organization of a classification or division essay:

For more on creating a graphic organizer, see Chapter 2.

- The **introduction** announces the topic, gives background information, and states the thesis.
- The **body paragraphs** explain the categories or parts and their characteristics.
- The **conclusion** brings the essay to a satisfying close by reinforcing the thesis and offering a new insight on the topic.

GRAPHIC ORGANIZER 16.1 The Basic Structure of a Classification or Division Essay

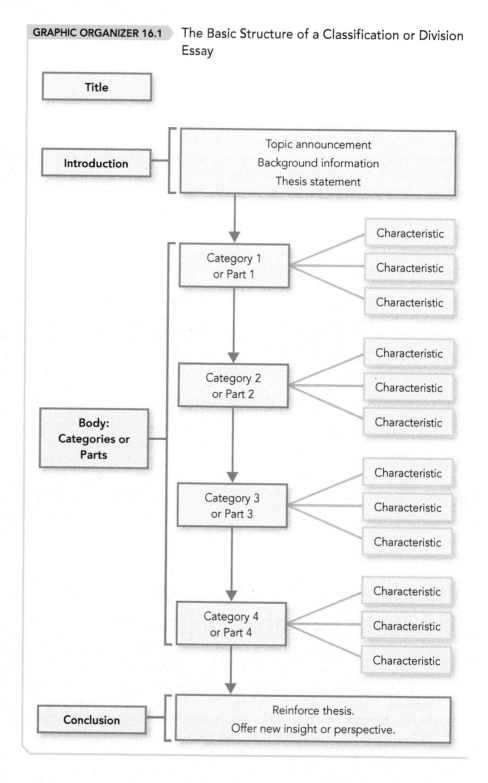

The Language of Junk Food Addiction: How to "Read" a Potato Chip

Michael Moss

Michael Moss is a Pulitzer Prize–winning investigative reporter for the *New York Times*, where he has worked since 2000. Before coming to the *Times*, he reported for publications including the *Daily Sentinel* (in Grand Junction, Colorado), the *Atlanta Journal-Constitution*, *New York Newsday*, and the *Wall Street Journal*. He has also published two books, *Palace Coup: The Inside Story of Harry and Leona Helmsley* (1989) and *Salt Sugar Fat: How the Food Giants Hooked Us* (2013). The interview from which this selection was taken was based on Moss's work for *Salt Sugar Fat*. **Before reading**, preview the selection and make connections by thinking about what you already know about junk food addiction. **While reading**, notice the parts the author divides the topic into and what his principle of division is. Then compare your notes with Graphic Organizer 16.2.

Betcha can't eat just one.   1

These five words captured the essence of the potato chip far better than   2
anyone at Frito-Lay could have imagined. In the '60s, the sentiment might have
seemed cute and innocent—it's hard not to pig out on potato chips, they're tasty,
they're fun. But today the familiar phrase has a sinister connotation because of our
growing vulnerability to convenience foods and our growing dependence on them.

As I researched *Salt, Sugar, Fat*, I was surprised to learn about the meticulously   3
crafted allure of potato chips (which I happen to love). When you start to
deconstruct the layers of the chip's appeal, you start to see why this simple little
snack has the power to make a profound claim on our attention and appetite.
"Betcha can't eat just one" starts sounding less like a lighthearted dare—and more
like a kind of promise. The food industry really is betting on its ability to override
the natural checks that keep us from overeating.

Here's how it works.   4

It starts with salt, which sits right on the outside of the chip. Salt is the first   5
thing that hits your saliva, and it's the first factor that drives you to eat and perhaps overeat. Your saliva carries the salty taste through the neurological channel
to the pleasure center of the brain, where it sends signals back: "Hey, this is really
great stuff. Keep eating."

The industry calls this salty allure a food's "flavor burst," and I was surprised   6
to learn just how many variations on this effect there are. The industry creates different varieties of salt for different kinds of processed foods: everything from fine
powders that blend easily into canned soups, to big chunky pyramid-shaped gran-
ules with flat sides that stick better to food (hollowed out on the inside for maximum contact with the saliva).

Then, of course, there's fat. Potato chips are soaked in fat. And fat is   7
fascinating because it's not one of the five basic tastes that Aristotle identified way
back when—it's a *feeling*. Fat is the warm, gooey sensation you get when you bite
into a toasty cheese sandwich—or you get just *thinking* about such a sandwich (if

you love cheese as much as I do). There's a nerve ending that comes down from the brain almost to the roof of the mouth that picks up the feel of fat, and the industry thus calls the allure of fat "mouthfeel."

The presence of fat, too, gets picked up by nerve endings and races along the neurological channel to the pleasure center of the brain. Which lights up, as strongly as it lights up for sugar. There are different kinds of fats—some good—but it's the saturated fats, which are common in processed foods, that are of most concern to doctors. They're linked to heart disease if over-consumed. And since fats have twice as many calories as sugar, they can be problematic from an obesity standpoint.   8

But potato chips actually have the entire holy trinity: They're also loaded with sugar. Not added sugar—although some varieties do—but the sugar in most chips is in the potato starch itself, which gets converted to sugar in the moment the chip hits the tongue. Unlike fat, which studies show can exist in unlimited quantities in food without repulsing us, we do back off when a food is too sweet. The challenge is to achieve just the right depth of sweetness without crossing over into the extreme. The industry term for this optimal amount of sugar is called the "bliss point."   9

So you've got all three of the big elements in this one product. But salt, sugar, and fat are just the beginning of the potato chip's allure. British researchers, for instance, have found that the more noise a chip makes when you eat it, the better you'll like it and the more apt you are to eat more. So chip companies spend a lot of effort creating a perfectly noisy, crunchy chip.   10

The chip has an amazing textural allure, too, a kind of meltiness on the tongue. The ultraprocessed food product most admired by food company scientists in this regard is the Cheeto, which rapidly dissolves in your mouth. When that happens, it creates a phenomenon that food scientists call "vanishing caloric density." Which refers to the phenomenon that as the Cheeto melts, your brain interprets that melting to mean that the calories in the Cheeto have disappeared as well. So they tend to uncouple your brain from the breaks that keep your body from overeating. And the message coming back from the brain is: "Hey, you might as well be eating celery for all I care about all the calories in those disappearing Cheetos. Go for it."   11

Then there's the whole act of handling the chip—the fact that we move it with our hand directly to the mouth. When you move a food directly to your mouth with your hand there are fewer barriers to overeating. You don't need to wait until you have a fork, or a spoon, or a plate to eat. You can eat with one hand while doing something else. These handheld products lead to what nutrition scientists call "mindless eating"—where we're not really paying attention to what we're putting in our mouths. This has been shown to be hugely conducive to over-eating. One recent example is the Go-Gurt yogurt that comes in a collapsible tube. Once you open it, you can just squeeze out the yogurt with one hand while you're playing a computer game with the other.   12

The bottom line, which everyone in the food industry will tell you, is taste. They're convinced that a good number of us will talk a good game on nutrition and health, but when we walk through the grocery store, we'll look for and buy the products that taste the best. And that's the cynical view: They will do nothing to improve the health profile of their products that will jeopardize taste. They're as hooked on profits as they are on salt, sugar, fat.   13

GRAPHIC ORGANIZER 16.2 The Structure of "The Language of Junk Food Addiction"

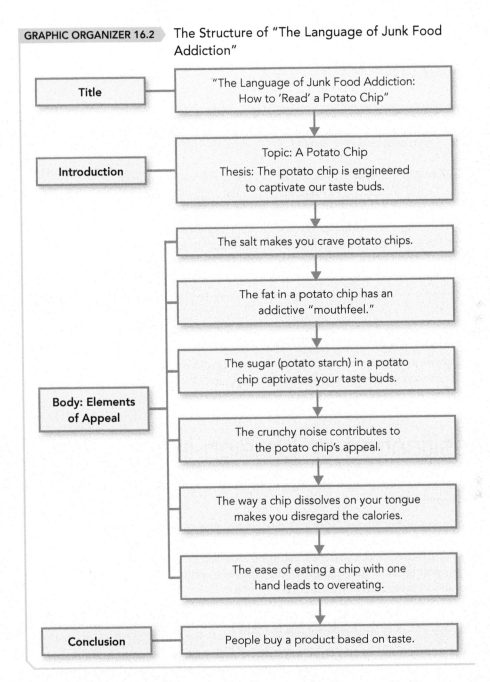

Title — "The Language of Junk Food Addiction: How to 'Read' a Potato Chip"

Introduction — Topic: A Potato Chip
Thesis: The potato chip is engineered to captivate our taste buds.

Body: Elements of Appeal —
The salt makes you crave potato chips.

The fat in a potato chip has an addictive "mouthfeel."

The sugar (potato starch) in a potato chip captivates your taste buds.

The crunchy noise contributes to the potato chip's appeal.

The way a chip dissolves on your tongue makes you disregard the calories.

The ease of eating a chip with one hand leads to overeating.

Conclusion — People buy a product based on taste.

EXERCISE 16.3   **DRAWING A GRAPHIC ORGANIZER**

Using Graphic Organizer 16.1 as a basis, draw a graphic organizer for "Reds, Blues, and Purples: Which Five TV Shows Bring Them All Together?"

THE READING PROCESS	STRATEGIES
BEFORE READING	**Preview** the essay to get an overview of its content and organization. **Make connections** by thinking about the categories or parts into which the topic could be grouped or divided.
AFTER READING	**Analyze and evaluate** the reading by answering the following questions: • What is the **principle of classification or division**? Is it appropriate given the writer's **purpose**? Does it reflect the writer's **biases**? How? • Does the classification or division omit any **significant categories or parts**? • Has the writer provided **sufficient detail** about each category? • How is the essay **relevant** to your own experience? Would you have divided or classified the subject differently?

EXERCISE 16.4 ▶ READING CRITICALLY

Apply the questions in the "How Writers Read" box to the selection "The Language of Junk Food Addiction: How to 'Read' a Potato Chip."

Integrate Classification or Division into an Essay

Classification and division are often used along with one or more other patterns of development.

- An essay that argues for stricter gun control may categorize guns in terms of their firepower, purpose, or availability.
- A narrative about a writer's frustrating experiences in a crowded international airport terminal may categorize the types of travel frustration or divide the airport into zones of frustration.

When incorporating classification or division into an essay based on another pattern of development, keep the following tips in mind:

1. **Avoid focusing on why the classification or division is meaningful.** When used as a secondary pattern, the significance of the classification or division should be clear from the context in which it is presented.
2. **State the principle of classification briefly and clearly.**
3. **Name the categories or parts.** In the sentence that introduces the classification or division, name the categories or parts to focus your readers' attention on the explanation that follows.

PREWRITING   DRAFTING   REVISING   EDITING & PROOFREADING

A Guided Writing Assignment*

CLASSIFICATION AND DIVISION

Your Essay Assignment

Write a classification or division essay on a topic that you believe would interest other students at your college or readers who share an interest or experience of yours. The following are some options for general topics:

Classification
- types of pets
- types of sports fans
- types of movies

Division
- your family
- a sports team or extracurricular club
- a public place (building, stadium, park)

1 Select a topic, devise a principle of classification or division, and list the categories of which it is made up or the parts into which it breaks down.

Choose a topic idea, and then try one of the following suggestions to generate ideas for categories or parts:

- **Start from the categories or parts:** Brainstorm, freewrite, or use another idea-generating strategy to generate details describing your topic. Then categorize the details into logical groups. Look for three or four groups or parts that share a common thread.

- **Start from a principle of classification or division:** Think about a trait or principle (like degrees of enthusiasm for sports fans or types of horror films) and then freewrite, brainstorm with a friend or classmate, or use another strategy to come up with the specific types or parts.

In small groups, **test your categories (classification)** or **parts (division)** to make sure that:

1. **all members** of a category **fit** *or* **no essential parts** have been **omitted**

2. **all categories are exclusive** (each group member fits in one category only) or **no parts overlap**

3. categories or parts will **engage your readers**

4. **names** of categories or parts describe them **accurately**, emphasizing their **distinguishing features**

*The writing process is *recursive*; that is, you may find yourself revising as you draft or prewriting as you revise. This is especially true when writing on a computer. Your writing process may also differ from project to project and from that of your classmates.

PREWRITING

2 Consider your purpose, audience, and point of view.

Ask yourself these questions:

- What is my **purpose**, and who is my **audience**? How do they affect my **topic**, my **principle of classification** or **division**, and my **categories** or **parts**?

    Example: To *inform* novice Snapchat users about the software, your parts and details must be straightforward and nontechnical.

- How might **additional patterns of development** help readers understand and appreciate my topic?

    Example: A classification essay might also compare and contrast types of sports fans.

- What **point of view** best suits my purpose and audience? **First person** (*I*, *we*) or **second person** (*you*) may be appropriate in **informal writing** if your audience has **personal knowledge** of or **experience** with the topic. **Third person** (*he, she, it, they*) is appropriate in more **formal writing** or for topics **less familiar** to your audience.

3 Generate supporting details.

Try one of the following suggestions for generating supporting details that will engage your readers and reinforce your purpose:

1. Alone or in pairs, visit a place where you can **observe your topic or the people associated with it**. For example, to generate details about pets, visit a pet store or an animal shelter. Make notes on what you see and hear. Record conversations, physical characteristics, behaviors, and so forth.

2. **Conduct research** to discover facts, examples, and other details about your topic.

3. **Use the patterns of development** to generate details. Ask yourself how the categories or parts are **similar or different (comparison and contrast)**, what **examples** you can use to illustrate the categories or parts **(illustration)**, what **stories or anecdotes** would help you distinguish categories or parts **(narration)**, or how you would **describe parts or group members** using **language that appeals to the senses (description)**.

4 Draft your thesis statement.

Your thesis statement should **identify your topic** and **reveal your principle of division or classification**. It should also suggest why your classification or division is **useful or important**. Notice how the following weak thesis is strengthened by showing both what the categories are and why they are important:

Weak
There are four types of insurance that most people can purchase.

Revised
Understanding the four common types of insurance will help you protect yourself, your family, and your property against disaster.

Working Together. In groups of two or three students, take turns reading your thesis aloud. As group members listen, have them:

1. list your categories/parts
2. write down why they matter

Finally, as a group, discuss how writers could make their categories or parts more distinctive and how they could show readers why these categories or parts are useful or important.

5 Choose a method of organization.

- **Least-to-most** and **most-to-least** work well in classification essays. You might arrange categories in increasing order of importance or from most to least common, difficult, or frequent.

  Example: In writing about the parts of a hospital, you might describe the most important areas first (operating rooms, emergency department) and then move to less important areas (waiting rooms, cafeterias).

- **Chronological order** works well when one category occurs or is observable before another.
- **Spatial order** works well in division essays when describing a place.

  Example: In describing the parts of a baseball stadium, you might move from stands to playing field.

Reviewing Chapter 7 may help you understand the methods of organization.

6 Draft your classification or division essay.

Use the following guidelines to keep your essay on track:

- The **introduction** should provide any **background** readers will need, include your **thesis statement**, and suggest why the classification or division is **useful** or **important**; it might also state your **principle of classification or division**.
- The **body paragraphs** should **name** and **elaborate on** your categories or parts, **explain the traits** they share, and **provide the details** readers need to understand and accept them. Be sure you devote roughly the **same amount of detail** to each category or part. **Headings** can help identify categories or parts discussed in multiple paragraphs; a **list** can help identify a large number of categories or parts; a **diagram** or **flowchart** may help make your system of classification or division clearer to readers. Include **transitions** such as *first, next, in contrast,* and *on the one/other hand* to keep readers on track as your essay moves from one category or part to another.
- The **conclusion** should bring your essay to a satisfying close, returning to your **thesis** and elaborating on why the classification or division is **useful** and **important** or **offering a new insight** or **perspective** on the topic.

7 Evaluate your draft and revise as necessary.

Use **Figure 16.1, "Flowchart for Revising a Classification or Division Essay,"** to evaluate and revise your draft.

FIGURE 16.1 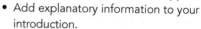 Flowchart for Revising a Classification or Division Essay

QUESTIONS   REVISION STRATEGIES

1. Highlight your thesis statement. Does it, along with the rest of your introduction, reveal your principle of classification or division and suggest why it is important?

 NO ▶

- Revise your thesis to make your justification stronger or more apparent.
- Add explanatory information to your introduction.

 YES ▼

2. *Write* the principle of classification you used at the top of your paper. Do you use this principle consistently throughout the essay? Does it fit your audience and purpose? Does it clearly relate to your thesis?

 NO ▶

- Brainstorm other possible principles of classification or division, and decide if one better fits your audience and purpose.
- Revise your categories and parts to fit either your existing principle or a new one, or rewrite your thesis to reflect your principle of classification/division.

 YES ▼

3. Underline the names of categories or parts. Do they cover all members of the group or all major parts of the topic? Are your categories or parts exclusive (not overlapping)?

 NO ▶

- Brainstorm or conduct research to add categories or parts.
- Revise your categories or parts so that each item fits into one group only.

 YES ▼

4. Place a ✔ beside the details that explain each category or part. Does your essay fully explain each one?

 NO ▶

- Brainstorm or do research to generate more details.
- Add examples, definitions, facts, and expert testimony to improve your explanations.

 YES ▼

5. *Write* the method of organization you used at the top of your essay. Is the organization clear? Does this method suit your audience and purpose? Have you followed it consistently?

 NO ▶

- Refer to Chapter 7 to discover a more appropriate organizing plan.
- Revise the order of your categories or parts.
- Add transitions to make your organization clear.

 YES ▼

QUESTIONS		REVISION STRATEGIES

6. <u>Underline</u> the topic sentence of each paragraph. Is each paragraph focused on a single category or part?

 NO ▶

- Consider splitting paragraphs that cover more than one category or part.
- Consider using headings to group paragraphs on a single category or part.

 YES ▼

7. Reread your conclusion. Does it offer a new insight or perspective on the topic or explain why your classification or division is useful or important?

 NO ▶

- Ask yourself: "So what? What is the point I'm trying to make?" Build your answers into the conclusion.

 8 Edit and proofread your essay.

Refer to Chapter 9 for help with

- **editing sentences** to avoid wordiness, make your verb choices strong and active, and make your sentences clear, varied, and parallel
- **editing words** for tone and diction, connotation, and concrete and specific language

Pay particular attention to the following:

1. Avoid **short, choppy sentences,** which can make a classification or division essay sound dull and mechanical. Try combining a series of short sentences and varying sentence patterns and lengths.

Example: Working dogs are another one of the American Kennel Club's breed categories. ~~These include German shepherds and sheepherding dogs.~~ **, such as German shepherds and sheepherding dogs,**

Example: One standard type of writing instrument, ~~is the fountain pen. It~~ is sometimes messy and inconvenient to use. **The fountain pen, one**

2. Add a comma after **opening phrases or clauses longer than four words**.

Example: When describing types of college students, be sure to consider variations in age.

Example: Although there are many types of cameras, most are easy to operate.

433

Readings: Classification and Division in Action

Science Fiction: Three Forms, Many Fans

Mya Nunnally

Mya Nunnally wrote the following essay in response to an assignment for her writing course, in which she was asked to write an essay about a genre of literature, explaining its various forms and the characteristics of each. As you read the essay, consider how effectively Nunnally explains her groupings. Does her principle of classification make sense? Does she provide enough detail to convince you that the groupings exist and that her topic is useful or important?

Title: Identifies subject

Introduction: Provides background; thesis identifies topic and principle of classification, and demonstrates the importance of the categories

Organization: Topic sentence introduces Category 1—books

Support: Examples show popularity of book form

Organization: Topic sentence identifies characteristics that drive Category 1's popularity

On a stormy night in 1816, Mary Shelley, her husband Percy Shelley, and their friend Lord Byron decided to have a contest to see who could write the best ghost story. Mary Shelley, inspired by a nightmare she had had the night before, wrote *Frankenstein*, a story in which a scientist uses electricity to bring a corpse back to life. It was at this moment that an eighteen-year-old teenager invented modern science fiction (Wolfe). Since *Frankenstein*, science fiction has exploded, becoming one of Western society's most popular art forms, available not only as books, but also as comics, graphic novels, movies, and television shows. The variety of forms in which science fiction is available contributes to its universal appeal.

1

The form that gave science fiction its start—books—began with classics such as *Frankenstein*, Aldous Huxley's *Brave New World* (1932), and Octavia Butler's *Kindred* (1979) defining the genre, and much science fiction content is still presented in book form. Series like *The Hunger Games* (2008–2010) and *Divergent* (2011–2013) have dominated the *New York Times* bestseller's list for years. Most recently, N. K. Jemisin's *Broken Earth* trilogy (2015–2017) has caught readers' imaginations, winning prestigious awards like science fiction's Hugo Award for Best Novel three years in a row.

2

Numerous features contribute to the popularity of science fiction in book form. Any science fiction novel can be checked out at a local library

3

or bought inexpensively on a used book website. Another characteristic contributing to the popularity of books is that fiction's prose allows the reader's imagination to run wild, creating a whole new world and characters in one's head. Because books do not supply visuals in the text as comics or film do, readers can create immersive worlds inside their own minds. Furthermore, because books started the science fiction genre in the early nineteenth century, there are decades of novels to choose from—hundreds and thousands of authors and series. However, books—which require a significant investment in time and imagination—can be an intimidating place to start. For this reason, novices may want to dive into science fiction in a more accessible form—film or television.

It was almost a century after *Frankenstein* before science fiction was introduced in another format—film—with *Charcuterie Mechanique* by Auguste and Louis Lumiere in 1895 and Georges Mélèis's *Le Voyage dans la Lune* (*The Trip to the Moon*) in 1902 (Fischer 9). Now, TV series like *Star Trek* and *Star Wars* are probably many people's first introduction to science fiction. Television shows like *Westworld* and *Black Mirror* cultivate faithful followings, and movies like *Men in Black* and *Pacific Rim* leave fans eager for the next installment. What makes film and television depictions of science fiction so popular? One characteristic is probably film's ability to mix language, images, and music to make a story come to life. Soundtracks can easily signal the mood or atmosphere of any scene, from screeching violins in a horror movie to a sweeping orchestra in a romantic comedy, which adds to the viewer's experience. Another aspect is science-fiction film's use of special effects, which make the imaginary seem real. George Mélèis introduced the use of stop-motion animation and double exposure in his groundbreaking film (Miller 13); his techniques may seem crude by today's standards, but they astounded viewers in 1902 (Miller 15). Today, CGI (computer-generated imagery) technology can bring any science fiction idea, from *Godzilla* to the humanistic apes in *Rise of the Planet of the Apes,* to life on screen. Film can create 3-D special effects (as in *Avatar,* 2009) that seem tangible in the world of the movie or television show, adding to the immersive aspect of this form.

Transitions: Transitions guide readers through characteristics of genre that explain popularity and connect to next form

4   **Organization:** Topic sentence introduces Category 2; transitions suggest method of organization in chronological order and introduce characteristics driving the Category 2's popularity

Movie posters for (*left*) *Le Voyage dans la Lune*, 1902, and (*right*) *Rise of the Planet of the Apes*, 2011. Both posters emphasize the films' powerful special effects that helped transport viewers to another world.

Very different is the two-dimensional visual story telling of science fiction's third form—comics. Comics use sequential art to tell a story, combining the illustrative talents of artists and the storytelling of writers to create a unique hybrid medium. Comics use many elements not found in books or films, such as panels, speech bubbles, and frames to tell a story. They come together to make an art form that allows for special storytelling capabilities. According to Scott McCloud, an inventive comic artist whose book *Understanding Comics* (1993) explains the magic of the form, says comics differ from traditional novels and films because they depend so much on the imagination of the reader to fill gaps between panels (94). Readers of comics construct a story out of the art, its sequence, and the dialogue and text found on the page. Another characteristic that sets comics apart is their unique blending of realism and the imaginary. Stories that might not have worked in any other form work in comics. Art Spiegelman's *Maus*, for example, retells the story of his father's time in the Holocaust through characters represented as

5

Illustration: Covers of two graphic works named show blending of "realism and the imaginary"

Book covers for (*left*) *Maus: A Survivor's Tale*, vol. 1, and (*right*) *Saga*, vol. 51, illustrate the species-bending possibilities that science fiction comics allow.

animals depending on their ethnicity. Science fiction comics such as Brian K. Vaughn's *Saga* and Shirow Masamune's *Ghost in the Shell*, a Japanese manga, take advantage of this form of storytelling to tell riveting tales.

Science fiction has come a long way from a teenage girl's story about a mad scientist and his creation. <u>It now comes in many forms, from classic novels to blockbuster movies to the latest illustrated comic.</u> Because it exists in so many different mediums, there are plenty of ways for everyone to experience it, no matter how big or how small one's budget and commitment to the genre. In the nineteenth century, there were only science fiction books, and people could hardly imagine the films and comics we have access to today. As technology progresses and creators develop even more ways to experience science fiction, perhaps another form will emerge—something unimaginable to everyone at the moment. What could it be?

6   **Conclusion:** Revisits background, restates <u>thesis</u>, and speculates about a future, as yet unknown, Category 4

Works Cited

Fischer, Dennis. *Science Fiction Film Directors, 1895–1998*. McFarland, 2011.

McCloud, Scott. *Understanding Comics: The Invisible Art*. Kitchen Sink Press, 1993.

Miller, Ron. *Special Effects: An Introduction to Movie Magic*. Twenty-First Century Books, 2006.

Wolfe, Gary K. "Mary Shelley and the Birth of Science Fiction." *The Great Courses Daily*, 2 Mar. 2017, www.thegreatcoursesdaily.com/mary-shelley-science-fiction.

Analyzing the Writer's Technique

1. **Summarize** According to Nunnally, why are books a popular format for science fiction?
2. **Organization** What principle of organization does Nunnally use to structure her essay? How effective is it?
3. **Introduction and Conclusion** Evaluate Nunnally's introduction and conclusion. How successful are they at engaging readers' interest? Does she convey to readers a sense of her topic's importance or a new insight or perspective? Why or why not?

Thinking Critically about Classification and Division

1. **Connotation** What is the connotation of the phrase "a sweeping orchestra" (para. 4)?
2. **Fact or Opinion** Reread the last sentence of paragraph 3. Is this fact or opinion? How can you tell?
3. **Sources** Evaluate Nunnally's use of sources. Are her sources convincing? What additional types of sources might have made her claims more convincing? Why?
4. **Tone** Consider Nunnally's tone. What kind of audience does she seem to be addressing?

Responding to the Essay

1. **Reaction** Nunnally says that "books—which require a significant investment in time and imagination—can be an intimidating place to start." Do you agree with this statement? Why or why not? In your opinion, what could make books a little less intimidating?
2. **Discussion** In the final sentence of her conclusion, Nunnally writes, "As technology progresses and creators develop even more ways to experience science fiction, perhaps another form will emerge—something unimaginable to everyone at the

moment. What could it be?" Use your imagination and discuss what form(s) might emerge.

3. **Journal** Write a journal entry describing your favorite work of science fiction and explaining why you like it.

4. **Essay** Nunnally's essay describes current forms of science fiction and the characteristics that give each form its appeal. Think of other ways you could classify or divide science fiction. For example, you might divide types of characters or themes, or you might classify the types of special effects. Once you have decided on the method and brainstormed for details, write an essay that includes the principle of classification or division, the categories or parts, the distinguishing characteristics, and examples. Use Nunnally's essay as a model for your writing.

> **READING**

Empower Pupils to Beat the Bullies

Ian Rivers

Ian Rivers is a professor of human development in the School of Sport and Education at Brunel University. This essay is based on his inaugural lecture, "A Land of Mythical Monsters and 'Wee Timorous Beasties': Reflections on Two Decades of Research on Bullying." **Before reading**, preview and make connections by thinking about situations in which you have observed or experienced bullying. What role, if any, did the bystanders play? **While reading**, notice how Rivers's classification essay also uses cause and effect to fully explain each category.

JUST-IN-TIME TIP Grouping or Dividing Ideas

"Empower Pupils to Beat the Bullies" categorizes bystanders by type, explains why they behave as they do, and reports the effects of their behavior. To help you organize all of this information, create a chart (like the one below) once you finish reading. As you read, highlight information to include in the chart.

Types of Bystander	Why They Do Not Act	Consequences of Their Behavior
The confederate		
The co-victim		
The isolate		

Expressing ideas in chart form (or by writing summary notes, if you prefer) will help you clarify relationships among ideas and help you see the "big picture." Creating the chart will also help you remember what you read. By identifying the reasons bystanders fail to act and the effects of their behavior in your own words, you are also consolidating key information.

See the Just-in-Time Guide, section 6a.

What are bystanders? Social psychology tells us that they are people who bear wit- 1
ness to an event and who, by their action or inaction, can change the outcome of
that event. Much of the research conducted on bystanders' behavior has cast them
as passive, almost anaesthetized, observers whose behavior is very much secondary to the "event" taking place. While there has been much more interest in the
role of bystanders in workplace bullying, it is only recently that school-based
research has moved away from looking at their behavior—or the lack of it—and
focused more on their own emotional well-being, in an attempt to understand why
they do not intervene.

Together with colleagues from Boston College in the United States (V. Paul 2
Poteat) and York St. John University in the United Kingdom (Nathalie Noret), I have
attempted to better understand the "mindset" of the bystander, in the hope that
it will provide me with further clues as to why bullying continues, despite forty
years of research and intervention. In essence, this research has resulted in a
recasting of the role of the bystander into three very distinct types of pupil: the
confederate, the co-victim, and the isolate. These three types are very different
from the pupil who does not engage; these are pupils who are desperate to avoid
the torment being meted out on their classmate. This is not rocket science, but
it does highlight a flaw in much of the research that has gone before: Without
taking into account the experiences of bystanders, we may have underplayed
the lasting impact that bullying can have on individuals and the school
community.

So what do we learn if we recast the bystander in these three roles? We learn 3
that the confederates of the bully may not be the mythical monsters we have
demonized, but pupils who experience a great deal of emotional turmoil, such
as feelings of self-loathing. This can lead to a series of harmful outcomes for
all involved, such as an escalation in violence perpetrated against the victim
(ironically to maintain a positive self-image), substance use, or truancy.

For the co-victim, clinical studies of community violence tell us that the 4
potential for long-term psychological harm is just as real, as if the bystander had
been the target of abuse. One systematic review of twenty-six studies of the
implications of exposure to community violence among urban adolescents
found a relationship between witnessing violence and poor mental health,
post-traumatic stress, and, surprisingly, aggression. In fact, there is increasing
anecdotal evidence to suggest that some of the most heinous acts of violence
perpetrated in schools have been carried out by young people who were themselves victims of bullying.

For the isolate—those who try to distance themselves—the story is less clear. 5
Very little is known about this group. Sometimes these pupils appear as reference
groups or control groups in studies because they report little or no involvement
in bullying. But if the fear of being humiliated or abused by others actively
encourages these pupils to hide away, this protective defense mechanism (albeit
effective in the short-term) may also have lasting detrimental effects. Isolating
oneself may reduce feelings of personal failure, but it can also result in
internalized hostility and self-loathing, which have been linked to depression
and self-harm. Furthermore, isolation itself may not be a useful long-term

strategy: It has been linked to unpopularity, especially among adolescents, and identifies isolates as potential bullying "targets" without friends to support or protect them.

So what can we do? As part of an expert panel convened in the United States, I reported on the findings from our study exploring correlations between being a bystander and contemplating suicide. One finding stood out from the others: Bystanders feel powerless. We need to empower pupils to stop bullying. But what does this mean? It means instilling in perpetrators a sense of disloyalty when they break the pupil code and victimize others. It means that every bully should know she or he has broken the code they have developed with their peers, that they have let themselves down and, more importantly, let everyone else down.   6

We do not need gimmicks, DVDs, complex strategies, or the myriad of for-profit resources that are out there. If we do need training in our schools, it is social skills training. As adults, we know how difficult it is to talk to strangers, and yet we presume that this comes naturally to children. Bullying is most prevalent in the first year of secondary school, we are told, so that may be a good place to reboot our efforts.   7

Understanding the Reading

1. **Background** According to Rivers, how has the focus of research on school bullying changed recently?
2. **Details** What actions does Rivers recommend to address the problem of school bullying?
3. **Details** Why does the author say isolation may not be a useful long-term strategy for coping with bullies?
4. **Vocabulary** Explain the meaning of each of the following words as it is used in the reading: *anaesthetized* (para. 1), *confederate* (2), *heinous* (4), *detrimental* (5), and *myriad* (7). Refer to your dictionary as needed.

Analyzing the Writer's Technique

1. **Introduction** Is it helpful or unnecessary for Rivers to give his reasons for conducting research into the mindset of bystanders?
2. **Title** What is the function of the essay's title?
3. **Audience and Purpose** What is Rivers's purpose in writing this essay? Who is his audience?
4. **Patterns** What other patterns of development does Rivers use in the essay?

Thinking Critically about the Text

1. **Connotation** What is the connotation of "bystander"?
2. **Support** What types of evidence does Rivers use to support his ideas? Does he provide sufficient detail in each category? What other kinds of details might be helpful or persuasive?

3. **Meaning** What does the author mean when he refers to confederates as "the mythical monsters we have demonized" (para. 3)?

4. **Tone** Describe the tone of the essay. What does it reveal about Rivers's attitude toward his subject?

Responding to the Reading

1. **Discussion** Have you observed students acting as bullies or as bystanders? What information in the essay reflects your own experience? What, if anything, conflicts with your experience?

2. **Journal** Write a journal entry exploring how you think schools should address bullying. Explain whether you agree with the author that the answer lies in empowering students in the way he describes.

3. **Essay** Consider what the author means by "the pupil code" (para. 6). In your opinion, what are the essential elements of a pupil code? Write an essay defining the term and dividing your code into its key components. (*Hint:* You might use the author's ideas as a starting point and include loyalty to peers and/or respect for others.)

> ### EXPLORE, RESEARCH, WRITE
>
> In "Empower Pupils to Beat the Bullies," Ian Rivers classifies bystanders by type and then uses cause-and-effect reasoning to explain how each type is affected by bullying. Many other reading selections also explore the roll of the bystander in bullying, including the following:
>
> - "Bystanders Are Essential to Bullying Prevention and Intervention," a factsheet developed by the U.S. Department of Health and Human Services
>
> - "Are Mindful Students Less Likely to Bully," by Tara Hornich-Lisciandro on the National Education Association's Web site *NEA Today*
>
> - "Bystanders Are the Key to Stopping Bullying," by Sharon Padgett and Dr. Charles E. Notar, Jacksonville State University (*Universal Journal of Educational Research*, vol. 1, no. 2 [2013], pp. 33–41)
>
> Using your own ideas and one or more of the selections included above, write a well-crafted classification essay in which you discuss at least two additional types of bystanders to bullying and their motivations. (As you will remember, Rivers identifies three types of bystanders—confederate, co-victim, and isolate—but other psychologists and mental health professionals may suggest other types and categories.) Be sure to incorporate at least one quotation from the readings and cite it correctly at the end of the essay.

The Guided Writing Assignment in this chapter can walk you through the process of writing a classification essay; for help with evaluating sources, see Chapter 21; for help choosing and synthesizing ideas from sources, see Chapter 22; for help with documenting sources, see Chapter 23.

Apply Your Skills: Additional Essay Assignments

Write a classification or division essay on one of the following topics, using what you learned about classification and division in this chapter. Depending on the topic you choose, you may need to conduct research.

For more on locating and documenting sources, see Part 5.

To Express Your Ideas

1. Explain whether you are proud of or frustrated with your ability to budget money. For example, you might classify budget categories that are easy to master versus those that cause problems.
2. Explain why you chose your career or major. Categorize the job opportunities or benefits of your chosen field, and explain why they are important to you.
3. Divide a store—such as a computer store, clothing store, or grocery store—into departments. Describe where you are most and least tempted to overspend.

To Inform Your Reader

4. Write an essay for the readers of your college newspaper classifying college instructors' teaching styles.
5. Explain the parts of a ceremony or an event you have attended or participated in.
6. Divide a familiar substance (like toothpaste) or object (like a Web page or a basketball team) into its component parts.

To Persuade Your Reader

7. Behavior in response to a natural disaster (such as a fire or flood) or health crisis (such as a measles epidemic or the Covid-19 pandemic) can vary from panic to a carefully thought out plan for action. Classify the responses to a crisis that you have seen or heard about, and then take a position as to which behaviors are helpful and productive and which are not.
8. In an essay that categorizes types of parenting skills and demonstrates how they are learned, develop the argument that effective parenting skills can be acquired through practice, training, or observation.

Cases Using Classification or Division

9. Write an essay for an introductory education class identifying a problem you have experienced or observed in the public education system. Divide public education into parts to better explain your problem.
10. You oversee the development of the annual catalog for a large community college, including the section describing the services offered to students. Decide how that section of the catalog should be organized, and then list the categories it should include. Finally, write a description of the services in one category.

SYNTHESIZING IDEAS   **FOOD**

Both "I'm Not Leaving until I Eat This Thing" (pp. 293–96) and "The Language of Junk Food Addiction: How to 'Read' a Potato Chip" (pp. 425–26) deal with food. "The Language of Junk Food Addiction" focuses on little-known facts about a well-known product—potato chips—while "I'm Not Leaving until I Eat This Thing" recounts the author's experience with a most unusual food—pickled pig lips.

Analyzing the Readings

1. What attitude did the two authors have toward the product they were describing?

2. Write a journal entry exploring the differences and/or similarities that exist between the production of the products, the elements of appeal, and the targeted market.

Essay Idea

Write an essay in which you analyze attitudes toward two or three different categories of foods—for example, organic food, gourmet food, and convenience food. You might consider value, cost, or availability.

17
Definition

Explaining What You Mean

Pawel Wewiorski/Moment Select/Getty Images

Writing Quick Start

ANALYZE Suppose your psychology instructor showed this photograph to the class and asked, "What type of human behavior is being exhibited here?" What would be your response? You might say the people in the photograph are demonstrating social distancing or cooperation, for example.

WRITE Compose a paragraph defining the motivation of the two people shown in the photograph. First choose a term that describes their motivation or behavior. Then write a brief definition of the term you chose and explain the qualities or characteristics of the motivation or behavior.

CONNECT The paragraph you have just composed is a good example of a definition paragraph.

Definition is a way of explaining the meaning of a term, often intended for those who are unfamiliar with the thing or idea being explained. In this chapter you will learn to use definition to explain. Often you will use other patterns, as well, to provide a complete explanation. For example, you might explain the term *koi* to someone unfamiliar with tropical fish by identifying their characteristics, but also describe their appearance or compare them to other types of tropical fish.

In this chapter you will learn to

- understand the purpose and function of definition essays

- use graphic organizers to visualize definition essays

- integrate definition into an essay

- read and think critically about definition

- plan, organize, draft, revise, and edit essays using definition

445

Definition is a powerful tool for writers, but it requires accuracy and precision. You must clearly distinguish the thing or idea from those that are similar, and you must provide enough characteristics so your reader fully understands the term. Definitions are useful in a variety of everyday and academic situations. For example, if you call a friend a *nonconformist*, she might ask you what you mean. In academic fields, definitions are often supplied to avoid confusion, misinterpretation, and misuse of information.

USING DEFINITION   IN COLLEGE AND THE WORKPLACE

- On an exam for a *health and fitness course*, the following short-answer question appears: "Define the term *wellness*."
- Your *psychology instructor* asks you to write a paper exploring classical conditioning. As part of the essay, you need to define the concept and provide examples from everyday life.
- As a *chemical engineer* responsible for your department's compliance with the company's standards for *safety* and *work efficiency*, you write a brief memo to your staff defining each term.

What Are the Characteristics of Extended Definitions?

If you wanted to define the term *happiness*, you would probably have trouble coming up with a brief definition because the emotion is experienced in a wide variety of situations, and the term may mean different things to different people. However, you could explore the term in an essay and explain what it means to you. Such a lengthy, detailed definition is called an **extended definition**.

Extended definitions are particularly useful in exploring a topic's various meanings and applications. Some extended definitions begin with a brief standard definition that anchors the essay's thesis statement. Other extended definitions begin by introducing a new way of thinking about the term. Whatever approach is used, the remainder of the extended definition then clarifies the term by using one or more other patterns of development.

An Extended Definition Is Focused and Detailed

An extended definition focuses on a specific term and discusses it in detail. In the first reading (pp. 450–53), for example, the author defines *freeganism*. To explain the concept, she explores the origin of the word *freegan*, describes the freegan philosophy, explains how and where freegans forage for their food, and discusses safety measures.

An Extended Definition Often Includes a Standard Definition of the Term

A **standard definition**, such as the kind found in a dictionary, consists of three parts:

- the *term* itself
- the *class* to which the term belongs
- the *characteristics or details* that distinguish the term from all others in its class

Here are two examples:

── term ──┐ ┌class┐┌──────── distinguishing characteristics ────────
A wedding band is a ring, often made of gold, that brides and grooms exchange

during a marriage ceremony.

┌─term─┐   ┌── class ──┐   ┌──── distinguishing characteristics ────
Dalmatian is a breed of dog that originated in Dalmatia; it has a short,

smooth coat with black or dark brown spots.

To write an effective standard definition, use the following guidelines:

1. **Describe the class as specifically as possible.** This will make it easier for your reader to understand the term you define. Notice, for example, that for *Dalmatian,* the class is not *animal* or *mammal* but rather a *breed of dog.*
2. **Do not use the term (or forms of the term) as part of your definition.** Do not write, "*Mastery* means that one has *mastered* a skill." In place of *mastered,* you could use *learned,* for example.
3. **Include enough distinguishing characteristics so that your readers will not mistake the term for something similar within the class.** If you define *a food processor* as "an appliance that purees food," your definition would be incomplete because a blender also purees food. A more complete definition would be "an appliance with interchangeable blades that shreds, dices, chops, or purees food."
4. **Do not limit the definition so much that it becomes inaccurate.** Defining *bacon* as "a smoked, salted meat from the side of a pig that is served at breakfast" would be too limited because bacon is also served at other meals. To make the definition accurate, you could either delete "that is served at breakfast" or add a qualifying expression like "usually" or "most often" before "served."

Look at the following definition of the term *bully,* taken from a magazine article on the topic. As you read it, study the highlighting and marginal notes.

The term *bully* does not have a standard definition, but Dan Olweus, professor of psychology at the University of Bergen, has honed the definition to three core elements—bullying involves a pattern of repeated aggressive behavior with negative intent directed from one child to another where there is a power difference. Either a larger child or several children pick on one child, or one child is clearly more dominant than the others. Bullying is not the same as

Term

Three characteristics

Distinguishes *bullying* from similar terms

garden-variety aggression; although aggression may involve similar acts, it happens between two people of equal status. By definition, the bully's target has difficulty defending him- or herself, and the bully's aggressive behavior is intended to cause distress.

— Hara Estroff Marano, "Big. Bad. Bully."

| EXERCISE 17.1 | WRITING STANDARD DEFINITIONS AND LISTING DISTINGUISHING CHARACTERISTICS |

Write a standard definition for two of the following terms, listing the distinguishing characteristics that you might use in building an extended definition:

1. hero
2. giraffe
3. science fiction
4. social media
5. friendship

An Extended Definition Makes a Point

The thesis of an extended definition essay conveys why the term is worth reading about. The following thesis statements include a brief definition and make a point about the term:

Informative thesis: Makes a point about hormones that most would find relevant

⎡— term —⎤   ⎡——— point ———⎤
Produced by the body, hormones are chemicals that are important to physical as

well as emotional development.

Persuasive thesis: Makes a judgment regarding an important issue about which readers are likely to care

⎡— term —⎤
Euthanasia, the act of ending the life of someone suffering from a terminal illness, is

——————————— point ———————————
an issue that should not be legislated; rather, it should be a matter of personal choice.

An Extended Definition Uses Other Patterns of Development

To explain the meaning of a term in an extended definition, you generally must integrate one or more other patterns of development into your essay. Suppose you want to define the term *lurking* as it is used in the context of the Internet, where it usually means reading postings or comments on an online forum without directly participating in the discussion. You could use

- **narration** (Chapter 11) to relate a story about learning something by lurking
- **description** (Chapter 12) to describe the experience of lurking
- **illustration** (Chapter 13) to give examples of typical situations involving lurking

- **process analysis** (Chapter 14) to explain how to lurk in an Internet chat room
- **comparison and contrast** (Chapter 15) to compare and contrast lurking to other forms of observation
- **classification and division** (Chapter 16) to classify the reasons people lurk—for information, entertainment, and so on
- **cause and effect** (Chapter 18) to explain the benefits or outcomes of lurking
- **argument** (Chapters 19 and 20) to argue that lurking is an ethical or unethical practice

EXERCISE 17.2 ▸ **USING ADDITIONAL PATTERNS OF DEVELOPMENT**

For one of the terms listed in Exercise 17.1, describe how you might use two or three patterns of development in an extended definition of the term.

An Extended Definition May Use Negation and Address Misconceptions

Your extended definition essay may use **negation**—explaining what a term is *not*—to show how the term is different from the other terms in the same class. For example, in an essay defining rollerblading (in-line skating), you might clarify how it is unlike roller skating, which uses a different type of wheeled boot that allows different kinds of motions.

You can also use negation to clarify personal meanings. In defining what you mean by *relaxing vacation*, you might include examples of what is *not* relaxing for you: the pressure to see something new every day, long lines, crowded scenic areas, and many hours in a car each day.

In addition, your extended definition may address popular misconceptions about the term being defined. In an essay defining *plagiarism*, for instance, you might correct the mistaken idea that plagiarism only means passing off an entire paper written by someone else as your own, explaining that plagiarism also includes using excerpts from other writers' work without giving them credit.

EXERCISE 17.3 ▸ **USING NEGATION AND ADDRESSING MISCONCEPTIONS**

For two of the following broad topics, select a narrowed term and develop a standard definition of it. Then, for each term, consider how you could address misconceptions and use negation in an extended definition of the term.

1. A type of dance
2. A play, call, or player position in a sport
3. A piece of clothing (hat, jacket, jeans)
4. A term related to a course you are taking
5. A type of business

The following readings demonstrate the techniques for writing effective extended definition essays discussed above. The first reading is annotated to point out how Jan Goodwin defines *freegan*. As you read the second essay, try to identify for yourself how Joseph Paul Forgas uses the techniques of extended definition to explain what *gullibility* means.

> **READING**

Freegans: They Live Off What We Throw Away

Jan Goodwin

Jan Goodwin is a senior fellow at Brandeis University's Schuster Center for Investigative Journalism and a Soros Foundation Media Fellow. The winner of three Amnesty International UK Media Awards and a World Hunger Award, Goodwin has long been an activist for human rights and social justice. She wrote about the threat of extremism in the Muslim world in her books *Price of Honor* (1994) and *Caught in the Crossfire* (1987) and was a reporter for Lifetime Television's documentary *Defending Our Daughters* (1998). This reading was published in 2009 in the magazine *Marie-Claire*, for which Goodwin was senior international editor.

Before Reading

1. **Preview:** Use the steps listed in Chapter 2.
2. **Connect:** What do you know about how and why some people scavenge for food or free merchandise?

While Reading Study the annotations to identify the characteristics of definition.

Focus: Activities and motivations of freegans, term to be defined

It's nearly closing time on a crisp Monday night at a Midtown Manhattan super-   1
market, when a burly crew begins tossing bulging black bags filled with the day's trash—crusty breads, salad-bar fixings, last week's fruits and vegetables—to the curb. Just then, a cadre of 15 jeans-and-sneakers-clad men and women turn the corner and quietly descend upon the heaps, gingerly opening and dissecting their contents. As they forage through the small mountains of discarded food, a 30-something woman sporting a green rain slicker calls out, "Over here, expensive

Narration: Anecdote demonstrates freegan foraging

Greek yogurt." Seconds later, a ponytailed guy wearing a backpack hollers, "Here's bacon and chicken for anyone who eats meat—and a perfect eggplant." Someone shouts a reminder not to tear the bags or leave litter on the ground, lest the store get fined. After less than 30 minutes, they excitedly depart the scene, each shouldering at least one tote bag filled with booty.

Negation: Uses negation to address misconceptions

Definition: Thesis identifies term, class ("radical environmentalists . . .") distinguishing characteristics

These urban foragers are neither homeless nor destitute. They are committed   2
freegans, radical environmentalists (typically vegan) who reject our wasteful consumer culture by living almost entirely on what others throw away. Freegans rarely go hungry thanks to the colossal amount of food Americans dump every day— 38 million tons annually, according to the Environmental Protection Agency. Here's another way to look at it: The United Nations says our leftovers could satisfy every single empty stomach in Africa. Those castoffs are composed, in part, of the less-than-perfect products consumers instinctively reject: bruised apples, wilted

One man's trash is another man's treasure. A "freegan" climbs into a dumpster behind a West Palm Beach supermarket in search of edible food. The Palm Beach Post/ZUMA Press/Alamy

lettuce, dented cans. Who hasn't passed on an entire carton of eggs after discovering a single slight fracture among the dozen? Supermarkets can't unload the quarts of milk tagged with yesterday's use-by date—which many of us interpret as a product's expiration but in fact refers to its period of peak flavor. Meaning, there's still plenty of life left in those quarts.

Freegans, like 24-year-old Leia MonDragon, a buxom Latina with a taste for heavy eye makeup, feast on those castoffs. "It's amazing what you can find and the good condition it's in," she exclaims, holding aloft a week's worth of produce, including watermelon, summer squash, kale, tomatoes, onions, and bananas. Though technically past their prime, they look pristine. MonDragon also scored half gallons of soy milk and lemonade, both unopened and still chilled, and bagels that only an hour earlier were for sale. "I once found 200 one-pound bags of organic fair-trade coffee beans just dumped outside a store with the trash," she brags, like a woman combing the racks at a Gucci clearance sale.

Aside from the $1600 a month in rent MonDragon pays for her two-bedroom Brooklyn apartment, which she shares with her boyfriend, Tate, their 1-year-old daughter, Uma, and her retired grandfather, just about everything she owns has been salvaged or handmade. She found her ivory faux-leather couch, dishes, and flatware on the street; many of Uma's clothes and toys were recovered from boxes abandoned on sidewalks and stoops, a common sight in New York, where apartment detritus—from halogen lamps to bed frames—is blithely left on the streets. MonDragon used to get around on a bicycle she and Tate cobbled together from discarded parts, but not long ago it was stolen. "So now I'm building another one," she says.

3   **Illustration:** Examples explain motivation of freegans

Narration, description: Tells story of one freegan; describes MonDragon so readers can visualize her

4

Though official figures are hard to come by, freegan ranks are believed to   5
be in the thousands, with an estimated 500 practitioners living in New York City
alone. Born of the extreme environmentalist and anti-globalization movements
of the '90s, freeganism is a wholly modern crusade whose followers live off the
grid while simultaneously exploiting it. Freegans gravitate toward cities—and
their relentless mounds of garbage; Web sites keep devotees in close contact
with each other so they can plan group foraging outings, recruit new members,
and spread word of upcoming events, like move-out day at a college dorm, a
veritable freegan Christmas. Using a discarded computer they restored, Mon-
Dragon and her boyfriend routinely scour Craigslist for freebies. (The Web connection comes from a cable package her grandfather pays for.) "The only thing I
don't have yet is a skillet. But I'll find one," MonDragon declares confidently, as
she ladles dinner—tofu-and-veggie stir-fry with lime zest—from a large
stockpot.

MonDragon first embraced freeganism five years ago as a student at a   6
Minnesota community college, where she met Tate. "We were broke, trying to find
the money for even a simple meal like rice and beans," she explains. "We saw a
freegan flyer and hooked up with some people who showed us how to do it. And
just like that, we had a source of free food. It was amazing." The more time the pair
spent with entrenched freegans, the more exposure they got to the movement's
renegade rhetoric. Since relocating to New York two years ago, they have become
ardent practitioners, positioning their lifestyle as a boycott of "corporate greed"
and an alternative to capitalism. "It's so wrong when people are losing their jobs,
struggling to survive, that stores are throwing out such vast quantities of good
food," MonDragon sighs, as Papo, her wiry gray mutt, nips the hem of her long
black skirt. She tosses him a roasted chicken leg, retrieved from her last
supermarket trash run.

MonDragon admits she was initially skeeved out by the prospect of eating   7
garbage—Dumpsters are a frequent freegan haunt—but says she was reassured
by the movement's common-sense safety measures. Some freegans show up for
Dumpster dives armed with rubber gloves and antibacterial lotion. Produce is
washed thoroughly, withered leaves discarded; baked goods bearing even a hint of
mold are tossed. Everything undergoes a basic smell test. (Tate says he once
scarfed down day-old sushi, despite its funky aroma, and ended up with food poisoning.) And since stores generally separate discarded food from, say, bathroom
trash bins, the ickiest finds are usually just putrid meats and dairy. MonDragon
decontaminates all salvaged housewares with a mixture of vinegar, baking soda,
and hydrogen peroxide and launders all of Uma's secondhand stuffed animals and
clothes. Though she draws the line at pre-owned underwear, instead buying new
pairs from discount stores, MonDragon makes her own reusable sanitary napkins
from cloth in much the same way women did a century ago. (Think that's hardcore? Some freegans squat in abandoned buildings and jerry-rig toilets that com-
post their own waste matter.) "People in this country are a lot more freaked out
about dirt than they need to be. We need a little dirt in our lives for our immune
systems to be strong," MonDragon says.

Background: Explains history of freeganism

Narration: Continues MonDragon's story

"Freegans have been living this way for years and are very healthy," says Dr. Ruth Kava, director of nutrition at the American Council on Science and Health. "In fact, a freegan's biggest risk may be falling headfirst into a Dumpster." That, or being slapped with a fine—or worse—for trespassing on private property to scavenge. It's not uncommon for store owners, mistaking freegans for homeless people or burglars, to call the police. Two years ago, a pair of freegans in Steamboat Springs, CO, were sentenced to six months in jail after jumping a fence and taking a couple of handfuls of fruit and vegetables from a grocery store's trash. For that reason, MonDragon confines her searches to whatever she finds on the street. She and Tate get by on less than $20,000 a year—he drives a taxi, and she clerks at a nonprofit during the summer. Their meager income is earmarked for inescapable expenses, like their tuition at a community college and rent. The couple qualifies for food stamps, which pay only for Uma's formula (MonDragon stopped breast-feeding once she started working).

Though she lives hand to mouth, MonDragon insists she wants for nothing. Her family eats three hearty meals a day; their closets are crammed with wool coats, shoes, shirts with tags still dangling from their sleeves. She's got an active social life, towing Uma to playdates with other freegan moms and fielding invitations to watch DVDs with freegan friends. A week earlier, she and Tate uncovered a hoard of unopened Chinese food inside a streetside trash can, still warm in its gleaming white containers. They took it to a friend's house for an impromptu dinner party. "We usually never take more than we need," she explains, unzipping her black Patagonia shell and tossing it onto her bed—everything from the taupe sheets to the queen-size mattress were recovered from the streets of Manhattan. "We don't need to. There will be more trash out there tomorrow."

8

Background: Explains risks of freeganism

Cause-effect: Explains why MonDragon restricts her searches to the street

9

Conclusion: Ends with quotation that demonstrates lack of want— negation from paragraph 2

Visualize an Extended Definition Essay: Create a Graphic Organizer

Graphic Organizer 17.1 shows the basic organization of an extended definition essay.

For more on creating a graphic organizer, see Chapter 2.

- The **introduction** announces the term, provides background information, and usually includes the thesis statement (which briefly defines the term and indicates its significance to readers).
- The **body paragraphs**, which use one or more patterns of development, present the term's distinguishing characteristics along with supporting details.
- The **conclusion** refers back to the thesis and brings the essay to a satisfying close.

GRAPHIC ORGANIZER 17.1 The Basic Structure of an Extended Definition Essay

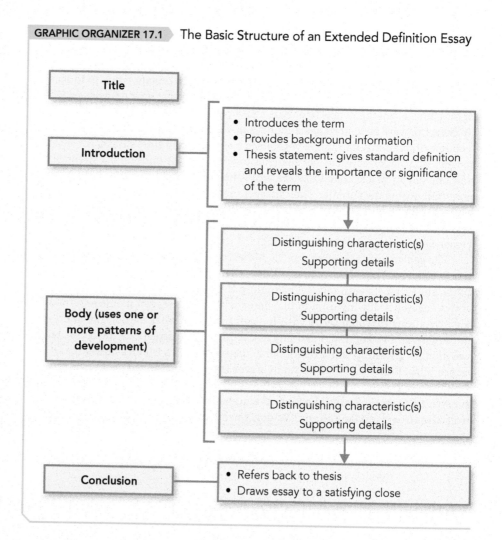

Title

Introduction
- Introduces the term
- Provides background information
- Thesis statement: gives standard definition and reveals the importance or significance of the term

Body (uses one or more patterns of development)

Distinguishing characteristic(s)
Supporting details

Distinguishing characteristic(s)
Supporting details

Distinguishing characteristic(s)
Supporting details

Distinguishing characteristic(s)
Supporting details

Conclusion
- Refers back to thesis
- Draws essay to a satisfying close

READING

Why Are Some People More Gullible Than Others?

Joseph Paul Forgas

Joseph Paul Forgas is the Scientia Professor of psychology at the University of New South Wales in Australia. His research—and he has published more than twenty books and two hundred articles—focuses on how cognition and emotion affect interpersonal communication. He is also the coeditor of the *Frontiers of Social Psychology* series. This article appeared in TheConversation.com on March 30, 2017—just before April Fool's Day. **Before reading**, preview the selection and make connections by thinking of situations in which you or others you know have heard or used the word *gullible*.

While reading, notice how the writer defines *gullibility* through examples, reasons, and an explanation of factors that contribute to gullibility.

Homo sapiens is probably an intrinsically gullible species. We owe our evolutionary success to culture, our unique ability to receive, trust and act on stories we get from others, and so accumulate a shared view about the world. In a way, trusting others is second nature. But not everything we hear from others is useful or even true. There are countless ways people have been misled, fooled and hoaxed, sometimes for fun, but more often, for profit or for political gain. Although sharing social knowledge is the foundation of our evolutionary success, in this age of unlimited and unfiltered information, it is becoming a major challenge to decide what to believe, and what to reject.   1

What Is Gullibility?

Gullibility is a tendency to be easily manipulated into believing something is true when it isn't. Credulity is closely related, a willingness to believe unlikely propositions with no evidence behind them. April Fool's tricks often work because they exploit our baseline inclination to accept direct communications from others as reliable and trustworthy. When a colleague tells you the boss wants to see you immediately, the first, automatic reaction is to believe them. Once we realize this is April 1, a more critical mindset will increase our threshold of acceptance and triggers more thorough processing. Rejection is then likely unless there is strong corroborating evidence.   2

Do We Want to Be Gullible?

So it seems that gullibility and credulity have to do with how we think and the level of proof we need before accepting information as valid. In most face-to-face   3

Classic April Fool's Day joke: the BBC's 1957 spaghetti harvest

situations, the threshold of acceptance is fairly low, as humans operate with a "positivity bias" and assume most people act in an honest and genuine way.

Of course, this is not always so. Others often want to manipulate us for their own purposes. For instance, we often prefer bare-faced flattery to truth, even when we know the communicator's ulterior motives. When the information is personally rewarding, we actually want to be gullible. We are also subject to a marked "confirmation bias." This is when we tend to prefer dubious information that supports our pre-existing attitudes and are more inclined to reject valid information that challenges our beliefs. A similar bias exists when passing on doubtful information to others. We tend to reshape rumor and gossip in ways that support our pre-existing stereotypes and expectations (Rosnow and Foster). Inconsistent details—even if true—are often changed or even omitted.

Gullibility in Public Life

Gullibility and credulity have become important issues as a deluge of raw, unverified information is readily available online. Consider how fake news during the U.S. presidential election influenced voters (Menn). Stories that generate fear and promote a narrative of corrupt politicians and media can be particularly effective. In Europe, Russian websites "reported" numerous false stories designed to undermine the E.U. and to bolster support for extreme right-wing parties (Janda and Sharibzhanov).

Credulity and gullibility are also of great commercial importance when it comes to marketing and advertising (Burkeman). For example, much brand name advertising subtly appeals to our need for social status and identity. Yet, we obviously cannot acquire real status or identity just by buying an advertised product. Even water, a freely available colorless, tasteless, transparent liquid is now successfully marketed as an identity product, a multi-billion dollar industry built mostly on misleading advertising and gullibility (Elmhirst). Dietary supplements are another large industry exploiting gullibility (Schwartz).

Explaining Gullibility

Gullibility occurs because we have evolved to deal with information using two fundamentally different systems, according to Nobel Prize winning psychologist Daniel Kahneman. System 1 thinking is fast, automatic, intuitive, uncritical and promotes accepting anecdotal and personal information as true. This was a useful and adaptive processing strategy in our ancestral environment of small, face-to-face groups, where trust was based on life-long relationships. However, this kind of thinking can be dangerous in the anonymous online world.

System 2 thinking is a much more recent human achievement; it is slow, analytical, rational and effortful, and leads to the thorough evaluation of incoming information. While all humans use both intuitive and analytic thinking, system 2 thinking is the method of science, and is the best available antidote to gullibility. So, education tends to reduce gullibility (Preece and Baxter), and those who receive scientific training in critical, skeptical thinking also tend to be less gullible and less easily manipulated.

Differences in trust can also influence gullibility. This may be related to early   9
childhood experiences, with the idea that trust in infancy sets the stage for a
lifelong expectation the world will be a good and pleasant place to live ("Trust").

Does Our Mood Make a Difference?

Many factors, including mood, influence how we process incoming information.   10
Positive mood facilitates system 1 thinking and gullibility, while negative mood
often recruits more careful, cautious and attentive processing. In several
experiments we found that people in a negative mood were less gullible
and more skeptical, and were actually better at detecting deception (Forgas
and East).

Although detecting deception was always important to human groups to   11
identify cheats and freeloaders, it has become much more critical in our modern
age. Given unlimited access to dubious information, combating gullibility and
promoting critical thinking is one of the major challenges of our age. There are
worrying signs that lack of education, poor ability to think rationally, and the
massive amount of doubtful and manipulative information we encounter may
combine to threaten our impressive cultural achievements.

Links

Burkeman, Oliver. "Exploiting Gullible People Is a Modern Form of Mining." *The Guardian*,
    7 Aug. 2015, www.theguardian.com/lifeandstyle/2015/aug/07/exploiting-gullible-people
    -modern-mining.

Elmhirst, Sophie. "Liquid Assets: How the Business of Bottled Water Went Mad." *The Guardian*,
    6 Oct. 2016, www.theguardian.com/business/2016/oct/06/liquid-assets-how-business
    -bottled-water-went-mad.

Forgas, Joseph P., and Rebekah East. "On Being Happy and Gullible: Mood Effects on Skepticism
    and the Detection of Deception." *Journal of Experimental Social Psychology*, vol. 44, no. 5 (2008),
    pp. 1362–67, doi.org/10.1016/j.jesp.2008.04.010.

Janda, Jakub, and Ilyas Sharibzhanov. "Six Outrageous Lies Russian Disinformation Peddled
    about Europe in 2016." *Atlantic Council*, 8 Feb. 2017, www.atlanticcouncil.org/blogs/
    ukrainealert/six-outrageous-lies-russian-disinformation-peddled-about-europe
    -in-2016.

Menn, Joseph. "U.S. Government Loses to Russia's Disinformation Campaign: Advisers."
    Reuters, 20 Dec. 2016, www.reuters.com/article/us-usa-russia-disinformation-analysis
    -idUSKBN1492PA.

Preece, Peter F. W., and John H. Baxter. "Scepticism and Gullibility: The Superstitious and
    Pseudo-scientific Beliefs of Secondary School Students." *International Journal of Science
    Education*, 16 July 2010, doi.org/10.1080/09500690050166724.

Rosnow, Ralph L., and Eric K. Foster. "Rumor and Gossip Research." American Psychological
    Association, *Psychological Science Agenda*, "Science Brief," April 2005, www.apa.org/science/
    about/psa/2005/04/gossip.

Schwartz, Larry. "Five Over-the-Counter Meds You Likely Use that Just Don't Work." *AlterNet*,
    www.alternet.org/2014/06/5-over-counter-meds-you-likely-use-just-dont-work.

"Trust: The Development of Trust." *Marriage and Family Encyclopedia*, Net Industries, 2019, family
    .jrank.org/pages/1713/Trust-Development-Trust.html.

EXERCISE 17.4 DRAWING A GRAPHIC ORGANIZER

Using Graphic Organizer 17.1 or 17.2 as a basis, draw a graphic organizer for "Freegans: They Live Off What We Throw Away."

GRAPHIC ORGANIZER 17.2 The Structure of "Why Are Some People More Gullible Than Others?"

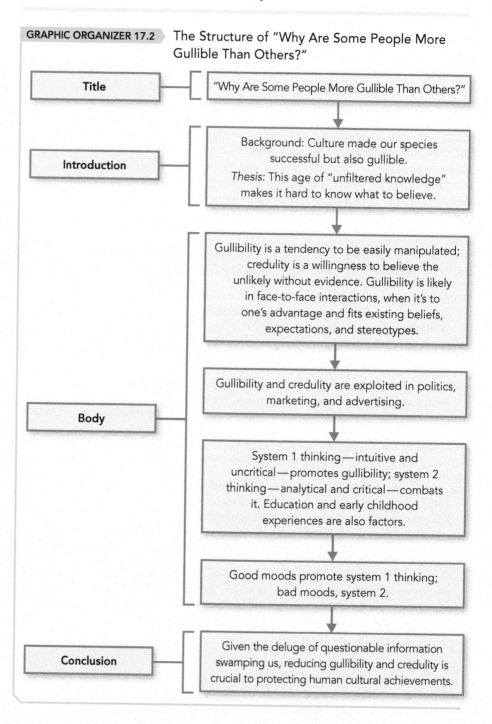

Title — "Why Are Some People More Gullible Than Others?"

Introduction — Background: Culture made our species successful but also gullible.
Thesis: This age of "unfiltered knowledge" makes it hard to know what to believe.

Body —
Gullibility is a tendency to be easily manipulated; credulity is a willingness to believe the unlikely without evidence. Gullibility is likely in face-to-face interactions, when it's to one's advantage and fits existing beliefs, expectations, and stereotypes.

Gullibility and credulity are exploited in politics, marketing, and advertising.

System 1 thinking—intuitive and uncritical—promotes gullibility; system 2 thinking—analytical and critical—combats it. Education and early childhood experiences are also factors.

Good moods promote system 1 thinking; bad moods, system 2.

Conclusion — Given the deluge of questionable information swamping us, reducing gullibility and credulity is crucial to protecting human cultural achievements.

DEFINITION

THE READING PROCESS	STRATEGIES
BEFORE READING	**Preview** the essay to get an overview of its content and organization. **Make connections** by thinking about what the term being defined means and how you would use it.
AFTER READING	**Analyze and evaluate** the reading by answering the following questions: • Does the writer effectively **distinguish the term** from other similar terms? (Give specific examples.) • Is each characteristic **understandable** and **distinct** (no overlap with other characteristics)? • Do the characteristics **cover all situations** and **uses** of the term? Is the term defined completely? • Is each characteristic **presented accurately** and in a way that is **consistent** with what you already know about the term and in a **fair** and **reasonable** way? • Does the author use language that has strong **connotations** or use language to **hide or mislead**? Does the definition seem to reflect **bias**?

EXERCISE 17.5 **READING CRITICALLY**

Apply the questions in the "How Writers Read" box to the selection "Why Are Some People More Gullible Than Others?"

Integrate Definition into an Essay

Including standard or extended definitions in writing that is based on other patterns of development is common. For example, you may need to include a definition in a response to an essay exam question. Definitions should also be included when terms are likely to be unfamiliar to the reader or when terms may be understood differently than intended. The following kinds of terms usually require definition:

- **Judgmental or controversial terms.** Define terms that imply a judgment or that may be controversial. If you describe a policy as "fiscally unsound," for example, make clear whether you mean "spending more money than we earn," "paying an interest rate that is too high," or something else.

- **Technical terms.** When writing for a general audience, define specialized terms that readers may find unfamiliar. In law, for example, you may need to define terms like *writ, deposition, hearing,* and *plea* for a general audience.
- **Abstract terms.** Terms that refer to ideas or concepts, such as *loyalty, heroism,* and *conformity,* may need to be defined because they can seem vague or mean different things to different people.

In general, if you are not sure whether a term needs a definition, include one.

You may choose to provide your definition in a separate sentence or section, or you can incorporate a brief definition or synonym into a sentence, using commas, dashes, or parentheses to set off the definition, as in the following examples.

┌──── term ────┐ ┌──────────────── definition ────────────────┐
Implicit memory, or the nonconscious retention of information about prior

└──────────────┘
experiences, is important in eyewitness accounts of crimes.

┌─ term ─┐ ┌──────────────── definition ────────────────
Empathy—a shared feeling of joy for people who are happy or distress for

└──────────────┘
people who are in pain—explains the success of many popular films.

PREWRITING	DRAFTING	REVISING	EDITING & PROOFREADING

A Guided Writing Assignment*

EXTENDED DEFINITION

The following guide will lead you through the process of writing an extended definition essay. Although the assignment focuses on definition, you will need to integrate one or more other patterns of development in order to develop your essay.

Your Essay Assignment

Write an extended definition essay on a term, activity, phenomenon, or object. You may choose something you are learning about, something you know well already, or something you or your fellow students are likely to be interested in. The following are some options:

---

* The writing process is *recursive*; that is, you may find yourself revising as you draft or prewriting as you revise. This is especially true when writing on a computer. Your writing process may also differ from project to project and from that of your classmates.

- a key concept from an introductory psychology, sociology, or economics course, such as ethnocentrism, diaspora, or monopoly capitalism
- a type of music, such as indie rock, free jazz, or hip hop
- an inappropriate behavior, such as distracted driving or stalking
- a type of television show, such as a situation comedy, game show, or reality TV show
- an unusual sport or leisure activity, such as curling or spelunking

1 Select a topic from the list above, or create one of your own.

Ask yourself these questions when choosing a topic:

- What do I **already know** about the topic? How much **research** will I have **time** to do?
- How much do **my readers** (other students at my college or university) **already know** about the topic?
- Will my readers be **interested** in the topic **already**, or will I need to **create interest**?

Collaborate: In small groups, take turns having other students tell you what they think your term means.

2 Narrow your topic to a more specific term to explore in your essay.

Use the following guidelines to narrow your general topic:

1. **Start general.** Use **branching** or **clustering** to come up with specific types of your general topic.

    Example: *Celebrity* is probably too broad a topic for a brief essay, but the topic could be narrowed to a particular type of celebrity, such as *a sports celebrity, a Hollywood celebrity, a local celebrity,* or *a political celebrity.*

2. **Start specific.** Think of a specific example of your topic and use that example as the focus of your definition essay.

    Example: You might choose Tom Brady or Serena Williams and use that person to identify the characteristics defining "sports celebrity."

3 Consider your purpose, audience, and point of view.

- If you were writing an essay that defines *search engines,* your **purpose** might be to **express** your frustration or success with using them to locate information, **inform** readers about the alternatives to Google, or **persuade** readers that Bing or Dogpile is superior to all others.
- What does my **audience already know**? What does the audience **need to know** to understand/accept my definition?
- What **point of view** best suits my purpose and audience? Most definition essays are written in the **third person** (*he, she, it, they*). **First person** (*I, we*) or **second person** (*you*) may be appropriate in **informal contexts** if you or your readers have **personal knowledge** of or **experience** with the topic.

PREWRITING

4 Identify distinguishing characteristics and supporting details.

Try one or more of the following:

1. **Discuss** the term with a classmate, making notes as you talk.

2. **Brainstorm** a list of (a) words that describe your term, (b) people and things that might serve as examples of the term, and (c) everything a person would need to know to understand the term.

3. **Observe** a person who is associated with the term or who performs some aspect of it. Take notes on your observations.

4. **Look up** the term's *etymology*, or origin, in the *Oxford English Dictionary*, *A Dictionary of American English*, or *A Dictionary of Americanisms*, all of which are available in the reference section of your library or an online database it subscribes to. Take notes; the word's etymology will give you some of its characteristics and details, and it might give you ideas on how to organize your essay.

5. **Think of incidents or situations** that reveal the meaning of the term.

6. **Think of similar and different terms** with which your reader is likely to be more familiar.

7. **Do a Google search** on your term. Visit three or four Web sites and take notes on what you discover. Keep track of your sources, so you can cite them later.

5 Generate supporting details.

Use the other patterns of development:

1. **Narration:** Think of incidents or situations that reveal the meaning of the term.

2. **Description:** Observe a person who is associated with the term and take notes on what that person looks like, sounds like, and so forth.

3. **Illustration:** Brainstorm a list of examples.

4. **Comparison and contrast:** Think of similar and different terms with which you can contrast it.

6 Draft your thesis statement.

Your thesis should

1. include a **brief definition** (including the class to which the term belongs and its key distinguishing characteristics)

2. convey why your extended definition might be **useful**, **interesting**, or **important** to readers

Notice how a weak thesis (in this case, a barebones definition) can be revised to reveal the writer's main point.

Example: Phishing ~~is a~~ , the fraudulent practice of sending seemingly legitimate emails to obtain personal information , is rampant and action is needed to control it.

Collaboration. In small groups, take turns reading your thesis aloud. Have classmates try to identify the following:

- the term, the class to which it belongs, and its distinguishing characteristics
- the writer's main point

Consider revising if

- the class is overly general
- the distinguishing characteristics lack specificity or are too limited
- group members cannot identify the main point

7 Choose a method of organization.

If you use **one main supporting pattern**, use the graphic organizers in the **related chapter** to organize your essay. If you use **several patterns of development**, use graphic organizers to **try out several organizations**, and then pick the most logical order.

8 Draft your extended definition essay.

Use the following guidelines to draft your essay:

- The **introduction** should **introduce the term**, provide any **background information** readers will need, and include your **thesis**. When introducing your term, it may be helpful to explain what the term is *not* as well as what it is or include a brief history of how your term has been used. But whatever you include, be sure you convey why your term is **worth reading about**.
- Each **body paragraph** should use one or more **patterns of development** (narration, description, or comparison and contrast, for example) to explain one of the term's distinguishing features. Be sure to include **enough details** for readers to understand each characteristic. Use **transitions** (such as *another*, *also*, or *in addition*) to guide readers as you move from characteristic to characteristic.

The **conclusion** should bring your essay to a satisfying close, revisiting your thesis and elaborating on **why understanding the term is useful**, **interesting**, or **important**.

9 Evaluate your draft and revise as necessary.

Use **Figure 17.1, "Flowchart for Revising an Extended Definition Essay,"** to guide your evaluation and revision:

1. Avoid the **awkward expressions** *is when or is where* in defining your term. Instead, name the class to which the term belongs.

   Example: Early bird specials ~~is when~~ restaurants ~~offer reduced-price dinners~~ late in the afternoon and early in the evening.

(are reduced-priced dinners offered in)

2. Make sure **subjects and verbs agree in number**. When two subjects are joined by *and*, the verb should be plural.

   Example: Taken together, the military and Medicare ~~costs~~ U.S. taxpayers an enormous amount of money.

(cost)

FIGURE 17.1 Flowchart for Revising an Extended Definition Essay

QUESTIONS

REVISION STRATEGIES

1. Highlight your thesis statement. Does it include a brief definition of the term? Does it indicate why your extended definition is useful, interesting, or important?

 ▶

- Identify the class and distinguishing characteristics of your term, and incorporate a standard definition into your thesis.
- Ask yourself, Why is this definition worth reading about? Add your answer to your thesis

 YES ▼

2. Place ✔ beside the distinguishing characteristics of your definition. Do they make your term distinct from similar terms? Is each characteristic true in all cases?

 ▶

- Do additional research or prewriting to discover more characteristics and details you can add to the definition.
- Eliminate characteristics and details that limit the definition too much.

 YES ▼

3. Write the name of the pattern(s) of development you used in your essay. Does each clearly connect your details and help explain the distinguishing characteristics of your term?

 ▶

- Review the list of patterns on pages 448–49 and consider substituting or adding one or more of them to clarify your definition.

 YES ▼

4. [Bracket] the sections where you use negation or address misconceptions. Does each section eliminate possible misunderstandings? Are other misunderstandings possible?

 ▶

- Revise your explanation of what your term is not.
- Add facts or expert opinion to correct readers' mistaken notions about the term.

 YES ▼

5. Reread your supporting paragraphs. Does each one have a clear topic sentence that focuses on a particular characteristic? Is each paragraph well developed?

 NO ▶

- Consider combining paragraphs that cover the same characteristic or splitting paragraphs that cover more than one.
- Add or revise topic sentences and supporting details that focus on the characteristic.

 YES
▼

6. Reread your introduction and conclusion. Does the introduction provide necessary background information and hint at the point that will make your definition worth reading? Does your conclusion bring the essay to a satisfying close?

 NO ▶

- Add background information that sets a context for the term you are defining and suggests the point you are making about the term.
- Revise your conclusion so that it lends closure, possibly by returning to the point you are making about the term.

10 Edit and proofread your essay.

Refer to Chapter 9 for help with

- **editing sentences** to avoid wordiness, making your verb choices strong and active, and making your sentences clear, varied, and parallel
- **editing words** for tone and diction, connotation, and concrete and specific language

Pay particular attention to the following:

- When two nouns are joined by *or*, the verb should agree with the noun closest to it.

  Example: For most birds, the markings or wing span ~~are~~ ^is^ easily observed with a pair of good binoculars.

- When the subject and verb are separated by a prepositional phrase, the verb should agree with the subject of the sentence, not with the noun in the phrase.

  Example: The features of a hot-air balloon ~~is~~ ^are^ best learned by studying the attached diagram.

Readings: Extended Definition in Action

Title: Identifies subject and creates interest

Guerrilla Street Art: A New Use of Public Space

Kate Atkinson

Kate Atkinson wrote the following essay for an assignment to write an extended definition of a specialized term related to one of her interests. Atkinson decided to write about guerrilla street art. As you read, note how Atkinson uses other patterns of development—such as description and illustration—to define guerrilla street art as a nontraditional art form growing in popularity.

Introduction: Provides background information on guerrilla street art and explains by example what it is

Distinguishing characteristics: Thesis statement offers brief definition and suggests value and importance of guerrilla street art (term to be defined)

Distinguishing characteristics: Presents first distinguishing characteristic and lists five examples. Topic sentence is supported by rest of paragraph—a pattern followed in next three paragraphs.

Guerrilla street art is everywhere, if you look for it. There are countless examples in the small college town where I grew up, where the dense population of college students and artists breeds creativity. Just around the corner from my school, stickers litter sign posts, colorful graffiti is scrawled on exposed brick walls, homemade posters advertise local bands at the bus stop, and a cheerful Dr. Seuss character is stenciled on the sidewalk. These small works of art can easily go unnoticed, but they bring an unexpected vibrancy to the city and raise the controversial question of what constitutes art. By taking art out of its traditional context, guerrilla street artists use public space to create controversy and intrigue while at the same time making art free and accessible to a broad audience. 1

Common forms used by street artists today include graffiti, stenciling, poster art, sticker art, scratchiti, and yarn bombing. Graffiti, the most prevalent form of guerrilla street art, is unauthorized writing or drawing on a public surface. It dates back centuries (see fig. 1), and artists have been known to use chalk, markers, paint, and even carving tools to inscribe their messages on public property. Graffiti is so common that it is difficult to travel far in most urban settings without coming across a word or image scrawled in spray paint on a public surface. Stenciling is simply a form of graffiti in which artists use precut stencils to guide their work. Posters and stickers are popular because they can be easily 2

Fig. 1. A graffiti-covered wall from Pompei, Italy. The explosion of the volcano Vesuvius preserved the ancient graffiti.

mass-produced and quickly applied. Posters are usually applied with a technique called "wheat pasting" — using a vegetable-based adhesive to attach posters to walls. Artists apply the clear paste with a roller in a thin layer to both sides of the poster, making it weather-proof and durable. Scratchiti is found almost everywhere there is glass. It became popular in the 1990s after New York City's Metropolitan Transportation Authority installed easily scratched, shatter-resistant glass in all its subway cars and clamped down on traditional aerosol graffiti. Scratchiti is popular because it is so easy to produce — all it requires is a knife, fingernail file, or even a key. But it is looked down upon as an art form, since doing more than scratching your initials or street name into the glass is difficult in this medium ("Scratchiti"). A less common street-art technique is "yarn bombing," in which craft artists knit colorful sheaths of wool and acrylic and wrap them around telephone poles and park benches. The finished pieces are eye-catching and unusual but not permanent or damaging to public property.

   The various motives behind guerrilla street art are as diverse as the artwork itself and range from social and political activism to self-promotion of the artist. Artists embellish telephone poles with colorful yarn and train carriages with ornate murals as a way to reclaim and beautify public space. Others use public space as a billboard to

Definition: Includes brief sub-definitions of *wheat pasting, yarn bombing*

Illustration: Offers examples of types of guerrilla street art

Support: Cites source in text

3   **Distinguishing characteristic:** Discusses motives of artists and offers examples

Photo: Leemage/Universal Images Group/Getty Images

Illustration: Provides example of political activism and documents source

advocate for a cause. An example of street art as political activism is artist Shepard Fairey's iconic image of Barack Obama (Wortham). The simple design combines a striking red, white, and blue portrait of Obama with the word "Hope." With the approval of Obama's 2008 campaign team, Fairey and his team dispersed and pasted, stenciled, or tacked the image onto countless public surfaces across the United States until it became an important facet of the campaign. The picture itself is powerful, but what made it even more effective as a campaign tool was the distribution of the image by supporters and the youth appeal that it garnered as a result.

Discusses appeal of street art and gives examples

Definition: Includes brief sub-definition of "tag"

Illustration: Provides example of using "tag" to gain fame; no source needed because fact widely reported

Street art has many appeals. It is an easy way for new artists to gain notoriety, and anyone with a spray can and a flair for creativity can partake. A tag, which is an artist's signature or symbol, is the most common type of graffiti. Before the Obama campaign, Shepard Fairey gained international acclaim for a sticker depicting wrestler Andre the Giant and the word "Obey." The image soon became his tag and can be found in almost all of his work, making it instantly recognizable. The anonymity of street art also gives artists the freedom to express themselves without fearing the judgment of their peers. At worst, this freedom can result in crude or offensive inscriptions on public property; but at best, it can produce bold, striking statements. Guerrilla street art is contemporary and can be enjoyed without a visit to a museum. It is free and encourages the belief that art should be accessible and available to everyone. It is also a movement that anyone can take part in and that challenges traditional standards of art.

Distinguishing characteristic: Discusses secrecy of artists

Illustration: Uses Banksy as example of secrecy

Due to the illicit nature of their art, the street artist community is shrouded in secrecy. In the film *Exit through the Gift Shop*, a documentary by notorious British street artist Banksy, hooded figures in ski masks are shown scaling buildings and perched precariously on ledges, armed with spray cans and buckets of industrial paste and always on the lookout for the police. Despite his celebrity, Banksy has managed to keep his identity anonymous, and his face is never shown in the film. It is common for street artists to be arrested for trespassing and vandalism, and the risk and intentional disobedience involved in street art adds to its appeal, especially among young people.

4

5

Guerrilla street art has blossomed from an underground movement to a cultural phenomenon. At the very least, it brings up the question of what constitutes art and whether public space is an appropriate place for it. Although it does not adhere to all traditional standards of art, guerrilla street art provokes thought, brings beauty and intrigue to urban spaces that would otherwise go unnoticed, and is a tool for artists to exercise freedom of speech and expression.

6 **Conclusion**: Comments on street art movement as cultural experience; explains its value

Works Cited

Exit through the Gift Shop. Directed by Banksy, performances by Banksy and Thierry Guetta, Paranoid Pictures, 2010.

"Scratchiti." *The Cyber Bench—Documenting New York City Graffiti,* @149st, 2003, www.at149st.com/scratch.html.

Wortham, Jenna. "'Obey' Street Artist Churns Out 'Hope' for Obama." *Wired,* 21 Sept. 2010, www.wired.com/2008/09/poster-boy-shep/.

Analyzing the Writer's Technique

1. **Definition** How does Atkinson define *guerrilla art*?
2. **Effectiveness** Evaluate the effectiveness of the title, introduction, and conclusion.
3. **Terms** Locate one of each of these in the essay—a judgment term, a technical term, an abstract term, and a controversial term.

Thinking Critically about Definition

1. **Bias** Atkinson is not neutral on the subject of this essay. Explain her bias. How does this affect the essay?
2. **Sources** What other types of sources could Atkinson have included to make her essay more comprehensive? What do her two sources reveal about her attitude about the topic?
3. **Connotation** Atkinson uses words such as *vibrancy* (para. 1) and *blossomed* (6) to describe guerrilla street art. What kind of connotation do these words have, and how do the connotations play into the overall tone of the essay?
4. **Euphemism** Is "guerrilla street art" a euphemism? Why or why not? If so, how would the same idea be expressed in more direct language?

5. **Evaluation** Atkinson limits her definition of guerrilla street art to items that have no commercial or financial purpose. She does not mention posters promoting businesses or paid entertainment, signs and banners used for fund-raising by organizations, and advertising flyers, even though these items also are often displayed in the same places as those she does discuss and with the same lack of legal permission. How are these items similar to and different from the kinds of items she includes in her definition?

Responding to the Reading

1. **Reaction** Have you ever created any graffiti? Discuss how doing it made you feel. If you have never created any, consider what situations, if any, might encourage you to do so.
2. **Discussion** Discuss the value of work like Shepard Fairey's, which takes political messages and conveys them in street art. Why is this strategy effective? How does it reach a broader audience than other methods of communication?
3. **Journal** Write a journal entry discussing whether guerrilla art adds value to public space or devalues the space. How should the answer to this question be determined?

READING ▸ **DEFINITION COMBINED WITH OTHER PATTERNS**

Dating on the Autism Spectrum

Emily Shire

Emily Shire has published articles in a number of publications, including *Slate*, *The Week*, the *New York Times*, and the *Daily Beast*. She is currently pursuing a law degree at Yale Law School. This essay appeared in *The Atlantic* in 2013. **Before reading,** preview the selection and make connections by thinking about what you already know about autism. **While reading,** notice how Shire uses examples and quotations from personal interviews to make her extended definition vivid and convincing.

JUST-IN-TIME TIP Identifying Types of Supporting Information

Shire uses numerous patterns to support her thesis. As you read, identify patterns other than definition, and highlight examples of each. Doing so will enable you to remember more of what you read and more effectively evaluate whether the author adequately supports her thesis. To organize your analysis, use a chart like this:

Pattern of Development	Examples
Process Analysis	Flirting (12)
Comparison and Contrast	
Illustration	

Some patterns you may see are listed, and one example has been done for you.

The way to Paulette Penzvalto's heart is through her Outlook calendar. "Honestly, if   1
you want to be romantic with me, send an email through Outlook and give me all
the possible dates, locations, and times, so that I can prepare," she said.

The former Miss America contestant and Juilliard-trained opera singer knew   2
she had a different conception of romance than her previous boyfriends had and,
for that matter, everyone else. "People tend to think of romance as spur of the
moment and exciting," she told me. "I think of romance as things that make sense
and are logical." However, she didn't know why until this year when, at the age of
31, she was diagnosed with autism.

The aspects of autism that can make everyday life challenging—reading   3
social cues, understanding another's perspectives, making small talk and exchang-
ing niceties—can be seriously magnified when it comes to dating. The American
Psychiatric Association defines autism as a spectrum disorder: Some people do not
speak at all and have disabilities that make traditional relationships (let alone
romantic ones) largely unfeasible, but there are also many who are on the
"high-functioning" end and do have a clear desire for dating and romance.

Autism diagnosis rates have increased dramatically over the last two decades   4
(the latest CDC reports show one in 50 children are diagnosed), and while much
attention has been paid to early-intervention programs for toddlers and younger
children, teens and adults with autism have largely been overlooked—especially
when it comes to building romantic relationships.

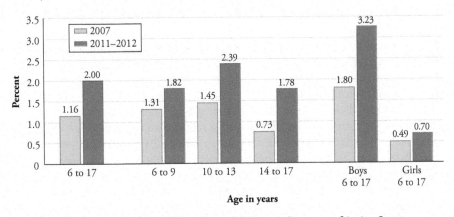

**Percentage of Children (Aged 6–17) Whose Parent(s) Report a Diagnosis of Autism Spectrum
Disorder.**

Data from CDC/NCHS, *National Survey of Children's Health,* 2007 and 2001–2012.

Certain characteristics associated with the autism spectrum inherently go against   5
typical dating norms. For example, while a "neuro-typical" person might think a bar is
a great place for a first date, it could be one of the worst spots for someone on the
spectrum. Dorsey Massey, a social worker who helps run dating and social programs
for adults with various intellectual disabilities, explained, "If it's a loud, crowded place,
an individual on the spectrum may be uncomfortable or distracted." Sensory issues
may also make certain lights and noises especially unpleasant.

Seemingly basic, non-sexual touching may be an issue, as well. "It may give them discomfort for someone to kiss them lightly or hold their hand," Massey said. "They need pressure, and that's not typically what you think of with tender, romantic love." 6

Perhaps because so much of their behavior runs counter to mainstream conceptions of how to express affection and love, people with autism are rarely considered in romantic contexts. A constant complaint among the individuals interviewed for this piece is the misconception that people with autism can't express love or care for others. "I think a lot of times someone will go out on a date with someone on the spectrum and think they're a robot," said Alex Plank, founder of WrongPlanet.net, a popular online autism community. "It's hard to read us if we don't explicitly say what we're feeling, but all the feelings are there." 7

In fact, people with autism may have greater emotional capacities. "Studies have shown that people with autism can have feelings that are stronger and deeper than those without autism," said John Elder Robison, bestselling author of *Look Me in the Eyes* and autism advocate. "Yet those feelings may be invisible to outsiders because we don't show them. Because we don't show them or the expected response, people make the wrong assumption about our depth of feeling about other people." 8

It's not that individuals on the spectrum do not have the same desire for love; they just may not know how to find it. Dr. Elizabeth Laugeson, an Assistant Clinical Professor at UCLA said, "If you asked a person with autism if they wanted a romantic relationship, they would probably say yes, but they would probably also say they don't know how to." 9

Partially from the emphasis on early intervention treatments, there's a dearth of dating skills programs, or, rather, effective ones for people on the spectrum. "Early intervention can significantly improve the outcome, but kids grow up, and we don't have the proper services," said Laugeson, who serves as director of UCLA PEERS, a program that teaches social, including romantic, interaction skills to teens and young adults on the spectrum. 10

Central to PEERS is the promotion of "ecologically valid" social skills, traits humans have been shown to exhibit in reality, rather than what we think we're "supposed" to do. "We know people with autism think very concretely," said Laugeson. "Social skills can be abstract behavior that's difficult to describe, but we try to break it into concrete steps." 11

For example, PEERS will take the seemingly mundane, but actually complex act of flirting and translate it into a step-by-step lesson. "First, a couple notices each other across the room. They make eye contact and look away, and they look again and they look away," said Laugeson. "The look away makes it known you're safe, but the common error someone with autism can make is to stare, which can seem predatory and scare a person." People with autism are also specifically instructed how to smile and for how long, since "another common mistake is to smile really big rather than giving a slight smile," said Laugeson. "A big smile can also be frightening." 12

Neuro-typical people often take flirting for granted as a fairly organic, coy, and even fun back-and-forth, but for someone with autism, it is really a complex, nonsensical interaction. "Flirting still doesn't make sense to me. It seems like a waste of time," said Plank, who worked on a video with Laugeson to teach his Wrong-Plank community members how to flirt. "If you think about it logically, you say 13 things you wouldn't normally say, so it's harder. There are a whole other set of things you have to deal with."

While he didn't have PEERS to guide him, in college, Plank studied guys who were always successful at picking up girls and started mimicking their behaviors. He quickly realized acting confident was the key to dating success, especially if you're a man.

However, maintaining that confidence may be the hardest part of dating for someone on the spectrum, because of their difficulty processing social cues from others. "We will constantly not be able to read whether someone is interested, so you can have an insecurity about whether the person you're dating likes you," said Plank.

In heterosexual courtships where men are still often expected to pursue women, males with autism are at a distinct disadvantage to their female counterpart. "For guys on the spectrum it's a one-way thing," said Robison. "We can be interested, but have no way to tell if they're interested in us."

Some women with autism may ultimately have an edge in the dating world. A common trait of people on the spectrum is being extremely logical and straightforward. A blunt man may repulse women or get a slap in the face; think of how a woman would react if a date told her yes, she did look fat in that dress, or consider the famous 1989 study where a female researcher received positive responses to her request for sex from men on the street 69 to 75 percent of the time compared to her male counterpart who received not a single yes. Women who are forward are prized for it. "Especially if they're really attractive, neuro-typical guys appreciate when women are blunt," said Plank.

While Penzvalto doesn't necessarily think women with autism have it easier than men, she has noticed that her neuro-typical dates have particularly valued many of her autistic traits. "I've found that people who are neuro-typical really appreciate the qualities that people on the spectrum possess: complete honesty and almost an inability to lie," she said.

However, both sexes on the spectrum struggle equally with the fear of rejection. Since so much of dating for adults with autism is trial by error, the risk of mistakes, and often embarrassing ones, is high. Jeremy Hamburgh, a dating specialist for people with special needs, including those on the autism spectrum, has noticed how hard his clients take initial failure with dating. "The risk and rewards are very different for people who are neuro-typical," he said. "The average neuro-typical person can go out and meet ten people, and do well with one, and feel success, but for those with special needs, who have been rejected all their lives, that can really hurt their self-esteem."

Plank has witnessed friends on the spectrum too quickly walk away from dating for fear of rejection. "It's a numbers game in many ways and because people on the spectrum use black-and-white thinking, they think they're doing something wrong," he said. "I wish more people on the spectrum knew you need to practice, you need to go out on more dates."

Worse, is that people on the spectrum may turn the blame on themselves for not exhibiting neuro-typical norms for dating and romance. While interviewing subjects on the spectrum for his documentary *Autism in Love*, filmmaker Matt Fuller noticed how, "When something is perceived as inappropriate, and it gets addressed, they will get embarrassed leading to a rabbit hole of self-deprecating thoughts." And Penzvalto, too, remembers feeling self-conscious and abnormal for her views of dating and romance. "I have struggled in the past with people telling me 'this is how it should be' and having sort of a crisis of maybe I just don't get it, maybe I'm wrong," she said.

In fact, it was during one of those types of fights in a relationship earlier this year that Penzvalto decided to be evaluated for autism. She realized past boyfriends' frustrations over her "rigid thinking" and "boundary issue" could be explained by autism, and a subsequent psychological evaluation confirmed it. However, rather than alarmed, she felt relief.   22

Perhaps because she had spent so much of her life trying to "act" normal and conform to others' expectations for romance, knowing she had autism has helped her become more comfortable with dating. It's a feeling not necessarily shared by all members on the spectrum, but realizing why she saw love and romance the way she does freed her from the pressure of neuro-typical standards. Now, she is following her own heart. "The number one freedom I found in the diagnosis is I don't need to really give into a partner's idea of what a relationship should or needs to look like," she said. "It's really liberating to know I've been living my life a certain way, and it turns out that that's okay."   23

Understanding the Reading

1. **Explanation** How do the needs of people on the autism spectrum differ from those of "neuro-typical" people (those not on the autism spectrum)?
2. **Cause** Why do uninformed people believe that an autistic person is incapable of having a romantic relationship?
3. **Characteristics** What characteristic(s) do autistic women possess that may give them an advantage in dating? How might this (these) characteristic(s) be advantageous?
4. **Vocabulary** Explain the meaning of each of the following words as it is used in the reading: *inherently* (para. 5), *dearth* (10), *mundane* (12), and *predatory* (12).

Analyzing the Writer's Technique

1. **Source** How does the author's decision to include a quotation from a former Miss America contestant affect the reader's response to the article?
2. **Thesis** Restate Shire's thesis in your own words. How effective is it as the thesis of an extended definition essay? If you were revising her thesis, how might you change it?
3. **Introduction** Does the introduction provide all the background information you need to understand the essay? If not, what else should the author have included?
4. **Conclusion** Is the essay's conclusion satisfying? Why or why not?

Thinking Critically about Text and Images

1. **Connotation** What connotation does the word *act* (para. 23) have? How does the use of quotation marks around it affect your understanding?
2. **Tone** Describe the tone of the essay. What does it reveal about Shire's attitude toward people on the autism spectrum?

3. **Sources** What types of sources does Shire use to support her thesis? What other types of sources might she have used to make her essay more convincing?

4. **Objectivity** How objective a view of people on the autism spectrum does Shire present? Identify any words, phrases, or examples that seem intended to influence the reader's emotional response to the article. Does her definition seem euphemistic or incomplete? Support your answers with evidence from the text.

5. **Visual** Examine the figure in the reading. Do you see any trends? What reasons, besides an actual increase in the number of children with autism spectrum disorder, may account for the apparent increase?

Responding to the Reading

1. **Discussion** Discuss the challenges flirting, asking someone out, or even joining a conversation present. What "'ecologically valid' social skills" (para. 11) have you observed or practiced in these contexts? How would you instruct a younger friend or family member in the fine art of asking someone out on a date or joining a conversation among people you don't know well?

2. **Journal** Write a journal entry describing a time you (or someone you know) were totally misjudged or your motives were misunderstood.

3. **Essay** Write an essay defining a perfect date for your classmates.

Working Together

With a small group of fellow students, write a thirty-second public service announcement (PSA) promoting a class in responsible dating to share with the class. Start by naming the class, then brainstorm ideas, and write the PSA.

EXPLORE, RESEARCH, WRITE

In "Dating on the Autism Spectrum," Emily Shire discusses the challenges and frustrations that individuals on the spectrum experience with dating. Other people have also studied this phenomenon. Some reports about this issue include the following:

- "How Does a Person with ASD Date Successfully?" by Maureen Bennie, founder of the Autism Awareness Centre and the mother of two children with autism (30 May 2015)

- "Romance 101: Dating for Adults with ASD," posted by the Center for Autism Research (CAR) and the Children's Hospital of Philadelphia (5 January 2017)

- "Ten Things I Wish Everyone Knew about Autism and Romantic Relationships" by Gwen Greenward, a young adult with Asperger's syndrome who started the Web site Seeing Double to help others understand the world from the point of view of those on the autism spectrum (21 October 2014)

Using your own ideas and one or more of the selections listed here, write an essay that defines a successful dating relationship for individuals on the autism spectrum. Be sure to include at least three characteristics of a successful dating relationship and incorporate at least two quotations (one from two different readings) and cite them correctly at the end of the essay.

The Guided Writing Assignment in this chapter can walk you through the process of writing a definition essay; for help with evaluating sources, see Chapter 21; for help choosing and synthesizing ideas from sources, see Chapter 22; for help with documenting sources, see Chapter 23.

Apply Your Skills: Additional Essay Assignments

For more on locating and documenting sources, see Part 5.

Write an extended definition essay on one of the following topics, using what you learned in this chapter. Depending on your topic, you may need to conduct research.

To Express Your Ideas

Choose a specific audience and write an essay defining and expressing your views on one of the following terms:

1. Parenting
2. Assertiveness
3. Sexual harassment

To Inform Your Reader

4. Write an essay defining a term from a sport, hobby, or form of entertainment for a classmate who is unfamiliar with the term.
5. Write an essay for your instructor defining the characteristics of the "perfect job" you hope to hold after graduation.
6. Write an essay defining an important concept in a field of study, perhaps from one of your other courses. Your audience consists of students not enrolled in the course.

To Persuade Your Reader

"Freegans: They Live Off What We Throw Away" (pp. 450–53) addresses the issue of consumer waste and excess. Write an essay for readers of your local newspaper in which you define one of the terms listed below and demonstrate that the problem is either increasing or decreasing in your community.

7. Racism or ethnic stereotyping
8. Sexual discrimination
9. Age discrimination

Cases Using Definition

10. You are a fifth-grade teacher working on a lesson plan entitled "What Is American Democracy?" How will you limit the term *American democracy* to define it for your audience? What characteristics and details will you include?
11. Write a press release for a new menu item as part of your job as public relations manager for a restaurant chain. First, choose the new menu item, and then define the item and describe its characteristics using sensory details.

SYNTHESIZING IDEAS   CULTURE

Both "Freegans: They Live Off What We Throw Away" and "Guerrilla Street Art" discuss the activities of a subculture: dumpster divers and graffiti artists.

Analyzing the Readings

1. In what ways does each self subgroup set itself apart from the larger society?

2. Write a journal entry exploring how some subgroups set themselves apart—for example, through dress, behavior, or language.

Essay Idea

Write an essay in which you explore a subgroup of college students, such as student democrats or vegans. Give examples of ways in which certain groups on campus set themselves apart through their language, their activities, or in some other way.

18

Cause and Effect

Using Reasons and Results to Explain

Bill Stormont/Alamy

In this chapter you will learn to

- understand the purpose and function of cause-and-effect essays
- use graphic organizers to visualize cause-and-effect essays
- integrate cause and effect into an essay
- read and think critically about cause and effect
- plan, organize, draft, revise, and edit essays using cause and effect

Writing Quick Start

ANALYZE   Assume you are a journalist for your local newspaper reporting on this natural disaster. Brainstorm to determine possible causes, both immediate and long-range, of this fire. Then consider the immediate effects and long-term effects.

WRITE   Your task is to draft a plausible account of the event to accompany the photograph shown here. In your paragraph, be sure to tell readers why the disaster occurred and what happened as a result of it.

CONNECT   The paragraph you wrote is an example of **cause-and-effect analysis** (or causal analysis) because it considered *causes* (why the disaster occurred), *effects* (what happened because of the disaster), or both. In this chapter you will learn to write effective causal analysis essays. You probably use causal analysis every day. If you decide to get a good night's sleep rather than pull an all-nighter because you know you do better on exams when you're well rested, that's cause-effect analysis. Causal analysis is frequently required in college classes too, where you might be asked to analyze and write about the causes of the Civil War or the effects of oxygen deprivation on the central nervous system.

Causal analysis is a useful and important method of organization and way of thinking because it promotes understanding and enables change, improvement, and innovation. It examines relationships that reveal why things happen and what occurs as a result of those events.

USING CAUSE AND EFFECT **IN COLLEGE AND THE WORKPLACE**

- For an essay exam in your *twentieth-century history course,* you are required to discuss the causes of U.S. involvement in the Korean War.
- For a *health and nutrition course*, you decide to write a paper on the relationship between diet and heart disease.
- For your job as an *investment analyst*, you need to explain why a certain company is likely to be profitable in the next year.

What Are the Characteristics of Cause-and-Effect Essays?

A successful causal analysis essay fully explains the causes or effects that are the focus of the essay's thesis and presents those causes or effects in a logical order.

Causal Analysis May Focus on Causes, Effects, or Both

Remember that *causes* are the reasons that something happened and *effects* are the results of the thing that happened. Some causes and effects are relatively easy to separate out.

Cause	Effect
You get a flat tire. ⟶	You are late for work.
You forget to mail a loan payment. ⟶	You receive a past-due notice.

EXERCISE 18.1 **IDENTIFYING CAUSES**

Alone or with a classmate, list one or more possible causes for each of the following events or phenomena:

1. You observe a peacock strutting down a city street.
2. The airline notifies you that the flight you had planned to take tonight has been canceled.
3. Your phone frequently rings once and then stops ringing.
4. Your town decides to fund a new public park.
5. A good friend keeps saying to you, "I'm too busy to get together with you."

EXERCISE 18.2   **IDENTIFYING EFFECTS**

Alone or with a classmate, list one or more possible effects for each of the following events:

1. You leave your backpack containing your wallet on the bus.
2. You decide to change your major.
3. Your spouse is offered a job in a city five hundred miles away from where you live now.
4. You volunteer as a Big Brother or Big Sister.
5. A close relative becomes very ill.

But causal analysis can be complex when it deals with an event or phenomenon that has multiple causes, multiple effects, or both. For example, you probably chose the college you attend (*one effect*) for a number of reasons (*multiple causes*).

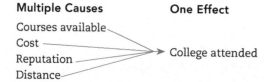

One cause may also have several effects. For instance, the decision to quit your part-time job (*one cause*) will have several results (*multiple effects*).

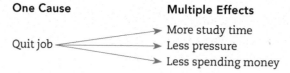

Related events or phenomena may have multiple causes and multiple effects. For instance, in urban areas, an increase in the number of police patrolling the street along with the formation of citizen watch groups (*multiple causes*) will result in less street crime and more small businesses moving into the neighborhood (*multiple effects*).

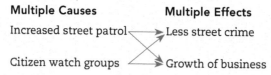

In some cases, a series of events forms a **chain of consequences**.

Cause	Effect	Effect	Effect
You cannot find your car keys. →	You are late for class. →	You miss a surprise quiz. →	Your A quiz average is lowered to a B average.
	Cause	**Cause**	

Once you clearly identify causes and effects, you can decide whether to focus on causes, effects, or both.

Causal Analysis Includes a Clear Thesis Statement

An effective thesis statement for a cause-and-effect essay does the following:

- It identifies the topic.
- It makes an assertion about that topic.
- It suggests whether the essay focuses on causes, effects, or both.

Causes
    ┌causes┐ ┌──── topic ────┐┌
The root causes of unsportsmanlike behavior lie in how society
──────── assertion ────────
elevates athletes to positions of fame and heroism, making them
unaccountable for their behavior.

Effects
    ┌effects┐ ┌──── topic ────┐┌
The negative effects of unsportsmanlike behavior impact fans,
──── assertion ────┐
players, and the institutions the players represent.

Causes and Effects
    ┌──── topic ────┐ ┌causes┐
Unsportsmanlike behavior has deep roots in society's inflated
──── assertion/effects ────
regard for athletes, producing negative effects on fans, other
players, and the institutions they represent.

Causal Analysis Is Logically Organized

A good cause-and-effect essay is organized logically and systematically. You may present causes or effects in any logical order, but these are the most commonly used:

- *Chronological order*, the order in which causes or effects happened

  Example: An essay about causes of rising college tuition costs might begin with reasons for tuition increases in the late 1990s and move chronologically to current increases.

- *Most-to-least* or *least-to-most order*

  Example: An essay about increased immigration to the United States might begin with more important causes and progress to less important ones.

Causal Analysis Explains Each Cause or Effect Fully

A causal analysis essay should present each cause or effect in a detailed and understandable way. For most cause-and-effect essays, you will need to research your topic to find evidence that supports your thesis. For instance, in an essay about the effects on children of viewing violence on television, you might conduct research to locate facts or statistics that document changes in children's behavior after watching violent programs or expert opinion supporting this claim.

You might use another pattern of development (such as illustrations, descriptions, or comparisons) to explain causes or effects. For example, an essay about why dishonesty and lying are common in social media may include reasons, but also give examples or narrate incidents of dishonesty, categorize the characteristics of the social media environment that make lying easy, or contrast face-to-face communication with online communication.

Causal Analysis May Challenge Readers' Assumptions or Offer Surprising Reasons

Cause-and-effect essays that merely repeat commonplace causes or effects will discourage the audience from reading on. Engaging causal analyses, in contrast, surprise readers by challenging popular assumptions, offering surprising reasons, or including interesting evidence. For example, an essay on the effects of capital punishment might attempt to dispel the notion that it deters crime, or it might surprise readers by contending that criminals are in fact deterred, but not for the reasons readers would be likely to assume.

Dealing with the causes or effects that readers assume to be primary is an effective strategy because it creates the impression that you have recognized other viewpoints and not overlooked important information. So essays that challenge readers' assumptions may first explain why the most popular explanation is false or inadequate before moving on to the writer's preferred cause or effect.

The following readings demonstrate the techniques for writing effective cause-and-effect essays. The first reading is annotated to point out how Alex Vitale explains the connection between police misconduct and the likelihood of indictment. As you read the second essay, try to identify for yourself how Adam Alter uses the techniques of causal analysis to support his claim that labels shape identity.

READING

Why the Police Are Rarely Indicted for Misconduct

Alex S. Vitale

Alex Vitale is an associate professor of sociology at Brooklyn College and the author of *City of Disorder: How the Quality of Life Campaign Transformed U.S. Politics*. Vitale has also published numerous articles for publications such as *The Nation, The Abolitionist*, and *Gotham Gazette*. The essay that appears below was originally published online by *Al Jazeera America*, a news and current events media outlet.

Before Reading

1. **Preview:** Use the steps listed in Chapter 2.
2. **Connect:** What incidences of perceived police misconduct have you read about in print or seen on television?

While Reading Study the annotations that accompany the reading to discover how the essay illustrates the characteristics of effective cause-and-effect writing.

On Monday evening, St. Louis County Prosecuting Attorney Robert P. McCulloch announced that a grand jury decided not to indict Ferguson, Missouri, police officer Darren Wilson for the August 9, 2015, shooting death of unarmed teenager Michael Brown. The announcement concluded a tumultuous summer of mass protests against police violence and racial discrimination. Although the decision will be a disappointment to many, those who follow prosecutions of police for use of excessive or unwarranted force say a decision not to indict Wilson is unsurprising.

1   **Introduction:** Grabs readers' attention with anecdote drawn from the headlines

There are major legal, institutional, and social impediments to prosecuting police. Thousands of officers are involved in shootings every year, resulting in about 400 deaths annually. However, successful criminal prosecution of a police officer for killing someone in the line of duty, if no corruption is alleged, is extremely rare. Even when officers are convicted, the charges are often minimal. For example, Coleman Brackney, a Bella Vista, Oklahoma, police officer who was convicted of misdemeanor negligent homicide in 2010 after shooting an unarmed teen to death while in custody in his cruiser, went on to rejoin the police and was recently appointed chief of police in Sulphur Springs, Oklahoma.

2   **Thesis:** Thesis forecasts multiple causes to explain a controversial effect

Effect

Structural Barriers

There are significant structural barriers to successful police indictment or prosecution. For one, investigations are usually conducted by a combination of police detectives and investigators from the prosecutors' office. Prosecutors tend to take a greater role when there is a reason to believe that the shooting might not be justified. However, they must rely on the cooperation of the police to gather necessary evidence, including witness statements from the officer involved and other officers at the scene. In some cases they are the only living witnesses to the event.

Heading: Signals Cause 1

3   Topic sentence for section 1

Transition

Explanation offers support

The close collaboration between police and prosecutors, which is an asset in homicide investigations, becomes a hindrance in police shooting cases. In most cases, the prosecutors' reliance on the cooperation of police creates a fundamental conflict of interest. As a result, prosecutors are often reluctant to aggressively pursue these cases.

4

Reasons offer support

Effect

Moreover, the local elected district attorneys often want to avoid being seen as inhibiting police power. Even in communities where distrust of police is common, no prosecutor ever got thrown out of office for defending the police. At its core, the public sees the DA's office as a defender of law and order and expects these officials to uphold them.

5

Reasons offer support

The way prosecutors handled the Wilson case illustrates this conflict of interest. It took prosecutors months to collect and present evidence to the grand jury. While this has the appearance of thoroughness, it also has the effect of creating a public cooling-off period as short-term demands for prosecution become muted. The radically different approach of the St. Louis County DA is telling. Typically, prosecutors make a short presentation to the grand jury in which they call for specific charges to be considered and then put on their best show of the evidence to see if it passes muster. Indictments occur in more than 90 percent of cases, owing to the low threshold of probable cause and the one-sided nature of the proceedings. In Wilson's case, however, the DA said he planned to provide the grand jury with all the evidence and allow them to decide, without any prompting, whether an indictment was justified and for what offense.

6   Example offers support

The DA hoped to accomplish two things. First, this approach allowed him to   7
absolve himself of any responsibility for the outcome. Second, it served to confuse
and undermine the confidence of the grand jury. Normally, the jury is given clear
guidance and overrules prosecutors only in extreme cases. By giving the jurors a
wide variety of conflicting evidence and little framework in which to evaluate it,
the DA is opening the door to a he said/he said dynamic in which they may err on
the side of caution and avoid an indictment.

Heading: Signals Cause 2

Topic sentence for section 2

Example offers support

Legal Hurdles

There are also huge legal hurdles to overcome. State laws that authorize police use   8
of force, which are backed up by Supreme Court precedent, give police significant
latitude in using deadly force. In the 1989 case *Graham v. Connor*, the Supreme
Court ruled that officers may use force to effect a lawful arrest or if they reasonably believe that the person represents a serious physical threat to the officer or
others. This means that police may use force over any resistance to arrest and that
if the resistance escalates, officers may escalate their force. The court also said
that the totality of circumstances must be judged with an understanding of the
split-second nature of police decision-making.

Transition

Effect

Furthermore, in Missouri and many other states, even a perceived effort to   9
take an officer's gun justifies the use of deadly force. Therefore, in judging the
reasonableness of the officer's actions, the jury may consider factors such as the
alleged perpetrator's size and previous actions as well as the officer's training and
guidance. All this creates numerous avenues for justifying police action based on the
officer's reasonable understanding of the situation rather than a more objective post
hoc assessment.

Reasons offer support

Juror mindset creates yet another challenge to successful indictments and   10
prosecutions. Grand juries and criminal court juries consist of local residents. Even
in periods of heightened concern about police misconduct, most citizens retain a
strong bias in favor of police. Popular culture and political discourse are suffused
with commentaries about both the central importance of police in maintaining the
basic structural integrity of society and the dangerous nature of their work. In
addition, the legal standard for judging police misconduct calls on jurors to put
themselves in the officers' shoes, further strengthening the tendency to identify
with the police.

Heading: Signals Cause 3

Topic sentence for section 3

Example offers support

Race Relations

Another important dynamic in police prosecutions is the state of race relations in   11
the United States. Despite the rhetoric about being a post-racial society, racial
divisions and bias remain omnipresent in American society and nowhere more
than in the realm of criminal justice. There is abundant evidence of jury bias in a
variety of racially disparate criminal justice outcomes, including false convictions,
application of the death penalty, and drug convictions. Research shows that whites
have a generally more positive view of the police than blacks do. The sad reality is
that white jurors are much more likely to side with police, regardless of the race of
the officer and the person killed. This was seen in the Rodney King prosecutions in
California, in which a mostly white suburban state court jury did not convict four
Los Angeles Police Department officers in the severe beating of King after a

high-speed car chase, despite the incident's being videotaped. (The jury acquitted three of the four officers and deadlocked on a charge of excessive force against one officer.) A more diverse federal jury later found two of the officers guilty of violating King's civil rights.

Regardless of what happens in Brown's case, there are no simple fixes for these problems. Advocates such as the Rev. Al Sharpton have called for a federal prosecution. Even if federal officials get involved, they must bring a different kind of charge, related to civil rights violations. While this legal twist of logic has been an important check on failed state legal processes going back to the civil rights fights of the 1950s and 1960s, it is not a substitute for local criminal prosecution, especially in an era of heightened resistance to federal legitimacy.

Internal administrative accountability is sorely lacking. In "Jammed Up: Bad Cops, Police Misconduct, and the New York City Police Department," Robert Kane and Michael White show that police rarely face internal disciplinary charges for use of force. Recent reports from Philadelphia and Seattle show that even when officers are subject to discipline, the majority of such cases end up being overturned by arbitrators or courts as a result of extensive due process protections for police officers.

Instead, states should create a police prosecutor's office, or blue desk, that is more removed from local politics. While relying on state attorneys general has its own challenges, the outcomes are likely to be viewed as more legitimate. These blue desks could become repositories of expertise on police prosecutions. Even if tied to state politics, they might be better able to insulate themselves from accusations of overly aggressive prosecutions as well as charges of not supporting the police.

Laws on the use of force need reform. Police shootings were much more common in the 1970s when regulations about the use of force were even looser. In response to public outcries and rioting in the 1960s and '70s, local police began to tighten up regulations and offer training to officers, resulting in significant reductions in shootings. The 1984 Supreme Court case *Tennessee v. Garner* institutionalized some of these changes nationally, including making it unlawful for police to shoot a fleeing suspect. Since then, however, the courts have mostly expanded police authorization to use force.

Finally, the U.S. needs to dial back the dramatic expansion of police power over the last forty years. For example, the growing prevalence of paramilitary SWAT teams and the ongoing war on drugs have significantly contributed to excessive use of force. In part this happened through the combined direct enforcement practices of these two types of policing. But they also contributed indirectly to a larger ethos of militarized patrolling that equates policing with the use of force and a war footing. The public and its representatives need to realize that there are better ways to prevent crime and serve the community than licensing excessive police force.

12   **Conclusion:** Refers back to example in introduction; reviews possible solutions (prosecute police misconduct on federal level) before offering solutions of his own in paragraphs 14–16

13

14   Transitions signal proposed solutions (creating a "blue desk," reforming laws on use of force, demilitarizing the police)

15

16

Visualize Cause-and-Effect Essays: Create Graphic Organizers

For more on creating a graphic organizer, see Chapter 2.

Graphic Organizers 18.1, 18.2, and 18.3 show the basic organization of three types of causal analysis essays.

- Graphic Organizer 18.1 shows the organization of an essay that examines either causes or effects.
- Graphic Organizer 18.2 shows the organization of an essay that examines a chain of causes and effects.
- Graphic Organizer 18.3 shows two possible arrangements for an essay that focuses on multiple causes and effects.

All three types of causal analyses include an introduction (which identifies the event, provides background information, and states a thesis) as well as a conclusion. Notice in Graphic Organizers 18.2 and 18.3 that causes are presented before effects. Although this is the typical arrangement, writers sometimes use the reverse organization, discussing effects first and then causes to create a sense of drama or surprise.

GRAPHIC ORGANIZER 18.1 The Basic Structure of an Essay on Causes or Effects

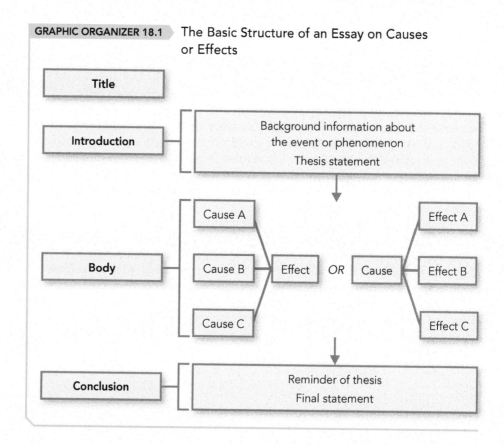

GRAPHIC ORGANIZER 18.2 The Basic Structure of an Essay on a Chain of Causes and Effects

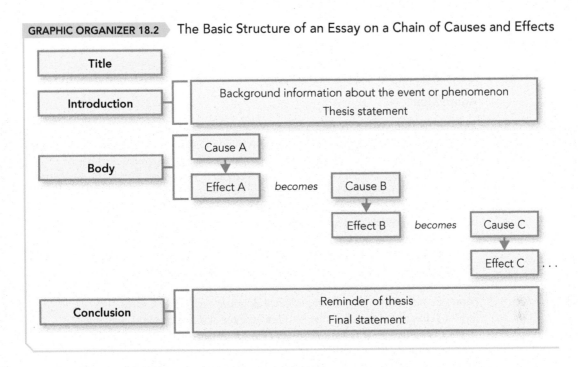

GRAPHIC ORGANIZER 18.3 The Basic Structure of an Essay on Multiple Causes and Effects

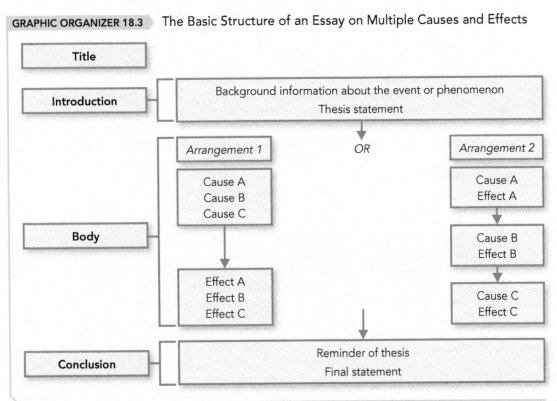

How Labels Like *Black* and *Working Class* Shape Your Identity

Adam Alter

Adam Alter is an associate professor of marketing and psychology at New York University. His research focuses on decision making, and he has published numerous articles in academic journals in psychology. He has also published a number of articles for general readers in publications such as the *New York Times*, the *Wall Street Journal*, and *Psychology Today*. This reading is from Alter's 2013 book *Drunk Tank Pink and Other Unexpected Forces That Shape How We Think, Feel, and Behave*. **Before reading**, preview the selection and make connections by thinking about the way labels affect how people are treated. Think of instances that illustrate or disprove this idea. **While reading**, highlight the effects Alter names as resulting from racial bias or social labeling. Then compare your notes with Graphic Organizer 18.4.

1   Long ago, humans began labeling and cataloguing each other. Eventually, lighter-skinned humans became "whites," darker-skinned humans became "blacks," and people with intermediate skin tones became "yellow-," "red-," and "brown-skinned." These labels don't reflect reality faithfully, and if you lined up 1,000 randomly selected people from across the earth, none of them would share exactly the same skin tone. Of course, the continuity of skin tone hasn't stopped humans from assigning each other to discrete categories like "black" and "white"—categories that have no basis in biology but nonetheless go on to determine the social, political, and economic well-being of their members.

2   Social labels aren't born dangerous. There's nothing inherently problematic about labeling a person "right-handed" or "black" or "working class," but those labels are harmful to the extent that they become associated with meaningful character traits. At one end of the spectrum, the label "right-handed" is relatively free of meaning. We don't have strong stereotypes about right-handed people, and calling someone right-handed isn't tantamount to calling them unfriendly or unintelligent.

3   In contrast, the terms "black" and "working class" are laden with the baggage of associations, perhaps some of them positive, but many of them negative. During the height of the civil-rights struggle, one teacher showed just how willingly children adopt new labels. On April 4, 1968, Martin Luther King Jr. was murdered, and the next day thousands of American children went to school with a combination of misinformation and confusion. In Riceville, Iowa, Stephen Armstrong asked his teacher, Jane Elliott, why "they shot that king." Elliott explained that the "king" was a man named King who was fighting against the discrimination of "Negroes." The class of white students was confused, so Elliott offered to show them what it might be like to experience discrimination themselves.

Elliott began by claiming that the blue-eyed children were better than the brown-eyed children. The children resisted at first. The brown-eyed majority was forced to confront the possibility that they were inferior, and the blue-eyed minority faced a crisis when they realized that some of their closest friendships were now forbidden. Elliott explained that the brown-eyed children had too much melanin, a substance that darkens the eyes and makes people less intelligent. Melanin caused the "brownies," as Elliott labeled them, to be clumsy and lazy. Elliott asked the brownies to wear paper armbands—a deliberate reference to the yellow armbands that Jews were forced to wear during the Holocaust. Elliott reinforced the distinction by telling the brown-eyed children not to drink directly from the water fountain, as they might contaminate the blue-eyed children. Instead, the brownies were forced to drink from paper cups. Elliott also praised the blue-eyed children and offered them privileges, like a longer lunch break, while she criticized the brown-eyed children and forced them to end lunch early. By the end of the day, the blue-eyed children had become rude and unpleasant toward their classmates, while even the gregarious brown-eyed children were noticeably timid and subservient.

News of Elliott's demonstration traveled quickly, and she was interviewed by Johnny Carson. The interview lasted a few brief minutes, but its effects persist today. Elliott was pilloried by angry white viewers across the country. One angry white viewer scolded Elliott for exposing white children to the discrimination that black children face every day. Black children were accustomed to the experience, the viewer argued, but white children were fragile and might be scarred long after the demonstration ended. Elliott responded sharply by asking why we're so concerned about white children who experience this sort of treatment for a single day, while ignoring the pain of black children who experience the same treatment across their entire lives. Years later, Elliott's technique has been used in hundreds of classrooms and in workplace-discrimination training courses, where adults experience similar epiphanies. Elliott's approach shows how profoundly labels shape our treatment of other people and how even arbitrary damaging labels have the power to turn the brightest people into meek shadows of their potential selves.

Four years before Jane Elliott's classroom demonstration, two psychologists began a remarkable experiment at a school in San Francisco. Robert Rosenthal and Lenore Jacobson set out to show that the recipe for academic achievement contains more than raw intellect and a dozen years of schooling. Rosenthal and Jacobson kept the details of the experiment hidden from the teachers, students, and parents; instead, they told the teachers that their test was designed to identify which students would improve academically over the coming year— students they labeled "academic bloomers." In truth, the test was an IQ measure with separate versions for each school grade, and it had nothing to do with academic blooming. As with any IQ test, some of the students scored quite well, some scored poorly, and many performed at the level expected from students of their age group.

The next phase of the experiment was both brilliant and controversial. Rosenthal and Jacobson recorded the students' scores on the test, and then labeled a randomly chosen sample of the students as "academic bloomers." The bloomers performed no differently from the other students—both groups had the same average IQ score—but their teachers were told to expect the bloomers to experience a rapid period of intellectual development during the following year.

When the new school year arrived, each teacher watched as a new crop of children filled the classroom. The teachers knew very little about each student, except whether they had been described as bloomers three months earlier. As they were chosen arbitrarily, the bloomers should have fared no differently from the remaining students. The students completed another year of school and, just before the year ended, Rosenthal and Jacobson administered the IQ test again. The results were remarkable.

The first and second graders who were labeled bloomers outperformed their peers by 10–15 IQ points. Four of every five bloomers experienced at least a 10-point improvement, but only half the non-bloomers improved their score by 10 points or more. Rosenthal and Jacobson had intervened to elevate a randomly chosen group of students above their relatively unlucky peers. Their intervention was limited to labeling the chosen students "bloomers," and remaining silent on the academic prospects of the overlooked majority.

Observers were stunned by these results, wondering how a simple label could elevate a child's IQ score a year later. When the teachers interacted with the "bloomers," they were primed to see academic progress. Each time a bloomer answered a question correctly, her answer seemed to be an early sign of academic achievement. Each time she answered a question incorrectly, her error was seen as an anomaly, swamped by the general sense that she was in the process of blooming.

During the year, then, the teachers praised these students for their successes, overlooked their failures, and devoted plenty of time and energy to the task of ensuring that they would grow to justify their promising academic labels. The label "bloomer" did not just resolve ambiguity, in other words—it changed the outcome for those students.

EXERCISE 18.3 **DRAWING A GRAPHIC ORGANIZER**

Using Graphic Organizer 18.3, draw a graphic organizer for "Why the Police Are Rarely Indicted for Misconduct."

GRAPHIC ORGANIZER 18.4   The Structure of "How Labels Like *Black* and *Working Class* Shape Your Identity"

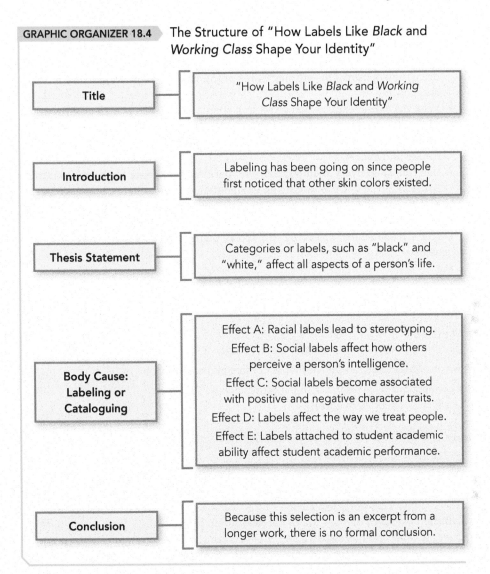

| Title | "How Labels Like *Black* and *Working Class* Shape Your Identity" |

| Introduction | Labeling has been going on since people first noticed that other skin colors existed. |

| Thesis Statement | Categories or labels, such as "black" and "white," affect all aspects of a person's life. |

| Body Cause: Labeling or Cataloguing | Effect A: Racial labels lead to stereotyping.
Effect B: Social labels affect how others perceive a person's intelligence.
Effect C: Social labels become associated with positive and negative character traits.
Effect D: Labels affect the way we treat people.
Effect E: Labels attached to student academic ability affect student academic performance. |

| Conclusion | Because this selection is an excerpt from a longer work, there is no formal conclusion. |

Integrate Cause and Effect into an Essay

Although some of your essays will focus solely on causal analysis, other essays will combine cause and effect with other patterns. For example, in an essay comparing two popular magazines that have different journalistic styles, you might explain the effects of each style on the reading experience. Use the following tips to integrate causal analyses into essays that rely on other patterns of development:

1. **Introduce the causal analysis.** Use transitional words and expressions to prepare readers for a causal explanation. For example, in writing about your college president's decision to expand the Career Planning Center, you might introduce your discussion of causes by writing, "Three primary factors were responsible for her decision."

2. **Keep the causal explanation direct and simple.** Since your overall purpose is not to explore causal relationships, an in-depth analysis of causes and effects will distract readers from your main point. So focus on only the most important causes and effects.

3. **Use causal analysis to emphasize why particular points or ideas are important.** For example, if you are writing an explanation of how to hold a successful yard sale, your readers are more likely to follow your advice to keep the house locked and valuables concealed if you include anecdotes and statistics that demonstrate the effects of not doing so (such as thefts and break-ins during such sales).

HOW WRITERS READ ▷ CAUSE AND EFFECT

THE READING PROCESS	STRATEGIES
BEFORE READING	**Preview** the essay to get an overview of its content and organization.
	Make connections by thinking about the causes behind the effects (or the effects resulting from causes).
AFTER READING	**Analyze and evaluate** the reading by answering the following questions:

- How is the essay **relevant** to your own experience? What are your **reactions** to the essay?
- What is the writer's **purpose** in offering this analysis of causes and/or effects?
- What **assumptions** underlie the explanation? Are they reasonable?
- How well does the writer **explain** the causal relationship? Has the writer provided **sufficient evidence** to make the causal relationship believable?
- Does the writer cover **all major causes** or **effects fairly**? Is anything important omitted?
- Has the writer avoided the **common errors of reasoning**, such as *confusing chronology with causation* (carrying a rabbit's foot does not cause good luck); *mistaking correlation with causation* (an increase in sales of shovels and mittens doesn't mean shoveling causes people to buy mittens); and/or *misidentifying causal relationships* (does failure in school cause personal problems or vice versa? Maybe both are caused by some third factor)?

EXERCISE 18.4

Apply the questions in the "How Writers Read" box to the selection "How Labels Like *Black* and *Working Class* Shape Your Identity."

A Guided Writing Assignment*

CAUSE AND EFFECT

Your Essay Assignment

Write a causal analysis essay on a topic that you believe would interest readers of your college newspaper. You may consider causes, effects, or both. The following are some options:

- the popularity (or lack of popularity) of a public figure
- cheating on college exams
- a current trend or fad
- a major change or decision in your life
- a problem or event on campus or in the community

1 **Select a topic from the list above, or create one of your own.**

Consider the **length** of your essay as you choose your **topic** and decide whether to write about **causes**, **effects**, or **both**.

Example: You couldn't explore fully both causes and effects of child abuse in a five-page paper.

2 **Consider your purpose and audience, and choose a point of view.**

Ask yourself these questions:

- What is my **purpose**? A cause-and-effect essay for a college course may be both **informative** and **persuasive**.

   Example: An essay on academic cheating could examine the causes (informative) and propose policies to help alleviate the problem (persuasive).

- Who is my **audience**? How much do my readers **already know** about the topic? If your readers are **unfamiliar** with the topic you are writing about (or if the topic is complex), limit your focus to **the most important**, **obvious**, and **easily understood** causes or effects. If your audience is **generally familiar** with your topic, then you can deal with **less obvious** or **more complex causes or effects**. Take into consideration what your readers will think are the most likely causes or effects.

* The writing process is *recursive*; that is, you may find yourself revising as you draft or prewriting as you revise. This is especially true when writing on a computer. Your writing process may also differ from project to project and from that of your classmates.

PREWRITING

- What **point of view** is most appropriate given my purpose and audience? Although academic writing usually uses the **third person** (*he, she, they*), you might use the **first person** (*I*) to relate relevant personal experiences.

3 Discover causes and effects.

Try one or more of the following idea-generating strategies:

- Write your topic in the middle of a page. Then alone or with a classmate, **brainstorm** possible causes and effects, listing causes on the left and effects on the right.
- **Replay the event in your mind.** Ask yourself, "Why did the event happen?" "What happened as a result of it?" Make notes on the answers.
- **Ask questions** (or have a friend ask the questions) about the problem or phenomenon and then write down answers. Did a chain of events cause the phenomenon? Try to identify causes and effects that are not obvious.
- **Research your topic.** Try Googling a keyword and making notes on possible causes and effects.

4 Identify primary causes and effects.

Review your prewriting, and highlight what you see as the **primary**, or most important, **causes and effects**. Ask yourself questions like these:

- What causes or effects are the most **obvious** and **immediate**?
- What cause(s) or effects are the **most serious**? **For whom**?
- What causes or effects will my readers **expect me to address**?

Example:

Topic	*Effects of television violence on young viewers*
Primary Effects	An increase in aggressive behavior
	A willingness to accept violence as normal
Secondary Effects	Learning inappropriate or offensive words

Work Together

In groups of two or three, test your causes or effects.

1. Take turns presenting your primary causes or effects to the group. First, state your cause(s) or effect(s), and then explain why you think they are important:

   Example: I think _____ caused/is an effect of _____ because _____.

2. Have each member of the group rank each cause or effect as

   (a) sufficient (enough) on its own

   (b) a contributing cause or minor effect

   (c) an unlikely cause or effect

3. Compare notes and discuss what might be the most interesting or persuasive causes or effects to focus on.

Hint: Do not assume that the most obvious or simplest explanation is the only one. If a child often reports to the nurse's office complaining of a stomachache, a parent may reason that the child has digestive problems, but a closer study of the symptoms may reveal that the stomachaches are the result of stress.

5 Gather evidence to support your thesis.

Compile evidence—**facts and statistics, expert opinion, personal observation**—to support each cause or effect you will include. (Conduct research as needed—Chapters 21 and 22 can help you find and select sources.) Alone or with another student, consider whether one or more of the other **patterns of development** would help you support your thesis effectively.

Examples:

- A **story** (narration) could demonstrate the effects a fad diet had on an individual.
- A **comparison** with a fad diet from an earlier era could show likely effects.
- **Examples** of earlier fads that have come and gone could show likely causes.

6 Draft your thesis statement.

An effective thesis statement should

- **State the cause-and-effect relationship.** Do not leave it to your reader to figure out.

> **Example:** Breathing paint fumes in a closed environment can be dangerous/ ~~People~~ suffering from
> *for people*
>
> asthma and emphysema ~~are particularly vulnerable.~~
> *because their lungs are especially sensitive to irritants.*

The word *because* makes the cause-and-effect connection explicit. Adding *their lungs are especially sensitive to irritants* makes the cause more specific and focused.

- **Avoid overly broad or absolute assertions.**

> **Example:** Drugs are ~~the root~~ cause of inner-city crime.
> *a major*

> **Example:** Overemphasizing competitive sports ~~is~~ harmful to the psychological development of
> *may be*
>
> young children.

- Avoid an overly assertive or dogmatic tone.

Example: ~~There is no question~~ that American youths have changed in response to the culture in

Substantial evidence suggests

which they live.

Working together. In groups of two or three students, take turns reading your thesis statements aloud. While they listen, have group members write down the **cause-effect relationship** and identify any **qualifications**. Then, as a group, discuss how writers could make the cause-effect relationship more **plausible** and **specific**.

7 Choose a method of organization.

- **Chronological order** works well when a clear sequence of events is apparent.
- **Most-to-least order** works well to highlight one or two particularly important causes.
- **Least-to-most order** works well to create suspense.

Review Graphic Organizers 18.1, 18.2, and 18.3 to find the graphic organizer that is closest to your essay's basic structure, or use the outline function in your word-processing program to create an outline for your essay.

8 Draft your cause-and-effect essay.

Use the following guidelines to keep your essay on track.

- Your **introduction** should **identify the topic** and **causal relationship** as well as draw your reader into the essay. Unless you want to give readers the sense of discovering the cause-effect relationship for themselves, you will likely include the **thesis statement** as well.
- Your **body paragraphs** should include a clear **topic sentence** and provide **sufficient evidence** (examples, statistics, expert opinion, comparisons, and so on). Use **transitional words** and **phrases** (such as *in addition, furthermore, more important,* or *finally*) as you move from one cause or effect to another, and use **transitional sentences** to alert readers that you are moving from discussing causes to discussing effects (or vice versa) or shifting to a different pattern of development. Use **qualifying words** and **phrases**, such as *perhaps, possible, it is likely,* and *most likely,* to limit your claims and avoid a dogmatic tone.
- Your **conclusion** should remind readers of your **thesis** and draw your essay to a **satisfying close.**

9 Evaluate your draft and revise as necessary.

Use **Figure 18.1, "Flowchart for Revising a Cause-and-Effect Essay,"** to evaluate and revise your draft.

FIGURE 18.1 Flowchart for Revising a Cause-and-Effect Essay

QUESTIONS

REVISION STRATEGIES

1. Highlight your thesis. Does it express a qualified, manageable assertion? (Can you prove your thesis?)

 ▷

- Use a branching diagram to narrow your topic (see Chapter 4).
- Focus on only primary causes or effects.
- Add qualifying words or phrases to your thesis.

YES ▼

2. Place a ✔ by each cause. Mark an ✘ by each effect. Does your essay clearly focus on causes, effects, or both?

 ▷

- Reconsider whether you want to explain causes, effects, or both. Will the essay be skimpy if you focus on only one? Will it be too long or too complicated if you discuss both?

YES ▼

3. [Bracket] the explanation for each cause or effect. Is each explained fully?

 ▷

- Add anecdotes, observations, or other details and examples.
- Do research to locate facts, research studies, statistics, and expert opinions.

YES ▼

4. Write the method of organization (chronological, least-to-most, or most-to-least) you used at the top of your essay. Is it clear and effective? Do your ideas progress logically?

 ▷

- Choose a different order if necessary.
- Rearrange your causes, effects, or both.

YES ▼

5. Circle any sections where you have recognized readers' assumptions and either supported or challenged them. Have you identified all likely preconceptions?

 ▷

- Brainstorm popular ideas readers might assume about your topic and either support or challenge them.

YES ▼

REVISING

(continued on next page) ▶

(Figure 18.1 continued)

QUESTIONS

REVISION STRATEGIES

6. <u>Underline</u> each topic sentence. Is each paragraph focused on a separate cause or effect?

 NO ▶

- Combine closely related paragraphs.
- Split paragraphs that cover more than one cause or effect.

YES
▼

7. Reread your introduction and conclusion. Do they provoke thought, engage readers, and provide a sense of completeness?

 NO ▶

- Revise your introduction so that it sets the tone of the essay, provides necessary background, and engages readers.
- Revise the conclusion so that it reaffirms your thesis and brings the essay to a satisfying close.

10 Edit and proofread your essay.

Refer to Chapter 9 for help with

- **editing sentences** to avoid wordiness, make your verb choices strong and active, and make your sentences clear, varied, and parallel
- **editing words** for tone and diction, connotation, and concrete and specific language

Watch out particularly for **wordy sentences** and **mixed constructions:**

1. Revise wordy sentences. Writers often use complex and compound-complex sentences to explain causal relationships. These sentences can sometimes become wordy and confusing, so look for ways to eliminate empty phrases and simplify your wording.

    Example: ~~As you are already well aware,~~ viruses ^Certain types of computer^ ~~of certain types in a computer file~~ often create

    errors that you cannot explain ~~in documents~~ and may eventually result in lost data.

2. Revise to eliminate mixed constructions. A mixed construction occurs when a writer connects phrases or clauses that do not fit together in a sentence.

    Example: ~~Samantha, although~~ ^Although^ she was late for work, ~~but~~ ^Samantha^ was not reprimanded by her boss.

Using both *although* and *but* makes this a mixed sentence. To avoid mixed constructions, check words that join your phrases and clauses. Pay attention to prepositions and conjunctions. Also, check to be sure that the subjects of your sentences can perform the actions described by the verbs. If not, revise the sentence to supply the appropriate verb.

    Example: The college ~~hopes~~ ^encourages^ all students ~~will~~ ^to^ take a freshman seminar.

Readings: Cause and Effect in Action

Why Ban Single-Use Plastics?

Thai Luong

Thai Luong was asked to write a cause-and-effect essay that identified the causes, effects, or both causes and effects related to a phenomenon that interested him. He decided to examine how banning single-use plastics is affecting individuals and the environment. As you read the essay, notice how he carefully presents both positive and negative effects.

Title: Identifies topic and indicates causal analysis

Recently, communities across the country from California to Maine and New York to Hawai'i have begun to pass laws that will eliminate the use of single-use plastic items, such as plastic straws and bags. Their goal is to reduce the plastic waste that clogs our landfills and pollutes our oceans. While some of the effects of such bans are positive, they may also have some surprising negative effects that need to be considered before the bans are introduced on a large scale.

1   **Introduction:** Provides background; concludes with thesis statement that identifies one cause and multiple effects (positive and negative), and suggests essay's organization

The ban of plastic straws will produce many positive effects on the environment. Single-use plastic straws are typically too small to be recycled because they fall through the machinery used to sort recyclables, so they end up in the trash (Stockton). Because they are so light, they often get pulled from trash cans and garbage trucks by the wind, carried into bodies of water, float downstream to oceans, and wash up on beaches. A 2015 article in *Science* magazine estimated that over 7 million plastic straws end up on U.S. beaches every year (qtd. in Stockton). For these reasons, many localities, such as New York, Seattle, and San Francisco, have established plastic straw bans ("Why"), and within two to three years, a number of large chains that serve food, including Starbucks, American Airlines, and Hyatt hotels, will follow suit, eliminating plastic straws and stirrers (Corbett). Banning single-use

2   **Cause 1:** Positive effects identified in topic sentence

Support: Uses evidence from sources to support positive effects (negative effects will be eliminated)

Topic sentence: Negative effects announced in topic sentence; transition emphasizes shift

Support: Uses evidence from sources to support negative effects

Cause 2: Positive effects identified in topic sentence; transition indicates second type of single-use plastic item

Support: Uses evidence from sources to support positive effects

Topic sentence: Negative effects announced in topic sentence; transition emphasizes shift

Support: Uses evidence from sources to support negative effects

plastic straws is one way that municipalities and businesses can positively impact the reduction of waste in landfills and bodies of water.

Unfortunately, eliminating plastic straws will also have an adverse effect on members of the disabled community, including individuals who have mobility and strength issues that make it difficult for them to hold a cup and those whose hands move or shake without warning (Vallely). Paper straws are not strong enough for these consumers, and reusable glass or bamboo straws need to be washed after every use (Isom and Shughart) and present a danger to disabled users who may break such straws by accident (Vigdor). According to Katherine Carroll of the Center for Disability Rights in New York, "Plastic straws are an accessible way for people with certain disabilities to consume food and drinks, and it seems the blanket bans are not taking into account that they need straws and also that plastic straw replacements are not accessible to people" (Martinez).

In addition to banning single-use plastic straws, communities across the country also are working to ban or tax single-use plastic bags because they can have a negative impact on the environment. These bags can choke birds and fish and float into tree branches where they are difficult to remove. In addition, the production of these bags, which are typically used for just twenty minutes, uses up precious fossil fuels (Gosden). So far, only California, Hawai'i, and New York have banned the use of plastic bags statewide, but cities such as Boston, Chicago, Seattle, and Washington, D.C., restrict their use or charge a per-bag fee ("State Plastic and Paper Bag"). The result of a ban on single-use plastic bags could be good news for the environment.

Although this kind of ban sounds like a sensible idea on the surface, eliminating plastic bags may actually have a negative effect on the environment by creating more trash and waste. According to Rebecca Taylor, an economist from the University of Sydney, California cities that implemented a ban on plastic bags could wind up having to get rid of 80 million more pounds of paper bags every year (Rosalsky). Taylor also estimates that many consumers end up replacing the free plastic bags they get from the grocery store with thicker garbage bags, leading to a 120 percent increase in sales of four-gallon bags (Rosalsky).

3

4

5

While the push to ban single-use plastic items is motivated by a worthy cause—to combat the growing mountain of plastics in landfills, waterways, and beaches—such bans often turn out to have surprising—and concerning—effects. Rather than focusing on banning plastic straws and bags, we need to find creative strategies to encourage people to adopt reusable substitutes or to find ways to recycle plastic materials effectively. Doing so would not only help Earth but also benefit the people that inhabit our planet.

6   **Conclusion:** Revisits cause and effects and lends closure by encouraging creative thinking for solutions

Works Cited

Corbett, Erin. "These Eight Companies Are Ditching Plastic Straws. Here's How They Are Replacing Them." *Fortune*, 11 July 2018, www.fortune.com/2018/07/11/ditching-plastic-straws-replacements.

Gosden, Emily. "Five Reasons Why Our Plastic Bag Habit Is Bad." *The Telegraph* [London], 24 July 2015, www.telegraph.co.uk/news/earth/environment/11759608/Five-reasons-why-our-plastic-bag-habit-is-bad.html.

Isom, Brian, and William F. Shughart II. "Replacements for Plastic Straws Have Their Own Problems." *Duluth News Tribune*, 11 Aug. 2018, www.duluthnewstribune.com/opinion/4484642-national-view-replacements-plastic-straws-have-their-own-problems. Letter.

Martinez, Gina. "'Disabled People Are Not Part of the Conversation.' Advocates Speak Out against Plastic Straw Bans." *Time*, 12 July 2018, www.time.com/5335955/plastic-straws-disabled.

Rosalsky, Greg. "Are Plastic Bag Bans Garbage?" *NPR*, 9 Apr. 2019, www.npr.org/sections/money/2019/04/09/711181385/are-plastic-bag-bans-garbage.

"State Plastic and Paper Bag Legislation." National Conference of State Legislatures, 2019, www.ncsl.org/research/environment-and-natural-resources/plastic-bag-legislation.aspx.

Stockton, Nick. "How Plastic Straws Slip through the Cracks of Waste Management." *Wired*, 26 July 2018, www.wired.com/story/how-plastic-straws-slip-through-the-cracks-of-waste-management.

Vallely, Erin. "Grasping at Straws: The Ableism of the Straw Ban." *Center for Disability Rights*, www.cdrnys.org/blog/disability-dialogue/grasping-at-straws-the-ableism-of-the-straw-ban. Accessed 23 July 2019.

Vigdor, Neil. "Fatal Accident with Metal Straw Highlights a Risk." *The New York Times*, 11 July 2019, www.nytimes.com/2019/07/11/world/europe/metal-straws-death.html.

"Why Plastic Straws Are Being Banned." *Town Square: Business Resource Center*, 2019, squareup.com/townsquare/why-plastic-straws-are-being-banned.

Analyzing the Writer's Technique

1. **Purpose** Describe Luong's purpose.
2. **Patterns** What other patterns of development does Luong use to support his thesis and maintain readers' interest?
3. **Introduction and Conclusion** Evaluate Luong's introduction and conclusion. How effectively do they stimulate the reader's interest and lend closure to the essay?

Thinking Critically about Cause and Effect

1. **Tone** Describe the tone of Luong's essay. What words and phrases suggest his attitude toward the banning of single-use plastics? Given his tone, who do you think was his audience?
2. **Sources** Evaluate Luong's use of sources. Are his sources convincing? What additional types of sources might have made his claims more convincing? Why?
3. **Objectivity** How objective does Luong seem in his presentation of information on the effects of banning single-use plastics? Use evidence from the essay to support your claim.

Responding to the Essay

1. **Discussion** Rate your level of concern (1 being the least concerned and 5 being the most concerned) about landfills being filled and oceans being polluted by single-use plastics. Share your rating with your peers and explain why you rated yourself as you did. Would you be in favor of banning plastic straws and bags in your community? Why or why not? How do you think most people would react to the ban? Would you be willing to pay for bags when you shop in an effort to reduce the number being used? If not, how could communities restrict the number of bags being used?
2. **Reaction** In paragraph 6, Luong states that adopting reusable substitutes or finding ways to recycle materials effectively "would not only help Earth but also benefit

the people that inhabit our planet." The benefits to the Earth are obvious, but how do you think the proposed strategies could benefit people?

3. **Journal** Luong focused on both the negative and the positive effects of banning single-use plastics. Write a journal entry on the following topic: How would your life be affected, both positively and negatively, by the banning of one of the following: firearms, video games, smoking, alcoholic beverages, or television?

Why Summer Makes Us Lazy

Maria Konnikova

Maria Konnikova is the author of several books, including *Mastermind: How to Think Like Sherlock Holmes* (2013), *The Confidence Game* (2016), and *The Biggest Bluff* (2020). She has published numerous articles for publications such as *Scientific American, The Atlantic, Slate,* and the *Wall Street Journal.* In addition, she hosts the podcast *The Grift,* about con artists. The essay that appears here was originally published in *The New Yorker*'s Elements blog in 2013. **Before reading,** preview and make connections by thinking about how seasons of the year affect your mood and performance. **While reading,** highlight the results of each scientific study that Konnikova uses to support the cause-and-effect relationship she proposes.

JUST-IN-TIME TIP   Organizing Cause-and-Effect Relationships

This reading explores detailed and complex cause-and-effect relationships. To strengthen your concentration, understanding, and recall, organize these causal relationships using a chart similar to the one below; the first entry is provided to help you get started.

Variable	Cause	Effect
Motivation and productivity (paras. 2–3)	• Bad weather • Good weather	• Motivation/productivity falls. • Motivation/productivity increases.
Quality of critical thinking (4)		
Mood (7–8)		
"Goldilocks" effect (9)		

Creating this chart will keep you focused as you read and make it easy to review the reading for class discussion and written response.

See Just-in-Time Guide, section 6a.

In his meticulous diaries, written from 1846 to 1882, the Harvard librarian John 1
Langdon Sibley complains often about the withering summer heat: "The heat
wilts & enervates me & makes me sick," he wrote in 1852. Sibley lived before the
age of air-conditioning, but recent research suggests that his observation is still
accurate: summer really does tend to be a time of reduced productivity. Our brains
do, figuratively, wilt.

One of the key issues is motivation: when the weather is unpleasant, no one 2
wants to go outside, but when the sun is shining, the air is warm, and the sky is
blue, leisure calls. A 2008 study using data from the American Time Use Survey
found that, on rainy days, men spent, on average, thirty more minutes at work
than they did on comparatively sunny days. In 2012, a group of researchers from
Harvard University and the University of North Carolina at Chapel Hill conducted a
field study of Japanese bank workers and found a similar pattern: bad weather
made workers more productive, as measured by the time it took them to complete
assigned tasks in a loan-application process.

When the weather improved, in contrast, productivity fell. To determine why 3
this was the case, the researchers assigned Harvard students data entry on either
sunny or rainy days. The students were randomly assigned to one of two conditions: before starting to work, they were either shown six photographs of outdoor
activities in nice weather, such as sailing or eating outdoors, or were asked to
describe their daily routines. The researchers found that participants were less
productive when they'd viewed pleasant outdoor photographs. Instead of focusing
on their work, they focused on what they'd rather be doing—whether or not it was
actually sunny or rainy outside (though the effect was stronger on sunny days).
The mere thought of pleasant alternatives made people concentrate less.

But each season has its share of attractive days—and a skier's mind would 4
likely have many opportunities to wander in the dead of winter. There's evidence,
however, that in summer, our thinking itself may simply become lazier. In 1994,
Gerald Clore, a pioneer in researching how ambient mood-altering phenomena
affect cognition and judgment, found that pleasant weather can often lead to a
disconcerting lapse in thoughtfulness. Clore's team approached a hundred and
twenty-two undergraduates on days with either good or bad weather and asked
them to participate in a survey on higher education. The better the weather, the
easier it was to get the students to buy into a less-than-solid argument: on days
that were sunny, clear, and warm, people were equally persuaded by both strong
and weak arguments in favor of end-of-year comprehensive exams. When the
weather was rainy, cloudy, and cold, their critical faculties improved: in that condition, only the strong argument was persuasive. Clore and his colleagues concluded
that pleasant weather led people to embrace more heuristic-based thinking—that
is, they relied heavily on mental shortcuts at the expense of actual analysis.

Summer weather—especially the muggy kind—may also reduce both our 5
attention and our energy levels. In one study, high humidity lowered concentration
and increased sleepiness among participants. The weather also hurt their ability to
think critically: the hotter it got, the less likely they were to question what they
were told.

The shift toward mindlessness may be rooted in our emotions. One common   6
finding is a link between relative sunshine and happiness: although people who
live in sunnier places, like Southern California, are no happier than those who live
in the harsher conditions of the Midwest, day-to-day variations in sunshine make
a difference. People get happier as days get longer and warmer in the approach to
the summer solstice, and less happy as days get colder and shorter. They also
report higher life satisfaction on relatively pleasant days. The happiest season,
then, is summer.

A good mood, generally speaking, has in turn been linked to the same type   7
of heuristic, relatively mindless thinking that Clore observed in his pleasant-
weather participants. On the flip side, a bad mood tends to stimulate more
rigorous analytical thought. Weather-related mood effects can thus play out in
our real-life decisions—even weighty ones. In one recent project, the psychologist Uri Simonsohn found that students were more likely to enroll in a university
that was famous for its academic rigor if they visited on days that were cloudy.
When the weather turned sour, he concluded, the value they placed on academics increased.

There's a limit, however, to heat's ability to boost our mood: when tempera-   8
tures reach the kind of summer highs that mark heat waves all over the world, the
effect rapidly deteriorates. In a 2013 study of perceived well-being, the economist
Marie Connolly found that on days when the temperature rose above ninety
degrees, the negative impact on happiness levels was greater than the consequences of being widowed or divorced.

Conversely, the effects of heat on our brains aren't entirely negative. Many   9
of the behaviors that psychologists study follow a so-called inverted-U pattern:
as one factor steadily increases, a related behavior improves, plateaus, and
then starts to deteriorate. A famous example of this is the Yerkes-Dodson
curve, which charts the effect of stress on how well someone performs a given
task. If we experience too little stress, or too much, our performance suffers.
Like Goldilocks, we want to get it just right. Similarly, our cognitive abilities
seem to improve up to a certain temperature, and then, as the temperature
continues to rise, quickly diminish. An early study suggested that the optimal
temperature hovered around seventy-two degrees Fahrenheit. A more recent
review of the literature shows a target of twenty-seven degrees Celsius, or
roughly eighty-one degrees Fahrenheit. (An important caveat, however, is that
neither of these studies take humidity or sunshine into account, two major
factors when it comes to assessing the influence of summer weather on
behavior.)

Maybe best of all, blistering heat does give us a perfectly good reason to eat ice   10
cream: studies have shown again and again that blood glucose levels are tied to
cognitive performance and willpower. A bite of something frozen and sweet, boosting depleted glucose stores, might be just what a brain needs as the temperature
spikes.

Understanding the Reading

1. **Summarizing** List the changes in behavior Konnikova contends are affected by summer weather.
2. **Details** On what segment of the population did Uri Simonsohn conduct his research? Why did he choose to use this particular group of people as his research subjects?
3. **Recommendations** According to Konnikova, what type of food might help to raise glucose level and boost brain function in the summertime?

Analyzing the Writer's Technique

1. **Thesis** Identify Konnikova's thesis statement.
2. **Evidence** The author includes evidence consisting of data from the American Time Use Survey and the results of a research study by Harvard and the University of North Carolina at Chapel Hill. Why do you think she includes these sources of information?
3. **Vocabulary** Explain the meaning of each of the following words as it is used in the reading: *meticulous* (para. 1), *enervates* (1), *ambient* (4), *cognition* (4), and *heuristic* (4).

Thinking Critically about Cause and Effect

1. **Evaluation** Konnikova cites research conducted in the United States and Japan but none conducted in Europe. She also includes studies that were conducted on very specific segments of the population. How might broadening her research help strengthen the essay?
2. **Tone** How would you describe the tone of the essay? Use examples from the text to support your answer.
3. **Fact or Opinion** In paragraph 10, Konnikova states, "A bite of something frozen and sweet, boosting depleted glucose stores, might be just what a brain needs as the temperature spikes." Is Konnikova's statement fact or opinion? How do you know?
4. **Purpose** What does Konnikova hope to accomplish by writing this essay?

Responding to the Reading

1. **Discussion** The results of research conducted by Harvard and the University of North Carolina suggest that bad weather makes workers more productive. As a student, have you found this to be true? Why or why not? What about workers in general? Are there certain factors—for example, type of work or type of worker—that might affect the veracity of this statement? What might those factors be?
2. **Journal** What is your favorite season of the year? Write a journal entry in which you explain why you favor this season over the other three.
3. **Essay** Write an essay in which you identify one or more surprising ways in which a person could improve his or her mental health.

Working Together

Using the information in Konnikova's essay, work with a partner to write an advertisement for ice cream as being the "magic bullet" for cognitive performance. Your ad must include both words and images. Try to capture the attention of your readers and leave them with a message they will remember. Be prepared to share your advertisement with the class.

> ### EXPLORE, RESEARCH, WRITE
>
> In "Why Summer Makes Us Lazy," Maria Konnikova uses information from scientific studies to support her thesis that warm summer weather causes laziness. Many other researchers have also explored the impact of weather and the seasons on our bodies and minds, including the following:
>
> - "Seasonal Affective Disorder," published by the U.S. National Institute of Mental Health (March 2016)
> - "Five Ways Change of Seasons Might Affect Your Mental Health," a blog post written by Joel L. Young, a psychiatrist and director of a center for behavioral medicine (*Psychology Today,* 20 October 2017)
> - "How Seasonal Changes Can Affect Your Body's Metabolism," published on the Humanitas University Web site (5 May 2017)
>
> Using your own ideas and one or more of the selections included here, write a thoughtful cause-and-effect essay in which you discuss the effects another of the seasons can have on the human mind or body. (The effects may be negative, positive, or a combination of the two.) Be sure to incorporate at least one quotation from the readings and cite it correctly at the end of the essay.

The Guided Writing Assignment in this chapter can walk you through the process of writing a cause-and-effect essay; for help with evaluating sources, see Chapter 21; for help choosing and synthesizing ideas from sources, see Chapter 22; for help with documenting sources, see Chapter 23.

READING

More Driving, More Dying

Joe Cortright

Joe Cortright is an economist and the president of Impresa, a consulting firm that specializes in urban economics. He also serves as a senior policy advisor for CEOs for Cities and was formerly the executive officer of the Oregon Legislature's Trade and Economic Development Committee. This reading originally appeared on CityObservatory.org, a Web site managed by Cortright and devoted to the analysis of issues, ideas, and policies that affect urban areas. **Before reading**, preview and make connections by thinking about the automobile accidents that you have heard and read about and the reasons that they occurred. **While reading**, highlight the reasons that the number of automobile injuries and fatalities is increasing.

See Just-in-Time Guide, section 4a.

> ## JUST-IN-TIME TIP   Reading Statistics
>
> This reading makes use of statistics to explain what causes and what does not cause traffic deaths. It is easy to get lost in the statistical details. They are important in supporting the author's thesis but not necessary to remember in and of themselves. More important is what each set of statistics contributes to the causal analysis. Write marginal notes next to reports of statistics so you do not have to reread them later to figure out, again, what they mean. For example, paragraph 3 cites statistics that support an effect—an increase in the number of traffic deaths; the cause of that increase is discussed later in the essay.

Four days before Christmas, on a Wednesday morning just after dawn, Elizabeth Meyers was crossing Sandy Boulevard in Portland, near 78th Avenue, just about a block from her neighborhood library. She was struck and killed, becoming Portland's 50th traffic fatality of 2017 (Ryan).   1

Vision Zero, a bold road-safety campaign with its origins in Scandinavia, has been sweeping through the US for the past decades, prompting all kinds of tough-talking, goal-setting traffic safety campaigns. And admirably, Vision Zero is designed to be a results-oriented, no-nonsense, and data-driven effort. Fair enough.   2

But judging by the grisly traffic statistics of 2017, we're failing. Almost everywhere you look, traffic injuries and crashes are increasing. The final national numbers aren't in, but the trend is clearly toward higher road deaths. To focus on Portland for a moment, where Elizabeth Meyers was killed, the 50 traffic deaths recorded in 2017 were the highest number in two decades. After years of declines, traffic deaths in Portland have spiked in the past three years (see Figure 1).   3

After averaging 31 traffic deaths per year between 2005 and 2014, traffic deaths have jumped 60% over the past three years.

There's a lot of finger-pointing about distracted driving (and red herrings, like distracted pedestrians), but there's a simpler explanation for what's at work here. Americans are driving more, and as a result, more people are dying on the roads. As the Victoria Transportation Policy Institute's Todd Litman noted, international comparisons make it clear that miles driven are a significant and independent risk factor that's much higher in the US than in other developed countries. As Litman puts it: 4

> . . . don't blame high traffic death rates on inadequate traffic safety efforts, blame them on higher per capita vehicle travel, and therefore automobile-dependent transportation planning and sprawl-inducing development policies; those are the true culprits.

The effects are big enough to show up in mortality statistics: American children are twice as likely to die in automobile crashes as are children in other advanced countries (Walker), which is a major contributor to the higher child mortality rate in the US.   5

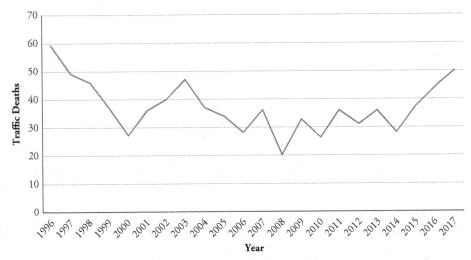

Fig. 1 Portland Traffic Deaths, 1996–2017 (Source: Portland Bureau of Transportation, press reports)

After more than a decade of moderation in driving (motivated largely by high   6
gas prices), driving in the US started increasing again when oil prices collapsed in
2014. Data from the U.S. Department of Transportation trace a clear uptick in driving in the past three years (Figure 2, Policy).

The result inevitably has been increased carnage on the highways.   7

There's some good news out of the Oregon Legislature in the past year. The   8
legislature gave the city permission to set lower speed limits on city streets, and
the city has just forwarded a new speed limit of 20 miles per hour that will apply
to many of the city's residential neighborhoods (Njus).

As important as this move is—excessive speed is a key contributor to   9
fatalities—it does nothing to address the conditions that led to the death of Elizabeth
Meyers. Sandy Boulevard is a multi-lane arterial street, the kind that the region's
safety analysis has determined to be the deadliest part of the roadway system
("Regional Transportation"). The city has been working on pedestrian improvements,
and efforts to reduce speeding and red-light running. But in the area just east of
where Meyers died, a section of roadway controlled by the Oregon Department of
Transportation, the state agency rejected city efforts to lower posted speeds:

> In response to a community request to reduce the posted 35 MPH speed on
> the east end of NE Sandy Blvd, traffic speed counts were taken east of 85th
> Avenue in early 2014 as part of the High Crash Corridor evaluation. 85th per-
> centile speeds were 40.3 MPH. The Oregon Department of Transportation
> (ODOT) reviews and makes decisions on posted speed reduction requests.
> ODOT will not consider speed reductions that are 10 MPH or more below the
> 85th percentile speed. Therefore, ODOT would not approve a speed reduction
> on outer NE Sandy Blvd near 85th Ave. (City of Portland, Bureau of Transporta-
> tion, NE Sandy Boulevard High Crash Corridor Safety Plan, 2014, page 5.)

Fig. 2 Traffic Volume Trends (Source: Policy and Governmental Affairs, Office of Highway Policy Information, U.S. Department of Transportation, Federal Highway Administration. "October 2017 Traffic Volume Trends. Figure 1—Moving 12-Month Total on All Highways." www.fhwa.dot.gov/policyinformation/travel_monitoring/17octtvt/figure1.cfm.)

The grisly trend indicated by the traffic death data of the past three years tells   10 us that as hard as we're trying to achieve Vision Zero, we're not trying hard enough. The biggest risk factor is just the sheer amount of driving we do, and with the boost to driving in recent years from lower fuel prices, it was predictable that deaths would increase. If we're serious about Vision Zero, we ought to be doing more to design places where people can easily live while driving less and where people can walk without regularly confronting speeding automobiles. We clearly have a lot of work to do.

Links

Litman, Todd. "A New Traffic Safety Paradigm." *Planetizen*, 18 Dec. 2017, www.planetizen.com/blogs/96324-new-traffic-safety-paradigm. Blog post.

Njus, Elliot. "Portland Poised to Drop Speed Limit to 20 mph on Residential Streets." *The Oregonian*, 15 Jan. 2018, www.oregonlive.com/commuting/2018/01/portland_poised_to_drop_speed.html.

"Regional Transportation Safety Strategy." 2018 Regional Transportation Plan, 6 Dec. 2018, oregonmetro.gov/safety. Resolution no. 18-4894, Metro Council, Portland, Oregon. https://www.oregonmetro.gov/sites/default/files/2019/01/29/2018-Regional-Transportation-Safety-Strategy_FINAL.pdf.

Ryan, Jim. "Police ID Woman Killed in NE Portland Crash." *The Oregonian*, 21 Dec. 2017, www
.oregonlive.com/portland/2017/12/police_id_woman_killed_in_ne_p.html.

Walker, Alissa. "U.S. Kids Die from Traffic Fatalities at Twice the Rate of Other
Wealthy Nations." *Curbed*, 10 Jan. 2018, www.curbed.com/2018/1/10/16871152/
traffic-deaths-children-vision-zero.

Understanding the Reading

1. **Effect** According to the author, what effect does the price of gasoline have on the number of traffic injuries and fatalities?
2. **Contrast** What difference does the author see in the automobile fatality rate of children in the United States as compared to other developed countries?
3. **Conclusion** What does the author conclude about our efforts to reduce traffic injuries and fatalities?

Analyzing the Writer's Technique

1. **Thesis** Identify Cortright's thesis statement. Is it stated or implied?
2. **Sources** The author includes several references to scientific studies. How do these references affect your reaction to his analysis? How do they affect the overall tone of the selection?
3. **Vocabulary** Explain the meaning of each of the following words as it is used in the reading: *grisly* (para. 3), *culprits* (4), *uptick* (6), *carnage* (7), and *arterial* (9).

Thinking Critically about Cause and Effect

1. **Meaning** In paragraph 4, Cortright mentions distracted pedestrians as a reason that some people use to explain the increase in traffic injuries and deaths. He refers to this reason as a *red herring*. What is the meaning of this term?
2. **Evidence** Cortright cites a number of sources that he regards as authorities on the topic. Based on the information in the references list, explain how you could determine whether the authors of those sources were in fact authorities. Going beyond the reference list, what other information could you use to determine whether a source was authoritative?

To learn more about evaluating sources, see Chapter 21.

3. **Purpose and Audience** Why do you think the author wrote this essay? Who do you think he expected to read this selection, and how might his intended audience have influenced the decisions he made as a writer?
4. **Tone** How would you describe the tone of the essay? Use examples from the text to support your answer.

Responding to the Reading

1. **Discussion** Do you agree with Cortright's thesis that the reason there are more highway deaths in the United States is that more people are driving? Why or why not?

2. **Journal** Are you a help or a hazard on the roads you travel? Write a journal entry in which you examine your driving habits and explain whether you are creating safe or dangerous situations for yourself and others on the road. Are there habits you need to change in order to make the roads safer for other drivers you encounter?

3. **Email** Using Cortright's research as your source, write an email to your city's transportation director in which you present a three-pronged plan for reducing the number of drivers on the streets of your city. Your email should be business-like and use standard email format.

Working Together

In the closing paragraph of "More Driving, More Dying," Cortright states that we need to design places where people can walk safely. Working with a small group of peers, research at least three ways that our cities could make streets safer for pedestrians. Once you have found the way that you think Cortright and your city officials would most favorably endorse, create a thirty-second television infomercial for it. Be sure to focus on the seriousness of the problem and the benefits of the plan. Be prepared to explain to the class the reason(s) Cortright and city officials would endorse the plan.

EXPLORE, RESEARCH, WRITE

In "More Driving, More Dying," Cortright uses research to support his claim that more people are dying on U.S. roads because Americans are driving more. Other researchers have also studied the reasons for the ever-increasing number of traffic fatalities. Some reports about this research include the following:

- "Motor Vehicle Crash Deaths" by the Centers for Disease Control and Prevention (6 July 2016)

- "Even as Cars Get Safer, Traffic Fatalities Still High" by David Schaper (NPR, 22 August 2018)

- "More Cars on the Road, and More Distracted Drivers, Lead to a Jump in U.S. Traffic Deaths" by Mary Wisniewski (NPR, 28 May 2018)

The Guided Writing Assignment in this chapter can walk you through the process of writing a cause-and-effect essay. For help with evaluating sources, see Chapter 21; for help choosing and synthesizing ideas from sources, see Chapter 22; for help with documenting sources, see Chapter 23.

Using your own ideas and one or more of the selections listed above, write a thoughtful cause-and-effect essay that goes beyond what the article tells and presents other reasons for the increase in deaths on U.S. roads. Be sure to include at least two supporting statistics from the readings and cite them correctly at the end of the essay.

Apply Your Skills: Additional Essay Assignments

Write a cause-and-effect essay on one of the following topics, using what you learned about causal analysis in this chapter. Depending on your topic, you may need to conduct research.

For more on locating and documenting sources, see Chapters 22 and 23.

To Express Your Ideas

1. Write an essay explaining the causes of a "bad day" you recently experienced.
2. Suppose you or a friend or relative won a large cash prize in a national contest. Write an essay about the effects of winning the prize.

To Inform Your Reader

3. Young children frequently ask "Why?" Choose a *why* question you have been asked by a child or think of a *why* question you have always wondered about (Examples: Why is the sky blue? Why are sunsets red? Why do parrots learn to talk?). Write an essay answering your question. Your audience is young children.
4. Write an essay explaining how you coped with a stressful situation.
5. Write a memo to your supervisor at work explaining the effects of requiring employees to work overtime.

To Persuade Your Reader

6. Write a letter to the dean of academic affairs about a problem at your school. Discuss causes, effects, or both and propose a solution to the problem.
7. Write a letter to the editor of your local newspaper explaining the possible effects of a proposed change in your community and urging citizens to take action for or against it.
8. Write a letter to the sports editor of your city's newspaper. You are a fan of a professional sports team, and you just learned that the team has been sold to new owners who may move the team to a different city. In your letter, explain the effects on the city and the fans if the team moves away.

Cases Using Cause and Effect

9. Your psychology professor invites you to participate in a panel discussion on the psychology of humor. You are required to research this question: What makes a joke funny? Conduct research on the topic and write a paper summarizing your findings for the panel discussion.
10. A controversy has arisen concerning the use of campus computer networks. Students use the college computer system for personal as well as course-related reasons, and some students have complained that the campus network is being used to post messages on social networking sites that defame the character of other

students. In a letter to the student newspaper, either defend the students' right to use the campus computer network to post such messages or call for a policy that limits such use. Give reasons in support of your position.

SYNTHESIZING IDEAS   DISCRIMINATION

Both "Right Place, Wrong Face" (pp. 243–45) and "How Labels Like *Black* and *Working Class* Shape Your Identity" (pp. 488–90) deal with the effects of discrimination.

Analyzing the Readings

1. While both authors address discrimination, they use two very different approaches: One focuses on a single personal experience; the other describes two experiments in detail. They also use two different points of view. Explain the advantages and disadvantages of each approach and point of view. To what type(s) of audience does each appeal?

2. Write a journal entry exploring whether you feel the incidents of discrimination in these two essays are typical and representative of discrimination in U.S. society.

Essay Idea

Write an essay in which you describe the effects of discrimination on a particular person or group with which you are familiar. Define what discrimination the group faces and propose solutions. (You need not limit yourself to racial discrimination; you might discuss age, sex, weight, or workplace discrimination, for example.)

PART FOUR

Reading and Writing Arguments

19
Reading Arguments

In this chapter you will learn to

- recognize the basic parts of an argument
- identify three types of claims
- understand the key elements of support in an argument: reasons, evidence, emotional appeals, and refutations
- identify the structure of an argument
- read, analyze, and think critically about arguments

Writing Quick Start

ANALYZE   The photograph on this page was taken on a state university campus in California where students were demonstrating against tuition increases. Although this sign is too small to list their reasons for opposing the increases, what do you think these students might say to support their position? Members of the faculty or administration may feel that the tuition increase is justified. How might they respond to the students' claims?

WRITE   Draft a paragraph that identifies your position, either for or against tuition increases, and offers reasons that others should accept your position. Be sure to consider what those who take a different view might find convincing.

CONNECT   The paragraph you just wrote is an example of a brief argument. An argument makes a claim and offers reasons and evidence in support of the claim. This chapter will show you how to read, analyze, and evaluate arguments, and in the next chapter you will learn strategies for writing effective argument essays.

Reading an argument effectively involves identifying and understanding the argument's basic parts and evaluating the effectiveness of each part.

READING ARGUMENTS ▸ IN COLLEGE AND THE WORKPLACE

- To prepare for a class discussion in a *sociology course,* you read and evaluate an essay proposing a solution to the gentrification of cities.

- In a *mass communication class,* your instructor assigns three articles that take different positions on the issue of whether journalists should provide graphic coverage of accidents and other human tragedies. Your instructor asks you to articulate your opinion on this issue.

- While working as a *purchasing agent* for a carpet manufacturer, you are listening to a sales pitch by a sales representative trying to convince you to purchase a new type of plastic wrapping used for shipping carpets.

What Are the Basic Parts of an Argument?

In everyday conversation, an argument can be a heated exchange of ideas between two people. College roommates might argue over who should clean the sink or who left the door unlocked the previous night. Colleagues in a company might argue over policies or procedures. However, there is a difference between an emotional, irrational argument and a rational, effective argument.

An effective argument is a logical, well-thought-out presentation of ideas that makes a claim about an issue and supports that claim with evidence. This does not mean that emotion has no place in an argument. In fact, many sound arguments combine emotion with logic.

Even a casual conversation can make a reasoned argument, as in the following:

Damon:	I've been called for jury duty. I don't want to go. They treat jurors so badly!
Maria:	Why? Everybody is supposed to do it.
Damon:	Have you ever done it? I have. First of all, they force us to serve, whether we want to or not. And then they treat us like criminals. Two years ago I had to sit all day in a hot, crowded room with other jurors while the TV was blaring. I couldn't read, study, or even think! No wonder people will do anything to get out of it.

Damon is arguing that jurors are treated badly. He offers two reasons to support his claim and uses personal experience to support the second reason (that jurors are treated "like criminals"), which also serves as an emotional appeal.

An effective argument must clearly state an *issue,* make a *claim,* and offer *support.* In many cases an argument also recognizes or refutes (argues against) opposing viewpoints.

Graphic Organizer 19.1 shows the basic components of an argument. Notice that unlike the graphic organizers in Part 3, the model graphic organizer showing the parts of an argument essay does not necessarily reflect the order in which the ideas are presented.

GRAPHIC ORGANIZER 19.1 The Basic Parts of an Argument Essay

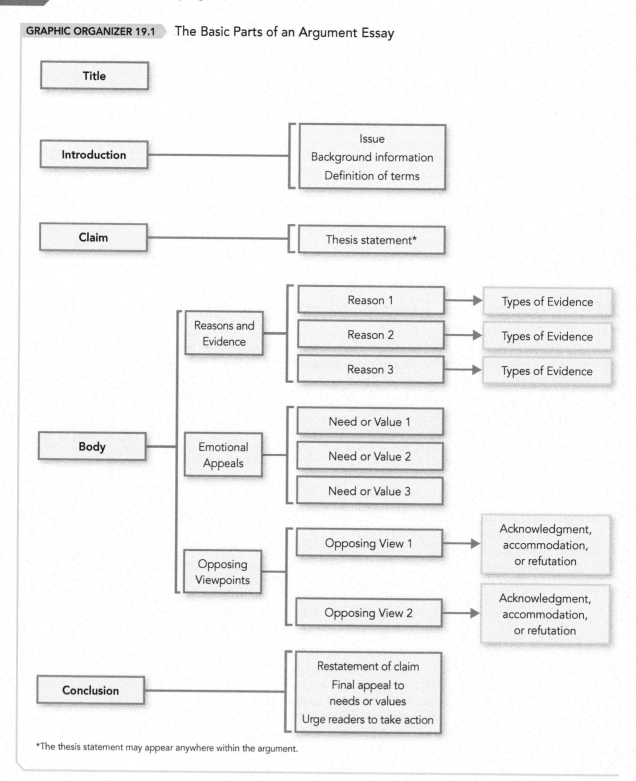

*The thesis statement may appear anywhere within the argument.

Rather, it provides a visual representation of the components of an argument. The arguments you read may address opposing views before presenting reasons and evidence in support of the writer's claim, for example.

The Issue Is a Controversial Topic

An argument is concerned with an **issue**—a controversy, a problem, or an idea about which people hold different points of view. In the exchange between Damon and Maria, the issue is "fairness of jury duty."

The Claim Is the Writer's Point

The claim is the point the writer tries to prove, usually the writer's view on the issue. In Damon and Maria's conversation, the claim is that "jury duty is unfair." The claim often appears as part of the thesis statement in an argument essay. In some essays, however, it is implied rather than stated directly.

There are three types of claims:

1. **Claims of fact** are statements that can be proved or verified. Of course, readers are not likely to be interested in arguments about long-established claims of fact, such as how far the moon is from the earth; instead, claims of fact in argument essays focus on facts that are in dispute or not yet well established.

   Example   Excessive use of the Internet has shortened college students' attention spans.

2. **Claims of value** are statements that express an opinion or judgment about whether one thing or idea is better or more desirable than other things or ideas. Issues involving questions of right or wrong, acceptable or unacceptable, often lead to claims of value. Since claims of value are subjective, they cannot be proved definitively.

   Example   Doctor-assisted suicide is a violation of the Hippocratic oath and therefore should not be legalized.

3. **Claims of policy** are statements offering one or more solutions to a problem. Often the verbs *should, must,* or *ought* appear in the claim. Like claims of value, claims of policy cannot be proved definitively.

   Example   The motion picture industry must accept greater responsibility for the consequences of violent films.

EXERCISE 19.1   **PREDICTING ISSUES AND CLAIMS**

For each of the following titles, predict the issue and the claim the essay would make:

1. "The Drugs I Take Are None of Your Business"
2. "Watch That Leer and Stifle That Joke at the Water Cooler"
3. "Crazy in the Streets: A Call for Treatment of Street People"
4. "Penalize the Unwed Dad? Fat Chance"
5. "A Former Smoker Applauds New Laws"

EXERCISE 19.2 **WRITING CLAIMS**

On your own or with one or two classmates, choose two of the following issues and write two different types of claims for each. For example, if one statement is a claim of value, the other should be a claim of policy or a claim of fact.

1. Legalization or decriminalization of marijuana
2. Stem cell research
3. Socially distant education
4. Protection for endangered species
5. College course requirements

The Support Includes Reasons, Evidence, and Appeals

The support in an argument consists of the ideas and information intended to convince readers that the claim is sound or believable. In Damon and Maria's conversation, Damon provides two key pieces of support:

1. People are forced to serve.
2. Potential jurors are treated like criminals.

Three common types of support are *reasons, evidence,* and *emotional appeals.*

Reasons. A **reason** is a general statement that backs up a claim. It explains why the writer's view on an issue is reasonable or correct. However, reasons alone are not sufficient support for an argument. Each reason must be supported by evidence and is sometimes accompanied by emotional appeals.

Evidence. The **evidence** provided in an argument usually consists of facts, statistics, examples, expert opinion, and observations from personal experience.

Claim	Reading aloud to preschool and kindergarten children improves their chances of success in school.
Facts	First-grade children who were read to as preschoolers learned to read earlier than children who were not read to.
Statistics	A 2010 study at the University of California–Davis found that having children read to shelter animals for 10 weeks improved the children's reading skills by about 30 percent.
Expert Opinion	Pam Allyn, author of over sixty educational publications and well-known childhood literacy advocate, urges parents to read aloud to their preschool children frequently.
Examples	Stories about unfamiliar places or activities increase a child's vocabulary. For example, reading a story about a farm to a child who lives in a city apartment will acquaint the child with such new terms as *barn, silo,* and *tractor.*
Personal Experience	When I read to my three-year-old son, I notice that he points to and tries to repeat words.

Emotional appeals.　Emotional appeals evoke the **needs** or **values** that readers are likely to share.

- **Appealing to needs:** People have both physiological **needs** (food and drink, health, shelter, safety, sex) and psychological needs (a sense of belonging or accomplishment, self-esteem, recognition by others, self-fulfillment). Your friends and family, people who write letters to the editor, personnel directors who write job listings, and advertisers all appeal to needs, directly or indirectly.
- **Appealing to values:** A **value** is a principle or quality that is considered important, worthwhile, or desirable, such as freedom, justice, loyalty, friendship, patriotism, duty, and equality. Arguments often appeal to values that the writer assumes most readers will share.

The public service announcement below appeals to both viewers' needs and values. The picture of the cute dog appeals to viewers' needs by evoking the emotional attachment to companion animals (either our own or other people's pets) that many of us share. The text, "a person is the best thing to happen to a shelter pet," also appeals

to viewers' need to be needed. The ad appeals to values as well by evoking the principle that caring for others, including animals, is important.

EXERCISE 19.3   **PROVIDING REASONS AND EVIDENCE**

Imagine you are the director of a day care center justifying expenditures to the board of directors. Choose two of the following items, and write a paragraph providing reasons for the purchases and offering evidence to show how each item would benefit the children:

1. Tropical fish tank
2. Microwave
3. Read-along books with audio recordings
4. Set of Dr. Seuss books
5. One or more tablet computers

The Refutation Responds to Alternative Viewpoints

A **refutation**, also called a *rebuttal*, recognizes and argues against opposing viewpoints. Refutation involves finding a weakness in the opponent's argument by casting doubt on the opponent's reasons or by questioning the accuracy, relevance, and sufficiency of the opponent's evidence.

Suppose you want to argue that you deserve a raise at work (your claim). To support your claim, you will remind your supervisor of the contributions and improvements you have made, your length of employment, your conscientiousness, and your promptness. But you suspect that your supervisor may still turn you down, not because you don't deserve the raise but because other employees might demand a similar raise. By anticipating this potential objection, you can build into your argument the reasons that the objection is not valid. You may have more time invested with the company and have taken on more responsibilities than the other employees, for example.

If an opponent's argument is too strong to refute, most writers will acknowledge or accommodate the opposing viewpoint in some way. They **acknowledge** an opposing view simply by stating it. They **accommodate** an opposing view by noting that it has merit and modifying their position or finding a way of addressing it. In an argument opposing hunting, for example, a writer might simply *acknowledge* the view that hunting bans would cause a population explosion among deer. The writer might *accommodate* this opposing view by stating that if a population explosion were to occur, the problem could be solved by reintroducing natural predators into the area.

The following readings illustrate the components of effective argument essays. The first reading, by student Suzanne Nguyen, is annotated to point out those components. As you read the second essay, try to identify for yourself the claim and the supporting reasons, evidence, and emotional appeals Howard Bryant includes. Look, too, for places where Bryant refutes, accommodates, or acknowledges opposing views.

Are Zoos the Best Answer for Animals?

Suzanne Nguyen

Suzanne Nguyen was a first-year student when she wrote the following essay for her composition course.

Title: Identifies issue, suggests claim, and engages readers with a rhetorical question

Zoo-goers gather in the African mammals corner of the park to admire three new lionesses. These lionesses, the guide explains, were recently rescued from an illegal animal trading ring and efforts are underway to rehabilitate them for release back into the wild. A visitor raises his hand, asks the guide for more details on their rehabilitation program, and is told that staff members implement enrichment activities that promote the animals' natural behaviors. There is no evidence of enrichment activity in the lionesses' exhibit and the guide does not offer specific examples. The other visitors look impressed, nonetheless, and filter out. A little girl runs back to the glass in front of the lionesses and bangs against it repeatedly, trying to elicit a response from the animals. Instead of stopping her, her mother smiles and snaps a few photos of her daughter next to the glass. One of the lionesses ignores the girl and tries to sleep; one licks its nearly hairless, chapped paws continuously; the other paces anxiously within its small enclosure and swipes at the glass in front of the girl. Many people have witnessed similar scenes at zoos and have become aware of the animals' sometimes subpar living conditions and the lackluster rehabilitation programs these institutions devise. While they seemingly offer a fun, family-friendly way to view and learn more about animals and their habitats, zoos too often prioritize entertainment over animal care and rehabilitation and, thus, should be abolished in favor of true wildlife preservation organizations.

Introduction: Engages readers with an anecdote and appeals to readers' concerns for animals

Claim: Thesis statement makes claims of value and policy

As the example of the lionesses suggests, captivity in zoos can take a severe toll on the emotional well-being of animals. The more time that animals spend in captivity, the more they demonstrate abnormal, repetitive behaviors, such as excessive licking, de-feathering, pacing, head bobbing, and so on. These abnormal behaviors stem from depression,

Reason 1: Topic sentence states first reason. Transition links paragraph to anecdote in introduction.

1

2

Support: Uses information from sources as supporting evidence

anxiety, and distress (Mason et al. 164). A captive animal must depend on its keepers to provide its mental, physical, and social needs. While many zoos try to design enrichment programs that discourage the adoption of abnormal repetitive behaviors, often entertainment is incorporated into these activities, and frequently, purposeful enrichment is replaced by gimmicks and animal shows that will attract more people to the institution. These ulterior motives often lead to animals' loss of sanity and do not accomplish their most important goal: preparing an animal for a life outside of captivity (Smith).

Reason 2: Topic sentence states second reason

Frequently, zoos advertise their rehabilitation programs and supposed success stories as reasons for their existence, but many do not adequately support reintegration of rescued animals into the wild. A 2008 reintegration study conducted by researchers at the University of Exeter showed that only 30 percent of animals released from zoos into the wild survived. Why? One reason is that zoo animals are not taught to fear and avoid humans, but instead learn to tolerate their presence, making the animals easy targets of poachers and fearful residents (Jule et al. 356). Another reason is that animals who live most of their lives in captivity for the purpose of viewing pleasure, especially animals that do not spend enough time with members of their own species, do not have the opportunity to develop the learned behaviors that will help them survive in their natural habitats (Jule et al. 357). As a result, many of the animals not killed by humans die of starvation or become prey themselves. Essentially, the majority of animals released from zoos perish because they are left without survival tools in an unfamiliar place.

Support: Statistics from a source provide evidence; rhetorical question ("Why?") engages readers

Reason 3: Topic sentence states third reason. Transition suggests organization from least to most important reason.

Perhaps the most important reason that zoos fail their animal inhabitants is that zoos prioritize their entertainment value to paying customers over their animals' welfare. Such institutions are more concerned with profits gained from tourist attractions (such as guided tours, food stands, souvenir shops, and other amusement park perks) than they are with pursuing the path to reintegration. The Columbus Zoo and Aquarium offers one such example. In an interview with the Columbus Zoo and Aquarium's director emeritus, Jack Hanna claims that conservation awareness is at the core of his work (McConnell). However, he spends most of the interview boasting about the zoo's revenue and

Support: Analysis of interview provides evidence to support claim stated in topic sentence

3

4

monetary growth, rather than about wildlife conservation work. In photographs published with the interview, Hanna is shown posing with a variety of wild animals at photo shoots—a practice condemned by many wildlife activists as animal exploitation. (See fig. 1.) In the past decade, this zoo has purchased a water park and golf course, and established additional food stands to accommodate the resulting influx of guests. While these changes have boosted park visitation and revenue, they do little to inspire confidence in their institutions' dedication to animal conservation.

Support: Photo provides evidence

Fig. 1. Jack Hanna poses with actress and singer Debbie Gibson and a lemur at the 2012 Daytime Emmy Awards.

Many zoo enthusiasts and supporters praise the improvements and successes zoos have achieved since their early days and choose to focus on an optimistic future for their animals instead of dwelling on the shortcomings they have yet to correct. Without zoos, they argue, how will the general public be exposed to wildlife, learn to value wild animals, and become supporters of conservation efforts? The answer is easy: through organizations such as sanctuaries and wildlife reservations. Reserves, such as the Chincoteague National Wildlife Refuge in Virginia, and sanctuaries, such as Big Cat Rescue in Florida, use a variety of resources to educate the public and promote conservation awareness. The proliferation of

5   **Conclusion: Acknowledges** and **rebuts** opposing view, and offers alternative to zoos

social media makes these organizations highly accessible, and donations benefit their animals directly instead of being funneled into snack bars and bathrooms. Living conditions for animals in reserves and sanctuaries are spacious and resemble more closely their natural environments. Enrichment activities are for the animals' benefit only, and do not take the form of cheap tricks designed to attract an audience. True wildlife preservation organizations have proven that it is possible to educate the public while providing safe, spacious, clean living environments for endangered animals, all without the need for mass attraction gimmicks. So who needs zoos?

Concludes with another rhetorical question

Works Cited

Jule, Kristen R., et al. "The Effects of Captive Experience on Reintroduction Survival in Carnivores: A Review and Analysis." *Biological Conservation*, vol. 141, no. 2, Feb. 2008, pp. 355–63. *Science Direct*, www.sciencedirect.com/science/article/pii/S0006320707004417.

Mason, G., et al. "Why and How Should We Use Environmental Enrichment to Tackle Stereotypic Behaviour?" *Applied Animal Behaviour Science*, vol. 102, no. 3–4, Feb. 2007, pp. 163–88. *Science Direct*, www.sciencedirect.com/science/article/pii/S0168159106001900.

McConnell, Kitty. "Q&A: The Columbus Zoo's Jack Hanna." *Columbus CEO*, Feb. 2014, www.columbusceo.com/content/roundup/2014/02/jack-hanna.html?page=all.

Smith, Laura. "Zoos Drive Animals Crazy." *Slate*, 20 June 2014, www.slate.com/blogs/wild_things/2014/06/20/animal_madness_zoochosis_stereotypic_behavior_and_problems_with_zoos.html.

EXERCISE 19.4 ▶ **WRITING A SUMMARY**

Check your understanding of the argument by writing a summary of "Are Zoos the Best Answer for Animals?"

EXERCISE 19.5 ▶ **DRAWING A GRAPHIC ORGANIZER**

Using Graphic Organizers 19.1 or 19.2 as a basis, draw a graphic organizer for "Are Zoos the Best Answer for Animals?"

> **READING**

Smoke Screen

Howard Bryant

Howard ("Howie") Bryant is a senior writer for ESPN.com and ESPN *The Magazine*. He is also a well-known radio personality and sports correspondent who appears regularly on ESPN Radio and National Public Radio. The following essay appeared in ESPN *The Magazine* in 2013.

Before Reading

1. **Preview:** Use the steps listed in Chapter 2.
2. **Connect:** Where do you stand on the issue of medical marijuana? Do you know anyone who uses it as a therapeutic alternative? Would you consider using it if you were in chronic pain?

While Reading Identify the reasons and evidence Bryant uses to support his claim. Check the reasons and evidence you identify against those listed in Graphic Organizer 19.2.

The truest way to see the NFL is not before the game, when the helmets are shiny   1
and the energy is high, but after the final whistle, when the bodies are bruised and the athletic tape is soiled with dirt and blood. Or at the practice facility the following day, when the players show up with crutches and walking casts, fingers in splints, arms in slings. Pain is the singular constant of the NFL. Maintenance of that pain is as vital to players as mastering the read-option*; whether through cortisone, painkillers or drugs and alcohol, they have always self-medicated to heal from the game that breaks their bodies. Which is why, more than any other sport, the NFL should lead the conversation on considering medicinal marijuana as a therapeutic alternative.

Medicinal marijuana is currently legal in twenty states, eight of which are home   2
to NFL teams, and it is almost universally accepted in the medical community as a safe and effective pain reliever. Yet there appears to be no plan to reassess marijuana's place on the NFL's list of banned substances, and according to the NFLPA, no player in the league has received an exemption to use pot for medicinal purposes.

*A common play in football.

That likely will not change tomorrow or even next year; the transition toward 3
legitimacy is tricky. States are decriminalizing marijuana even as it remains illegal
federally. Where marijuana can be obtained with a license, it still violates numerous federal drug-free-zone school statutes. If you are caught boarding a plane with
marijuana or putting it in the mail, you will likely face arrest, whether you have a
license exemption or not.

Decriminalization is one thing; mainstream acceptance is something else. In a 4
recent Gallup poll, for the first time, a majority of Americans (58 percent) said that
the drug should be legal. Still, as much as the awareness of marijuana's medicinal
benefits is growing, the racial and cultural stigmas attached to it are far stronger,
at least for now. (Remember Charles Oakley once saying that the NBA had "guys
out there playing high every night," or the ridicule snowboarding takes for being a
"stoner sport.") So marijuana appears destined to join Sudafed in the gray area of
sport: a legal substance that athletes are banned from using.

It does not have to be this way. The NFL has been defined this season by its 5
unwilling place at the front of cultural transitions in sports. Its ironclad codes of
masculinity are being challenged, first through grudging acknowledgment of the
vulnerabilities of the human body, and second, from a re-examination—again
unwillingly—of the locker room environment, as ignited by Richie Incognito and
Jonathan Martin.* But now the league has an opportunity to actually lead, to open
a discussion about medicinal marijuana and about the culture of pain maintenance among its players.

No one can pretend this is an easy conversation to have, with the inevitable 6
discomfort that comes from recognizing America's utterly failed war on drugs. And
the path of least resistance would be for the league, with its corporate caution, to
back away and wait until the states and the federal government can reconcile local
decriminalization with federal statutes, to find a dozen easy and obvious ways to
stifle discussion. But what was illegal yesterday may be legal tomorrow. And
because football players deal with pain management more acutely than athletes
from other sports, a more virtuous and forward-thinking approach for the NFL
would be to stimulate discussion of marijuana use. This is a league in which the
locker room culture still demands that athletes play through it all. And given that
marijuana is a legitimate pain reliever—especially for the migraines that can be a
byproduct of head trauma—and is far less dangerous and potentially addictive
than, say, OxyContin, it is almost immoral to deny players the right to use it.

Whether it is the military or construction work or playing left tackle, pain— 7
and not politics or culture—is the real issue. And if the NFL is serious about
making the game both safer and better to play, it should be a leader on a difficult
topic, to contribute to an honest dialogue and, more important, to make life a little
more comfortable for its broken warriors.

---

*In 2013, an investigation by the Miami Dolphins found that Richie Incognito and other players bullied their
teammate Jonathan Martin (and others). Martin decided to leave the Dolphins and was traded to the San
Francisco 49ers. Incognito was suspended and later released by the Dolphins.

GRAPHIC ORGANIZER 19.2   The Structure of "Smoke Screen"

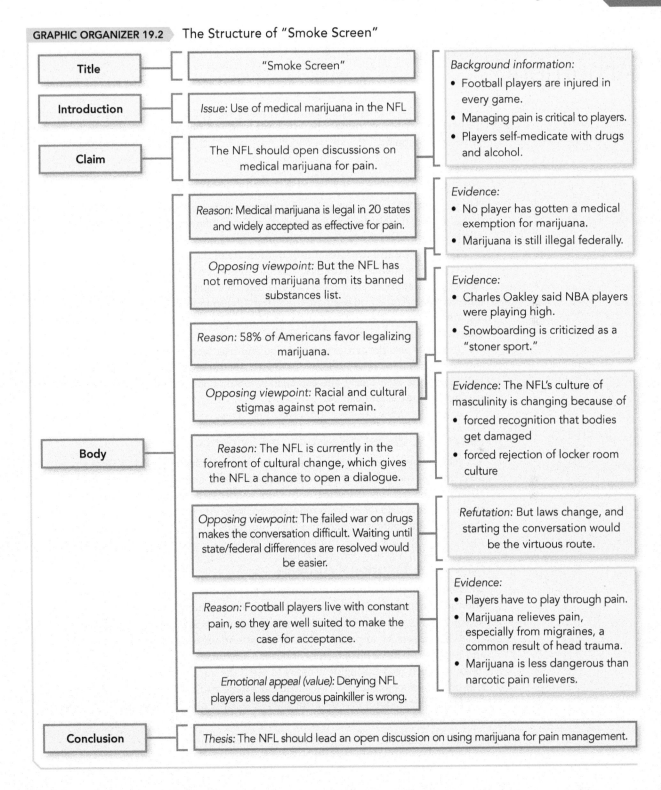

Title	"Smoke Screen"
Introduction	*Issue:* Use of medical marijuana in the NFL
Claim	The NFL should open discussions on medical marijuana for pain.

Background information:
- Football players are injured in every game.
- Managing pain is critical to players.
- Players self-medicate with drugs and alcohol.

Body

Reason: Medical marijuana is legal in 20 states and widely accepted as effective for pain.

Evidence:
- No player has gotten a medical exemption for marijuana.
- Marijuana is still illegal federally.

Opposing viewpoint: But the NFL has not removed marijuana from its banned substances list.

Evidence:
- Charles Oakley said NBA players were playing high.
- Snowboarding is criticized as a "stoner sport."

Reason: 58% of Americans favor legalizing marijuana.

Opposing viewpoint: Racial and cultural stigmas against pot remain.

Evidence: The NFL's culture of masculinity is changing because of
- forced recognition that bodies get damaged
- forced rejection of locker room culture

Reason: The NFL is currently in the forefront of cultural change, which gives the NFL a chance to open a dialogue.

Opposing viewpoint: The failed war on drugs makes the conversation difficult. Waiting until state/federal differences are resolved would be easier.

Refutation: But laws change, and starting the conversation would be the virtuous route.

Reason: Football players live with constant pain, so they are well suited to make the case for acceptance.

Evidence:
- Players have to play through pain.
- Marijuana relieves pain, especially from migraines, a common result of head trauma.
- Marijuana is less dangerous than narcotic pain relievers.

Emotional appeal (value): Denying NFL players a less dangerous painkiller is wrong.

Conclusion	*Thesis:* The NFL should lead an open discussion on using marijuana for pain management.

Analyze the Basic Components of an Argument

For more on evaluation, see Chapters 3, 5, and 21.

As you read an argument, consider the basic aspects of all persuasive writing: the author's credibility, purpose, and audience, and the reasons and evidence he or she provides as support.

Analyze the Writer's Credibility, Purpose, and Audience

Ask yourself: Why does the writer want to convince me of this? What does he or she stand to gain, if anything? Be particularly skeptical if a writer stands to profit personally from your acceptance of an argument.

Use the tone and the formality or informality of the author's language to figure out the type of audience—receptive, hostile, interested but skeptical—the author is expecting to address. How receptive the intended audience is expected to be might help you understand and evaluate the writer's argument. For example, writers addressing a receptive audience may not argue as carefully for their claims as would writers addressing a skeptical or hostile audience.

Consider also the writer's knowledge and trustworthiness. Ask yourself whether the writer has a thorough understanding of the issue, acknowledges opposing views and represents them fairly, and establishes common ground with readers by acknowledging their needs and values.

Assess the Writer's Reasons and Evidence

To assess the reasons and evidence, ask yourself questions like these: Does the writer offer enough reasons, do those reasons make sense, and are they relevant? Does the author supply enough evidence, and is that evidence accurate, complete, representative, up-to-date, and taken from reputable sources? Are the authorities cited experts in their field? Are sources cited formally or informally?

Assess the Emotional Appeals

Emotional appeals are a legitimate part of an argument. However, writers should not attempt to manipulate readers' emotions to distract them from the issue and the evidence. Table 19.1 presents some common unfair emotional appeals.

When assessing appeals to values, pay attention to the language the author uses and how he or she defines terms. Underline any terms that can have more than one meaning. Then read through the essay to see if the author defines these terms clearly and uses them consistently. Pay particular attention to words that appeal to values, and remember that not everyone considers the same principles or qualities important or agrees on their definition.

TABLE 19.1 Common Unfair Emotional Appeals

Unfair Emotional Appeal	Example
Name-calling: Using an emotionally loaded term to create a negative response	"That reporter is an *egotistical bully.*"
Ad hominem: Attacking the opponent rather than his or her position on the issue	"How could anyone who didn't fight in a war criticize the president's foreign policy?"
False authority: Quoting the opinions of celebrities or public figures about topics on which they are not experts	"According to singer Jennifer Hope, entitlement reform is America's most urgent economic problem."
Plain folks: Urging readers to accept an idea or take an action because it is suggested by someone who is just like they are	"Vote for me. I'm just a regular guy."
Appeal to pity: Arousing sympathy by telling hard-luck or excessively sentimental stories	"Latchkey children come home to an empty house or apartment, a can of soup, and a note on the refrigerator."
Bandwagon: Appealing to readers' desire to conform ("Everyone's doing it, so it must be right")	"It must be okay to exceed the speed limit, since so many people speed."

Evaluate Opposing Viewpoints

If an argument essay takes into account opposing viewpoints, you must evaluate how the writer presents them. Ask yourself the following questions:

- **Does the author state the opposing viewpoint clearly?**
- **Does the author present the opposing viewpoint fairly and completely?** That is, does the author treat the opposing viewpoint with respect or attempt to discredit or demean those holding the opposing view? Does the author present all the major parts of the opposing viewpoint or only those parts that he or she is able to refute?
- **Does the author clearly show why he or she considers the opposing viewpoint wrong or inappropriate?** Does the author apply sound logic? Does the author provide reasons and evidence?
- **Does the author acknowledge or accommodate points that cannot be refuted?**

Detect Faulty Reasoning

In some arguments, a writer may commit **fallacies,** errors in reasoning or thinking. Fallacies can weaken an argument, undermine a writer's claim, and call into question the relevancy, believability, or consistency of supporting evidence. Table 19.2 provides a brief review of the most common types of faulty reasoning.

For more on reasoning, see Chapter 20.

TABLE 19.2 Common Fallacies

Fallacy	Example
Circular reasoning (begging the question): Using the claim (or part of it) as evidence by simply repeating the claim in different words	"*Cruel* and unusual experimentation on helpless animals is *inhumane.*"
Hasty generalization: Drawing a conclusion based on insufficient evidence or isolated examples	"Based on the three chocolate cakes I just tasted, I can tell you that chocolate cake is overly sweet."
Sweeping generalization: Claiming that something applies to all situations or instances without exception	"All TV remotes are easy to use."
False analogy: Comparing two situations that are not sufficiently similar. Just because two items or events are alike in some ways does not mean they are alike in all ways.	"A human body needs rest after strenuous work, and a car needs rest after a long trip."
Non sequitur ("It does not follow" in Latin): Joining two or more ideas when no logical relationship exists between them	"Because my sister is financially independent, she will make a good parent."
Red herring: Distracting readers from the main issue by raising an irrelevant point	In an argument about banning advertisements for alcohol on TV, mentioning that some parents give their children sips of alcohol could distract readers from the main issue.
Post hoc fallacy ("after this, therefore because of this" in Latin): Assuming that event A caused event B simply because B followed A	"Student enrollment fell dramatically this semester because of the recent appointment of the new college president." (Other factors may have contributed to the decline in enrollment.)
Either-or fallacy (false dilemma): Arguing that there are only two sides to an issue and that only one of them is correct	"Marijuana must be *either* legalized *or* banned." (A third alternative is to legalize marijuana for medical use, such as to reduce nausea for those undergoing chemotherapy.)

EXERCISE 19.6 **EVALUATING AN ARGUMENT**

Working in a group of two or three students, analyze one of the reading selections in this or the next chapter by analyzing its basic components listed in the previous section.

HOW WRITERS READ ▶	ARGUMENT
THE READING PROCESS	**STRATEGIES**
BEFORE READING	**Preview** the essay to get an overview of its content and organization. **Make connections** by thinking about what claim the author is likely to make, given the title and how you feel about the issue.
WHILE READING	**Analyze and evaluate** the reading by answering the following questions: • What **issue** is the writer tackling? What is the **claim**, or position, on the issue? • What are the author's main **reasons**, and what **evidence** does the author offer? • What **needs** or **values** does the author seem to be appealing to? • Does the author present and respond to **opposing views** fairly?
AFTER READING	**Analyze and evaluate** the reading by answering the following questions: • What are the author's **credentials**? Many books and magazine articles will include a headnote or minibiography, or you can Google the author's name. (Be sure you're selecting the correct person, especially if the writer has a common name.) Is the writer an **authority** on the topic? • Does the author provide **compelling and relevant reasons** to support the claim? Is the evidence **accurate**, **complete**, **representative**, **up-to-date**, and **sufficient** to make the claim convincing? • Does the author use **emotional appeals fairly**? • Has the writer avoided the **common errors of reasoning**, such as *circular reasoning*, *sweeping generalization*, or the *either-or fallacy*?

EXERCISE 19.7 ▶ READING CRITICALLY

Apply the questions in the "How Writers Read" box to the selection "Smoke Screen."

Readings: Arguments in Action

READING

The Case for Free Money

James Surowiecki

James Surowiecki is a finance journalist. From 2000 to 2017, he wrote "The Financial Page" column for *The New Yorker*. Prior to 2000, he wrote the Moneybox column for *Slate* and worked as the business columnist for *New York* magazine. In 2018 he became a senior producer on HBO's *Vice News Tonight*. **Before reading**, preview and make connections by thinking about this question: What would you do if some of your basic needs were taken care of? **While reading**, notice the many examples the author provides. What is the cumulative effect of all these examples?

JUST-IN-TIME **TIP** Evaluating Evidence

The key to evaluating an argument is to examine whether the reasons the writer offers are adequately supported. Charts like the one below (and on p. 537) can help you identify and organize reasons and evaluate the evidence offered in support. The first reason is filled in for you. Be sure to conclude with an overall statement of how well you feel the author provides supporting evidence.

Reason	Evidence	Evaluation and Questions
Para. 3: Support for basic income comes from both left and right.		
Para. 4:		
Para. 5:		
Para. 6:		
Para. 7:		

In the mid-nineteen-seventies, the Canadian province of Manitoba ran an unusual experiment: it started just handing out money to some of its citizens. The town of Dauphin, for instance, sent checks to thousands of residents every month, in order to guarantee that all of them received a basic income. The goal of the project, called Mincome, was to see what happened. Did people stop working? Did poor people spend foolishly and stay in poverty? But, after a Conservative government ended the project, in 1979, Mincome was buried. Decades later, Evelyn Forget, an economist at the University of Manitoba, dug up the numbers. And what she found was that life in Dauphin improved markedly. Hospitalization rates fell. More teenagers stayed in school. And researchers who looked at Mincome's impact on work rates discovered that they had barely dropped at all. The program had worked about as well as anyone could have hoped.

Mincome was a prototype of an idea that came to the fore in the sixties, and that is now popular again among economists and policy folks: a basic income guarantee. There are many versions of the idea, but the most interesting is what is called a universal basic income: every year, every adult citizen in the U.S. would receive a stipend—ten thousand dollars is a number often mentioned. (Children would receive a smaller allowance.)

One striking thing about guaranteeing a basic income is that it's always had support both on the left and on the right—albeit for different reasons. Martin Luther King embraced the idea, but so did the right-wing economist Milton

Friedman, while the Nixon Administration even tried to get a basic-income guarantee through Congress. These days, among younger thinkers on the left, the U.B.I. is seen as a means to ending poverty, combatting rising inequality, and liberating workers from the burden of crappy jobs. For thinkers on the right, the U.B.I. seems like a simpler, and more libertarian, alternative to the thicket of anti-poverty and social-welfare programs.

There are signs that the U.B.I. may be an idea whose time has come. Switzerland held a referendum on a basic income last week (though it lost badly); Finland is going to run a U.B.I. experiment next year; and Y-Combinator, a Silicon Valley incubator firm, is sponsoring a similar test in Oakland. Why now? In the U.S., the new interest in the U.B.I. is driven in part by anxiety about how automation will affect workers. Bhaskar Sunkara, the publisher of the socialist magazine *Jacobin* told me, "People are fearful of becoming redundant, and there is this sense that the economy cannot be built to provide jobs for everyone." In the short run, concerns about robots taking all our jobs are probably overstated. But the appeal of a basic income—a kind of Social Security for everyone—is easy to understand. It is easy to administer; it avoids the paternalism of social-welfare programs that tell people what they can and cannot buy with the money they're given; and, if it is truly universal, it could help destigmatize government assistance. As Sunkara puts it, "Universal programs build social solidarity, and they become politically easier to defend."

The U.B.I. is often framed as a tool for fighting poverty, but it would have other important benefits. By providing an income cushion, it would increase workers' bargaining power, potentially driving up wages. It would make it easier for people to take risks with their job choices, and to invest in education. In the U.S. in the seventies, there were small-scale experiments with basic-income guarantees, and they showed that young people with a basic income were more likely to stay in school; in New Jersey, kids' chances of graduating from high school increased by twenty-five per cent.

Critics of the U.B.I. argue that handing people cash, instead of targeted aid (like food stamps), means that much of the money will be wasted, and that a basic income will take away the incentive to work, lowering G.D.P. and giving us a nation of lazy, demoralized people. But the example of the many direct-cash-grant programs in the developing world suggests that, as the Columbia economist Chris Blattman puts it, "the poor do not waste grants." As for the work question, most of the basic-income experiments suggest that the disincentive effect would not be large; in Manitoba, working hours for men dropped by just one per cent. It is certainly true that the U.B.I. would make it easier for people to think twice about taking unrewarding jobs. But that is a good consequence, not a bad one.

A basic income would not be cheap—depending on how the program was structured, it would likely cost at least twelve to thirteen per cent of G.D.P. And, given the state of American politics, that renders the U.B.I. politically impossible for the time being. Yet the most popular social-welfare programs in the U.S. all seemed utopian at first. Until the nineteen-twenties, no state in the union offered any kind of old-age pension; by 1935, we had Social Security. Guaranteed health care for seniors was attacked as unworkable and socialist; now Medicare is uncontroversial. If the U.B.I. comes to be seen as a kind of insurance against a radically changing job market, rather than simply as a handout, the politics around it will change. When this happens, it is easy to imagine a basic income going overnight from completely improbable to totally necessary.

Understanding the Reading

1. **Summary** Summarize Surowiecki's opinion regarding universal basic income and quote one or more sentences from the essay that concisely express his opinion.
2. **Evidence** What type of evidence does Surowiecki rely on primarily?
3. **Reasons** List at least three reasons that Surowiecki provides to support the idea that universal basic income may be beneficial.
4. **Vocabulary** Explain the meaning of each of the following words as it is used in the reading: *prototype* (para. 2), *stipend* (2), *thicket* (3), *redundant* (4), *paternalism* (4), *incentive* (6).

Analyzing the Writer's Technique

1. **Issue and Claim** What specific issue does Surowiecki discuss? What type(s) of claim does he make?
2. **Audience** Who is Surowiecki's intended audience?
3. **Appeals** To what emotions does Surowiecki appeal in the essay?
4. **Title** Why do you think the author entitled the reading "The Case for Free Money"? What does the title reveal about the author's attitude toward a universal basic income?

Thinking Critically about Argument

1. **Tone** Describe Surowiecki's tone. Highlight key words or phrases that reveal this tone.
2. **Sources** Discuss the author's use of sources. Has he consulted a reasonable number of sources? How does his engagement (or lack of engagement) with sources affect the credibility of his argument?
3. **Connotation** What connotation does the word *thicket* (para. 3) have in Surowiecki's article?
4. **Refutation and Opposing Viewpoints** Does Surowiecki present opposing viewpoints? If so, how does he present them and what is his response to them?

Responding to the Reading

1. **Reaction** What is your response to Surowiecki's examples and his argument? Do you find yourself basically agreeing with him or basically disagreeing with him about the feasibility of a universal basic income plan for U.S. citizens?
2. **Rebuttal** Imagine that you must respond to Surowiecki's article. List at least three reasons why universal basic income would not be beneficial.

3. **Journal** In your journal, compile a list of the concerns and questions that you have about instituting a universal basic income.

4. **Essay** Write an essay in which you examine a federal antipoverty program, such as School Lunch program, SNAP (food stamps), or TANF (Temporary Assistance for Needy Families). How effective has this program been in fighting poverty? How is the program administered? What are some of its pros and cons? How could the program better help the needy rise above poverty? Be sure to include evidence from sources and a correctly formatted Works Cited page.

READING

Five Reasons Why Universal Basic Income Is a Bad Idea

Ian Goldin

Ian Goldin is a professor of globalization and development at the University of Oxford in England. Born in South Africa, he held a number of important positions before becoming a professor at Oxford, including serving as a principal economist for the European Bank for Reconstruction and Development, chief executive of the Development Bank of South Africa, adviser to President Nelson Mandela, and vice president of the World Bank. He is also a prolific writer of books and journal articles. **Before reading,** preview and make connections by thinking about how work will change as artificial intelligence (AI) becomes more sophisticated. How might lost jobs be replaced? **While reading,** notice how Goldin recognizes and responds to alternative views.

JUST-IN-TIME TIP   Evaluating Types of Evidence

This reading offers five reasons why UBI is not feasible. The author needs to provide solid evidence to support the viewpoints offered. Charts like the one below (and on p. 534) will help you examine and evaluate the evidence provided (or not provided). The first reason is filled in for you. Be sure to conclude with a statement providing your overall assessment of the author's use of supporting evidence.

Reason	Evidence	Evaluation and Questions
Para. 2: One third of jobs are threatened.		
Para. 3:		
Para. 4:		
Para. 5:		
Para. 6:		
Para. 7:		
Para. 8:		

As the scale of the potential job losses arising from the artificial intelligence and robotics revolution becomes clearer, a chorus of otherwise disconnected billionaires, trade unionists and others are calling for universal basic income. Recognizing the threat posed by these dislocations is welcome and timely, but seeking solace in UBI is a bad idea.

At least one in three jobs is vulnerable to AI and robotics, with routine and repetitive tasks in manufacturing, administration and call centers most easily substituted. Research at the Oxford Martin School estimates that over the next 20 years, up to 47 per cent of U.S. jobs, around 40 per cent of UK and European jobs and a higher share of jobs in many developing countries including China, could be replaced by machines. The exponential increase in computing power and machine learning will intensify these vulnerabilities. It is misleading to think of this as yet another industrial revolution and take comfort in the fact all previous industrial revolutions have resulted in more and better-quality jobs. This time is different, both in the pace and the reach of change. The growth of new jobs is slower than the destruction of old jobs and their quality in many cases is inferior, as full-time career employment gives way to gig work or contingency contracts.

The places most vulnerable are also geographically isolated from the dynamic cities experiencing record earnings growth and low unemployment. Moving to these cities is increasingly difficult, as soaring housing and commuting costs reduce employment mobility. The result is rising geographical concentration of poverty and inequality in places left behind by change. The political reverberations are already being felt. The legitimate concerns of vulnerable workers must be addressed. But UBI is a red herring for five reasons.

First, UBI is financially irresponsible. *Universal* means everyone gets it. Even in the richest societies, if UBI was set at a level to provide a modest but decent standard of living it would be unaffordable and lead to ballooning deficits. To close the UBI budget black hole, much higher taxes or reallocation of resources from other areas such as health and education would be needed.

Second, UBI will lead to higher inequality and poverty. It typically aims to replace existing unemployment and other benefits with a simple universal grant. As shown by the OECD, the Paris-based club of mostly rich nations, by reallocating welfare payments from targeted transfers (such as unemployment, disability or housing benefits) to a generalized transfer to everyone, the amount that goes to the most deserving is lower. Billionaires get a little more.

Third, UBI will undermine social cohesion. Individuals gain not only income, but meaning, status, skills, networks and friendships through work. Delinking income and work, while rewarding people for staying at home, is what lies behind social decay. Crime, drugs, broken families and other socially destructive outcomes are more likely in places with high unemployment, as is evident in the drug pandemic in the U.S.

Fourth, UBI undermines incentives to participate. Stronger safety nets are vital. No decent society should tolerate dire poverty or starvation. But for those who are able, help should be designed to get individuals and families to participate in society; to help people overcome unemployment and find work, retrain, move cities. Wherever possible, safety nets should be a lifeline towards meaningful work and participation in society, not a guarantee of a lifetime of dependence.

Fifth, UBI offers a panacea to corporate and political leaders, postponing a discussion about the future of jobs. The demographic pressures in rich countries, and the deep challenge AI poses to development prospects in poor ones, adds to the need for this conversation. There must be more part-time work, shorter weeks, and rewards for home work, creative industries and social and individual care.   8

Forget about UBI; to reverse rising inequality and social dislocation we need to radically change the way we think.   9

Understanding the Reading

1. **Definition** What is a *red herring?*
2. **Reasons** What are the five reasons that Goldin gives to prove his claim that UBI is a red herring?
3. **The Larger Issue** In the title of the essay, Goldin hints that because of the distraction caused by the idea of UBI, a larger issue is not being addressed. What is the larger issue?
4. **Vocabulary** Explain the meaning of each of the following words as it is used in the reading: *solace* (para. 1), *contingency* (2), *reverberations* (3), *cohesion* (6), *pandemic* (6), *panacea* (8).

Analyzing the Writer's Technique

1. **Claim** What is Goldin's claim? Is it a claim of fact, value, or policy? Explain how you know.
2. **Appeals** What types of emotional appeals does Goldin make? Identify the needs and values to which he appeals.
3. **Evidence** What types of evidence does Goldin use to support his claim?
4. **Reasoning** Are there any errors in reasoning? If so, explain.

Thinking Critically about Argument

1. **Opposing Viewpoints** Does the author discuss, acknowledge, or rebut opposing viewpoints? If so, how? Are these opposing viewpoints representative of the arguments in favor of UBI?
2. **Fact or Opinion** Is Goldin relying on fact, opinion, or both to support his argument? Identify passages that support your answer.
3. **Tone** Describe Goldin's tone. Highlight several words or phrases that reveal this tone.
4. **Figurative Language** Explain what the author means when he speaks of the "budget black hole" (para. 4).

Responding to the Reading

1. **Reaction** What is your reaction to Goldin's article? How, if at all, did Goldin's article affect your thinking or change your opinion?

2. **Discussion** The author mentions the "political reverberations" (para. 3) related to inequality and poverty in areas left behind because of changes in the job market. Bring to class several examples of issues that are politically divisive. What are the various sides of each issue, what types of claims (fact, value, policy) are made for each? What criteria would you use to judge which side of the argument you favor?

3. **Journal** What jobs in your community have fallen victim to the artificial intelligence and robotics revolution? Of the jobs that remain, which ones do you think will continue to be viable in the future? How do you think the job you hope to have in the future will be affected by artificial intelligence and robotics?

4. **Essay** Write an essay in which you argue for or against one of the following:

   - a shorter work week
   - replacing unemployment benefits with UBI
   - free tuition at state colleges and universities
   - funding UBI with reallocated funds from health and education
   - setting an earnings cap on UBI distribution

SYNTHESIZING IDEAS   **UNIVERSAL BASIC INCOME**

"The Case for Free Money: Why Don't We Have Universal Basic Income?" and "Five Reasons Why Universal Basic Income Is a Bad Idea" take opposing viewpoints on the topic of universal basic income.

Analyzing the Readings

1. Having read these two essays, which do you think more effectively acknowledges and accommodates opposing viewpoints, and how does this affect whether you accept the writer's position?

2. One of the essays has information related to experimental projects and quotes from expert economists, while the other relies heavily on the author's own opinions as a renowned economist. Which makes a more compelling case? Which do you think would provide a better model for your own writing, and why?

Essay Idea

Write an essay in which you refute either Surowiecki's or Goldin's main claim. Use evidence from the essays in this chapter to support your position, and conduct research as needed.

Tuition-free college education for all has been proposed by politicians, legislators, and educators, and even implemented in a few places. But it has not become the norm in the United States. The readings that follow offer a representative sample of opinions in favor of and opposed to tuition-free college for all:

- "The Argument for Tuition-Free College" by U.S. Representative Keith Ellison of Minnesota (*The American Prospect*, 14 April 2016)

- "Make College Free for All" by Vermont Senator Bernie Sanders (*Washington Post*, 22 October 2015)

- "College Doesn't Need to Be Free" by Charles Lane, an editorial writer on fiscal policy (*Washington Post*, 21 May 2015)

Using what you learned in this chapter about reading and evaluating arguments, answer the following questions for each of the readings:

- What specific issue does the author discuss?

- What is the claim? State it in your own words.

- What type of evidence does the author rely on primarily to support his claim?

- To which values does the author appeal?

- Does the author present opposing viewpoints? If so, what are they?

After answering the questions for each reading, write a paragraph for each reading that analyzes the effectiveness of the author's argument. Be sure to consider the author's credibility, purpose, and audience, and the reasons and evidence he provides as support.

20
Writing Arguments

John Sommers II/Getty Images

Writing Quick Start

ANALYZE   The photograph above emphasizes the importance of voter turnout—getting qualified voters to the polls. Some people take the position that voter turnout could be dramatically increased if voting were made more convenient and accessible through online voting.

WRITE   Draft a brief argument (one to three paragraphs) that either agrees or disagrees with the position that online voting should be readily available.

Be sure to

▶ identify the issue

▶ state your position on the issue (your claim)

▶ offer at least one reason why your position is reasonable and should be accepted

Then, alone or with one or two classmates, revise your argument to appeal to an audience that disagrees with your position. How would your original argument have to change? What needs or values could you use to appeal to this new group? What ideas and attitudes would you need to acknowledge, accommodate, or refute?

CONNECT   By following the steps listed, you started to build a sound argument: You made a claim, supported it with evidence, and refuted or accommodated opposing views. The ability to construct sound arguments is an important skill. Many political, social, and economic issues are resolved through public and private debate that involves argument.

In this chapter you will learn to write effective arguments, modeling the characteristics of effective arguments you learned in Chapter 19 and following the detailed guidelines offered in this chapter.

> **USING ARGUMENT**   **IN COLLEGE AND THE WORKPLACE**
>
> - In a *health science course*, you are part of a group working on an argument essay claiming that the results of genetic testing, which can predict a person's likelihood of contracting serious diseases, should be confidential.
> - As a student member of the *affirmative action committee* on campus, you write a letter to the editor of the campus newspaper defending the committee's recently drafted affirmative action plan for minorities and women.
> - As a *lawyer* representing a client whose hand was seriously injured on the job, you argue to a jury that your client deserves compensation for the work-related injury.

What Are the Characteristics of Argument Essays?

In developing an argument essay, you need to select a controversial issue, make a clear and specific claim that takes a position on the issue, and give reasons and evidence to support the claim that will appeal to your audience. In addition, you should follow a logical line of reasoning; use emotional appeals appropriately; and acknowledge, accommodate, or refute opposing views.

Arguments Focus on Arguable, Narrowly Defined Issues

An **issue** is a controversy, problem, or idea about which people disagree. When writing an argument, be sure your issue is controversial. For example, *free public education* is an important topic, but it is not particularly controversial. (Most people would be in favor of at least some forms of free public education.) Instead, you might choose the issue *free public college education* or *universal, free prekindergarten education*.

Depending on the issue you choose and the audience you write for, a clear definition of the issue may be required. In addition, your readers may need background information. For example, in an argument about awarding organs for transplantation, you may need to give general readers information about the scarcity of organ donors versus the number of people who need transplants.

The issue you choose should be narrow enough to deal with adequately in an essay-length argument. For a brief (three- to five-page) essay on organ transplants, for instance, you could narrow your focus to transplants of a particular organ or to one aspect of the issue, such as who should and should not receive them. A narrow focus will allow you to offer more detailed reasons and evidence and respond to opposing viewpoints more effectively.

EXERCISE 20.1   **LIMITING A TOPIC AND PROVIDING BACKGROUND INFORMATION**

Working alone or with a partner, choose two of the following issues. For each issue, use two or more strategies from Chapter 4 to limit the topic. Then list the background information readers might need to understand the issue.

1. Virtual learning and access to education
2. Social media and the right to privacy
3. Speech codes on campus
4. Religious symbols on public property
5. Mandatory drug testing

An Argumentative Thesis Makes a Specific Claim and May Call for Action

For more on types of claims, see Chapter 19.

To build a convincing argument, you need to make a clear and specific **claim**, one that states your position on the issue precisely. To keep your essay on track, state your claim in a strong thesis in the introduction or early in the essay. As you gain experience in writing arguments, you can experiment with placing your thesis later in the essay.

Here are a few examples of how general claims can be narrowed to create clear and specific thesis statements:

Statewide   regulate the child-to-caregiver ratio and the qualifications of workers
More standards are needed to ~~protect children~~ in day care centers.

testing of cosmetics and skin-care products on
The ~~use of~~ animals ~~in testing~~ should be prohibited.

While all arguments make and support a claim, some, like claims of policy, also call for a specific action to be taken. An essay opposing human cloning might urge readers to voice their opposition in letters to congressional representatives, for example.

Be careful about the way you state your claim. In most cases, avoid an absolute statement that applies to all cases; your claim will be more convincing if you qualify, or limit, it by using words and phrases like *probably, often,* and *for the most part.* For example, the claim, "Single-sex educational institutions are *always* more beneficial to girls than coeducational schools are," could easily be undermined by a critic by citing a single exception. If you qualify your claim—"Single-sex educational institutions are *often* more beneficial to girls than are coeducational schools"—then an exception would not necessarily weaken the argument.

EXERCISE 20.2 **MAKING CLAIMS AND CALLING FOR ACTION**

Choose two of the following issues. For each issue, write two thesis statements—one that makes a claim and contains a qualifying term and another that makes a claim and calls for action.

1. Controlling pornography on the Internet
2. Limiting immigration
3. Limiting political campaign spending
4. Restricting testing of beauty products on animals
5. Promoting competitive sports for young children

Effective Arguments Are Logical

The reasons and evidence in an argument should follow a logical line of reasoning. The most common types of reasoning are induction and deduction (see Figure 20.1). **Inductive reasoning** begins with evidence and moves to a conclusion; **deductive reasoning** begins with a commonly accepted statement, or *premise*, and shows how a conclusion follows from it. You can use one or both types of reasoning to keep your argument on a logical path.

FIGURE 20.1 Inductive and Deductive Reasoning

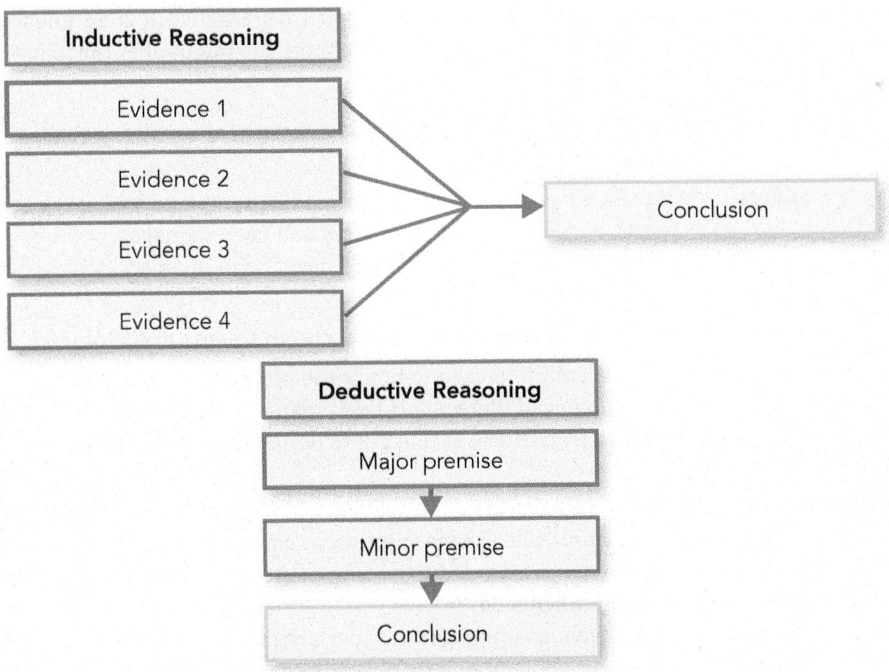

Inductive reasoning.   Think of inductive reasoning as a process of coming to a conclusion after observing a number of examples. For example, suppose you go shopping for a new pair of sneakers. You try on one style of Nikes. The sneakers don't fit, so you try a different style. That style doesn't fit either. You try two more styles, neither of which fits. Finally, because of your experience, you draw the conclusion that either you need to remeasure your feet or Nike does not make a sneaker that fits your feet.

When you use inductive reasoning, you make an *inference*, or guess, about the cases that you have not experienced. In doing so, you run the risk of being wrong. When building an inductive argument, be aware of some potential pitfalls.

- Consider as many possible explanations for the cases you observe as you can. In the sneaker example, perhaps the salesperson brought you the wrong size.
- Be sure that you have *sufficient* and *typical* evidence on which to base your conclusion. Suppose you learn that one professional athlete was involved in a driving-while-intoxicated incident and that another left the scene of an auto accident. If, from these limited observations, you conclude that professional athletes are irresponsible, your reasoning is faulty because these two cases may not be typical of all professional athletes and are not sufficient for drawing a conclusion. (If you draw a conclusion based on insufficient evidence or isolated examples, you have committed the fallacy of **hasty generalization**. You may also have committed a **sweeping generalization**—drawing a conclusion that applies to all cases without exception.)

For more on common fallacies, see Chapter 19, Table 19.2.

When you use inductive reasoning in an argument essay, the conclusion becomes the claim, and the specific pieces of evidence support your reasons for making the claim. For example, suppose you make a claim that Pat's Used Cars is an unethical business from which you should not buy a car. As support you might offer the following reasons and evidence:

Reason	Pat's Used Cars does not provide accurate information about its products.
Evidence	My sister's car had its odometer reading tampered with. My best friend bought a car whose chassis had been damaged, yet the salesperson claimed the car had never been in an accident.
Reason	Pat's Used Cars doesn't honor its commitments to customers.
Evidence	The dealership refused to honor the ninety-day guarantee for a car I purchased there. A local newspaper recently featured Pat's in a report on businesses that fail to honor guarantees.

Deductive reasoning.   Deductive reasoning begins with **premises**—statements that are generally accepted as true. Once the premises are accepted as true, the conclusion must also be true. The most common deductive argument is a **syllogism**, which consists of two premises and a conclusion.

When you use deductive reasoning, putting your argument in the form of a syllogism will help you write your claim, then organize and evaluate your reasons and evidence. Suppose you want to support the claim that state funding for Kids First, an early

Syllogism	Definition	Example
Major premise	A general statement about a group	Food containing dairy products makes you ill.
Minor premise	A statement about an individual belonging to that group	Frozen yogurt contains dairy products.
Conclusion	Logically necessary result	Frozen yogurt will make you ill.

childhood program, should remain intact. You might use the following syllogism to build your argument:

Major Premise	State-funded early childhood programs have increased the readiness of at-risk children to attend school.
Minor Premise	Kids First is a popular early childhood program in our state, where it has had many positive effects.
Conclusion	Kids First is likely to increase the readiness of at-risk children to attend school.

Your thesis statement would be "Because early childhood programs are likely to increase the readiness of at-risk children to attend school, state funding for Kids First should be continued." Your evidence would be information demonstrating the effectiveness of Kids First, such as the school performance of at-risk students who attended Kids First versus the school performance of at-risk students who did not and the cost of remedial education in later years versus the cost of Kids First.

Effective Arguments Depend on Careful Audience Analysis

To build a convincing argument, you need to know your audience. Analyze your audience to determine their education, background, and experience. Then also consider the following:

For more on audience analysis, see Chapter 4.

- how familiar your audience is with the issue
- whether your audience is likely to agree, be neutral or wavering, or disagree with your claim

This knowledge will help you select reasons and evidence and choose appeals that your readers will find compelling.

Agreeing audiences.   Agreeing audiences are the easiest to write for because they already accept your claim. When you write for an audience that is likely to agree with your claim, the focus is usually on urging readers to take a specific action. Instead of having to offer large amounts of facts and statistics as evidence, you can concentrate on reinforcing your shared viewpoint and building emotional ties with your audience. By doing so, you encourage readers to act on their beliefs.

Neutral or wavering audiences. Although they may be somewhat familiar with the issue, neutral or wavering audiences may have questions about, misunderstandings about, or no interest in the issue. When writing for this type of audience, emphasize the importance of the issue or shared values, and clear up misunderstandings readers may have. Your goals are to make readers care about the issue, establish yourself as a knowledgeable and trustworthy writer, and present solid evidence in support of your claim.

Disagreeing audiences. The most challenging audience is one that holds viewpoints in opposition to yours. The people in such an audience may have strong feelings about the issue and may distrust you because you don't share their views. In writing for a disagreeing audience, your goal is not necessarily to persuade readers to adopt your position but rather to convince them to consider your views. To be persuasive, you must follow a logical line of reasoning. Rather than stating your claim early in the essay, it may be more effective to build slowly to your thesis, first establishing **common ground**, a basis of trust and goodwill, by mentioning shared values, interests, concerns, and experiences.

> **EXERCISE 20.3** **DEVELOPING AN ARGUMENT FOR A SPECIFIC AUDIENCE**

Choose one of the following claims and discuss how you would argue in support of it for (a) an agreeing audience, (b) a neutral or wavering audience, and (c) a disagreeing audience:

1. Public school sex education classes should be mandatory because they help students make important decisions about their lives.
2. Portraying the effects of violent crime realistically on television may help reduce the crime rate.
3. Children who spend too much time interacting with a computer may fail to learn how to interact with people.

Effective Arguments Present Reasons and Evidence Readers Will Find Compelling

In developing an argument, you need to provide reasons for making a claim. A **reason** is a general statement that backs up a claim; it answers the question "Why do I have this opinion about this issue?" You also need to support each reason with evidence.

Suppose you want to argue that high school uniforms should be mandatory. You might give three reasons:

1. Uniforms reduce clothing costs for parents.
2. They help eliminate distractions in the classroom.
3. They reduce peer pressure.

You would need to support each of your reasons with some combination of evidence, such as facts, statistics, examples, personal experience, or expert testimony. Carefully linking your evidence to reasons helps your readers see how the evidence supports your claim.

Choose reasons and evidence that will appeal to your audience. In the argument about mandatory school uniforms, high school students would probably not be impressed by your first reason, but they might be persuaded by your second and third reasons if you cite evidence that appeals to them, such as personal anecdotes from other students. For an audience of parents, facts and statistics about reduced clothing costs and improved academic performance would be appealing types of evidence.

Effective Arguments Appeal to Readers' Needs and Values

Although an effective argument relies mainly on credible evidence and logical reasoning, **emotional appeals** to readers' needs and values can help support and strengthen a sound argument. **Needs** can be biological or psychological (food and drink, sex, a sense of belonging, self-esteem). **Values** are principles or qualities that readers consider important, worthwhile, or desirable. Examples include honesty, loyalty, privacy, and patriotism.

For more on emotional appeals, see Chapter 19.

Effective Arguments Recognize Alternative Views

Recognizing and countering alternative perspectives on an issue forces you to think hard about your claims. When you anticipate readers' objections, you may find reasons to adjust your reasoning and develop a stronger argument. Readers will also be more willing to consider your claim if you take their point of view into account.

You can recognize alternative views in an argument by acknowledging, accommodating, or refuting them.

1. **Acknowledge** an alternative viewpoint by admitting that it exists and showing that you have considered it.

   Example   Readers opposed to mandatory high school uniforms may argue that a uniform requirement will not eliminate peer pressure because students will use other objects to gain status, such as backpacks, iPads, and smartphones. You could acknowledge this viewpoint by admitting that there is no way to stop teenagers from finding ways to compete for status.

2. **Accommodate** an alternative viewpoint by acknowledging readers' concerns, accepting some of them, and incorporating them into your argument.

   Example   In arguing for mandatory high school uniforms, you might accommodate readers' view that uniforms will not eliminate peer pressure by arguing only that uniforms will eliminate one major and expensive means of competing for status.

3. **Refute** an opposing viewpoint by demonstrating the weakness of the opponent's argument.

   Example   To refute the viewpoint that uniforms force students to give up their personal style, you can argue that the majority of students' lives are spent outside school, where uniforms are not necessary and where each student is free to express his or her individuality.

The following readings demonstrate the techniques for writing effective argument essays discussed above. The first reading is annotated to point out how Noah Smith makes an arguable claim, provides reasons and evidence in support of his claim, and responds to alternative views. As you read the second essay, pay particular attention to the logic of the argument and the strategies S.K. uses to appeal to readers.

READING ▸

Tipping Has Hidden Benefits for Servers and Customers

Noah Smith

Noah Smith is an opinion columnist for Bloomberg News, a blogger, and an assistant professor of finance at Stony Brook University. The essay below appeared in the South Carolina *Post and Courier* in 2015.

Before Reading

1. **Preview:** Use the steps listed in Chapter 2.
2. **Connect:** As a customer, do you like or dislike tipping? Why?

While Reading Study the annotations that accompany the reading to discover how the essay illustrates the characteristics of effective cause-and-effect writing.

Title: Clearly identifies issue

Introduction: Presents issue (tipping), establishes anti-tipping position, and hints at own view that "hidden" issues are at stake

Thesis

Topic sentence: Introduces reasons to like tipping

Reason 1 to like tipping; anti-tipping response follows

Topic sentence: Reason 2 to like tipping, supported by evidence: facts from federal law

1 If you want to get economics pundits excited, bring up the issue of tipping. Most of my fellow pundits despise tipping, the way they despise the electoral college and the penny. Well, the pundits are sure to be rejoicing: Danny Meyer's Union Square Hospitality Group, which runs more than a dozen restaurant chains, recently said it will eliminate tipping at all of its establishments. The end of tipping would bring American restaurant culture closer to the global standard. But the celebration in the press may be premature. The issue of tipping is a lot more complicated than it seems, and it is not clear that its death would be a good thing.

2 Basic economic theory gives us several reasons to like tipping. First, tips are under the table, which allows restaurants, servers and customers all to dodge a little bit of taxes. Since taxes distort the economy to some degree, theoretically this means that tipping increases efficiency. Of course, it is unfair to allow certain types of businesses, such as restaurants, hotels and taxicabs, to selectively evade taxation.

3 Another good thing about tipping is that it can make minimum wage laws less burdensome. Federal law allows restaurants to pay a lower minimum wage, a break known as a tip credit, if wait staff are expected to make up the difference in gratuities. When economists looked at what happened when the tip credit was decreased, they found that employment went down for servers. So the end of

tipping culture will mean minimum wage laws take a bigger bite out of employment. That is something to think about as the nationwide campaign for $15 minimum wages gathers force.

A third reason to like tipping is that it can be used as a reward for good service. That would be a form of pay for performance—customers would give bigger tips to better wait staff, which would incentivize better service and draw better servers into the industry. The trouble is, both casual experience and data suggest that tips are pretty random and unfair.

> Anti-tipping response follows with evidence (from experts— "economists")

> 4   **Topic sentence:** Reason 3 to like tipping
>
> **Transition:** Introduces reasons for anti-tipping view

Most of the tips we leave are determined by social convention. In the past, the standard was 15 percent. These days, it is 20 percent. That number has nothing to do with how good a server is. In addition, percentage tips are grossly unfair, since it pays lots of money to a server at an expensive restaurant and very little money to one at a cheap restaurant, even though these two servers often provide exactly the same quality of service.

> 5   **Topic sentence:** Reason 1 for anti-tipping view

Tips are also affected by random factors such as whether the customer is paying by cash or by credit or debit card. For these reasons, many economists claim that tip size is only very weakly related to the quality of service.

> 6   **Topic sentence:** Reason 2 for anti-tipping view

So tips may seem unfair, but probably give the restaurant industry—and wait staff employment—a boost. But here is where things get complicated. Tipping also probably has a number of effects that are not captured by this tradeoff, or by standard economic theory.

> 7   Transition: Introduces writer's view
>
> **Thesis**

Economists typically assume that when you pay for a service, the way you pay does not make a difference to you. That assumption is probably wrong in the case of tipping. When customers leave a tip, they often get a sense of satisfaction from the idea that they gave money directly to a poor, hard-working person instead of to a big faceless corporation. Many of us like knowing that some of the money we pay will go directly into the server's pocket, instead of going through the vast, complex machinery of corporate accounting.

> 8   **Topic sentence:** Introduces refutation of economists' view
>
> "Hidden" reason 1 for writer's pro-tipping view

Econ 101 just does not deal with the personal bond that buyers and sellers can feel as the result of a transaction. But in the real world, that can make a big difference. Research shows that servers who draw smiley faces on checks get higher tips. Those customers are not tipping for a smiley face—they are tipping because it feels good to pay money to another human being with whom they feel they have shared a personal interaction.

> 9   **Topic sentence:** "Hidden" reason 2 for pro-tipping view
>
> **Evidence:** Support based on interpretation of fact

I believe that economics has made a big mistake by ignoring the utility humans get from the method of exchange. Tipping is just one tiny example. Personal relationships between sales workers and customers, or between purchasers and suppliers, or between bosses and employees, are emotionally important to us. A huge amount of economic activity is probably driven by that emotional importance. There is no reason economics couldn't take that into account, but it is almost always ignored.

> 10   **Conclusion:** Goes beyond thesis to make broader claim of fact and value

So I think tipping is a more complicated phenomenon than the pundits believe. Standard economics simply doesn't give us the answer. The real solution is for some businesses, such as Union Square Hospitality Group, to experiment with no-tip service, and see whether customers like it.

> 11   Returns to tipping and offers solution

Visualize an Argument Essay: Create a Graphic Organizer

For more on creating a graphic organizer, see Chapter 2.

Graphic Organizer 20.1 will help you analyze arguments as well as plan those that you write. Unlike the graphic organizers in Part 3, this organizer does not necessarily show the order in which an argument is presented. Some arguments, for example, may begin with a claim, whereas others may start with evidence or opposing viewpoints. In addition, not every element will appear in every argument. Thus you will likely need to adapt this organizer to fit the essays you analyze and write.

> READING

The Case against Tipping

S.K.

The essay that follows first appeared as a blog post on the Web site of the *Economist*, a weekly British publication devoted to keeping its readers well-informed about global news, especially economic news. Subscribing to the idea that what is written is more important than the person who writes it, and because many of its articles are debated and edited by many, the newspaper does not identify its journalists. It identifies writers of blog posts only to avoid confusion if posts adopt differing positions on the same issue. Thus, we know only the initials of the author of "The Case against Tipping." **Before reading**, preview and make connections by thinking about your tipping habits. Why do you tip a server? How do you determine how much to tip? **While reading**, notice how S.K. provides reasons for abolishing tipping and anticipates possible counterarguments.

Would you like a smile with your burger and fries? That will be 15% extra. These days anything less in America will earn you either shame or a pointed question from an irate server. But on October 14th Danny Meyer, head of Union Square Hospitality, a restaurant group, announced that he would put an end to tips in his eateries (B.R). This will not affect his customers' wallets; prices will rise to offset the banned tips. But it is good news for America.   1

Mr. Meyer is going against a trend that started in America just after the civil war. Tipping first caught on in Europe, where guests in fancy British houses would be threatened with gravy on their breeches if they failed to tip the footman. It spread across the pond as American holiday-makers returned to show off exotic European fashions. Once employers responded by slashing wages, workers worked hard to make sure they got their tips. In 1918, 100 waiters were arrested for poisoning the soup of prominent anti-tippers.   2

Today, tipping is entrenched. According to the Economic Policy Institute, 4.3 million Americans rely on the generosity of tippers to scrape a living. The idea seems like a good one. If the customer knows best, then who better to monitor and reward the performance of the servers? Without a tip on offer, waiters might be reluctant to fetch endless glasses of tap water with a smile.   3

But the system is flawed. Tips are paid after the service is provided, allowing opportunistic stingies to scarper, free-riding on the generosity of others. Society   4 tries to stop this by imposing a strong social norm on diners—tip much less than 15–20% and either be engulfed with shame, or face disapproval from your date. But this strong social norm undermines the original rationale for tips as a way to incentivize excellent service. Studies of tipping have found that diners do part with more cash when they feel they have been better served, but not much. A study from 2000 (Lynn and McCall) found that differences in customer-service ratings accounted for only 1–5% of the variation in dining parties' tips. So much for performance-related pay. A country like Japan, where tipping is seen as rude and the service is excellent, shows that you don't need to tip to be well-looked-after.

As well as not taking their motivational duties seriously, customers reward waiters for all manner of arbitrary things. Studies suggest that tips are larger when diners are presented with a good weather forecast, when the bill is presented on a tray embossed with a credit card insignia, when their waitress is blonde (Guéguen), and (as found in France) when she is wearing a red top. A recent study found that attractive servers earned $1,261 more in tips per year than unattractive ones. Worse, tipping is a vehicle for customers' prejudices to infiltrate into pay. Gender and race influence the size of tips; black servers are tipped less (Lynn et al.), and a study in 2011 found that for anything less than "exceptional service," women's tips were smaller. Even if tipping does lead to better service, letting discrimination sneak round the law is wrong.

Mr. Meyer's motive for scrapping tips was the bind they put him in when setting pay. Laws limit what greedy managers can siphon off for themselves, but also the extent to which chefs and other back-room staff—who play just as big a part in the meal waiters do—can share the customers' cash. No wonder there are chef shortages in New York. Managers are right to demand to set pay as they please.

Americans are caught in a nasty cycle of low pay justifying tips and tips justifying low pay. It is time to break out. Restaurateurs are best placed to lead the way. Laws passed in the 1900s to ban tipping were repealed as they were unenforceable. And a diner's lone act of defiance will only sap the income of the hard-working waiter. Servers scared of being stiffed can take comfort from the knowledge that Mr. Meyer banned smoking in his restaurants long before a general prohibition was passed. And who knows, customers might even find the human service sweeter when it does not have to be bought.

Links

B.R. "A New York Restaurateur Bans Tipping." *The Economist*, 15 Oct. 2015, www.economist.com/gulliver/2015/10/15/a-new-york-restaurateur-bans-tipping.

Guéguen, Nicolas. "Hair Color and Wages: Waitresses with Blond Hair Have More Fun." *The Journal of Socio-Economics*, vol. 41, no. 4 (2012), pp. 370–72, doi.org/10.1016/j.socec.2012.04.012.

Lynn, Michael, and Michael McCall. "Gratitude and Gratuity: A Meta-analysis of Research on the Service-Tipping Relationship." *The Journal of Socio-Economics*, vol. 29, no. 2 (2000), pp. 203–14, scholarship.sha.cornell.edu/articles/152.

Lynn, Michael, et al. "Consumer Racial Discrimination in Tipping: A Replication and Extension." *Journal of Applied Social Psychology*, vol. 28, no. 4, pp. 1045–60, scholarship.sha.cornell.edu/articles/27.

EXERCISE 20.5 DRAWING A GRAPHIC ORGANIZER

Using Graphic Organizer 20.1 or 20.2 as a basis, draw a graphic organizer for "Tipping Has Hidden Benefits for Servers and Customers."

GRAPHIC ORGANIZER 20.1   The Basic Structure of an Argument Essay

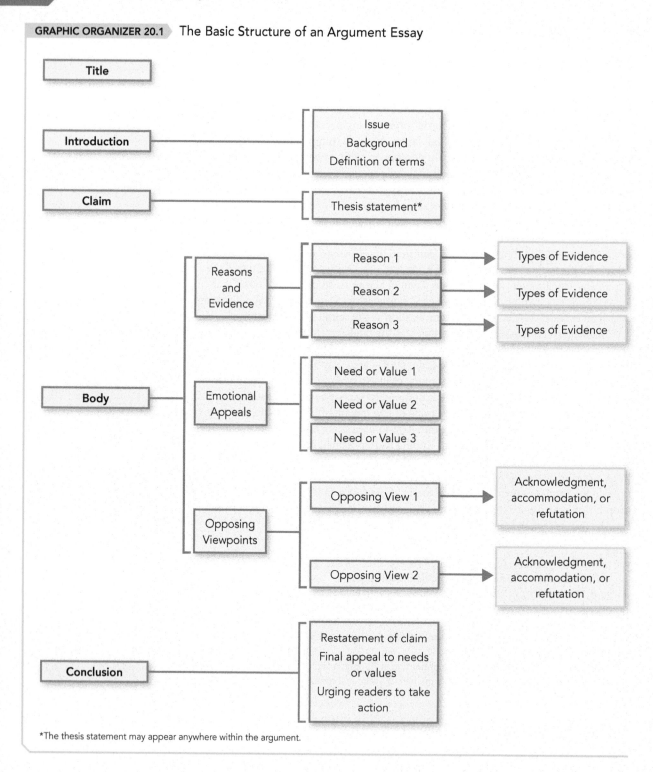

*The thesis statement may appear anywhere within the argument.

GRAPHIC ORGANIZER 20.2 The Structure of "The Case against Tipping"

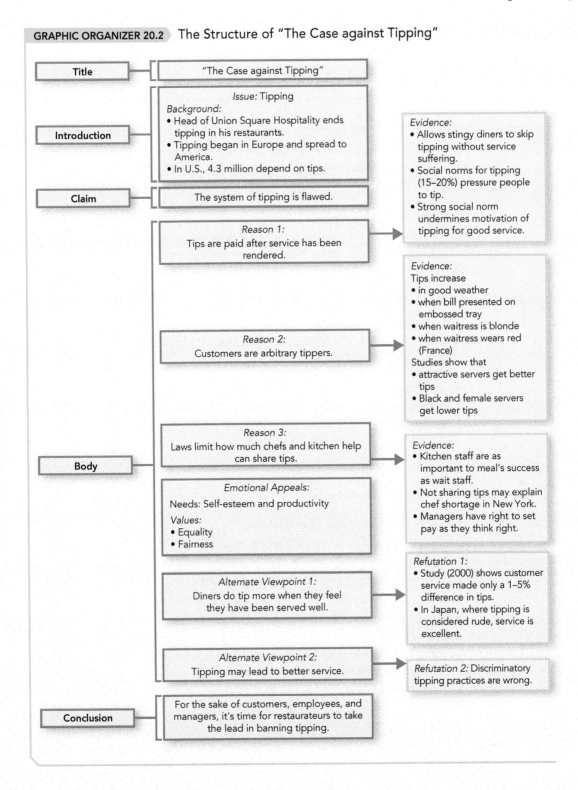

Title
"The Case against Tipping"

Introduction
Issue: Tipping
Background:
- Head of Union Square Hospitality ends tipping in his restaurants.
- Tipping began in Europe and spread to America.
- In U.S., 4.3 million depend on tips.

Evidence:
- Allows stingy diners to skip tipping without service suffering.
- Social norms for tipping (15–20%) pressure people to tip.
- Strong social norm undermines motivation of tipping for good service.

Claim
The system of tipping is flawed.

Body

Reason 1:
Tips are paid after service has been rendered.

Reason 2:
Customers are arbitrary tippers.

Evidence:
Tips increase
- in good weather
- when bill presented on embossed tray
- when waitress is blonde
- when waitress wears red (France)
Studies show that
- attractive servers get better tips
- Black and female servers get lower tips

Reason 3:
Laws limit how much chefs and kitchen help can share tips.

Evidence:
- Kitchen staff are as important to meal's success as wait staff.
- Not sharing tips may explain chef shortage in New York.
- Managers have right to set pay as they think right.

Emotional Appeals:
Needs: Self-esteem and productivity
Values:
- Equality
- Fairness

Alternate Viewpoint 1:
Diners do tip more when they feel they have been served well.

Refutation 1:
- Study (2000) shows customer service made only a 1–5% difference in tips.
- In Japan, where tipping is considered rude, service is excellent.

Alternate Viewpoint 2:
Tipping may lead to better service.

Refutation 2: Discriminatory tipping practices are wrong.

Conclusion
For the sake of customers, employees, and managers, it's time for restaurateurs to take the lead in banning tipping.

PREWRITING ⟩ DRAFTING ⟩ REVISING EDITING & PROOFREADING ⟩

A Guided Writing Assignment*

ARGUMENT

The following guide will lead you through the process of writing an argument essay. Although the assignment focuses on argument, you will probably need to use one or more other patterns of development in order to argue effectively for your position.

Your Essay Assignment

Take a position on a controversial issue and write an argument that makes a narrowly focused arguable claim, offers logical supporting reasons and evidence that readers will find convincing, appeals to readers' needs and values, and takes alternative viewpoints into consideration. You may choose an issue that interests you or your readers or select one from the following list:

- virtual learning replacing traditional face-to-face classes
- quotas to increase the number of men admitted to colleges
- paying college athletes
- providing a free college education to prisoners
- donating kidneys to save the lives of others
- an environmental problem or issue in your community
- mandatory drug testing for high school extracurricular activities

1 Choose and narrow a controversial issue.

To check whether an issue is controversial, try the following:

- Alone or with a classmate, brainstorm different sides of the issue.
- Draw an idea map of the issue, connecting ideas as they come to mind.
- Talk with experts; ask them to give you a sense of the main positions on the issue.
- Google your issue plus *blog*. Then scan your results to get a sense of the positions expressed.

The issues listed in the assignment, and most of the issues you are likely to come up with initially, are very broad. Try one or more of these strategies to **narrow** the issue you have chosen:

- **Use a branching diagram.** Type your issue at the left, and then subdivide the topic into three or more categories on the right. Choose a subcategory and repeat the process.
- **Ask yourself** the *who*, *what*, *where*, *when*, *why*, and *how* **questions** to focus your attention on particular aspects of the issue.
- **Freewrite** about your topic, and then read what you've written.

Then consider whether you can explore your topic fully in a brief essay. If not, try another narrowing strategy.

* The writing process is *recursive*; that is, you may find yourself revising as you draft or prewriting as you revise. This is especially true when writing on a computer. Your writing process may also differ from project to project or from that of your classmates.

PREWRITING

2 Consider your purpose, audience, and point of view.

Use appropriate **idea-generating strategies** to generate evidence and appeals that will be most effective given your readers. For example, you may wish to freewrite, create lists or columns, or discuss these issues with classmates.

Purpose: What do you want to **happen as a result** of your argument?

    . . . change readers' minds?

    . . . make readers more certain of their beliefs?

    . . . encourage readers to consider your point of view?

    . . . inspire readers to take a specific action?

Audience: Who are your **readers**, and how best can you **tailor your argument** to them? **Ask yourself questions like these:**

- What do my readers **already know** about the issue?
- Is my audience likely to **agree, be neutral/wavering**, or **disagree** with my position?
- What **needs** are likely to affect my readers' position on the issue? What **values** do my readers hold that are likely to affect their views? What shared needs or values can I use to establish **common ground** with my readers?

Point of view: What point of view is most appropriate to **your position** and **purpose** and to your **relationship with your readers**?

- The **first person** will help your readers feel close to you and accept you or your experiences as part of your argument.
- The **second person** may help you establish a familiarity with your audience.
- The **third person** works well when you want to establish an objective, impersonal tone.

3 Explore your issue.

To come to a more nuanced understanding, explore your issue thoroughly before taking a position:

1. Make a **tentative claim** and list reasons that support it. Then **switch sides**, and brainstorm reasons and evidence to support an alternative view.
2. Create a table with three columns. In the center column, type your issue; in the first column **list pros** and in the third, **cons**.
3. Conduct a **mock argument** with a classmate. Choose opposing views on the issue and defend your positions.

Use the ideas you come up with when drafting your argument.

4 Research your issue.

- Find **books** from reliable publishers on your issue.
- Find **articles** in academic journals and well-respected magazines and newspapers on your issue.
- Search **YouTube** to find news programs and documentaries on your issue.
- Search your issue on **Google Scholar** and examine the first few pages of results.

Then take notes on the most relevant sources to use when drafting your argument. (**Hint:** Sources can not only provide evidence to support your position; they can also provide background information and deepen your insight into a range of viewpoints.)

Note: To avoid **accidental plagiarism**, be sure to enclose quotations in quotation marks and use your own words and sentences when summarizing and paraphrasing information from sources. Also record all publication details you will need to cite your sources (author, title, publisher and site, publication date, page numbers, and so on).

5 Consider alternative viewpoints.

Drawing on your research, brainstorm reasons those holding **alternative positions** would be likely to offer. Choose the reasons your readers are likely to find most persuasive, and then decide whether you should **acknowledge**, **accommodate**, or **refute** those reasons:

- **Acknowledge** an opposing viewpoint by mentioning it in your claim.

    ┌──────────── acknowledges alternative view ────────────┐
    Example: Although speed-limit laws are intended to save lives, the conditions that apply to

    specific highways should be taken into account when enforcing them.

    Doing so shows that you take the view seriously but that you think your claim outweighs it.

- **Accommodate** an alternative viewpoint by finding a portion of the opposing argument that you can build into your argument.

    ┌──────────── accommodates alternative view ────────────┐
    Example: Clearly, poor instruction in high school must take some of the blame for so many high

    school graduates being unprepared for college. But with class sizes in many high schools

    in our district now exceeding thirty-five, even the most conscientious teachers struggle

    to educate all of their students.

- **Refute** an alternative viewpoint by pointing out problems or flaws in your opponent's reasoning or evidence. You could do the following:

    - **Give a counterexample** (an exception to the opposing view).
    - **Question the opponent's facts** by presenting alternative facts or statistics or an alternative interpretation.
    - **Question the credibility of "experts."**
    - **Question outdated examples, facts, or statistics.**
    - **Present the full context of statistics or quotations.**
    - **Point to any examples of faulty or fallacious reasoning**, such as examples that are not representative (sweeping generalization) or conclusions based on too little evidence (hasty generalization). (For more on fallacious reasoning, see Table 19.2.)

Collaboration. In small groups, take turns offering examples that show how each member plans to acknowledge, accommodate, or refute opposing views; critique those strategies; and suggest more effective approaches. Then work independently to list opposing viewpoints for your own argument and develop strategies for dealing with the opposition.

6 Draft your thesis statement.

Be sure your **thesis**

- makes an **arguable claim**

    Unarguable Fact   In recent years, U.S. consumers have experienced an increase in credit card fraud.

- is **specific** enough to explore fully

    Too General   Many problems that U.S. consumers complain about are mostly their own fault.

- avoids **absolutes**

    Too Absolute   U.S. consumers have no one but themselves to blame for the recent increase in credit card fraud.

Here is an example of a thesis that is **arguable**, **specific**, and appropriately **limited**:

Although the carelessness of merchants and electronic tampering contribute to the problem, U.S. consumers are largely to blame for the recent increase in credit card fraud.

7 Choose a line of reasoning and a method of organization.

Choose a line of reasoning that best suits your audience:

- **Inductive reasoning** allows readers to draw their own conclusions based on the evidence you present and so **may work best with readers who disagree with your position**.
- **Deductive reasoning** may work best with readers who agree or are neutral or wavering; readers who disagree with your position may feel railroaded by this approach.

Here are four common ways to organize an argument:

Method 1 (deductive)	Claim/thesis	Reasons/evidence	Alternative viewpoints
Method 2 (deductive)	Claim/thesis	Alternative viewpoints	Reasons/evidence
Method 3 (inductive)	Reasons/evidence	Alternative viewpoints	Claim/thesis
Method 4 (inductive)	Alternative viewpoints	Reasons/evidence	Claim/thesis

Method 1 works best with agreeing audiences, methods 2 and 3 with neutral or wavering audiences, and method 4 with disagreeing audiences.

Also decide how to **arrange your reasons and evidence** as well as the **alternative views** you canvass: From strongest to weakest? Most to least obvious? Most to least familiar? Draw graphic organizers or make outlines to try out each alternative.

8 Draft your argument essay.

Use the following guidelines to keep your essay on track:

- Your **introduction** should identify the **issue**, offer needed **background**, define **terms** that may be misunderstood, engage **readers**, and create **goodwill**. (Try opening with an attention-getting fact, statistic, or quotation; an engaging anecdote or story; or counterarguments your readers are likely to accept.) Most argument essays also include a thesis statement in which the writer states her or his **claim.**

- Your **body paragraphs** should state your **reasons** (one per paragraph) and provide appropriate **supporting evidence**. Body paragraphs should also **acknowledge**, **accommodate**, or **refute** compelling alternatives.

- Use **transitions** such as *also* and *in addition* to move clearly from reason to reason; use **transitional sentences** such as, "Those opposed to the death penalty claim . . . ," to introduce an opposing viewpoint and, "Contrary to what those in favor of the death penalty maintain . . . ," to signal a refutation.

    Cite sources of all **quotations**, **summaries**, or **paraphrases** of ideas or information, using an appropriate citation style. (See Chapter 23.)

    Finally, establish an appropriate **tone**: For a serious issue, use a serious, even somber, tone; for a call to action, use an energetic, enthusiastic tone; with a disagreeing audience, use a friendly, nonthreatening tone. Avoid statements that allow no room for other viewpoints ("It is obvious that . . .") and language that may insult your reader ("Anybody who thinks differently does not understand the issue").

- Your **conclusion** should remind readers of your **thesis**. Depending on your readers, you might also make a final appeal to **values**, urge readers to take **a specific action**, project what **might happen in the future**, or call for **further research**.

9 Evaluate your draft and revise as necessary.

Use **Figure 20.2, "Flowchart for Revising an Argument Essay,"** to evaluate and revise your draft.

FIGURE 20.2 Flowchart for Revising an Argument Essay

QUESTIONS | REVISION STRATEGIES

1. Circle the section of your essay where you introduce the issue. Do you define the issue clearly and limit it sufficiently? Do you provide enough background information?

 NO

- Use a branching diagram or questioning to limit your issue. (See Chapter 4.)
- Ask friends unfamiliar with the issue to read this section and tell you what else they need to know.

 YES

2. Highlight your thesis. Does it make a clear, specific claim? Does it take a stand on a controversial issue?

 NO

- Replace vague or overly broad words with more specific ones.
- Limit the claim to a more specific issue.
- Add a qualifying word or phrase (such as *may* or *possibly*) to limit your claim.

 YES

3. Describe briefly your intended audience. Do you take into account readers' knowledge of and attitude toward the issue? Do you appeal to readers' needs and values?

 NO ▶

- Add background information.
- Brainstorm to discover needs, values, and experiences you share with your readers.
- Add reasons and evidence based on those needs, values, and experiences.

 YES
▼

4. Place a ✔ by each supporting reason and an ✘ by each piece of evidence that supports a reason. Do you have enough reasons and evidence?

 NO ▶

- Brainstorm to discover compelling reasons.
- Conduct research to find solid evidence.

 YES
▼

5. Label the parts of your argument. Does each step follow logically from the one before and lead logically to the one after? Is your reasoning free of errors? Does the order make sense given your audience?

 NO ▶

- Create an outline or graphic organizer using inductive or deductive reasoning.
- Adjust your organization to appeal to your readers—agreeing, neutral, or disagreeing. (See Step 7 of the Guided Writing Assignment.)
- Check for and correct faulty reasoning and fallacies. (See Chapter 19.)

 YES
▼

6. [Bracket] sections where you present opposing viewpoints. Do you effectively acknowledge, accommodate, or refute the most important opposing viewpoints?

 NO ▶

- Conduct research to get a clearer understanding of opposing viewpoints.
- Modify your claim to accommodate an alternative viewpoint.
- Identify and refute weaknesses in opposing viewpoints.
- Point out unfair uses of appeals or faulty reasoning.

 YES
▼

7. Review your introduction and conclusion: Does the introduction identify the issue, define terms, provide background, and engage readers? Does your conclusion appeal to values or inspire action?

 NO ▶

- Revise your introduction to start with a compelling anecdote, fact, or commonly held misconception.
- Revise your conclusion to refer back to the introduction, make a strong emotional appeal, or urge readers to take a specific action.

REVISING

10 Edit and proofread your essay.

Refer to Chapter 9 for help with

- **editing sentences** to avoid wordiness, make your verb choices strong and active, and make your sentences clear, varied, and parallel
- **editing words** for tone and diction, connotation, and concrete and specific language

Watch out particularly for **ambiguous pronouns** and **problems with the subjunctive mood**.

1. **Look for and correct ambiguous pronouns.** A pronoun must refer to another noun or pronoun, called its *antecedent.* The pronoun's antecedent should be clearly named, not just implied.

   Example: Children of divorced parents are often shuttled between two homes, and that can be

   this lack of stability

   confusing and disturbing to them.

2. **Use the subjunctive mood correctly.** In an argument, you often write about what would or might happen in the future. When you use the verb *be* to speculate about future conditions, use *were* in place of *was.*

   Example: If all animal research was outlawed, progress in the control of human diseases would be

   were

   slowed dramatically.

Reading: Argument in Action

Pull the Plug on Explicit Lyrics

James Sturm

Title: Indicates Sturm's position on the issue of explicit lyrics

James Sturm wrote this essay when he was a student at Kalamazoo College, where he graduated with a degree in international and area studies. As you read, notice how Sturm uses comparison and contrast as well as illustration to strengthen his argument.

> Many kids pass through a rebellious phase in middle school. If the teacher asks them to stop throwing pencils, they toss one more. If the sign reads "No Trespassing," they cross the line. If they hear their father

1

listening to classical music, they tune in to rap and hardcore. Unfortunately, the lyrics in rap and hardcore can be quite explicit and may have a negative effect on impressionable youngsters. <u>For this reason, music with explicit lyrics should be off-limits until the age of sixteen.</u>

2   Currently, the government takes a rather laissez-faire attitude with regard to the music industry. Thousands of songs are readily available to young people regardless of explicit content. In fact, the main control mechanism for protecting youthful consumers from harmful content comes from the recording companies themselves. Under the Parental Advisory campaign of the Recording Industry Association of America (RIAA), it is the responsibility of artists and record labels themselves to decide if songs should receive the infamous "Parental Advisory: Explicit Content" label. Children are allowed to listen to such songs regardless ("Parental Advisory").

3   <u>This lack of regulation</u> would not be a problem if the music did not produce negative effects on its listeners. Although it is difficult to prove statistically that music full of hateful content fuels similar attitudes in its listeners, it requires only common sense to recognize that such an influence is likely: People are influenced by what they think about. If a child thinks, for example, that he is unimportant or unloved, then he will act out in various ways to gain attention from his peers. Problem thinking is a result of a variety of influences, including friends, parents, and the media. Negative music, if listened to frequently enough, naturally implants negative thoughts in the minds of its listeners.

4   <u>Furthermore,</u> consider the unique influence of music as opposed to other forms of media. Unlike movies, video games, and magazines, music has a way of saturating one's mind. Everyone knows the feeling of having a song "stuck" in their head, repeating itself throughout the day. Unlike a movie, which is seen once, discussed among friends, and then forgotten, a song can remain lodged in one's mind for weeks on end. And if the songs are steeped in content such as violence against women, happiness found in harmful drugs, and hatred of the police, these themes will continue reverberating in the minds of the listener, slowly desensitizing them to

Introduction: Sturm captures readers' interest by talking about youthful rebellion. In his <u>thesis statement</u>, he clearly states his claim of policy.

Background: Sturm offers background information about government regulation and record labeling, providing a source citation.

Reason 1: After providing a <u>transition</u> and accommodating an opposing viewpoint, Sturm presents his first reason and supports it with a hypothetical example.

Reason 2: Sturm presents his second reason and supports it by establishing common ground with his audience. Here and in the next paragraph, he includes <u>transitions</u> between his reasons.

otherwise repulsive ideas. Becoming numb to such ideas is the first step toward passively agreeing with them or even acting upon them.

Reason 3: Sturm presents his third reason and **accommodates two opposing viewpoints;** he refers back to the previous paragraph to create coherence.

Whereas adults can usually listen to such music with no behavioral ramifications, children are far more susceptible to its subtle influence. With less experience of life, a lower level of maturity, and a lack of long-term thinking, young people are prone to make impulsive decisions. Providing them with access to music that fuels negative and harmful thoughts is a dangerous decision. We live in an age where violent tragedies such as school shootings are increasingly commonplace. Although various factors contribute to such acts of violence, hatred-themed music is likely a part of the equation. Therefore, given the influential power of music and the heightened effect it can have on those still in the developmental stage of their lives, young people should have limited access to music with explicit lyrics.

5

Sturm offers an explanation for choosing sixteen as an age cutoff.

Sixteen years of age would be a reasonable cut-off. Until children reach that age, they should not be allowed to consume music with a Parental Advisory label. At sixteen, they are becoming young adults and making more and more of their own decisions. Before sixteen, they are weathering the turbulent transition from middle school to high school. This transition should not be accompanied by music that promotes rebellion as a means of coping with stress and difficulty. After reaching age sixteen, however, most young people will have obtained a driver's license, and the freedom that it allows eliminates the possibility of protecting youth from certain music. Those with a driver's license can seek out their own venues (such as streaming services or concerts) in which to hear explicit content.

6

Opposing viewpoints: In this paragraph and the next two, Sturm **recognizes three opposing viewpoints and accommodates each of them.** Notice that he cites a source for the first viewpoint and includes transitions between them.

The main critique of efforts to curtail young teens' access to explicit music is not new. Many say that it's pointless to censor music's explicit content because, as the RIAA's Web site contends, "music is a reflection, not a cause; it doesn't create the problems our society faces, it forces us to confront them" ("Freedom of Speech"). It is true that music reflects our culture. But it is also true that music fuels the perpetuation of that culture, for better or for worse. Guarding youth from explicit music does not equate to ignoring the issues raised in the music. It merely delegates that task to adults rather than to children.

7

Another critique says that limiting youth access to explicit music would take a financial toll on the music industry. This is true, but it would also

8

force the music industry to adapt. We can either allow the youth of our nation to adapt to the music industry, or we can force the industry to adapt to an impressionable generation of kids.

A third critique is that even if explicit music were restricted to those of a certain age, younger kids would find access to it anyway. This is a legitimate concern, especially given the explosion of music-streaming services. But if not only record companies but also streaming services such as YouTube, Spotify, and iTunes were included in the regulations, progress would surely come.

9

Hip-hop artist Ja Rule has spoken in favor of the current Parental Advisory system, saying, "That's what we can do as musicians to try to deter the kids from getting that lyrical content." But he added, "I don't think it deters the kids—it's just another sticker on the tape right now" (Bowes). Even some hip-hop artists agree that protecting the minds of our youth is a necessity. But until laws are passed to restrict access to this music, the "Parental Advisory" label will just be another logo.

10

Conclusion: Sturm quotes a hip-hop artist (and cites the source) to offer final support for his claim.

Works Cited

Bowes, Peter. "Spotlight on Explicit Lyrics Warning." *BBC News World Edition*, 27 May 2002, news.bbc.co.uk/2/hi/entertainment/2010641.stm.

"Freedom of Speech." *Recording Industry Association of America*, riaasalestool.shoshkey.com/aboutus.php?content_selector=Freedom -Of-Speech. Accessed 18 Sept. 2015.

"Parental Advisory." *Recording Industry Association of America*, 2016, www.riaa.com/resources-learning/parental-advisory-label/.

Analyzing the Writer's Technique

1. **Thesis** Analyze Sturm's thesis statement. What does it suggest about the organization of the essay? What aspect of the essay does it give no hint about?
2. **Evidence** What additional types of evidence could Sturm have used to support his reasons?
3. **Definition** How precisely does Sturm define the term *explicit lyrics*? Does his definition need to be more precise? Why or why not?

Thinking Critically about Argument

1. **Author's Attitude** What is Sturm's attitude toward explicit lyrics? Highlight words and phrases that reveal it.
2. **Fact or Opinion** Is Sturm relying on fact, opinion, or both to support his argument? Identify passages that support your answer.
3. **Audience** Who is Sturm's main audience? How do you know?
4. **Euphemism** What is "explicit music" a euphemism for?
5. **Needs and Values** To what needs and values does Sturm appeal?

Responding to the Reading

1. **Discussion** Discuss Sturm's proposal to ban the sale of "explicit music" to children. How are other media, such as books, movies, magazines, and TV shows, treated similarly or differently when it comes to children?
2. **Journal** What is the benefit, if any, of having explicit lyrics in music? Why are they needed, or why should they be allowed at all?
3. **Essay** Write an essay discussing the following dilemma: A middle school student wants to listen to explicit music, but it is not legally available to her age group. Her parents do not want her to have access to such music. Is there a compromise position? What advice would you offer to each side?

The Guided Writing Assignment in this chapter can walk you through the process of writing an argument essay; for help with evaluating sources, see Chapter 21; for help choosing and synthesizing ideas from sources, see Chapter 22; for help with documenting sources, see Chapter 23.

EXPLORE, RESEARCH, WRITE

In Chapter 19, you explored the topic of tuition-free college and evaluated and wrote an analysis of these three readings:

- "The Argument for Tuition-Free College" by Minnesota Congressman Keith Ellison (*The American Prospect*, 14 April 2016)
- "Make College Free for All" by Vermont senator and 2016/2020 presidential candidate Bernie Sanders (*The Washington Post*, 22 October 2015)
- "College Doesn't Need to Be Free" by Charles Lane, an editorial writer on fiscal policy (*The Washington Post*, 21 May 2015)

Now put your knowledge to work by using these readings to write an essay. First, revisit the readings to make sure you understand them. Then take a position on the issue of tuition-free college. Finally, write an argument that

- makes an arguable claim
- offers logical supporting evidence
- appeals to readers' needs and values
- addresses opposing viewpoints

Be sure to incorporate at least two quotations from the readings and cite them correctly at the end of the essay.

Apply Your Skills: Additional Essay Assignments

To Persuade Your Reader

Write an argument essay on one of the following issues:

1. Professional sports
2. E-waste (electronic waste)
3. Alternative energy options
4. Genetic testing
5. Presidential campaigns

Narrow the issue to one that is arguable, such as a problem that could be solved by reforms or legislation. Narrow the issue to one that can be addressed in a brief paper (3–5 pages). Depending on the issue you choose, you may need to conduct research. Your audience is your classmates and instructor.

Cases Using Argument

1. Write an essay for a sociology course, arguing your position on the following statement: The race of a child and that of the prospective parents should /should not be taken into consideration in making adoption decisions.
2. For a public health class you are taking, you have been asked to research and write a paper making recommendations about how the state can best prepare for the next pandemic. Propose steps that should be taken and explain why you recommend them. Use sources to support your proposal.
3. You have a job as a copyeditor at a city newspaper. Write a proposal that explains and justifies your request to work at home one day per week. Incorporate into your argument the fact that you could use your home computer, which is connected to the newspaper's computer network.

PART FIVE

Writing with Sources

Planning a Research Project and Evaluating Sources

fatihhoca/Getty Images

Writing Quick Start

ANALYZE Suppose you are enrolled in a public speaking class. Your instructor has chosen the topic of preschool and will divide the class into two teams. One team will argue for free, public preschool, and the other team will argue against it. At this point, you don't know which team you'll be on.

WRITE Draft a brief statement summarizing what you think the pros and cons of free public preschool are. Then indicate what further information you would need in order to defend either position.

CONNECT Before planning a speech or writing in detail about the pros or cons of public preschool, you would probably need to consult several sources to learn more about it. What information would you need to support your ideas? What types of sources would be useful? How would you be sure the information contained in your sources is relevant and reliable? How would you detect whether a source exhibits bias?

This chapter will answer these and other questions about choosing and evaluating useful sources. It will also lead you through the process of planning a project with sources. Graphic Organizer 21.1 lists the research skills covered in this chapter, placing them within the context of the process of writing a research project as a whole.

GRAPHIC ORGANIZER 21.1   Writing a Paper with Sources

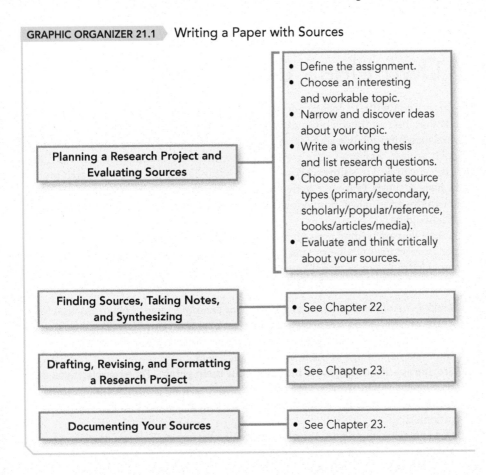

Planning a Research Project and Evaluating Sources
- Define the assignment.
- Choose an interesting and workable topic.
- Narrow and discover ideas about your topic.
- Write a working thesis and list research questions.
- Choose appropriate source types (primary/secondary, scholarly/popular/reference, books/articles/media).
- Evaluate and think critically about your sources.

Finding Sources, Taking Notes, and Synthesizing
- See Chapter 22.

Drafting, Revising, and Formatting a Research Project
- See Chapter 23.

Documenting Your Sources
- See Chapter 23.

USING RESEARCH   **IN COLLEGE AND THE WORKPLACE**

- *For an astronomy course,* you are asked to write a two-page report on black holes. Your textbook contains basic information on the subject, but you need to consult other sources to complete the assignment.

- *For a political science class,* you need to write a five-page research project on a current issue (such as Internet-based voting or government shutdowns), explaining the issue and reporting on current developments.

- *You are a journalist* and will interview your state governor. You need background information on the governor's position on several issues of local concern. You also need to interview politicians or local groups who may disagree with the governor's positions.

Write from Sources: Use Sources to Make Your Own Ideas Convincing

To learn more about documenting sources in MLA and APA style, see Chapter 23.

The papers you write in college are intended to be serious works of scholarship. This means that instructors will often expect you to support your own ideas with convincing evidence from reliable sources and to document those sources. When you write a research project, you don't simply glue together the facts, statistics, information, and quotations you find in sources. Like any other essay-length writing, a research project must have a thesis that your body paragraphs support with reasons and evidence. Although the information from outside sources is not your own, the interpretation you give it should be.

When you are writing a research project, instructors will expect you to use information from sources whenever your topic demands more factual information than you can provide from your personal knowledge and experience. For example, use information from sources to do the following:

- **Make general comments more specific.** For example, instead of writing that "the crime rate in Boston has decreased over the past few years," specify the years over which the decrease has occurred, and use official police statistics to show the exact percentage of the decrease in each year.
- **Provide specific examples to illustrate your main points.** For example, if you are writing about why some online companies charge a restocking fee for returns made after thirty days, locate a business with such a policy and find out its rationale.
- **Use sources to supply technical information.** For example, if you are writing about a drug that lowers high blood pressure, gather information about its manufacturer, ingredients, effectiveness, cost, and side effects so that you can make informed, accurate comments.
- **Support opinions with concrete evidence.** To support the claim that more federal assistance is needed for public education, you might provide facts and statistics showing how much less federal assistance is provided now than was provided in earlier decades, or you could quote education experts to support your position.
- **Provide historical information or context.** If you are writing about space stations, for example, find out when the first one was established, what country launched it, and what it has been used for. These details add useful background information to your research project.
- **Compare information about similar events or ideas with those you are discussing.** For example, if you are writing about a president's intervention in a labor strike, find out if other presidents have intervened in similar strikes. You can then point out similarities and differences.

For more on synthesizing, see Chapters 2 and 22.

Instructors will also expect you to **synthesize**, or make connections, among sources. When you synthesize information and ideas, you engage in a kind of conversation with your sources, making connections among ideas and information that reinforce or challenge each other to create new meaning of your own. Synthesis allows you to do the following:

- **Explore different points of view.** For example, in a paper about the consequences of divorce on children, you might use some sources that discuss the negative consequences and others that discuss the benefits.
- **Review key ideas on a topic.** For example, in a paper for an economics class explaining the reasons for increased income disparity in the past ten years, you might begin by reviewing the main reasons others have offered and respond to ideas you agree or disagree with.
- **Understand your topic in depth.** For example, synthesizing information and ideas from a variety of sources on global warming will help you see the issue from a variety of perspectives, leading you to think more deeply about the issue.

Plan Your Research Project

The best place to start a research project is at your desk. There you can think about the assignment and devise a plan for completing it. This section describes several tasks that you should accomplish *before* you begin your research. (See Graphic Organizer 21.1.)

Define the Assignment

Before you begin researching an assigned topic, be sure you understand your instructor's expectations. Often the assignment will be written on the syllabus. Read the assignment carefully, noting all the requirements, which may include the following:

- the length and due date of the final paper
- the number and types of sources you must use
- the purpose of the assignment—**informative** projects ask you to *explain* a topic (for example, "Explain the treatment options for breast cancer") or *explore* an issue (for example, "Examine the pros and cons of legalizing casino gambling"); **persuasive** projects ask you to *defend* or *argue for* a position (for example, "Argue for or against your college's proposal to eliminate athletic scholarships")
- the genre of the assignment and the format you must follow (for example, are you writing a case study? a lab report? an evaluation?)
- any limitations placed on the research (for example, "No citations from Wikipedia," "No sources published before 2010," "No citations from for-profit organizations")
- the documentation style you are required to follow (See Chapter 23.)

If your instructor announces the assignment in class, write down what he or she says, including as many details as possible. Sometimes instructors make sample papers available for students to consult. Don't miss any opportunity to learn from, and be inspired by, these models.

Often major research projects are announced the first week of class. As you proceed through the course, create a schedule for deciding on a topic, conducting the research, writing your first draft, revising your paper, ensuring your citations follow the required format exactly, and polishing your paper. You might build time into your schedule to share your drafts with friends or classmates or to get feedback from a writing center tutor.

Do not wait until the last minute to begin a research project! It is likely to be a large part of your final grade, so devote the time necessary to making it the best it can be.

Choose an Interesting and Workable Topic

Too many students waste hours researching a topic that they finally realize is too difficult, broad, or ordinary. The following tips will help you avoid such pitfalls:

1. **Choose a topic that interests you.**
2. **Choose a manageable topic.** Make sure you can adequately cover the topic within the assigned length of your paper.
3. **Avoid ordinary topics.** Familiar subjects that have been thoroughly explained in many sources seldom make good topics. For example, the subjects of "childhood obesity" and "reality TV" have been thoroughly discussed in many newspapers and magazines and *ad nauseam* on Web sites.
4. **Choose a practical topic.** Make sure information on the subject is readily available and is not too technical.

Narrow and Discover Ideas about Your Topic

For more on narrowing a topic and discovering ideas, see Chapter 4.

The following techniques will help you narrow your topic as well as discover ideas about it.

Do some preliminary reading. To get a sense of the scope, depth, and breadth of your topic, as well as to identify more manageable subtopics, you might skim an article on your topic in a general encyclopedia, such as *Encyclopaedia Britannica*, or in a specialized encyclopedia, such as *The McGraw-Hill Encyclopedia of Science and Technology*. Searching for your topic in your library's holdings, in a specialized database such as the weekly *CQ Researcher* (which contains thousands of articles on current topics), or even Google can also help you identify the subtopics into which a topic can be broken. You can also ask a reference librarian for assistance.

Try prewriting. To uncover an interesting angle on your topic or to narrow a broad topic, use one or more prewriting techniques. A branching diagram may be particularly helpful in narrowing a topic. The questioning technique, which challenges you to see your topic from different perspectives—psychological, sociological, scientific or technical, historical, political, and economic—can help you find an interesting subtopic or get an interesting angle. Here is how one student used questioning to analyze different perspectives on television advertising:

Topic: Television Advertising

Perspective	Questions
Psychological	• How does advertising affect people? • Does it affect everyone the same way? • What emotional appeals are used, and how do they work?
Sociological	• Do different age groups respond differently to ads? • Is advertising targeted toward specific racial and ethnic groups?
Scientific or technical	• How are ads produced? • Who writes them? • Are the ads tested before they are broadcast?
Historical	• What is the history of advertising? • When and where did it begin?
Political	• What legislation affects the content of advertising? • Why are negative political advertisements effective?
Economic	• How much does a television ad cost? • Is the cost of advertising added to the price of the product?

This list of questions yielded a wide range of interesting subtopics about advertising, including emotional appeals, targeting ads to specific racial or ethnic groups, and negative political advertising. You might work with a friend or classmate to devise and answer questions.

EXERCISE 21.1 ▶ NARROWING A TOPIC FOR A RESEARCH PROJECT

Working with one or two classmates, narrow each of the following topics until you reach a topic that would be manageable for a five- to ten-page research project:

1. Taxes
2. Changes in the workplace
3. Health care reform
4. Drones
5. Alternative energy sources

RESEARCH PROJECT IN PROGRESS 1

Choose a broad topic for your research project. Come up with one on your own, or choose one of the broad topics below. Your audience consists of your classmates. Begin by using one or more prewriting techniques to generate ideas and narrow your focus. Then reread your work and highlight useful ideas.

1. Extreme sports
2. Adopting children from foreign countries
3. Employer-employee relations
4. Identity fraud
5. Piracy of intellectual property (books, music, etc.)

Feel free to consult with your instructor about your topic. Your instructor may suggest a way to narrow your topic, recommend a useful source, or offer to review your outline.

Write a Working Thesis and List Research Questions

For more on drafting and revising a thesis statement, see Chapter 5.

Once you have chosen and narrowed a topic, try to determine, as specifically as possible, the kinds of information you need to know about it. Begin by writing a working thesis for your paper and listing the research questions you need to answer.

For example, one student working on the general topic of child abuse used prewriting and preliminary reading to narrow his focus to physical abuse and its causes. Since he already had a few ideas about possible causes, he used those ideas to write a working thesis. He then used his thesis to generate a list of research questions. Notice how the student's questions follow from his working thesis.

Working Thesis	The physical abuse of children often stems from parents' emotional instability and a family history of child abuse.
Research Questions	If a person was physically abused as a child, how likely is that person to become an abusive parent?
	What kinds of emotional problems seem to trigger the physical abuse of children?
	Which cause is more significant—a family history of abuse or emotional problems?
	Is there more physical abuse of children now than there was in the past, or is more abuse being reported?

A working thesis and a list of research questions will help you approach your research in a focused way. Instead of running helter-skelter from one aspect of your topic to another, you will be able to identify the specific information you need from sources.

EXERCISE 21.2   **WRITING A WORKING THESIS AND RESEARCH QUESTIONS**

For one of the following topics, write a working thesis and four or more research questions:

1. Methods of controlling pornography online
2. The possibility that some form of life has existed (or currently exists) on other planets
3. The rise of celebrity worship in the United States (or in any other country)
4. Benefits of tracing your family's genealogy (family tree)
5. Ways that personal freedoms should (or should not) be curtailed in a pandemic

---

RESEARCH PROJECT IN PROGRESS 2

Review the list of ideas you generated in Research Project in Progress 1. Underline the ideas for which you need further details or supporting evidence, and list the information you need. Then, using the preceding guidelines, write a working thesis and a list of research questions.

Consider Source Types

Once you have a working thesis and a list of research questions, stop for a moment. Think about which kinds of sources will be most useful, appropriate, relevant, and reliable. Keep in mind that you are unlikely to find all the sources you need online. Researchers must be equally skilled at locating sources in print and in electronic formats.

The types of sources that you will be expected to use will vary from discipline to discipline and assignment to assignment. The sources that are most appropriate will depend on your writing situation:

To learn more about the writing situation, see Chapter 4.

- the assignment
- your purpose for writing
- your audience
- the genre (or type) of writing you are expected to produce

For example, if you were writing a research project (genre) for a history class (audience: your instructor) in which you argued (purpose) that skilled military commanders enabled the South to prolong the American Civil War, you might consult diaries or letters written by Union and Confederate generals, scholarly books and journal articles on Civil War battles and strategy, and maps showing troop movements.

Use Primary and Secondary Sources

The examples above mention primary (or firsthand) sources, such as interviews, letters, and diary entries, as well as secondary sources, such as books and articles. **Primary sources** include the following:

- historical documents (letters, diaries, speeches)
- literary works, autobiographies
- original research reports
- eyewitness accounts
- your own interviews, observations, or correspondence

For example, a report on a study of heart disease written by the researcher who conducted the study is a primary source, as is a novel by William Faulkner. In addition, what you say or write can be a primary source. Your own interview with a heart attack survivor for a paper on heart disease is a primary source.

Secondary sources, in contrast, report or comment on primary sources. A journal article that reviews several previously published research reports on heart disease is a secondary source. A book written about William Faulkner by a literary critic or biographer is a secondary source.

Depending on your topic, you may use primary sources, secondary sources, or both. For a research project comparing the speeches of Abraham Lincoln with those of Franklin D. Roosevelt, you would probably read and analyze the speeches and listen to recordings of Roosevelt delivering his speeches (primary sources). But to learn about Lincoln's and Roosevelt's domestic policies, you would probably rely on several histories or biographies (secondary sources).

Use Scholarly, Popular, and Reference Sources

For more on using a database to narrow sources by type, see Chapter 22 (Figure 22.2).

In addition to primary and secondary, sources can also be classified as scholarly, reference, and popular sources. **Scholarly sources** are written by professional academics and scientific researchers and include both books by university presses or professional publishing companies and articles in discipline-specific academic journals that are edited by experts in the field. University presses include Oxford University Press, Princeton University Press, and the University of Nebraska Press (among many others).

There are thousands of highly regarded academic journals, ranging from *Nature* (a key journal in biology and the life sciences) to the *Lancet* (an important medical journal) to *American Economic Review* (a key journal for economists). Articles in academic journals often fall into two main categories:

1. Reports on original research conducted by the writer
2. Surveys of previous research on a topic to identify key areas of agreement, which then become part of the accepted body of knowledge in the discipline

Many scholarly sources are **peer reviewed**, which means the articles and books undergo a rigorous process of review by other scholars in the same discipline before they are accepted for publication. For these reasons, scholarly resources are accepted as accurate and reliable, and they usually form the basis of most research in academic papers.

Reference works are well-organized compendiums of facts, data, and information. They are intended to be consulted to answer specific questions rather than to be read from beginning to end. Dictionaries, encyclopedias, and thesauruses are common reference works.

Students and researchers frequently use discipline-specific reference works. For example, students of literature might consult *Gale Artemis Literary Sources* or *The Oxford Companion to English Literature*. Like scholarly resources, reference works are checked closely for accuracy, which makes them reliable sources of information. Many reference works also include suggestions for further reading, which can help researchers in their quest for additional resources. While reference works are a handy place to look up background information, they are not appropriate sources on which to base a research project.

Popular sources (newspapers, magazines, and general-interest nonfiction books) typically discuss what is going on in the "real world." One type of popular source, known as a **trade journal**, is aimed at people in specific professions. Trade journals provide the latest information on new ideas, products, personnel, events, and trends in an industry.

For more on evaluating sources, see "Evaluate Sources" on pp. 580–84.

"Popular" does not necessarily mean unreliable. For example, a serious newspaper (like the *Wall Street Journal*) or magazine (like *Time* or *Scientific American*) can be a good source of information. The articles they publish are written by journalists who are trained in methods of research. Some popular magazines such as *Scientific American* and the *Economist* are quite serious indeed. Check with your instructor to find out whether serious popular sources are acceptable.

Table 21.1 summarizes some of the differences between scholarly and popular sources. For most college research projects, consulting and citing more serious popular

TABLE 21.1 A Comparison of Scholarly Journals and Popular Sources

	Scholarly Journals	Popular Sources
Who reads it?	Researchers, professionals, students	General public
Who writes it?	Researchers, professionals	Reporters, journalists, freelance writers
Who decides what to publish in it?	Other researchers (peer reviewers)	Editors, publishers
What kind of information does it contain?	Results of research studies and experiments, statistics and analysis, in-depth evaluations of specialized topics, overviews of all the research on a subject (literature review), technical vocabulary, bibliographies and references	Articles of general interest, easy-to-understand language, news items, interviews, opinion pieces, no bibliographies (sources cited informally within the article)
How often is it published?	Mostly quarterly (every three months)	Daily (newspapers), weekly, or monthly (magazines)
What are some examples?	*Journal of Bioethics, American Journal of Family Law, Film Quarterly*	*Chicago Tribune, Miami Herald, Popular Science, Psychology Today, The Week*

sources is acceptable, but academic research projects generally do not rely solely on popular sources. Distinguishing among scholarly, popular, and reference sources when they are accessed through a database can be tricky, since visual cues, like the glossy paper and splashy photographs, that distinguish popular sources from scholarly ones may be missing. Instead, you can use database tools or consult a reference librarian to help you determine source type.

Use Books, Articles, and Media Sources

Books often take years of study to produce and are often written by authorities on the subject, so they are likely to offer the most in-depth, comprehensive discussions of topics. Most scholarly books also provide pages and pages of research citations to help you dig further into any topic you find interesting or useful. Printed books provide an index to help you locate specific topics; e-books allow you to conduct keyword searches.

Articles tend to be more focused than books, exploring just one or two key points. They may also be more up-to-date, since they can be written and produced more rapidly than books can.

Most of the articles you access through your library's databases begin with an **abstract**, or brief summary. Reading the abstract can help you determine whether the article will be useful to your research. Keyword searches in electronic articles can help

For more on keyword searching, see Chapter 22.

you locate the topics you are researching, and many academic databases use keywords to link you to other articles that may be useful in your research.

Media sources, such as photographs and information graphics, documentaries, podcasts, or works of fine art, can be useful sources of ideas and information. While in popular sources, media items may be used to illustrate a text simply to attract readers, in academic texts, media must play a more substantial role. Use images in printed texts, or video and sound files in online texts, to illustrate a concept or to provide an example, but do not include illustrations merely for window dressing. Finally, keep in mind that documentaries may include fictional elements. Evaluate media sources carefully before including them as sources.

As you seek answers to your research questions, you will likely need to consult various types of sources. Let's suppose you are writing a research project about narcissistic personality disorder (NPD), a recognized psychological disorder in which a person is obsessively concerned with ideas of his or her own personal superiority, power, and prestige. Through the process of narrowing your topic, you have decided to focus your paper on the behaviors associated with the disorder. What types of sources might you use?

- To help your readers understand exactly what NPD is, you might look to a reference book, such as the *Diagnostic and Statistical Manual of Mental Disorders,* 5th edition (DSM-V), a key reference work in psychology. The DSM is published by the American Psychological Association, which makes it a reliable resource.
- To research the real-world behaviors of people with NPD, you might consult several types of books. Scholarly books written by psychologists and published by university presses might offer case studies of people with NPD. You will likely also find books written by people who have NPD, in which they talk about their experiences and feelings. By using both types of sources, you can explore two sides of the issue: not only the clinical, diagnostic side of NPD but also the human side of it.
- To get your audience interested in your topic, you might begin by talking about celebrity behaviors that may reveal NPD. If you can find videos of celebrity interviews in which the celebrity exhibits behaviors associated with NPD, you will have found a good, reliable source to cite.

Evaluate Sources

Evaluating sources is an essential part of writing a paper using research. Unless you locate solid, relevant, and reliable sources and think critically about the ideas presented in each, your essay will lack academic rigor and credibility.

Choose Relevant Sources

A *relevant* source contains information that helps you answer one or more of your research questions. Ask yourself the following questions to determine whether a source is relevant:

1. **Is the source appropriate for your intended audience, or is it too general or too specialized?**

2. **Is the source up-to-date or recent enough for your purposes?** In rapidly changing fields of study, outdated sources are not useful unless you need to give a historical perspective.

Choose Reliable Sources

A *reliable* source is honest, accurate, and credible. Ask the following questions to help you determine whether a source is reliable:

1. **Is the source scholarly?** Although scholars often disagree with one another, they make a serious attempt to present accurate information.
2. **Does the source have a solid reputation?** Some news sources—magazines such as *Time* or *Wired* and newspapers such as the *Washington Post* and the *New York Times*—are known for responsible reporting, whereas other newspapers and magazines have a reputation for sensationalism or bias. Such sources may be useful when you are exploring multiple perspectives on an issue, but be careful about interpreting articles in these publications as "the truth."
3. **What is the publication's purpose?** Why was the source published? In the case of general-interest magazines like the *Week*, which summarizes many articles from magazines and newspapers around the world, the purpose is clear: to provide readers with a wide variety of perspectives on issues of local and global importance. The purpose of a flyer left in your mailbox may be to introduce a new business in your neighborhood or to get you to convert to a new religion. To determine purpose, look for a link on the publication's Web site labeled "About Us" or "Mission Statement."
4. **Is the source professionally edited and presented?** Professionally published, reliable sources are generally free of typographical errors. Materials with obvious mistakes, as well as amateur typesetting or design, are often unreliable. Blogs may be good sources of viewpoint pieces, but a blog may just be one person's online diary. Such blogs may be subject to heavy bias as well as possible factual errors.
5. **Is the author an expert in the field?** Check the author's credentials. Information about authors may be given in a headnote, in a link to the author's biography, in the preface, or elsewhere. You might also check a reference work such as *Contemporary Authors* or Google the author to verify credentials.
6. **Does the author approach the topic fairly and objectively?** A writer who states a strong opinion is not necessarily biased. However, a writer who ignores opposing views, distorts facts, or ignores information that does not fit his or her opinion is presenting a biased and incomplete view of a topic.
7. **Can the content be verified?** The content in reliable sources can be verified in other reliable sources. Be cautious about using a piece of information you can find in only one source. Also be skeptical of any source that purports to summarize research or cite facts but does not provide a list of works cited (or, in the case of popular sources, attribution within the article or in footnotes or links).

For more on evaluating sources, see Chapter 3.

| **EXERCISE 21.3** | **EVALUATING THE RELEVANCE AND RELIABILITY OF SOURCES** |

Working in a small group, discuss the context in which the sources listed for each topic below would or would not be considered appropriate sources.

1. Topic: Caring for family members with Alzheimer's disease
   a. Introductory health and nutrition textbook
   b. Article in *Woman's Day* titled "Mother, Where Are You?"
   c. Article from a gerontology journal on caring for aging family members
2. Topic: Analyzing the effects of heroin use on teenagers
   a. Newspaper article written by a former heroin user
   b. Article from the *Journal of Neurology* on the biochemical effects of heroin on the brain
   c. Web page on teenage drug use published by the National Institutes of Health
3. Topic: Implementing training programs to reduce sexual harassment in the workplace
   a. Article from the *Christian Science Monitor* titled "Removing Barriers for Working Women"
   b. Personal Web site or blog relating an incident of harassment on the job
   c. Training manual for employees of General Motors

Evaluate Resources in the Digital Landscape

Use special care in evaluating the quality of the electronic materials you consult. In addition to the guidelines listed above, consider the following:

- If you accessed the source through a library database or found the source through your college library's catalog, it is most likely reliable.
- If the source is an electronic version of a respected print publication (such as the *New York Times* or the *Boston Globe*), the source is likely reliable. Be careful, however, about distinguishing between content that is edited and checked by the publication (and is therefore reliable) and links to other sources or any comments posted by readers.
- If the source does not specify its authorship or does not provide any information about the author's qualifications, proceed with caution.
- If the source contains factual errors, poor layout or design, too many photos and not enough words, or highly charged or emotional language, these are all signs that the source may be biased and lack credibility.

See also "Detect Disinformation" in Chapter 3.

Think Critically about Sources

As you select sources for possible use in your paper, it is important to think critically about each. The following list of questions will help you analyze and evaluate sources:

For more on identifying bias by examining the writer's use of language, assumptions, generalizations, or omissions, see Chapter 3.

- **Analyze the author's ideas.** Does the author make reasonable inferences, use reliable evidence, and make it clear when he or she is expressing an opinion?
- **Analyze the author's language.** Does the author's use of connotation and figurative language reveal bias? What does the tone indicate about the author's

attitude? Does the author use euphemisms to hide something or to spare feelings?

- **Analyze the author's assumptions, generalizations, and omissions.** Are the author's assumptions and generalizations fair and reasonable? Are they supported by evidence? Do they reinforce or challenge social standards? Does any information seem to be omitted or treated in a less than thorough or complete way?

The way authors present ideas and use language and the assumptions, generalizations, and omissions that they make may all help you detect bias. **Bias** refers to publishers' or writers' views or particular interest in a topic. A biased source is not necessarily unreliable, but you need to recognize bias when you see it and find additional sources that present other points of view. Pay particular attention to tone.

Many relevant and reliable sources demonstrate bias. Some provide only a portion of the information you need for your paper. For example, if you are writing an essay on problems in the nursing profession, the *American Journal of Nursing* might be a reliable source, but it would probably not contain articles that are critical of nurses.

Other sources may have a strong opinion and present information from that point of view. For example, suppose you are writing an essay on home schooling for an introductory education class, and you find a book titled *The Home Schooling Movement: What Children Are Missing.* The author taught at a public high school for thirty years. This book may offer valuable information, but you need to recognize that its author supports classroom instruction and so may emphasize the shortcomings of home schooling or downplay its advantages. To use a biased source effectively, take the author's point of view into consideration as you evaluate the evidence the source provides.

EXERCISE 21.4   EXAMINING SOURCES FOR BIAS

Examine each of the following sources and their annotations. Discuss whether the source is likely to be objective (O), somewhat biased (SB), or heavily biased (HB).

1. Eboch, M. M. (editor). *Immigration and Travel Restrictions.* Greenhaven Publishing, 2019. Introducing Issues with Opposing Viewpoints.
    This book contains several articles that present the pros and cons of different issues relating to immigration and travel restrictions. The articles are written by experts and give bibliographic references.
2. Malcolm *X. The Autobiography of Malcolm X.* Ballantine Books, 1965.
    Malcolm X tells his life story in this autobiography, which was published just before his death.
3. Adams, Liam. "Called to Missions. Held Back by Student Loans." *Christianity Today,* 20 Apr. 2020, https://www.christianitytoday.com/ct/2020/may-june/rising-student-debt-missions.html.
    This article describes the difficulties student debt can present to students applying for missionary posts.
4. Fath, Brian D. *Encyclopedia of Ecology.* 2nd ed., Elsevier, 2018.
    In-depth coverage of ecology, with data from experts in the environmental and life sciences.

The following worksheet can help you evaluate the relevance and reliability of sources:

Worksheet: Evaluating Sources

Title: _____

Author: _____

Author's qualifications or experience: _____

Publication information (journal, volume, issue; publisher, URL):

_____

Month, date, and year of publication: _____

Is this source up-to-date? ☐ yes   ☐ no

Type of source: ☐ primary   ☐ secondary   ☐ multimedia
                ☐ book   ☐ article   (specify: _____)
                ☐ scholarly work   ☐ reference work   ☐ popular source

Is the source appropriate for your audience? ☐ yes ☐ no

Does the source have a good reputation? ☐ yes ☐ no

  Does the source exhibit bias? ☐ yes ☐ no

  What evidence do you have that the source is biased?

  _____

  _____

  Are opinions clearly stated as such? ☐ yes ☐ no

What is the purpose of the source? _____

  Who publishes the source? _____

  What are the publisher's goals? _____

Are the visual aids included with the source useful and credible? ☐ yes ☐ no

Is the source professionally presented and edited? ☐ yes ☐ no

Does the source contain any factual errors? ☐ yes ☐ no

Does the source provide documentation for all of its cited sources, either within the text or in a Works Cited/References section (or both)? ☐ yes ☐ no

Are there any hints that information has been omitted? ☐ yes ☐ no

If yes, describe: _____

22
Finding Sources, Taking Notes, and Synthesizing Ideas

Writing Quick Start

ANALYZE Suppose you are doing a unit on fads, trends, and communities in an introductory sociology class. Your instructor gives the class a number of photographs and directs students to choose one and write a paper about the trend it portrays.

WRITE Draft a brief statement describing the global trend the photograph above illustrates. Consider where you might go to learn about why people take and share selfies and their impact on communication and interpersonal relationships. Make a list of the sources you would consult.

CONNECT What did you learn about this trend? What sources of information did you list? This chapter will show you how to find and evaluate a variety of sources; how to conduct field research; and how to record, connect, and make sense of what you learn from sources. To do all this effectively, you must approach the research process in a systematic way. Graphic Organizer 22.1 lists the research skills you will need to develop, placing the skills covered in this chapter within the context of the process of writing a research project as a whole.

In this chapter you will learn to

- use keywords effectively to find sources using your library's catalog and databases and Internet search engines

- conduct field research: interviews, surveys, and observations

- take effective notes: annotating and highlighting, summarizing, and paraphrasing information

- evaluate your research

- synthesize information and ideas from sources

- create an annotated bibliography

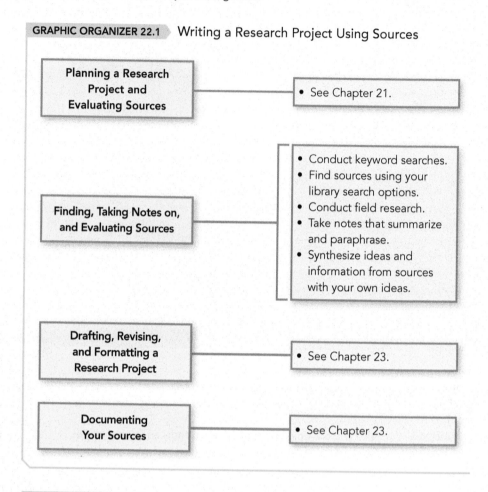

GRAPHIC ORGANIZER 22.1   Writing a Research Project Using Sources

| Planning a Research Project and Evaluating Sources | • See Chapter 21. |

| Finding, Taking Notes on, and Evaluating Sources | • Conduct keyword searches.
• Find sources using your library search options.
• Conduct field research.
• Take notes that summarize and paraphrase.
• Synthesize ideas and information from sources with your own ideas. |

| Drafting, Revising, and Formatting a Research Project | • See Chapter 23. |

| Documenting Your Sources | • See Chapter 23. |

USING RESEARCH   IN COLLEGE AND THE WORKPLACE

- For an *anthropology course,* you are asked to write a research project in which you analyze the differences between the religious practices of two cultures.

- For an *art history course,* you must write a biography of a famous Renaissance artist as a final research project.

- As *supervisor* of a health care facility, you decide to conduct a survey of the staff to determine employees' interest in flexible working hours.

Get an Overview of Library Sources

Your college library is an immense collection of print, media, and online sources. Learning your way around the library is the first step in locating sources effectively.

Learn Your Way around the Library

It is a good idea to become familiar with your college library *before* you need to use it. The following are two ways to do so:

1. **Take a tour of the library.** Check the library for places to study, such as a library carrel or cubicle or a room where you can collaborate with classmates.
2. **Take a tour of your library's Web site.** Most college libraries provide access to rich resources through the library's Web site (see Figure 22.1). Often students can search for books, articles, multimedia sources, and more; access citation (or reference) managers (to help you manage sources and create lists of works cited

FIGURE 22.1 ▸ Sample Library Home Page

The Montgomery College Library home page allows students to search for books, articles, and other resources all through a single portal. The home page also provides access to a wealth of other useful information.

or references); request sources through interlibrary loan; or ask a reference librarian for help. Visit your library's Web site to find out what services are available online as well as face-to-face.

Make Use of Reference Librarians

Reference librarians can help you at any stage in the research process, advising you about what sources to use and where to locate them. For example, reference librarians can help you do all of the following:

- Use library resources to make a topic broader, narrower, or more relevant.
- Get you started by steering you toward reference resources or basic books and articles that provide background information on your topic.
- Identify other libraries or special collections that might be relevant to your research, then help you request those materials through interlibrary loan.
- Help you decide which search terms to use, identify appropriate specialized databases, and learn how to search those databases most efficiently.
- Obtain the full text of articles for which you have only summary information (abstracts).
- Show you how to use various citation management systems such as EndNote, Zotero, and RefWorks. (Citation management systems allow you to store and format bibliographic material from your sources in a number of popular citation styles.)

In short, reference librarians can often save you time, so don't hesitate to ask them for help.

Use Keywords Effectively

Whether you use your library's search options or Google, you will use **keywords**, words or phrases that describe your topic, to search for information. You type your keywords into a search box and hit "Enter," and the search engine scans all the items in its index for those that include your keywords. In other words, to search effectively, you must figure out which words your sources are likely to use and use those as your keywords. The following tips can help improve your search results:

- **More specific terms yield more relevant results.** For example, if you were writing about alternative political parties in the United States, using keywords like *politics* or even *political parties* would be too broad. Searching on phrases like *third parties in the United States* would reduce the number of hits and make those hits more relevant. If you are having difficulty coming up with keywords, use a reference resource, like a specialized encyclopedia, to find the terms those writing about a topic would be likely to use.

- **Include synonyms.** To make sure your search yields the best results, brainstorm a list of synonyms for your keywords and search for those terms as well. For example, if you are searching for information on *welfare reform*, you might also search for *entitlement programs*, *government benefits*, and *welfare spending*.
- **Use full names and titles.** If the name is common, add other pieces of information, such as the college or university where the person teaches.
- **Use the advanced search functions.** For example, Google's advanced search feature allows you to search for an exact phrase and to exclude words that should not appear in your search results (among other options). Google also allows you to filter your results by language, reading level, date, region, and several other criteria. Library catalogs and databases also allow you to narrow your results, for example, to scholarly articles or to books published within a specific timeframe, in a specific language, or on a specific subject.
- **Use subject headings.** Most libraries and database vendors (such as EBSCO or LexisNexis) use standard subject headings to index their contents. To generate more relevant search results, make sure your keywords match the Library of Congress subject headings, or use the Thesaurus or Subject Terms link on the search page to check and refine your list of keywords. For instance, checking the thesaurus for a medical database may reveal that the ideal search term is not *heart attack* but *myocardial infarction*.

If your keyword searches are returning too many results or too many irrelevant results, try the following:

- Combine keywords to make your search terms more specific, or remove search terms to broaden your results.
- Once you find a relevant source, look at the subject terms associated with it, and use those for subsequent searches.
- Conduct a new search using a specialized database.
- Read the tool's search tips or FAQs for specific advice on how to improve your results.

Keep in mind that effective research requires ingenuity and persistence, so don't give up too easily.

Use Appropriate Search Tools

As you analyze your writing assignment, you will likely find yourself wondering where to begin. The key entry portal for research is your library's homepage. Student researchers may also benefit from using **research**, or **subject, guides**, discipline- and course-specific lists of useful resources. Each research guide has been created by a librarian and is tailored to the kinds of assignments that college students get regularly.

Search for Books and Other Library Holdings

Libraries own a variety of source types: books and e-books, magazines and newspapers (in print), some printed government documents, special collections and rare books and manuscripts, and multimedia items such as video and audio recordings. Researchers identify relevant items in the library's collection by accessing a computerized catalog, which allows users to search online for sources by keyword, title, author, subject, or the first portion of the call number. Some systems, like the one shown in Figure 22.2, allow users to narrow a search by subject, author, publication

FIGURE 22.2   Library Catalog Search Results

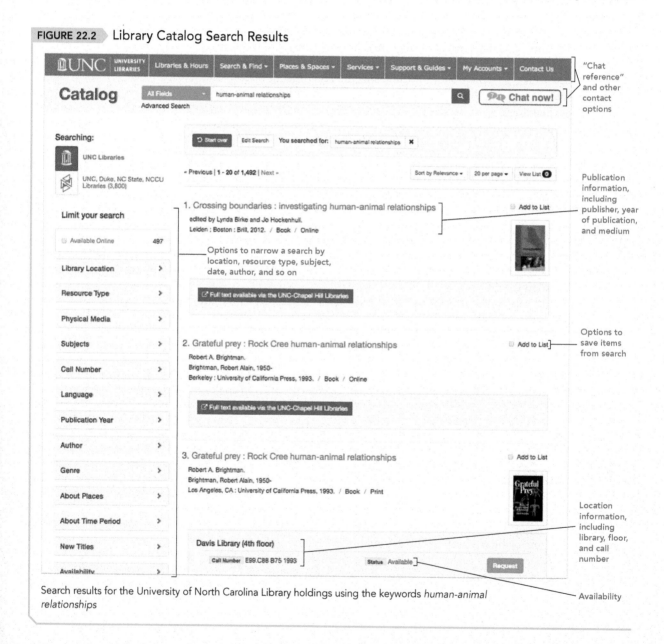

Search results for the University of North Carolina Library holdings using the keywords *human-animal relationships*

date, and other options. Often the catalog will indicate not only where an item is shelved, but also whether it has been checked out and when it is due back.

Once you have a specific call number, use a library floor plan and the call number guides posted on shelves to locate the appropriate section of the library and the book you need. While looking for your book, be sure to scan the surrounding books, which are usually on related topics. You may discover other useful sources that you overlooked in the catalog.

Search for Articles in Your Library's Databases

College libraries subscribe to databases that list articles in **periodicals**, publications that are issued at regular intervals (daily, weekly, monthly, or quarterly), such as scholarly journals, magazines, and newspapers. Database entries usually include an **abstract**, or brief summary of the article, as well as information about the article itself (title, author, publishing information, and keywords used in the article). As with library catalogs, databases allow users to refine their searches by limiting results by date or publication type, for example. They also may allow you to email, print, or save relevant articles.

Many articles will be available through the database in full text. They may appear in PDF format, which usually shows the article just as it appeared in the periodical, or in HTML format, which is usually text only. For articles that are not available in full text, a librarian can help you request them via interlibrary loan.

Your library probably subscribes to general databases and specialized ones. **General databases** list articles on a wide range of subjects in both popular magazines and scholarly journals. Academic Search Premier (Figure 22.3), for example, offers the full text of articles in over 3,000 of those periodicals.

FIGURE 22.3   Academic Search Premier: Sample Search Results

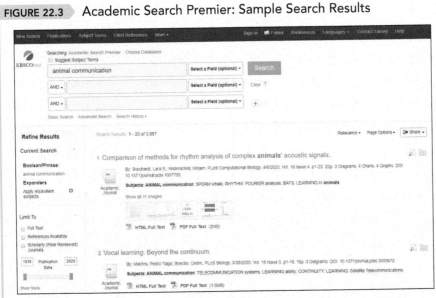

Search results on the keywords *animal communication*

Specialized databases index either articles within specific academic disciplines or fields, or particular types of articles, such as book reviews, abstracts of doctoral dissertations, and articles and essays published in books. Some examples of specialized databases are *Book Review Digest Plus, Dissertation and Theses, PsycArticles, Web of Science,* and *Sociological Abstracts.*

Note: Names of databases may change, the number of sources a database indexes or includes full text for may change, and database vendors may make different packages of databases available at different times, so consult a reference librarian if you are not sure which database to use.

Use the Internet for Research, with Caution

The Internet provides access to millions of Web sites, but you need to use a search engine to find them. **Search engines** allow you to find information by typing a keyword or phrase into a search box. Google is such a popular search engine that you might have never used anything else, but other excellent search engines exist, and some of them are listed below. Because different search engines may generate different results, it is a good idea to try your search on more than one search engine.

For more on evaluating sources, see Chapter 3 and Chapter 21.

Search Engine	Why try it?
Bing.com	Bing provides a list of results in the main column but also includes a list of "Related searches," which may help you refine your search strategy.
Dogpile.com	Dogpile is a metasearch engine; in other words, it draws its results from a variety of other search engines.
DuckDuckGo.com	DuckDuckGo allows users to search anonymously and lists all results on a single page, making less clicking necessary.

While the Internet is an amazing resource for researchers, the quality of the content you will find varies wildly. As a result, researchers must evaluate content very carefully before relying on it.

News sites. Newspapers, television and radio networks, and magazines have companion Web sites that provide current information and late-breaking news stories. Some of the most useful are listed below. (Some may require a subscription, but your library may allow access through a database. Check with a librarian.)

BBC	www.bbc.co.uk
CNN	www.cnn.com
Wall Street Journal	www.wsj.com
New York Times	www.nytimes.com
National Public Radio	www.NPR.org
Washington Post	www.washingtonpost.com

General reference sites.   Reference works are available online, through the Web or through the databases your library subscribes to. Some of the most useful general reference sites are listed below.

Britannica Online	www.eb.com
Encyclopedia.com	www.encyclopedia.com
Encyclopedia Smithsonian	www.si.edu/encyclopedia
Merriam-Webster Online	www.merriam-webster.com

Some of these sites may not be available for free through Google; check to find out if your college library provides access to these or other general reference sources.

Government documents.   The federal government makes hundreds of thousands of documents freely available online every year on a vast range of subjects. Some government sites that students find particularly useful are listed below.

U.S. Bureau of Labor Statistics	www.bls.gov
U.S. Census Bureau	www.census.gov
The Central Intelligence Agency's World Fact Book	www.cia.gov/library/publications/resources/the-world-factbook/index.html
Data.gov	www.data.gov
Library of Congress	www.loc.gov
National Institutes of Health	www.nih.gov

In addition, you can access many useful government documents through library databases such as *CQ Press Library*.

Conduct Field Research

Depending on your research topic, you may need—or want—to conduct field research to collect original information. This section discusses three common types of field research:

1. Interviews
2. Surveys
3. Observation

For more about primary vs. secondary sources, see Chapter 21.

All of these methods generate primary source material.

Conduct Interviews

An **interview** allows you to obtain firsthand information from a person who is knowledgeable about your topic. For example, if the topic of your research project is *treatment of teenage alcoholism*, it might be a good idea to interview an experienced substance abuse counselor who works with teenagers. Use the following suggestions to conduct effective interviews:

1. **Choose interviewees carefully.** Be sure your interviewees work in the field you are researching or are experts on your topic.
2. **Arrange your interview by phone or email well in advance.** Describe your project and purpose, explaining that you are a student working on an assignment, and indicate the amount of time you think you'll need.
3. **Plan the interview.** Do some research to make sure the information you need is not already available through more traditional sources. Then devise a list of questions you want to ask. Try to ask *open questions*, which generate discussion, rather than *closed questions*, which can be answered in a word or two. For example, "Do you think your company has a promising future?" could be answered yes or no, whereas "How do you account for your company's turnaround last year?" might spark a detailed response. Open questions usually encourage people to open up and reveal attitudes as well as facts.
4. **Take notes during the interview.** Write the interviewee's responses in note form and ask whether you may quote him or her directly. If you want to record the interview, be sure to ask the interviewee's permission.
5. **Evaluate the interview.** As soon as possible after the interview, reread your notes and fill in information you did not have time to record. Also write down your reactions while they are still fresh in your mind.

Conduct Surveys

A **survey** is a set of questions designed to elicit information quickly from a large number of people. Surveys are often used to assess people's attitudes or intentions. They can be conducted face-to-face, by phone, or online.

Use the following suggestions to prepare effective surveys:

1. **Clarify the purpose of the survey.** Prepare a detailed list of what you want to learn from the survey.

2. **Design your questions.** A survey can include closed or open questions or both, but most surveys use mostly closed questions (either multiple-choice or ranking), so responses can be tabulated easily.

3. **Test your survey questions.** Try out your questions on a few classmates, family members, or friends to be sure they are clear, unambiguous, and easily understood.

4. **Select your respondents.** Your respondents—the people who provide answers to your survey—must be *representative* of the group you are studying and must be *chosen at random*. One way to draw a random sample is to give the survey to every fifth or tenth name on a list or to every fifteenth person who walks by.

5. **Summarize and report your results.** Tally the results and look for patterns in the data. In your project, discuss your overall findings, and explain the purpose of the survey as well as how you designed it. Include a copy of the survey and tabulations in an appendix.

Conduct Observations

An **observation** (of an event, a scene, or an activity) can be an important primary source in a research project. For instance, you might observe children at play to analyze differences in play between boys and girls. Firsthand observation can yield valuable insights on the job as well. You might, for example, need to observe and report on the condition of hospital patients or the job performance of your employees.

Use the following tips to conduct observations effectively:

1. **Arrange your visit in advance.** Make the purpose of your visit clear when arranging your appointment.

2. **Take detailed notes on what you observe.** Write down the details you will need to describe the scene vividly in your paper. Observe the scene from different angles or perspectives.

3. **Create a dominant impression.** As soon as possible after your visit, evaluate your observations. Think about what you saw and heard. Then describe your dominant impression of what you observed and the details that support it.

For more on creating a dominant impression, see Chapter 12.

Work with Sources: Take Notes, Summarize, and Paraphrase

Reading sources involves some special skills. You can often read sources selectively, previewing the source to identify relevant sections and reading just those sections.

For more on previewing, see Chapter 2.

Take Effective Notes

As you conduct research, your ideas will develop, and you will generate topic sentences to support your thesis based on a synthesis of sources that you've read.

For more on creating entries in a works-cited or references list, see Chapter 23.

Because you must give credit to those who informed your thinking, be particularly cautious when cutting and pasting source materials into your notes. Always place quotation marks around anything you have cut and pasted. Be sure to clearly separate your ideas from the ideas you found in sources. If you copy an author's exact words, place the information in quotation marks, and write the term *direct quotation* as well as the page number(s) in parentheses after the quotation. If you write a summary note or paraphrase, write *paraphrase* or *summary* and the page number(s) of the source. Be sure to include page numbers; you'll need them to double-check your notes against the source and to create an in-text citation. Be sure to record all the information you will need to create a complete works-cited or reference entry.

Note-taking tools.   Many students use a series of computer folders or a notebook for their research, organized into subfolders or dividers.

While many students prefer to take notes in computer files or notebooks, some researchers still like to use index cards for note-taking. (There are also programs available that allow you to create computerized note cards.) Note cards allow you to arrange and rearrange the material to experiment with different ways of organizing your project. If you decide to use note cards, put information from only one source or about only one subtopic on each card. At the top of the card, indicate the author of the source and the page numbers on which the information appears, and note the subtopic that the note covers. Use a separate set of note cards or a separate section of your notebook or computer file to list the bibliographic information you will need to cite the source. (See Figure 22.4 for a worksheet to help you record the information you will need.)

Citation (or reference) managers—programs like EndNote, RefWorks, and Zotero—can be useful tools throughout the research process because they allow you to save sources, take notes, and incorporate those notes into your research project as you write. They may also help you format your works cited or reference list entries.

FIGURE 22.4   Bibliographic Information Worksheet

Author(s) _____
Title and subtitle of source _____
Title of work source appears in (if any): Journal/anthology/Web site _____
Other contributors: Editor/translator/director _____
Version: Edition/director's cut _____
Volume/issue _____
Publisher/sponsor _____
Publication date _____
Location: Pages/URL/DOI (digital object identifier) _____

Summarize

As you write summary notes, keep in mind that everything you put in summary notes must be *in your own words and sentences*. Your summary notes should accurately reflect the relevant main points of the source. Use the following guidelines to write effective summary notes:

1. **Write notes that condense the author's ideas into your own words.** Include key terms and concepts or principles, but omit specific examples, quotations, your opinion, or anything else that is not essential to the author's main point. (You can write comments in a separate note.)

2. **Record the ideas in the order in which they appear in the original source.** Reordering ideas might affect the meaning.

3. **Record the complete publication information for the sources you summarize.** Unless you summarize an entire book or poem, you will need to include page references when you write your paper and prepare a works-cited list.

A sample summary appears in Chapter 2 on pages 42–43.

For more on summarizing, see Chapter 2.

Paraphrase

When you paraphrase, you restate the author's ideas *in your own words and sentences*. You do not condense ideas or eliminate details as you do in a summary; instead, you keep the author's intended meaning but express that meaning in different sentence patterns and vocabulary. In most cases, a paraphrase is approximately the same length as the original material.

When paraphrasing, be careful not to *plagiarize*—that is, do not use an author's words or sentence patterns as if they were your own. Merely replacing some words with synonyms is not enough; you must also use your own sentence structures and may want to reorganize the presentation of ideas. Reading the excerpt from a source below and comparing it, first, with the acceptable paraphrase that follows and then with the example that includes plagiarism will help you see what an acceptable paraphrase looks like.

For more on avoiding plagiarism, see Chapter 23.

Excerpt from Original

Learning some items may interfere with retrieving others, especially when the items are similar. If someone gives you a phone number to remember, you may be able to recall it later. But if two more people give you their numbers, each successive number will be more difficult to recall. Such proactive interference occurs when something you learned earlier disrupts recall of something you experienced later. As you collect more and more information, your mental attic never fills, but it certainly gets cluttered.

—David G. Myers, *Psychology*

Acceptable Paraphrase

According to David Myers, *proactive interference* means that things you have already learned make it harder for you to dredge up things you learn later.

In other words, details you learn first may make it harder to recall closely related details you learn subsequently. Myers compares memory with an attic. You can always add more junk to it, but the messier it gets, the harder it becomes to find anything. He also gives an example: the first new phone number you learn makes it harder to remember the next one.

Unacceptable Paraphrase — Includes Plagiarism

Replaces terms with synonyms

Copied terms and phrases

When you learn some things, it may interfere with your ability to remember others. This happens when the things are similar. Suppose a person gives you a phone number to remember. You probably will be able to remember it later. Now, suppose two persons give you their numbers. Each successive number will be harder to remember. Proactive interference happens when something you already learned prevents you from recalling something you experience later. As you learn more and more information, your mental attic never gets full, but it will get cluttered.

The unacceptable paraphrase does substitute some synonyms—*remember* for *retrieving*, for example—but it is still an example of plagiarism. Not only are some words copied directly from the original, but also the structure of the sentences is nearly identical to the original.

Paraphrasing can be tricky, because letting an author's language creep in is easy. These guidelines will help you paraphrase without plagiarizing:

1. **Read first; then write.** To avoid copying an author's words, cover up the passage you are paraphrasing (or switch to a new window on your computer), and then write.

2. **Use synonyms that do not change the author's meaning or intent, and if you must use distinctive wording of the author's, enclose it in quotation marks.** Note that for some specialized terms and even for some commonplace ones, substitutes may not be easy to come by. In the acceptable paraphrase above, the writer uses the key term *proactive interference*, as well as the everyday word *attic*, without quotation marks. However, if the writer paraphrasing the original were to borrow a distinctive turn of phrase, this would need to be in quotation marks. If you are not sure, using quotation marks is never wrong.

For more on varying sentence structure, see Chapter 9.

3. **Use your own sentence structure.** Using an author's sentence structure can be considered plagiarism. If the original uses lengthy sentences, for example, your paraphrase may use shorter sentences. If the original phrases something in a compound sentence, try recasting the information in a complex one.

4. **Rearrange the ideas if possible.** If you can do so without changing the sense of the passage, rearrange the ideas. In addition to using your own words and sentences, rearranging the ideas can make the paraphrase more your own. Notice that in the acceptable paraphrase above, the writer starts by introducing the term *proactive interference*, whereas in the original source, this term is not used until the fourth sentence.

Be sure to record the publication information (including page numbers) for the sources you paraphrase. You will need this information to document the sources in your paper.

EXERCISE 22.1   WRITING A PARAPHRASE

Write a paraphrase of the following excerpt from a source on animal communication:

> Another vigorously debated issue is whether language is uniquely human. Animals obviously communicate. Bees, for example, communicate the location of food through an intricate dance. And several teams of psychologists have taught various species of apes, including a number of chimpanzees, to communicate with humans by signing or by pushing buttons wired to a computer. Apes have developed considerable vocabularies. They string words together to express meaning and to make and follow requests. Skeptics point out important differences between apes' and humans' facilities with language, especially in their respective abilities to order words using proper syntax. Nevertheless, these studies reveal that apes have considerable cognitive ability.
>
> —David G. Myers, *Psychology*

EXERCISE 22.2   EVALUATING A PARAPHRASE FOR PLAGIARISM

The piece of student writing below is a paraphrase of a source on the history of advertising. Working with another student, evaluate the paraphrase and discuss whether it would be considered an example of plagiarism. If you decide the paraphrase is plagiarized, rewrite it so that it is not.

Original Source

> Everyone knows that advertising lies. That has been an article of faith since the Middle Ages—and a legal doctrine, too. Sixteenth-century English courts began the Age of Caveat Emptor by ruling that commercial claims—fraudulent or not—should be sorted out by the buyer, not the legal system. ("If he be tame and have ben rydden upon, then caveat emptor.") In a 1615 case, a certain Baily agreed to transport Merrell's load of wood, which Merrell claimed weighed 800 pounds. When Baily's two horses collapsed and died, he discovered that Merrell's wood actually weighed 2,000 pounds. The court ruled the problem was Baily's for not checking the weight himself; Merrell bore no blame.
>
> —Cynthia Crossen, *Tainted Truth*

Paraphrase

> It is a well-known fact that advertising lies. This has been known ever since the Middle Ages. It is an article of faith as well as a legal doctrine. English courts in the sixteenth century started the Age of Caveat Emptor by finding that claims by businesses, whether legitimate or not, were the responsibility of the consumer, not the courts. For example, there was a case in which one person (Baily) used his horses to haul wood for a person named Merrell. Merrell told Baily that the wood weighed 800 pounds, but it actually weighed 2,000 pounds. Baily discovered this after his horses died. The court did not hold Merrell responsible; it stated that Baily should have weighed the wood himself instead of accepting Merrell's word.

Record Quotations

For more on how to adjust a quotation to fit your sentence, see Chapter 23.

When writing your paper, you may adjust a quotation to fit your sentence, so long as you do not change the meaning of the quotation, but when taking notes, be sure to record the quotation precisely as it appears in the source. Also provide the page number(s) on which the material being quoted appears in the original source. In your notes, be sure to indicate that you are copying a direct quotation by including quotation marks, the term *direct quotation*, and the page number(s) in parentheses.

Keep Track of Sources

For more on citing sources, see Chapter 23.

Using a form like the one shown in Figure 22.4 (p. 596) can help you make sure you record all the information you will need. Using a citation manager can also help.

Work with Sources: Evaluate Your Notes and Synthesize

Before you begin drafting, you'll need to make sense of the information you've gathered by synthesizing information and ideas. **Synthesis** means "a pulling together of information to form a new idea or point." You synthesize information every day. For example, after you watch a preview of a movie, talk with friends who have seen the film, and read a review of it, you then pull together the information you have acquired and come up with your own idea—that the movie is your cup of tea, or that you will probably not like it.

You often synthesize information for your college courses. In a biology course, for instance, you might evaluate your own lab results, those of your classmates, and the data in your textbook or another reference source to reach a conclusion about a particular experiment.

Synthesis involves putting ideas together to see how they agree, disagree, or otherwise relate to one another. When working with sources, ask yourself the following questions:

- Do my sources reinforce or contradict one another?
- How do their claims and lines of reasoning compare?
- Do they make similar or dissimilar assumptions and generalizations?
- Is their evidence alike in any way?

For more on evaluating the reliability of sources, see Chapters 3 and 21.

Before you begin the synthesis process, however, you must evaluate the sources you've consulted in terms of how well they suit your purposes and audience.

Evaluate Your Research

Before you began researching your topic, you most likely wrote a *working thesis*—a preliminary statement of your main point about the topic—and a list of research questions you hoped to answer. Then, as you researched your topic, you may have discovered facts, statistics, or experts' ideas about the topic that surprised you.

As you evaluate your research notes, keep the following questions in mind:

1. What research questions did I begin with?
2. What answers did I find to those questions?
3. What other information did I discover about my topic?
4. What conclusions can I draw from what I've learned?
5. How does my research affect my working thesis?

In many cases, the answers to these questions will influence your thinking on the topic, requiring you to modify your working thesis. If you can't answer these questions in a way that you find satisfactory, you will need to conduct more research to clarify or refine your thinking. In some cases, you may even need to rethink the direction of your research project.

The process of evaluating your research will often result in decisions not to use specific sources in your final paper. Perhaps the source does not provide any new or relevant information; perhaps it comes from a source that you decide is unreliable; perhaps you have too much information to fit in the length of your assignment, and you need to narrow your focus. View this research as information that has contributed to your understanding of the topic, and then set aside the note cards or move the information to a separate notebook section or file where it will not get in your way.

Use Categories to Synthesize Information from Sources

In order to make sense of what you've learned, you will need to find patterns in the information you have gathered. One way to find patterns is to categorize information according to your research questions. For example, one student found numerous sources on and answers to his research question "What causes some parents to abuse their children physically?" After rereading his research notes, he realized the information could be divided into three categories:

Category	Sources
1. Lack of parenting skills	Lopez, Wexler, Thomas
2. Emotional instability	Wexler, Harris, Thompson, Wong
3. Family history of child abuse	Thompson, Harris, Lopez, Strickler, Thomas

Evaluating his research in this way made him see that he needed to revise both his working thesis and the scope of his paper to include lack of parenting skills as a major cause of child abuse. Notice how he modified his working thesis accordingly:

- ~~The main reasons that~~ ^{Some} children are physically abused ~~are~~ ^{because of} their parents' emotional instability, ~~and~~ family history of child abuse[,] ^{and lack of parenting skills.}

For controversial topics, you may want to categorize the information you've gathered in terms of each position on the issue (pro, con, or somewhere in between). Alternatively, you could categorize information in terms of the reasons sources offer to support their positions. On the issue of gun control legislation, for example, some sources may favor it for national security reasons: Gun control makes it harder for terrorists to acquire guns. Others may favor it for statistical reason: Statistics prove that owning a gun does not prevent crime. Still others may favor it for emotional reasons: A loved one was injured or killed by a firearm.

If your research project focuses on comparing or contrasting two things (for example, communism and capitalism), you could categorize the information you found on each subtopic separately, and then use that organized information to prepare an outline or graphic organizer of your paper.

Draw a Graphic Organizer to Synthesize Sources

Drawing a graphic organizer can help you identify patterns as well as show you how main ideas and supporting details connect. Suppose, for example, that you are arguing in favor of adopting voluntary simplicity—the minimizing of personal possessions and commitments to create a happier, more manageable life. You have located three reliable and relevant sources on voluntary simplicity, but each develops the idea somewhat differently:

1. Source 1 (Walker) is a practical how-to article that includes some personal examples.
2. Source 2 (Parachin) offers a theoretical look at statistics about workloads and complicated lifestyles and the reasons that voluntary simplicity is appealing.
3. Source 3 (Remy) presents some strategies for simplifying but emphasizes the values of a simplified life.

Graphic Organizer 22.2 presents a sample organizer that synthesizes information from these three sources.

Depending on the types of information you uncover, you can use a variety of organizer formats: If all your sources compare and contrast the same things, such as the policies and effectiveness of two U.S. presidents, you could adapt one of the graphic organizers for comparison and contrast shown in Chapter 15. If most of your sources focus on effects, such as the effects of a recession on retail sales and employment, you could adapt one of the cause-and-effect graphic organizers shown in Chapter 18. Whatever style of organizer you use, be sure to keep track of the sources for each idea and to include them in your organizer.

Create an Annotated Bibliography

As part of the process of writing a research project, some instructors may require you to create an **annotated bibliography,** a list of sources that includes both publication information and a brief summary for each source. Annotated bibliographies are useful ways to document your research process, so they include all the sources you consulted in researching your topic.

GRAPHIC ORGANIZER 22.2   Synthesizing Sources

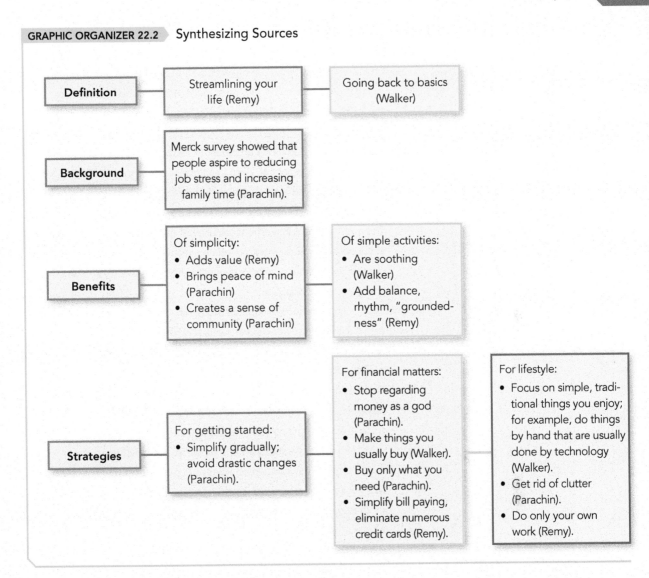

Your writing situation will influence the information you include in your annotations, but for most college research projects, the annotations should summarize the main point of the source. They may also evaluate the source in terms of how it relates to your thesis. For example, does it provide useful background information or supporting examples, or does it represent a popular alternative viewpoint? A sample annotated bibliography for researching the use of digital textbooks and e-learning in college classrooms appears below. It uses MLA-style citations.

Sample Annotated Bibliography

Bajarin, Ben. "Reinventing the Book for the Digital Age." *Time*, 12 Nov. 2013,
techland.time.com/2013/11/12/reinventing-the-book-for-the-digital-age/.

> This article from a general-interest magazine describes the features
> that e-books provide while suggesting even more ideas for future
> e-books.

deNoyelles, Aimee, et al. "Exploring Students' E-Textbook Practices in Higher
Education." *Educause Review*, 2015, er.educause.edu/articles/2015/7/
exploring-students-etextbook-practices-in-higher-education.

> This scholarly article reports results from a two-year study by the authors.
> The authors found that e-textbook use has grown over the course of the
> study period because e-textbooks are cheaper and more convenient than
> print textbooks, but instructors are not keeping pace with students'
> appetites for e-textbooks.

Falc, Emilie O. "An Assessment of College Students' Attitudes towards Using an
Online E-Textbook." *Interdisciplinary Journal of E-Learning and Learning
Objects*, vol. 9, 2013, pp. 1–12, www.ijello.org/Volume9/IJELLOv9p001
-012Falc831.pdf.

> This article from a scholarly journal reports on research studying student
> experiences with e-textbooks. Recommendations are given for faculty to
> guide their students on effective use of e-textbooks.

Keengwe, Jared. *Research Perspectives and Best Practices in Educational
Technology Integration*. Information Science Reference, 2013.

> This book provides research-based information on how e-learning can be
> integrated into the college classroom in ways that make technological,
> practical, and educational sense.

Tichi, Cecelia. "What the E-Book Should Be." *The Chronicle of Higher Education*,
15 Apr. 2016, chronicle.texterity.com/chronicle/20160415b?folio=B25.

> This article from a periodical aimed at college faculty discusses the way
> e-books should change in relation to students' study habits.

▶ RESEARCH PROJECT IN PROGRESS 3 ▶

For the topic you worked on in Research Projects in Progress 1 and 2 in Chapter 21,
locate a minimum of six sources that answer one or more of your research questions.
Your sources should include at least one book, one magazine article, one scholarly
journal article, one Internet source, and two other sources of any type. On a scale of
1 to 5 (where 1 is low, 5 is high), rank the relevance and reliability of each source you

located using the guidelines provided in Chapter 21. Use the following chart to structure your responses:

Source	Relevancy Rating	Reliability Rating
1. _____	_____	_____
2. _____	_____	_____
3. _____	_____	_____
4. _____	_____	_____
5. _____	_____	_____
6. _____	_____	_____

RESEARCH PROJECT IN PROGRESS 4

For the three most relevant and reliable sources you identified in Research Project in Progress 3, use the suggestions in the section "Work with Sources: Take Notes, Summarize, and Paraphrase" (pp. 595–600) to take notes on your sources. Your goal is to provide information and support for the ideas you developed earlier. Choose a system of note-taking, writing summary notes and paraphrases, annotating and underlining, and recording quotations as needed. As you work, try to answer your research questions and keep your working thesis in mind.

RESEARCH PROJECT IN PROGRESS 5

For the three sources you worked with in Research Project in Progress 4, use the suggestions in the section "Work with Sources: Evaluate Your Notes and Synthesize" (pp. 600–602) to synthesize your notes using categories or a graphic organizer. As you work, keep your research questions and working thesis in mind. After synthesizing, consider whether you need to alter your working thesis or conduct additional research.

23

Drafting, Revising, and Formatting a Research Project

ANGELA WEISS/AFP/Getty Images

In this chapter you will learn to

- organize and draft your research project

- avoid plagiarism by understanding what to document and giving credit to all your sources

- integrate sources into your research project effectively with signal phrases (attributions) and in-text citations

- follow the proper guidelines for integrating quotations into your research project

- revise and prepare a final draft of your research project

- document your sources in MLA or APA format

Writing Quick Start

ANALYZE   Suppose you were assigned to write a research project for a mass communication course on a topic related to human communication involving two or more people. You decided to write about issue-oriented art, examining how artists make political or social statements through their art. After reviewing numerous sources, you decided to focus on one artist—Eduardo Kobra. You drafted a working thesis, examined Kobra's works, and synthesized commentaries on and evaluations of Kobra's art. Now you are ready to revise your thesis, organize your ideas, and begin drafting your essay.

WRITE   Based on what you have learned about drafting and revising from earlier chapters and from your instructor, write a paragraph describing how you will follow through on the process of drafting and revising your research project. Also consider how writing and revising a research project might differ from writing a paper that does not rely on outside sources.

CONNECT   In this chapter you will learn detailed information about the process of creating a research paper. You will see that writing a research paper has much in common with other kinds of writing you have already done. Both require you to work through the writing process, while considering your writing situation.

In Chapter 21 you learned how to plan a project using sources and how to choose and evaluate useful information. Chapter 22 gave you advice on finding sources, taking notes, making sense of information from sources, and synthesizing sources as you prepare to compose your research project. This chapter continues the research process by showing you how to organize, draft, revise, and document a research project using sources. Graphic Organizer 23.1 presents an overview of the process.

GRAPHIC ORGANIZER 23.1   Writing a Paper Using Sources

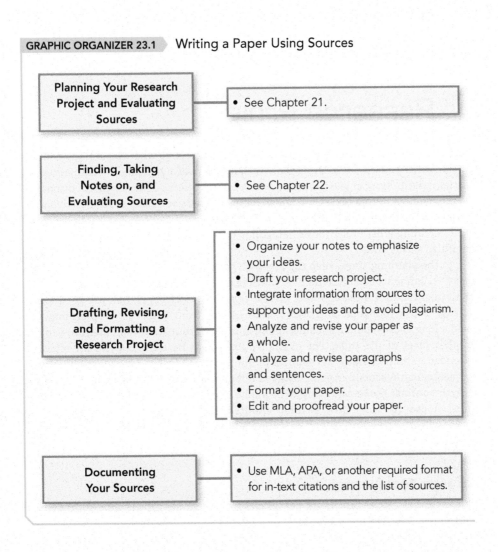

Planning Your Research Project and Evaluating Sources

- See Chapter 21.

Finding, Taking Notes on, and Evaluating Sources

- See Chapter 22.

Drafting, Revising, and Formatting a Research Project

- Organize your notes to emphasize your ideas.
- Draft your research project.
- Integrate information from sources to support your ideas and to avoid plagiarism.
- Analyze and revise your paper as a whole.
- Analyze and revise paragraphs and sentences.
- Format your paper.
- Edit and proofread your paper.

Documenting Your Sources

- Use MLA, APA, or another required format for in-text citations and the list of sources.

Organize Your Research Project

For more on using categories or a graphic organizer to synthesize ideas, see Chapter 22.

Your first step in organizing your research project is deciding what you will say and the order in which you will say it. Think about which pattern of organization—chronological, spatial, most-to-least or least-to-most, or one of the patterns of development discussed in Parts 3 and 4 of this text—will allow you to convey your ideas most effectively. As you plan your organization, think about the best ways to use sources to support those ideas. Creating a list of synthesis categories or a synthesis graphic organizer can be helpful in this regard.

In the planning stage, keep the research project's required length in mind. Many essay assignments can be completed in three or four pages, but your research assignment might require a paper of ten, fifteen, or even twenty pages. Can you get enough mileage out of your topic and organization? If you think your current plan may not yield a long enough paper, consider using another pattern of development to explore another facet of the topic. For example, you might be able to write an effective extended definition essay on the topic of home-schooling, but for a lengthy research project on home-schooling you may need not only to define the term but also to compare or contrast home-schooling with public education, to explore the reasons parents choose to home-school their children or the effects of home-schooling (cause-effect), and so on. Below are some additional guidelines for organizing your research paper.

Arrange Your Notes

Start by considering your thesis or the categories you identified while synthesizing your notes. Then list the subtopics you want to explore in your research project, and arrange your research notes into these categories. For example, files for the thesis "Pre-kindergarten programs provide children with long-lasting educational advantages" might be sorted by type of educational advantage, such as reading readiness, social skills, and positive self-image.

If you used . . .	then . . .
computer files	copy and paste notes into folders by subtopic.
a citation (or reference) manager	save notes and sources in separate subfolders for each subtopic.
a research notebook	pull out pages and keep the notes on each subtopic in a separate manila folder.
photocopies of sources	attach sticky notes to indicate the subtopic and place copies in separate manila folders for each subtopic.
note cards	sort them into piles by subtopic or category.

Regardless of the medium in which you worked, be careful to keep track of which material belongs to which source as you rearrange your notes. Once your notes are organized by subtopic, you are ready to develop your outline or graphic organizer.

Develop an Outline or Graphic Organizer

Use an outline or a graphic organizer to show how you plan to arrange the divisions and subdivisions you intend to use. Preparing such a plan is especially important for a research project because you are working with a substantial amount of information. Without something to follow, it is easy to get lost and write an unfocused paper.

For more on creating outlines and graphic organizers, see Chapter 7.

Writing an outline or sketching a graphic organizer can help you test several different organizations. Be sure to save your original outline or graphic organizer and any revised versions as separate files in case you need to return to earlier versions.

RESEARCH PROJECT IN PROGRESS 6

Using the synthesis categories or graphic organizer that you developed for Research Project in Progress 5 (at the end of Chapter 22), sort your notes into categories and evaluate your working thesis. Then prepare an outline or a graphic organizer for your research project.

Avoid Plagiarism

After you have decided what source information to use, you will need to build that information into your essay. Three common methods for extracting information—summarizing, paraphrasing, and quoting—are discussed in Chapter 22. In general, paraphrasing or summarizing is better than quoting unless the wording is unusual or beautiful, or if you want to provide an expert's exact words on the topic. Quotations are also appropriate when discussing works of literature and historical (primary) sources. (More information on integrating quotations into your paper appears in the section "Use In-Text Citations to Integrate Source Information" on pp. 613–16.)

Regardless of how you integrate sources, be sure to acknowledge and document all ideas or information you have borrowed from sources that is not common knowledge. Remember that you must cite your sources regardless of whether you are using direct quotations, paraphrases, or summaries and regardless of whether the information or ideas came to you from a book, an article, a Web site, or even a conversation. Failing to cite a source, even by mistake, may be considered plagiarism.

What Is Plagiarism?

Plagiarism is the use of someone else's ideas, wording, organization, or sentence structure without acknowledging the source. At most schools, both intentional (deliberate) plagiarism and unintentional (accidental) plagiarism are considered serious forms of cheating and carry the same academic penalties—generally a failing grade or even permanent expulsion. Buying a paper and submitting it as your own work is plagiarism, but so is copying text from a source into your notes and then incorporating it into your essay as if it were your own idea, because you no longer realize that it is another writer's work.

Instructors may use Internet tracking resources like Turnitin.com, or they may paste a student's paper into a Google search box to check for plagiarism, so managing the information you have borrowed from sources is crucial. The quick reference guide below can help you determine if you have plagiarized.

Quick Reference Guide to Plagiarism

You have plagiarized if you

- copied information word for word without using quotation marks, whether or not you acknowledge the source
- paraphrased information (put it in your own words and sentences) without acknowledging the source
- borrowed someone else's organization, sentence structure, or sequence of ideas without acknowledging the source
- reused someone else's visual material (graphs, tables, charts, maps, diagrams, and so on) without acknowledging the source
- submitted another writer's paper as your own

How Can You Avoid Plagiarism?

Plagiarism is a serious matter, but it can be avoided if you follow these tips:

- **Take careful notes.** Place anything you copy directly in quotation marks. Record the source for any information you quote, paraphrase, summarize, or even comment on.
- **Be sure to separate your own ideas from ideas expressed in the sources you are using.** Use different colors, different font sizes, different sections of a notebook, or different computer files to distinguish your ideas from those of others. Or take

notes in two columns, with ideas and information from sources in one column and your own comments in another.

- **Never copy and paste directly from an online source into your paper.** Instead, cut and paste information you want to save into a separate file. Enclose the material you pasted in quotation marks to remind yourself that it is someone else's wording, and record the source information.
- **Paraphrase information from sources carefully.** Paraphrasing is an effective way to test your understanding of sources and to avoid overquoting, but be careful that when you paraphrase, you restate the author's ideas in your own words and sentences.
- **Record all the information you will need to access and cite the source.** Include the name of the site, the URL, your date of access, and so on.

For detailed instructions on how to paraphrase without plagiarizing, see Chapter 22. See also the bibliographic worksheet in Figure 22.4, which can help you record all the information you need to cite your sources fully.

What Sources Do You Need to Document?

You must document all information and ideas you get from a source unless that information is common knowledge. But what is common knowledge, and how can you tell? **Common knowledge** is information that is widely available and undisputed. The fact that George Washington was the United States' first president is common knowledge; so is the fact that the earth revolves around the sun. A good rule of thumb is that if a piece of information is available in a minimum of three reliable sources, then it is considered common knowledge. Of course, you will never be wrong if you cite the source, and you can always ask your instructor or a reference librarian if you are unsure about whether to document something. Table 23.1 also summarizes the types of material that *do* and *do not* require documentation.

TABLE 23.1 What Does and Does Not Require Documentation

Documentation Required	Documentation Not Required
• Summaries, paraphrases, and quotations from sources • Obscure or recently discovered facts (such as a little-known fact about Mark Twain or a recent discovery about Mars) • Others' opinions • Others' field research (results of opinion polls, case studies, statistics) • Quotations or paraphrases from interviews you conduct • Others' visuals (photographs, charts, maps, Web images) • Information from others that you use to create visuals (data you use to construct a table, graph, or other visual)	• Common knowledge (George Washington was the first U.S. president, the earth revolves around the sun) • Facts that can be found in numerous sources (winners of Olympic competitions, names of Supreme Court justices) • Standard definitions of academic terms • Your own ideas or conclusions • Your own field research (surveys or observations) • Your own visuals (such as photographs you take)

Draft Your Research Project

When drafting your research project, keep the following guidelines in mind:

For more about audience, see Chapter 4; for more about tone, see Chapter 3.

1. **Remember your audience.** Academic audiences will expect you to take a serious, academic tone and may expect you to use the third person (*he, she, they*). The third person is more impersonal, sounds less biased, and may lend credibility to your ideas. Although your instructor may know a great deal about your topic, he or she may want you to demonstrate that you understand key terms and concepts, so definitions and explanations may be required.

For more about placing the thesis statement, see Chapter 5; for more about introductions and conclusions, see Chapter 7.

2. **Follow the introduction, body, and conclusion format, and for most research projects, place your thesis in the introduction.** A straightforward organization, with your thesis in the introduction, is usually the best choice for a research project, since it allows readers to see from the outset how your supporting reasons relate to your main point. However, for projects analyzing a problem or proposing a solution, placing your thesis near the end may be more effective. For example, if you were writing an essay proposing stricter traffic laws on campus, you might begin by documenting the problem—describing accidents that have occurred and detailing their frequency. You might conclude your essay by suggesting that your college lower the speed limit on campus and install two new stop signs.

3. **Follow your outline or graphic organizer, but feel free to make changes as you work.** You may discover a better organization, think of new ideas about your topic, or realize that a subtopic belongs in a different section. Do not feel compelled to follow your outline or organizer to the letter, but be sure to address the topics you list.

4. **Refer to your source notes frequently as you write.** If you do so, you will be less likely to overlook an important piece of evidence. If you suspect that a note is inaccurate in some way, check the original source.

For more on writing and placing topic sentences, see Chapter 6; for more on supporting your ideas with evidence, see Chapter 5.

5. **State and support the main point of each paragraph.** Use your sources to substantiate, explain, or provide detail to support your main points. Make clear for your readers how your paragraph's main point supports your thesis as well as how the evidence you supply supports your paragraph's main point. Support your major points with evidence from a variety of sources. Doing so will strengthen your position. Relying on only one or two sources may make readers think you did insufficient research. But remember that your research project should not be just a series of facts, quotations, and statistics taken from sources. The basis of the paper should be *your* ideas.

For more on using transitions, see Chapter 6.

6. **Use strong transitions.** Because a research project may be lengthy or complex, readers need strong transitions to guide them from paragraph to paragraph and section to section. Make sure your transitions help readers understand how you have divided the topic and how one point relates to another.

7. **Use source information in a way that does not mislead your readers.** Although you are presenting only a portion of someone else's ideas, make sure you are not using information in a way that is contrary to the writer's original intentions.

8. **Include source material only for a specific purpose.** Just because you discovered an interesting statistic or a fascinating quote, do not feel that you must use it. Information that does not support your thesis will distract your reader and weaken your paper. Images may add interest, but in most academic disciplines, use visuals only for a useful purpose (such as to provide evidence or to analyze, as for an art history project).

9. **Incorporate in-text citations for your sources as you draft.** Whenever you paraphrase, summarize, or quote a source, be sure to include an in-text citation. The sections "Use In-Text Citations to Integrate Source Information" (pp. 613–16), "Use MLA Style for In-Text Citations" (pp. 623–27), and "Use APA Style for In-Text Citations" (pp. 648–51) can help you incorporate in-text citations effectively.

Use Research to Support Your Ideas

Supporting paragraphs in research projects have three parts:

- **Topic sentence.** Identifies the paragraph's topic, offers reasons to believe thesis, and provides a transition from the previous paragraph.
- **Supporting evidence.** Offers examples, facts, statistics, definitions, and other evidence to support the topic sentence; it may also include supporting summaries, paraphrases, or quotations from sources with in-text citations to identify those sources.
- **Analysis.** Explains how the evidence supports the paragraph's main point and provides a transition to the next paragraph.

Each of these three parts is crucial: Without a topic sentence, readers are left to wonder what the main point is. Without the evidence, readers are left to wonder whether the main point is supported. Without the analysis, readers are left to make sense of the evidence and figure out how the evidence supports the topic on their own. Of course, transitions are also needed to connect the parts within the paragraph and connect the paragraph to the rest of the essay. The paragraph in Figure 23.1 shows this three-part structure at work. (The essay from which it was taken appears later in the chapter.)

For more about creating a research "sandwich," see Chapter 6.

Use In-Text Citations to Integrate Source Information

When writing a research project, the goal is to support your own ideas with information from sources and to integrate that information so that you achieve an easy-to-read flow. Along with transitions and strategic repetition, **in-text citations** (brief references to sources in the body of your paper) make this seamless flow possible. These in-text citations direct readers to the list of works cited (or references) at the end of the research project, where they can find all the information they need to locate the sources for themselves. When used effectively, in-text citations also mark where the writer's ideas end and information from sources begins.

Many academic disciplines have a preferred format, or style, for in-text citations and lists of works cited (or references). In English and the humanities, the preferred

FIGURE 23.1

Transitions

Topic sentence

Supporting evidence

Writer's analysis

One of the major reasons that research into animal emotions was traditionally avoided is that scientists fear being accused of *anthropomorphism*—the act of attributing human qualities to animals. To do so is perceived as unscientific and has been cause for much debate in the scientific community (Bekoff, *Emotional Lives* 124–25). However, Frans de Waal, of the Yerkes Regional Primate Research Center in Atlanta, argues that if people are not open to the possibility of animals having emotions, they may be overlooking important information about both animals and humans. He defends his position in his book, *Primates and Philosophers*. The term *anthropodenial*, which he coined, "denotes willful blindness to the human-like characteristics of animals, or the animal-like characteristics of ourselves" (65). De Waal proposes that because humans and animals are so closely related, it would be impossible for one not to have some characteristics of the other. He contends, "While it is true that animals are not humans, it is equally true that humans are animals. Resistance to this simple yet undeniable truth is what underlies the resistance to anthropomorphism" (65). If de Waal is correct, then we should see animal emotions as on a continuum with humans' and can infer the existence of animal emotions through their behavior, just as we infer the emotions of fellow humans.

documentation format is usually that of the Modern Language Association (MLA) and is known as **MLA style**. In the social sciences, the guidelines of the American Psychological Association (APA) are often used; these guidelines are called **APA style**. These are the two most widely used formats and are discussed in detail later in this chapter. A third popular style, which many scientists follow, was created by the Council of Science Editors (CSE); you can find a book detailing CSE style in your college library; citation managers, like RefWorks or EndNote, can also help you format citations in CSE style.

In MLA style, an in-text citation usually includes the author's last name and the page number(s) on which the information appeared in the source. (Use just the author's name for one-page sources and online sources, like Web pages, that do not have page numbers.) This information can be incorporated in two ways:

1. In a signal, or attribution, phrase
2. In a parenthetical citation

Using a signal phrase.   When using a **signal phrase**, include the author's name with an appropriate verb before the borrowed material, and put the page number(s) in parentheses at the end of the sentence.

┌────── signal phrase ──────┐   page number
As Jo-Ellan Dimitrius observes, big spenders often suffer from low self-esteem (143).

Using a signal phrase before and a page number after borrowed material also helps readers clearly distinguish *your* ideas from those of your sources. Notice how the writer in Figure 23.1 uses in-text citations to make clear where information from sources begins and ends.

Often, providing some background information about the author the first time you mention a source is useful to readers, especially if the author is not widely known.

—————————— relevant background information ——————————
Jo-Ellan Dimitrius, a jury-selection consultant whose book *Reading People* discusses

methods of predicting behavior, observes that big spenders often suffer from low

self-esteem (143).

Such information helps readers understand that the source is relevant and credible.

Using a signal phrase will help you integrate information from sources smoothly into your paper. Most summaries and paraphrases and *all* quotations need such an introduction. Compare the paragraphs below.

Quotation Not Integrated

Anecdotes indicate that animals experience emotions, but anecdotes are not considered scientifically valid. "Experimental evidence is given almost exclusive credibility over personal experience to a degree that seems almost religious" (Masson and McCarthy 3).

Quotation Integrated

Anecdotes indicate that animals experience emotions, but anecdotes are not considered scientifically valid. Masson and McCarthy, who have done extensive field observation, comment, "Experimental evidence is given almost exclusive credibility over personal experience to a degree that seems almost religious" (3).

In the first example paragraph, the quotation is merely dropped in. In the second, the signal phrase, including background information on the source authors, smooths the connection.

When writing signal phrases, vary the verbs you use and where you place the signal phrase. The following verbs are useful for introducing many kinds of source material:

advocates	contends	insists	proposes
argues	demonstrates	maintains	shows
asserts	denies	mentions	speculates
believes	emphasizes	notes	states
claims	explains	points out	suggests

In most cases, a neutral verb such as *states*, *explains*, or *maintains* will be most appropriate. Sometimes, however, a verb such as *denies* or *speculates* may more accurately reflect the source author's attitude.

Using a parenthetical citation. When you are merely citing facts or have already identified a source author, a **parenthetical citation** that includes the author's last name and the page number may be sufficient.

> Some behavioral experts claim that big spenders often suffer from low
>
> parenthetical citation
> self-esteem (Dimitrius 143).

Integrate Quotations into Your Research Project

Although quotations can lend interest to your research project and provide support for your ideas, they must be used appropriately. The following sections answer some common questions about the use of quotations. (The in-text citations below follow MLA style. See pp. 648–51 for creating in-text citations in APA style.)

Using quotations. Do not use quotations to reveal ordinary facts and opinions. Rather, quote only when:

- The author's wording is unusual, noteworthy, or striking. The quotation "Injustice anywhere is a threat to justice everywhere" from Martin Luther King Jr.'s "Letter from Birmingham Jail" is probably more effective than any paraphrase.
- The original words express the exact point you want to make, and a paraphrase might alter or distort the statement's meaning.
- The statement is a strong, opinionated, exaggerated, or disputed idea that you want to make clear is not your own.

Formatting long quotations. Both MLA and APA style require indenting lengthy quotations as a block by half an inch, but the two styles differ in terms of what is considered lengthy. In MLA style, quotations of more than three lines of poetry or more than four lines of prose get indented as a block; in APA style, quotations of forty or more words get indented as a block. Like a shorter quotation in the main text, always introduce a block quotation with a signal phrase. Use a colon at the end of the signal phrase if it is a complete sentence, as in the following example:

> . . . In her book *Through a Window,* which elaborates on her thirty years of experience studying and living among the chimps in Gombe, Tanzania, Jane Goodall gives the following account of Flint's experience with grief:
>
> > Flint became increasingly lethargic, refused most food and, with his immune system thus weakened, fell sick. The last time I saw him alive, he was hollow-eyed, gaunt and utterly depressed, huddled in the vegetation close to where Flo had died. . . . The last short journey he made, pausing to rest every few feet, was to the very place where Flo's body had lain. There he stayed for several hours, sometimes staring and staring into the water. He struggled on a little further, then curled up—and never moved again. (196–97)

Unlike a shorter quotation in the main text, the page numbers in parentheses appear *after* the final sentence period. (For a short quotation within the text, the page numbers within parentheses *precede* the period.)

Punctuating quotations.   There are specific rules and conventions for punctuating quotations. The most important rules are listed below.

1. **Use single quotation marks to enclose a quotation within a quotation.**

   Coleman and Cressey argue that "concern for the 'decaying family' is nothing new" (147).

2. **Use a comma after a verb that introduces a quotation.** Begin the first word of the quotation with a capital letter (enclosed in brackets if it is not capitalized in the source).

   As Thompson and Hickey report, "There are three major kinds of 'taste cultures' in complex industrial societies: high culture, folk culture, and popular culture" (76).

3. **When a quotation is not introduced by a verb, it is not necessary to use a comma or capitalize the first word.**

   Buck reports that "pets play a significant part in both physical and psychological therapy" (4).

4. **Use a colon to introduce a quotation preceded by a complete sentence.**

   The definition is clear: "Countercultures reject the conventional wisdom and standards of the dominant culture and provide alternatives to mainstream culture" (Thompson and Hickey 76).

5. **For a paraphrase or quotation integrated into the text, punctuation *follows* the parenthetical citation; for a block quotation, the punctuation *precedes* the parenthetical citation.**

   Integrated

   Scientists who favor a related scientific theory called *mutual altruism* believe that animals help each other because, when they themselves need help, they would like to be able to count on reciprocal assistance (Hemelrijk 480).

   Block

   Franklin observed the following scene:

   > Her unhappy spouse moved around her incessantly, his attention and tender cares redoubled. . . . At length his companion breathed her last; from that moment he pined away, and died in the course of a few weeks. (qtd. in Barber 116)

6. **Place periods and commas inside quotation marks.**

   "The most valuable old cars," notes antique car collector Michael Patterson, "are the rarest ones."

7. **Place colons and semicolons outside quotation marks.**

> As Buck demonstrates, "Petting a dog increases mobility of a limb or hand" (4);
> petting a dog, then, can be a form of physical therapy.

8. **Place question marks and exclamation points inside quotation marks when they are part of the original quotation; place them outside when they belong to your own sentence.**

> The instructor asked, "Does the text's description of alternative lifestyles agree with
> your experience?"

> Is the following definition accurate: "Sociolinguistics is the study of the relationship
> between language and society"?

Adapting quotations.   Use the following guidelines when adapting quotations to fit in your own sentences:

1. **You must copy the spelling, punctuation, and capitalization exactly as they appear in the original source, even if they are in error.** (See the last item on this list, item 5, for the only exception.) If a source contains an error, copy it with the error and add the word *sic* (Latin for "thus") in brackets immediately following the error.

> According to Bernstein, "The family has undergone rapid decentralization since
> Word [sic] War II" (39).

2. **You can emphasize words in a quotation by italicizing them.** However, you must add the notation *emphasis added* in parentheses at the end of the sentence to indicate the change.

> "In *unprecedented* and *increasing* numbers, patients are consulting practitioners of
> every type of complementary medicine" (Buckman and Sabbagh 73; emphasis added).

3. **You can omit part of a quotation, but you must add an ellipsis—three spaced periods (. . .)—to indicate that material has been deleted.** You may delete words, sentences, paragraphs, or entire pages as long as you do not distort the author's meaning by doing so.

> According to Buckman and Sabbagh, "Acupuncture . . . has been rigorously tested
> and proven to be effective and valid" (188).

When an omission falls at the end of a quoted sentence, use the three spaced periods after the sentence period.

> Thompson maintains that "marketers need to establish ethical standards for
> personal selling. . . . They must stress fairness and honesty in dealing with
> customers" (298).

If you are quoting only a word or phrase from a source, do not use an ellipsis before or after it because it will be obvious that you have omitted part of the original sentence. If you omit the beginning of a quoted sentence, you need not use an ellipsis unless what you are quoting begins with a capitalized word and appears to be a complete sentence.

4. **You can add words or phrases in brackets to make a quotation clearer or to make it fit grammatically into your sentence.** Be sure that in doing so you do not change the original sense.

> Masson and McCarthy note that the well-known animal researcher Jane Goodall finds that "the scientific reluctance to accept anecdotal evidence [of emotional experience is] a serious problem, one that colors all of science" (3).

5. **You can change the first word of a quotation to a capital or lowercase letter to fit into your sentence.** If you change it, enclose it in brackets.

> As Aaron Smith said, "The . . ." (32).
>
> Aaron Smith said that "[t]he . . ." (32).

RESEARCH PROJECT IN PROGRESS 7

Using your research notes, your revised thesis, and the organizational plan you developed for your research project, write a first draft. Be sure to integrate sources carefully and to include in-text citations. (See "Document Your Sources: MLA Style," pp. 623–27, for MLA style guidelines for in-text citations; see "Document Your Sources: APA Style," pp. 648–51, for APA style.)

Revise Your Research Project

Revise a research project in two stages. First, focus on the project as a whole; then consider individual paragraphs and sentences for effectiveness and correctness. If time allows, wait at least a day before rereading your research project.

For more on revision, see Chapter 9.

Analyze and Revise Your Project as a Whole

Begin by evaluating your project as a unified piece of writing. Focus on general issues, overall organization, and the key points that support your thesis. Use the flowchart in Figure 23.2 to help you discover the strengths and weaknesses of your research project as a whole. You might also ask a classmate to review your draft by using the questions in the flowchart.

Analyze and Revise Paragraphs and Sentences

After evaluating your project as a whole, check each paragraph to be sure that it supports your thesis and integrates sources appropriately. Then check your sentences for correct structure, transitions, and in-text citation format. Use your earlier work with Figure 23.1 to guide your analysis.

RESEARCH PROJECT IN PROGRESS 8

Using the questions in Figure 23.2, revise the first draft of your research project.

FIGURE 23.2   Flowchart for Revising a Research Project

QUESTIONS	REVISION STRATEGIES

1. Highlight your thesis statement. Is it clear and specific? Is the assertion based on some of your own (and not just the sources') ideas about the subject?

 NO ▶

- Delete your thesis statement. Then have a peer read the paper and tell you what he or she believes the thesis is.
- Brainstorm about the main point you want to make.
- Review the guidelines for writing a thesis in Chapter 5.

YES ▼

2. Underline the topic sentence of each paragraph. Does each topic sentence make a point that supports your thesis? Does each topic sentence express your own ideas?

 NO ▶

- Revise any topic sentences that do not support the thesis.
- Revise any topic sentences that rely too heavily on ideas from sources.
- Eliminate any points that do not truly support the thesis.

YES ▼

3. [Bracket] the information and ideas that support each topic sentence. Do you analyze or explain how this information supports your point? Do you use a variety of sources? Do you avoid strings of quotations?

 NO ▶

- Rewrite to show how source material supports your point.
- Replace some quotations with summaries or paraphrases, so more of your research project is in your own words.

YES ▼

4. Draw a circle around terms that are essential to your thesis or that your audience might not know. Is each defined?

 NO ▶

- Add definitions where necessary.
- Read the circled terms and definitions to one or more classmates and ask if they understand them.
- Ask one or more classmates to read your project and circle any terms they do not understand.

YES ▼

QUESTIONS	REVISION STRATEGIES

5. Place a checkmark ✔ next to each idea that came from an outside source. Do you give credit to each source in an in-text citation? Is it clear where source material begins and ends?

NO ▶

- Add in-text citations wherever you need them for all paraphrases, summaries, and quotations. Include a signal phrase (*Dr. X argues, Professor Y claims*) and follow the source material with a page reference (see "Use In-Text Citations to Integrate Source Information," pp. 613–16).
- Vary the verbs you use and the placement of signal phrases to avoid ineffective repetition (see "Use In-Text Citations to Integrate Source Information").

YES ▼

6. Draw a box around your introduction and conclusion. Does the introduction provide a context for your research? Is the conclusion satisfying and relevant?

NO ▶

- Revise your introduction to provide background or to capture your readers' attention with a dramatic anecdote or quotation.
- Revise your conclusion to propose action or a way of thinking that is appropriate in light of the research.
- Review the strategies for introductions and conclusions in Chapter 7.

Prepare Your Final Draft

After you have revised your project and compiled a list of references or works cited, you are ready to prepare the final draft. Following are some guidelines to help you format, edit, and proofread your final paper. For an example of an essay in MLA style, see "Do Animals Have Emotions?" by Nicholas Destino (pp. 641–48). For an example of an essay in APA style, see "Schizophrenia: Definition and Treatment" by Sonia Gomez (pp. 659–64).

Format Your Research Project

Academic papers should follow a standard format that meets the expectations of the genre in which you are writing. For example, if you are writing a research report for a psychology class, you will probably be expected to include a title page, an abstract (if your instructor requests one), and headings for each of your main sections. If you are writing a research paper for a literature class, in contrast, no title page or abstract is typically required, and headings are considered necessary only in lengthy essays.

The following guidelines are common for writing projects in the humanities. If your instructor suggests or requires a different format, be sure to follow it. If your instructor does not recommend a format, these guidelines would likely be acceptable.

1. **Paper.** Use 8½- by 11-inch white paper. Use a paper clip; do not staple or use a binder.
2. **Your name and course information.** Position your name at the left margin one inch from the top of the page. Underneath it, on separate lines, list your instructor's name, your course name and number, and the date. (If you are following APA style, include this information and your title on a title page. See "Schizophrenia: Definition and Treatment" by Sonia Gomez on p. 659 for an example.)
3. **Title.** Place the title one double-spaced line below the date, and center it. Capitalize the first and last words and all other important words (all except articles, coordinating conjunctions, and prepositions). Do not underline or italicize your title or put quotation marks around it. Start your paper one double-spaced line below the title.
4. **Margins, spacing, and indentation.** Use one-inch margins. Double-space your paper (including your name and course information, your title, block quotations, and works-cited entries). Indent block quotations and the first line of each paragraph half an inch, and use a **hanging indent** (first line flush left, subsequent lines indented half an inch) in the list of works cited.
5. **Numbering of pages.** Number all pages using arabic numerals (1, 2, 3) in the upper-right corner. Place the numbers half an inch below the top of the paper. (If you include a title page, do not number it and do not count it in your numbering, unless you are following APA style.) Precede each page number with your last name, leaving a space between your name and the number.
6. **Headings.** The system recommended by the American Psychological Association (APA) should work for most research projects. Main headings should be centered and boldface; subheadings should be boldface and begin at the left margin. Capitalize first, last, and other important words.
7. **Visuals.** If you include tables and figures (graphs, charts, maps, photographs, and drawings) in your paper, label each table or figure with an arabic numeral (*Table 1, Table 2; Fig. 1, Fig. 2*) and give it a title. Place the table number and title on separate lines above the table. Place the figure number and title below the figure. Capitalize figure and table titles as you would any other title.

For more on editing and proofreading, see Chapter 9.

Edit and Proofread Your Research Project

As a final step, edit and proofread your revised paper for errors in grammar, spelling, punctuation, mechanics, and documentation style. As you edit and proofread, check for the types of errors you commonly make, and watch for these ten common problems:

1. **Long, cumbersome sentences.** Try splitting them into separate sentences.
2. **Incomplete sentences.** Correct sentence fragments (a group of words that cannot stand alone as a sentence because it is missing a subject, a complete verb, or both), comma splices (two or more independent clauses linked by a comma but without a coordinating conjunction), and run-on (or fused) sentences (two or more independent clauses joined without a punctuation mark or coordinating conjunction).

3. **Verb problems.** Avoid tense shifts (from present to past or future) unless there is a good reason to do so. Also, make sure the subjects and verbs in all your sentences agree in person (*first*: I, we; *second*: you; *third*: he/she/it/they) and number (singular/plural). Be particularly careful when words come between the subject and verb. But note that MLA and APA styles now recommend using *they* with a singular verb to refer to a person when you do not know the preferred pronoun.

4. **Wordiness.** Avoid wordy expressions (*at this particular point in time* rather than simply *now*), redundancy (*dashing quickly*), intensifiers (such as *very* or *really*), and weak verb-noun combinations (*wrote a draft* rather than *drafted*).

5. **Inappropriate tone/level of diction.** Avoid slang, abbreviations, and emoticons (☺). Aim for a clear and direct tone, and use words with appropriate connotations.

6. **Incorrect in-text citations.** Make sure you punctuate and format them to conform to MLA style, APA style, or that of another system of documentation.

7. **Inaccurate direct quotations.** Check quotations carefully against the original source for accuracy, and double-check your use of quotation marks, capital letters, commas, and ellipses.

8. **Plagiarism.** Avoid plagiarism by carefully quoting, paraphrasing, and summarizing the ideas of others, and citing your sources for all ideas and opinions and all facts except those that are common knowledge.

9. **Incorrect formatting.** Check that you have formatted your paper consistently, following these or your instructor's instructions. Check the citations in your list of works cited carefully against the models provided later in this chapter.

10. **Incomplete list of works cited/references.** Make sure all sources cited in your paper are included in the list in alphabetical order.

For MLA-style works-cited models, see pp. 627–41; for APA-style reference list models, see pp. 651–58.

> **RESEARCH PROJECT IN PROGRESS 9**

Edit and proofread your research project, paying particular attention to the questions in the preceding list.

Document Your Sources: MLA Style

The system described in this section is recommended by the Modern Language Association (MLA) and is described in detail in the *MLA Handbook*, Eighth Edition (available from most libraries). MLA style uses in-text citations within the text of a research project and a list of works cited at the end to document the sources used. If you are unsure whether to use MLA style, check with your instructor.

　　The first student paper at the end of this section ("Do Animals Have Emotions?") models the use of MLA style.

Use MLA Style for In-Text Citations

Your paper must include in-text citations—either signal phrases (attributions) or parenthetical citations—for all material you paraphrase, summarize, or quote from sources. Many instructors prefer that you use signal phrases rather than parenthetical citations in most places because signal phrases allow you to put sources in context.

For more about using signal phrases and parenthetical citations, see "Use In-Text Citations to Integrate Source Information" on pp. 613–16.

For either type of citation, use the following rules:

- Omit the word *page(s)* or the abbreviation *p.* or *pp.*
- Place the sentence period after the closing parenthesis unless the citation follows a block quotation. (See "Punctuating Quotations," pp. 617–18.)
- If a quotation ends the sentence, insert the closing quotation mark before the parentheses enclosing the page reference.

Examples showing in-text citations in MLA style follow.

Directory of MLA In-Text Citation Models

1. **One author**

    In his classic analysis of post-war advertising techniques, Vance Packard claims that . . . (58).

    . . . (Packard 58).

2. **Two authors.** Include both authors' names, in either a signal phrase or a parenthetical citation.

    Marquez and Allison assert . . . (74).

    . . . (Marquez and Allison 74).

3. **Three or more authors.** Include the first author's last name followed by *et al.*, which means "and others" in Latin.

    Hong et al. maintain . . . (198).

    . . . (Hong et al. 198).

4. **Two or more works by the same author(s).** When citing two or more sources by the same author or group of authors, include the full title in a signal phrase, or a brief version of the title in a parenthetical citation.

    In *For God, Country, and Coca-Cola*, Pendergrast describes . . . (96).

    . . . (Pendergrast, *For God* 96).

5. **Corporate or organizational author.** Use the group's full name in the signal phrase; you may abbreviate common words when providing a parenthetical citation.

> The American Diabetes Association estimates that the cost of diagnosed diabetes in the United States in 2012 was $245 billion.

> The cost of diagnosed diabetes in the United States in 2012 was estimated at $245 billion (Amer. Diabetes Assn.).

(There is no page number in these in-text citations because the information comes from an unpaginated digital source. See "16. Digital source," pp. 626–27.)

6. **No author named.** If the author is unknown, use the full title in a signal phrase or a shortened form in parentheses.

> According to the article "Medical Mysteries and Surgical Surprises," . . . (79).

> . . . ("Medical Mysteries" 79).

7. **Authors with the same last name.** Include the first initial of these authors in all parenthetical citations. Use the complete first name if both authors have the same first initial.

> John Dillon proposes . . . (974).

> . . . (J. Dillon 974).

8. **Two or more sources in the same citation.** When citing two or more sources of one idea in parentheses, list the authors (or titles) in alphabetical order, and separate the citations with a semicolon.

> . . . (Breakwater 33; Holden 198).

9. **Entire work.** When referring to an entire work, name the author in a signal phrase or parentheses.

> In *For God, Country, and Coca-Cola*, Pendergrast presents an unauthorized history of Coca-Cola, the soft drink and the company that produces it.

10. **Chapter in an edited book or work in an anthology.** An *anthology* is a collection of writings (articles, stories, poems) by different authors. In the in-text citation, name the author who wrote the work (not the editor of the anthology) and include the page number(s) from the anthology. The corresponding entry in the list of works cited begins with the author's last name; it also names the editor of the anthology.

In-Text Citation

> According to Ina Ferris . . . (239).

> . . . (Ferris 239).

Works-Cited Entry

> Ferris, Ina. "The Irish Novel 1800–1829." *Cambridge Companion to Fiction in the Romantic Period*, edited by Richard Maxwell and Katie Trumpener, Cambridge UP, 2008, pp. 235–49.

11. **Multivolume work.** When citing two or more volumes of a multivolume work, indicate the volume number, followed by a colon and the page number.

> Terman indicates . . . (2: 261).
>
> . . . (Terman 2: 261).

When you cite only one volume in your research project, create an in-text citation as you would for any other single-volume work.

12. **Indirect source.** Use the abbreviation *qtd. in* to indicate that you are using a source that is cited in another source.

> As Arthur Miller says, "When somebody is destroyed everybody finally contributes to it, but in Willy's case, the end product would be virtually the same" (qtd. in Martin and Meyer 375).

13. **Personal communication (interview, letter, email, conversation).** Name the person in your text, and mention the type of communication (interview, letter, and so on).

> In an interview with Professor Emilio Lopez, . . .

14. **Literary work.** Readers may find it helpful if you include information that will help them locate the material in any edition. For novels, cite the page and chapter number: (109; *ch.* 5). For plays, cite the act and/or scene number: (35; *sc.* 1). For poetry, cite the book or part number and line numbers: (6.129–30). If you are citing lines of poetry only, use the word *line* or *lines* in the first reference and then just the line numbers in subsequent references:

First Reference   (lines 12–15)

Later References   (16–18)

15. **Encyclopedia or dictionary entry.** Mention the word or entry in your text in italics. If more than one definition is given in the dictionary, include the definition number in your in-text citation.

> The term *prion* was coined by Stanley B. Prusiner from the words *proteinaceous* and *infectious* plus *-on* ("Prion," def. 2).

16. **Digital source.** In general, a digital source is cited like its printed counterpart. Give enough information in the citation so that readers can locate the source in your list of works cited. If the digital source provides page numbers, you should provide them too. If the source uses another ordering system, such as paragraph (*par.* or *pars.*), section (*sec.*), or screen (*screen*) numbers, provide those instead.

> Brian Beckman argues that "centrifugal force is a fiction" (par. 6).
>
> . . . (Beckman, par. 6).

If the source does not have paragraph or page numbers, which is often the case, do not add them. Instead, just cite the work by author, title, or whatever begins your entry in the list of works cited.

Author

> Teresa Schmidt discusses . . .
>
> . . . (Schmidt).

Title

> The "Band of Brothers" section of the History Channel site . . .
>
> . . . ("Band").

Use MLA Style for the List of Works Cited

Follow these general guidelines when preparing your list of works cited:

1. Include only the sources that you paraphrase, summarize, or quote in your research project. If you consulted a work but did not cite it, do not include it in the list of works cited.
2. Put the list on a separate page at the end of your paper. Type *Works Cited*, centered, at the top of the page; do not use quotation marks, italics, or boldface for the heading.
3. Alphabetize the list by the first important word in each citation, usually the author's last name. (Ignore articles: *A, An,* or *The.*)
4. Capitalize the first and last word of each title and all words except for articles (*a, an, the*), coordinating conjunctions (*and, but, for, nor, so, yet*), and prepositions (*in, of, on, off, up,* and so on).
5. Format the list with a hanging indent (usually a setting on the ruler or on the paragraph tab), so the first line is flush with the left margin and subsequent lines are indented by half an inch.
6. Double-space the whole list.

GENERAL GUIDELINES FOR CREATING ENTRIES IN THE WORKS-CITED LIST

An MLA-style citation includes the following:

▶ *The author (if named) + period.* The first author's name appears last name first, with a comma between first and last names.

▶ *The title + period.* Titles of self-contained works, such as books, Web sites, and television series, are italicized; titles of works contained within other works, such as articles from magazines or journals, are enclosed in quotation marks.

▶ *"Container" information.* The MLA calls any work a "container" that is made up of other works, so a journal is a container because it "contains" articles; a television series is a container because it is made up of episodes. Follow the container title and all but the last item of information about the container with a comma. End the container section with a period. If a source appears in multiple containers—for example, you cite an article that appears in a journal (container 1) via a database (container 2)—include information about the second container after the first.

- **The title of the "container" + comma.** Titles of containers (books, periodicals, databases, and so on) are typically italicized.
- **Other contributors + comma.** Other contributors may include the editor, translator, producer, actor, illustrator, and so on.

- **Version + comma.** The version may be the edition number (seventh edition) or name (revised edition, abridged edition, director's cut, and so on).
- **Number + comma.** The number may be the volume number of a multivolume work, volume and issue number of a journal, or disk number of a set of DVDs.
- **Publication information + comma.** Publication information may include the name of the publisher, government agency, or site sponsor. The MLA does not require the place of publication.
- **Publication date + comma.** The publication date will be a year for movies and books; a month, year, and season for most journals; a month and year for monthly magazines; and a day, month, and year for weekly magazines and daily newspapers.
- **Source location + period.** The source location may be page numbers for a printed text, a URL or DOI (digital object identifier, a permanent code) for an online text, or a time stamp for an online video, audio file, blog post, and so on.

▶ *Additional information + period.* You may decide to include original publication information for a reprinted book (if relevant to your readers), an access date for an undated online source, or a label for an unusual source type or a source type readers will not be able to identify based solely on the citation (such as a letter to the editor, a typescript, or a lecture).

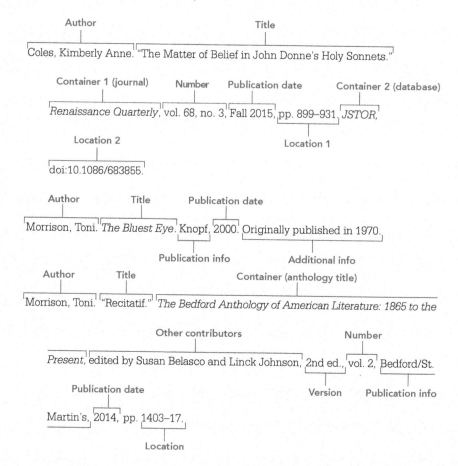

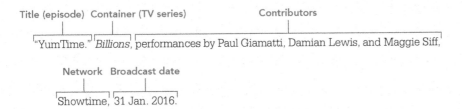

Title (episode) Container (TV series)   Contributors

"YumTime." *Billions*, performances by Paul Giamatti, Damian Lewis, and Maggie Siff,

Network Broadcast date

Showtime, 31 Jan. 2016.

A variety of models for different types of sources follow. However, you may need to combine information from one or more models to create a citation for a work you are using. (Some models included here are created by applying the MLA's rules to create citation models they do not supply.)

For instance, to cite a reading from this textbook, you would need to treat it as a work in an edited book or anthology in an edition other than the first:

> Goleman, Daniel. "His Marriage and Hers: Childhood Roots." *Successful College Writing*, by Kathleen T. McWhorter, 8th ed., Bedford/St. Martin's, 2021, pp. 403–8.

Directory of MLA Works-Cited Models

Authors

1. **One author.** Give the author's last name first, followed by a comma. End with a period.

   Rybszynski, Witold.

2. **Two authors.** List the names in the order they appear in the source. Do not reverse the order of the second author's names.

   Botkin, Daniel B., and Diana Pérez.

3. **Three or more authors.** List the first author, last name first, followed by *et al.* (which means "and others" in Latin).

   Lewin, Benjamin, et al.

4. **Corporation, organization, or governmental body as author.** List the organization or corporation as the author, omitting any initial article (*A, An,* or *The*). If author and publisher are the same, omit the author and include the publisher following the title.

   National Kidney Foundation.

   United States, Government Accountability Office.

5. **No author named.** Begin with the title. If the source is a self-contained work, such as a book, italicize the title; if the source is part of another, larger work (for example, if the work is an article in a newspaper or magazine), set it in quotation marks.

   Go Ask Alice.

   "California Sues EPA over Emissions."

6. **Author using a pseudonym.** Use the name as it appears in the source; if you know the author's real name, insert it following the pseudonym, in parentheses.

   Atrios (Duncan Black).

7. **Two or more works by the same author(s).** Alphabetize the works by title, ignoring the article (*A, An,* or *The*). For entries after the first, replace the author's name with three hyphens followed by a period.

   Coates, Ta-Nehisi. *The Beautiful Struggle: A Father, Two Sons, and an Unlikely Road to Manhood.* Spiegel and Grau, 2008.

   ---. *Between the World and Me.* Spiegel and Grau, 2015.

Books and Other Self-Contained Works. Most of the information you will need to cite a book appears on the book's title page and copyright page (see Figure 23.3). In printed books, these two pages appear toward the beginning of the text; in e-books, they may appear elsewhere.

FIGURE 23.3 Where to Find Documentation Information for a Book

CITING A BOOK

▶ *Author.* Begin with the author's name, last name first.

▶ *Title.* Provide the full title and subtitle in italics.

▶ *Publisher.* Use the full name of the publisher (*Houghton Mifflin* or *Basic Books*). Omit business words or abbreviations, such as *Company, Ltd.,* or *Inc.* Standardize punctuation, using the word *and* in place of & (ampersand). For university presses, use the abbreviations *U* (for *University*) and *P* (for *Press*).

▶ *Date.* Use the most recent publication year listed on the book's copyright page.

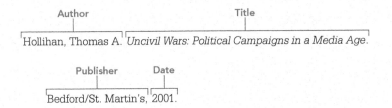

Author   Title

Hollihan, Thomas A. *Uncivil Wars: Political Campaigns in a Media Age.*

Publisher   Date

Bedford/St. Martin's, 2001.

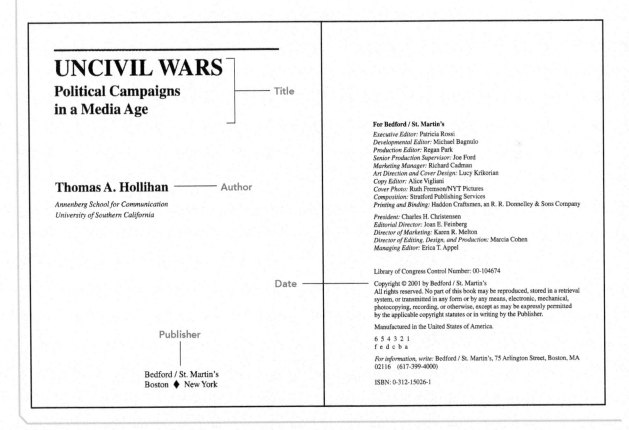

8. **Basic format for a book.** Include the author (last name first), title, publisher, and publication date. If you are citing an e-book, add information about the e-reader used. If you are citing an online book, add information about the second, digital "container," including the name of the Web site on which the online book appears and the permalink URL.

Print

> Ward, Jesmyn. *Sing, Unburied, Sing*. Scribner, 2017.

E-Book

> Larson, Steig. *The Girl with the Dragon Tattoo*. Alfred A. Knopf, 2008. Kindle.

Online

> Dickens, Charles. *Great Expectations*. Estes, 1881. *Google Books*, play.google.com/
> store/books/details?id=fhUXAAAAYAAJ&rdid=book-fhUXAAAAYAAJ&rdot=1.

9. **Edited book or anthology.** In the author position, list the editor's name followed by a comma and the word *editor* (or *editors*).

> Szeman, Imre, and Timothy Kaposy, editors. *Cultural Theory: An Anthology*.
> Wiley-Blackwell, 2011.

For a model for a chapter from an edited book, a work in an anthology, or an introduction, preface, foreword, or afterword, see page 638.

10. **Translated book.** After the title, include the phrase *Translated by*, followed by the first and last names of the translator.

> Kawakami, Hiromi. *Manazuru*. Translated by Michael Emmerich, Counterpoint
> Press, 2010.

11. **Edition other than the first.** Indicate the number of the edition following the title.

> Barker, Ellen M. *Neuroscience Nursing*. 3rd ed., Mosby-Elsevier, 2008.

12. **Multivolume work.** If the reference is to all the volumes in a multivolume work, give the number of volumes at the end of the citation.

> Stark, Freya. *Letters*. Edited by Lucy Moorehead, Compton Press, 1974–82. 8 vols.

If the reference is to one volume in a multivolume work, give the number of the volume you used before the publisher.

> Stark, Freya. *Letters*. Edited by Lucy Moorehead, vol. 5, Compton Press, 1978.

13. **Encyclopedia or dictionary entry**

Print

> Robinson, Lisa Clayton. "Harlem Writers Guild." *Africana: The Encyclopedia of
> the African and African American Experience*, 2nd ed., Oxford UP, 2005,
> p. 163.

Online

"House Music." *Wikipedia*, 7 Mar. 2020, en.wikipedia.org/wiki/House_music.

14. **Entire Web site or blog.** You may not be able to find all the information for a Web site or blog that you would typically include for a book. If you cannot find all the information you need to create a complete citation, include as much as you can. If the Web site lacks an update or publication date, include an access date at the end of your citation. If the title of the Web site is very similar to the name of the organization that publishes the Web site, you may omit the name of the publisher.

LaMoreaux, Andrew M., editor. *The Huntington Archive of Buddhist and Related Art.* The Ohio State U, 2020, www.huntingtonarchive.osu.edu/.

Railton, Stephen. *Mark Twain in His Times.* U of Virginia Library, 2012, twain.lib .virginia.edu/.

Transparency International: The Global Coalition against Corruption, 2018, www .transparency.org/.

The Newton Project. U of Sussex, 2020, http://www.newtonproject.ox.ac.uk/.

Bae, Rebecca. Home page. Iowa State U, 2015, www.engl.iastate.edu/ rebecca-bae-directory-page/.

Kiuchi, Tatsuro. *Tatsuro Kiuchi: News & Blog*, tatsurokiuchi.com/. Accessed 3 Mar. 2019.

15. **Government document.** If a specific author is listed, include the information about the government, department, and agency that produced the document following the title, in the publisher position. If no author is listed, begin with the government, department, and agency. If the author and publisher are the same, begin the citation with the title.

Gilder, Carrie. *Space Station Leaves "Microbial Fingerprint" on Astronauts.* NASA, 6 May 2020, https://www.nasa.gov/mission_pages/station/research/ news/microbiome-space-station-leaves-microbial-fingerprint-on-astronauts.

Federal Student Loans: Repaying Your Loans. United States, Department of Education, Federal Student Aid, 2015, studentaid.ed.gov/sa/sites/default/files/ repaying-your-loans.pdf.

Eligibility Manual for School Meals: Determining and Verifying Eligibility. United States, Department of Agriculture, Food and Nutrition Service, Child Nutrition Programs. July 2015, www.fns.usda.gov/sites/default/files/cn/SP40_CACFP18 _SFSP20-2015a1.pdf.

16. **Film, DVD, or streamed video.** Begin with the title, unless you are focusing on the work of the director or another contributor, in which case list that person in the author position. Include the name of the production company in the publisher position and the release date in the publication date position. For supplementary material on a DVD, include the title of that information, along with the information for the movie; at the end of the citation include the disc number if there was more than one disc. If you watched the video online, include the URL.

Film

> *La La Land.* Directed by Damien Chazelle, performances by Ryan Gosling and Emma Stone, Summit Entertainment, 2016.

> Scott, Ridley, director. *The Martian.* Performances by Matt Damon, Jessica Chastain, Kristen Wiig, and Kate Mara, Twentieth Century Fox, 2015.

DVD

> "Sweeney's London." *Sweeney Todd: The Demon Barber of Fleet Street,* directed by Tim Burton, produced by Eric Young, DreamWorks, 2007, disc 2.

Streamed

> Lewis, Paul. "Citizen Journalism." *YouTube,* 14 May 2011, www.youtube.com/watch?v=9APO9_yNbcg.

17. **Music recording.** Begin with the composer or performer, unless you are focusing on the work itself. Include the composer or performer and the title of the recording or composition as well as the production company, and the date. Titles of recordings should be italicized, but titles of compositions identified by form (for example, Symphony No. 5) should not. (See "21. Live performance," p. 635.)

> Blige, Mary J. "Don't Mind." *Life II: The Journey Continues (Act 1),* Geffen, 2011.

> Bizet, Georges. *Carmen.* Performances by Jennifer Larmore, Thomas Moser, Angela Gheorghiu, and Samuel Ramey, Bavarian State Orchestra and Chorus, conducted by Giuseppe Sinopoli, Warner, 1996.

18. **Pamphlet**

> Rainie, Lee, and Maeve Duggan. *Privacy and Information Sharing.* Pew Research Center, 14 Jan. 2016, www.pewinternet.org/files/2016/01/PI_2016.01.14 _Privacy-and-Info-Sharing_FINAL.pdf.

19. **Lecture or public address.** Begin with the person who delivered the address, the title of the speech (if any) in quotation marks, the lecture's sponsor, the date, and the place where the lecture occurred.

> Eugenides, Jeffrey. Portland Arts and Lectures, 30 Sept. 2003, Arlene Schnitzer Concert Hall, Portland, OR.

> Burden, Amanda. "How Public Spaces Make Cities Work." *TED.com,* Mar. 2014, www.ted.com/talks/amanda_burden_how_public_spaces_make_cities_work.

If the fact that the source is a lecture is unclear from the information provided, you may want to include the label *Lecture* or *Speech* at the end of the citation.

20. **Personal interview.** Begin with the name of the person interviewed, the words *Personal interview*, and the date on which the interview took place.

> Freedman, Sasha. Personal interview. 10 Nov. 2014.

21. **Live performance.** Include the title of the work performed and the names of the writer, composer, or performers; the theater or location of the performance; and the date of the performance.

> Piano Concerto no. 3. By Ludwig van Beethoven, conducted by Andris Nelsons,
>
> performances by Paul Lewis and Boston Symphony Orchestra, Symphony Hall,
>
> Boston, 9 Oct. 2015.

Articles in Periodicals and Other Works Contained in Longer Works. A periodical is a publication that appears at regular intervals: Newspapers generally appear daily, magazines weekly or monthly, and scholarly journals quarterly. In periodicals, the information you will need to cite may appear on the first page of the article (see Figure 23.4), the database entry, or a combination of places (the first page of the article, the cover of the periodical, the Web page or Web site on which the article appears, and so on).

FIGURE 23.4 Where to Find Documentation Information for a Periodical

CITING AN ARTICLE IN A PERIODICAL

▶ *Author.* Begin with the author's name; the first author is cited last name first.

▶ *Article title.* Provide the full title of the article, including the subtitle, in quotation marks.

▶ *Periodical title.* Give the full title of the magazine, journal, or newspaper that "contains" the article, including any initial *A, An,* or *The.* Italicize the periodical title.

▶ *Number and/or date.* For scholarly journals, give the volume and issue numbers and date of publication (often a season and year or just a year): *vol. 54, no. 1, Autumn 2012.* For newspapers and magazines, give the date: day, month, year (or month, year, for monthly magazines); abbreviate the names of months except for *May, June,* and *July.*

▶ *Location.* For a print publication, include page numbers; for an online publication, include the DOI (digital object identifier, a permanent code) or URL (permalink preferred). If pages are not consecutive, include the first page number and a plus sign (+).

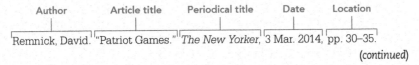

Author	Article title	Periodical title	Date	Location

Remnick, David. "Patriot Games." *The New Yorker,* 3 Mar. 2014, pp. 30–35.

(continued)

Article title

Author

LETTER FROM SOCHI

PATRIOT GAMES

Vladimir Putin lives his Olympic dream.

BY DAVID REMNICK

A quarter century ago, as jubilant citizens took sledgehammers to the Berlin Wall, Vladimir Vladimirovich Putin, an officer in the Dresden station of the K.G.B., fed a raging furnace with the documentary evidence of Soviet espionage activities in East Germany. Putin was grateful for his Dresden posting. He had grown up in a pretty wife and two young daughters, and enough leisure to play Ping-Pong, fish in the rivers outside town, and drink beer in the city's pubs and breweries. He drank so much beer that he gained twenty-five pounds. Now the happy days were ending. The Wall had been breached, and Putin was shovelling top-secret files into the fire so few months, Putin slipped back home to Leningrad and took a position as "vice-rector"—the residential spy—at the local university.

As the Soviet Union began to unravel, there was a pervasive mood of desperation in its most repressive offices. Occasionally, that desperation took on comic dimensions. One fall morning in 1990, when I was working as a Moscow correspondent, I was reading a stack of newspapers—a requirement of the job—and came across an article of tangy interest in *Komsomolskaya Pravda*. The headline read "MISS K.G.B."; below was a photograph of a woman in her twenties, named Katya Mayorova, provocatively adjusting the strap of her bulletproof vest. She had, it seemed, won a beauty

Putin's aim was to put on a display of renewed national confidence and modernity. "Russia is back," officials kept insisting.

Leningrad, an uneven student with early dreams of serving the state. One of his grandfathers was a cook for Lenin and Stalin. His father was an undercover operative during the war. Putin's parents barely survived the Nazi siege; an older brother did not. After a rough upbringing, Putin had enjoyed a halcyon four years in Dresden. He had quickly, he recalled in a book-length interview, that "the furnace burst." This was early in November, 1989. Later, angry Germans threatened to break into the K.G.B. compound. Putin's superiors called Moscow for reinforcements, but, he says, "Moscow was silent." The state was failing even its most resolute foot soldiers. Within a contest at Lubyanka, the K.G.B. headquarters. This was new. I took a sip of coffee. The article described how Comrade Mayorova wore her vest with "exquisite softness, like a Pierre Cardin model." Beyond "mere beauty," her talents included the ability to deliver a karate kick "to her enemies' head." I called Lubyanka, which, by now, had a press

30   THE NEW YORKER, MARCH 3, 2014

PASCAL LE SEGRETAIN/GETTY

Location   Periodical title   Date

22. Article in a magazine. Provide the complete publication date of the magazine—day, month, and year for weekly magazines and month and year for monthly magazines. For an online version of a magazine, replace the page numbers with the URL. If you accessed the article through a database, add information about the database (the second "container") to the end of the citation.

Print

> Butler, Kiera. "Works Well with Others." *Mother Jones*, Jan./Feb. 2008, pp. 66–69.

Online

> Seabrook, John. "Behind the Cellar Door." *The New Yorker*, 23 Jan. 2017, www
> .newyorker.com/magazine/2017/01/23/behind-the-cellar-door.

Database

> Sharp, Kathleen. "The Rescue Mission." *Smithsonian*, Nov. 2015, pp. 40–49. *OmniFile*
> *Full Text Select*, web.b.ebscohost.com.ezproxy.bpl.org/.

23. **Article in a newspaper.** Include the full title of the newspaper, including any initial
    A, *An*, or *The*. If the newspaper article does not appear on consecutive pages, give
    the first page number followed by a plus sign. If an edition name (*National ed.*)
    appears on the newspaper's first page, include it after the date. If you read a
    newspaper article online, replace page numbers with a permalink URL.

Print

> Sherry, Allison. "Volunteers' Personal Touch Turns High-Tech Data into Votes." *The*
> *Denver Post*, 30 Oct. 2012, pp. 1A+.

> Urbina, Ian. "Gas Wells Recycle Water, but Toxic Risks Persist." *The New York Times*,
> 2 Mar. 2011, late ed., pp. A1+.

Online

> Capuzzo, Jill P. "What about the Plants?" *The New York Times*, 22 May 2020,
> https://nyti.ms/3bNsRjX.

24. **Article in a scholarly journal.** Give the volume and issue number and the month
    or season (if provided). If you accessed the article online, replace page numbers
    with the permalink URL or DOI (digital object identifier, a permanent code). If you
    accessed the journal through a database your school's library subscribes to, add
    the information about that database at the end of the citation.

Print

> Matchie, Thomas. "Law versus Love in *The Round House*." *Midwest Quarterly*,
> vol. 56, no. 4, Summer 2015, pp. 353–64.

Online

> Bryson, Devin. "The Rise of a New Senegalese Cultural Philosophy?" *African Studies*
> *Quarterly*, vol. 14, no. 3, Mar. 2014, pp. 33–56, asq.africa.ufl.edu/files/Volume-14
> -Issue-3-Bryson.pdf.

Database

> Coles, Kimberly Anne. "The Matter of Belief in John Donne's Holy Sonnets." *Renaissance*
> *Quarterly*, vol. 68, no. 3, Fall 2015, pp. 899–931. *JSTOR*, doi:10.1086/683855.

25. **Editorial or letter to the editor.** Cite the editorial or letter beginning with the
    author's name (if provided), and add the word *Editorial* or *Letter* followed by a

period at the end of the citation. Often editorials are unsigned, and letters to the editor omit titles.

Editorial

"Reopening: A Time to Celebrate Cautiously." *The San Diego Union-Tribune*, 22 May 2020, p. B1. Editorial.

Letter to the Editor

Ginn, Lee. *Wired*, Dec. 2008, p. 19. Letter.

26. **Chapter in an edited book or work in an anthology.** List the author and title of the work, followed by the title and editor of the anthology. (Include the words *edited by* before the editor's name.) Publisher, date, and the pages on which the work appears follow.

Riss, Jacob. "How the Other Half Lives." *The Affordable Housing Reader*, edited by J. R. Tighe, Routledge, 2013, pp. 6–13.

27. **Introduction, preface, foreword, or afterword**

Aaron, Hank. Foreword. *We Are the Ship: The Story of Negro League Baseball*, by Kadir Nelson, Disney Publishing, 2008, p. vi.

28. **Book or film review.** List the reviewer's name and title of the review. After the title, add *Review of* and give the title and author of the book. For a film review, replace *by* with *directed by*. Include publication information for the review itself, not for the material reviewed.

Peters, Justin. "Original Sin." Review of *Spam: A Shadow History of the Internet*, by Finn Brunton, *Columbia Journalism Review*, vol. 52, no. 3, 2013, pp. 58–59.

29. **Published interview.** Start with the person interviewed; include the title of the interview (if any), followed by the person conducting the interview. End with the publication information for the source in which the interview appeared.

Blume, Judy. "Judy Blume in Conversation with Lena Dunham." Interview by Lena Dunham. *The Believer*, vol. 12, no. 1, Jan. 2014, pp. 39+.

FIGURE 23.5   Where to Find Documentation Information for a Source on a Web Site

CITING A DOCUMENT ON A WEB SITE

▶ *Author.* Include the name of the author, if provided. If the author is an organization, include the name only if it is substantially different from the name of the Web site. Otherwise, begin with the title of the source.

▶ *Web page and Web site title.* Enclose the titles of Web pages in quotation marks; italicize the titles of Web sites and other self-contained works.

▶ *Site sponsor.* Include the site sponsor (or publisher) of a Web site only if the name of the sponsor is substantially different from the name of the Web site.

▶ *Date of publication.* Give the most recent date of publication. It may appear on the home page or at the bottom of the Web page.

▶ **Location.** Give the permalink URL, if available; if a permalink URL is not available, give the site's URL.

Author Web page title Web site title

Sirhindi, Marcella. "Jamini Roy: Bengali Artist of Modern India." The Huntington Archive

Date Location

of Buddhist and Asian Art, 2017, huntingtonarchive.org/Exhibitions/JaminiRoy.php.

Location Web site title

Courtesy The John C. and Susan L. Huntington Photographic Archive of Buddhist and Asian Art

30. **Document on a Web site.** Include an access date if no date of publication is provided.

> Gallagher, Sean. "The Last Nomads of the Tibetan Plateau." *Pulitzer Center on Crisis*
> *Reporting*, 25 Oct. 2012, pulitzercenter.org/reporting/china-glaciers-global
> -warming-climate-change-ecosystem-tibetan-plateau-grasslands-nomads.
>
> "Social and Historical Context: Vitality." *Arapesh Grammar and Digital Language*
> *Archive Project*, Institute for Advanced Technology in the Humanities, www
> .arapesh.org/socio_historical_context_vitality.php. Accessed 6 May 2020.

31. **Posting to an online discussion list or newsgroup.** For a discussion group, include the author's name or handle (if both are available, include the handle with the name in parentheses), the title or subject line enclosed in quotation marks, the name of the Web site on which the group is found, the site sponsor (if substantially different from the name of the Web site), the date of posting, and the URL. If possible, cite an archived version. If the posting has no title, label it *Online posting.*

> Yen, Jessica. "Quotations within Parentheses (Study Measures)." *Copyediting-L*,
> 18 Mar. 2016, list.indiana.edu/sympa/arc/copyediting-l/2016-03/msg00492.html.

32. **Twitter post (tweet).** Include the name or handle (if you know both, include the name in parentheses after the handle); the whole post; any hashtags; the site name, date, and time; and URL.

> @grammarphobia (Patricia T. O'Conner and Steward Kellerman). "Is 'if you will,' like, a
> verbal tic? http://goo.gl/oYrTYP #English #language #grammar #etymology #usage
> #linguistics #WOTD." *Twitter*, 14 Mar. 2016, 9:12 a.m., twitter.com/grammarphobia.

33. **Episode of a television or radio program.** Include the episode title, the program title (in italics), key contributors (writer, director, performers), the network, and the date of the broadcast. If you streamed the broadcast, include the URL.

Broadcast

> "Free Speech on College Campuses." *Washington Journal*, narrated by Peter Slen,
> C-SPAN, 27 Nov. 2015.

Streamed

> "I'm Not Paying Attention to Any Polls." *The Rush Limbaugh Show*, narrated by Rush
> Limbaugh, Premiere Radio Networks, 21 May 2020, www.rushlimbaugh.com/
> daily/2020/05/21/im-not-paying-any-attention-to-any-polls/.

34. **Interview on a television or radio program.** Begin with the name of the person interviewed, the words *Interview by*, and the interviewer's name, if relevant. End with information about the program (as in an episode of a television or radio program).

> Schulte, Brigid. Interview by Terry Gross. *Fresh Air*, WNYC, 21 May 2020.

35. **Episode on a podcast.** Cite an episode of a podcast as you would a short work from a Web site.

McDougall, Christopher. "How Did Endurance Help Early Humans Survive?" *TED*

  Radio Hour, National Public Radio, 20 Nov. 2015, www.npr.org/2015/11/20/

  455904655/how-did-endurance-help-early-humans-survive.

36. **Short online audio or video segment.** Cite a short online audio segment or video
    as you would a short work from a Web site.

    Nayar, Vineet. "Employees First, Customers Second." *YouTube*, 9 June 2015,

      www.youtube.com/watch?v=cCdu67s_C5E.

    Fletcher, Antoine. "The Ancient Art of the Atlatl." *Russell Cave National Monument*,

      narrated by Brenton Bellomy, National Park Service, 12 Feb. 2014, www.nps

      .gov/media/video/view.htm?id=C92C0D0A-1DD8-B71C-07CBC6E8970CD73F.

RESEARCH PROJECT IN PROGRESS 10

For the final paper you prepared in Research Project in Progress 9, prepare a list of
works cited in MLA style.

STUDENTS WRITE

The following research project was written by Nicholas Destino for his first-year writing course while he was a student at Niagara County Community College. Destino
used MLA style for documenting his sources and formatted his research project using
the "Prepare Your Final Draft" instructions in this chapter (pp. 621–23). Notice how he
uses in-text citations and quotations to provide evidence that supports his thesis.

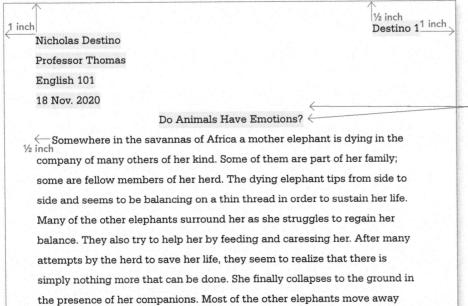

1 inch

½ inch
Destino 1 1 inch

Header: Student's name and
page number

Nicholas Destino

Professor Thomas

English 101

18 Nov. 2020

Double-spaced identification:
Writer's name, instructor's name,
course title, and date

Do Animals Have Emotions?

Title: Centered and
double-spaced

Somewhere in the savannas of Africa a mother elephant is dying in the
½ inch
company of many others of her kind. Some of them are part of her family;

some are fellow members of her herd. The dying elephant tips from side to

side and seems to be balancing on a thin thread in order to sustain her life.

Many of the other elephants surround her as she struggles to regain her

balance. They also try to help her by feeding and caressing her. After many

attempts by the herd to save her life, they seem to realize that there is

simply nothing more that can be done. She finally collapses to the ground in

the presence of her companions. Most of the other elephants move away from the scene. There are, however, two elephants who remain behind with the dead elephant—another mother and her calf. The mother turns her back to the body and taps it with one foot. Soon the other elephants call for them to follow and eventually they do (Masson and McCarthy 95). These movements, which are slow and ritualistic, suggest that elephants may be capable of interpreting and responding to the notion of death.

The topic of animal emotions is one that, until recently, has rarely been discussed or studied by scientists. However, since the now-famous comprehensive field studies of chimpanzees by the internationally renowned primatologist Jane Goodall, those who study animal behavior have begun to look more closely at whether animals feel emotions. As a result of their observations of various species of animals, a number of these researchers have come to the conclusion that animals do exhibit a wide range of emotions, such as grief, sympathy, and joy.

One of the major reasons that research into animal emotions was traditionally avoided is that scientists fear being accused of *anthropomorphism*—the act of attributing human qualities to animals. To do so is perceived as unscientific and has been cause for much debate in the scientific community (Bekoff, *Emotional Lives* 124–25). However, Frans de Waal, of the Yerkes Regional Primate Research Center in Atlanta, argues that if people are not open to the possibility of animals having emotions, they may be overlooking important information about both animals and humans. He defends his position in his book, *Primates and Philosophers*. The term *anthropodenial*, which he coined, "denotes willful blindness to the human-like characteristics of animals, or the animal-like characteristics of ourselves" (65). De Waal proposes that because humans and animals are so closely related, it would be impossible for one not to have some characteristics of the other. He contends, "While it is true that animals are not humans, it is equally true that humans are animals. Resistance to this simple yet undeniable truth is what underlies the resistance to anthropomorphism" (65). If de Waal is correct, then we should see animal emotions as on a continuum with humans' and can infer the existence of animal emotions through their behavior, just as we infer the emotions of fellow humans.

In many instances, their behaviors (and presumably, therefore, their emotions) are uncannily similar to the behaviors of humans. Consider grief: In

Citation: Parenthetical in-text citation of a work with 2 authors

Sources: Abbreviated title included because another work by this author cited earlier

Sources: Signal phrase, with author background, establishes author credentials and introduces paraphrase and quotation; **page number** follows quotation

Destino 3

"Animal Emotions: Exploring Passionate Natures," Marc Bekoff provides several examples of animals who exhibit behaviors that can only reflect their grief. He notes that sea lions wail at the loss of their young, dolphins struggle to save their babies, and orphaned elephants who have witnessed their mothers' deaths have been observed to wake up screaming (866). In his book *The Emotional Lives of Animals*, he includes a description from Cynthia Moss's *Elephant Memories* about elephants suffering the loss of one of their group:

½ inch

> They stood around Tina's carcass, touching it gently. . . . Because it was rocky and the ground was wet, there was no loose dirt; but they tried to dig into it . . . and when they managed to get a little earth up they sprinkled it over the body. Trista, Tia, and some of the others went off and broke branches from the surrounding low brushes and brought them back and placed them on the carcass. . . . By nightfall they had nearly buried her with branches and earth. Then they stood vigil over her for most of the night and only as dawn was approaching did they reluctantly begin to walk away. (qtd. in Bekoff, *Emotional Lives* 66–67)

Diane Ackerman, a columnist for *The New York Times* who writes regularly about the intersection of human and animal worlds, notes that "[b]iologists tell of sea lions wailing when their babies have been mutilated by killer whales, of grief-stricken monkey mothers carrying dead infants around for days, of geese singing both halves of a duet when their partners have died."

Perhaps the most extreme case of grief experienced by an animal is exemplified by the story of Flint, a chimp, when Flo, his mother, died. In her book, *Through a Window*, which elaborates on her thirty years of experience studying and living among the chimps in Gombe, Tanzania, Jane Goodall gives the following account of Flint's experience with grief.

> Flint became increasingly lethargic, refused most food and, with his immune system thus weakened, fell sick. The last time I saw him alive, he was hollow-eyed, gaunt and utterly depressed, huddled in the vegetation close to where Flo had died. . . . The last short journey he made, pausing to rest every few feet, was to the very place where Flo's body had lain. There he stayed for several hours, sometimes staring and staring into the water. He struggled on a little further, then curled up—and never moved again. (196–97)

Sources: Titles included because 2 works by this author are cited

Quotation: Quote longer than four lines indented half an inch and not enclosed in quotation marks; period precedes citation

Sources: Citation for indirect source

Quotation: First letter of a quotation changed to lowercase to fit into sentence

Sources: Author's credentials included within the text

Sources: Page number follows quotation

Destino 4

Of course, animal emotions are not limited to sadness and grief. Indeed, evidence indicates that animals also experience happier emotions, such as sympathy and joy. Many scientists who study animal behavior have found that several species demonstrate sympathy for one another. In other words, they act as if they care about one another. It is probably safe to assume that no animal displays behaviors more closely associated with sympathy than chimpanzees. Those who have studied apes in the wild, including de Waal, have observed that animals who had been fighting make up with one another by kissing and hugging. Chimps have also been found to console the loser of a fight or try to restore peace (Wilford).

Sympathy and caring have been noted in non-primate species as well. Researchers have found that young barn owls are "impressively generous" toward each other, saving portions of their food for smaller and hungrier owls (Angier). Likewise, the *Nature* episode "Animal Odd Couples" documents a number of instances in which animals of one species have cared for animals of another. In one example (00:25:26-00:31:41), Jack, a goat, led Charlie, a blind horse, around the ranch where they lived *every day for sixteen years,* until Jack's death (fig. 1). The animals' caretaker even compared Jack to the television character Lassie, describing how Jack got

Fig. 1. Seeing is believing: Jack leading Charlie (a blind horse). Film still from "Animal Odd Couples" (00:27:23).

Sources: Information at beginning of this paragraph can be found in many sources, so does not need to be documented

Sources: Information from a source paraphrased, **no page number** because source is an online newspaper

Source: Title of television program and episode used in signal phrase; **time stamp** given for episode described, and information from source summarized

Illustration: Figure number included in text and caption

Destino 5

human help to rescue Charlie after he became trapped in a grove of trees following a microburst of wind.

What makes this example particularly noteworthy is that the animals were of different species. Had the goat been helping another goat, it would be easy to assume that the act of caring was the result of what scientists call *genetic altruism,* animals helping others of their own species because there is something in it for them—namely, the assurance that their kin (and, therefore, their genes) will continue. This theory certainly provides an adequate, unbiased scientific explanation for why animals might care for others. However, if animals really help each other out only when doing so will perpetuate their species, then Jack would have had no genetic reason to help Charlie.

There is another popular explanation for why an animal would help another from a different species. Scientists who favor a related scientific theory called *mutual altruism* believe that animals will help each other because, when they themselves need help, they would like to be able to count on reciprocal assistance (Hemelrijk 480). This theory is a plausible, nonanthropomorphic explanation for why animals show sympathy, regardless of whether they actually feel sympathy. This point is crucial because, after all, humans cannot actually observe how an animal feels; we can only observe how it behaves. It is then up to the observer to draw some logical conclusions about why animals behave in the ways they do.

The mutual altruism theory, however, can also be disputed. In many cases, animals have helped others even when the receiver of the help would probably never be in a position to return the favor. For example, there are many accounts of dolphins helping drowning or otherwise endangered swimmers. Phil Mercer, on the BBC Web site, reported that dolphins stopped a shark from attacking swimmers off the coast of New Zealand. The animals surrounded the swimmers for about forty minutes while the great white shark circled. When the swimmers reached the shore, they remarked that they were sure that the dolphins acted deliberately to save them. Marathon swimmer Matril Strel also believes that he was deliberately helped by pink dolphins during his 2007 swim of the

Source: Citation of a Web page includes only author's name and site's sponsor; no page numbers available

entire Amazon River, even believing that he heard them communicating (Butler).

Not only do animals show sympathy, but they are also clearly able to express joy. For example, Takahisa Matsusaka, a primatologist, has found that when chimpanzees demonstrate "panting" while tickling or chasing each other, the chance of such play becoming aggressive is reduced (222). Dog laughter has been observed to soothe other dogs, even when the other dogs are not playing (Bekoff, *Emotional Lives* 56). According to Jaak Panksepp, an author at J. P. Scott Center for Neuroscience, Mind, and Behavior, "Research on rough-housing play in mammals, both sapient and otherwise, clearly indicates that the sources of play and laughter in the brain are both instinctual and subcortical," meaning that many animals, and not just humans, are evolutionarily hardwired to laugh. Panksepp reports that rats who are tickled emit high-frequency chirps, and the process socially bonds them so that they want to spend time with other rats who chirp (62).

The actions of animals who are not able to laugh uproariously also indicate that they feel joy. John Webster, a professor of animal husbandry at the University of Bristol, said the following about joy:

> Sentient animals have the capacity to experience pleasure and are motivated to seek it. . . . You only have to watch how cows and lambs both seek and enjoy pleasure when they lie with their heads raised to the sun on a perfect English summer's day. (qtd. in Bekoff, *Emotional Lives* 55)

In short, animals exhibit a large number of behaviors that indicate that they possess not only the capacity to feel but the capacity to express their feelings in some overt way, sometimes through vocalizations, but most often through body language. If these are not proof enough that animals have emotions, people need look no further than their own beloved cat or dog. Pets are so frequently the cause of joy, humor, love, sympathy, empathy, and even grief that it is difficult to imagine that animals could elicit such emotions in humans without actually having these emotions themselves. The question, then, is not, *do* animals have emotions? but *which* emotions do animals have and *to what degree* do they feel them?

Destino 7

Works Cited

Ackerman, Diane. "The Lonely Polar Bear." *The New York Times*, 2 July 2011,
    www.nytimes.com/2011/07/03/opinion/sunday/03gus.html?_r=0.

Angier, Natalie. "The Owl Comes into Its Own." *The New York Times*, 25
    Feb. 2013, www.nytimes.com/2013/02/26/science/long-cloaked-in
    -mystery-owls-start-coming-into-full-view.html?.

"Animal Odd Couples." *Nature*, PBS, 7 Nov. 2012, www.pbs.org/wnet/
    nature/animal-odd-couples-full-episode/8009/.

Bekoff, Marc. "Animal Emotions: Exploring Passionate Natures." *Bioscience*,
    vol. 50, no. 10, Oct. 2000, pp. 861–70, bioscience.oxfordjournals.org/
    content/50/10/861.full.

---. *The Emotional Lives of Animals*. New World Library, 2007.

Butler, Rhett A. "Marathon Swimmer: An Interview with the First Man to
    Swim the Length of the Amazon." *Mongabay.com*, 23 Jan. 2011, news
    .mongabay.com/2011/01/marathon-swimmer-an-interview-with-the-first
    -man-to-swim-the-length-of-the-amazon/.

de Waal, Frans. *Primates and Philosophers*. Princeton UP, 2006.

Goodall, Jane. *Through a Window: My Thirty Years with the Chimpanzees
    of Gombe*. Houghton Mifflin, 1990.

Hemelrijk, Charlotte K. "Support for Being Groomed in Long-Tailed
    Macaques, *Macaca Fasciularis*." *Animal Behaviour*, vol. 48, no. 2, Aug.
    1994, pp. 479–81.

Masson, Jeffrey Moussaieff, and Susan McCarthy. *When Elephants Weep:
    The Emotional Lives of Animals*. Dell Publishing, 1995.

Matsusaka, Takahisa. "When Does Play Panting Occur during Social Play in
    Wild Chimpanzees?" *Primates*, vol. 45, no. 4, Oct. 2004, pp. 221–29.
    SpringerLink, doi:10.1007/s10329-004-0090-z.

Mercer, Phil. "Dolphins Prevent NZ Shark Attack." *BBC News*, 23 Nov. 2004,
    news.bbc.co.uk/2/hi/asia-pacific/4034383.stm.

Panksepp, Jaak. "Beyond a Joke: From Animal Laughter to Human Joy?"
    Science, vol. 308, no. 5718, 1 Apr. 2005, pp. 62–63. *JSTOR*, doi:10.1126/
    science.1112066.

Works Cited: List appears on a new page; heading is centered; entries are double spaced

Works Cited: Entries alphabetized by author's last name

Works Cited: First line of each entry is flush left with margin; subsequent lines indented half an inch

Destino 8

Wilford, John Noble. "Almost Human, and Sometimes Smarter." *The New York Times*, 17 Apr. 2007, www.nytimes.com/2007/04/17/science/17chimp.html?_r=0.

Document Your Sources: APA Style

The system described in this section is recommended by the American Psychological Association (APA) and is described in detail in *The Publication Manual of the American Psychological Association*, Seventh Edition (available from most libraries). APA style uses in-text citations within the text of a research project and a list of references at the end to document the sources used. If you are unsure whether to use APA style, check with your instructor. The student paper that appears at the end of this section ("Schizophrenia: Definition and Treatment," pp. 658–64) uses APA style.

Use APA Style for In-Text Citations

Your paper must include in-text citations for all material you summarize, paraphrase, or quote from sources. There are two basic ways to write an in-text citation:

1. **Use a signal phrase (attribution) and publication date (in parentheses).** Mention the author's name in a phrase or sentence introducing the material, include the year of publication in parentheses immediately following the author's name, and a page number or other locator, such as a heading, paragraph number (even if you have to count the paragraphs yourself), or figure, table, or slide number.
2. **Use a parenthetical citation.** In parentheses, include the author's last name, the year of publication, and a page number or other locator (separated by commas).

APA style requires only that you include a page number or other locator for quotations, but it recommends using a locator for paraphrases and summaries as well, so make sure you ask your instructor before omitting them. Signal phrases allow you to put your sources in context, so use a signal phrase for most citations. APA style generally requires that you use the past tense (*showed*) or present perfect tense (*has shown*) for signal verbs. Only use the present tense to discuss results or widely accepted information. For either type of citation, follow these rules:

- Place the sentence period after the closing parenthesis. When a quotation ends the sentence, insert the closing quotation mark before the opening parenthesis. Block quotations are an exception to these rules; see "Punctuating Quotations" (pp. 617–18).

- For direct quotations, include the page number or other locator after the year, separating it from the year with a comma. Use the abbreviation "p." or "pp." followed by a space and the page number. Use another word or abbreviation (such as "para." for "paragraph") depending on the locator type you used.

Signal Phrase

Avery and Ehrlich (2008) said "nasal sounds are made with air passing through the nose" (p. 21).

Parenthetical Citation

Snorts, snores, and other such sounds are created "with air passing through the nose" (Avery & Ehrlich, 2008, p. 21).

The following section provides guidelines for formatting APA-style in-text citations.

Directory of APA In-Text Citation Models

1. One author

Zhang (2019) showed that "when academics are strongly motivated to teach and are satisfied with and take pride in their teaching," their feeling of affiliation with the schools at which they teach increases (p. 1325).

(Zhang, 2019, p. 1325).

2. Two authors.

Include both authors' last names and the year in a signal phrase or parenthetical citation. In parenthetical citations, replace the word *and* with an ampersand (&).

Bloomberg and Pope (2017) have argued that with global warming we are facing a "*kairos*: a supreme moment at which one simply must act, however implausible or inconvenient" (p. 12).

Some have argued that we are facing a watershed moment, or "*kairos*," in the fight against global warming (Bloomberg & Pope, 2017, p. 12).

3. **Three or more authors.** For works with three or more authors, list just the first author plus "et al." in each in-text citation.

> Similarly, as Belenky et al. (1986) showed, examining the lives of women expands our understanding of human development.

> Examining the lives of women expands our understanding of human development (Belenky et al., 1986).

4. **Two or more works by the same author(s).** Cite the works chronologically, in order of publication.

> Gaerlan (2001, 2011) believed that . . .

> . . . (Gaerlan, 2001, 2011).

5. **Two or more works by the same author in the same year.** Add the lowercase letter "a" after the publication year for the first source as it appears alphabetically by title in your reference list. Add the letter "b" to the publication year for the source that appears next, and so forth. Include the years with the corresponding lowercase letters in your in-text citations. (See "Two or more works by the same author in the same year," p. 653, for the corresponding reference-list entries.)

> Soot-free flames can be produced by stripping the air of nitrogen and then adding that nitrogen to the fuel (Conover, 2019b).

6. **Authors with the same last name.** Use each author's first initial(s) with the last name.

> K. Yi (2019) has demonstrated . . .

> D. Yi (2017) has shown that . . .

7. **No author named.** Use the first few words of the title and the year in the signal phrase or parenthetical citation. Italicize a book title; put the title of a journal article in quotation marks. Unlike the entry in the list of references, use standard capitalization in the in-text citation. (See "Work with no author named," p. 653.)

> As noted in "Gluten Free Recipes" (2009), . . .

> . . . ("Gluten Free Recipes," 2009).

8. **Two or more sources in the same citation.** When citing two or more sources in parentheses, put a semicolon between them and list them in alphabetical order.

> . . . (Hoffman, 2011; Murphy, 2009).

9. **Specific part of a work.** When quoting, paraphrasing, or summarizing a passage, include the page number on which the passage appears. If the work does not have page numbers, use paragraph numbers, if provided (with the abbreviation "para."), or the heading of the section in which the material appears.

> Pinker (2007) offered an explanation for why swearing occurs across cultures: Obscenities "may tap into deep and ancient parts of the emotional brain" (p. 331).

> If obscenities "tap into deep and ancient parts of the emotional brain" (Pinker, 2007, p. 331), then it makes sense that swearing occurs across cultures.

10. **Chapter in an edited book or work in an anthology.** An *anthology* is a collection of writings by different authors. In the in-text citation, name the author who wrote the work (*not* the editor of the anthology) and give the year the anthology was published. (See "Chapter in an edited book or work in an anthology," p. 654, for the corresponding entry in the list of references.)

> As Pedelty (2010) noted . . .

> . . . (Pedelty, 2010).

11. **Multivolume work.** When you cite one volume of a multivolume work, include the year of publication for that volume.

> Terman (2008) indicated . . .

> . . . (Terman, 2008).

When you cite two or more volumes of a multivolume work, give inclusive years for the volumes.

> Terman (2008–2011) indicated . . .

12. **Indirect sources.** When you quote a source indirectly (rather than from the original source), include the words *as cited in* along with the information for the source in which you found the quote.

> According to Ephron, . . . (as cited in Thomas, 2009, p. 33).

13. **Personal interviews, letters, emails, and conversations.** Give the last name and initial of the interview subject or correspondent, the type of communication, and the exact date. Do not include these sources in the list of references.

> . . . (J. Lopez, personal communication, October 30, 2011).

14. **Internet sources.** For direct quotations, give the author, year, and page or paragraph number (or other locator) in the signal phrase or parenthetical citation.

> Stevens (2011, para. 5) has maintained . . .

> . . . (Stevens, 2011, para. 5).

Use APA Style for the List of References

Follow these general guidelines for preparing the list of references.

1. List only the sources you cite in your paper. If you consulted a source but did not cite it in your paper, do not include it in the list of references.
2. Put the list on a separate page at the end of your paper. The heading *References*, in boldface type, should be centered an inch below the top of the page.
3. Alphabetize the list by the entry's first important word (author's last name or, if no author is named, first key word of the title). Give the author's last name, followed by a comma and his or her initial or initials (not the full first name) and a space between initials: *Myers, D. G.* For works with multiple authors, list up to twenty authors' names in inverted order with an ampersand (&) before the last author's name.

4. Put the publication date in parentheses after the author's name.
5. For titles of books and articles capitalize the first word, the first word following a colon, and any proper nouns (names). For titles of periodicals, capitalize all important words.
6. Include the word *A*, *An*, or *The* at the beginning of titles.
7. Italicize titles of books and names of journals, newspapers, and magazines. Do not italicize, underline, or use quotation marks with article titles.
8. For magazine and journal articles, italicize the volume number.
9. Indent the second and all subsequent lines half an inch—hanging indent style.
10. Double-space the entire list.

A variety of models for different types of sources follow. However, you may need to combine information from one or more models to create a citation for a work you are using. For instance, to cite a reading from this textbook, you would need to treat it as a work in an anthology (p. 654) in an edition other than the first (p. 654):

Goleman, D. (2017). His marriage and hers: Childhood roots. In K. T. McWhorter, *Successful college writing* (8th ed.), pp. 403–08. Bedford/St. Martin's.

Directory of APA Reference Models

Authors

1 One author 653

2 More than one author 653

3 Two or more works by the same author(s) 653

4 Two or more works by the same author in the same year 653

5 Work with no author named 653

6 Agency or corporation as author 653

Books and Other Long Works

7 Edited book or anthology 654

8 Chapter in an edited book or work in an anthology 654

9 Translated book 654

10 Edition other than the first 654

11 Article from an encyclopedia or dictionary 654

12 Multivolume work 655

13 One volume in a multivolume work 655

14 Government publication 655

Articles in Periodicals

15 Article in a scholarly journal 656

16 Article in a magazine (print, online) 656

17 Article in a newspaper (print, online) 657

18 Editorial or letter to the editor 657

19 Book or film review 657

Other Sources

20 Document posted on a Web site 657

21 Film, video, or DVD 658

22 Television program 658

23 Mobile application software (app) 658

Authors

1. **One author.** Put the author's last name first, followed by her or his initials. If the author has more than one initial, include a space in between.

   Myers, W. D.

2. **More than one author.** Use inverted order (last name, initial) for all authors' names. Separate names with commas and use an ampersand (&) before the last author's name.

   Myers, W. D., & Myers, C.

   Wiegand, I., Seidel, C., & Wolfe, J.

   For citations with up to twenty authors, include all the authors listed. For citations with twenty-one or more authors, list the first nineteen (in the order they appear on the title page), an ellipsis (. . .), and then the last author's name.

3. **Two or more works by the same author(s).** Begin each entry with the author's name. Arrange the entries in chronological order of publication.

   Pollan, M. (2006).

   Pollan, M. (2008).

4. **Two or more works by the same author in the same year.** Arrange the works alphabetically by title; then assign a lowercase letter (*a, b, c*) to the year of publication for each source. (See "Chapter in an edited book or work in an anthology," p. 651, for the corresponding in-text citation.)

   Folger, T. (2014a). Beyond the Higgs Boson. . . .

   Folger, T. (2014b). Melting away. . . .

5. **Work with no author named.** Start the entry with the title; alphabetize it by the first important word (ignore *A, An,* or *The*).

   Go ask Alice. (1971). Avon Books.

6. **Agency or corporation as author.** List the agency as the author. If the publisher is the same as the author, omit the publisher.

   Bill and Melinda Gates Foundation. (2013). *Feedback for better teaching: Nine principles for using measures of effective teaching.*

Books. Most of the information you will need to cite a book appears on the book's title page and copyright page. (See Figure 23.3.) In printed books, these two pages appear toward the beginning of the text; in e-books, they may appear elsewhere.

CITING A BOOK

▶ *Author.* Begin with the author's surname and initial(s): *Myers, D. G.*

▶ *Year.* Include the year of publication, in parentheses. Use the most recent copyright year if more than one appears on the copyright page: *(2016).*

▶ *Title.* Italicize the title of the book. Capitalize only the first word of the title and subtitle (if any) and any proper nouns (*Juan*) or adjectives (*French*).

▶ *Publisher.* Include the full name of the publisher, followed by a period. Set the publisher's name as it appears on the copyright page. For example, if the publisher's name is spelled in all caps on the copyright page, include it in all caps in the list of references. Omit only business terms like *Ltd.* or *Inc.*

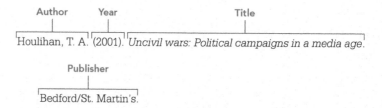

Books and Other Long Works

7. **Edited book or anthology.** List the editor's or editors' names, followed by the abbreviation *Ed.* or *Eds.* in parentheses and a period.

> Bradley, B., Feldman, F., & Johansson, J. (Eds.). (2013). *The Oxford handbook of the philosophy of death.* Oxford University Press.

8. **Chapter in an edited book or work in an anthology.** List the author of the work first and then the date the anthology was published. The title of the work follows. Then name the editor of the anthology (not in inverted order), give the title of the anthology (italicized), and insert the inclusive page numbers in parentheses for the work (preceded by *pp.*). The publication information follows in normal order.

> Pettigrew, D. (2018). The suppression of cultural memory and identity in Bosnia and Herzegovina. In J. Lindert & A. T. Marsoobian (Eds.), *Multidisciplinary perspectives on genocide and memory* (pp. 187–198). Springer.

9. **Translated book.** After the title, include the initial(s) and last name of the translator followed by a comma and *Trans.*

> Calasso, R. (2019). *The unnamable present* (R. Dixon, Trans.). Farrar, Straus and Giroux. (Original work published 2017)

10. **Edition other than the first**

> Dessler, A. E., & Parson, E. A. (2019). *The science and politics of global climate change: A guide to the debate* (3rd ed.). Cambridge University Press.

11. **Article from an encyclopedia or dictionary**

> Brue, A. W., & Wilmshurst, L. (2018). Adaptive behavior assessments. In B. B. Frey (Ed.), *The SAGE encyclopedia of educational research, measurement, and evaluation* (pp. 40–44). SAGE Publications. https://doi.org/10.4135/9781506326139.n21

Merriam-Webster. (n.d.). Adscititious. In *Merriam-Webster.com dictionary*. Retrieved

September 5, 2019, from https://www.merriam-webster.com/dictionary/

adscititious

12. **Multivolume work.** Give the volume numbers in parentheses after the title. If all volumes were not published in the same year, the publication date should include the range of years.

Zeigler-Hill, V., & Shackelford, T. K. (Eds.). (2018). *The SAGE handbook of personality*

and individual differences (Vols. I–III). SAGE Publications.

13. **One volume in a multivolume work.** Include the publication date for the individual volume following the editor's name. The number and title of the volume follow the title of the multivolume work.

Zeigler-Hill, V., & Shackelford, T. K. (Eds.). (2018). *The SAGE handbook of*

personality and individual differences: Vol. II. Origins of personality and

individual differences. SAGE Publications.

14. **Government publication.** If no author is given, list the most specific agency as the author and the broader organization as the publisher. Include any document or publication number if available.

National Park Service. (2019, April 11). *Travel where women made history: Ordinary*

and extraordinary places of American women. U.S. Department of the Interior.

https://www.nps.gov/subjects/travelwomenshistory/index.htm

Berchick, E. R., Barnett, J. C., & Upton, R. D. (2019, September 10). *Health*

insurance coverage in the United States: 2018 (Report No. P60-267). U.S.

Census Bureau. https://www.census.gov/library/publications/2019/demo/

p60-267.html

Articles in Periodicals. A periodical is a publication that appears at regular intervals: Newspapers generally appear daily, magazines weekly or monthly, and scholarly journals quarterly. In periodicals, the information you will need to cite may appear on the first page of the article (see Figure 23.4), or you may need to look at a combination of places (the first page of the article, the cover of the periodical, the database you used, the Web page or Web site on which the article appears, and so on).

CITING AN ARTICLE IN A PERIODICAL

▶ *Author.* Follow the basic format for listing authors' names. If no author is listed, begin with the article title and alphabetize the entry by its title (ignoring the words *A, An,* or *The*).

▶ *Date.* For articles in journals, the year of publication appears in parentheses following the author's name. For articles in newspapers and magazines, the month and day, if relevant, follow the year.

▶ *Article title.* Do not enclose article titles in quotation marks. Capitalize only the first word of the article title, along with any proper nouns or proper adjectives (*American*) and the first word following a colon.

▶ *Periodical title.* Italicize the name of the periodical. Use standard capitalization.

▶ *Volume/issue number.* For scholarly journals and magazines, give the volume number in italics; include the issue number in parentheses, not in italics, for all periodicals that offer them.

▶ *Pages.* Include the page numbers, but do *not* use *p.* or *pp.*

▶ *DOI/URL.* If a DOI (digital object identifier) is available, include it at the end of the citation with no period at the end. If there is no DOI but you can supply a direct-link URL, do so; if not, omit the URL. Include DOIs as links, using the format "https://doi.org/" and adding the DOI number for the specific work. Include a retrieval statement ("retrieved [month, day, year] from") before URLs only when the online source is designed to be regularly updated. If a DOI or URL is lengthy, you can include a shortened form by using a site like shortdoi.org or bitly.com. If your word processor inserts line breaks automatically or moves a DOI or URL to its own line, you can accept that formatting.

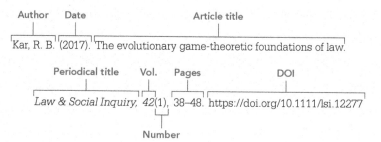

15. **Article in a scholarly journal.** Provide issue numbers for all journals that offer them. If the journal article has been assigned a DOI (digital object identifier), include it. If there is no DOI, you can provide a direct-link URL, but do not include URLs that lead to databases readers can't access.

> Ganegoda, D. B., & Bordia, P. (2019). I can be happy for you, but not all the time: A contingency model of envy and positive empathy in the workplace. *Journal of Applied Psychology, 104*(6), 776–795. https://doi.org/10.1037/apl0000377

16. **Article in a magazine.** Include the day, month, and year or month and year of the publication as applicable. If you accessed the magazine online, provide the DOI or a direct-link URL.

Print

> Koch, C. (2019, October). Is death reversible? *Scientific American, 321*(4), 34–37.

Online

> Talbot, M. (2020, May 18). The rogue experimenters. *The New Yorker*. https://www.
>
> newyorker.com/magazine/2020/05/25/the-rogue-experimenters

17. **Article in a newspaper.** Include the year, month, and day in parentheses following the author's name. If you accessed the article from a database, omit the URL; if you accessed it through a Web site, include it.

Print

> Finucane, M. (2019, September 25). Americans still eating too many low-quality
>
> carbs. *The Boston Globe*, B2.

Online

> Daly, J. (2019, August 2). Duquesne's med school plan part of national trend to train
>
> more doctors. *Pittsburgh Post-Gazette*. https://www.post-gazette.com/news/
>
> health/2019/08/02/Duquesne-med-school-national-trend-doctors-osteopathic-
>
> medicine-pittsburgh/stories/201908010181

If the direct-link URL is lengthy, you can include a shortened form.

> Daly, J. (2019, August 2). Duquesne's med school plan part of national trend to train
>
> more doctors. *Pittsburgh Post-Gazette*. https://bit.ly/2Vzrm2l

18. **Editorial or letter to the editor.** Cite the editorial or letter beginning with the author's name (if available). If the author's name is not available, begin with the title. Include *Editorial* or *Letter to the editor* in brackets following the title (if any).

> Gavin Newsom wants to stop rent gouging. Will lawmakers finally stand up for
>
> tenants? [Editorial]. (2019, September 4). *Los Angeles Times*. https://lat.
>
> ms/2lBlRm1

> Doran, K. (2019, October 11). When the homeless look like grandma or grandpa
>
> [Letter to the editor]. *The New York Times*. https://nyti.ms/33foD0K

19. **Book or film review.** List the reviewer's name, the date, and the title of the review (if any). In brackets, give a description of the work reviewed, including the medium (*book* or *motion picture*), title, and the author for a book or the director for a film.

> Hall, W. (2019). [Review of the book *How to change your mind: The new science of*
>
> *psychedelics*, by M. Pollan]. *Addiction, 114*(10), 1892–1893. https://doi.
>
> org/10.1111/add.14702

Other Sources

20. **Document posted on a Web site.** Many documents published on Web sites fall into other categories and can be cited using models in other sections. For articles in an online newspaper, for example, follow item 17, "Article in a newspaper"

(p. 657), and for an entry in an online dictionary, follow item 11, "Article from an encyclopedia or dictionary" (pp. 654–55). Use one of the models below only when your source does not fit in any other category. In these items, the Web site name follows the title unless the author and Web site name are the same. If you access the source online, include a direct-link URL. When no publication date is available, use "n.d." ("no date"). Include a retrieval statement ("retrieved [month, day, year] from") before URLs only when the online source is designed to be regularly updated.

> Albright, A. (2019, July 25). *The global education challenge: Scaling up to tackle the learning crisis*. The Brookings Institution. https://www.brookings.edu/wp-content/uploads/2019/07/Brookings_Blum_2019_education.pdf
>
> National Institute of Mental Health. (2016, March). *Seasonal affective disorder*. National Institutes of Health. https://www.nimh.nih.gov/health/topics/seasonal-affective-disorder/index.shtml
>
> BBC News. (2019, October 31). *Goats help save Ronald Reagan Presidential Library*. https://bbc.com/news/world-us-canada-50248549

21. Film, video, or DVD

> Peele, J. (Director). (2017). *Get out* [Film]. Universal Pictures.

22. Television program

> Waller-Bridge, P. (Writer), & Bradbeer, H. (Director). (2019, March 18). The provocative request (Season 2, Episode 3) [TV series episode]. In P. Waller-Bridge, H. Williams, & J. Williams (Executive Producers), *Fleabag*. Two Brothers Pictures; BBC.

23. Mobile application software (app)

> Google LLC. (2019). *Google earth* (Version 9.3.3) [Mobile app]. App Store. https://apps.apple.com/us/app/google-earth/id293622097

RESEARCH PROJECT IN PROGRESS 11

For the final paper you prepared in Research Project in Progress 10, prepare a list of references in APA style.

STUDENTS WRITE

The following research project was written by Sonia Gomez for her introductory psychology course. She used APA style for formatting her paper and documenting her sources. Notice her use of in-text citations and paraphrases and summaries of sources to provide evidence in support of her thesis.

1

Schizophrenia: Definition and Treatment

Sonia Gomez

Department of Psychology, Santa Teresa College

Psychology 101: Introduction to Psychology

Professor McCombs

January 22, 2020

Title Page: Page number at top right

Identification: Double-space and include on title page: title of the paper (centered, bold), writer's name, department and school, course number and name, instructor's name, and assignment due date.

Information on title page should be centered; begin 3–4 double spaces from top margin (not shown here).

2

Abstract

Schizophrenia is a mental/brain disorder that affects about 1% of the population. The five types of schizophrenia include paranoid, disorganized, catatonic, undifferentiated, and residual. There are three categories of symptoms—positive, disorganized or cognitive, and negative. The causes of schizophrenia are not well known, but there is likely a genetic component and an environmental component. The structure of the brain of schizophrenics is also unusual. Treatments include drug therapy with typical and atypical anti-psychotics and psychosocial and cognitive-behavioral therapies.

Abstract: Include an abstract (or brief summary) only if requested by instructor; heading centered, bold

Formatting: Double-space essay; leave one-inch margins on all sides

3

Title: Repeat full title just before text of paper begins; title centered, bold

Schizophrenia: Definition and Treatment

The disorder schizophrenia comes with an ugly cultural stigma. There is a common belief that all schizophrenics are violent. In fact, they are more a danger to themselves than to others because they often commit suicide. Many of the movies, books, and TV shows in our culture do not help to diminish this stigma. The movie *A Beautiful Mind*, for example, featured a paranoid schizophrenic who came close to harming his family and others around him because of his hallucinations and delusions. He believed that the government was out to get him (Grazer & Howard, 2001). Many people are afraid of schizophrenics and believe their permanent home should be in a mental hospital or psychiatric ward. This paper helps to dispel misperceptions of the disorder by providing facts about and treatments of the disorder.

Introduction: Presentation of the topic researched by Gomez

Sources: Authors named in **parenthetical citation**; ampersand (&), not the word *and*, between names

What Is Schizophrenia?

Schizophrenia is a mental/brain disorder that affects about 1% of the population or 2.2 million Americans (National Institutes of Mental Health, 2016). This disease can be very disruptive in people's lives. It causes problems with communication and maintaining jobs. It is a widely misunderstood disease; many people believe schizophrenics to be dangerous. There is no cure for schizophrenia, but it can often be successfully treated (National Institutes of Mental Health, 2016). Schizophrenia does not seem to favor a specific gender or ethnic group. The disease rarely occurs in children. Hallucinations and delusions usually begin between ages sixteen and thirty (National Alliance on Mental Illness, 2017).

Heading: First-level heading centered, bold

Sources: No individual author named, so **Web site sponsor** listed as author

Types of Schizophrenia

There are five types of schizophrenia—paranoid, disorganized, catatonic, undifferentiated, and residual. People with paranoid schizophrenia are illogically paranoid about the world around them. They often hold false beliefs about being persecuted. People with disorganized schizophrenia are confused and incoherent and jumble their speech. People with disorganized schizophrenia often show symptoms of schizophasia—creating their own words and using them in a word salad, a jumbling of coherent and noncoherent words.

Heading: Second-level heading at left margin, bold

4

People with catatonic schizophrenia are usually immobile and unresponsive to everything around them. Undifferentiated schizophrenia is diagnosed when the patient does not fit into the other three categories. Residual schizophrenia occurs when schizophrenic symptoms have decreased but still exist (WebMD, 2017).

Symptoms of Schizophrenia

The symptoms of schizophrenia are separated into three categories—positive, disorganized or cognitive, and negative. Positive symptoms include hallucinations and delusions (WebMD, 2017). Barch (2003) has described those with disorganized or cognitive symptoms as unable to think clearly. Disorganized or cognitive symptoms include difficulty communicating, use of nonsense words, inability to focus on one thought, slow movement, inability to make decisions, forgetfulness and losing of things, repetitive movements, inability to make sense of everyday events, and problems with memory. Negative symptoms are an absence of normal behavior (WebMD, 2017). They include a lack of emotion or inappropriate emotions, isolation, lack of energy and motivation, loss of interest or pleasure in life, problems functioning in everyday life (such as bad hygiene), rapid mood changes, and catatonia (remaining in the same position for a long time) (WebMD, 2017).

The diagnosis of schizophrenia is often difficult because it can be confused with a number of other mental disorders including bipolar disorder. The process of diagnosis begins with an interview by a psychiatrist. The patient is usually tested for other physical illnesses using various blood tests. If the symptoms last for at least six months and there is seemingly no other cause of the problem, the person is considered to have schizophrenia (National Alliance on Mental Illness, 2017).

Causes of Schizophrenia

No one is completely sure of the causes of schizophrenia. Most scientists believe that genetics are involved, and it seems that there is either a genetic mutation in DNA or a gene that can be activated by a number of situations. Scientists are close to determining the exact chromosome where the gene

Sources: Author named in text; date follows in parentheses

5

for schizophrenia might be located (Conklin & Iacono, 2002). The circumstances surrounding birth may have a great effect on whether the child's schizophrenic gene becomes activated or not. For example, if a fetus is exposed to viruses or malnourished before birth or if there are complications during birth, the gene may be activated. Conklin and Iacono (2002) reported a link between schizophrenia and complications during birth that result in lack of oxygen (hypoxia). Also, Bower (2008) observed that poor children or children who deal with highly stressful situations may be more likely to develop the disorder.

Besides all of these factors, the brains of people with schizophrenia seem to be different from other people's. People with schizophrenia have an imbalance of dopamine and glutamate in their brains. The ventricles at the center of the brain seem to be larger, and there appears to be a loss of brain tissue (Figure 1).

Figure 1.
Brain-tissue loss.

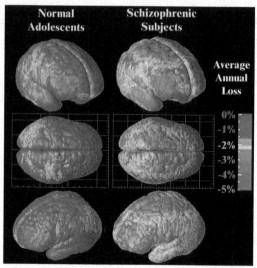

Note: Thompson et al. (2001). Mapping adolescent brain change reveals dynamic wave of accelerated gray matter loss in very early-onset schizophrenia. *Proc Natl Acad Sci USA 98*(20): 11650–11655. Copyright © (2001) National Academy of Science, USA.

Sources: Authors named in text, so *and,* not ampersand (&), used between names

Illustration: The figure is referred to in the text; the word *Figure* and a figure number and title appear above the figure.

6

Also, some areas of the brain seem to have more or less activity than normal brains do. Conklin and Iacono (2002) have shown that these abnormalities in the brain appear to be preexisting rather than caused by the disease. Schizophrenia tends to appear during puberty because of hormonal interactions occurring in the brain (WebMD, 2017).

Treatment

There is a wide variety of treatments for schizophrenia. Typical antipsychotic drugs, such as chlorpromazine and perphenazine, are an obvious choice, especially for people with hallucinations and delusions. They can help to clear up thinking problems. However, many of these drugs cause unpleasant side effects such as nausea and anxiety. Because of this, schizophrenics may stop taking or refuse to take their medication. Many of these antipsychotic drugs have not changed since the 1950s. In the 1990s, a new set of drugs—atypical antipsychotics—was developed. Clozapine was one of these drugs, and it was deemed very effective. However, it can cause agranulocytosis, a loss of white blood cells. Between the constant testing for agranulocytosis and the cost of clozapine, many with schizophrenia disliked the drug (National Institutes of Mental Health, 2017).

Other treatments do not rely on medication. Psychosocial and cognitive-behavioral therapies are often used. People with schizophrenia can learn illness-management skills. They can go to rehabilitation, and their families can be educated about how to care for them. Self-help groups are also common. However, if the disease becomes unmanageable, the person with schizophrenia may end up in the hospital. Electroconvulsive therapy, in which seizures are induced, is one of the more extreme treatments for schizophrenia. It is often used to treat catatonia. If the schizophrenia is still unmanageable, a lobotomy may be performed. A lobotomy is surgery in which the connections to and from the prefrontal cortex are cut. Lobotomies cause severe personality changes; they were used much more often in the 1950s than they are today (National Alliance on Mental Illness, 2017).

People with schizophrenia are very susceptible to substance abuse. Many schizophrenics have severe drinking problems, and tobacco addiction is also

7

common. It is harder for them than most people to break this addiction. If they combine substance abuse treatment with the other treatments for their disease, they get much more beneficial results (WebMD, 2017).

Conclusion

As scientists begin to understand schizophrenia, better treatments are becoming available. There is starting to be a better outlook for those with schizophrenia, and because of this, the public might develop a more sympathetic view of those with the disorder.

Conclusion: Conclusion is indicated by heading (bold and centered). Gomez references her introduction in her conclusion.

8

References

References: Heading centered, bold; list appears on a new page.

DOI: The DOI is provided when available for printed and online works.

Formatting: Double-spaced throughout

Entries: Alphabetize entries by first important word (author's last name or first key word of title if no author named). Only the first word and proper nouns/adjectives are capitalized in titles of shorter works (such as articles in a periodical, or Web pages on a Web site). First, last, and all key words are capitalized in titles of longer, stand-alone works (such as books, periodicals, films, Web sites).

URLs: The direct-link URL is provided for Web sites and Web pages.

Barch, D. (2003). Cognition in schizophrenia: Does working memory work? *Current Directions in Psychological Science, 12*(4), 146–150. https://doi.org/10.1111/1467-8721.01251

Bower, B. (2008). Rare mutations tied to schizophrenia. *Science News, 173*(14), 222.

Conklin, H., & Iacono, W. (2002). Schizophrenia: A neurodevelopmental perspective. *Current Directions in Psychological Science, 11*(1), 33–37.

Grazer, B. (Producer), & Howard, R. (Director). (2001). *A beautiful mind* [Film]. Universal Pictures.

National Alliance on Mental Illness. (2017). Schizophrenia. In *Mental health conditions.* https://www.nami.org/Learn-More/Mental-Health-Conditions/Schizophrenia

National Institutes of Mental Health. (2016, February). Schizophrenia. In *Health topics.* http://www.nimh.nih.gov/health/topics/schizophrenia/index.shtml

Thompson, P. M., Vidal, C., Giedd, J. N., Gochman, P., Blumenthal, J., Nicolson, R., Toga, A. W., & Rapoport, J. L. (2001). Mapping adolescent brain change reveals dynamic wave of accelerated gray matter loss in very early-onset schizophrenia. *Proceedings of the National Academy of Science 98*(20): 11650–11655.

WebMD. (2017). Schizophrenia guide. In *Mental health center.* http://www.webmd.com/schizophrenia/guide/default.htm

PART SIX

Academic and Business Applications

24

Reading and Writing about Literature

WATFORD/Mirrorpix/Getty Images

In this chapter you will learn to

- **develop a general approach to reading literature**
- **understand the language of literature**
- **analyze short stories**
- **analyze poetry**
- **write a literary analysis**

Writing Quick Start

ANALYZE Suppose your American literature instructor asks you to read carefully "The Bean Eaters," a poem by Gwendolyn Brooks (1917–2000). Brooks was a major American writer of poetry as well as fiction and nonfiction prose. She was the first African American woman to win a Pulitzer Prize for poetry (for *Annie Allen*, 1949). "The Bean Eaters" was originally published in 1960, in a collection of poems of the same title.

WRITE After reading "The Bean Eaters," how would you describe the life of the elderly couple shown in the photo on this page? (Note that the couple in the photo is not the couple described in the poem.) Using information about the life of the elderly couple presented in "The Bean Eaters," as well as your own experience with elderly people, write a paragraph describing what you think the couple's relationship might be like. How does Brooks's description of one elderly couple help you understand other elderly people like the man and woman in the photo?

CONNECT This writing task requires you to analyze and respond to a piece of literature. In this chapter you will learn skills to enable you to evaluate and write in response to literature.

The first half of this chapter offers a general approach to reading and understanding literature. The second half focuses on the characteristics of literary analysis and provides a Guided Writing Assignment. Although literature can take many forms—including poetry, short stories, biography, autobiography, drama, essays, and novels—this chapter concentrates on two literary genres: short stories and poetry.

The Bean Eaters

Gwendolyn Brooks

> They eat beans mostly, this old yellow pair.
> Dinner is a casual affair.
> Plain chipware on a plain and creaking wood,
> Tin flatware.
> Two who are Mostly Good.   5
> Two who have lived their day,
> But keep on putting on their clothes
> And putting things away.
> And remembering . . .
> Remembering, with twinklings and twinges,   10
> As they lean over the beans in their rented back room that
> is full of beads and receipts and dolls and cloths,
> tobacco crumbs, vases and fringes.

Both "The Bean Eaters" and the paragraph you wrote in the Writing Quick Start paint a picture of an elderly couple. Through carefully selected details, the poem describes the couple's daily activities, memories of the past, and current economic situation ("They eat beans mostly," "Plain chipware," and "rented back room" reveal that the couple is poor). The poem also suggests that routine is important to the couple ("But keep on putting on their clothes / And putting things away") and that their memories of the past are both good ("twinklings") and bad ("twinges").

"The Bean Eaters" suggests an answer to a question many students ask: "Why should I read or write about literature?" This poem, like all other literature, is about the experiences people share. Literature often deals with large issues: What is worthwhile? What is moral? What is beautiful? When you read and write about literature, you gain insights into many aspects of human experience and thereby enrich your own life.

LITERATURE IN COLLEGE AND THE WORKPLACE

- Your *art history professor* asks you to read Ernest Hemingway's *For Whom the Bell Tolls* (a novel set during the Spanish Civil War) and to write a paper discussing its meaning in conjunction with Picasso's *Guernica*, a painting that vividly portrays a scene from that war.

- In a *film class*, you watch *Romeo and Juliet*, directed by Franco Zeffirelli. Your instructor asks you to read excerpts from Shakespeare's *Romeo and Juliet* and write a paper evaluating how successfully the film portrays Juliet.

- You work at a local public library. Your supervisor has asked you to read several children's books that she is considering featuring during story hour and to write an evaluation of each.

A General Approach to Reading Literature

Textbooks focus primarily on presenting factual information, but works of literature are concerned with interpreting ideas, experiences, and events. Literature uses facts, description, and details to convey larger meanings.

The following general guidelines will help you read literary works effectively:

For more on previewing, see Chapter 2.

1. **Preview the work before reading it.** Be ready to respond to the work; don't make up your mind about it before you study the work in earnest. Read background information about the author and the work and study the title. Read the first few and last few paragraphs of a short story, and quickly skim the pages in between to notice the setting, the names of the characters, and the amount of dialogue. Read poems through once to get an initial impression.

2. **Read to establish the literal meaning first.** During the first reading of a work, establish its literal meaning. Who is doing what, when, and where? Identify the general subject, specific topic, and main character. What is happening? Describe the basic plot, action, or sequence of events. Establish where and during what time period the action occurs.

3. **Reread slowly and carefully to study the language.** Works of literature use language in unique and creative ways, requiring you to read them slowly. Interact with the work by jotting down your reactions as you read. Include hunches, insights, feelings, and questions. Highlight or underline key words, phrases, or actions that seem important or that you want to reconsider later. Mark interesting uses of language, such as striking phrases or descriptions, as well as sections that hint at the deeper meaning of the work. Note that literature often bends the rules of grammar and usage. Writers of literature may use sentence fragments, ungrammatical dialogue, or unusual punctuation to create a particular effect. When you encounter such instances, remember that most writers bend the rules for a purpose. Ask yourself what that purpose is.

4. **Reread once again to identify themes and patterns and piece together your interpretation.** Study your annotations to identify the conflict and discover how the ideas in the work link together to suggest a theme. **Themes** are large or universal topics that are important to nearly everyone. For example, the theme of a poem or short story might be that independence is a crucial component of true happiness or that growing up involves a loss of innocence. Think of the theme as the main point a poem or short story makes. To understand the work's theme, consider why the writer wrote the work and what message, view, or lesson about human experience the writer is trying to communicate. (For more about themes, see the section "Analyze Short Stories," pp. 670–79.)

5. **Write one or more paragraphs identifying the conflict and how it gets resolved, and stating what you think is the main theme.** Concluding your study of a work of literature with your own statement will help you move from comprehension of the work to your own interpretation and analysis of its significance.

Literary works are complex; you should not expect to understand a poem or short story immediately. You will need to reread parts or the entire work several times; its meanings will often come clear only gradually.

Understand the Language of Literature

Many writers, especially writers of literary works, use figures of speech to describe people, places, or objects and to communicate ideas. Figurative language is language used in a nonliteral way; it makes sense imaginatively or creatively but not literally. Three common figures of speech—*similes, metaphors,* and *personification*—make comparisons. Writers often use another literary device, *symbols,* to suggest larger themes. In addition, some writers use *irony* to convey the incongruities of life.

For more on figures of speech, see Chapter 9 and Chapter 12.

Similes, Metaphors, and Personification

Similes and metaphors are comparisons between two unlike things that have at least one common trait. A **simile** uses the word *like* or *as* to make a comparison, whereas a **metaphor** states or implies that one thing is another thing. If you say, "My father's mustache is a house painter's brush," your metaphor compares two dissimilar things—a mustache and a paintbrush—that share a common trait: straight bristles. If you say, "Martha's hair looks like she just walked through a wind tunnel," your simile creates a more vivid image of Martha's hair than if you simply stated, "Martha's hair is messy." Here are some additional examples from literary works:

Simile

My soul has grown deep like the rivers.

—Langston Hughes, "The Negro Speaks of Rivers"

Metaphor

Time is but the stream I go a-fishing in.

—Henry David Thoreau, *Walden*

When writers use **personification**, they attribute human characteristics to objects or ideas, as in this Emily Dickinson poem in which the poet likens death and immortality to passengers in a carriage: "Because I could not stop for Death— / He kindly stopped for me— / The carriage held but just Ourselves— / and Immortality." Like similes and metaphors, personification often creates a strong visual image.

Symbols

A **symbol** suggests more than its literal meaning. The sun breaking through the clouds, for instance, might suggest hope; the color white often suggests innocence and purity (or mourning in many Asian cultures). Because the writer does not directly state the abstract idea that a symbol represents, a symbol may suggest more than one meaning.

A white handkerchief, for example, might symbolize retreat in one context but good manners in another. Some literary critics believe the white whale in Herman Melville's novel *Moby-Dick* symbolizes evil, whereas others see the whale as representing the forces of nature.

To recognize symbols in a literary work, look for objects that are given a particular or unusual emphasis. The object may be mentioned often, may be suggested in the title, or may appear at the beginning or end of the work. Also be on the lookout for familiar symbols, such as flowers, doves, and colors.

Irony

Irony is literary language or a literary style in which actions, events, or words are contrary to what readers expect. For example, a prizefighter cowering at the sight of a spider is ironic because you expect prizefighters to be brave, a fire station burning down is ironic because you expect that a firehouse would be protected against fires, and a student saying that she is glad she failed an important exam is ironic because you expect the student to be upset that she failed the exam.

EXERCISE 24.1 **FIGURES OF SPEECH IN EVERYDAY LANGUAGE**

Working with another student, make a list of common metaphors and similes; examples of personification; and symbols you have heard or seen in everyday life, in films or television programs, or in works of literature.

Analyze Short Stories

A **short story** is a brief fictional narrative. Short stories are shorter than novels, and their scope is much more limited. For example, a short story may focus on one event in a person's life, whereas a novel may chronicle the events in the lives of an entire family. Like a novel, a short story makes a point about some aspect of the human experience.

When analyzing short stories, pay particular attention to five key elements:

1. Setting
2. Characters
3. Point of view
4. Plot
5. Theme

A worksheet later in the chapter will help you analyze short stories in terms of these five elements.

Read "The Story of an Hour" before continuing with this section of the chapter. The sections that follow will explain these five key elements and how each of them works in this short story.

The Story of an Hour

Kate Chopin

Kate Chopin (1850–1904), a nineteenth-century American writer, is best known for her novel *The Awakening* (1899), which outraged early literary critics with its portrayal of a woman in search of sexual and professional independence. As you read the following short story, originally published in *Vogue* magazine in 1894, look for, highlight, and annotate the five primary elements of short stories discussed in this chapter.

Knowing that Mrs. Mallard was afflicted with a heart trouble, great care was taken to break to her as gently as possible the news of her husband's death. [1]

It was her sister Josephine who told her, in broken sentences, veiled hints that revealed in half concealing. Her husband's friend Richards was there, too, near her. It was he who had been in the newspaper office when intelligence of the railroad disaster was received, with Brently Mallard's name leading the list of "killed." He had only taken the time to assure himself of its truth by a second telegram, and had hastened to forestall any less careful, less tender friend in bearing the sad message. [2]

She did not hear the story as many women have heard the same, with a paralyzed inability to accept its significance. She wept at once, with sudden, wild abandonment, in her sister's arms. When the storm of grief had spent itself she went away to her room alone. She would have no one follow her. [3]

There stood, facing the open window, a comfortable, roomy armchair. Into this she sank, pressed down by a physical exhaustion that haunted her body and seemed to reach into her soul. [4]

She could see in the open square before her house the tops of trees that were all aquiver with the new spring life. The delicious breath of rain was in the air. In the street below a peddler was crying his wares. The notes of a distant song which someone was singing reached her faintly, and countless sparrows were twittering in the eaves. [5]

There were patches of blue sky showing here and there through the clouds that had met and piled one above the other in the west facing her window. [6]

She sat with her head thrown back upon the cushion of the chair, quite motionless, except when a sob came up into her throat and shook her, as a child who has cried itself to sleep continues to sob in its dreams. [7]

She was young, with a fair, calm face, whose lines bespoke repression and even a certain strength. But now there was a dull stare in her eyes, whose gaze was fixed away off yonder on one of those patches of blue sky. It was not a glance of reflection, but rather indicated a suspension of intelligent thought. [8]

There was something coming to her and she was waiting for it, fearfully. What was it? She did not know, it was too subtle and elusive to name. But she felt it, [9] creeping out of the sky, reaching toward her through the sounds, the scents, the color that filled the air.

Now her bosom rose and fell tumultuously. She was beginning to recognize this thing that was approaching to possess her, and she was striving to beat it back with her will—as powerless as her two white slender hands would have been. 10

When she abandoned herself a little whispered word escaped her slightly parted lips. She said it over and over under her breath: "Free, free, free!" The vacant stare and the look of terror that had followed it went from her eyes. They stayed keen and bright. Her pulses beat fast, and the coursing blood warmed and relaxed every inch of her body. 11

She did not stop to ask if it were not a monstrous joy that held her. A clear and exalted perception enabled her to dismiss the suggestion as trivial. 12

She knew that she would weep again when she saw the kind, tender hands folded in death; the face that had never looked save with love upon her, fixed and gray and dead. But she saw beyond that bitter moment a long procession of years to come that would belong to her absolutely. And she opened and spread her arms out to them in welcome. 13

There would be no one to live for during those coming years; she would live for herself. There would be no powerful will bending her in that blind persistence with which men and women believe they have a right to impose a private will upon a fellow creature. A kind intention or a cruel intention made the act seem no less a crime as she looked upon it in that brief moment of illumination. 14

And yet she had loved him—sometimes. Often she had not. What did it matter! What could love, the unsolved mystery, count for in face of this possession of self-assertion which she suddenly recognized as the strongest impulse of her being. 15

"Free! Body and soul free!" she kept whispering. 16

Josephine was kneeling before the closed door with her lips to the keyhole, imploring for admission. "Louise, open the door! I beg; open the door—you will make yourself ill. What are you doing, Louise? For heaven's sake open the door." 17

"Go away. I am not making myself ill." No; she was drinking in a very elixir of life through that open window. 18

Her fancy was running riot along those days ahead of her. Spring days, and summer days, and all sorts of days that would be her own. She breathed a quick prayer that life might be long. It was only yesterday she had thought with a shudder that life might be long. 19

She arose at length and opened the door to her sister's importunities. There was a feverish triumph in her eyes, and she carried herself unwittingly like a goddess of Victory. She clasped her sister's waist, and together they descended the stairs. Richards stood waiting for them at the bottom. 20

Some one was opening the front door with a latchkey. It was Brently Mallard   21
who entered, a little travel-stained, composedly carrying his gripsack and
umbrella. He had been far from the scene of the accident, and did not even know
there had been one. He stood amazed at Josephine's piercing cry; at Richards' quick
motion to screen him from the view of his wife.

But Richards was too late.   22

When the doctors came they said she had died of heart disease—of joy that   23
kills.

Setting

The **setting** of a short story is the time, place, and circumstance in which the story
occurs. The setting provides the framework and atmosphere in which the plot develops
and characters interact. For example, Charles Dickens's "A Christmas Carol" is set in
nineteenth-century London in December. When analyzing setting, consider other
events that might have occurred in that place and time and how those events might
affect the story.

The setting of "The Story of an Hour" is the Mallards' home, and the events take
place during the course of one hour. The place and time are unclear, but the events
seem to be taking place in the past, before women commonly worked outside the home
or could divorce easily.

Characters

The **characters** are the actors in the story. They reveal themselves through dialogue,
actions, appearance, thoughts, and feelings. Drawing a character map (Figure 24.1) can
help you understand the relationships among characters. On a blank piece of paper,
write the main character's name inside a circle. Then add other characters' names,

FIGURE 24.1 Sample Character Map for "The Story of an Hour"

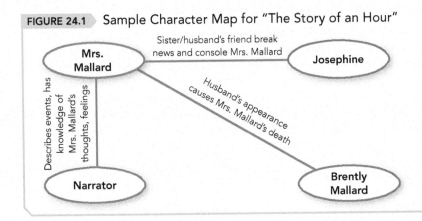

connecting them with lines to the main character. On the connecting lines, briefly describe the relationships between characters and the events or other factors (such as emotions) that affect their relationship.

The **narrator**, the person who tells the story, may also comment on or reveal information about the characters. The narrator is not necessarily the author of the story. The narrator can be one of the characters in the story or an onlooker who observes but does not participate in the action. Think critically about what the narrator reveals about the personalities, needs, and motives of the characters and whether the narrator's opinions may be colored by his or her perceptions and biases.

"The Story of an Hour" is centered on one principal character, Louise Mallard; Brently Mallard, a secondary character, is her husband, whose reported death and reappearance are the focus of Mrs. Mallard's thoughts, feelings, and actions. The narrator describes but does not participate in the action.

Point of View

The **point of view** is the perspective from which the story is told. There are two common points of view: first person and third person.

- In the **first-person** (*I, we*) point of view, the narrator tells the story as he or she sees or experiences it ("*I* saw the crowd gather at the cemetery"). A first-person narrator may be one of the characters or someone observing but not participating in the story.
- In the **third-person** (*he, she, they*) point of view, the narrator tells the story as if someone else is experiencing it ("*Laura* saw the crowd gather at the cemetery"). Third-person narrators fall into three categories:
  1. The narrator reports only the actions that can be observed from the outside but does not know or report the characters' thoughts.
  2. The narrator enters the minds of one or more (but not all) characters and writes about their thoughts and motives.
  3. The *omniscient*, or all-knowing, third-person narrator is aware of and reports on the thoughts and actions of all characters in the story.

To identify the point of view, consider who is narrating the story and what the narrator knows about the characters' actions, thoughts, and motives. "The Story of an Hour" is told by an omniscient narrator who is not directly involved in the story. The narrator is knowledgeable about Mrs. Mallard's actions and feelings, and seems to report them sympathetically. Rather than present her as an uncaring or even cruel woman actively planning her life after her husband's death, the narrator establishes her as helpless and acted upon. Mrs. Mallard perceives that something "was approaching to possess her," powerless to "beat it back with her will" (para. 10).

Plot

The **plot** is the basic story line — that is, the sequence of events and actions through which the story's meaning is expressed. (See Figure 24.2.) The plot often centers on a **conflict** — a problem or clash between opposing forces — and the resolution of the

FIGURE 24.2 The Plot Structure of a Story

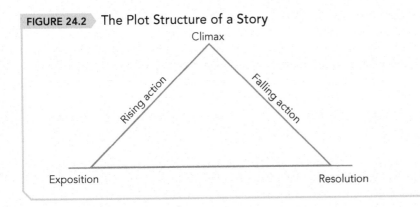

conflict. Once the scene is set and the characters are introduced (the **exposition**), a problem or conflict arises. Suspense and tension build as the conflict unfolds (**rising action**) and the characters wrestle with the problem. The events come to a **climax**, or turning point. Finally, the conflict is resolved and the story concludes (**falling action** and **resolution**). For stories with complicated plots that flash backward and forward in time, creating a time line, a chronological listing of events, may be helpful.

The plot of "The Story of an Hour" is straightforward: Mrs. Mallard is told that her husband was killed in a railroad accident and then discovers that he is still alive. The important part of the story occurs in Mrs. Mallard's mind and bodily responses, as she grasps the meaning of her husband's death and looks ahead to life without him.

Theme

The **theme** of a story is its central or dominant idea—the main point the author makes about the human experience. (Recall that themes are large or universal topics that are important to nearly everyone.) Readers do not always agree about a story's theme. Therefore, in analyzing a short story, you must give evidence to support your interpretation of the theme. The following suggestions will help you uncover clues:

1. **Study the title.** What meanings does it suggest?
2. **Analyze the main characters.** Do the characters change? If so, how, and in response to what?
3. **Look for broad statements about the conflict.** What do the characters and narrator say about the conflict or their lives?
4. **Look for symbols, figures of speech, and meaningful names** (Young *Goodman* Brown, for example).

Once you uncover a theme, try expressing it in a sentence rather than as a single word or brief phrase. For example, saying that a story's theme is "dishonesty" or "parent-child relationships" does not reveal the story's full meaning. When expressed as a sentence, however, a story's theme becomes clear: "Dishonesty sometimes pays" or "Parent-child relationships are often struggles for power and control."

One possible theme of "The Story of an Hour" is that independence is key to human happiness: When Mrs. Mallard learns that she is free of her husband, she becomes elated and looks forward to the years of freedom ahead of her. She dies when she realizes that her newfound freedom was illusory; her husband is alive. Another possible theme is that things are not always as they seem: Mrs. Mallard foresees an independent life ahead of her but is forced to realize that she is not free after all.

EXERCISE 24.2   **IDENTIFYING THE ELEMENTS OF A TV PROGRAM**

Working in groups of two or three, choose a television situation comedy and watch one episode, either together or separately. After viewing the program, identify each of the following elements: setting, characters, point of view, and plot. Then consider whether you think the episode has a theme.

Use the worksheet below to guide your analysis of the short story "Love in L.A." (pp. 677–79).

Worksheet for Analyzing Short Stories

Author:

Title:

Year of Publication:

Publisher:

Medium:

Setting: Time

1. In what time period (century or decade) does the story take place?
2. What major events (wars, revolutions, famines, political or cultural movements) occurred during that time, and what bearing might they have on the story?

Setting: Place

1. In what geographic area does the story take place? (Try to identify the country and the city or town, as well as whether the area is an urban or rural one.)
2. Where does the action occur? (For example, does it occur on a battlefield, in a living room, or on a city street?)
3. Why is the place important? (Why couldn't the story occur elsewhere?)

Characters

1. Who are the main characters in the story?
2. What are the distinguishing qualities and characteristics of each character?
3. Why do you like or dislike each character?
4. How and why do characters change (or not change) as the story progresses?

Point of View

1. Is the narrator a character in the story or strictly an observer?
2. Is the narrator knowledgeable about the motives, feelings, and behavior of any or all of the characters?
3. Does the narrator affect what happens in the story? If so, how? What role does the narrator play?

Plot

1. What series of events occurs? Summarize the action.
2. What is the conflict? Why does it occur? How does it build to a climax?
3. How is the conflict resolved?
4. Is the *resolution,* or outcome, satisfying? Why or why not?

Theme

1. What is the theme? What broad statement about life or the human experience does the story suggest?
2. What evidence from the story supports your interpretation of the theme?

SHORT STORY ‹ READING

Love in L.A.

Dagoberto Gilb

Dagoberto Gilb (b. 1950) was born in Los Angeles to an undocumented mother from Mexico and a father who moved to Los Angeles from Kentucky as a child. After high school, Gilb worked full time while attending community college. Later, he attended the University of California, Santa Barbara, where he earned a BA and MA. He worked in construction until 1992. His first book of stories, *The Magic of Blood* (from which "Love in L.A." is taken), was published in 1993. Gilb has won several literary awards, including the prestigious PEN/Faulkner Award, for his fiction, which focuses on the Latino experience in America. He is currently the director of CentroVictoria, a center for Mexican American literature and culture in Houston.

Jake slouched in a clot of near-motionless traffic, in the peculiar gray of concrete, smog, and early morning beneath the overpass of the Hollywood Freeway on Alvarado Street. He didn't really mind because he knew how much worse it could be trying to make a left onto the onramp. He certainly didn't do that every day of his life, and he'd assure anyone who'd ask that he never would either. A steady occupation had its advantages and he couldn't deny thinking about that too. He needed an FM radio in something better than this '58 Buick he drove. It would have crushed velvet interior with electric controls for the L.A. summer, a nice warm heater and defroster for the winter drives at the beach, a cruise control for those longer trips, mellow speakers front and rear of course, windows that hum closed, snuffing out that nasty exterior noise of freeways. The fact was that he'd probably

1

have to change his whole style. Exotic colognes, plush, dark nightclubs, maitais and daiquiris, necklaced ladies in satin gowns, misty and sexy like in a tequila ad. Jake could imagine lots of possibilities when he let himself, but none that ended up with him pressed onto a stalled freeway.

Jake was thinking about this freedom of his so much that when he glimpsed its green light he just went ahead and stared bye bye to the steadily employed. When he turned his head the same direction his windshield faced, it was maybe one second too late. He pounced the brake pedal and steered the front wheels away from the tiny brakelights but the smack was unavoidable. Just one second sooner and it would only have been close. One second more and he'd be crawling up the Toyota's trunk. As it was, it seemed like only a harmless smack, much less solid than the one against his back bumper.

Jake considered driving past the Toyota but was afraid the traffic ahead would make it too difficult. As he pulled up against the curb a few carlengths ahead, it occurred to him that the traffic might have helped him get away, too. He slammed the car door twice to make sure it was closed fully and to give himself another second more, then toured front and rear of his Buick for damage on or near the bumpers. Not an impressionable scratch even in the chrome. He perked up. Though the car's beauty was secondary to its ability to start and move, the body and paint were clean except for a few minor dings. This stood out as one of his few clearcut accomplishments over the years.

Before he spoke to the driver of the Toyota, whose looks he could see might present him with an added complication, he signaled to the driver of the car that hit him, still in his car and stopped behind the Toyota, and waved his hands and shook his head to let the man know there was no problem as far as he was concerned. The driver waved back and started his engine.

"It didn't even scratch my paint," Jake told her in that way of his. "So how you doin'? Any damage to the car? I'm kinda hoping so, just so it takes a little more time and we can talk some. Or else you can give me your phone number now and I won't have to lay my regular b.s. on you to get it later."

He took her smile as a good sign and relaxed. He inhaled her scent like it was clean air and straightened out his less-than-new but not unhip clothes.

"You've got Florida plates. You look like you must be Cuban."

"My parents are from Venezuela."

"My name's Jake." He held out his hand.

"Mariana."

They shook hands like she'd never done it before in her life.

"I really am sorry about hitting you like that." He sounded genuine. He fondled the wide dimple near the cracked taillight. "It's amazing how easy it is to put a dent in these new cars. They're so soft they might replace waterbeds soon." Jake was confused about how to proceed with this. So much seemed so unlikely, but there was always possibility. "So maybe we should go out to breakfast somewhere and talk it over."

"I don't eat breakfast."

"Some coffee then." 14

"Thanks, but I really can't." 15

"You're not married, are you? Not that that would matter that much to me. I'm 16
an openminded kinda guy."

She was smiling. "I have to get to work." 17

"That sounds boring." 18

"I better get your driver's license," she said. 19

Jake nodded, disappointed. "One little problem," he said. "I didn't bring it. I just 20
forgot it this morning. I'm a musician," he exaggerated greatly, "and, well, I dunno, I
left my wallet in the pants I was wearing last night. If you have some paper and a
pen I'll give you my address and all that."

He followed her to the glove compartment side of her car. 21

"What if we don't report it to the insurance companies? I'll just get it fixed for 22
you."

"I don't think my dad would let me do that." 23

"Your dad? It's not your car?" 24

"He bought it for me. And I live at home." 25

"Right." She was slipping away from him. He went back around to the back of 26
her new Toyota and looked over the damage again. There was the trunk lid, the
bumper, a rear panel, a taillight.

"You do have insurance?" she asked, suspicious, as she came around the back 27
of the car.

"Oh yeah," he lied. 28

"I guess you better write the name of that down too." 29

He made up a last name and address and wrote down the name of an insur- 30
ance company an old girlfriend once belonged to. He considered giving a real
phone number but went against that idea and made one up.

"I act too," he lied to enhance the effect more. "Been in a couple of movies." 31

She smiled like a fan. 32

"So how about your phone number?" He was rebounding maturely. 33

She gave it to him. 34

"Mariana, you are beautiful," he said in his most sincere voice. 35

"Call me," she said timidly. 36

Jake beamed. "We'll see you, Mariana," he said holding out his hand. Her hand 37
felt so warm and soft he felt like he'd been kissed.

Back in his car he took a moment or two to feel both proud and sad about his 38
performance. Then he watched the rear view mirror as Mariana pulled up behind
him. She was writing down the license plate numbers on his Buick, ones that he'd
taken off a junk because the ones that belonged to his had expired so long ago. He
turned the ignition key and revved the big engine and clicked into drive. His sense
of freedom swelled as he drove into the now moving street traffic, though he
couldn't stop the thought about that FM stereo radio and crushed velvet interior
and the new car smell that would even make it better.

Analyze Poetry

Poetry is written in lines and stanzas instead of in sentences and paragraphs. Because of the genre's unique format, poets often express ideas in compact and concise language, and reading and analyzing a short poem may take as much time and effort as analyzing an essay or a short story. To grasp the meaning of a poem, pay attention to the sound and meaning of individual words and consider how the words work together to convey meaning. The worksheet (pp. 681–82) can serve as a guide as you analyze poetry.

Use the following general guidelines to read and analyze poetry effectively:

1. **Read the poem through once, using the poem's punctuation as a guide.** Try to get a general sense of what the poem is about. If you come across an unfamiliar word or a confusing reference, keep reading. Although poetry is written in lines, each line may not make sense by itself. Meaning often flows from line to line, and a single sentence can be composed of several lines. Use the poem's punctuation to guide you. If there is no punctuation at the end of a line, read the line with a slight pause at the end and with an emphasis on the last word. Think about how the poet breaks lines to achieve a certain effect.

2. **Read the poem several more times, annotating as you read.** The meaning of the poem will become clearer with each successive reading. At first you may understand some parts but not others. If you find certain sections of the poem difficult or confusing, read these sections aloud several times. You might try copying them, word for word. Look up the meanings of any unfamiliar words in a dictionary.

   As you read, highlight striking elements (figures of speech, symbols, revealing character descriptions, striking dialogue, and the like) and record your reactions. (A sample annotated passage appears in Figure 24.3, p. 683.) Pay particular attention to the following:

   - **The speaker and tone.** Try to understand the speaker's viewpoint or feelings. How would you describe the speaker's personality? (Hint: Analyzing the vocabulary might help.) Also consider the speaker's tone: Is it serious, challenging, sad, frustrated, joyful? To determine the tone, read the poem aloud. Your emphasis on certain words or the rise and fall of your voice may provide clues to the tone; you may "hear" the poet's anger, despondency, or elation.
   - **To whom the poem is addressed.** Is it written to a person, the reader, an object? Consider the possibility that the poet may be writing to work out a personal problem or express strong emotions.
   - **Allusions.** Look up unfamiliar **allusions**, or references, to people, objects, or events outside the poem. If you see Oedipus mentioned in a poem, for example, you may need to use a dictionary or encyclopedia to learn that he was a figure in Greek mythology who unwittingly killed his father and married his mother. Your knowledge of Oedipus would then help you interpret the poem.

- **The language of the poem.** Consider the *connotations*, or shades of meaning, of words in the poem. Study the poem's use of descriptive language, similes, metaphors, personification, and symbols.
- **The poem's theme.** What does the title of the poem mean? What can it tell you about the poem's theme? Does the poem's overall meaning involve a feeling, a person, a memory, or an argument? Paraphrase the poem; express it in your own words and connect it to your own experience. Then link your ideas together to discover the poem's overall meaning. Ask yourself: What is the poet trying to tell me? What is the theme?

For more on connotations, see Chapters 3 and 9; for more on descriptive language, see Chapter 12.

3. **Write a response.** Copying passages from the poem and responding to those passages in writing can help you explore your reaction to the poem and grasp its meaning. Choose quotations from the poem that convey a main point or opinion, reveal a character's motives, or say something important about the plot or theme. Describe your reaction to each quotation, interpreting, disagreeing with, or questioning it. Comment on the language of the quotation and relate it to other quotations or elements in the work. Here is a sample response to Frost's "Two Look at Two":

"With thoughts of the path back, how rough it was" (line 5)	The couple's past has been difficult; returning to daily life may be difficult, too. Nature is rough and challenging.
. . . "This is all," they sighed, "Goodnight to woods.". . . (lines 13–14)	The couple will soon come to the end—of their relationship or their lives.

Worksheet for Analyzing Poetry

Poet:

Poem:

Year of Publication:

Source:

Medium:

Speaker, Tone, and Addressee

1. Who is the speaker? What do you know about him or her? What tone does the speaker use? To whom is he or she speaking?
2. What emotional atmosphere or mood does the poet create? Do you sense, for example, a mood of foreboding, excitement, or contentment?
3. Does the poem express emotion? If so, for what purpose?
4. How does the poem make you feel—shocked, saddened, angered, annoyed, happy? Write a sentence or two describing your reaction.

Allusions

1. Does the poem make references to people, events, or other works of art or literature?
2. How do these allusions affect the tone or meaning of the poem?

Language

1. How does the poet use language to create an effect? Does the poet use similes, metaphors, personification, or symbols?
2. Does the poem rhyme? If so, does the rhyme affect the meaning? (For example, does the poet use rhyme to emphasize key words or phrases?)

Theme

1. What is the meaning of the poem's title?
2. What is the theme of the poem?

READING POEM

Two Look at Two

Robert Frost

Robert Frost (1874–1963) is a major American poet whose work often focuses on familiar objects, natural scenes, and the character of New England. In his early life Frost was a farmer and teacher; later he became a poet in residence at Amherst College and taught at Dartmouth, Yale, and Harvard. Frost was awarded Pulitzer Prizes for four collections of poems: *New Hampshire* (1923), from which "Two Look at Two" is taken; *Collected Poems* (1930); *A Further Range* (1936); and *A Witness Tree* (1942). As you read the selection, use the questions in the preceding worksheet to think critically about the poem.

Love and forgetting might have carried them
A little further up the mountain side
With night so near, but not much further up.
They must have halted soon in any case
With thoughts of the path back, how rough it was   5
With rock and washout, and unsafe in darkness;
When they were halted by a tumbled wall
With barbed-wire binding. They stood facing this,
Spending what onward impulse they still had
In one last look the way they must not go,   10
On up the failing path, where, if a stone
Or earthslide moved at night, it moved itself;
No footstep moved it. "This is all," they sighed,
"Good-night to woods." But not so; there was more.
A doe from round a spruce stood looking at them   15
Across the wall, as near the wall as they.
She saw them in their field, they her in hers.
The difficulty of seeing what stood still,
Like some up-ended boulder split in two,
Was in her clouded eyes: they saw no fear there.   20
She seemed to think that two thus they were safe.
Then, as if they were something that, though strange,

She could not trouble her mind with too long,
She sighed and passed unscared along the wall.
"*Th*is, then, is all. What more is there to ask?"   25
But no, not yet. A snort to bid them wait.
A buck from round the spruce stood looking at them
Across the wall, as near the wall as they.
This was an antlered buck of lusty nostril,
Not the same doe come back into her place.   30
He viewed them quizzically with jerks of head,
As if to ask, "Why don't you make some motion?
Or give some sign of life? Because you can't.
I doubt if you're as living as you look."
Thus till he had them almost feeling dared   35
To stretch a proffering hand—and a spell-breaking.
Then he too passed unscared along the wall.
Two had seen two, whichever side you spoke from.
"This *must* be all." It was all. Still they stood,
A great wave from it going over them,   40
As if the earth in one unlooked-for favor
Had made them certain earth returned their love.

The poem takes place on a mountainside path, near dusk. A couple walking along the path finds a tumbled wall. Looking beyond the wall, the couple encounters first a doe and then a buck. The doe and buck stare at the human couple and vice versa; hence the title "Two Look at Two." The action is described by a third-person narrator

---

FIGURE 24.3   **A Sample Annotated Passage from "Two Look at Two"**

Love and forgetting might have carried them

A little further up the mountain side

With night so near, <u>but not much further up</u>. ⟵——————————————— *limitations of humans*

They must have halted soon in any case

With <u>thoughts of the path back</u>, how rough it was ⟵————————— *road of life?*
                                                                                      difficulty of life

With rock and washout, and unsafe in darkness;

When they were halted by a <u>tumbled wall</u> ⟵——————————— *separates man and nature—*
                                                                                      Why is it tumbled?

With <u>barbed-wire</u> binding. They stood facing this, ⟵——————— *sharp, penetrating*

Spending what onward impulse they still had

In one last look the way <u>they must not go</u>, ⟵————————— *prohibited from crossing*

who can read the thoughts of the humans. The speaker creates an objective tone by reporting events as they occur.

In "Two Look at Two," Frost considers the relationship between humans and nature. The wall is symbolic of the separation between them. Beyond the wall the couple looks at "the way they must not go" (line 10). Although humans and nature are separate, they are also equal and in balance. These qualities are suggested by the title as well as by the actions of both couples as they observe each other in a nonthreatening way. The third-person point of view contributes to this balance in that the poem's narrator is an outside observer rather than a participant. One possible theme of the poem, therefore, is the balance and equality between humans and nature.

As you read the following poem, use the guidelines and worksheet for reading a poem to help you analyze its elements and discover its meaning.

READING ▸ POEM

Famous

Naomi Shihab Nye

Naomi Shihab Nye (b. 1952) is an American poet and songwriter and the author of books for children and young adults. The daughter of an American mother and a Palestinian father, she has lived in both America and Jerusalem, and much of her work reflects the cultural differences that she has experienced throughout her life. Nye is the author of numerous collections of poetry, including *Different Ways to Pray* (1980); *Hugging the Jukebox* (1982), which won the Voertman Poetry Prize; and *Words under the Word: Selected Poems* (1995), in which "Famous" appeared. Her most recent work is *The Tiny Journalist* (2019).

> The river is famous to the fish.
> The loud voice is famous to silence,
> which knew it would inherit the earth
> before anybody said so.
> The cat sleeping on the fence is famous to the birds   5
> watching him from the birdhouse.
> The tear is famous, briefly, to the cheek.
> The idea you carry close to your bosom
> is famous to your bosom.
> The boot is famous to the earth,   10
> more famous than the dress shoe,
> which is famous only to floors.
> The bent photograph is famous to the one who carries it
> and not at all famous to the one who is pictured.
> I want to be famous to shuffling men   15
> who smile while crossing streets,
> sticky children in grocery lines,
> famous as the one who smiled back.
> I want to be famous in the way a pulley is famous,
> or a buttonhole, not because it did anything spectacular,   20
> but because it never forgot what it could do.

A Guided Writing Assignment*

LITERARY ANALYSIS

A **literary analysis** essay, sometimes called *literary criticism* or a *critique*, analyzes and interprets one or more aspects of a literary work. As with other types of essays, writing a literary analysis involves generating ideas through prewriting, developing a thesis, collecting supporting evidence, organizing and drafting, analyzing and revising, and editing and proofreading.

Keep in mind that a literary analysis does not merely summarize the work, but rather analyzes and interprets it. In a literary analysis, you take a position on some aspect of the work and support your position with evidence. In other words, you assume the role of a literary critic, in the same way that a film critic argues for his or her judgment of a film rather than simply reporting its plot.

A literary analysis has the following characteristics:

- It makes a point about one or more elements of a literary work.
- It includes and accurately documents evidence from the work. (It may also include evidence from outside sources.)
- It assumes that the audience is somewhat familiar with the work but not as familiar as the writer of the analysis.
- It has a serious tone and is written in the present tense.

Your Essay Assignment

Write a literary analysis of a poem or short story, focusing on one element of the work. You may analyze a work of your own choosing, a work your instructor assigns, or one of the works reprinted in this chapter.

- Gwendolyn Brooks, "The Bean Eaters"
- Kate Chopin, "The Story of an Hour"
- Dagoberto Gilb, "Love in L.A."
- Robert Frost, "Two Look at Two"
- Naomi Shihab Nye, "Famous"

---

* The writing process is recursive; that is, you may find yourself revising as you draft or prewriting as you revise. This is especially true when writing on a computer. Your writing process may also differ from project to project and from that of your classmates.

1 Read and analyze your writing assignment carefully.

Ask yourself these questions about your **writing situation**:

- What is my **purpose** for writing? To explain one element of the work? To argue for my interpretation?
- What are my **instructor's expectations**? What will he or she be looking for?
- Given my and my instructor's goals for the assignment, how much should I assume that **my readers already know** about the author, genre, or literary work?
- Am I allowed to do **research** to find out what others have said about the work or to find background information about the author?
- How will I use **additional patterns of development** within my literary analysis? For example, you will likely use illustration to cite examples to support your analysis. In addition, you might compare or contrast two main characters or analyze a plot by discussing causes and effects.

2 Explore the work of literature and generate ideas.

Try one or more of the following suggestions to devise **a focus** and generate **ideas**:

- **Highlight** and **annotate** the work. Focus on striking details, such as figures of speech, symbolic images, actions and reactions of characters, repetition, and so on.
- **Freewrite.** Explore your reaction to the work or use a word or image from the work as a jumping off point.
- **Discuss the literary work with classmates.** Move from general meaning to a more specific paragraph-by-paragraph or line-by-line examination. Then discuss your interpretation of the work's theme.
- **Write a summary.** Doing so may lead you to raise and answer questions about the work.
- **Draw a time line or a character map.** For stories with plots that flash back or forward in time, a time line can help you envision the sequence of events. A character map can help you understand characters' relationships.

3 Conduct background research.

If your instructor allows it, you may develop an interesting focus by putting the work into **context**.

- **Read about the author's background.** Look for connections between the work and the author's life. For example, writing an interpretation of Charles Dickens's "A Christmas Carol" might be easier if you understand the author's own impoverished childhood.
- **Explore the historical context.** Research the historical, social, economic, and political context of the work. Understanding conditions of the poor in nineteenth-century England might help you understand Dickens's portrayal of the Cratchit family.
- **Discover parallel works or situations.** Compare the work to a film or television show or to your own experience to develop insight.
- **Apply theories you have learned about in other classes.** Theories from your psychology class may help you understand Mrs. Mallard's reaction to the news of her husband's death in "The Story of an Hour."

4 Evaluate your ideas and choose an approach to your literary analysis.

Here are several **possible approaches** you might choose to take in a literary analysis:

- **Evaluate symbolism.** Discuss how the author's use of images and symbols creates a particular mood and contributes to the overall meaning of the work.
- **Analyze conflicts.** Focus on their causes, effects, or both.
- **Evaluate characterization and interpret relationships.** Discuss how characters are presented; analyze how their true nature is revealed or how they change in response to circumstances.
- **Explore themes.** Discover an important point or theme the work conveys, and back up your ideas with examples from the work.

5 Draft your thesis statement.

Your **thesis** should

- include the **author's name** and the **work's title**
- indicate the **element** of the work you will analyze (its theme, characters, or use of symbols, for example)
- state the **main point** you will make about that element

Notice how the writers include all three elements in these two example thesis statements:

Example: Flannery O'Connor's short story "A Good Man Is Hard to Find"
uses color to depict various moods throughout the story.

Example: In Susan Glaspell's play *Trifles*, the female characters are treated condescendingly

by the males, and yet the women's interest in so-called trivial matters leads them to

interpret the "trivial" pieces of evidence that solve the murder mystery.

Working Together. In groups of two or three students, take turns presenting your thesis statements and main supporting evidence. As group members listen, have them note the element you will analyze and your main point. They should be able to restate your main point in their own words; if they can't, your main point may not be clear. Brainstorm as a group to

- clarify your thesis
- add a missing element
- identify evidence or insights the writer may have overlooked

6 Choose a method of organization.

One of these **methods of organization** may work well in a literary analysis:

- Use **least-to-most** order to highlight one or more important reasons or causes.
- Use **chronological order** to explore events as they occur in the work of literature or the process by which an author makes events or connections clear.
- Use **point-by-point** or **subject-by-subject** order to compare or contrast characters or works of literature.

7 Draft your literary analysis.

Use the following guidelines to keep your essay on track:

- The **introduction** should name the **author** and **title**, present your **thesis,** and suggest why your analysis is **useful** or **important.** Try to engage **readers' interest** by including a meaningful **quotation** or a comment on the **universality** of a **character** or **theme**, for example.

- Each **body paragraph** should include a **topic sentence** that states your main point, a point that supports your thesis and enough **evidence** to support your main point. Include **quotations** or **paraphrases** from the work of literature as support, identified by **page numbers** (for a short story) or **line numbers** (for a poem). Include a **works-cited entry** at the end of your paper indicating the edition of the work you used. Use plot summary only where necessary to make the analysis clear. Write in the **"literary present" tense** (see step 9 below), except when discussing events that occur before the story or poem begins.

- The **conclusion** should **reaffirm your thesis** and give the essay a sense of **closure.** You may want to tie your conclusion to your introduction or offer a final word on your main point.

8 Evaluate your draft, and revise as necessary.

Use **Figure 24.4, "Flowchart for Revising a Literary Analysis Essay,"** to help you discover the strengths and weaknesses of your draft. You might also ask a classmate to review your draft using the questions in the flowchart.

FIGURE 24.4 Flowchart for Revising a Literary Analysis Essay

QUESTIONS   REVISION STRATEGIES

1. Highlight your thesis statement. Does it identify the work, the one aspect of it you are analyzing, and the main point of your analysis?

NO ▶
- Revise your thesis so that all of these items are included.
- Ask a classmate to read your thesis and convey his or her understanding of your main point.

YES
▼

2. Place a ✔ by the evidence from the literary work that supports your thesis. Is all of your evidence relevant to your thesis? Is there enough evidence?

NO ▶
- Delete examples that do not support your thesis or that might be confusing to readers.
- Add relevant quotations, paraphrases, and summaries.
- Explain how the examples support your point.

YES
▼

| QUESTIONS | REVISION STRATEGIES |

3. [Bracket] each quotation from the work. Do you cite each quotation so readers can locate it in the work of literature?

 ▶

- Include paragraph, page, or line numbers for each quotation.
- Include a works-cited entry for the edition of the work you used.

4. Review your assignment. Does your essay achieve your and your instructor's goals?

 ▶

- Add information about the author, plot, characters, or other elements as needed.
- Make sure you go beyond summary to interpret and analyze the work of literature.

5. Circle each verb. Have you used the present tense appropriately?

 ▶

- Use the present tense to discuss the writing of the story or events within it.
- Use the past tense to discuss events that occurred before the action of the story begins.

6. Place an ✗ next to words that reveal your feelings or judgments about the work. Does your tone suggest a serious, objective view of the work?

 ▶

- Tone down or eliminate any overly critical or enthusiastic statements.
- Avoid slang or overly casual language.

7. Review each body paragraph. Does each have a clear topic sentence? Does each focus on one main point or idea?

 ▶

- Be sure each paragraph has a clear topic sentence that supports your thesis statement.
- Combine closely related paragraphs or split paragraphs that cover two or more main points or ideas.

(continued on next page) ▶

REVISING

(Figure 24.4 continued)

QUESTIONS		REVISION STRATEGIES

8. Reread your introduction and conclusion. Does the introduction suggest the importance of your thesis and engage your readers' interest? Does your conclusion lend closure?

- Ask yourself why your audience would be interested in your thesis, and incorporate the answer in your introduction.
- End by referring back to your introduction or showing why the work of literature is relevant or important.
- Use the guidelines in Chapter 7.

9 Edit and proofread your essay.

Refer to Chapter 9 for help with

- **editing sentences** to avoid wordiness, make your verb choices strong and active, and make your sentences clear, varied, and parallel
- **editing words** for tone and diction, connotation, and concrete and specific language

Pay particular attention to the following:

1. **Use the literary present tense.** Even though the poem or short story was written in the past, as a general rule write about the events in it and the author's writing of it as if they were happening in the present. An exception to this rule occurs when you are referring to a time earlier than that in which the narrator speaks, in which case a switch to the past tense is appropriate.

   Example: Keats in "Ode on a Grecian Urn" ~~referred~~ ^{refers} to the urn as a "silent form" (line 44).

   Example: In "Two Look at Two," it is not clear why the couple decided to walk up the mountainside path. The couple made the decision before the action in the poem began.

2. **Punctuate quotations correctly.** Direct quotations from a literary work, whether spoken or written, must be placed in quotation marks. Omitted material should be marked by an ellipsis (. . .). The lines of a poem when they are run together in an essay are separated by a slash (/).

   Example: In "Two Look at Two," Frost concludes that the earth in one unlooked-for favor / Had made them certain earth returned their love (lines 41–42).

   Periods and commas appear within quotation marks. Question marks and exclamation points precede or follow quotation marks, depending on the meaning of the sentence. In the example below, the question mark goes inside the closing quotation marks because it is part of Frost's poem (line 32). Notice, too, that double and single quotation marks are required for a quotation within a quotation. (See Chapter 23 for more on incorporating quotations into your writing.)

   Example: The buck seems "to ask, 'Why don't you make some motion'?" (line 32).

The Short, Happy Life of Louise Mallard

Irina Dudnik

Irina Dudnik wrote this literary analysis for her first-year writing class. As you read the essay, notice her thesis. How does she use quotations from the story to support her claim? How does she weave those quotations into her essay?

"There was something coming to her and she was waiting for it, fearfully. What was it? She did not know, it was too subtle and elusive to name" (671). So writes the narrator about Louise Mallard, the main character in Kate Chopin's short story "The Story of an Hour." Set toward the end of the nineteenth century, the story follows Mrs. Mallard's reaction to the news of her husband's death, which develops from grief to a state of suspended emotion to a sense of utter freedom. Chopin's tale delivers a powerful message about the repression that women like Mrs. Mallard suffered under the cultural institution of marriage built on male dominance. What makes this message so powerful is the fact that Louise Mallard's sense of freedom isn't immediate or simple, but once it develops, there's no going back.

When her sister breaks the news that her husband is dead, Mrs. Mallard bursts into "a storm of grief" (671), weeping in her sister's arms, and then retreats to her room. Ironically, it is here in her room, in an armchair facing an open window, that Mrs. Mallard develops her sense of freedom. It is first revealed in the contrast between the way she sits down, "pressed down by a physical exhaustion that haunted her body and seemed to reach into her soul" (671), and in the freshness she sees through the open window, in which "the tops of trees . . . were all aquiver with the new spring life" (671), the open window symbolizing a means of escape and a pathway to a fresh life. Chopin takes care that the first signals of Mrs. Mallard's repression come through her senses, so that readers can learn with Mrs. Mallard just how deeply she has internalized the effects of marriage.

Like Mrs. Mallard, readers only become aware of the character's newfound sense of freedom gradually. They share her experience as she

1   **Introduction:** Begins with a quotation that suggests main point, identifies page

Identifies setting and shows relevance

Thesis: Thesis focuses on Mrs. Mallard's developing sense of liberation

2   **Organization:** Uses chronological organization, following Mrs. Mallard's developing response

Support: Uses quotations to support claim about Mrs. Mallard's changing feelings

Interpretation: Explains meaning of quotations and symbolism

3   **Paragraph:** Topic sentence makes point of paragraph clear

Evidence: Quotations support point topic sentence makes

stares out the window with eyes that reflect "a suspension of intelligent thought" (671). This "subtle and elusive" feeling doesn't come in words or accusations. It comes through her senses, "the sounds, the scents, the color" (672) showing that her confinement is so penetrating that it has mapped itself onto the way she experiences the world around her.

The fact that readers can't name the feeling Louise Mallard has until she can name it herself effectively conveys how deep her sense of captivity has been. At last, Mrs. Mallard names how she feels — "[f]ree, free free!" (672) — and she (and her readers) begin to see more than just an open window. She can envision the freedom that window represents, the "years to come that would belong to her absolutely" (672). And Chopin emphasizes Mrs. Mallard's bodily feeling of freedom just as much as her mental understanding: "Now her bosom rose and fell tumultuously . . . her pulses beat fast, and the coursing blood warmed and relaxed every inch of her body" (672). The fact that it takes a while to name her freedom, and to recognize the sensations in her body as relief and joy, shows that the kind of repression Mrs. Mallard felt in her marriage worked on a deep, psychological level.

Interpretation: Explains meaning of quotations, how they support thesis

Transitions: Uses transitional words and phrases to show that she is moving to another reason

But this is not the only reason that this kind of confinement is so difficult to identify. By showing readers how Mrs. Mallard grapples with her husband's death, Chopin shows them not only how much harm has been caused by lack of self-determination but also that the harm can coexist with affection, kindness, and even love. The story makes clear that Mr. Mallard was no monster: His "face . . . had never looked save with love upon her" (672). Here, Chopin challenges the notion that physical or verbal harm are the only kinds that can cause suffering or that oppression has to be inflicted on purpose. Mr. Mallard loved his wife, and she had at times even loved him, but here she is whispering, "Free! Body and soul free!" (672), and readers know that her happiness is not a matter of love (or the lack of it). Her happiness at the end of the story is about life's possibilities and how rich they can feel to a person who can now make decisions for herself: "What could love . . . count for in the face of this possession of self-assertion which she suddenly recognized as the strongest impulse of her being?" (672). By leading readers away from the

4

5

picture of her husband as a cruel tyrant, Chopin helps them understand that relationships not only need to be free of violence but also need to be built on mutual independence.

When Mrs. Mallard is given even an hour-long understanding of what living for herself feels like, she can't survive a return to dependency: Brently Mallard, whose death was misreported, walks in the front door, and his wife collapses, dead. After watching Mrs. Mallard come to understand just what her husband's absence means, readers can now understand what her husband's presence means. The power of this story is in the way it uncovers the complicated relationship between repression and love and the way this understanding is felt in the body. Chopin's brilliant story sheds light on the underbelly of marital bliss, but more importantly, it implores her readers to recognize and reject repression, in whatever form it takes, before it is too late.

6 **Conclusion:** Shows how dramatic ending relates to thesis, title of essay

Work Cited

Chopin, Kate. "The Story of an Hour." *Successful College Writing*, 8th ed., by Kathleen McWhorter, Bedford/St. Martin's, 2021, pp. 671–73.

Works cited: Cites edition of story used

Analyzing the Writer's Technique

1. **Thesis** Does Dudnik provide sufficient evidence to support her thesis? Choose one example Dudnik offers and evaluate its effectiveness.
2. **Introduction and Conclusion** Evaluate Dudnik's introduction and conclusion. In what ways could they be improved?
3. **Development** Which paragraphs are particularly well developed? Which, if any, need further development?

Responding to the Essay

1. **Discussion** How does Dudnik's interpretation of "The Story of an Hour" compare with yours?
2. **Journal** Dudnik discusses the issue of marriage and repression as it existed in the nineteenth century. Write a journal entry exploring whether and how this issue has changed in the time that has elapsed since then.

25

Essay Examinations and Portfolios

Oogy flunks his cave drawing final—

Randall McIlwaine/CartoonStock

Writing Quick Start

ANALYZE   The cartoon on this page humorously comments on the process of taking tests. No doubt you have taken tests throughout your school years, and they are an important part of college classes as well.

WRITE   Assume you are taking a short, fifteen-minute, timed writing test. Write about your experiences with taking tests. You might write about how you prepare for exams or share test-taking tips, for example. You have fifteen minutes to complete the writing test.

CONNECT   In completing this timed writing test, did you feel pressured by the fifteen-minute limit? How did you decide what to write about? Did you have as much time as you would have liked to organize, plan, develop, and revise your ideas? Probably not.

Essay exams require students to use more advanced thinking skills than they use when taking a multiple-choice or short-answer test. For instance, an essay exam for a history course might require you to pull ideas together to analyze historical trends or compare two political figures.

This chapter will help you prepare for the timed essay exams you will encounter in college as well as the other kinds of writing assignments you need to complete under time pressure. This chapter will also help you prepare a portfolio of your writing.

- For the midterm exam in your *philosophy of religion course,* you have one hour to answer the following essay question: "Contrast the beliefs of Islam with those of either Judaism or Christianity."
- For a *business communication class,* you are asked to assemble a portfolio that illustrates your mastery of the six course objectives.
- As a *freelance artist,* you need to prepare a portfolio of your illustration styles to help art directors evaluate your work.

Prepare for and Take Essay Examinations

Doing well on essay examinations involves not only preparing for the exam, but also analyzing and answering the exam's questions clearly and fully.

Prepare for Essay Exams

Because essay exams require you to produce a written response, the best way to prepare for them is by organizing and writing.

Create study sheets to synthesize information. Most essay exams require you to *synthesize,* or pull together, information. To prepare for this task, try to identify the key topics in a course, and then create a **study sheet** for each main topic. Study sheets help you organize, consolidate, and study complex or detailed information.

For more on synthesizing sources, see Chapter 22.

To prepare a study sheet, draw on information from your textbook as well as from class notes, handouts, previous exams (look for emphasized topics), and assigned readings. You can organize a study sheet in a variety of ways. For example, you might

- draw a graphic organizer to create a visual study sheet
- create a timeline to connect historical events
- write an outline to organize information
- construct a comparison-and-contrast chart to see relationships among different topics
- develop a list of categories and use them to organize information

Whatever method of organization you use for your study sheet, be sure to include key information about each topic: definitions, facts, principles, theories, events, research studies, and the like.

Here is part of one student's study sheet for a speech communication course on the topic *audience analysis*:

Sample Study Sheet

Topic: Audience Analysis

1. Demographic characteristics
   —Age and gender
   —Educational background (type and level of education)
   —Group membership (people who share similar interests or goals)
   —Social and religious activities
   —Hobbies and sports
2. Psychological characteristics
   —Beliefs (about what is true or false, right or wrong)
   —Attitudes (positive or negative)
   —Values (standards for judging worth of thoughts and actions)

EXERCISE 25.1 **PREPARING A STUDY SHEET**

Use the preceding guidelines to prepare a study sheet on a general topic that you expect will be covered on an upcoming exam in one of your courses.

Predict essay exam questions. Once you prepare study sheets for a particular course, the next step is to predict questions that might be asked on an essay exam. Although essay exam questions usually focus on general topics, themes, or patterns, these questions generally also require you to supply details in your response. For example, an essay question on a psychology exam might ask you to compare and contrast the James-Lange and Cannon-Bard theories of motivation. Your answer would focus on the similarities and differences between these key theories, incorporating relevant details where necessary.

Use the following strategies to help you predict the types of questions you might be asked on an essay exam:

1. **Group topics into categories.** Review your textbook, class notes, and study sheets to devise categories. For example, if you find a chapter on kinship in your anthropology textbook and several entries in your class notes on this topic, a question on kinship is likely to appear on an essay exam for the course.
2. **Study your syllabus and objectives.** These documents contain important clues about what your instructors want you to learn during the course.
3. **Study previous exams.** Notice which key ideas are emphasized in previous exams. If you had to explain the historical significance of the Boston Tea Party on

your first American history exam, you can predict that future exams will ask you to explain the historical significance of other events.

4. **Listen to your instructor's comments.** When instructors announce or review material for an upcoming essay exam, pay close attention to the key topics they reveal or to the areas they suggest that you study.

5. **Draft possible essay questions.** Use Table 25.1 (p. 700) to draft possible essay questions using key verbs that hint at how you must answer effectively.

EXERCISE 25.2 ▸ **PREDICTING ESSAY QUESTIONS FOR A COLLEGE COURSE**

For an upcoming essay exam in one of your courses, predict and write at least three possible questions your instructor might ask about the course material.

Draft answers in outline form.   After you predict several possible essay exam questions, the next step is to write a brief, rough outline of the information that answers each question. Be sure each outline responds to the *wording* of the question; that is, it should *explain*, *compare*, *describe*, or do whatever else the question asks (see Table 25.1). Writing a rough outline will strengthen your recall of the material. It will also save you time during the actual exam because you will have already spent some time thinking about, organizing, and writing about the material.

Here is a sample essay question and an informal outline written in response to it:

Essay Question

Explain how material passes in and out of cells by crossing plasma membranes.

Informal Outline

Types of Transport

1. Passive—no use of cellular energy; random movement of molecules
   a. Diffusion—molecules move from areas of high to areas of low concentration (example: open bottle of perfume, aroma spreads)
   b. Facilitated diffusion—similar to simple diffusion; differs in that some kinds of molecules are moved more easily than others (helped by carrier proteins in cell membrane)
   c. Osmosis—diffusion of water across membranes from area of lower to area of higher solute concentration
2. Active—requires cellular energy; usually movement against the concentration gradient
   a. Facilitated active transport—carrier molecules move ions across a membrane
   b. Endocytosis—material is surrounded by a plasma membrane and pinched off into a vacuole
   c. Exocytosis—cells expel materials

> **EXERCISE 25.3** **PREPARING AN INFORMAL OUTLINE**
>
> For one of the questions you predicted in Exercise 25.2, prepare a brief informal outline in response to the question.

Reduce informal outlines to key-word outlines. To help you recall your outlined answer during the exam, reduce it to a brief key-word outline or list of key topics. Here is a sample key-word outline for the essay question about cells:

Key-Word Outline

Types of Transport

1. Passive
   — Diffusion
   — Facilitated diffusion
   — Osmosis
2. Active
   — Facilitated active transport
   — Endocytosis
   — Exocytosis

> **EXERCISE 25.4** **PREPARING A KEY-WORD OUTLINE**
>
> Reduce the outline answer you wrote in Exercise 25.3 to a key-word outline.

Take Essay Exams

Once prepared, you should be more confident about taking an essay exam. The following general guidelines will help you when you confront the exam itself:

1. **Arrive at the exam room or log on with the exam link a few minutes early.** You can use this time to collect your thoughts and get organized.
2. **Choose your work area carefully.** For in-person exams, sit at the front of the room, where you will be less distracted. For online exams, choose a quiet place that has good reception, where you are unlikely to be interrupted.
3. **Read the directions carefully.** Some exams may direct you to answer only one of three questions, whereas other exams may ask you to answer all questions.
4. **Consider your audience and purpose.** For most essay exams, your instructor is your audience. Since your instructor is already knowledgeable about the topic, your purpose is to demonstrate what you know about the topic. Therefore, you should write thorough and complete answers, pretending that your instructor knows only what you tell him or her.

5. **Preview the exam and plan your time carefully.** Read through the whole exam to get a complete picture of the task at hand and then plan how you will complete the exam within the allotted time. If you have fifty minutes, spend roughly ten minutes planning; thirty minutes writing; and ten minutes editing, proofreading, and making last-minute changes. Begin by writing a brief thesis statement. Then jot down the key supporting points and number them in the order you will present them. Leave space under each supporting point for your details. If the question is one you had predicted, write down your keyword outline. If an idea for an interesting connection or an effective example comes to mind, jot it down as well. At the end of your allotted time for writing, reread your essay and correct surface errors.

6. **Notice the point value of each question.** If your instructor assigns points to each question, use the point values to plan your time. For example, spend more time answering a 30-point question than a 10-point question.

7. **Choose topics or questions carefully.** Often you will have little or no choice of topic or question. If you do have a choice, choose the topics or answer the questions that you know the most about. If the question asks you to write about a broad topic, such as a current social issue, narrow the topic to one you can write about in the specified amount of time.

8. **Answer the easiest question first.** Answering the easiest question first will boost your confidence and allow you to spend the remaining time working on the more difficult questions. Generally if an exam contains both objective and essay questions, get the objective questions out of the way first.

9. **Remember that your first draft is your final draft.** Plan on writing your first draft carefully and correctly so that it can serve as your final copy. However, you can always make minor changes and additions as you write or edit and proofread.

Analyze Essay Exam Questions

Essay exam questions are often concise, but if you read them closely, you will find that they *do* specifically tell you what to write about. Consider the following sample essay question from a sociology exam:

Choose a particular institution, define it, and identify its primary characteristics.

The question tells you exactly what to write about—*a particular institution* (you get to choose one). In addition, the key verbs *define* and *identify* tell you how to approach the subject. To get full credit for this essay question, then, you would have to give an accurate definition of the institution you chose and discuss its primary characteristics.

Table 25.1 lists key verbs commonly used in essay exam questions along with sample questions and tips for answering them. As you study the list, notice that many of the verbs suggest a particular pattern of development. For example, *trace* suggests using a narrative sequence, and *justify* suggests using argumentation. For key verbs such as *explain* or *discuss*, you might use a combination of patterns.

TABLE 25.1 Responding to Key Verbs in Essay Exam Questions

Key Verbs	Sample Essay Questions	Tips for Answering Questions
Compare	Compare the poetry of Judith Ortiz Cofer with that of Julia Alvarez.	Show how the poems are similar as well as different; use details and examples.
Contrast	Contrast classical and operant conditioning.	Show how the two types of conditioning are different; use details and examples.
Define	Define *biofeedback* and describe its uses.	Give an accurate explanation of the term with enough detail to demonstrate that you understand it.
Discuss	Discuss the halo effect, and give examples of its use.	Consider important characteristics and main points; include examples.
Evaluate	Evaluate the accomplishments of the feminist movement over the past fifty years.	Assess merits, strengths, weaknesses, advantages, or limitations.
Explain	Explain the functions of amino acids.	Use facts and details to make the topic or concept clear and understandable.
Illustrate	Illustrate with examples from your experience how culture shapes human behavior.	Use examples that demonstrate a point or clarify the idea.
Justify	Justify laws outlawing smoking in federal buildings.	Give reasons and evidence that support the action, decision, or policy.
List	List the advantages and disadvantages of sales promotions.	List or discuss one by one; use most-to-least or least-to-most organization.
Summarize	Summarize Maslow's hierarchy of needs.	Briefly review all the major points.
Trace	Trace the life cycle of a typical household product.	Describe its development or progress in chronological order.

Write Essay Answers

Use the following guidelines to write the answers to essay questions:

1. **Since your first-draft essay exam is also your final draft, write in complete and grammatically correct sentences from the start.** Supply sufficient detail and follow a logical organization. It is acceptable to cross out words or sentences neatly and indicate corrections in spelling or grammar.

2. **Add ideas neatly.** If you think of an idea you would like to add to your answer, write the sentence at the top of the paper and draw an arrow to indicate where it should be inserted.

3. **Provide a brief introduction and, in some cases, a conclusion.** Depending on how much time you have, the introduction may consist of only your thesis statement, or it may also include necessary background information on the topic. Write a conclusion only if the question seems to require a final evaluative statement.

4. **If you run out of time, jot the unfinished portion of your outline at the end of the essay.** Your instructor may give you partial credit.

Write your thesis statement. Your thesis statement should be clear and direct. Identify your subject and suggest your approach to the topic. Often the thesis statement answers the essay exam question. Consider the following examples:

For more on writing a thesis, see Chapter 5.

Essay Exam Question	Thesis Statement
Explain how tides are produced in the Earth's oceans. Account for seasonal variations.	The Earth's gravitational forces are responsible for producing tides in the Earth's oceans.
Distinguish between bureaucratic agencies and other government decision-making bodies.	Bureaucratic agencies are distinct from other government decision-making bodies because of their hierarchical organization, character, culture, and professionalism.

Your thesis may also suggest the organization of your essay. For example, if the question asks you to explain the differences between primary and secondary groups, you might state your thesis as follows: "Primary groups differ from secondary groups in their membership, purpose, level of interaction, and level of intimacy." Your essay would then discuss membership first, purpose second, and so on.

EXERCISE 25.5 ▸ **WRITING THESIS STATEMENTS FOR ESSAY EXAM QUESTIONS**

Write thesis statements for two of the following essay exam questions:

1. Define and illustrate the meaning of the term *freedom of the press*.
2. Distinguish between the medical care provided by private physicians and that provided by medical clinics.
3. Choose a recent television advertisement and describe its rational and emotional appeals.
4. Evaluate an episode of a current political podcast in terms of its breadth and depth of coverage, objectivity, and political and social viewpoints.

Develop supporting details. Write a separate paragraph for each of your key points. For example, in an essay answer distinguishing primary from secondary groups, devote one paragraph to each distinguishing feature: membership, purpose, level of

For more on topic sentences, see Chapter 6.

interaction, and level of intimacy. The topic sentence for each paragraph should identify and briefly explain the key point. For example, a topic sentence for the first main
point about groups might be: "Membership, or who belongs, is one factor that distinguishes primary from secondary groups." The rest of the paragraph would explain
membership: what constitutes membership, what criteria are used to decide who
belongs, and who decides.

Whenever possible, supply examples to make it clear that you can apply the information you have learned. Keep in mind that your goal is to demonstrate your knowledge and understanding of the material.

For more on editing and proofreading, see Chapter 9.

Reread and proofread your answer. Leave enough time to reread and proofread
your essay answer. First, reread to make sure you have answered all parts of the question. Then reread your answer, checking it for content. Add missing information, correct vague or unclear sentences, and add facts or details. Next, proofread for errors in
spelling, punctuation, and grammar. A clear, nearly error-free essay makes a positive
impression on your instructor and identifies you as a serious, conscientious student.
An error-free essay may also improve your grade.

EXERCISE 25.6 **WRITING A COMPLETE ESSAY EXAM ANSWER**

For the essay question you worked on in Exercise 25.5, use the preceding guidelines
to write a complete essay answer.

STUDENTS WRITE

Essay Exam Response

Ronald Robinson

A model essay exam response was written by Ronald Robinson for his introductory
sociology course. First read the exam question below and then read Robinson's essay
exam, which follows. As you read, consider how effectively and fully Robinson has
answered the exam question. The essay has been annotated to point out its key
features.

Essay Exam Question

Distinguish between fads and fashions, explaining the characteristics of
each type of group behavior and describing the phases each usually goes
through.

Essay Exam Answer

<u>Fashions and fads, types of collective group behavior, are distinct from one another in terms of their duration, their predictability, and the number of people involved. Each type follows a five-stage process of development.</u>

A fashion is a temporary trend in behavior or appearance that is followed by a relatively large number of people. Although the word *fashion* often refers to a style of dress, there are fashions in music, art, and literature as well. Trends in clothing fashions are often engineered by clothing designers, advertisers, and the media to create a particular "look." The hip-hop look is an example of a heavily promoted fashion. Fashions are more universally subscribed to than fads. Wearing athletic shoes as casual attire is a good example of a universal fashion.

A fad is a more temporary adoption of a particular behavior or look. Fads are in-group behaviors that often serve as identity markers for a group. Fads also tend to be adopted by smaller groups, often made up of people who want to appear different or unconventional. Unlike fashions, fads tend to be shorter-lived, less predictable, and less influenced by people outside the group. Examples of recent fads are face tattoos, lab-created meat, and wearable technology. Fads are usually harmless and have no long-range effects.

Fashions and fads each follow a five-phase process of development. In the first phase, latency, the trend exists in the minds of a few people but shows little evidence of spreading. In the second phase, the trend spreads rapidly and reaches its peak. After that, the trend begins a slow decline (phase three). In the fourth phase, its newness is over and many users drop or abandon the trend. In its final phase, quiescence, nearly everyone has dropped the trend, and it is followed by only a few people.

Introduction: Includes only the thesis statement

Body paragraph 1: Definition and characteristics of *fashion*

Body paragraph 2: Definition and characteristics of *fad*

Body paragraph 3: Description of 5-phase process

Create Portfolios

A **portfolio** is a collection of materials that represents a person's work. It may be a digital file or a print collection of materials. It often demonstrates or exemplifies skill, talent, or proficiency. Architects create portfolios that contain drawings and photographs of buildings they have designed. Sculptors' portfolios may include photographs of their sculptures, as well as copies of reviews, awards, or articles about their work.

Similarly, your writing instructor may ask you to create a portfolio that represents your skill and proficiency as a writer. Think of your portfolio as a summary of your development as a writer over time.

Understand Your Purposes for Creating a Writing Portfolio

Instructors assign writing portfolios for two main reasons:

- **Grading and assessment.** Your instructor may use your collection of writing to evaluate your mastery of the objectives outlined in the course syllabus. That evaluation will become part of your final grade in the course.
- **Learning, reflection, and self-assessment.** Building a portfolio makes you think about yourself as a writer. By building a writing portfolio, you learn a great deal about the writing process, assess your strengths and weaknesses as a writer, and observe your own progress as you build writing proficiency.

Think of your writing portfolio as an opportunity to present yourself in the best possible way—highlighting the work you are proud of and demonstrating the skills you have mastered. It is also an opportunity, as you track your progress, to realize that your hard work in the course has paid off.

Decide What to Include in Your Portfolio

Instructors often specify what their students' portfolios should include. If you are uncertain about what to include, ask your instructor. You might ask to see a sample of a portfolio that meets your instructor's expectations.

To get the best grade on your portfolio, be sure you can answer each of the following questions about the portfolio and its contents:

- How many writing projects should I include? Are there limits to what I can include?
- Should the portfolio include only writing done in the course, or can I include materials I wrote for other courses or outside school (work-related email or service-learning projects, for example)?
- What version(s) should be included—drafts, outlines, and revisions or just the final drafts?
- Should writing projects be based on personal experience, research, or some combination of these?
- Is the portfolio limited to essays, or can multimedia projects (such as timelines or presentation slides), research notes, or completed class exercises also be included?
- How should the portfolio be organized?
- What type of introductory letter or essay is required? What length and format are appropriate?
- How much does the portfolio count in my grade?
- What is the due date, or is the portfolio to be submitted at various intervals throughout the term?
- How will it be graded? That is, is the grade based on improvement or only on the quality of the work included?

Use Your Course Syllabus as a Guide

Your course syllabus is an important guide to deciding what to include in your portfolio. If it contains objectives, which outline what your instructor wants you to learn in the course, you can use several or all of these objectives to structure your portfolio. If an objective states, "Students will demonstrate control over errors in sentence structure, spelling, and punctuation," you would want to include examples of essays in which you identified and corrected these types of errors. You might also include a list of exercises you completed to develop mastery.

Organize and Prepare to Present Your Portfolio

Begin collecting materials for your portfolio as soon as your instructor assigns it. If you wait until the due date to assemble what you need, you may have already discarded or misplaced important prewriting, revision materials, or drafts.

Use physical or online folders divided into sections to hold any of your prewriting, outlines, or graphic organizers. If you are including research materials, include your notes and annotated sources. Also keep peer-review comments as well as papers with your instructor's comments. Save backup copies of your files on a thumb drive or to the cloud.

Use the following suggestions to present a well-organized portfolio.

- **Cover page.** Include a cover or title page that provides your name, course number, instructor's name, and date. (Ask your instructor if you're not sure a title page is required.)
- **Table of contents.** Include a table of contents that identifies the elements in the portfolio and the page number (or a link) on which each piece begins. Number the portfolio consecutively from beginning to end. Since your essays may already have page numbers, put the new page numbers in a different position or use a different color font. If your instructor has not indicated how the contents should be sequenced, choose a method of organization that presents your work and skill development in the best possible way. For example, if you are including two writing projects to demonstrate your effective use of narration, you might present the better one first, thereby making the strongest possible first impression. If you are trying to show growth in your ability to use narration, you might present the stronger writing project second. Use Table 25.2 to guide your selection and sequence.
- **Reflective letter or essay.** Most instructors will expect you to include an essay or a letter that reflects on your development as a writer. This essay is the key to the portfolio, since it reflects on and explains the portfolio's contents. It should explain how your portfolio is organized and give an overview of its contents and why you chose them. It should also include an appraisal of what you learned in the course and discuss your strengths, weaknesses, and development as a writer. Point out specific examples in the portfolio to support your claims.
- **Drafts.** Attach earlier drafts to the final draft, or place all drafts in a single subfolder, clearly labeling each draft. Date and label each piece, identifying its place within your growth process so that your instructor knows what

TABLE 25.2 Guidelines for Building a Writing Portfolio

If you are asked to . . .	Include . . .
demonstrate your growth as a writer	• weak writing projects from early in the semester and your best writing projects from later in the semester • an essay that demonstrates major changes from first to final draft
demonstrate your ability to approach writing as a process	• work you did for topic selection, generating ideas, drafting, revising, and proofreading • first and final drafts that show your writing project gradually developing and evolving as you worked
feature your best work of the semester	• writing projects that solidly exemplify the method of organization you are using • writing projects that demonstrate your ability to develop and support ideas • writing projects that demonstrate thoughtfulness and creativity
demonstrate your ability to write for a variety of audiences and purposes	• writing projects for courses in different areas of study • pieces that use widely different tones or levels of diction • non-course-related, nonacademic, and multimedia compositions, if allowed
demonstrate your ability to use library and Internet sources	• research projects that cite sources accurately in a list of works cited or references • research projects that use both library and Internet sources rather than one or the other

it demonstrates. For example, if an essay demonstrates your ability to use narration, label it as such.

Your portfolio represents you. Be sure it is neat, complete, and carefully assembled.

What Should You Avoid?

Here are a few things to avoid when building your portfolio:

- **Avoid writing about writing in general.** Instead, write about what you learned about *your* writing. That is, do not repeat points from the textbook about the writing process. Instead, explain how you used that information to become a better writer.
- **Do not exaggerate your progress or say what you think the instructor wants to hear.** Instead, be honest and forthright in assessing your progress.
- **Avoid flattery or praise of the instructor or the course.** Most instructors will give you a separate opportunity to evaluate the course and their teaching methods.

Portfolio Contents and Reflective Letter

Bryan Scott

The portfolio assignment below was given to Bryan Scott, a nursing student and former Marine, for his first-year writing course.

Portfolio Assignment

For your final assignment you will submit a portfolio containing the following:

- A table of contents listing the titles and page numbers of all included writing pieces
- A reflective letter that introduces your portfolio
- One series of writing pieces (prewriting, outlines, drafts) that demonstrates your ability to move successfully through the steps in the writing process
- At least two pieces of writing that demonstrate your growth as a writer
- One piece of writing done this term for another class
- Essays that demonstrate your ability to use various methods of organization
- A limited number of materials of your own choice

In your reflective letter, include answers to the following questions.

1. What are your current strengths and weaknesses as a writer?
2. What specific writing skills have you developed?
3. How have you changed as a writer?
4. What critical reading and thinking skills have you learned, *or* in what ways have you strengthened your critical reading and thinking skills?

Scott organizes his reflective letter using the principles of good writing he learned in the course. Within this organization, he is able to identify his strengths and weaknesses as a writer throughout the letter and analyze his essays. Compare the assignment Scott received with his table of contents and reflective letter.

Scott 1

Bryan Scott

May 16, 2020

Final Portfolio

English 109

From the Marines to the Writing Classroom

I enrolled in this course because it was a required course in my
nursing curriculum, but I can now say that I am glad that it was required.
As a former Marine, I had little experience with writing, other than
writing emails and texts to my wife and parents. Now, as I prepare for a
career as a nurse, I realize that writing is an important communication
skill. Writing reports about patients, such as "Nursing Care Plan: Patient
4," requires me to present clear, precise, and accurate information about
patients and their care. Through this course I have learned to do so.
Although I improved in almost every area of writing, my greatest
improvements were in approaching writing as a process, moving from
personal to informative writing, and developing an awareness of
audience.

Through this course I have learned to view writing as a process rather
than a "write-it-once-and-I-am-done" activity. As shown in the packet of
writing for "The Wall at Sunset," I have discovered the value of prewriting
as a way of coming up with ideas. Before I started writing this essay,

1

2

I knew that visiting the Vietnam Veterans Memorial had been an emotional experience for me, but I found that mapping helped me define and organize my feelings. My first draft in the packet demonstrates my ability to begin with a thesis statement and build ideas around it. My second draft shows how I added detail and arranged my impressions into an organized essay. My final draft shows my ability to catch most errors in spelling, grammar, and punctuation.

Moving from personal writing to informative writing was a valuable learning experience that is essential for my career. My first essay, "The Wall at Sunset," was a very personal account of my visit to the Vietnam Veterans Memorial, as was the essay "How the Marines Changed My Life," a personal account of life in the U.S. Marine Corps. While I had a lot to say about my own experiences, I found it difficult to write about topics that did not directly involve me. I found that learning to use sources, especially online sources, helped me get started with informative writing. By visiting news Web sites, doing online and library research, and reading blogs, I learned to move outside of myself and begin to think about and become interested in what other people were saying and thinking. My essay "Miracle in the Operating Room" demonstrates my ability to use sources, both print and digital, to learn how kidney transplants are done.

As I moved from personal to informative writing, I found that the patterns of development provided a framework for developing and organizing informative writing. Process seemed to be an effective way to present information for the essay "Miracle in the Operating Room." My essay "Emotional Styles of Athletes" initially contained a lot of my own personal impressions (see the first draft that I have included), but by using classification, I was able to focus on characteristics of athletes rather than on my opinions of them.

Before I took this course, I had no idea that I should write differently for different audiences. My essay "How the Marines Changed My Life"

Scott 3

was written for my classmates, many of whom had no military experience. I found I had to explain things about chain of command, regimentation, and living conditions—all things that I and other Marines are familiar with. In my case report for my nursing class, "Nursing Care Plan: Patient 4," my audience was other nurses and medical staff, even doctors. Because I was writing for a specialized audience, I could mention medical terms, procedures, and medications freely without defining them. However, in "Miracle in the Operating Room," I was writing for a general, nonspecialized audience, so I realized it was necessary to explain terms such as *dialysis*, *laparoscopy*, and *nephrectomy*. This essay and my nursing case report demonstrate my ability to write in a clear, direct, and concise manner in my chosen field for different audiences.

While I developed many strengths as a writer, I am still aware of many weaknesses. I have difficulty with descriptive writing; I just cannot come up with words to paint a visual picture as effectively as I would like. Fortunately, nursing will not require much creative description. I also have difficulty choosing a topic. Although I found the suggestions in our textbook helpful, I still feel as if I am overlooking important or useful topics. Finally, I have not benefited from peer review as much as others have. I still find myself uncomfortable when accepting criticism and revision ideas from other students. Perhaps my military training to look to authority for direction is still getting in the way.

6

As I developed strengths as a writer, I also became a more critical reader and thinker. I am enclosing my annotations for the professional essay "Bad Conduct, by the Numbers." These annotations demonstrate my ability to ask questions and challenge the author. I also found enlightening discussions in the text on connotative language, bias, and fact and opinion. These are things I had never thought much about, and now I find myself being aware of these things as I read. Overall, by taking this course, I have become a more serious and aware writer and have come to regard writing as a rewarding challenge.

7

26
Multimedia Presentations and Business Writing

Writing Quick Start

ANALYZE   The photograph on this page depicts a speaker making a presentation on the topic of refugees entering countries via boat. Imagine you are making a presentation on this issue. What information would you need to speak clearly and effectively to your audience?

WRITE   Draft a list of questions that you would need answered before preparing your presentation.

CONNECT   In addition to questions about refugee immigration, you would need to define your purpose and understand the makeup of your audience. You might also ask what multimedia options are available. Success in college and on the job depends on your ability to speak effectively to your audience and to communicate clearly, correctly, and concisely. In college, your professors may use oral presentations to assess their students' understanding of a topic or issue. On the job, presentations are used to sell products, make proposals, and respond to issues and problems. In this chapter you will learn to make effective multimedia presentations. You will also learn other important business-related skills, including creating a résumé, writing a job application letter, and using electronic media in the workplace.

In this chapter you will learn to

- **prepare and deliver multimedia presentations**
- **create a résumé and job application letter**
- **use electronic media for workplace communication**

Both college and the workplace demand strong oral and digital communication skills. In college, your grades may depend on them; in the workplace, your career success may hinge upon them.

> **MULTIMEDIA PRESENTATIONS** ▶ **IN COLLEGE AND THE WORKPLACE**
>
> - For a *sociology class*, you conduct field research on college students' attitudes about a particular trend and report your findings.
> - For a *public speaking class*, you make a presentation about learned helplessness, an important concept in your first-year psychology class.
> - As a *sales representative* for a Web site design company, you create and give a presentation to a group of restaurant owners to demonstrate how revamping their Web sites with photographs and customer reviews can increase their visibility and profitability.

Develop and Deliver Multimedia Presentations

A **multimedia presentation** is a presentation to an audience—either face-to-face or online—using visual aids. The visual aids may be a simple prop or poster or presentation slides that may include graphics, video, sound files, animation, and other media. By learning to give a presentation to an audience, you will gain self-confidence and become a more effective communicator.

Plan Your Presentation

The more carefully you plan your presentation, the more comfortable you will be in delivering it. The sections that follow detail the steps to follow in planning a presentation.

For more on choosing and narrowing a topic, see Chapter 4.

Select your topic. First, make sure you understand the assignment and the type of presentation you are to give. Then consider your audience: What topics are important to your listeners and will sustain their interest? Here are a few suggestions for choosing a topic:

- **Choose a topic that you find interesting or know something about.** You will find it easier to exude and generate enthusiasm if you speak about a topic that is familiar and that you enjoy.
- **Choose a topic that is appropriate and of value to your audience.** Learning how to choose a day care center may be of value to young parents, but you may have difficulty sustaining the interest of average college students with such a topic. Trivial topics such as how to create a particular hairstyle or a report about characters on a soap opera are unlikely to have sufficient merit for college instructors.

- **Choose a topic you can explain fully in the time allotted.** If your topic is too broad, your presentation will go over time, or you may resort to generalities that lack supporting evidence.

Identify your purpose.   Determine whether your purpose is to express, inform, or persuade. Then define your purpose more specifically. For a persuasive presentation, for example, do you want to convince the audience that a change in policy is needed or simply to encourage them to consider the issue with an open mind?

For more information on determining your purpose, see Chapter 4.

Research your topic.   Unless your presentation is to be based on your personal knowledge or experience, you will need to research your topic.

For more on researching, see Chapters 21 and 22.

Consider what type of visual aids are appropriate.   Visual aids, from maps and photographs to Prezi or PowerPoint presentation slides with embedded sound and video files, add interest to your presentation and can be used to reinforce your message and make your ideas clear and concrete. Use flip charts or presentation slides to show your main points in outline form, which may make your presentation easier to follow. Presentation programs also allow you to integrate sound, photo, and video files into your presentation seamlessly. Ask your instructor what is permissible and what media are available for classroom use.

Some speakers find that using visual aids builds their confidence and lessens their apprehension. Such aids distract speakers from thinking about themselves and how they look, and lessen concerns that speakers will forget what they were planning to say to their audience. However, presentation slides must be used effectively to avoid "Death by PowerPoint."

To learn more about using presentation slides effectively, see the section "Create Presentation Slides" later in this chapter.

Draft Your Presentation

Once you have made a plan, begin drafting your presentation.

Develop a thesis and generate supporting ideas.   Based on your research, create a working thesis. Use idea-generating strategies to develop a variety of supporting reasons, and consider which will be most effective, given your purpose and audience.

For idea-generating strategies, see Chapter 4; for more about developing and supporting a thesis, see Chapter 5.

Organize your presentation.   Using one of the patterns of organization from Parts 3 and 4 will make your presentation easier for your audience to follow and for you to remember the order of your main points. For example, you could use classification to organize a presentation on types of procrastinators, providing four main categories of procrastinators with descriptive details to explain each. When organizing, consider saving your most convincing evidence or examples for last, as audience members are likely to recall the end of your presentation more clearly than the beginning.

For more on organizing, see Chapter 7. Also see the chapters in Part 3 for planning presentations using one of the patterns of development.

Draft the body of your presentation.   When you write an essay, your readers can reread if they miss a point. When you give a presentation, your listeners do not have that option, so reiterate your thesis frequently to make your presentation easier to follow, and use plenty of transitions to ensure that your listeners do not get lost.

(Presentation slides showing your main points in the order you present them can also help your audience follow along.)

Select evidence that your audience would find convincing. Including different types of evidence that reinforce one another, such as statistics to support the examples you include, will help listeners recall your main points. Emotional appeals can be more memorable for an audience than statistics, but reinforce any emotional appeals you make with concrete evidence. Including meaningful evidence adds credibility to your presentation.

To learn more about emotional appeals, see Chapter 19.

Work references to your sources into your presentation.   Use signal phrases to incorporate references to authors or works (or both), and include background information about the author or work, to provide context. If you use quotations, avoid tedious expressions such as "I quote here" or "I want to quote an example." Instead, integrate your quotations into your speech as you would integrate quotations into an essay.

To learn more about using signal phrases and integrating quotations, see Chapter 23.

Draft your introduction and conclusion.   Your introduction should grab your audience's attention, introduce your topic, and establish a relationship between you and your audience. To build a relationship with your audience, try to make connections with them. You might mention others who are present; refer to a shared situation (a previous class or another student's presentation); or establish common ground by referring to a well-known event, personality, or campus issue.

To learn more about writing introductions and conclusions, see Chapter 7.

Your conclusion is a crucial part of your presentation because it is your last opportunity to leave a strong impression on your audience. You should summarize your speech and let the audience know your presentation is ending. The conclusion should also remind listeners of the importance of your topic. Consider closing with a powerful quotation or anecdote that reinforces your main point.

Create Presentation Slides

Presentation software, like PowerPoint and Prezi, allows you to list or summarize your main points and to embed multimedia evidence—audio, video, and image files—in support of your claims. While PowerPoint allows a linear presentation of electronic slides, Prezi allows zooming in and out of specific parts of your presentation. (**Hint:** To create a presentation using Prezi, start by drawing an idea map and use that map to plan an easy-to-follow path through the presentation.)

- **Use presentation software to aid understanding.** Project key words or concepts you want to emphasize or provide an outline so your audience can follow your main points.
- **Use a design template that suits your audience and purpose.** A simple color scheme with a sharp contrast between text and background will be easiest to read. Avoid using reds and greens if differences between the two colors are significant, because color-blind members of the audience will not be able to differentiate between them. Use subdued color schemes and easily readable fonts (such as Arial or Verdana) for business or academic presentations. For PowerPoint slides, use just a few animation schemes (how text enters and leaves a slide) consistently.

- **Format your slides so they are easily readable.** Use a large point size (usually 24 points or greater) so everyone in the audience can read the text easily. Keep the number of words per slide low: Slides crammed with text are difficult to read, and if audience members are busy reading lengthy slides, they are not listening to what you are saying. A good rule of thumb is to use no more than six bullet points per slide, with no more than six words per bullet point. (If you can do so clearly, use just words and phrases rather than complete sentences.)
- **Use presentation software to display visuals and graphics.** Photos, cartoons, graphics, and embedded videos can convey your message in a memorable way. They also keep your audience interested and alert. But keep graphics simple, so the audience can take them in at a glance, and use visuals and graphics only when they are relevant to your point, not just as decoration.
- **Edit your slides carefully.** Check for errors in spelling, grammar, and formatting as well as other kinds of typos. Run the entire slide show for yourself several times before presenting it to correct any errors you find.

On the next page is a sample Prezi presentation designed by student Nicholas Destino, whose research project appears in Chapter 23. He used his research to create this presentation for his first-year composition class. This introductory slide shows all the slides at once; as he navigates through his presentation, the Prezi zooms in on each circle, enlarging it, so audience members can easily read the text. Destino included a list of works cited at the end of his presentation to document the sources he used.

Rehearse Your Presentation

Practice is the key to comfortable and effective delivery. The following tips can help you rehearse effectively:

- **Practice giving the entire presentation, not just parts of it.** Rehearse at least three or four times, using your visual aids. Try to improve your presentation with each rehearsal.
- **Time yourself.** If you are over or seriously under the time limit, make necessary cuts or additions, and edit your presentation slides accordingly.
- **If possible, rehearse the presentation in the room in which you will give it.** This will make you more comfortable on the day of the presentation and gives you an opportunity to find out in advance if the room can support the technology you plan to use.
- **Rehearse in front of an audience of a few friends or classmates.** Ask them for constructive criticism. Some students record their presentations on their smart phones to build their confidence and identify areas that need improvement.

Overcome Stage Fright

Many students are nervous about making presentations. Often called *stage fright*, this apprehension is normal. You can often overcome presentation anxiety by following these suggestions:

- **Prepare thoroughly.** Knowing you have put together a solid, interesting presentation can build your self-confidence.

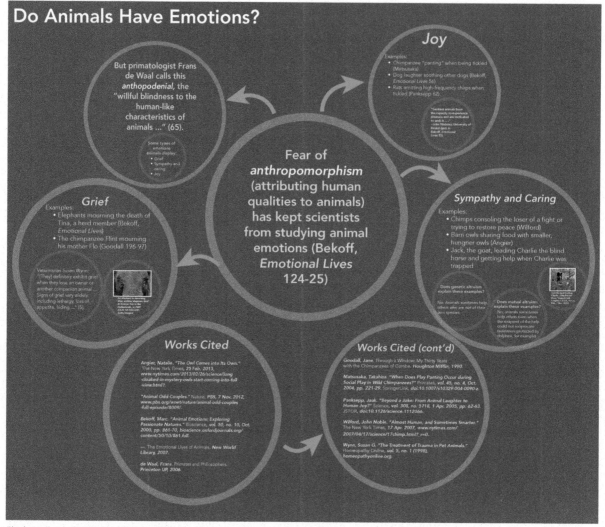

Do Animals Have Emotions?

Joy

Examples:
• Chimpanzee "panting" when being tickled (Matsusaka)
• Dog laughter soothing other dogs (Bekoff, Emotional Lives 56)
• Rats emitting high-frequency chirps when tickled (Panksepp 62)

"Sentient animals have the capacity to experience pleasure and are motivated to seek it ..."
—John Webster, University of Bristol (qtd. in Bekoff, Emotional Lives 55)

But primatologist Frans de Waal calls this *anthropodenial*, the "willful blindness to the human-like characteristics of animals ..." (65).

Some types of emotions animals display:
• Grief
• Sympathy and caring
• Joy

Fear of *anthropomorphism* (attributing human qualities to animals) has kept scientists from studying animal emotions (Bekoff, *Emotional Lives* 124-25)

Sympathy and Caring

Examples:
• Chimps consoling the loser of a fight or trying to restore peace (Wilford)
• Barn owls sharing food with smaller, hungrier owls (Angier)
• Jack, the goat, leading Charlie the blind horse and getting help when Charlie was trapped

Does genetic altruism explain these examples?

No. Animals sometimes help others who are not of their own species.

Does mutual altruism explain these examples?
No, animals sometimes help others even when the recipient of the help could not reciprocate (swimmers protected by dolphins, for example).

Grief

Examples:
• Elephants mourning the death of Tina, a herd member (Bekoff, Emotional Lives)
• The chimpanzee Flint mourning his mother Flo (Goodall 196-97)

Veterinarian Susan Wynn: "[They] definitely exhibit grief when they lose an owner or another companion animal ... Signs of grief vary widely, including lethargy, loss of appetite, hiding ..." (5).

An elephant in mourning. Mike and her elephant died at Science Tree in the Netherlands, in 2007. OLAF KRAAK/AFP, Getty Images

Works Cited

Angier, Natalie. "The Owl Comes into Its Own." *The New York Times*, 25 Feb. 2013, www.nytimes.com/2013/02/26/science/long-cloaked-in-mystery-owls-start-coming-into-full-view.html?.

"Animal Odd Couples." *Nature*, PBS, 7 Nov. 2012, www.pbs.org/wnet/nature/animal-odd-couples-full-episode/8009/.

Bekoff, Marc. "Animal Emotions: Exploring Passionate Natures." *Bioscience*, vol. 50, no. 10, Oct. 2000, pp. 861-70, bioscience.oxfordjournals.org/content/50/10/861.full.

— The Emotional Lives of Animals. *New World Library*, 2007.

de Waal, Frans. *Primates and Philosophers*. Princeton UP, 2006.

Works Cited (cont'd)

Goodall, Jane. *Through a Window: My Thirty Years with the Chimpanzees of Gombe*. Houghton Mifflin, 1990.

Matsusaka, Takahisa. "When Does Play Panting Occur during Social Play in Wild Chimpanzees?" *Primates*, vol. 45, no. 4, Oct. 2004, pp. 221-29. SpringerLink, doi:10.1007/s10329-004-0090-z.

Panksepp, Jaak. "Beyond a Joke: From Animal Laughter to Human Joy?" *Science*, vol. 308, no. 5718, 1 Apr. 2005, pp. 62-63. JSTOR, doi:10.1126/science.1112066.

Wilford, John Noble. "Almost Human, and Sometimes Smarter." *The New York Times*, 17 Apr. 2007, www.nytimes.com/2007/04/17/science/17chimp.html?_r=0.

Wynn, Susan G. "The Treatment of Trauma in Pet Animals." *Homeopathy Online*, vol. 5, no. 1 (1998), homeopathyonline.org.

Elephant photo: OLAF KRAAK/Stringer/Getty Images

- **Practice, practice, practice.** To reduce the newness of the task, practice your presentation several times. (See the previous section on rehearsal.)
- **Use desensitization.** If someone is afraid of snakes, a therapist might begin by showing the person a photograph, then a video, then a small snake at a distance, and so forth, gradually building up the person's tolerance. You can use the same technique to overcome your fear of oral presentations. Begin by asking or answering a question in class. Then try practicing your speech on a group of friends. Eventually you will become more comfortable with public speaking and ready to make a presentation to the class.

- **Use visualization.** Visualization involves imagining yourself successfully completing a task. For a presentation, create a mental recording that begins with your arrival at the classroom and takes you through each step: confidently walking to the front of the room, beginning your presentation, engaging your audience, handling your notes, and so on. Visualize the presentation positively, and avoid negative thoughts, to create the image of yourself as a successful speaker. Review your visualized performance often, especially on the day of your presentation. As you give your presentation, try to model the look and feel of your visualization.
- **Imagine a friend in the audience.** If you feel conspicuous, try to imagine that you are talking to one friend or one friendly and supportive classmate. Looking directly at one member of the audience at the beginning of your presentation can help.

Deliver an Effective Presentation

The delivery of your presentation ultimately determines its effectiveness. Use the suggestions below, as well as Table 26.1, to improve the delivery of your presentation:

- **Avoid using too many notes or a detailed outline.** Instead, construct a key-word outline that will remind you of major points in the order you wish to present them.

TABLE 26.1 Frequently Asked Questions for Making Presentations

Question	Suggested Solutions
What should I do if I go blank?	Refer to your notes or presentation slides.
	Ask if there are any questions. Even if no one asks any, the pause will give you time to regroup.
What should I do if classmates are restless, uninterested, or even rude?	Make eye contact with as many members of the class as possible as you speak.
	For a particularly troublesome person, you might lengthen your eye contact.
	Change the tone or pitch of your voice.
	Try to make your speech more engaging by asking questions or using personal examples.
What should I do if I accidentally omit an important part of the presentation?	Go back and add it in. Say something like, "I neglected to mention . . ." and present the portion you skipped.
What if I realize that my speech will be too short or too long?	If you realize it will be too short, try to add examples, anecdotes, or more detailed information.
	If you realize it will be too long, cut out examples or summarize instead of fully explaining sections that are less important.

- **Make eye contact with your audience.** Make the audience part of your presentation.
- **Move around a little rather than standing stiffly.** Use gestures to add an expressive quality to your presentation.
- **Speak slowly.** Speaking too fast is a common mistake, but try not to overcompensate by speaking so slowly that your audience loses interest.

Prepare and Deliver Online Presentations

At some point in your education or career, you may be asked to use an online meeting application, such as GoToMeeting or WebEx, which allows you to conduct virtual meetings with instructors, colleagues, clients, and vendors. These applications allow others to view what you have on your computer screen, so you can pull up documents, spreadsheets, presentation slides, and anything else for everyone to look at together in real time. You may communicate by phone, with Zoom, or via Google Hangouts or another online system. The following tips will help you give an effective Web-based presentation:

- **Become familiar with the technology in advance.** Your audience may become restless if you cannot resolve technical difficulties quickly.
- **Review all documents and materials prior to the meeting.** Be sure you know where to find the documents you need to display.
- **Prepare thoroughly, but be ready to adjust your presentation in response to questions from the audience.** You should know the content well enough to respond to a question or comment that draws you away from your prepared remarks.
- **Turn off all notifications and programs that are running on your computer.** You do not want an email from a friend popping up on your screen while you are delivering a presentation.

Create Effective Business Documents

Business writing will be an important part of your life after college. Good business writing is concise and correct. It is often more direct than some forms of academic or personal writing. Because you are judged on the business documents that you write, prepare materials that will present you and your accomplishments in the best light possible.

Prepare a Résumé and Job Application Letter

A **résumé** (Figure 26.1) is a complete listing of your education, training, and work experience in an easy-to-read format. A **job application (or cover) letter** (Figure 26.2) highlights the qualifications that make you right for the job and convinces the employer that you are an excellent candidate for the opening. Because your application packet will determine whether a potential employer will interview you, tailor each one to the job for which you are applying.

FIGURE 26.1   Sample Résumé

Martin Simms

20600 Main Street • Silver Spring, MD 20906

301-555-5555 • martin.simms@gmail.com

Objective

A marine science internship at Phillips Wharf Environmental Center

Education

B.S., Biology (GPA 3.5)   Expected May 2020
    University of Maryland, College Park

A.S., Science (GPA 3.7)   May 2018
    Montgomery College, Rockville Campus

Volunteer Experience

Guide, Underground Railroad Experience Hike   2017–Present
    Woodlawn Manor Culture Park
    Montgomery County, MD

Coordinator, Green Club   2016–2017
    Oak View Elementary School
    Silver Spring, MD

Relevant Skills

Completed Science and Math Coursework

- Proficient at applying mathematics in a laboratory setting
- Completed calculus for life sciences, principles of genetics, principles of chemistry II (3.8 average)

Works Well in a Group

- Effectively collaborate with a diverse group of people
- Ensure work is split equally and fairly among teammates
- Maintain a constant pace when working with a group

Experienced in Interacting with the Public

- Succinctly convey a message to people, regardless of their background knowledge
- Ensure audience stays engaged by reading nonverbal cues from patrons
- Remain positive when faced with a difficult patron
- Tailor lessons to meet the needs of different audiences

Works Well with Children

- Vary content to suit a child's age and interest levels
- Devise fun activities suitable to children of different ages

References

Available on request

Contact information: Displayed at the top of the page

Headings: Boldfaced type used to make résumé easy to read

Organization: Reverse chronological order used for information under Education and Volunteer Experience, so most recent item listed first

Student currently with little experience, so skills categorized by topic

Key words: Key words from job advertisement used so skills and experience match words in employer's electronic job database

Proofreading: Résumé proofread carefully to correct spelling, punctuation, and capitalization errors

FIGURE 26.2   Sample Job Application Letter

Block style: Standard block style used (double line space between paragraphs, type aligned at left edge)

Formatting: Return address appears at top of page

Formatting: Inside address follows the date

Salutation: Letter begins with salutation ("Dear Ms. Cannon:")

Content: Opening paragraph identifies desired position; second and third paragraphs describe relevant details of Martin Simms's volunteer experience, not everything in résumé

Content: Fourth paragraph provides contact information

Closing: The letter ends with standard closing: "Sincerely"; signature follows closing, with name typed below

---

20600 Main Street
Silver Spring, MD 20906

February 29, 2020

Ms. Melissa Cannon, Administrator
Phillips Wharf Environmental Center
6129 Tilghman Island Road
Tilghman, MD 21671

Dear Ms. Cannon:

I am writing in response to your advertisement for a marine science intern. I believe that I am an ideal applicant: Not only am I a biology major, but I also have volunteer experience educating the public (both adults and children).

As a volunteer on the Underground Railroad Experience Hike, I work closely with another guide to write and deliver a coordinated, professional presentation simulating the Underground Railroad experience. Our presentation explains how those seeking freedom found their way north and survived on the trail and is tailored to the audience. (We highlight different elements for an audience of Cub Scouts than we do for a group of seniors from Leisure World.)

Interacting with children is a particular strength of mine: As coordinator of the Oak View Elementary School Green Club, I created entertaining activities for children in grades three through five that taught them about the importance of environmental preservation while also engaging their attention.

I believe that my skills meet the needs of your internship, especially regarding my proven ability to work with children. I would welcome the opportunity to discuss at your convenience how my qualifications can meet your needs. I can be contacted at 301-944-2222 or at martin.simms@gmail.com.

Thank you for considering my application. I look forward to hearing from you.

Sincerely,

Martin Simms

Martin Simms

Most employers invite applicants to upload résumés and job application (or cover) letters to their Web sites or to send the application letter as an email message with the résumé attached. If you are sending a hard copy résumé and job application letter, print both documents on good-quality white paper.

Follow these tips when preparing your résumé:

- **Tailor your résumé.** Do not create a one-size-fits-all résumé. Instead, tailor it to the specific job you are applying for. Use key words from the advertisement (such as *marine science intern*) and active verbs (*collaborate, devise*) to show what you can do.

- **Simple is best.** Prepare your résumé as a document with an unlined, white background, as if you were going to print it on 8½- x 11-inch paper. Leave 1-inch margins on all sides. Do not include graphics, colors, or elaborate underlining and formatting. If possible, save your résumé in PDF format. Be sure to check it carefully before sending.

- **Display your name, address, and contact information at the top of the page.** Check that your contact information is correct. (A computer's spell-check function will not identify such mistakes.)

- **Fit your résumé onto a single page whenever possible.** If providing a printed copy, use only one side of an 8½- x 11-inch sheet of paper. Write clearly and concisely, and use categories (such as "Education," "Experience," and "Skills") so that potential employers can scan your résumé quickly.

- **List education and experience, in reverse chronological order.** Include dates you attended school or received a degree, listing your most recent education and experience first. If your relevant experience is scant (as it is for many new college graduates), include a section highlighting your skills.

- **Specify how the employer can obtain your references.** This is usually done by stating, "References are available on request," but be prepared to supply references by asking instructors or previous employers whether they are willing to give you a good recommendation and whether you can share their contact information with prospective employers.

- **Proofread carefully.** Résumés must be clear, concise, and free of errors in grammar, punctuation, mechanics, and spelling.

For more about proofreading, see Chapter 9.

Follow these tips when writing a job application letter or email:

- **Use standard business formats.** Block-style business letters have one-inch margins on all sides and are single-spaced, with an extra line space between paragraphs. All type is aligned at the left edge of the page. (The sample job application letter in Figure 26.2 is in block style.) Use letterhead or list your address at the top of the page. The date should appear below your address, and the address of the person to whom you are writing should appear below the date. Job applications, like résumés, should be prepared with a white, unlined background.

- **Include a formal salutation and closing.** Begin with "Dear Ms._____:" or "Dear Mr. _____:" and call the company for a name if you are unsure to whom you should address your letter. Close with "Sincerely," or "Yours truly," followed by your signature. Formal salutations and closings are appropriate, even when sending a job application by email.

- **Include key information in the body.** If submitting your job application letter by email, use the subject line to identify the job you are applying for. In both job application emails and letters, identify the job you are applying for in the opening paragraph. You may also indicate where you learned about the position or where it was posted or listed. The middle paragraphs should briefly state the skills and experiences that make you especially qualified. (Do not repeat everything you have listed in your résumé.) At the end of the letter, indicate that you are available for an interview at the employer's convenience or specify when you are available.
- **Proofread carefully.** If job application letters or emails are not clear, concise, and free of errors in grammar, punctuation, mechanics, and spelling, they are likely to wind up in the "reject" pile.
- **Follow instructions for uploading your documents.** If you are applying by email, be sure to double-check that you have attached your résumé before hitting "send."

Use Electronic Media for Business Writing

In your career, you will likely use digital media—email (Figure 26.3) but perhaps also Slack, Twitter, LinkedIn, and interoffice information management systems—as your main means of communication. Follow the tips below to communicate effectively with supervisors, colleagues, clients, and other business contacts.

For more about writing concisely, see Chapter 9.

- **Keep it brief and get right to the point.** Typically the most important information is in the first paragraph. Paragraphs are usually only one to three sentences long, and wordiness is frowned upon. Messages overall are usually brief (just a few paragraphs), so they can be scanned quickly for important information. If more detail is required, supporting documents may be attached.
- **Do not say anything you do not want shared.** Online communications can easily be forwarded to others. Remember at all times that you are representing your employer and serving as the voice of your company. Do not say anything in an email that you would not say to your entire company and all your clients.
- **Use a specific and relevant subject line.** Using a specific and relevant subject line is crucial, not only so recipients can know how to prioritize the communications they receive, but also to locate important messages later. Without a subject line that clearly references a client, case number, file name, or other specific identifier, a message can be impossible to retrieve. Be particularly careful when replying that you adjust the subject line as needed.

For more about tone and level of diction, see Chapter 9.

- **Write in complete words and sentences and with a moderately formal tone.** Avoid online slang (such as *LOL* and *OMG*) and emoticons (such as the smiley face), avoid writing in all capital or all lowercase letters, and always reread messages to be sure the tone is cordial and professional. Abbreviations are acceptable, but only if your recipient will understand them.
- **Copy only people who need to be informed about the topic.** Do not automatically "carbon copy" (cc) your boss or everyone else in your company on every message. Avoid "Reply all" unless the content of your reply is truly relevant to "all."
- **Remember to attach relevant files.** It makes more work for everyone if you forget to include the attachment.

FIGURE 26.3 Sample Business Email

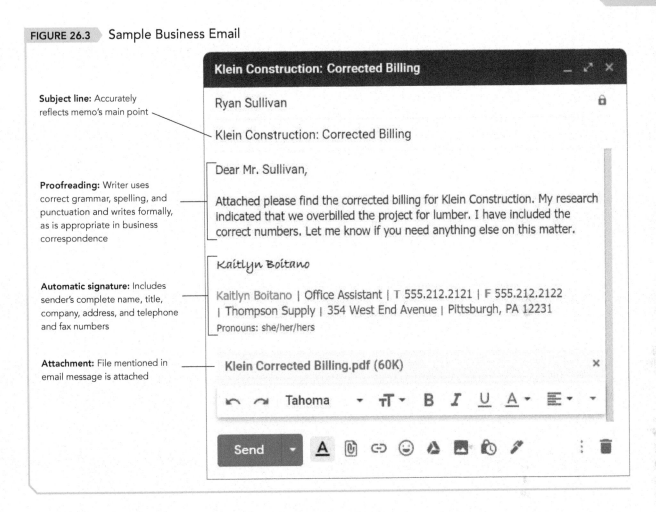

Subject line: Accurately reflects memo's main point

Proofreading: Writer uses correct grammar, spelling, and punctuation and writes formally, as is appropriate in business correspondence

Automatic signature: Includes sender's complete name, title, company, address, and telephone and fax numbers

Attachment: File mentioned in email message is attached

Klein Construction: Corrected Billing

Ryan Sullivan

Klein Construction: Corrected Billing

Dear Mr. Sullivan,

Attached please find the corrected billing for Klein Construction. My research indicated that we overbilled the project for lumber. I have included the correct numbers. Let me know if you need anything else on this matter.

Kaitlyn Boitano

Kaitlyn Boitano | Office Assistant | T 555.212.2121 | F 555.212.2122 | Thompson Supply | 354 West End Avenue | Pittsburgh, PA 12231
Pronouns: she/her/hers

Klein Corrected Billing.pdf (60K)

Tahoma   B *I* U A ▼

Send

- **Use an automatic signature file.** An automatic signature should include your name, title, company address, and telephone and fax numbers so that people can contact you easily. Some companies may also require the writer to include preferred pronouns.
- **Proofread carefully.** You are a representative of your business, so take the time to communicate concisely and professionally, and proofread your messages carefully before sending.

PART SEVEN

Handbook: Writing Problems and How to Correct Them

Review Basic Grammar

1   Parts of Speech

Each word in a sentence acts as one of eight parts of speech: *nouns, pronouns, verbs, adjectives, adverbs, conjunctions, prepositions,* and *interjections*. These building blocks of our language are summarized in Table H1.1. Often, to revise your writing or to correct sentence errors, you need to understand how a word or phrase functions in a particular sentence.

TABLE H1.1 ▶ Parts of Speech

Part of Speech	Definition/Primary Function	Examples
Noun	Names a person, place, thing, or idea	

	A **proper noun** refers to a specific person, place, thing, or idea and should be capitalized.	• Proper nouns:
		  • Person: *Jane Smith*
		  • Place: *Texas*
		  • Thing: *Xbox*
		  • Idea: *Marxism*

	A **common noun** refers to a person, place, thing, or idea in general and should not be capitalized.	• Common nouns:
		  • Person: *waiter*
		  • Place: *classroom*
		  • Thing: *textbook*
		  • Idea: *excitement*

	A **count noun** names items that can be counted.	• Count nouns: *artist, bike, town*
	A **noncount noun** names items that cannot easily be counted.	• Noncount nouns: *rain, traffic, mail*
Pronoun	Takes the place of a noun	Pronouns: • *I, me, my, mine* • *You, your, yours* • *He, his, she, her, hers, it, its, they, their, theirs*
	The noun to which a pronoun refers is called its **antecedent**. *Note:* Individuals may prefer a gender-neutral pronoun, such as *zie* or *ve* (for *he/she*) or *hir* or *vir* (for *him/her*). Both MLA and APA styles endorse respecting this preference and suggest using *they* in a gender-neutral way (such as *Nik called their parents last week*) if a person's preferred pronoun is unknown.	• *I* have several questions about the job. • *You* really should try to help *your* father more. • The *managers* believe *they* are being true to *their* values, but *their* stubbornness will be *their* undoing. • Is this iPad *mine* or *yours*?

(continued on next page) ▶

TABLE H1.1 Parts of Speech (continued)

Part of Speech	Definition/Primary Function	Examples
Verb	Shows action, occurrence, or a state of being **Types of verbs:**	
	• **Action verbs** express physical or mental activities.	Action verbs: *grows, grew, thinks, thought*
	• **Linking verbs** show existence, explaining what something is, was, or will become.	Linking verbs: *am, is, are, was, were, be, being, been, appear, become, feel, grow, look, prove, remain, seem, smell, sound, stay, taste*
	• **Helping verbs (plus action or linking verb)** indicate tense, mood, or voice.	Verb phrases (with helping verbs in italics): • *can* help, *could* go • *have* seen, *had* created • *may* visit, *might have* cried • *shall* meet, *should* plan • *will* live, *would* awaken
	Verb tenses:	
	• **Simple tenses** indicate when an action occurs (past, present, future).	Simple tenses: • Present: He *performs* his own stunts. • Past: The doctor *treated* him and *sent* him home. • Future: The play *will begin* on time.
	• **Perfect tenses** indicate that an action was or will be finished before some other action.	Perfect tenses: • Present: The mayor *has followed* their progress closely. • Past: The birds *had eaten* all the berries before we knew they were ripe. • Future: By next year, the apprentice *will have become* an expert.
	• **Progressive tenses** indicate that the action does, did, or will continue.	Progressive tenses: • Present: The governor *is considering* a Senate campaign. • Past: They *were expecting* guests. • Future: It is a long flight; we *will be sitting* for hours.
Adjective	Modifies a noun or pronoun by describing it, limiting it, or giving more information about it Answers one of these questions:	
	• Which one? • What kind? • How many?	• The *cutest* puppy belongs to the neighbors. • Use only *academic* sources for the paper. • *Japanese* tourists are visiting by the busload. • *Several* friends are visiting for the weekend. • He read *eight* books by Stephen King.
	Some are combined with specific prepositions *Note:* Articles (*a, an, the*) are considered adjectives.	Common adjective/preposition pairs: *interested in, afraid of, full of, proud of, suspicious of, tired of, grateful for (thing), responsible for (thing or action), sorry for, grateful to (person), responsible to (person), satisfied with*

Part of Speech	Definition/Primary Function	Examples
Adverb	Modifies a verb, adjective, other adverb, or entire sentence.	
	Often end in -ly	
	Answers one of these questions:	
	• How?	• The Rolling Stones performed *brilliantly*.
	• When?	• *Later*, they met to discuss the proposal.
	• Where?	• The taxi driver headed *downtown*.
	• How often?	• The bobcat is *rarely* seen in the wild.
	• To what extent?	• He agreed to cooperate *fully* with the investigation.
	Appear in a specific order:	
	• Possessives before numbers	• *Anita's three papers* were accepted.
	• Ordinal numbers before cardinal numbers	• *James's first three requests* were denied.
	• Descriptive adjectives in order as numbered:	• *Beautiful large white horse*
	1. Article/possessive noun: *an, Joe's, these*	• *Juan's nasty old gray tweed coat*
	2. Opinion: *favorite, hideous*	• *An expensive, new red British sports car*
	3. Size: *huge, tiny*	
	4. Shape: *round, square*	
	5. Age: *teenaged, three-year-old*	
	6. Color: *blue, green*	
	7. National origin: *English, Vietnamese*	
	8. Religion: *Catholic, Jewish, Muslim*	
	9. Matter or substance: *crystal, tweed*	
	10. Noun as adjective: *book* jacket, *picture* frame	
Conjunction	Connects words, **phrases** (groups of words that lack a subject, a predicate, or both—see Section 2b), or **clauses** (groups of words that contain both a subject and a predicate—see Section 2c)	
	• **Coordinating conjunctions** connect words, phrases, or clauses of the same kind.	Coordinating conjunctions: *and, but, for, nor, or, so, yet*
	• **Correlative conjunctions** are used in pairs.	Correlative conjunctions: *either . . . or, neither . . . nor, not only . . . but also, whether . . . or*
	• **Subordinating conjunctions** connect ideas of unequal importance.	Subordinating conjunctions: *after, because, before, even if, even though, if, in order to, since, so that, unless, until, when, whether, while*

(continued on next page) ▶

TABLE H1.1   Parts of Speech (continued)

Part of Speech	Definition/Primary Function	Examples
Preposition	Links and relates a noun or a pronoun to the rest of the sentence; may be a word or a phrase	Prepositions: *about, according to, along, as, as well as, at, below, by, despite, for, in, in spite of, near, on, onto, out, over, past, through, to, under, until, up, with, without, with regard to*
	Uses *in*, *on*, and *at* before nouns or pronouns to indicate time or location	• *In*: with months, years, seasons, time of day, geographic places: *In April, in 2020, in the spring, in the morning, in San Francisco, in rural areas* • *On*: with days of the week, dates, surfaces, forms of public transit, street names: *On Tuesday, on June 1, on a shelf, on the bus, on Main Street, on the fourth floor, on the Gulf Coast* • *At*: with specific times or parts of the day, specific addresses and named locations, some general locations and locations with specific functions: *At 8 p.m., at dawn, at 130 Ash Street, at Juan's house, at the college, at the library*
	A **prepositional phrase** includes the preposition along with its object and modifiers.	Prepositional phrases: *in the deep blue sea, on top of the high mountain, alongside the rugged Atlantic coast*
Interjection	Expresses surprise or some other strong feeling; often followed by an exclamation point	• *Ouch!* • *No way!* • *Oh,* it wasn't important.

2   Sentence Structure

2a   Sentence Parts

A **sentence** is a group of words that expresses a complete thought about something or someone. Every sentence must contain two basic parts: a subject and a predicate.

Subjects.   The **subject** of a sentence names a person, place, or thing and tells whom or what the sentence is about. It identifies the performer or receiver of the action expressed in the predicate.

▶ *Lady Gaga*, the flamboyant performer, has made savvy decisions about her career.

▶ The *clock* on the mantel was given to the children by their grandmother.

The noun or pronoun that names what the sentence is about is called the **simple subject**.

▶ *Mozart* began composing at the age of four.

▶ The postal *worker* was bitten by a dog.

The simple subject of an imperative sentence is understood as *you*, but *you* is not stated directly.

▶ Be quiet.

  The sentence is understood as [*You*] *be quiet*.

The **complete subject** is the simple subject plus its modifiers—words that describe, identify, qualify, or limit the meaning of a noun or pronoun.

```
          ┌──── complete subject ────┐
```
▶ A series of very bad *decisions* doomed the project.

```
              ┌──── complete subject ────┐
```
▶ There are too many *books* to fit on the shelves.

A sentence with a **compound subject** contains two or more simple subjects joined by a coordinating conjunction (*and, but, for, nor, or, so,* or *yet*).

▶ Joel <u>and</u> Ethan Coen produce and direct their films.
▶ A doctor <u>or</u> a physician's assistant will explain the results.

Predicates.   The **predicate** of a sentence indicates what the subject does, what happens to the subject, or what is said about the subject. The predicate, then, can indicate an action or a state of being.

Action   Plant respiration *produces* oxygen.

State of Being Stonehenge *has existed* for many centuries.

The **simple predicate** is the main verb along with its helping verbs.

▶ Reporters *should call* the subjects of their stories for comment.
▶ A snow bicycle for Antarctic workers *has been developed*.

The **complete predicate** consists of the simple predicate plus its modifiers and any objects or complements.

```
                      ┌──────── complete predicate ────────┐
```
▶ The growth of Los Angeles *depended* to a large extent on finding a way to get

```
  ┌───────────────┐
```
  water to the desert.

```
                  ┌──────── complete predicate ────────┐
```
▶ Watching fishing boats *is a relaxing and pleasant way to spend an afternoon.*

A **compound predicate** contains two or more predicates that have the same subject and that are joined by *and, but, or, nor,* or another conjunction.

▶ AIDS drugs *can save many lives* <u>but</u> *are seldom available in poor countries that need them desperately.*
▶ President Johnson <u>neither</u> *wanted to run for a second term* <u>nor</u> *planned to serve if elected.*

Objects.   A **direct object** is a noun or pronoun that receives the action of a verb. A direct object answers the question, What? or Whom?

▶ The Scottish fiddler played a lively *reel*.

  The noun *reel* answers the question, What did he play?

A **helping verb** (also called an **auxiliary verb**) combines with a main verb to indicate tense, mood, or voice or to add further information.

A **complement** is a word or group of words that describes or renames a subject or an object.

▶ The crowd in the stadium jeered the *quarterback*.

The noun *quarterback* answers the question, Whom did they jeer?

An **indirect object** is a noun or pronoun that names the person or thing to whom or for whom something is done.

▶ Habitat for Humanity gave *them* an award for *their* work.
▶ A child on a bench tossed the *ducklings* some crumbs.

Complements.   A **complement** is a word or group of words that describes a subject or object and completes the meaning of the sentence. There are two kinds of complements: subject complements and object complements.

A **linking verb** (such as *be, become, feel, seem,* or *taste*) connects the subject of a sentence to a **subject complement**, a noun, a noun phrase, or an adjective that renames or describes the subject.

▶ Aretha Franklin was a *much-loved performer*.
▶ She was *too sick to finish her tour*.

An **object complement** is a noun, a noun phrase, or an adjective that modifies or renames the **direct object**. Object complements appear with transitive verbs (such as *name, find, make, think, elect, appoint, choose,* and *consider*), which express action directed toward something or someone.

> A **direct object** receives the action of the verb: *He drove me home.*

▶ The council appointed Nik as *its new vice president*.
▶ The undercooked meat made several children *sick*.

2b Phrases

A **phrase** is a group of related words that lacks a subject, a predicate, or both. A phrase cannot stand alone as a sentence. There are four common types of phrases: prepositional phrases, verbal phrases, appositive phrases, and absolute phrases. Phrases can appear at the beginning, middle, or end of a sentence and can help make your writing more detailed and interesting.

Prepositional phrases.   A **prepositional phrase** consists of a preposition (such as *in, above, with, at, behind*), the object of the preposition (a noun or pronoun), and any modifiers of the object. Prepositional phrases usually function as adjectives or adverbs to tell more about people, places, objects, or actions. They can also function as nouns. A prepositional phrase generally adds information about time, place, direction, or manner.

Adjective Phrase	The plants *on the edge of the field* are weeds.
	On the edge and *of the field* tell *where.*
Adverb Phrase	New Orleans is very crowded *during Mardi Gras.*
	During Mardi Gras tells *when.*
Noun Phrase	*Down the hill* is the shortest way to town.
	Down the hill acts as the subject of the sentence.

Each of the following sentences has been edited to include a prepositional phrase or phrases that expand the meaning of the sentence by adding detail:

▶ He fell/ ^on the icy sidewalk.

▶ The ship suddenly appeared/ ^through the mist near the shore.

Verbal phrases. A **verbal** is a verb form used as a noun (the *barking* of the dog), an adjective (a *barking* dog), or an adverb (continued *to bark*). It cannot be used alone as the verb of a sentence, however. The three kinds of verbals are participles, gerunds, and infinitives. A **verbal phrase** consists of a verbal and its modifiers.

Participles and participial phrases. All verbs have two participles: present and past. The **present participle** is the *-ing* form of a verb (*being, hoping, studying*). The **past participle** of most verbs ends in *-d* or *-ed* (*hoped, consisted*). The past participle of irregular verbs has no set pattern (*been, ridden*). Both the present participle and the past participle can function as adjectives modifying nouns and pronouns.

▶ The planes flew over the foggy airport in a *holding* pattern.

▶ The pot was made of *molded* clay.

A **participial phrase**, which consists of a participle and its modifiers, can also function as an adjective in a sentence.

▶ The suspect, *wanted for questioning* on robbery charges, had vanished.

Gerunds and gerund phrases. A **gerund** is the present participle, or *-ing* form, of a verb that functions as a noun in a sentence.

▶ *Driving* can be a frustrating activity.
▶ The government has not done enough to build *housing*.

A **gerund phrase** consists of a gerund and its modifiers. Like a gerund, a gerund phrase is used as a noun and can therefore function in a sentence as a subject, a direct object, an indirect object, an object of a preposition, or a subject complement.

Subject	*Catching the virus* can be dangerous.
Direct Object	All the new recruits practiced *marching*.
Indirect Object	One director gave his *acting* a chance.
Object of a Preposition	An ambitious employee may rise by *impressing* her boss.
Subject Complement	The biggest thrill was the *skydiving*.

Infinitives and infinitive phrases. An **infinitive** is the base form of a verb preceded by *to*: *to study, to sleep.* An **infinitive phrase** consists of the infinitive plus any modifiers or objects. An infinitive phrase can function as a noun, an adjective, or an adverb.

Subject	*To become* an actor is my greatest ambition.
Adjective	She had a job *to do.*
Adverb	The weary travelers were eager *to sleep.*

Sometimes the *to* in an infinitive phrase is understood but not written.

▶ Her demonstration helped me learn the software.

Note: Be sure to distinguish between infinitive phrases and prepositional phrases beginning with the preposition *to.* In an infinitive phrase, *to* is followed by a verb (*to paint*); in a prepositional phrase, *to* is followed by a noun or pronoun (*to a movie*).

Appositive phrases. An **appositive** is a word that explains, restates, or adds new information about a noun. An **appositive phrase** consists of an appositive and its modifiers.

▶ Ben Affleck, *a famous actor,* is active in trying to improve conditions in the Congo.

The appositive phrase adds information about the noun *Ben Affleck*.

Absolute phrases. An **absolute phrase** consists of a noun or pronoun and any modifiers, usually followed by a participle. An absolute phrase modifies an entire sentence, not any particular word or words within the sentence. It can appear anywhere in a sentence and is set off from the rest of the sentence with commas.

▶ *Their shift completed,* the night workers walked out at sunrise.
▶ *An unsuspecting insect clamped in its mandible,* the praying mantis, *its legs folded piously,* appears serenely uninvolved.

2c Clauses

A **clause** is a group of words that contains a subject and a predicate. A clause is either independent (also called *main*) or dependent (also called *subordinate*). An **independent clause** can stand alone as a grammatically complete sentence.

▶ Einstein was a clerk at the Swiss Patent Office.
▶ Ethnic disputes followed the disintegration of Yugoslavia.

A **dependent clause** has a subject and a predicate, but it cannot stand alone as a grammatically complete sentence because it does not express a complete thought. A dependent clause usually begins with either a **subordinating conjunction** (such as *although, because, before, if,* or *whether;* see Table 9.3, p. 207) or a **relative pronoun** (see Table H2.1) that connects it to an independent clause. Subordinating conjunctions connect less important ideas (expressed in a dependent clause) to more important ideas

TABLE H2.1   Relative Pronouns

Relationship Shown	Relative Pronouns	Example
Reference to people	*who, whoever, whom, whomever, whose*	Sylvia Plath was married to Ted Hughes, *who later* became poet laureate of England.
Reference to things	*that, what, whatever, which, whose*	The research *that* caused the literacy-test controversy was outdated.

(expressed in an independent clause). Relative pronouns introduce dependent clauses that function as adjectives and refer back to a noun or pronoun that the clause modifies.

The following examples show subordinating conjunctions and relative pronouns and their use in dependent clauses:

dependent clause beginning with a subordinating conjunction

▶ *When the puppies were born*, the breeder examined them carefully.

dependent clause beginning with a subordinating conjunction

▶ Van Gogh's paintings began to command high prices *after he died*.

dependent clause beginning with a relative pronoun

▶ Isadora Duncan, *who personified modern dance*, died in a bizarre accident.

2d   Types of Sentences

For coverage of sentence types, see Chapter 9, pp. 204–8.

Write Grammatically Correct Sentences

3   Sentence Fragments

A **sentence fragment** is a group of words that cannot stand alone as a complete sentence.

> A **sentence** is a group of words that must include at least one independent clause (a subject and a verb that express a complete thought).

3a   Recognize fragments.

A fragment is often missing a subject, a complete verb, or both.

Fragment   Are hatched in sand.

> This group of words does not tell *who* or *what* are hatched in sand. It lacks a subject.

	Fragment	Especially his rebounding ability.

This group of words has a subject, *his rebounding ability*, but lacks a verb.

Fragment	To notice a friendly smile.

This group of words lacks both a subject and a verb. *To notice* is not a complete verb. It is an infinitive.

A group of words can have both a subject and a verb but still be a fragment because it does not express a complete thought.

$$\text{subject} \qquad \text{verb}$$

Fragment	Because the *number* of voters *has* declined.

This group of words does not tell what happened as a result of the voter decline. Its meaning is incomplete.

For a list of common subordinating conjunctions, see Table 9.3 (p. 207). For a list of relative pronouns, see Table H2.1.

Notice that the preceding fragment begins with the subordinating conjunction *because*. A clause that begins with a subordinating conjunction cannot stand alone as a complete sentence. Word groups that begin with a relative pronoun (*that, which, who*) are also not complete sentences.

$$\text{subject} \quad \text{verb}$$

Fragment	Which *scientists studied* for many years.

The group of words does not tell *what* the scientists studied.

Finally, when a word group begins with a transitional word or phrase (*for example, also*), make sure that it includes both a subject and a verb.

$$\text{subject}$$

Fragment	For example, *the Gulf Coast of Florida*.

Use Figure H3.1, "How to Identify a Fragment," to help you decide whether a particular word group is a complete sentence or a sentence fragment. Then use Figure H3.2 for how to correct any fragments you identify.

3b Correct fragments.

A sentence fragment can be revised in two general ways:

1. Joining it to a nearby sentence
2. Adding the parts that are missing

The method you choose depends on the element the fragment lacks as well as your intended meaning.

▶ Certain turtle eggs are ~~Are~~ hatched in sand.

▶ Jamal is a basketball player of many talents, ~~E~~especially his rebounding ability.

▶ Sam was too busy to ~~To~~ notice a friendly smile.

▶ The ~~Because the~~ number of voters has declined.

FIGURE H3.1   How to Identify a Fragment

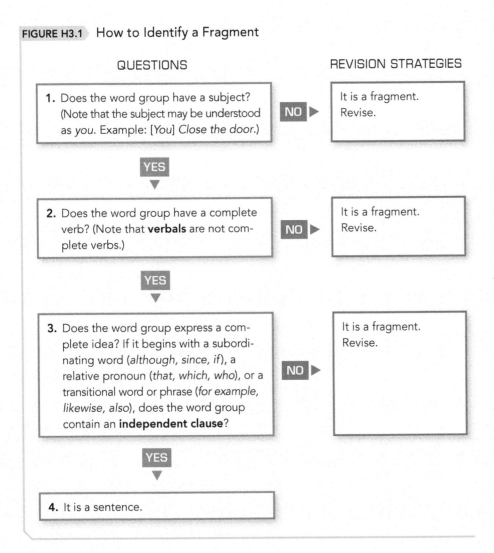

QUESTIONS

REVISION STRATEGIES

1. Does the word group have a subject? (Note that the subject may be understood as *you*. Example: [*You*] *Close the door.*)

NO ▶ It is a fragment. Revise.

YES ▼

2. Does the word group have a complete verb? (Note that **verbals** are not complete verbs.)

NO ▶ It is a fragment. Revise.

YES ▼

3. Does the word group express a complete idea? If it begins with a subordinating word (*although, since, if*), a relative pronoun (*that, which, who*), or a transitional word or phrase (*for example, likewise, also*), does the word group contain an **independent clause**?

NO ▶ It is a fragment. Revise.

YES ▼

4. It is a sentence.

3c Recognize intentional fragments.

Professional writers sometimes use sentence fragments intentionally to achieve special effects, particularly in works of fiction or articles written for popular magazines. An *intentional* fragment may be used to emphasize a point, answer a question, recreate a conversation, or make an exclamation. However, you should avoid using intentional fragments in academic writing. Instructors and other readers may find the fragments distracting or too informal, or they may assume you used a fragment in error.

TABLE H3.2 Correcting Sentence Fragments

Lacks a subject: Join the fragment to another sentence or add a subject.	▶ Jessica speaks Spanish fluently/~~And~~ ^{and} reads French well. ▶ Jessica speaks Spanish fluently. ~~And~~ ^{She also} reads French well.
Lacks a complete verb: Add a helping verb. (Verb forms ending in *-ing* need helping verbs, which can be forms of *do*, *be*, and *have* or words such as *will*, *can*, *could*, *shall*, *should*, *may*, *might*, and *must*.)	▶ The college ^{is} installing a furnace to heat the library.
Lacks a subject and a verb: Join the fragment to another sentence, or add the missing subject and verb. (Infinitives such as *to hope*, *to walk*, and *to play* and *-ed* or *-ing* forms are not complete verbs.)	▶ I plan to transfer next semester/~~To~~ ^{to} live closer to home. ▶ Generals Lee and Grant met on April 9, 1865/, ~~Bringing~~ ^{bringing} an end to the Civil War. ▶ Linda was reluctant to go out alone at night. ^{She was unwilling to} ~~To~~ walk across campus from the library. ▶ Kyle was determined to do well on his math exam. ^{He studied} ~~Studied~~ during every available hour.
Begins with a transitional word or phrase: Join the fragment to the previous sentence.	▶ Annie has always wanted to become an orthopedist/ ^{—that} ~~That~~ is, a bone specialist.
Begins with a subordinating word: Join the fragment to another sentence, or drop the subordinating word.	▶ The students stared spellbound/~~While~~ ^{while} the professor lectured. ▶ Until Dr. Jonas Salk invented a vaccine/, ~~Polio~~ ^{polio} was a serious threat to public health. ▶ ~~Because the~~ ^{The} 800 area code for toll-free dialing is overused. New codes—888 and 877—have been added.
Begins with a relative pronoun: Join the fragment to another sentence, or rewrite it as a complete sentence. (Relative pronouns include *who*, *whom*, *whose*, *whoever*, *whomever*, *what*, *whatever*, *which*, and *that*.)	▶ My contemporary fiction instructor assigned a novel by Stephen King/, ~~Whose~~ ^{whose} work I admire. ▶ The dodo is an extinct bird. ~~That~~ ^{It} disappeared in the seventeenth century.

Correct any fragments in the following sentences. Some groups of sentences may be correct as written.

▶ More people are going to college every year. ~~Especially~~ young women.
                                         , especially

1. The number of students in college. Increased greatly in the years after World War II.
2. Because federal funding from the 1944 GI Bill made it possible. Millions of returning veterans attended colleges.
3. Many people credit this program with helping to create a strong middle class. In the United States during the 1950s and 1960s.
4. Now, about two-thirds of high school graduates will attend college. Because, on average, those with bachelor's degrees earn over $20,000 more a year than people with only high school diplomas do.
5. However, as education costs continue to rise. Some wonder whether a traditional four-year college is always worth the expense.

Rewrite the following passage as needed to eliminate sentence fragments.

▶ How much and what kind of intervention should be undertaken/ ~~On~~ behalf of endangered species?
                                                            on

    Gila trout are endangered in some stretches of water. That are managed as designated wilderness. A hands-off policy would be their doom. Because exotic trout species now swim in the same streams. Gila trout can survive the competition and the temptation to interbreed only if they swim in isolated tributaries. In which a waterfall blocks the upstream movement of other fish. Two decades ago, one such tributary was fortified. With a small concrete dam. In other words, a dam deliberately built in the wilderness. It is often difficult to choose the right way. To manage a wilderness area. A scientific grasp of the way the ecosystem works is essential. Yet not always available.

4   Run-on Sentences and Comma Splices

A **run-on sentence** occurs when two or more independent clauses are joined without a punctuation mark or a coordinating conjunction. Run-on sentences are also known as **fused sentences**.

Run-on Sentence
                     ┌────────── independent clause ──────────┐ ┌──────── independent
                     A television addict is dependent on television I have suffered this
                     clause ──────────┐
                     addiction for years.

A **comma splice** occurs when two or more independent clauses are joined with a comma but without a coordinating conjunction (such as *and, or,* or *but*).

**Comma
Splice**

—————— independent clause —————— ┌── independent

A typical magic act includes tricks and illusions, both depend on

clause ——┐
deception.

Notice that only a comma separates the two independent clauses, causing the comma splice.

Another type of comma splice occurs when a word other than a coordinating conjunction is used with a comma to join two or more independent clauses.

**Comma
Splice**

—————— independent clause —————— ┌——

A typical magic act includes tricks and illusions, however, both

independent clause ——┐
depend on deception.

In the preceding sentence, *however* is a conjunctive adverb, not a coordinating conjunction. There are only seven coordinating conjunctions: *and, but, for, nor, or, so,* and *yet.*

4a Recognize run-on sentences and comma splices.

Many students have difficulty spotting run-on sentences and comma splices in their own writing. Use the flowchart in Figure H4.1 to help you identify these types of errors in your sentences.

4b Correct run-on sentences and comma splices.

There are five basic ways to correct a run-on sentence or comma splice (Table H4.1). Choose the method that best fits your sentence or intended meaning.

FIGURE H4.1   How to Identify a Run-on Sentence or Comma Splice

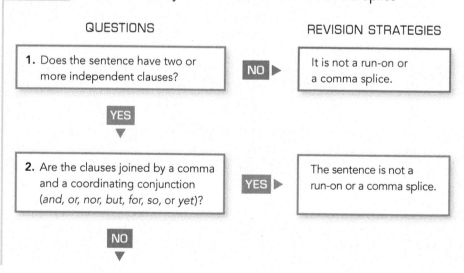

QUESTIONS   REVISION STRATEGIES

1. Does the sentence have two or more independent clauses?

NO ▶ It is not a run-on or a comma splice.

YES ▼

2. Are the clauses joined by a comma and a coordinating conjunction (*and, or, nor, but, for, so,* or *yet*)?

YES ▶ The sentence is not a run-on or a comma splice.

NO ▼

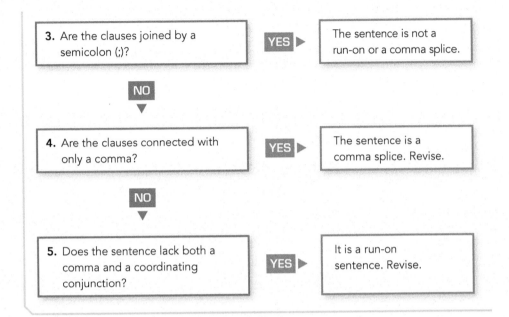

EXERCISE 4.1

Correct any run-ons or comma splices in the following sentences.

▶ A deadly nerve poison is found on the skin of some Amazon tree frogs/; native
tribes use the poison on the tips of their arrows when they hunt.

1. Nearly every American child dreams of going to Disney World, it has become one
of the most popular family vacation destinations.
2. Openness is one way to build trust in a relationship another is to demonstrate
tolerance and patience.
3. In the 1960s some Americans treated Vietnam veterans disrespectfully this
situation has changed dramatically since that time.
4. With large bodies and tiny wings, bumblebees have long been a puzzle, how do
they fly?
5. Restoring a painting is, indeed, delicate work too much enthusiasm can be
dangerous.

TABLE H4.1 ▸ Correcting Run-on Sentences and Comma Splices

Create two separate sentences.	**Run-on Sentence**	A résumé should be directed to a specific audience. ~~it~~ _{It} should emphasize the applicant's potential value to the company.
	Comma Splice	To evaluate a charity, you should start by examining its goals~~,~~. ~~then~~ _{Then} you should investigate its management practices.
Join the two independent clauses with a semicolon (;). (You may want to follow the semicolon with a conjunctive adverb—such as *also, however, still,* or *as a result.* See the second example.)	**Run-on Sentence**	Specialty products are unique items that consumers take time purchasing; these items include cars, parachutes, and skis.
	Comma Splice	Studies show that male and female managers often have different leadership styles; as a result, workers may respond differently to each.
Join the two independent clauses with a comma and a coordinating conjunction (*and, but, for, nor, or, so,* or *yet*).	**Run-on Sentence**	Closed-minded people often refuse to listen to opposing views, _{and} they reject ideas without evaluating them.
	Comma Splice	Some educators support home schooling, _{but} others oppose it.
Add a subordinating conjunction (such as *because* or *although*) to turn one of the independent clauses into a dependent clause.	**Run-on Sentence**	_{Because facial} ~~Facial~~ expressions are very revealing, they are an important communication tool.
	Comma Splice	_{Although the} ~~The~~ remote fishing lodge has no flush toilet or electricity, ~~nevertheless~~ it is a popular vacation spot.
Turn one independent clause into a phrase.	**Run-on Sentence**	Distributors open big-budget movies late in the week, _{hoping} ~~they hope~~ moviegoers will flock to theaters over the weekend.
	Comma Splice	Medieval peasants in Europe ate a simple, hearty diet, _{relying} ~~they relied~~ almost totally on agriculture.

EXERCISE 4.2

Correct any run-on sentences and comma splices in the following paragraph. Some sentences may be correct as written.

▶ Some people believe dreams are revealing,^but others think the brain is simply unloading excess information.

  Throughout recorded history, people have been fascinated by dreams, they have wondered what meaning dreams hold. Whether the dreams are ominous or beautiful, people have always wanted to understand them. There are many ancient stories about dream interpretation one of these is the biblical story of Daniel. Daniel is able to interpret a ruler's dream, this power to interpret convinces the ruler that Daniel is a prophet. Other early writers considered the topic of dream interpretation, to Latin writers, some dreams were meaningful and some were not. Meaningful dreams could reveal the future, these writers argued, but other dreams were simply the result of eating or drinking too much. Sigmund Freud, the founder of psychoanalysis, dramatically changed the field of dream interpretation he believed that dreams come from the subconscious. According to Freud, ideas too frightening for the waking mind often appear in dreams, patients in Freudian therapy often discuss dream images. Today, not everyone agrees with Freud, scientists trying to understand the brain still pay attention to dreams. They are certain that dreams reflect modern life more and more people today dream about computers.

5   Subject-Verb Agreement

Subjects and verbs must agree in person and number. **Person** refers to the forms *I* or *we* (first person), *you* (second person), and *he, she, it,* and *they* (third person). **Number** shows whether a word refers to one thing (singular) or more than one thing (plural). In a sentence, subjects and verbs need to be consistent in person and number: *I drive, you drive, she drives, they drive.*

  Subject-verb agreement errors often occur in complicated sentences, in sentences with compound subjects, or in sentences where the subject and verb are separated by other words or phrases. The following sections will help you look for and revise common errors in subject-verb agreement.

5a Make sure the verb agrees with the subject, not with words that come between the subject and verb.

▶ The *number* of farm workers *has* remained constant over several decades.

  The subject *number* is singular and requires a singular verb, even though the words *of farm workers* appear between the subject and verb.

5b Use a plural verb when two or more subjects are joined by *and*.

▶ A dot and a dash represents the letter A in Morse code.

▶ Basketball star Shaquille O'Neal, comedian D. L. Hughley, and actor Tom
Arnold ~~was~~ all born on March 6.

^were^

5c Revise to make the verb agree with the subject closest to it when two or more subjects are joined by *or, either . . . or,* or *neither . . . nor*.

When two or more singular subjects are joined by *or, either . . . or,* or *neither . . . nor*, use a singular verb.

▶ *Math* or *accounting appears* to be a suitable major for you.
▶ Either the *waiter* or the *customer has* misplaced the bill.
▶ Neither the *doctor* nor the *patient is* pessimistic about the prognosis.

When one singular and one plural subject are joined by *or, either . . . or,* or *neither . . . nor*, the verb should agree in number with the subject nearest to it.

▶ Neither the *sailors* nor the *boat was* harmed by the storm.

▶ Neither the *boat* nor the *sailors were* harmed by the storm.

▶ Either my daughters or my wife water that plant daily.

^s^

5d Use a singular verb with most collective nouns, such as *family, couple,* and *class*.

When a **collective noun** refers to a group as one unit acting together, use a singular verb. When the members of the group are acting as individuals, use a plural verb. To make their meaning clearer and avoid awkwardness, writers often add *members* or a similar noun.

▶ The school *committee has* voted to increase teachers' salaries.
> The committee is acting as a unit.

▶ The family ~~are~~ living in a cramped apartment.

^is^

▶ The *team members are* traveling by train, bus, and bike.
> The team members are acting individually.

▶ The members of the jury ~~is~~ divided and unable to reach consensus.

^are^

5e Use a singular verb with most indefinite pronouns, such as *anyone, everyone, each, every, no one,* and *something.*

Indefinite pronouns do not refer to a specific person, place, or object. They refer to people, places, or things in general. Singular indefinite pronouns include the following: *each, either, neither, anyone, anybody, anything, everyone, everybody, everything, one, no one, nobody, nothing, someone, somebody, something.*

▶ Everyone in this room is welcome to express an opinion.

▶ Neither of the candidates ~~have~~ ^has^ run for office before.

Other indefinite pronouns, such as *several, both, many,* and *few,* take a plural verb.

▶ Every year *many succeed* in starting new small businesses.

▶ Several of you jog~~s~~ at least three miles a day.

Some indefinite pronouns, such as *all, any, more, most, some,* and *none,* take either a singular or a plural verb depending on the noun they refer to. To decide which verb to use, follow this rule: Treat the indefinite pronoun as singular if it refers to something that cannot be counted and as plural if it refers to more than one of something that can be counted.

▶ Most of the water go^es^ into this kettle.

   You cannot count water.

▶ Some of the children in the study choose~~s~~ immediate rather than delayed rewards.

   You can count children.

5f Revise to make verbs agree with the antecedents of *who, which,* and *that.*

When a **relative pronoun** (*who, which, that*) refers to a singular noun, use a singular verb. When it refers to a plural noun, use a plural verb.

▶ Toni Morrison, *who enjoyed* unique success as both a popular and a literary author, won the Nobel Prize in literature in 1993.

   Who refers to Toni Morrison, and because *Toni Morrison* is singular, the verb *enjoys* is singular.

▶ Look for *stores that display* this sign.

   That refers to *stores,* a plural noun, so the verb *display* is plural.

Using *one of the* often leads to errors in subject-verb agreement. The phrase *one of the* plus a noun is plural.

▶ A pigeon is *one of the two birds that drink* by suction.

   That refers to *birds,* and since *birds* is plural, the verb *drink* is plural.

However, *only one of the* plus a noun is singular: *The cheetah is the only one of the big cats that has nonretractable claws.*

An **antecedent** is the noun or pronoun to which a pronoun refers.

A **relative pronoun** introduces a dependent clause that functions as an adjective: *the patient who injured her leg.*

5g Revise to make the verb agree with a subject that follows it.

When a sentence begins with either *here* or *there* (which cannot function as a subject) or with a **prepositional phrase**, the subject often follows the verb. Look for the subject after the verb and make sure the subject and verb agree.

▶ There is a false *panel* somewhere in this room.

▶ Under the stairs *lurks* a solitary *spider*.

5h Make sure a linking verb agrees with its subject, not a word or phrase that renames the subject.

Linking verbs, such as forms of *be* and *feel, look,* and *taste,* connect a subject with a word or phrase that renames or describes it. In sentences with linking verbs, the verb should agree with the subject.

▶ The *bluebell* is any of several plants in the lily family.

▶ The *issue* discussed at the meeting *was* the low wages earned by factory workers.

5i Use a singular verb when the subject is a title.

▶ *Gulliver's Travels* ~~are~~ is a satire by the eighteenth-century British writer Jonathan Swift.

5j Use singular verbs with singular nouns that end in *-s,* such as *physics* and *news.*

▶ *Linguistics deals* with the study of human speech.

EXERCISE 5.1

Correct any sentences with subject-verb agreement errors in the following paragraph. Some sentences may be correct as written.

Everyone in the colder climates want to know whether the next winter will be severe. The National Weather Service, however, usually predict the weather only a short time in advance. Another method of making weather predictions are popular with many Americans. According to folklore, there is a number of signs to alert people to a hard winter ahead. Among these signs are the brown stripe on a woolly bear caterpillar. If the brown stripe between the caterpillar's two black stripes are wide, some people believe the winter will be a short one. Another of the signs that indicate a hard winter is a large apple harvest. And, of course, almost everyone in the United States have seen news stories on February 2 about groundhogs predicting the end of winter. Folk beliefs, which are not based on science, seems silly to many people. Neither the National Weather Service nor folklore are always able to forecast the weather accurately, however.

6 ▶ Verb Forms

Except for *be*, all English verbs have five forms.

Base Form	Past Tense	Past Participle	Present Participle	-s Form
move	moved	moved	moving	moves

- ▶ Many designers *visit* Milan for fashion shows each year.
- ▶ Sarah *visited* her best friend in Thailand.
- ▶ Students have *visited* the state capital every spring for decades.
- ▶ His cousin from Iowa is *visiting* this week.
- ▶ Maria *visits* her grandmother in Puerto Rico as often as possible.

6a Use *-s* or *-es* endings for present tense verbs that have third-person singular subjects.

The *-s* form is made up of the verb's base form plus *-s* or *-es*.

- ▶ Mr. King *teaches* English.

A third-person singular subject can consist of a singular noun, a singular pronoun (*he, she*, and *it*), or a singular indefinite pronoun (such as *everyone*).

Singular Noun	The flower opens.
Singular Pronoun	He opens the door.
Singular Indefinite Pronoun	Everybody knows the truth.

- ▶ She ~~want~~ to be a veterinarian.
  ^wants^
- ▶ None of the townspeople ~~understand~~ him.
  ^understands^

6b Do not omit *-ed* endings on verbs.

For regular verbs, both the past tense and the past participle are formed by adding *-ed* or *-d* to the base form of the verb.

- ▶ She *claimed* to be the czar's daughter, Anastasia.
- ▶ The defendant *faced* his accusers.

Some speakers do not fully pronounce the *-ed* endings of verbs (*asked, fixed, supposed to, used to*). As a result, they may unintentionally omit these endings in their writing.

- ▶ He ~~talk~~ to the safety inspectors about plant security.
  ^talked^
- ▶ They ~~use~~ to order lattes every morning.
  ^used^

Individuals may prefer a gender-neutral pronoun (*zie* for *he/she* or *hir* for *him/her*). Others may prefer to use *they* in a gender-neutral way (such as *Nik called their parents last week*). Respect the choices of those to whom you refer. Note, however, that instructors may want to ensure that you understand and can apply the traditional rules, so consult your instructor before using plural pronouns in a singular sense.

For more on verb tense, see Table H1.1, p. 727.

6c Use the correct form of irregular verbs such as *lay* and *lie*.

The verb pairs *lay* and *lie* and *sit* and *set* have similar forms and are often confused. Each verb has its own meaning: *lie* means to recline or rest on a surface, and *lay* means to put or place something; *sit* means to be seated, as in a chair, and *set* means to place something on a surface.

> ▶ Our dog likes to ~~lay~~ *lie* on the couch all afternoon.

> ▶ Let me ~~set~~ *sit* in this chair for a while.

6d Use the active and passive voice appropriately.

When a verb is in the **active voice**, the subject performs the action.

    Active Voice   The Mississippi River flows into the Gulf of Mexico.

When a verb is in the **passive voice**, the subject receives the action.

    Passive Voice   The computer file was deleted.

        Notice that the sentence in the passive voice does not tell *who* deleted the file.

The active voice expresses ideas more vividly and emphatically than does the passive voice. Whenever possible, use the active voice in your sentences.

> ▶ The colonists threw tea
> ~~Tea was thrown~~ into Boston Harbor ~~by the colonists.~~

> ▶ No one is allowed to sell illegal
> ~~Illegal~~ drugs ~~are not allowed to be sold.~~

Sentences in the passive voice may seem indirect, as if the writer is purposely withholding information. In general, use the passive voice sparingly. There are two situations in which it is the better choice, however:

1. When you do not know or do not want to reveal who performed the action of the verb:

    Passive   Several historic buildings had been torn down.

2. When you want to emphasize the object of the action rather than the person who causes the action:

    Passive   The poem "My Last Duchess" by Robert Browning was discussed in class.

        In this sentence, the title of the poem is more important than the people who discussed it.

6e Use the present tense when writing about literary works, even though they were written in the past.

> ▶ Chaucer's *Canterbury Tales* ~~depicted~~ *depicts* a tremendously varied group of travelers.

6f Be sure to distinguish between the immediate past and the less immediate past.

Use the past perfect form of the verb, formed by adding *had* to the past participle, to indicate an action that was completed before another action or a specified time.

Unclear   Roberto finished three research papers when the semester ended.

Roberto did not finish all three right at the end of the semester.

Revised   Roberto had finished three research papers when the semester ended.

For more on verb tense, see Table H1.1, p. 727.

EXERCISE 6.1

Correct the errors in verb form in the following paragraph. Some sentences may be correct as written.

>   contains
> ▶ Walt Whitman's *Leaves of Grass* ~~contain~~ long, informally structured poems.
>   ^

Walt Whitman was usually considered one of the greatest American poets. He spent almost his whole life in Brooklyn, New York, but he like to write about all of America. He was fired from several jobs for laziness and admitted that he liked to lay in bed until noon. But he had a vision: He wanted to create an entirely new kind of poetry. Rhyme was considered unimportant by him, and he did not think new American poetry needed formal structure. Unfortunately for Whitman, his great masterpiece, *Leaves of Grass*, was not an overnight success. Ralph Waldo Emerson admire it, but Whitman sold very few copies. He revise it continuously until his death. Today, people admires *Leaves of Grass* for its optimism, its beautiful language, its very modern appreciation of the diversity of America, and its astonishing openness about sexuality. Whitman's body of work still move and surprise readers.

---

7   Pronoun Problems

Pronouns are words used in place of nouns. They provide a quick, convenient way to refer to a word that has already been named. Common problems in using pronouns include problems with pronoun reference, agreement, and case.

Pronoun Reference

A pronoun should refer clearly to its **antecedent**, the noun or pronoun for which it substitutes.

If an antecedent is missing or unclear, the meaning of the sentence is also unclear. Use the following guidelines to make certain your pronoun references are clear and correct.

7a Make sure each pronoun refers clearly to one antecedent.

▸ The hip-hop radio station battled the alternative rock station for the highest ratings.

▸ Eventually, ~~it~~ ^{the hip-hop station} won.

The revised sentence makes it clear which station won: the hip-hop station.

7b Be sure to check for vague uses of *they*, *it*, and *you*.

They, *it*, and *you* often refer vaguely to antecedents in preceding sentences or to no antecedent at all.

Omitted Antecedent	On the Internet, they claimed that an asteroid would collide with Earth.
	On the Internet does not explain what *they* refers to.
Clear	On the Internet, a blog claimed that an asteroid would collide with Earth.
	Adding the noun *a blog* clears up the mystery.

▸ When political scientists study early political cartoons, ~~it provides~~ ^{they gain} insight into historical events.

▸ In Florida, ~~you often hear~~ ^{people often talk} about hurricane threats of previous years.

7c Make sure pronouns do not refer to adjectives or possessives.

Pronouns must refer to nouns or other pronouns. Adjectives and possessives cannot serve as antecedents, although they may seem to suggest a noun the pronoun *could* refer to.

▸ He became so depressed that ~~it made him~~ ^{he was} unable to get out of bed.

The pronoun *it* seems to refer to the adjective *depressed*, which suggests the noun *depression*. This noun is not in the sentence, however.

▸ The stock market's rapid rise made ~~it~~ ^{stocks} appear to be an attractive investment.

The pronoun *it* seems to refer to *stock market's*, which is a possessive, not a noun.

7d Make sure the pronouns *who*, *whom*, *which*, and *that* refer to clear, specific nouns.

▸ Lake-effect storms hit cities along the Great Lakes. ~~That makes~~ ^{These storms make} winter travel treacherous.

> **EXERCISE 7.1**

Correct any errors in pronoun reference in the following sentences.

> ▶ Innovative codes are important because ~~it means that~~ they ~~will be~~ are hard to break.

1. A country at war must be able to convey information to military personnel. That is always a challenge.
2. The information's importance often requires it to be transmitted secretly.
3. During World War II, U.S. government code specialists hired Navajo Indians because it is a difficult and little-studied language.
4. The Nazis' Enigma code was extremely difficult to crack. This was an enormous problem for the Allied forces.
5. Alan Turing's mathematical genius saved the day. He was a British civil servant who finally solved the Enigma code.

Pronoun-Antecedent Agreement

Pronouns and **antecedents** must agree in **person, number,** and **gender.** The most common agreement error occurs when pronouns and antecedents do not agree in number. In general, if the antecedent is singular, use a singular pronoun; if the antecedent is plural, use a plural pronoun. But note that English may be in transition. Many authorities, including the Modern Language Association (MLA), now accept *they, their, them,* and *theirs* as singular pronouns. However, instructors may want to know that you understand the traditional rules and can apply them, so consult your instructor before using plural pronouns in a singular sense.

7e Use singular pronouns to refer to indefinite pronouns that are singular in meaning.

Singular indefinite pronouns include the following:

another	anywhere	everyone	none	other
anybody	each	everything	no one	somebody
anyone	either	neither	nothing	someone
anything	everybody	nobody	one	something

> ▶ *Each* of the experiments produced *its* desired result.

> ▶ If *anyone* wants me, give *him or her* my email address.

> ▶ *Everyone* in America should exercise *their* right to vote so *their* voice can be heard.

An **antecedent** is the noun or pronoun to which a pronoun refers.

Person indicates whether the subject is speaking (first person: *I, we*), is being spoken to (second person: *you*), or is being spoken about (third person: *he, she, it, they*).

Number is a term that classifies pronouns as singular (*I, you, he, she, it*) or plural (*we, you, they*).

Gender is a way of classifying pronouns as masculine (*he, him*), feminine (*she, her*), or neuter (*it, its*).

An **indefinite pronoun** does not refer to a specific person, place, or object. It refers to people, places, or things in general (*anywhere, everyone, everything*).

If the pronoun and antecedent do not agree, change either the pronoun or the indefinite pronoun to which it refers.

> ▶ ~~Everyone~~ should check their credit card statements monthly.

(People written above Everyone)

If you must use a singular pronoun, you may want to use *he or she* or *him or her* to avoid sexism.

> ▶ Everyone should check ~~their~~ credit card statement monthly.

(his or her written above their)

Note: Overuse of *him or her* and *his or her* can create awkward sentences. To avoid this problem, you can revise your sentences in one of two ways: by using a plural antecedent and a plural pronoun or by omitting the pronouns altogether.

Alternatively, if your instructor agrees, you may be able to use *they* or *their* in a singular sense.

> ▶ Everyone should check their credit card statement monthly.

> ▶ No one should lose ~~their~~ job because of family responsibilities.

(a written above their)

The indefinite pronouns *all, any, more, most,* and *some* can be either singular or plural, depending on how they are used in sentences. When an indefinite pronoun refers to something that can be counted, use a plural pronoun to refer to it. When an indefinite pronoun refers to something that cannot be counted, use a singular pronoun to refer to it.

> ▶ Of the tropical plants studied, *some* have proven *their* usefulness in fighting disease.

Because the word *plants* is a plural, countable noun, the pronoun *some* is plural in this sentence.

> ▶ The water was warm, and *most* of it was murky.

Water is not countable, so *most* is singular.

7f Use a plural pronoun to refer to a compound antecedent joined by *and*.

> ▶ The *walrus and the carpenter* ate *their* oysters greedily.

Exception: When the singular antecedents joined by *and* refer to the same person, place, or thing, use a singular pronoun.

> ▶ As *a father and a husband, he* is a success.

Exception: When *each* or *every* comes before the antecedent, use a singular pronoun.

> ▶ *Every* nut and bolt was in *its* place for the inspection.

When a compound antecedent is joined by *or* or *nor*, the pronoun should agree with the noun closer to the verb.

> ▶ Either the panda or the sea otters should have ~~its~~ ^their^ new habitat soon.

7g Use a singular or plural pronoun to refer to a collective noun, depending on the meaning.

A **collective noun** names a group of people or things acting together or individually (*herd, class, team*) and may be referred to by a singular or plural pronoun depending on your intended meaning. When you refer to a group acting together as a unit, use a singular pronoun.

> ▶ The *wolf pack* surrounds *its* quarry.
>
>   The pack is acting as a unit.

When you refer to the members of the group as acting individually, use a plural pronoun.

> ▶ After the false alarm, *members* of the bomb squad returned to *their* homes.
>
>   The members of the squad acted individually.

EXERCISE 7.2

Correct any errors in pronoun-antecedent agreement in the following sentences. Some sentences may be correct as written.

> ▶ A team of researchers might disagree on ~~its~~ ^their^ conclusion about the disappearance of the dinosaur.

1. Neither the many species of dinosaurs nor the flightless dodo bird could prevent their own extinction.
2. Every scientist has their own ideas about the state of the environment.
3. However, most believe that their findings indicate the dodo died out because of competition from other species.
4. In one way, animals resemble plants: Some are "weeds" because it has the ability to thrive under many conditions.
5. Any species that cannot withstand their competitors may be doomed to extinction.
6. When a "weed" and a delicate native species compete for its survival, the native species usually loses.
7. If the snail darter and the spotted owl lose their fight to survive, should humans care?
8. Everyone should be more concerned about the extinction of plants and animals than they seem to be.
9. Every extinction has their effect on other species.
10. The earth has experienced several mass extinctions in its history, but another would take their toll on the quality of human life.

Pronoun Case

Most of the time you will automatically know which form, or *case*, of a pronoun to use: the **subjective**, **objective**, or **possessive** case. A pronoun's case indicates its function in a sentence. When a pronoun functions as a subject in a sentence, the subjective case (*I*) is used. When a pronoun functions as a **direct object**, an **indirect object**, or an **object of a preposition**, the objective case (*me*) is used. When a pronoun indicates ownership, the possessive case (*mine*) is used.

A **direct object** receives the action of the verb: *Pat drove me home.*

An **indirect object** indicates to or for whom an action is performed: *I gave her the keys.*

An **object of a preposition** is a word or phrase that follows a preposition: *with me, above the table.*

Subjective Case	Objective Case	Possessive Case
I	me	my, mine
we	us	our, ours
you	you	your, yours
he, she, it	him, her, it	his, her, hers, its
they	them	their, theirs
who	whom	whose

Use the following guidelines to correct errors in pronoun case.

7h **Read the sentence aloud without the noun and the word** *and* **to decide which pronoun to use in a compound construction (***Yolanda and I, Yolanda and me***).**

Incorrect   Yolanda and me graduated from high school last year.

If you mentally delete Yolanda and, the sentence sounds wrong: Me graduated from high school last year.

Revised   Yolanda and I graduated from high school last year.

If you mentally delete Yolanda and, the sentence sounds correct: I graduated from high school last year.

Incorrect   The mayor presented the citizenship award to Mrs. Alvarez and I.

If you delete Mrs. Alvarez and, the sentence sounds wrong: The mayor presented the citizenship award to I.

Revised   The mayor presented the citizenship award to Mrs. Alvarez and me.

If you delete Mrs. Alvarez and, the sentence sounds correct: The mayor presented the citizenship award to me.

7i **Read the sentence aloud using the pronoun as the subject when a pronoun follows a form of the verb** *be* **(***is, are, was, were***).**

Incorrect   The leader is him.

If you swap him with the leader, the sentence sounds wrong: Him is the leader.

Revised   The leader is he.

> If you swap *he* with *the leader*, the sentence sounds correct: *He is the leader.*

▶ The best singer in the group is ~~her.~~ ^she.^

7j Read the sentence aloud without the noun to determine whether *we* or *us* should come before a noun.

▶ If we hikers frighten them, the bears may attack.

> If you mentally delete *hikers*, the sentence sounds correct: *If we frighten them, the bears may attack.*

▶ The older children never paid attention to us kindergarteners.

> If you mentally delete *kindergarteners*, the sentence sounds correct: *The older children never paid attention to us.*

7k Choose the correct pronoun form for a comparison using *than* or *as* by mentally adding the verb that is implied.

▶ Diedre is a better athlete than I [am].
▶ The coach likes her better than [he likes] me.

> An **object** is the target or recipient of the action described by the verb: *I gave her the keys.*

7l Use *who* or *whoever* when the pronoun functions as the subject of a sentence. Use *whom* or *whomever* when the pronoun functions as the object of a verb or preposition.

To decide whether to use *who* or *whom* in a particular question, answer the question yourself by using the words *he* or *him* or *she* or *her*. If you use *he* or *she* in the answer, you should use *who* in the question. If you use *him* or *her* in the answer, use *whom* in the question.

> An **object of a preposition** is a word or phrase that follows a preposition: *with him, above the table.*

Question	(*Who, Whom*) photocopied the article?
Answer	*She* photocopied the article.
Correct Pronoun	*Who* photocopied the article?
Question	To (*who, whom*) is that question addressed?
Answer	It is addressed to *him.*
Correct Pronoun	To *whom* is that question addressed?

Similarly, to decide whether to use *who* or *whom* in a **dependent clause**, turn the dependent clause into a question. The pronoun you use to answer that question will tell you whether *who* or *whom* should appear in the clause.

> A **dependent clause** contains a subject and a verb but does not express a complete thought.

▶ Aphra Behn's *Oronooko* dramatizes the life of an enslaved man ~~whom~~ ^who^ came from African royalty.

> If you ask the question (*Who, whom*) *came from African royalty?*, the answer, *He came from African royalty*, indicates that the correct pronoun is *who*.

shift

The leader ~~who~~ we seek must unite the community.
               ^whom

> If you ask the question (*Who, whom*) *do we seek?*, the answer, *We seek her*, indicates that the correct pronoun is *whom*.

7m Use a possessive pronoun to modify a gerund.

▶ *His moralizing* has never been welcome.

> The possessive pronoun *his* modifies the gerund *moralizing*.

Gerunds are often confused with **participles** because both end in -*ing*.

Participle	Teenagers across the United States watched *her singing* on *American Idol*.
	The teenagers watched her, not the singing.
Gerund	The professor discovered *their cheating* on the final exam.
	The cheating was discovered, not the students doing the cheating.

A **gerund** is an -*ing* form of a verb that functions as a noun (*complaining, jogging*).

A **participle** is an -*ing* or -*ed* form of a verb that is used as an adjective (*the terrifying monster*) or with a helping verb to indicate tense (*he was running away*). Pronouns used with participles should be in the objective case; pronouns used with gerunds should be in the possessive case.

EXERCISE 7.3

Correct any errors in pronoun reference, agreement, and case in the following paragraph. Some sentences may be correct as written.

▶ ~~Her~~ and her husband married for love, which was unusual at the time.
   ^She

> Lady Mary Wortley Montagu, whom was a wealthy aristocrat, was one of the eighteenth century's most interesting characters. Few women then were as well educated as her. Every parent wanted their daughter to be charming, not intellectual, so Lady Mary secretly taught herself Latin. When her husband was appointed ambassador to Turkey, she and he traveled there together. Her letters to friends in London, which were later published, were filled with detail. She described a Turkish bath's atmosphere so vividly that it became a popular setting for paintings and literature. She also learned that smallpox was rare in Turkey. Of the Turkish people she met, most had gotten his or her immunity to smallpox from a kind of inoculation. This had an effect on Lady Mary herself. Lady Mary's children were among the first British citizens who were inoculated against it.

8   Shifts and Mixed Constructions

A **shift** is a sudden, unexpected change in point of view, verb tense, voice, mood, or level of diction that may confuse your readers. Shifting from a direct to an indirect question or quotation can also confuse readers. A **mixed construction** is a sentence containing parts that do not sensibly fit together. This chapter will help you identify and correct shifts and mixed constructions in your sentences.

Shifts

8a Refer to yourself, your audience, and the people you are writing about in a consistent way.

Person shows the writer's point of view. Personal pronouns indicate whether the subject is the speaker (first person: *I, we*), the person spoken to (second person: *you*), or the person or thing spoken about (third person: *he, she, it, they, one*).

For more on point of view, see Chapter 4, p. 109.

Inconsistent   I discovered that *you* could touch some of the museum exhibits.

> Notice that the writer shifts from first-person *I* to the second-person *you*.

Consistent   I discovered that I could touch some of the museum exhibits.

> The writer uses the first-person *I* consistently within the sentence.

▶ When people study a foreign language, ~~you~~ ^{they} also learn about another culture.

8b Maintain consistency in verb tense throughout a paragraph or an essay unless the meaning requires you to change tenses.

Inconsistent   The virus *mutated* so quickly that it *develops* a resistance to most vaccines.

> The sentence shifts from past to present.

Revised   The virus *mutates* so quickly that it *develops* a resistance to most vaccines.

Shifts between the present and past tense are among the most common shifts writers make.

▶ The city's crime rate continues to drop, but experts disagree~~d~~ on the reasons.

8c Change verb tense when you want to indicate an actual time change.

Use the present tense for events that occur in the present; use the past tense for events that occurred in the past. When the time changes, be sure to change the tense. Notice the intentional shifts in the following passage (the verbs are in italics):

> Every spring migratory birds *return* to cooler climates to raise their young. This year a pair of bluejays *is occupying* a nest in my yard, and I *spy* on them. The hatchlings *are growing* larger and *developing* feathers. Last spring, robins *built* the nest that the jays now *call* home, and I *watched* them every morning until the young birds *left* home for the last time.

As the events switch from this year (present) to the previous year (past), the writer changes from the present tense (*is occupying*) to the past tense (*built*).

For more on verb tense, see Table H1.1, p. 727.

In the **active voice**, the subject of the sentence performs the action.

In the **passive voice**, the subject receives the action.

For more on voice, see 6d.

8d Use a consistent voice.

Needless shifts between the **active voice** and the **passive voice** can disorient readers and create wordy sentences.

> The researchers gave one
> ▶ ~~One~~ group of volunteers ~~was given~~ a placebo, and ~~the researchers~~ treated
>   ^   they
>
> another group with the new drug.

>   the specter of starvation forced
> ▶ Drought and windstorms made farming impossible, and many families ~~were~~
>   ^
> ~~forced~~ to leave Oklahoma.~~by the specter of starvation.~~
>   ^

To change a sentence from the passive voice to the active voice, make the performer of the action the subject of the sentence. The original subject of the sentence becomes the direct object. Delete the form of the verb *be*.

| **Passive** | The restraining order was signed by the judge. |
| **Active** | The judge signed the restraining order. |

8e Avoid sudden shifts from indirect to direct questions or quotations.

An indirect question tells what a question is or was.

| **Indirect Question** | The defense attorney asked where I was on the evening of May 10. |
| **Direct Question** | "Where were you on the evening of May 10?" |

Avoid shifting from direct to indirect questions.

>   he
> ▶ Sal asked what could ~~I~~ do to solve the problem.
>   ^

8f Use a consistent mood throughout a paragraph or an essay.

Mood indicates whether the sentence states a fact or asks a question (**indicative mood**); gives a command or direction (**imperative mood**); or expresses a condition contrary to fact, a wish, or a suggestion (**subjunctive mood**). The subjunctive mood is also used for hypothetical situations or impossible or unlikely events.

Inconsistent

You shouldn't expect to learn ballroom dancing immediately, and remember that even Fred Astaire had to start somewhere. First, find a qualified instructor. Then, you should not be embarrassed even if everyone else seems more graceful than you are. Finally, keep your goal in mind, and you need to practice, practice, practice.

This paragraph contains shifts between the indicative and imperative moods.

Consistent

Don't expect to learn ballroom dancing immediately, and remember that even Fred Astaire had to start somewhere. First, find a qualified instructor. Then, don't be embarrassed if everyone else seems more graceful than you are. Finally, keep your goal in mind, and practice, practice, practice.

This revised paragraph uses the imperative mood consistently.

8g Use a consistent level of diction.

Your level of diction can range from formal to informal. The level you choose should be appropriate for your audience, your subject matter, and your purpose for writing. As you revise your essays, look for inappropriate shifts in diction, such as from a formal to an informal tone or vice versa.

William H. Whyte's studies of human behavior in public space yielded a number of surprises. Perhaps most unexpected was the revelation that people seem to be drawn toward, rather than driven from, crowded spaces. They tend to congregate near the entrances of stores or on street corners. Plazas and shopping districts crowded with pedestrians attract more pedestrians. For some reason, people seem to ~~get a charge out of hanging out where lots of other folks are hanging out, too.~~ enjoy gathering together in public spaces.

For more on levels of diction, see Chapter 9, pp. 215–17.

For academic writing, including class assignments and research papers, use formal language.

EXERCISE 8.1

Correct the shifts in person, verb tense, voice, mood, and level of diction in the following paragraph.

▶ Some artists long ago used techniques that still ~~surprised~~ surprise modern students of their work.

Museum visitors can see paintings by the seventeenth-century Dutch artist Jan Vermeer, but you cannot see how he achieved his remarkable effects. Most of his paintings showed simply furnished household rooms. The people and objects in these rooms seem so real that the paintings resembled photographs. Vermeer's use of perspective and light would also contribute to the paintings' realism. Some art historians believe he used a gizmo called a *camera obscura*. This machine projected an image onto a flat surface so you could draw it. For most experts, Vermeer's possible use of technological aids does not make his totally fabulous results less impressive. It is agreed by art historians that the paintings are masterpieces. Vermeer's paintings are admired even more now than they are in his own lifetime.

Mixed Constructions

8h Make sure clauses and phrases fit together logically.

A **mixed construction** contains phrases or clauses that do not work together logically and that cause confusion in meaning.

Mixed	The fact that the marathon is twenty-six miles, a length that explains why I have never finished it.

The sentence starts with a subject (*The fact*) followed by a dependent clause (*that the marathon is twenty-six miles*). The sentence needs a predicate to complete the independent clause; instead it includes a noun (*a length*) and another dependent clause (*that explains why I have never finished it*). The independent clause that begins with *The fact* is never completed.

Revised	The marathon is twenty-six miles long, which is why I have never finished it.

In the revision, the parts of the sentence work together.

To avoid mixed constructions in your writing, it often helps to check the words that connect clauses and phrases, especially prepositions and conjunctions.

8i Make subjects and predicates consistent.

Faulty predication occurs when a subject does not work grammatically with its predicate.

Faulty	The most valued trait in an employee is a person who is loyal.

A person is not a trait.

Revised	The most valued trait in an employee is loyalty.

▶ Rising health-care costs decrease health insurance. ~~for many people.~~

             the number of people who can afford

Costs do not decrease health insurance.

8j Avoid the constructions *is when, is where,* and *reason . . . is because.*

Faulty	Indigestion is when you cannot digest food.
Revised	Indigestion is the inability to digest food.

▶ Gravitation is ~~where~~ one body ~~is being attracted by~~ another.

         the attraction of   to

▶ ~~The reason~~ I enjoy jogging ~~is~~ because it provides outdoor exercise.

EXERCISE 8.2 ▶

Correct the mixed constructions in the following sentences.

▶ ~~The reason~~ internships are valuable ~~is~~ because they give students real-world experience.

1. Surveys showing that college graduates who intern receive higher salary offers than their classmates who do not.
2. The fact that students must be careful, as all internships are not created equal.
3. A good internship is when the intern gains knowledge and skills in a professional environment.
4. Other companies may use unpaid interns that is free labor instead of hiring full-time employees.
5. Companies do not meet federal requirements, because they must pay minimum wage or face lawsuits.

9 Adjectives and Adverbs

Adjectives and adverbs are powerful. Used appropriately, they can add precision and force to your writing, as the following excerpt demonstrates:

> Seated cross-legged on a brocade pillow, wrapped in burgundy robes, was a short, rotund man with a shiny pate. He looked very old and very tired. Chhongba bowed reverently, spoke briefly to him in the Sherpa tongue, and indicated for us to come forward.
>
> —Jon Krakauer, *Into Thin Air*

Adjectives modify nouns or pronouns and indicate which one, what kind, or how many. **Adverbs** modify verbs, adjectives, other adverbs, clauses, or entire sentences and indicate how, when, where, how often, or to what extent. (See also Table H1.1, p. 727.)

The two most common errors involving adjectives and adverbs occur when writers use (1) an adjective instead of an adverb (or vice versa) and (2) the wrong form of an adjective or adverb in a comparison. Use the following guidelines to identify and correct these and other common errors in your writing.

9a Use adverbs, not adjectives, to modify verbs, adjectives, or other adverbs.

Although in conversation you may often use adjectives in place of adverbs, you should be careful in your writing to use adverbs to modify verbs, adjectives, or other adverbs.

▶ Those pants are ~~awful~~ ^{awfully} expensive.

▶ The headlights shone ~~bright~~ ^{brightly.}

9b Use adjectives, not adverbs, after linking verbs.

Linking verbs, often forms of *be* and other verbs such as *feel*, *look*, *make*, and *seem*, express a state of being. A linking verb takes a **subject complement**—a word group that completes or renames the subject of the sentence. Verbs such as *feel* and *look* can also be action verbs. When they function as action verbs in a sentence, they may be modified by an adverb.

If you are not sure whether a word should be an adjective or adverb, determine how it is used in the sentence. If the word modifies a noun, it should be an adjective.

Adjective   Our *waiter* looked *slow*.

Slow (an adjective) modifies the word *waiter,* a noun. In this sentence, *looked* is a linking verb.

Adverb   Our waiter *looked slowly* for some menus.

In this sentence, *looked* is expressing an action and is not a linking verb; *slowly* (an adverb) modifies *looked*.

9c Use *good* and *bad* as adjectives; use *well* and *badly* as adverbs.

▶ Einstein was not a *good student*.

The adjective *good* modifies the noun *student*.

▶ Einstein did not *perform well* in school.

The adverb *well* modifies the verb *perform*.

▶ He did ~~bad~~ badly on an entrance exam.

The adverb *badly* modifies the verb *did*.

When you are describing someone's health, *well* can also function as an adjective.

▶ The disease was in remission, but the *patients* were not yet *well*.

9d Be careful not to use adjectives such as *real* and *sure* to modify adverbs or other adjectives.

▶ The produce was crisp and ~~real~~ really fresh.

The adverb *really* modifies the adjective *fresh*.

9e Avoid double negatives.

A sentence with two negative words or phrases contains a **double negative**, which conveys a positive meaning. Do not use two negatives in a sentence unless you want to express a positive meaning (for example, *not uncommon* means "common").

▶ The company is not doing ~~nothing~~ anything to promote its incentive plan.

▶ No one under eighteen ~~can't~~ can vote in the presidential election.

Positive Meaning Intended

▶ Athletic sportswear is not uncommon as casual attire.

9f Use the comparative form of adjectives and adverbs to compare two things; use the superlative form to compare three or more things.

Adjectives and adverbs can be used to compare two or more persons, objects, actions, or ideas. The **comparative** form of an adjective or adverb compares two items. The **superlative** form compares three or more items. Use the list below to check the comparative and superlative forms of most regular adjectives and adverbs in your sentences.

	Comparatives	**Superlatives**
One-syllable adjectives and adverbs	Add -er: *colder, faster*	Add -est: *coldest, fastest*
Two-syllable adjectives	Add -er: *greasier**	Add -est: *greasiest**
Adjectives with three or more syllables or adverbs ending in -ly	Add *more* in front of the word: *more beautiful, more quickly*	Add *most* in front of the word: *most beautiful, most quickly*

Irregular adjectives and adverbs form their comparative and superlative forms in unpredictable ways, as the following list illustrates.

	Comparative	**Superlative**
Adjectives		
good	better	best
bad	worse	worst
little	less	least
Adverbs		
well	better	best
badly	worse	worst
Words That Function as Adjectives and Adverbs		
many	more	most
some	more	most
much	more	most

Do not use comparative or superlative forms with absolute concepts, such as *unique* and *perfect*. Something cannot be more or less unique, for example; it is either unique or not unique.

▶ This is ~~the most~~ ^a unique solution to the pollution problem.

9g Check your comparisons to be sure they are complete when using comparative and superlative forms.

An incomplete comparison can leave your reader confused about what is being compared.

Incomplete   The Internet works more efficiently.

Revised   For sending correspondence and documents, the Internet works more efficiently than the postal service.

*To form the comparative and superlative forms of adjectives ending in -y, change the y to i and add -er or -est.

| Incomplete | The catcher sustained the most crippling knee injury. |
| Revised | The catcher sustained the most crippling knee injury of his career. |

9h Do not use *more* or *most* with the *-er* or *-est* form of an adjective or adverb.

▶ The hypothesis must be ~~more~~ clearer.

EXERCISE 9.1

Correct any errors involving adjectives and adverbs in the following paragraph. Some sentences may be correct as written.

▶ Originating in China, *feng shui* is a traditional~~ly~~ art of balancing elements to achieve harmony.

     Feng shui is taken very serious in many Asian societies. Some Hong Kong business executives, for example, will not feel comfortably working in an office until it has been approved by a *feng shui* master. Other people are more interested in *feng shui* for its elegance. A room designed with this idea in mind looks tranquilly. The name *feng shui* means "wind and water," and balancing elements is the more important aspect of the art. Some people believe that this balance brings good luck. Others will admit only that surroundings can have a psychologically effect. It is easier to feel comfortable in a room designed according to *feng shui* principles. The placement of doors, windows, and furnishings contributes to the peaceful effect. Whether *feng shui* is magic or simple great interior design, something about it seems to work.

---

10   Misplaced and Dangling Modifiers

A **modifier** is a word or group of words that describes, changes, qualifies, or limits the meaning of another word or group of words in a sentence.

▶ The contestant *smiled delightedly.*

The adverb *delightedly* modifies the verb *smiled.*

▶ *Pretending to be surprised, he* greeted the guests.

The adjective phrase *Pretending to be surprised* modifies the pronoun *he.*

Modifiers that are carefully placed in sentences give your readers a clear picture of the details you want to convey. However, when a sentence contains a **misplaced modifier**, the reader must determine which word or group of words the modifier is supposed to be describing.

10a Place modifiers close to the words they describe.

Misplaced   The mayor *chided* the pedestrians for jaywalking *angrily*.

The adverb *angrily* should be closer to the verb it modifies, *chided*. Here, the adverb appears to be modifying *jaywalking*, so the sentence is confusing.

Revised   The mayor *angrily chided* the pedestrians for jaywalking.

Misplaced   The press *reacted* to the story leaked from the Pentagon *with horror*.

The adverb phrase *with horror* should explain how the press reacted, not how the story was leaked, so the modifier should be closer to the verb *reacted*.

Revised   The press *reacted with horror* to the story leaked from the Pentagon.

10b Make sure each modifier clearly modifies only one word or phrase in a sentence.

When a modifier is placed near or next to the word or phrase it modifies, it may also be near another word it could conceivably modify. When a modifier's placement may cause such ambiguity, rewrite the sentence, placing the modifier so that it clearly refers to the word or phrase it is supposed to modify.

Unclear   The film's attempt to portray war accurately depicts a survivor's anguish.

Does the film attempt to portray war accurately, or does it accurately depict a survivor's anguish? The following revisions eliminate the uncertainty.

Revised   ~~The film's~~ In its attempt to portray war accurately ∧ , the film depicts a survivor's anguish.

Revised   The ~~film's attempt to portray war~~ film ∧ accurately depicts a survivor's anguish*I* ∧ in its attempt to portray war realistically.

10c Revise a dangling modifier by rewriting the sentence.

A **dangling modifier** is a word or phrase that does not modify or refer to anything in a sentence. Instead, it seems to modify something that has been left out of the sentence. A dangling modifier can make the meaning of a sentence unclear, inaccurate, or even comical. Most dangling modifiers appear at the beginning or end of sentences.

Dangling   After singing a thrilling ballad, the crowd surged toward the stage.

This sentence suggests that the crowd sang the ballad.

Dangling   Laying an average of ten eggs a day, the farmer is proud of his henhouse.

This sentence suggests that the farmer lays eggs.

To revise a sentence with a dangling modifier, follow these steps:

1. Identify the word or words that the modifier is supposed to modify.
2. Revise the sentence to correct the confusion either by changing the modifier into a clause with its own subject and verb or by rewriting the sentence so that the word being modified becomes the subject.

▶ After ~~singing~~ _{Adele sang} a thrilling ballad, the crowd surged toward the stage.

▶ Laying an average of ten eggs a day, the ~~neighboring~~ farmer ~~is~~ proud of his henhouse.

EXERCISE 10.1

Correct any misplaced or dangling modifiers in the following paragraph. Some sentences may be correct as written.

▶ The measurement is now based on atomic vibrations. ~~of one second.~~

Making sure standard weights and measures are the same all over the world is an important task. To trade internationally, a kilogram in Mexico must weigh the same as a kilogram in Japan. In the past, countries set standards for weighing and measuring individually. One English king declared a yard to be the distance from his nose to his thumb egotistically. Weight was once measured in barleycorns, so unethical merchants soaked barleycorns to make them heavier in water. Today, the metric system is the worldwide standard, and the weight of the U.S. pound is based even on the standard kilogram. In France, a cylinder is the world standard kilogram made of platinum. Securely, this official kilogram is kept in an airtight container. Nevertheless, losing a few billionths of a gram of weight each year, world standards might eventually be affected. Hoping to find a permanent solution, scientists want to base the kilogram measurement on an unchanging natural phenomenon.

Use Punctuation Correctly

11 End Punctuation

The end of a sentence can be marked with a period (.), a question mark (?), or an exclamation point (!).

11a Use a period to mark the end of a sentence that makes a statement, gives an instruction, or includes an indirect question; use periods with most abbreviations.

Writers seldom omit the period at the end of a sentence that makes a statement or gives directions.

Statement   Amnesty International investigates human-rights violations.

Instruction   Use as little water as possible during the drought.

Writers sometimes mistake an indirect question for a direct one, however.

> ▶ Most visitors want to know where the dinosaur bones were found?.
>
> This sentence states what question was asked; it does not ask the question directly.

An **indirect question** is a statement that reports what was asked or is being asked: *He asked where the classroom was.*

Many abbreviations use periods (*Mass., Co., St.,*). If you are not sure whether an abbreviation should include periods, check a dictionary.

When an abbreviation that uses periods ends a sentence, an additional period is not needed.

> ▶ My brother works for Apple Computer, Inc./

Note, however, that the Modern Language Association (MLA) recommends omitting periods in abbreviations that consist of capital letters (*IBM, USA, BC*) but including periods in abbreviations that consist of lowercase letters (*a.m.*).

11b Use a question mark to end a sentence that asks a direct question.

Direct Question   Why was the flight delayed?

When a question is also a quotation, the question mark is placed within the quotation marks (see also 14d).

> ▶ "What did she want"? Marcia asked.

11c Use an exclamation point to end a sentence that expresses a strong emotion or a forceful command.

> ▶ Altering experimental results to make them conform to a hypothesis is never ethical!

Use exclamation points sparingly; they lose their impact when used too frequently.

> ▶ Government officials immediately suspected terrorism!.

EXERCISE 11.1

Correct any errors in the use of end punctuation marks in the following sentences. Some sentences may be correct as written.

> ▶ Is it possible that hemophilia in the Russian czar's family contributed to the Russian Revolution/?

1. When the daughters of Queen Victoria of England, who carried the gene for hemophilia, married royalty in Germany and Russia, those royal families inherited hemophilia as well?

2. The Russian czar's only son and heir to the throne suffered from hemophilia.

3. You might ask if internal bleeding can occur when a hemophiliac receives a bruise?

4. Czar Nicholas and his wife Alexandra often saw their little boy in terrible pain!

5. A phony monk named Rasputin eased the child's pain, but was he a gifted healer or just a con man.

12 ▸ Commas

A **comma** (,) is used to separate parts of a sentence from one another. Commas, when you use them correctly, make your sentences clear and help readers understand your meaning.

12a Use a comma before a coordinating conjunction (*and, but, for, nor, or, so, yet*) that joins two independent clauses.

> An **independent clause** contains a subject and verb and can stand alone as a sentence.

▸ The ball flew past the goalie, but the score did not count.

▸ Her dog was enormous, so many people found it threatening.

12b Use a comma to separate three or more items in a series.

A **series** is a list of three or more items—words, phrases, or clauses.

▸ Dancing, singing, and acting are just a few of her talents.

▸ Sunflowers grew on the hillsides, along the roads, and in the middle of every pasture.

Some writers omit the comma before a coordinating conjunction (such as *and, but, for, or, nor, so, yet*) in a brief series when using a casual or journalistic style. Occasionally this omission can create confusion, so it is better to include the final comma.

Confusing   She insured her valuable heirlooms, watches and jewelry.

   Do her heirlooms consist entirely of watches and jewelry, or did she insure three kinds of items?

Clear   She insured her valuable heirlooms, watches, and jewelry.

A comma is not used after the last item in a series.

> See also 13c on when to use semicolons to separate items in a series.

▸ Aphids, slugs, and beetles/can severely damage a crop.

12c Use a comma to separate two or more adjectives that modify the same noun when they are not joined by a coordinating word.

▸ Rescue workers found the frightened, hungry child.

To be sure a comma is needed, try reversing the two adjectives. If the phrase still sounds correct when the adjectives are reversed, a comma is needed. If the phrase sounds wrong, a comma is not needed.

▶ The airy, open atrium makes visitors feel at home.

The phrase *open, airy atrium* sounds right, so a comma is needed.

▶ Local businesses donated the bright red uniforms.

The phrase *red, bright uniforms* sounds wrong because *bright* modifies *red uniforms* in the original sentence. A comma is not needed.

12d Use a comma to separate introductory words, phrases, and clauses from the rest of a sentence.

Introductory Word	Above, the sky was a mass of clouds.
	Without the comma, this sentence would be confusing.
Introductory Phrase	At the start of the project, the researchers were optimistic.
Introductory Clause	When alcohol was outlawed, many solid citizens broke the law.

Exception: A comma is not needed after a single word or short phrase or clause when there is no possibility of confusion.

▶ Then a rainbow appeared.

12e Use a comma to set off a nonrestrictive word group from the rest of the sentence.

A **nonrestrictive word group** describes or modifies a word or phrase in a sentence, but it does not change the meaning of the word or phrase. To decide whether a comma is needed, read the sentence without the word group. If the basic meaning is unchanged, a comma is needed.

▶ Most people either love or hate fruitcake, *which is a traditional holiday dessert.*

The meaning of *fruitcake* is not changed by the relative clause *which is a traditional holiday dessert,* so the word group is **nonrestrictive** and a comma is needed.

▶ The child *wearing a tutu* delights in ballet lessons.

The phrase *wearing a tutu* identifies which child delights in ballet lessons, so the word group is **restrictive**—necessary to explain what the word it modifies means—and a comma is not needed.

12f Use a comma to set off parenthetical expressions.

A **parenthetical expression** provides extra information. It can also be a transitional word or phrase (*however, for example, at the beginning*) that is not essential to the meaning of the sentence.

▶ *Furthermore,* his essay had not been proofread.
▶ Islamic countries were, *in fact,* responsible for preserving much classical scientific knowledge.

12g Use commas with dates, addresses, titles, and numbers.

▶ She graduated on June 8, 2020.

When you give only a month and year, a comma is not needed.

▶ She graduated in June 2020.

Place a comma after the date when it appears before the end of the sentence.

▶ The 2018 Winter Olympics began on February 9, 2018, in Pyeongchang, South Korea.

When you give an address within a sentence, do not place a comma between the state and the ZIP code.

▶ Send the package to PO Box 100, McPherson, Kansas 67460.

Separate a name from a title with a comma.

▶ The featured speaker was Kate Silverstein, Ph.D.

Use commas in numbers that have more than four digits.

▶ Estimates of the number of protesters ranged from 250,000 to 700,000.

In a number with four digits, the comma is optional: 1500 or 1,500.

12h Use a comma to separate a direct quotation from the words that explain it.

▶ She asked, "What's the score?"

Place the comma before the closing quotation mark.

▶ "Wait and see," was his infuriating response.

12i Use commas to set off the name of someone directly addressed, to set off an echo question, and with a "not" phrase.

Direct Address	"James, answer the question concisely." "Bail has not been granted, your honor."
Echo Question	More development will require a more expensive infrastructure, won't it?
"Not" Phrase	Labor Day, not the autumnal equinox, marks the end of summer for most Americans.

A **direct quotation** gives a person's *exact* words, either spoken or written, set off by quotation marks.

See also 14b.

12j Omit unnecessary commas.

Keep the following rules in mind as you edit and proofread your papers for common errors in comma usage:

Omit a comma between a subject and verb.

```
     ┌────── subject ──────┐ ┌─ verb ─┐
```
▶ The poet Wilfred Owen⁄was killed a week before World War I ended.

Omit a comma between a verb and complement.

> A **complement** is a word or group of words that describes or renames a subject or object.

```
                ┌── verb ──┐ ┌── complement ──┐
```
▶ The school referendum is considered⁄very likely to pass.

Omit a comma between an adjective and the word it modifies.

```
              adjective  noun modified
              ┌─┐  ┌─────┐
```
▶ A growing family needs a large⁄house.

Omit a comma between two verbs in a compound predicate.

```
   compound predicate
   ┌──────────────┐
```
▶ We sat⁄and waited for our punishment.

Omit a comma between two nouns or pronouns in a compound subject.

```
        ┌────── compound subject ──────┐
```
▶ Harold Johnson⁄and Margaret Simpson led the expedition.

Omit a comma before a coordinating word joining two dependent clauses.

```
              ┌ dependent clause ┐     ┌ dependent clause ┐
```
▶ The band began to play before we arrived⁄but after the rain stopped.

Omit a comma after *than* in a comparison.

▶ The Homestead Act made the cost of land to pioneers less than⁄the price the government had paid.

Omit a comma after *like* or *such as*.

▶ Direct marketing techniques such as⁄mass mailings and telephone solicitations can be effective.

Omit commas after a question mark, exclamation point, or dash; before an opening parenthesis; or with a set of parentheses.

▶ "Where have you been?⁄" she would always ask.
▶ "Stop!⁄" the guard shouted.
▶ Keep spending to a minimum⁄—our resources are limited—and throw nothing away.
▶ Fast food⁄(which is usually high in fat)⁄is growing in popularity all over the world.

Omit commas around words that rename and restrict another word before them.

If the words are **restrictive**—necessary to explain what the word they modify means—do not enclose them with commas.

▶ The man/who brought his car in for transmission work/is a lawyer.

EXERCISE 12.1

Correct any errors in the use of commas in the following sentences. Some sentences may be correct as written.

▶ After slavery was abolished in New York in 1827, several black settlements were established in what is now New York City.

1. Seneca Village a crowded shantytown on the Upper West Side was the home of many poorer black New Yorkers.
2. The land became part of Central Park and everyone, who lived there, had to leave in the 1850s.
3. In present-day Brooklyn, there was once a middle-class black settlement, called Weeksville.
4. Susan Smith McKinney-Steward, was born in Weeksville, and was the valedictorian of New York Medical College in 1870.
5. Weeksville was a success story, for some of the houses survived into the twentieth century and have been preserved as historical monuments.

EXERCISE 12.2

Correct any errors in the use of commas in the following paragraph. Some sentences may be correct as written.

▶ In June/ 1998, fifty years after Korczak Ziolkowski began sculpting the Crazy Horse monument, the face of Crazy Horse was unveiled.

A monument to the Lakota Sioux warrior, Crazy Horse, is under construction in the Black Hills of South Dakota. Korczak Ziolkowski a sculptor, who also worked on Mount Rushmore, began the project in 1948. Ziolkowski was born on September 6, 1908, —thirty-one years to the day after Crazy Horse died. A Sioux chief asked Ziolkowski, if he would create a monument to honor Crazy Horse, and other Indian heroes. Ziolkowski designed a sculpture of Crazy Horse on horseback that, when it is completed, will be the largest statue in the world. The sculpture is being shaped from Thunderhead Mountain a six-hundred-foot granite rock. Tons of rock have been blasted, from the mountain. The sculptor died in 1982 but his widow, children, and grandchildren have carried on the work. There has been no government funding so, they have paid for the work entirely with donations and admission fees. By the middle of the twenty-first century the statue should be finished, and will depict the great Sioux hero pointing at the hills he loved.

13 Semicolons and Colons

Semicolons and colons send subtle messages to your reader about the relationship between the material that precedes and follows the punctuation mark.

Semicolons

13a Use a semicolon to join two closely related independent clauses.

> In January and February, sunny days are rare and very short in northern countries; winter depression is common in the north.

An **independent clause** contains a subject and a verb and can stand alone as a sentence.

13b Use a semicolon to join two independent clauses linked by a conjunctive adverb or transitional expression.

> The stunt pilot had to eject from the cockpit; nevertheless, he was not injured.

> Mass transit is good for the environment; for example, as many people can fit in a bus as in fifteen cars.

A **conjunctive adverb** is a word (such as *also, however,* or *still*) that links two independent clauses.

13c Use semicolons to separate items in a series if commas are used within the items.

Semicolons help prevent confusion in a sentence that contains a series of items with one or more commas within the items.

> Fairy tales inspire children by depicting magical events, which appeal to their imaginations; clever boys and girls, who encourage young readers' problem-solving skills; evil creatures, who provide thrills; and good, heroic adults, who make the childhood world seem safer.

Also use a semicolon to separate a series of independent clauses that contain commas.

> He is stubborn, selfish, and conservative; she is stubborn, combative, and liberal; and no one is surprised that they do not get along.

See also 12b on when to use commas to separate items in a series.

13d Do not use a semicolon to introduce a list or to separate a phrase or dependent clause from the rest of the sentence.

> A growing number of companies employ prison inmates for certain jobs; selling magazines, conducting surveys, reserving airplane tickets, and taking telephone orders.

> On the other hand; taking risks can bring impressive results.

> I'll always wonder; if things could have been different.

For more on introducing lists, see 13e.

Correct any errors in the use of semicolons in the following sentences. Some sentences may be correct as written.

▶ Myths and stories about vampires have been around for centuries*/*;however, Bram Stoker's 1897 novel *Dracula* is probably the most famous fictional account of these monsters.

1. In the years since Stoker's novel, vampires have become a movie fixture; in America and throughout the world.
2. Actor Bela Lugosi played Count Dracula as more of a romantic figure than a monster in the 1931 film *Dracula*; this depiction provided the standard image of the vampire as a sexy fiend.
3. The vampire tale was adapted to the American movie western; for example, in *Billy the Kid vs. Dracula* in 1966.
4. The popular *Blacula* (1972); which recast the vampire as an African prince in 1970s Los Angeles; inspired a series of black-themed "blaxploitation" horror movies.
5. In the late 1990s, *Buffy the Vampire Slayer* was revived as a popular TV series; starring Sarah Michelle Gellar.

Correct any errors in the use of semicolons in the following paragraph. Some sentences may be correct as written.

▶ The word *placebo* is Latin for "I will please*,*"; placebos have long been used in medical experiments.

    In medicine, a placebo is a substance; often a sugar pill, that has no medicinal use. Placebos alone cannot cure any medical problem, nevertheless, many patients improve when taking them. Because patients who receive placebos do not know that the pills are useless, they think they are getting help for their condition; and they get better. This strange but true fact—recognized by doctors; pharmacists; and other professionals—is called the placebo effect. Chemically, a placebo does nothing, theoretically, the patient should not respond, but somehow this trick works on many people. The placebo effect is often seen in patients; but it is not widely understood.

Colons

You can use a **colon** (:) to introduce a list, an explanation, an example, or a further thought within a sentence. The information following the colon should clarify or offer specifics about the information that comes before it.

13e Use a colon to introduce a list or a series.

When you use a **colon** to introduce a list, make sure the list is preceded by a complete sentence.

▶ The archaeologists uncovered several items: pieces of pottery, seeds, animal bones, and household tools.

                                                              common childhood illnesses
▶ All students must be immunized against: measles, mumps, and rubella.
                                                           ^

13f Use a colon to introduce an explanation, an example, or a summary.

▶ In many ways Hollywood is very predictable: Action movies arrive in the summer, dramas in the fall.
▶ One tree is particularly famous for its spectacular autumn colors: the sugar maple.
▶ Disaster relief efforts began all over the country: Volunteers raised $40 million.

If the group of words following a colon is a complete sentence, the first word can begin with either a capital or a lowercase letter. Whichever option you choose, be consistent throughout your paper.

13g Use a colon to introduce a word or phrase that renames another noun.

▶ A hushed group of tourists stared at the most famous statue in Florence: Michelangelo's *David*.

13h Use a colon to introduce a lengthy or heavily punctuated quotation.

A quotation that is more than one or two lines long or that contains two or more commas can be introduced by a colon.

▶ Without pausing for breath, the campaign manager intoned the introduction: "Ladies and gentlemen, today it is my very great privilege to introduce to you the person on whose behalf you have all worked so tirelessly and with such impressive results, the person who is the reason we are all here today—the next president of the United States."
▶ The instructions were confusing: "After adjusting toggles A, B, and C, connect bracket A to post A, bracket B to post B, and bracket C to post C, securing with clamps A, B, and C, as illustrated in figure 1."

13i Use a colon to separate hours and minutes, in salutations for business letters, between titles and subtitles, and in ratios.

Hours and Minutes	9:15 a.m.
Salutations	Dear Professor Sung:
Titles and Subtitles	*American Sphinx: The Character of Thomas Jefferson*
Ratios	7:1

13j Use a colon only at the end of an independent clause.

A colon should always follow an independent clause, which could stand on its own as a complete sentence. Do not use a colon between a verb and its object; between a preposition and its object; or before a list introduced by such words as *for example, including, is,* and *such as.*

▶ A medieval map is hard to read: The top of the map points to the east, not the north.

A medieval map is hard to read is an independent clause.

▶ Even a small garden can produce: beans, squash, tomatoes, and corn.
▶ My cat had hidden a ball of twine under: the sofa.
▶ Bird-watchers are thrilled to spy birds of prey such as: peregrine falcons, red-tailed hawks, and owls.

EXERCISE 13.3

Correct any errors in the use of colons in the following sentences. Some sentences may be correct as written.

▶ Young, impeccably dressed couples participated in the latest craze: swing dancing.

1. The ceremony is scheduled for precisely 10.00 a.m.
2. The proposed zoning change was defeated by a margin of 2/1.
3. On early rap records, listeners heard percussion from unusual sources such as: turntables, microphones, and synthesizers.
4. To find out whether a film is historically accurate, consult *Past Imperfect: History According to the Movies.*
5. He believes that the most American of all sports is: baseball.

14   Quotation Marks, Ellipses, and Brackets

Quotation marks, ellipses, and brackets are frequently used together. Quotation marks indicate that you are borrowing someone's exact words, and ellipses and brackets are used to indicate changes within a quotation.

Quotation Marks

A **direct quotation** gives a person's *exact* words, either spoken or written, set off by quotation marks. Quotation marks are always used in pairs. The opening quotation mark (") appears at the beginning of a word or quoted passage, and the closing mark (") appears at the end. Quotation marks are also used with titles of short works and to mark words used as words.

14a Use quotation marks around direct statements from other speakers or writers.

Be careful to include the *exact* words of the speaker or writer within the quotation marks.

▶ Lincoln recalled that the United States was "dedicated to the proposition that all men are created equal."

> Because *dedicated to the proposition that all men are created equal* repeats Lincoln's exact words, quotation marks are required.

In dialogue, place quotation marks around each speaker's words. Every time a different person speaks, begin a new paragraph.

> He said, "Sit down."
> "No, thank you," I replied.

For details on quoting from original sources using MLA or APA style, see Chapter 23.

14b Place commas and periods inside the quotation marks.

▶ "Play it, Sam," Rick tells the piano player in *Casablanca*.

▶ Willie Sutton robbed banks because "that's where the money is."

14c Place colons and semicolons *outside* the quotation marks.

▶ The marching band played "Seventy-Six Trombones"; the drum major's favorite song.

▶ A new national anthem should replace "The Star-Spangled Banner"; no one can sing that song.

14d Place question marks and exclamation points according to the meaning of the sentence.

If the quotation is a question or exclamation, place the question mark or exclamation point *within* the closing quotation mark. If the punctuation mark comes at the end of a sentence, no other end punctuation is needed.

▶ "How does the bridge stand up?" the child wondered.

▶ Poe's insane narrator confesses, "It is the beating of his hideous heart!"

If the entire sentence, of which the quotation is part, is a question or exclamation, the question mark or exclamation point goes *outside* the closing quotation mark at the end of the sentence.

▶ Was Scarlett O'Hara serious when she said, "Tomorrow is another day"?

14e Use a comma to separate a short quotation from a signal phrase, such as *he replied* or *she said*.

▶ "Video games improve eye-hand coordination," he replied.

▶ "The homeless population," she reported, "grew steadily throughout the 1980s."

14f Use single quotation marks (' ') to indicate a quotation or title within a quotation.

▶ The mysterious caller repeatedly insists, "Play 'Misty' for me."

14g Place quotation marks around the titles of works within longer works.

Section of a Book	Chapter 1, "Ozzie and Harriet in Spanish Harlem"
Poem in a Collection	"Ode on a Grecian Urn"
Short Story	"The Yellow Wallpaper"
Essay or Article in a Newspaper or Magazine	"Their Malcolm, My Problem"
Song	"Bad Romance"
Episode of a Television Program	"Larry's Last Goodbye"

14h Do not use quotation marks to call attention to words or phrases.

▶ The manager who was originally in charge of the project "jumped ship" before the deadline.

Quotation marks can be used to mark words used as words (as an acceptable alternative to italics).

▶ The word "receive" is often misspelled.

EXERCISE 14.1

Correct any errors in the use of quotation marks in the following sentences. Some sentences may be correct as written.

▶ The hotel has an excellent restaurant specializing in "fresh" fish.

1. Her essay was entitled ""To Be or Not to Be": Shakespeare and Existentialism."
2. Why did the professor assign "To an Athlete Dying Young?"
3. A movie line many teenagers imitated was "Hasta la vista, baby".
4. After September 11, 2001, President Bush said he was going to "fight terror".
5. "I have a dream," Martin Luther King Jr. told the civil rights marchers.

Ellipses and Brackets

14i Use an ellipsis (. . .) to indicate an omission.

An **ellipsis** (. . .) is written as three equally spaced periods. Use an ellipsis to shorten a quotation so that it includes just the parts you want or need to quote.

Original Quotation	"The prison, a high percentage of whose inmates are serving life sentences, looked surprisingly ordinary."
Shortened	"The prison . . . looked surprisingly ordinary." Notice that the two commas were also omitted when the quotation was shortened.

When you shorten a quotation, be careful not to change the meaning of the original passage. Do not omit any parts that will alter or misrepresent the writer's intended meaning.

Original	"Magicians create illusions, but sometimes audience members want to believe that magic is real."
Meaning Altered	"Magicians . . . want to believe that magic is real."

When you omit the last part of a quoted sentence, add a period, for a total of four dots (the ellipsis plus a period).

Original Quotation	"In the sphere of psychology, details are also the thing. God preserve us from commonplaces. Best of all is to avoid depicting the hero's state of mind; you ought to try to make it clear from the hero's actions. It is not necessary to portray many characters. The center of gravity should be in two persons: him and her." —Anton Chekhov, Letter to Alexander P. Chekhov
Shortened	"God preserve us from commonplaces. Best of all is to avoid depicting the hero's state of mind. . . . It is not necessary to portray many characters. The center of gravity should be in two persons: him and her."

An ellipsis is not needed to indicate that the quoted passage continues after the last sentence you quote ends.

▶ He is modest about his contributions to the abolitionist cause: "I could do but little; but what I could, I did with a joyful heart⌣" (Douglass 54).

No ellipsis is needed at the beginning of a quotation, even though material in the original comes before it.

Original Quotation	"As was the case after the recent cleaning of the Sistine Chapel, the makeover of the starry ceiling in Grand Central Station has revealed surprisingly brilliant color."
Shortened	"[T]he makeover of the starry ceiling in Grand Central Station has revealed surprisingly brilliant color."

Note: The first word of a quoted sentence should be capitalized. If you change from a lowercase to a capital letter, enclose the letter in brackets (see Section 14j).

14j Use brackets to indicate changes in quotations and to enclose words already in parentheses.

Brackets ([ ]) are used within quotations and within parentheses.

Use brackets to add information or indicate changes you have made to a quotation.

▶ Whitman's preface argued, "Here [the United States] is not merely a nation but a teeming nation of nations."

The explanation tells where *here* is.

▶ "Along came a spider and sat down beside [Miss Muffett]," who apparently suffered from a phobia.

The bracketed name replaces *her* in the original.

Use brackets to enclose the word *sic* when signaling an error in original quoted material.

▶ The incumbent's letter to the editor announced, "My opponent's [sic] claims regarding my record are simply not true."

The Latin word *sic* lets your readers know that the misspelled word or other error in the quoted material is the original author's error, not yours.

Use brackets to enclose parenthetical material in a group of words already enclosed in parentheses.

▶ The demonstrators (including members of the National Rifle Association [NRA]) crowded around the candidate.

EXERCISE 14.2

Shorten each of the following quotations by omitting the underlined portion and adding an ellipsis and brackets where appropriate.

▶ "Some people who call themselves vegetarians still eat ~~less cuddly~~
    ^
~~creatures such as~~ chicken and fish."

1. "The structure of DNA, <u>as Watson and Crick discovered,</u> is a double helix."
2. "<u>Although African Americans had won Academy Awards before,</u> Halle Berry was the first African American woman to win the Academy Award for Best Actress."
3. "Cole Porter cultivated a suave, sophisticated urban persona <u>even though he came from a small town in Indiana.</u>"
4. "<u>Many Americans do not realize that</u> people of all classes receive financial help from the government."
5. "<u>Although</u> saltwater aquariums <u>are beautiful, they</u> are difficult and expensive to maintain."

15 ▸ Apostrophes

An **apostrophe** (') has three functions: to show ownership or possession, to indicate omitted letters in contractions, and to form some plurals.

15a Use an apostrophe to indicate possession or ownership.

Add -'s to make a singular noun possessive, including nouns that end with s or the sound of s and **indefinite pronouns** (*anyone, nobody*).

> ▶ The *fox's* prey led it across the field.
> ▶ Whether she can win the nomination is *anybody's* guess.

An **indefinite pronoun** does not refer to a specific person, place, or object. It refers to people, places, or things in general (*anywhere, everyone, everything*).

Note that the possessive forms of personal pronouns do not take apostrophes: *mine, yours, his, hers, ours, theirs, its.*

> ▶ Each bee has *its* function in the hive.

The possessive form of *who* is *whose* (not *who's*).

> ▶ Marie Curie, *whose* work in chemistry made history, discovered radium.

Add an apostrophe to a plural noun to make it possessive, or add -'s if the plural noun does not end in s.

> ▶ Both *farms'* crops were lost in the flood.
> ▶ Our *children's* children will reap the benefits of our efforts to preserve the environment today.

To show individual possession by two or more people or groups, add an apostrophe or -'s to each noun.

> ▶ Sam is equipment manager for both the *boys'* and the *girls'* basketball teams.
>
>   Sam works for two different teams.

To show joint possession by two people or groups, add an apostrophe or -'s to the last noun.

> ▶ The *coaches and players'* dream came true at the end of the season.

Add -'s to the last word of a compound noun to show possession.

> ▶ My *father-in-law's* boat needs a new engine.
> ▶ We were ushered into the *chairman of the department's* office.

15b Use an apostrophe to indicate the omitted letter or letters in a contraction.

> ▶ I*'ve* [I have] seen the answers.
> ▶ Jason *didn't* [did not] arrive last night.

15c Use an apostrophe to form the plural of a number, letter, symbol, abbreviation, or word treated as a word.

> ▶ There are three 5*'s* on the license plate.
> ▶ She spells her name with two C*'s*.
> ▶ The ?*'s* stand for unknown quantities.
> ▶ Using two *etc.'s* is unnecessary.
> ▶ Replace all *can's* in the contract with *cannot's*.

In the sentences above, note that numbers, letters, and words used as themselves are in italics. The -s ending should not be italicized, however.

When referring to the years in a decade, no apostrophe is used.

▶ The fashions of the 1970s returned in the 1990s.

Apostrophes are used, however, to signal the omission of the numerals that indicate the century.

the class of '03   music of the '20s

15d Avoid using apostrophes to form plurals and to form possessives for personal pronouns.

▶ The trapper̸s came to town to trade.
▶ She paid for my lunch as well as her̸s.

EXERCISE 15.1

Correct the errors in the use of apostrophes in the following sentences. Some sentences may be correct as written.

▶ As newer forms of communication like Twitter, Facebook, and text messaging take over our lives, we should ask whether we're becoming more connected or less connected with other people.

1. Our's is a society almost too willing to share.
2. We probably know more about the day-to-day lives of other's than ever before, as the details of our many friend's days are recorded in online status report's.
3. Its unclear, however, whether anyone is truly benefiting from all this sharing of private information, even as the various social networking sites privacy settings reveal more and more about user's.
4. Todays parents' can find out about their sons and daughters personal live's online, but they have less face-to-face contact with their children.
5. Of course, theyll have to figure out the meaning of all the LOLs', BTWs, and other shorthand slang in their kids online and text messages.

16 Parentheses and Dashes

Parentheses—( )—are used to separate nonessential information from the rest of a sentence or paragraph. A **dash** (—), or a pair of dashes, is (are) used to separate parts of a sentence. A dash suggests a stronger separation than a comma, colon, or semicolon does.

Parentheses

16a Use parentheses to add words, phrases, or sentences that expand on, clarify, or explain material that follows.

Words, phrases, or sentences that expand on, clarify, or explain material that precedes or follows should be set off with parentheses.

▶ The EPA (Environmental Protection Agency) is responsible for developing water-pollution standards.

▶ The application fee for the four-day workshop (a total of $500, including the registration fee) is due Friday.

Be sure to use parentheses sparingly; they can clutter your writing.

16b Use parentheses to insert dates or abbreviations.

▶ Elizabeth Cady Stanton (1815–1902) helped organize the first American women's rights convention.

▶ Guidelines for documenting research papers in the humanities are published by the Modern Language Association (MLA).

16c Check the placement of other punctuation used with parentheses.

Parenthetical information that appears at the end of a sentence should be inserted before the period that ends the sentence.

▶ Ballroom dancing has become popular in the United States (probably because of the success of *Dancing with the Stars*).

When parenthetical information appears after a word that would be followed by a comma, the comma is always placed after the closing parenthesis.

▶ He called when his plane landed (or so he said), but no one answered.

When a complete sentence appears within parentheses, punctuate the sentence as you would normally.

▶ Timber companies propose various uses for national forests. (Public land can be leased for commercial purposes.)

Exception: If the material within the parentheses is a question, it should end with a question mark.

▶ A few innocent-looking plants (have you heard of the Venus flytrap?) capture and eat insects and animals.

—

Dashes

16d Use a dash or dashes to emphasize a sudden shift or break in thought or mood.

▶ Computers have given us instant communication—and electronic junk mail.

16e Use a dash or dashes to introduce an explanation, an example, or items in a series.

▶ The tattoo artist had completed a large body of work—Fred's!
▶ The tattoo artist had seen everything—a full-size bear claw on a back, bleeding heart on a bicep, even an Irish cross on the tip of a nose.

When the added thought appears in mid-sentence, use two dashes to set it off.

▶ The tattoo artist—who would prefer to remain nameless—thinks tattoos are a waste of money.

16f Use dashes sparingly.

A **conjunction** is a word or words used to connect clauses, phrases, or individual words.

Dashes are emphatic. Do not overuse them, or they will lose their effectiveness. Also be careful not to use a dash as a substitute for a conjunction or transition.

▶ Einstein's job in Switzerland was dull—it offered him plenty of time to
    , but
think—he came up with the theory of relativity.
    ; while working there

EXERCISE 16.1

Correct the errors in the use of parentheses or dashes in the following sentences. Some sentences may be correct as written.

▶ Typhoid Mary would probably not have infected so many victims if she had stopped working (she was a cook).

1. In the 1960s, frozen foods—icy blocks of corn, peas, and string beans—were popular—and convenient—alternatives to fresh produce.
2. The Committee for Scientific Investigation of Claims of the Paranormal (CSICOP) tests claims of supernatural abilities.
3. Malcolm X 1925–1965 was an American political figure assassinated in the 1960s.
4. The invention of anesthesia made possible many advances in medicine (including lengthy surgery.)
5. In the 1990s, people in Great Britain were alerted to a new danger, mad cow disease.

Manage Mechanics and Spelling

17 Capitalization

Capitalize the first word of a sentence, **proper nouns**, and the pronoun I.

A **proper noun** names a particular person, place, thing, or group.

17a Capitalize the first word in a sentence and in a direct quotation.

▶ ᴿ̬revision is important.

Capitalize the first word in a direct quotation unless it is incorporated into your own sentence or it continues an earlier quotation.

▶ The union representative said, "ᵀ̬that meeting did not take place."

▶ Sam Verdon complained that "ⁿ̬No one takes college athletes seriously."

▶ "I prefer not to interpret my paintings," replied the famous watercolorist, "ᵇ̬Because they should speak for themselves."

17b Capitalize proper nouns, including the names of specific people, places, things, and groups.

People and Animals	Franklin Roosevelt, his dog Fala
Cities, States, Nations	St. Paul, Minnesota, the United States
Geographic Regions	the Gulf Coast, the U.S. Southwest
Government Offices, Departments, Buildings	the Pentagon, the Supreme Court, the Puck Building
Organizations (Cultural, Political, etc.)	League of Women Voters, National Basketball Association
Months, Days, Holidays	February, Thursday, Labor Day
Chapter or Section Titles in Books	"Why America Has Changed"
Nationalities and Languages	Ethiopian, Dutch
Religions and Sacred Books	Judaism, the Quran
Trade Names	Coca-Cola, Brillo
Historic Events	the Treaty of Versailles, Reconstruction
Specific Course Titles	Organic Chemistry 101

17c Do not capitalize common nouns.

Family Members	my uncle, his father
General Areas of the Country	southwestern United States

Subjects	my chemistry class
Centuries	seventeenth-century England
Geographical Areas	the lake in the park

17d Capitalize the titles of literary and other works, such as books, articles, poems, plays, songs, films, and paintings.

Capitalize the first and last words of the title, the first word following a colon, and all other words except **articles**, **coordinating conjunctions**, and **prepositions**.

Articles are the words *a, an,* and *the.*

Coordinating conjunctions (*and, but, for, nor, or, so, yet*) connect sentence elements that are of equal importance.

Prepositions (such as *before, on,* and *to*) are used before a noun or pronoun to indicate time, place, space, direction, position, or some other relationship.

Book	*The Fault in Our Stars*
Article	"Making History at Madison Park"
Poem	"Aunt Jennifer's Tigers"
Play	*A Raisin in the Sun*
Song	"Hello"
Film	*La La Land*
Painting	*The Starry Night*

17e Capitalize a personal title only when it directly precedes a person's name.

▶ Vice President Maria Washington briefed the stockholders.
▶ Maria Washington was hired from a rival company to be the new vice president.

It is acceptable to capitalize the titles of certain high government officials regardless of whether they precede a name: *the President of the United States.*

EXERCISE 17.1

Correct the capitalization errors in the following paragraph.

▶ The u̲nited n̲ations meets at its headquarters in New York City.

During world war II, the governments of twenty-six countries pledged their willingness to continue fighting on behalf of the Allies. United States president Franklin Roosevelt came up with a name for the group: the united nations. The "Declaration By United Nations" promised the support of those twenty-six governments for the war effort. The Nations signed this document on New Year's day of 1942. By 1945, the number of countries involved in the united nations had grown to fifty-one. From April through June of that year, fifty Representatives attended the united nations Conference on International Organization in San Francisco. There, the Nations debated the contents of a charter. Although the War was nearing an end, the governments foresaw a need to continue international cooperation. The charter was ratified on October 24, 1945, by China, France, The Soviet Union, The United Kingdom, The United States, and a majority of the other Nations. Every year since then, October 24 has been known as united nations day.

18 Numbers

As a general rule, use numbers according to the rules of your field of study. Be sure to represent numbers as numerals or as words consistently.

18a Spell out numbers that begin sentences.

> Two hundred ten
> ▶ ~~210~~ students attended the lecture.
>   ^

18b Spell out numbers that can be written in one or two words.

twenty-six checks   two hundred women
sixty students   one thousand pretzels

Use numerals for numbers that cannot be spelled out in one or two words.

>   375
> ▶ There are ~~three hundred seventy-five~~ students enrolled this fall.
>   ^

Use numerals for all numbers in a sentence if one of the numbers needs to be written in numerals.

>   28
> ▶ Of the 420 students in my school, only ~~twenty-eight~~ have a driver's license.
>   ^

When two numbers appear in succession, spell out one and use numerals for the other.

>   3
> ▶ Each counselor is in charge of nine ~~three~~-year-olds.
>   ^

18c Use numerals according to convention.

Dates	January 10, 2017; the 1990s
Decimals, Percentages, Fractions	56.7, 50% or 50 percent, 1¾ cups
Exact Times	9:27 a.m.
Pages, Chapters, Volumes	page 27, chapter 12, volume 4
Addresses	122 Peach Street
Exact Amounts of Money	$5.60, $1.3 million
Scores and Statistics	23–6 victory, a factor of 12

> EXERCISE 18.1

Correct the errors in the use of numbers in the following sentences. Some sentences may be correct as written.

>   77.
> ▶ The quotation you're looking for is on page ~~seventy-seven.~~
>   ^

1. 77% of those responding to the poll favored increased taxes on cigarettes.
2. The estimated cost was too low by eighty-seven dollars and fourteen cents.
3. Each window is composed of 100s of small pieces of colored glass.
4. All traffic stopped as a 90-car train went slowly past.
5. February twenty-two is George Washington's birthday, but Presidents' Day is always celebrated on a Monday.

19 Italics

Italic or *slanted type* is used for emphasizing particular words or phrases. It is also used to set off titles of longer works or works that contain other works (such as anthologies, Web sites, and magazines), names of vehicles, non-English words, and words deserving special emphasis. Most word-processing programs provide italic type on the font or format tabs.

19a Italicize titles of works published separately.

Books	*Great Expectations*
Plays and Musicals	*Hamilton*
Long Poems	*The Iliad*
Magazines and Journals	*Entertainment Weekly; New York Review of Books*
Newspapers	*Columbus Dispatch*
Movies and DVDs	*The Twilight Saga: Eclipse*
Long Musical Works, Recordings	*Exile on Main St.*
Television and Radio Series	*The Walking Dead*
Works of Art	*Birth of Venus; The Starry Night*
Blogs and Web Sites	*Gen Y Girl; Spotify*

For more about quotation marks with titles, see 14g.

The titles of shorter works, such as the titles of articles, short stories, and songs, should be enclosed in quotation marks.

19b Italicize the names of ships, trains, aircraft, and spacecraft.

Titanic	*Spirit of St. Louis*
Orient Express	space shuttle *Challenger*

19c Italicize non-English words not in everyday use.

Words from other languages should be italicized unless they have become a part of the English language, such as "chic" or "burrito." If you are unsure, check an English dictionary. If the word is not listed, it should be italicized.

▶ Our instructor lectured on the technique of *Verstehen*.
▶ Tacos are now as much a part of American cuisine as pizza.

19d Italicize numbers, letters, words, or phrases called out for special emphasis.

Use italics for numbers, letters, or words used as terms.

▶ Every bottle has *33* on the label.
▶ Hester Prynne is forced to wear a scarlet *A*.
▶ Today, *ain't* is listed in most dictionaries.

Italicize a word or phrase that is being defined or emphasized.

> ▶ *Alliteration*—the same sounds repeated at the beginning of each word in a group—can be an effective literary device.

Use italics for emphasis sparingly. When you italicize too many words in a sentence or paragraph, the emphasis is lost.

> (no italics)
> ▶ The U.S. National Park system is *extremely important* because it protects some of
> (no italics)   (no italics)
> the most *beautiful* and *unusual* parts of this country.

EXERCISE 19.1

Correct the errors in the use of italics in the following sentences. Some sentences may be correct as written.

> ▶ *Oedipus*, written by Sophocles in the fifth century BC, is possibly the most famous play of the classical period.

1. The exchange student greeted everyone with a hearty *"Kon'nichiwa!"*
2. His professor insisted that Soap Opera Digest was not an acceptable research source.
3. Cartoons like The Simpsons have become surprisingly popular with adult audiences.
4. The first European settlers at Plymouth arrived on the Mayflower.
5. His book is discussed in depth in the article *Africa: The Hidden History*.

20 Hyphens

A **hyphen** (-) is used to join compound words, to connect parts of words, and to split words at the end of typewritten lines of text.

20a Use a hyphen to join words that function as a unit.

Some compound nouns and verbs are spelled as one word (*download*), some are spelled as two words (*washing machine*), and some are spelled using hyphens (*foul-up*). Check a dictionary when you are unsure; if you do not find the compound listed in your dictionary, spell it as two words.

Use a hyphen to join words that together modify a noun.

> ▶ An *icy-fingered* hand tapped her shoulder.

However, when the first word of the compound ends in -ly or when the compound adjective follows the noun it modifies, no hyphen is used.

> ▶ The guard found a *clumsily hidden* duplicate key.
> ▶ Her voice was *well trained*.

20b Use a hyphen with some prefixes (*all-*, *ex-*, *great-*, *self-*) and suffixes (*-elect*).

▶ Most Americans' parents, grandparents, or *great-grandparents* came from another country.
▶ The *governor-elect* made a stirring victory speech.

Use a hyphen for clarity to prevent confusion with certain combinations of prefixes and base words.

▶ She wants the taxpayers to approve the funding for her ~~recreation~~ re-creation of the demolished town hall.

    Recreation has a different meaning from *re-creation*.

20c Use a hyphen when spelling out fractions and the numbers *twenty-one* to *ninety-nine*, in word-number combinations, and to indicate inclusive numbers.

two-thirds finished   *twenty-two* sources

▶ The 675-*yard* path winds through a landscaped garden.
▶ Pages 99–102 cover the military campaigns.

20d Use a hyphen between syllables to split a word at the end of a typewritten or handwritten line.

Although most word-processing programs automatically break the line before a long word and move the word to the next line, in typewritten or handwritten text, you should use a hyphen to divide any words that fall at the end of a line. Divide words between syllables; never break a one-syllable word. Divide a compound word between its parts. Words can also be divided between a prefix and root or between a root and suffix. Check your dictionary if you are uncertain about where to break a word.

> Viking invaders failed to conquer Ireland because the country was governed by a number of petty kings rather than by a central authority that could be effectively overthrown; however, by the tenth century this situation began to change.

EXERCISE 20.1

Correct the errors in the use of hyphens in the following sentences. If you are not sure about a word, check your dictionary. Some sentences may be correct as written.

▶ Does any ~~teen-ager~~ teenager really need liposuction?

1. Adolescents today who are unhappy with their looks can turn to the increasingly-popular option of plastic surgery.
2. For many selfconscious teens and young adults, surgery seems to be the perfect solution.

3. Until recently, very few sixteen year olds considered making permanent surgical changes.
4. But as more adults pay for nose-jobs and tummy tucks, more teens are expressing interest.
5. Are images of people with apparently perfect bodies and faces unduly influencing less-than-perfect young Americans?

21 Spelling

Misspelled words are among the most common errors for many student writers. Be sure to pay attention to spelling as you edit and proofread your papers, and keep a dictionary close at hand. Misspellings can make your paper appear carelessly written. Use the tips in the box below to help improve your spelling.

Tips for Improving Your Spelling

- **Purchase a collegiate dictionary and take the time to look up the correct spellings of unfamiliar words.**
- **Use your word processor's spell-checker function.** Be sure to take advantage of the spell-checker as you edit and proofread your drafts. However, keep in mind that this function will not catch all spelling errors; for example, it cannot detect the incorrect use of *it's* versus *its* or of homonyms such as *there* versus *their* and *weather* versus *whether*.
- **Proofread your drafts for spelling errors.** To avoid being distracted by the flow of ideas in your essays, proofread them backward, from the last word to the first, looking only for misspellings. For words that sound alike but have different spellings (*to/too/two, their/there*), stop to check their use in the sentence and determine whether you have used the correct word.
- **Keep a list of words you commonly misspell.** The best way to learn tricky words is to make a list of the words that give you trouble and refer to it often, especially as you proofread. Use your dictionary to locate the correct spelling and pronunciation of each word in the list. Review your list of words periodically, and practice pronouncing and writing the words until you master their spellings.
- **Develop a spelling awareness.** As you read and write, pay attention to words and how they are spelled. When you encounter a new word, pronounce it slowly and carefully while taking note of its spelling. Pay particular attention to words with similar-sounding endings (*-able/-ible, -cede/-sede*), doubled letters (*embarrassment, personnel*), several similar-sounding vowels (*cemetery*), words that seem to be missing necessary letters (*knowledge, privilege*), words from the same root but with different spellings (*heir, heredity*), and words with silent letters (*aisle, pneumonia*).

EXERCISE 7.1, P. 751

Possible Revisions

2. Because of the importance of the information, it often must be transmitted secretly.
4. The Nazis' enigma code was extremely difficult to crack. Its complexity was an enormous problem for the Allied forces.

EXERCISE 7.2, P. 753

2. Every scientist has their own ideas about the state of the environment. [Correct, or may be changed to "Every scientist has his or her own ideas . . ."]
4. In one way, animals resemble plants: Some are "weeds" because they have the ability to thrive under many conditions.
6. When a "weed" and a delicate native species compete for their survival, the native species usually loses.
8. People should be more concerned about the extinction of plants and animals than they seem to be.
10. The earth has experienced several mass extinctions in its history, but another would take its toll on the quality of human life.

EXERCISE 8.2, P. 760

Possible Revisions

2. Students must be careful, as all internships are not created equal.
4. Other companies may use unpaid interns for free labor instead of hiring full-time employees.

EXERCISE 11.1, P. 767

2. The Russian czar's only son and heir to the throne suffered from hemophilia. [Correct]
4. Czar Nicholas and his wife Alexandra often saw their little boy in terrible pain.

EXERCISE 12.1, P. 772

2. The land became part of Central Park, and everyone who lived there had to leave in the 1850s.
4. Susan Smith McKinney-Steward was born in Weeksville and was the valedictorian of New York Medical College in 1870.

EXERCISE 13.1, P. 774

2. Actor Bela Lugosi played Count Dracula as more of a romantic figure than a monster in the 1931 film *Dracula*; this depiction provided the standard image of the vampire as a sexy fiend. [Correct]
4. The popular *Blacula* (1972), which recast the vampire as an African prince in 1970s Los Angeles, inspired a series of black-themed "blaxploitation" horror movies.

EXERCISE 13.3, P. 776

2. The proposed zoning change was defeated by a margin of 2:1.
4. To find out whether a film is historically accurate, consult *Past Imperfect: History According to the Movies*. [Correct]

EXERCISE 14.1, P. 778

Possible Answers

2. Why did the professor assign "To an Athlete Dying Young"?
4. After September 11, 2001, President Bush said he was going to "fight terror."

EXERCISE 14.2, P. 780

Possible Answers

2. "Halle Berry was the first African American woman to win the Academy Award for Best Actress."
4. "[P]eople of all classes receive financial help from the government."

EXERCISE 15.1, P. 782

2. We probably know more about the day-to-day lives of others than ever before, as the details of our many friends' days are recorded in online status reports.
4. Today's parents can find out about their sons and daughters' personal lives online, but they have less face-to-face contact with their children.

EXERCISE 16.1, P. 784

2. The Committee for Scientific Investigation of Claims of the Paranormal (CSICOP) tests claims of supernatural abilities. [Correct]
4. The invention of anesthesia made possible many advances in medicine (including lengthy surgery).

EXERCISE 18.1, P. 787

2. The estimated cost was too low by $87.14.
4. All traffic stopped as a ninety-car train went slowly past.

EXERCISE 19.1, P. 789

2. His professor insisted that *Soap Opera Digest* was not an acceptable research source.
4. The first European settlers at Plymouth arrived on the *Mayflower*.

EXERCISE 20.1, P. 790

2. For many self-conscious teens and young adults, surgery seems to be the perfect solution.
4. But as more adults pay for nose jobs and tummy tucks, more teens are expressing interest.

Acknowledgments

Alter, Adam. "How Labels Like 'Black' and 'Working Class' Shape Your Identity." *The Week*, May 4, 2013. From *Drunk Tank Pink: And Other Unexpected Forces That Shape How We Think, Feel, and Behave.* Copyright © 2013 by Adam Alter. Used by permission of Penguin Press, an imprint of Penguin Publishing Group, a division of Penguin Random House LLC. All rights reserved.

Beato, Greg. "Internet Addiction." From *Reason Magazine*, July 1, 2010. Copyright © 2010 by Reason Foundation. Used with permission.

Blakley, Johanna. "Liberals and Conservatives Have Wildly Different TV-Viewing Habits but These 5 Shows Bring Everyone Together." From *The Conversation*, July 1, 2019. Copyright © 2019 by Johanna Blakley. Used with permission.

Brooks, Gwendolyn. "The Bean Eaters." Copyright © by Gwendolyn Brooks. Reprinted by consent of Brooks Permissions.

Bryant, Howard. "Smoke Screen." From *ESPN*, December 10, 2013. Copyright © 2013 by ESPN. Reprinted courtesy of ESPN .com.

Cortright, Joe. Modified from "2017 Year-in-Review: More Driving, More Dying." From *CityCommentary*, January 16, 2018. Licensed under CC License Attribution 4.0 International (CC by 4.0).

Didion, Joan. Excerpt from "Los Angeles Notebook." From *Slouching towards Bethlehem* by Joan Didion. Copyright © 1966, 1968, renewed 1996 by Joan Didion. Reprinted by permission of Farrar, Straus and Giroux.

Diehm, Jan, and Amber Thomas. "Pockets" (originally "Someone Clever Once Said Women Were Not Allowed Pockets"). From *The Pudding*, August 2018. Copyright © 2018 by The Pudding. Used with permission.

Edge, John T. "I'm Not Leaving until I Eat This Thing." From *The Oxford American*, September/October 1999. Used with permission of John T. Edge.

Fassler, Joe, and Michael Moss. "The Language of Junk Food Addiction." From *The Atlantic*, April 30, 2013. Copyright © 2013 by Joe Fassler. Used with permission.

Forgas, Joseph Paul. "Why Are Some People More Gullible Than Others?" From *The Conversation*, March 30, 2017. Copyright © 2017 by Joseph Paul Forgas. Used with permission.

Gilb, Dagoberto. "Love in L.A." Copyright © 2016 by Dagoberto Gilb. Used with permission.

Goldin, Ian. "Five Reasons Why Universal Basic Income Is a Red Herring." From *Financial Times*, February 19, 2018. Copyright © 2018 by Financial Times. Used under license from the Financial Times. All Rights Reserved.

Goleman, Daniel. Excerpt(s) from "Intimate Enemies." From *Emotional Intelligence: Why It Can Matter More Than IQ*, copyright © 1995 by Daniel Goleman. Used by permission of Bantam Books, an imprint of Random House, a division of Penguin Random House LLC. All rights reserved.

Goodwin, Jan. "She Lives Off What We Throw Away." From *Marie Claire*, March 11, 2009. Copyright © 2009 by Jan Goodwin. Used with permission.

Gottfried, Martin. "Rambos of the Road." From *Newsweek*, September 8, 1986. Copyright © 1986 by IBT Media. Used with permission.

Jabr, Ferris. "Why Walking Helps Us Think." From *The New Yorker*, September 3, 2014. Copyright © 2014 by Condé Nast Publications, Inc. Used with permission.

Jarrett, Christian. "The Psychology of Stuff and Things." From *The Psychologist*, vol. 26, no. 8 (2013). Copyright © 2013 by The British Psychological Society. Used with permission of the Licensor through PLSclear.

Jensen, Derrick. "Against Forgetting: Where Have All the Animals Gone?" From *Orion Magazine*, July/August 2013. Copyright © 2013 by Orion Magazine. Used with permission.

K., S. "The Case against Tipping." From *The Economist*, October 26, 2015. Copyright © 2015 by The Economist Group Limited, London. Used with permission.

Kiely, Eugene, and Lori Robertson. "How to Spot Fake News." From *FactCheck.org*, November 18, 2016. Copyright © 2018 by FactCheck.org, a project of the Annenberg Public Policy Center. Used with permission.

Konnikova, Maria. "Why Summer Makes Us Lazy." From *The New Yorker*, July 22, 2013. Copyright © 2013 by Condé Nast Publications, Inc. Used with permission.

Lamott, Anne. "Shitty First Drafts." From *Bird by Bird: Some Instructions on Writing and Life*, by Anne Lamott, copyright © 1994 by Anne Lamott. Used by permission of Pantheon Books, an imprint of the Knopf Doubleday Publishing Group, a division of Penguin Random House LLC. All rights reserved.

McCullough, Gretchen. "Children Are Using Emoji for Digital-Age Language Learning." From *WIRED*, January 1, 2019. Copyright © 2019 by WIRED. Used with permission.

Morris, Toby. "On a Plate." From *The Wireless*, 2015. Copyright © 2015 by Toby Morris. Used with permission.

Index

Handbook Contents